CD-ROMs to accompany this book available from Library Issue Desk

3D Games

Animation and Advanced Real-time Rendering

VOLUME TWO

We work with leading authors to develop the
strongest educational materials in computer science,
bringing cutting-edge thinking and best
learning practice to a global market.

Under a range of well-known imprints, including
Addison-Wesley, we craft high-quality print and
electronic publications which help readers to understand
and apply their content, whether studying or at work.

To find out more about the complete range of our
publishing, please visit us on the World Wide Web at:
www.pearsoneduc.com

3D Games

Animation and Advanced Real-time Rendering

ALAN WATT AND
FABIO POLICARPO

 ADDISON-WESLEY

An imprint of **Pearson Education**

Harlow, England • London • New York • Boston • San Francisco • Toronto • Sydney • Singapore • Hong Kong
Tokyo • Seoul • Taipei • New Delhi • Cape Town • Madrid • Mexico City • Amsterdam • Munich • Paris • Milan

Pearson Education Limited
Edinburgh Gate
Harlow
Essex CM20 2JE
England

and Associated Companies throughout the world

Visit us on the World Wide Web at:
www.pearsoneduc.com

First published 2003

© Pearson Education Limited 2003

The programs in this book have been included for their instructional value. They have been
tested with care but are not guaranteed for any particular purpose. The publisher does not
offer any warranties or representations nor does it accept any liabilities with respect to the
programs.

Many of the designations used by manufacturers and sellers to distinguish their products
are claimed as trademarks. Pearson Education has made every attempt to supply trademark
information about manufacturers and their products mentioned in this book. A list of the
trademark designations and their owners appears below.

Trademark notice

The following designations are trademarks or registered trademarks of the organisations whose names
follow in brackets:

Alias, Maya, Wavefront (Alias/Wavefront, a division of Silicon Graphics Limited); DirectX, Visual C++
(Microsoft Corporation); GeForce3 (NVIDIA Corporation); Open GL (Silicon Graphics, Inc.); Pentium
(Intel Corporation); RenderMan (Pixar).

ISBN 0 201 78706 7

British Library Cataloguing-in-Publication Data
A catalogue record for this book is available from the British Library

Library of Congress Cataloging-in-Publication Data
A catalog record for this book is available from the Library of Congress

10 9 8 7 6 5 4 3 2 1
07 06 05 04 03

Cover designed by Dionea Watt
Typeset in 9/12pt Stone Serif by 35
Printed and bound in Great Britain by Biddles Ltd, Guildford and King's Lynn

Para meus queridos pais, Fernando e Wania, que apesar das inevitáveis diferenças, sempre me apoiaram para conquistar meu espaço (3D) pelo meu próprio trabalho e dedicação . . . muito obrigado por tudo, Fabio.

Contents

Real-time rendering

Animation

Preface

The aim of this book is to address advanced techniques in games technology. These we divide into three main categories:

(1) generic processes, which consist of:
   - the build processes – the offline processing required in a game system;
   - real-time processes – the application-independent processes executed by a game engine;
   - software design – how everything fits together in a clean design and how applications integrate with the engine;

(2) real-time rendering processes. This is approached by considering both the underlying theory and, in a separate chapter, the current practice involved in real-time rendering. Another chapter deals with the important and somewhat neglected topic of geometry processing or the theory of polygon meshes;

(3) the theory and practice of character animation.

The treatment of these topics in the text is built around a specific games system, Fly3D SDK 2. Here the aim is to root as many as possible of the techniques described in the text in a practical games system. Because the treatment is intended to be both theoretical and practical, we have by necessity to choose a particular design approach. We hope that this specialisation does not detract much from the reader's ability to perceive the general principles involved.

Not all of the techniques described in the text have been implemented in Fly3D and some of the chapters are theoretical. However, even in the theoretical chapters most of the important methods have been implemented on a stand-alone basis. In this respect we hope that sufficient information has been given to enable interested readers to implement the technology in the supplied engine; or indeed in their own.

At the time of writing (August 2002), the potential of games to embrace other applications is strong. High scene complexity allied with low processing costs is now achievable. And one of the aims of the developments described in the text is to build facilities that can be applied to applications other than games.

An engine is the system that executes a game and the utilities are tools like editors, BSP builders etc. which enable a game to be designed and which perform the necessary pre-processing operations that prepare the game data for real-time processing by the engine. The game engine executes the game, exploiting the efficiency structures that have been set up in the off-line phase. As well as efficiently rendering static content, the engine must deal with the interaction of dynamic objects and player interaction.

A basic BSP engine and the associated BSP theory was described in [WATT01]. In the text we look at more advanced techniques that are implemented as Fly3D Version 2. These developments represent an evolution of experience and new approaches to optimisation. We hope that the results represent a state-of-the-art games system.

The features of the system are:

- –/+ Complete plug-in directed
- –/+ BSP/PVS render management supporting both complex landscapes and closed environments. Generic recursion of BSP
- + Automatic path finding through a level using the pseudo-portals of convex volumes and A*
- + Fixed functionality shaders with up to eight passes
- – Multi-texture support
- + Hardware vertex and pixel programming integrated into the shaders
- –/+ Light maps for static geometry with soft shadows
- – Volumetric fog with fog maps
- – Dynamic coloured lights with distance attenuation updating light maps and dynamic objects
- + Animated meshes (vertex morph with animation blending)
- + Animated meshes with skeleton (bone/skin with animation blending)
- + MoCap retargeting using IK
- 0 Mesh file formats supporting shaders (.F3D)
- 0 Skeleton animated mesh file format (.K3G)
- + Several face types: large face (more than three vertices), tri-strip, tri-fan, tri-soup and curved patch
- – Dynamic LOD for curved faces using bi-quadric Bézier patches
- + Hardware rendering options including cartoon/silhouette rendering
- – Dynamic shadows – using stencil shadow volumes
- – Multi-player support with client/server architecture (using DirectPlay)
- 0 Stereo and 3D sound support (using DirectSound)
- – Mouse and keyboard input (using DirectInput)
- – Intel Pentium3 vector and matrix math optimisation
- 0 Direct loading of all data from zip files
- + Script editor for .fly files with real-time preview
- + Shader editor for .shr files with real-time preview
- 0 3D Studio MAX ver 2, 3 and 4 plug-ins for exporting .F3D and .K3G files with any number of animations each with any number of keys

0   3D Studio MAX ver 3 and 4 plug-ins for importing and exporting .FMP (Fly3D Map) level files

0   flyBuild map processing utility and flyBuilder build front-end

0   Quake3 level converter allows the use of Quake3-compatible level editors.

– signifies material described in [WATT01]
+ signifies material covered in this text
0 mainly routine utilities that are not described in the text but are generally covered on the CD-ROM.

The engine and SDK feature list is intended to provide developers with advanced visual effects at the lowest possible processing cost. The evolution of development and art production tools is an important aspect of modern games as it leaves designers and artists free to concentrate on creation. It also separates the programmer's and artist's role in the game production process. We give examples of typical utilities in Chapter 3.

With the ongoing increase in hardware power and the development of more advanced management and rendering applications, high complexity is possible and has opened up many more potential applications for games engines other than games. The engine has now been used in the following applications:

- **3D games** Two game genres are used extensively as examples throughout the text:
  - the common first-person shooter type where a user navigates in a complex environment;
  - a non-linear character animation genre where an avatar is directed by a user to navigate an environment autonomously and interact with objects.

- **3D Internet applications/games** ActiveX control is provided, including all Fly3D functionality. Real-time 3D simulation on the Internet is straightforward. Intended applications include 3D shopping, 3D browsing and 3D marketing applications.

- **3D architectural real-time walkthrough for CAAD** Another of the games engine's potential applications is real-time interior visualisation of buildings and interiors. Figure P.1 (also Colour Plate) shows the games engine being used as a CAAD tool in shopping mall and apartment design.

- **Generic 3D visualisation** Complexity is manifested both by geometric complexity and the demand for advanced rendering techniques. We develop an example of a demanding landscape – a high polygon representation of part of the surface of Mars (see Figure 1.7).

Figure P.1
Showing the engine being
used for non-game
applications.

For additional resources specific to this book, visit www.booksites.net/watt_3d
or www.fly3d.com.br

Acknowledgements

People

We thank the following people who contributed work and resources to this book and to the demos included with the Fly3D 2.0 CD:

In Brazil:

- Althayr Rodrigues for the ship game demo sound effects and the Theme mp3 used on the menu level.
- Alexandre Barros for his hard work modelling the Apartamento2 architecture demo.
- Daniel Bezerra for helpful technical discussions, insights and some of the algorithm implementations, such as the lightmap packing and console code.
- Edison Bezerra for the help on the Fly3D documentation layout and design.
- Elisa Gomes for the excellent architecture demo Apartamento and all its textures.
- Flavio Ramos for the modelling and texture mapping of several of the demos and 3D models, especially the ones on Ship_SP1, Ship_MP1 and Apartamento2.
- Francisco Meirelles (chico) for the design of some of the demo maps, including the Tutorial, Gallery and Apartamento2.
- Gilliard Lopes (glopes) for the long-term work on all Fly3D engine areas and especially the AI, Documentation, Shader Editor, utility modules and the NewWaveFly midi sound used on the Ship_SP1 demo.
- Henrique Vidinha for the ship, weapon and powerup models used on the ship demo games.
- Marcos Bezerra for several texture maps used on the demos and the Apartamento architecture demo.
- Marina Morato for the design and implementation of the Fly3D Web Site.

In England:

- Dionea, as always, for the cover design work.
- Emanuel Tanguy for the facial animation contribution to the Animface demo.
- Mark Eastlick for contributions to Chapter 6.
- James Edge for contributions to the facial animation material (Chapter 9).
- Michael Meredith for contributions to Chapter 10.

All over the world:

- Marco Mustapic and Flavia Paganelli for the Boids contribution.
- Daniel Benmergui and Nicolás Vinacur for the FireFly contribution.
- Andreas Endres (padman) for the PadGarden contribution.
- Lukas Kwiatkowski for the TPPWalk contribution.
- Netvir for the Water Yard contribution.
- Juan Pineda for the Joystick contribution integrated into the Fly3D engine core.

Companies

We thank the following companies for the contributions in knowledge, hardware and investment that took this project into a higher level of quality.

- ATI (www.ati.com) for the impressive 3D video cards and very useful developer sample applications.
- INTEL (www.intel.com) for the excellent technical support and the very fast machines that we used in the development of this work.
- KELSEUS (www.kelseus.com) for the investment, support and development specially relating to the skeleton character animation system.
- NVIDIA (www.nvidia.com) for the excellent 3D video cards, the best OpenGL drivers ever and very good documentation.
- PARALELO (www.paralelo.com.br) for the people, time and money invested in this project.

Publisher's acknowledgements

We are grateful to the following for permission to reproduce copyright material:

Figure 4.4 from Appearance-preserving simplification in *Proceedings SIGGRAPH 98*, ACM Publications, Cohen, J., Olano, M. and Manocha, D. (1998), Figure 4.5 from Displaced subdivision surfaces in *Proceedings SIGGRAPH 00*, ACM Publications, Lee, A., Moreton, H. and Hoppe, H. (2000) and Figure 6.15 from View-dependent refinement of progressive meshes in *Proceedings SIGGRAPH 97*, ACM Publications, Hoppe, H. (1997), reprinted by permission; Figure 9.14 from *Tin Toy* (1988) reproduced with permission from Pixar Animation Studios; Figure 10.8 reproduced with permission from Charles F. Rose III.

In some instances we have been unable to trace the owners of copyright material, and we would appreciate any information that would enable us to do so.

1 The anatomy of an advanced game system I
The build process and static lighting

Off-line processes are usually known as building. Utilities are used to build a file which the engine accesses to execute its real-time processes – the game itself. The overall build process proceeds as:

(1) Convert the output from the content builder into a *map* file with optimum data structures.
(2) Build the BSP structures.
(3) Build the light map, which itself splits into three steps:
    (a) generating the light map coordinates;
    (b) light map packing;
    (c) illuminating the light map.
(4) Build the Potentially Visible Set (PVS).

The BSP build occurs first because the light map and PVS build can exploit the BSP for efficiency. Thus the BSP management functions both during the build process and when the game is played.

1.1   Data structures

The build process begins with the output from the contents building software converted into a representation which is optimal for our requirements. Data structures are of critical importance for efficient execution of a game that contains complex levels. Efficiency considerations need to address both the way we store the geometry and the use of graphics hardware – in particular, new extensions. We first consider storing vertices – the lowest level of the data structure.

1.1.1   Vertices

The conventional way to store the vertices is by using the following specification (note that the class has several methods not listed here).

```
class FLY_ENGINE_API flyVertex
{
public:
    vector pos;
    vector texcoord;
    vector normal;
    unsigned color;
};
```

This puts all vertices' properties in a single structure. Note that the *texcoord* vector stores texture coordinates and light map coordinates (two floats, x,y, are the texture coordinates and the two other floats, z,w, are the light map coordinates). This means that if two vertices share the same position in space, but possess different normals, colours or texture coordinates, then they cannot be shared (two different vertices must be created to represent them).

Thus we store a vertex array that will contain all vertices used in the level. In general, a vertex entity will appear many times with the same positional coordinates but different texture coordinates, colour etc.

```
flyVertex *vert=new flyVertex[nvert];
```

Each face will use a fixed number of vertices that must be consecutive entries in the vertex array. This means that the first *n* vertices will be for face 0, the next *m* vertices for face 1, etc. and no face shares a vertex with another face. This allows the use of vertex arrays that are always enabled. If any of the above information is stored in the face structure we will not be able to use vertex arrays because the displacement between consecutive entries will not be constant. For example, in the case of triangles we could have three texture coordinates for each face. That would allow different faces to share the same vertex, but would not allow the use of vertex arrays because the texture coordinates would not be spaced a fixed number of bytes from each other. There would be three consecutive texture coordinates, then a space and three more.

Faces

Faces are separated into five types:

(1) a large polygon (polygon with n vertices);

(2) a Bézier patch ($npu \times npv$ vertices defining its control mesh);

(3) triangle 'soup' (n vertices defining a mesh of triangles);

(4) triangle strip (tri-strip);

(5) triangle fan (tri-fan).

An important consideration is whether to use a variable or fixed length face structure. A fixed length structure is better. A variable structure would be required if we had an unorganised vertex array – the face would then require a variable length list of pointers into the vertex array.

As we are using an organised vertex array the face structure requires only two integers (the vertex index followed by number of vertices). The face structure will then have a fixed size regardless of the number of vertices it is referencing.

The following is the class definition for the face class:

```
class FLY_ENGINE_API flyPlane
{
   public:
      vector normal; // plane normal
      float d0;       // the perpendicular distance
                      // from the plane to the origin

   // computes the perpendicular distance from a point
   // to the plane

   inline float distance(vector &v)
      { return vec_dot(normal,v)-d0; }
};

class FLY_ENGINE_API flyFace : public flyPlane
{
   public:
      int facetype; // face type (1,2,3,4,5)

      int sh;        // shader
      int lm;        // light map

      int nvert;       // number of vertices
      int vertindx; // first vertex

      int patch_npu;    // only facetype==FACETYPE_PATCH
      int patch_npv;
      flyBezierPatch *patch;
```

```
    int ntriface;        // only facetype==FACETYPE_TRUSURF
    int ntrivert;
    int *trivert;
}
```

The first five variables are present in all face types. Some face types need more data. For faces with type 1 (polygons), all vertices must be coplanar and the polygon must be convex. It is important to use large polygons as much as possible. Consider just a rectangle – four vertices. Represented by triangles, we would have to pass six vertices to the graphics hardware.

We draw polygons using the following OpenGL command (which draws a polygon starting with vertex *vertindx* and consisting of *nvert* vertices).

```
glDrawArrays(GL_POLYGON,vertindx,nvert);
```

For faces of type 2 (bi-quadratic Bézier surface), we need to specify two more integers (the number of control vertices in each direction *u,v* (*npu,npv*)). The vertices of each control point are stored in the vertex array – just as for other types. The product of *npu* and *npv* gives the number of control points, represented as vertices, in the array.

We build a patch object using the control points starting at vertex *vertindx* and using *nvert* vertices:

```
nvert=npu*npv;
patch=new flyBezierPatch;
patch->set_control_points(npu,npv,&vert[vertindx]);
```

To draw a patch, we use triangle strips. Bézier patches have the advantage that they can be used as an easy LOD facility [WATT01]. Effectively they are uniformly subdivided based on a geometric error factor, to the highest level of detail. At render time an LOD appropriate to the viewing distance is obtained by skipping rows and columns in the triangle strip. To draw the patch model with dynamic LOD we use the *draw()* method from the *flyBezierPatch* class.

Faces of type 3 (triangle soups) are used to model the level detail (lamps, statues, etc. . . .). They need to specify a new integer which defines the number of triangular faces (*ntriface*) and an array of *3*ntriface* integers that indexes the face vertices which build the triangles. Note that such faces can share vertices between triangles. A distinction is made between large polygons comprising the architecture of a level and small objects that may appear as part of, say, a wall. These are subsequently treated differently by the BSP scheme. Only faces of type 1 can be used as partitioning planes for the BSP. Objects represented by type 3 are detailed small objects and they appear in all the BSP nodes they clip. Faces of type 3 require an extra array of integers that define the triangulation between the vertices. For each triangle there are three integers in the array indexing the vertices:

```
ntrivert=ntriface*3;
trivert=new int[ntrivert];
```

For this type of face we have n vertices creating m triangular faces (faces can share the same vertex here). To draw it we use the following OpenGL command:

```
glDrawElements(GL_TRIANGLES, ntrivert,GL_UNSIGNED_INT,trivert);
```

Faces of type 4 (tri-strips) represent a single triangle strip sequence. If the face includes n vertices, $n - 2$ triangles are represented. Tri-strips are drawn by:

```
glDrawElements(GL_TRIANGLE_STRIP,ntrivert,GL_UNSIGNED_INT,trivert);
```

Faces of type 5 (tri-fans) represent a single triangle fan sequence. If the face includes n vertices, $n - 2$ triangles are represented. Tri-fans are drawn by:

```
glDrawElements(GL_TRIANGLE_FAN,ntrivert,GL_UNSIGNED_INT,trivert);
```

1.1.3   Bounding boxes

All static faces and all dynamic objects are enclosed in axis-aligned bounding boxes (AABBs). As we shall see, these are used in many different optimisation contexts, including collision detection and view frustum culling.

1.2   The build process

We now examine the sequence of operations required to prepare the scene geometry for use in the game and to light it. The scene geometry is modelled in an editor and saved in a file that we refer to as the map file. This consists of the raw scene geometry – a list of faces and their vertices in the previously described format. This is the main input to the build program. This program generates the BSP file, the PVS file, the light maps and the games script. The games script is based on the game entities defined in the level and the type of game to be played.

1.2.1   Creating the BSP tree from the scene geometry

A good way to build a BSP tree is first to elaborate the level geometry to distinguish between structural faces and detail faces. Structural faces are large polygons, like those that represent walls, and they are distinguished because they are used as splitting planes in the BSP tree. Such faces form themselves into a single concave volume – the entire games scene (Figure 1.1 (also Colour Plate)).

Detail faces belong to small objects that are contained by such a volume. The overall aim of the strategy is to split a scene into the minimum number of convex volumes. This approach is much better than simply considering any face to possess the same status as any other. Such an approach results in

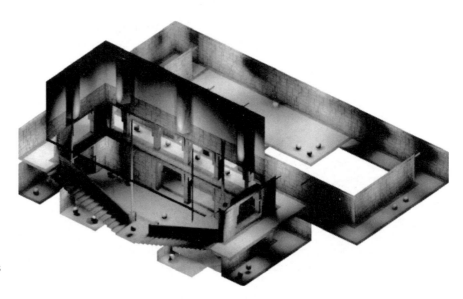

Figure 1.1
A view of an entire games level.

situations where the faces of small elements become splitting planes. Figure 1.2 (also Colour Plate) shows a level implemented in the games engine for a Computer Aided Architectural Design (CAAD) application. Here the walls of the apartment form structural faces and all the furniture, paintings on the wall etc. are categorised as detail faces which cannot function as splitting planes in the BSP build process and are thus contained within BSP leaf nodes that they clip.

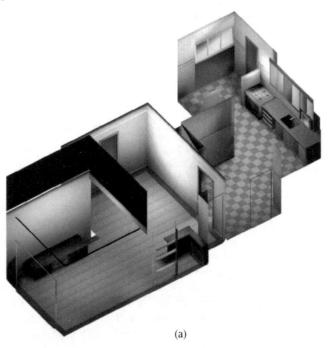

Figure 1.2
(a) Structural elements in a CAAD application used as BSP splitting planes.

(a)

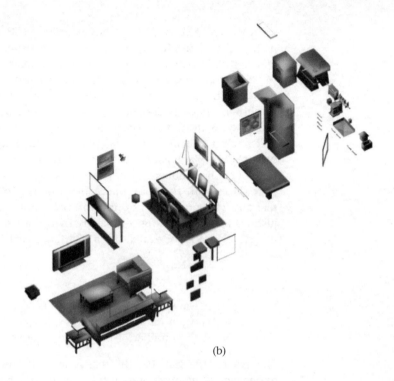

(b)

Figure 1.2 *continued*
(b) Detail elements in a
CAAD application. (c) The
entire apartment scene
showing both structural
and detail elements.

(c)

In the BSP tree every node has associated with it a list of faces and a list of planes. The planes have been derived from structural faces and the number of planes will, in general, be less than the number of faces. A recursive function is called to process the node. This function will decide which of the available planes is the best candidate for the next split. If there are no more planes in the list the node is designated as a leaf node. Also, if the node has no faces associated with it, it is discarded.

To select the best splitting plane in the node we consider all available planes. Each plane is examined to determine the result of its use. A count can be kept of the number of faces on the positive and negative side and the number of faces split. The optimum plane exhibits a balanced splitting and no intersections. This process is not linear in the number of planes per node – another justification for reducing complexity by using BSP sectors, as we describe next. A useful formula for evaluating a metric for each plane is:

$$N1 - N2 + 4N3$$

where

$N1$ is the number of positive splits
$N2$ is the number of negative splits
$N3$ is the number of face intersections

This reflects the fact that the cost of an imbalance of four faces is equivalent to one face being duplicated in the two children because it has been intersected.

The selected plane creates two children and every face is tested to determine whether it is one side of the plane or the other or is itself intersected by the plane. Intersected faces are split and are added to both children. The selected plane is removed from the plane list of the current node. A plane is only added to the child plane list if it has not already been used. Thus as the tree grows, nodes will contain fewer and fewer faces and fewer and fewer planes (Figure 1.3).

The following table describes the statistics for the apartment level:

Data

No. of vertices:	11975
No. of faces:	2652
No. of unique planes required to contain the faces:	339
Bounding box size:	706.00 1197.00 460.00

Selected cell size: 1024.00

BSP statistics

BSP sectors:	2
No. of leaf faces:	4913
No. of leaves:	628 (409 positive side, 219 negative side)
No. of nodes:	936

In the above, the bounding box size relates to the entire level. This is used in a further elaboration, which is to divide the scene into BSP sectors each of which

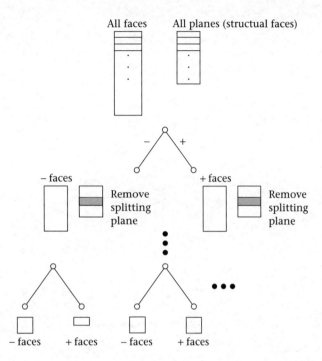

All faces   All planes (structural faces)

− faces

+ faces

Remove splitting plane

Remove splitting plane

− faces   + faces   − faces   + faces

Figure 1.3
BSP strategy: each
(non-leaf) node has a
list of faces and a list of
candidate splitting planes.

has its own BSP tree. In the above example we have used just two sectors. The BSP build process is non-linear in complexity as a function of the number of splitting planes required, and for extremely complex levels, like landscapes, further elaboration is necessary. This can be done by defining a maximum BSP cell size – a subdivision of the landscape bounding box. The entire level is then divided with axis-aligned planes until the cell dimension is smaller than the pre-defined size. These cells are then subject to the previously described algorithm. In effect the cell subdivisions form structural faces and we presume that as a first approximation the spatial density of polygons is constant and so uniform subdivision is a sensible strategy.

Figure 1.4(a) shows the plan of a simple level. This consists of 12 faces for the walls plus 3 faces each for the floor and the ceiling. The method then splits this into 3 convex volumes as shown, which form the leaf nodes. The structure consists of 18 convex polygons (quads) and 10 planes. Consider Figure 1.4(b) which demonstrates the recursive build process for this level, considering the walls only. The root node chooses plane a. Subsequent child nodes choose planes b, c and d. Each of these generate children with empty negative nodes and the recursion continues to generate leaf 1. Leaf 1 is then the convex volume to the left of plane a. This volume contains all the faces belonging to this convex volume. The process continues in a similar manner to generate two more leaf nodes.

The following code implements a basic BSP build. It loads a map file, creates a root node, and adds all face pointers to the root node list of faces and all

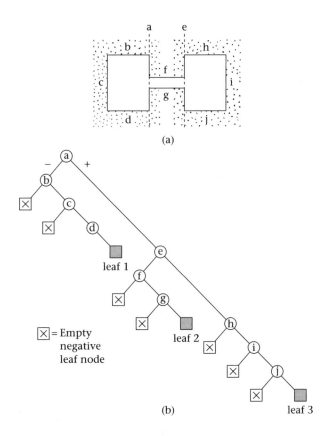

Figure 1.4
Building a BSP tree for
a level which results in
convex volumes at each
leaf. (a) Plan view of
simple level. (b) The BSP
build for the simple level.

structural face planes to the root node list of planes. It then calls the *split_axis*
method which initially divides the scene into BSP sectors.

```
int flyEngineBuild::build_bsp(const char *fmpfile)
{
    if (load_fmp(str)==0)
        return 0;

    flyBspNodeBuild *bspb=new flyBspNodeBuild;

    int i;
    for( i=0;i<nfaces;i++ )
    {
        if (faces[i].flag==FLY_FACEFLAG_STRUCTURAL)
            bspb->add_plane(faces[i].normal,faces[i].d0);
        bspb->faces.add(&faces[i]);
    }

    bspb->split_axis();

    save_bsp(str))

    return 1;
}
```

Split_axis starts by calculating the bounding box of the faces contained in the node. If any of the dimensions of the bounding box in each of the axes is larger than the grid size it will then split in a plane aligned with the axis. The plane is positioned to cut through the middle of the box. All faces are then assigned to child nodes and the method is called recursively for each of the children. When the node bounding box, in every axis, is smaller than the grid size, the node is processed. For a landscape level, at this step, all faces are transformed into a triangle mesh which shares vertices. For a closed level environment the standard BSP *split* is called, which builds the convex volumes inside the BSP sector.

```
void flyBspNodeBuild::split_axis()
{
   int i,j;

   bbox.reset();
   for( i=0;i<faces.num;i++ )
     if (faces[i]->facetype==FLY_FACETYPE_LARGE_POLYGON &&
        faces[i]->flag && faces[i]->sortkey)
        for( j=0;j<faces[i]->nvert;j++ )
          bbox.add_point(faces[i]->vert[j]);

   for( i=0;i<3;i++ )
     if (bbox.max[i]-bbox.min[i]>bspgridsize)
        break;

   if (i==3)
   {
      bsp_sectors++;
      if (landscape==0)
        split();
      else
        trimesh_landscape();
   }
   else
   {
      normal.vec(0,0,0);
      normal[i]=1;
      d0=((bbox.max[i]-bbox.min[i])*0.5f+bbox.min[i]);

      child[0]=new flyBspNodeBuild;
      child[1]=new flyBspNodeBuild;

      for( i=0;i<faces.num;i++ )
      {
        j=classify_face(faces[i]);
        if (j==-1)
        {
           child[0]->faces.add(faces[i]);
           child[1]->faces.add(faces[i]);
           child[0]->add_plane(faces[i]);
        }
```

```
         else
         {
            child[j]->faces.add(faces[i]);

            child[0]->add_plane(faces[i]);
         }
      }

      faces.clear();
      planes.clear();

      child[0]->split_axis();
      child[1]->split_axis();
   }
}
```

The standard BSP *split* method finds the best candidate, based on the available planes, and is then recursively called until every plane has been used.

```
void flyBspNodeBuild::split()
{
   if (planes.num==0)
      return;

   int p=find_split_plane();
   if (p==-1)
      return;

   normal=planes[p].normal;
   d0=planes[p].d0;
   planes.remove(p);

   child[0]=new flyBspNodeBuild;
   child[1]=new flyBspNodeBuild;

   side=-1;
   child[0]->side=0;
   child[1]->side=1;

   float f1,f2;
   int i,j,n,flag;
   flyFace *face;

   for( i=0;i<faces.num;i++ )
   {
      face=faces[i];
      flag=0;
      for( j=0;j<face->nvert;j++ )
      {
         f1=distance(face->vert[j]);
         if (f1>-0.01f && f1<0.01f)
            continue;

         if (flag==0)
```

```
                  {
                     f2=f1;
                     flag=1;
                  }
                  else
                     if  (f2*f1<0)
                        break;
               }
               if  (flag==0)
                  n=0;
               else
               if  (j==face->nvert)
                  if  (f2>=0)
                     n=0;
                  else
                     n=1;
               else
                  n=-1;

               if  (face->flag==FLY_FACEFLAG_STRUCTURAL)
                  j=find_plane(face->normal,face->d0);
               else j=-1;

               if  (n!=-1)
               {
                  child[n]->faces.add(face);
                  if  (j!=-1)
                     child[n]->add_plane(planes[j].normal,planes[j].d0);
               }
               else
               {
                  child[0]->faces.add(face);
                  child[1]->faces.add(face);
                  if  (j!=-1)
                  {
                     child[0]->add_plane(planes[j].normal,planes[j].d0);
                     child[1]->add_plane(planes[j].normal,planes[j].d0);
                  }
               }
            }

   faces.clear();
   planes.clear();

   if  (child[0]->faces.num)
      child[0]->split();
   else
   {
      delete  child[0];
      child[0]=0;
   }

   if  (child[1]->faces.num)
      child[1]->split();
```

```
        else
        {
          delete child[1];
          child[1]=0;
        }
}
```

Convex volumes for path planning and PVS calculation

The final aim of the process is to achieve a partitioning into convex volumes and if this is possible then there will only ever be positive leaf nodes, as shown in Figure 1.4. Such a partitioning scheme can then be used in path planning (Section 2.5). However, to achieve this implies constraints in the level modelling process. Consider the statistics for the game level shown in Figure 1.1.

Data

No. of vertices:	3635
No. of faces:	733
No. unique planes required to contain the faces planes:	166
Bounding box size:	1120.00 1630.00 677.00

Selected cell size: 1532.00

BSP statistics

BSP sectors:	2
No. of leaf faces:	1615
No. of leaves:	295 (207 positive side, 88 negative side)
No. of nodes:	505

These show 88 negative leaf nodes which in this case originate from the stair structures. Convex volumes can only be constructed if polygons are joined edge to edge. If we have a polygon edge abutting another polygon face this condition is not met (Figure 1.5). In the stair structure in the level we would have to subdivide the wall polygon onto which the stairs join. Alternatively, the stairs can be given detail status but to close the level they need to be backed by a sloping ramp which should not be rendered. Such modelling constraints, however, are context dependent and somewhat inconvenient.

Figure 1.6 (also Colour Plate) shows a level that has no negative volumes, designed by attending to the modelling constraints required such that the BSP tree produces no negative nodes.

Data

No. of vertices:	1827
No. of faces:	440
No. of unique planes required to contain the faces:	76
Bounding box size:	2176.00 2304.00 1664.00

Selected cell size: 1532.00

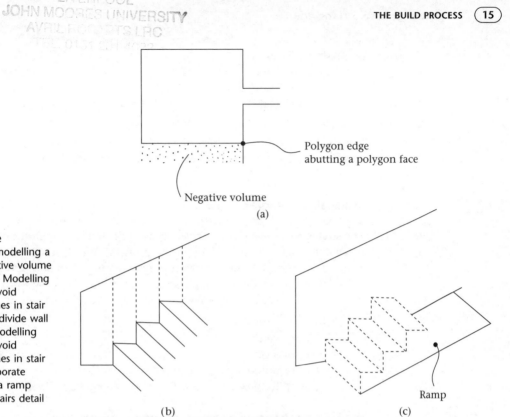

Polygon edge
abutting a polygon face

Negative volume

(a)

Figure 1.5
Convex volume
constraints in modelling a
level. (a) Negative volume
generation. (b) Modelling
constraint to avoid
negative volumes in stair
structure – subdivide wall
polygon. (c) Modelling
constraint to avoid
negative volumes in stair
structure – elaborate
structure with a ramp
and give the stairs detail
status.

(b)

(c)

Ramp

Figure 1.6
A level modelled so as to
produce no negative
nodes.

BSP statistics

BSP sectors:	7
No. of leaf faces:	637
No. of leafs:	131 (131 positive side, 0 negative side)
No. of nodes:	375

Negative nodes can be either tolerated or deleted. If we intend to construct a closed level, they represent volumes of space into which the player can never go.

1.2.3 Processing complex landscapes

The strategy we have just described is also sufficient to cope with complex landscape data. Figure 1.7 (also Colour Plate) shows a fly through a landscape with a high (for current games practice) polygon count (133,000 polygons). This is part of the surface of Mars and is rendered from NASA data. Also shown are the contents of a single subdivision cell. The statistics for this example are:

Data

No. of vertices:	400866
No. of faces:	133622
No. of unique planes required to contain the faces:	108325
Bounding box size:	400000.00 400000.00 40235.29

Figure 1.7
(a) A complex landscape – part of the Martian surface.

(a)

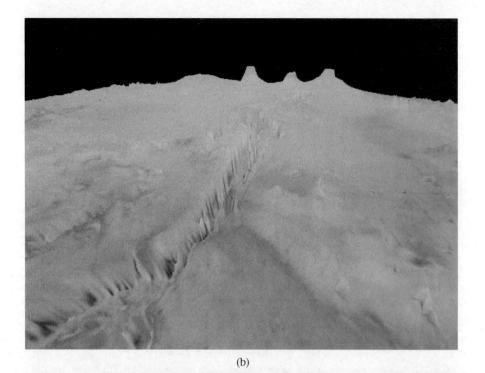

(b)

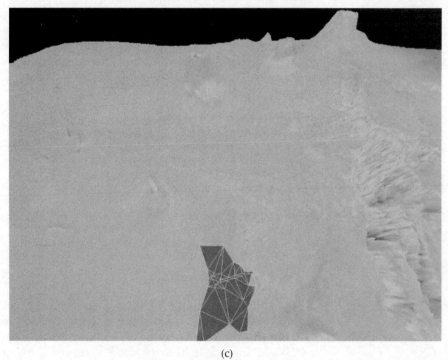

Figure 1.7 *continued*
(b) A closer view showing
the high level of detail.
(c) The contents of a
single BSP sector.

(c)

Selected cell size:	20000.00

BSP statistics

BSP sectors:	1014 (= no of leaves in the case of a landscape)
No. of leaf faces:	149188
No. of leaves:	1014 (509 positive side, 505 negative side)
No. of nodes:	1013

Note that in this case the number of BSP sectors is now equal to the number of leaves. The landscape contains no natural structure that we can use as structural elements and so we choose a cell size much smaller than the scene dimension, resulting in 10^3 sectors.

Another elaboration necessary for landscapes is to consider the representation of the contents of a single BSP sector or cell (Figure 1.7(c)). We could proceed as before and apply the standard strategy but this is extremely wasteful. In effect we have to consider individual landscape triangles as structural faces for splitting. By definition, structural faces cannot share vertices and we would end up storing three times as many vertices as faces – a very large number in our Mars example. This is shown in the above statistics where there are 400×10^3 vertices for 133×10^3 faces. To solve this problem we can consider the triangles in each sector to be a triangle mesh (face type 3). This means that we can make all triangles within a sector share their vertices, drastically reducing the number of vertices within a sector. For example, in a regular grid (ignoring borders) each vertex is shared by six faces. However, in the case of a landscape with different texture maps in the same sector, a vertex accessing different texture maps cannot be collapsed. In this case we have to construct as many faces in a sector as there are texture maps. Each face will contain all the triangles belonging to the sector and having the same material.

The statistics for the sample landscape with this elaboration are:

BSP statistics

BSP sectors:	1014 (= no of leaves in the case of a landscape)
No. of leaf faces:	1014
No. of leaves:	1014 (509 positive side, 505 negative side)
No. of nodes:	1013
No. of vertices:	92546
No. of faces:	1014

reducing the number of faces per leaf to 1 and reducing the number of vertices by a large factor.

Faces in BSP leaf nodes

Finally we consider how the faces contained in the BSP tree are to be processed. Each BSP leaf node includes a list of the faces associated with it. One face can be present in more than one BSP leaf node because partitioning planes crossed it. When drawing, lighting or colliding using the BSP tree, we need to mark the faces already processed (drawn, intersected, . . .) so that when testing another leaf, we do not repeat the computation in the same face more than once.

⟨1.2.5⟩

Finding leaf convex volumes

We now come to discuss the motivation for convex volumes. An important element of the previously described BSP strategy is the creation of closed convex volumes. In descending the tree from root to any leaf node we have, from each node, a set of planes which form themselves into a convex volume. This volume is formed both by the structural elements such as level walls and splitting planes (which may cross empty space). Nevertheless we have guaranteed, through modelling constraints, say, that such volumes exist and are convex and closed. We can use these volumes for the vitally important process of PVS calculation and also as a basis for path planning.

For PVS calculations and path planning we need to explicitly find the convex volume associated with each leaf node. That is, we have to find the polygons that make up the convex volume. This is straightforward and proceeds in four stages:

(1) Find the planes that form the convex volume.

(2) Find the vertices of the intersection of these planes.

(3) Find the vertices that contribute to each face.

(4) Order the vertices to define the polygons.

The first step is to find those planes that contain the convex volume faces. These are easily obtained by traversing the tree from the leaf to the root and collecting every node plane. The next step is to find the vertices of the convex volume which are formed by the intersection of these planes. To do this we form every possible combination of three planes in the set. These are then examined in turn to find those planes that intersect at a point. Such intersection points are potential vertices. The potential vertices are then tested to see if they belong to the convex volume. Figure 1.8(a) shows how this is done: a potential vertex is tested against all other planes in the set and is verified as a vertex if the distance to all other planes in the set is positive.

The following code finds the convex volume vertices that form the planes. For every leaf there is an array of planes. The plane normal of each of the three selected planes is stored in a 3×3 matrix. Each plane is defined by its normal N_x, N_y, N_z and its displacement D. To find the intersection we need to solve the following equation:

$$\begin{bmatrix} N1_x & N1_y & N1_z \\ N2_x & N2_y & N2_z \\ N3_x & N3_y & N3_z \end{bmatrix} \begin{bmatrix} x \\ y \\ z \end{bmatrix} = \begin{bmatrix} D1 \\ D2 \\ D3 \end{bmatrix}$$

using a matrix inversion.

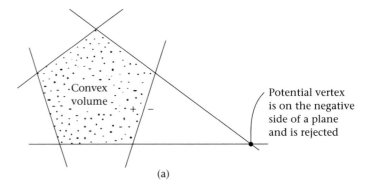

(a)

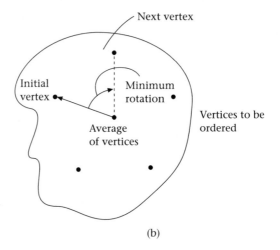

Figure 1.8
Finding the polygons that
make up a leaf convex
volume.

(b)

```
void flyEngineBuild::build_leaf_vertices()
{
   int p[3],n,i;
   flyVector mat[3],m[3],v;
   float f1,f2;

   #define MAT_DET(mat)
(mat[0][0]*mat[1][1]*mat[2][2]+mat[0][1]*mat[1][2]*mat[2][0]+mat[0]
[2]*mat[1][0]*mat[2] [1]-mat[0][0]*mat[1][2]*mat[2][1]-
mat[0][1]*mat[1][0]*mat[2][2]-mat[0][2]*mat[1][1]*mat[2][0])

   for( n=0;n<nleaf;n++ )
   {
      for( p[0]=0;p[0]<leafplanes[n].num-2;p[0]++ )
      for( p[1]=p[0]+1;p[1]<leafplanes[n].num-1;p[1]++ )
      for( p[2]=p[1]+1;p[2]<leafplanes[n].num;p[2]++ )
      {
         mat[0]=leafplanes[n][p[0]].normal;
         mat[1]=leafplanes[n][p[1]].normal;
         mat[2]=leafplanes[n][p[2]].normal;
         f1=MAT_DET(mat);
```

```
    if(f1>=-0.01f && f1<=0.01f)
      continue;
    for( i=0;i<3;i++ )
    {
       m[0]=mat[0]; m[1]=mat[1]; m[2]=mat[2];
       m[0][i]=leafplanes[n][p[0]].d0;
       m[1][i]=leafplanes[n][p[1]].d0;
       m[2][i]=leafplanes[n][p[2]].d0;
       f2=MAT_DET(m);
       v[i]=f2/f1;
    }
    for( i=0;i<leafverts[n].num;i++ )
      if ((v-leafverts[n][i]).length2()<0.01f)
        break;
    if (i<leafverts[n].num)
      continue;
    for( i=0;i<leafplanes[n].num;i++ )
      if (leafplanes[n][i].distance(v)<-0.01f)
        break;
    if (i<leafplanes[n].num)
      continue;
    leafverts[n].add(v);
  }
 }
}
```

Having built a list of vertices we now have to find the polygons formed by these vertices; in other words, find what vertices belong to each plane. Finally, finding the ordering of each vertex set defines each convex volume polygon. This final process is demonstrated in Figure 1.8(b). To find each ordering we:

(1) calculate the average of the vertices. Because we know that each polygon is convex, the average of the vertices must be a point contained within the polygon;

(2) define a vector from this average to any of the vertices. The next vertex in the sequence is given by that vertex which defines the minimum rotation of the vector.

The following code implements the ordering of a set of unordered vertices forming a convex polygon. It uses the notion of a clockwise dot product that returns a value from –3 to 1 (Figure 1.9).

```
float clockwise_dot(const flyVector &v1,const flyVector &v2,const
flyVector &normal)
{
   float dot=FLY_VECDOT(v1,v2),f;
   flyVector v;
   v.cross(v1,v2);
   f=FLY_VECDOT(v,normal);

   if(FLY_FPSIGNBIT(f))
     dot=-dot-2;
```

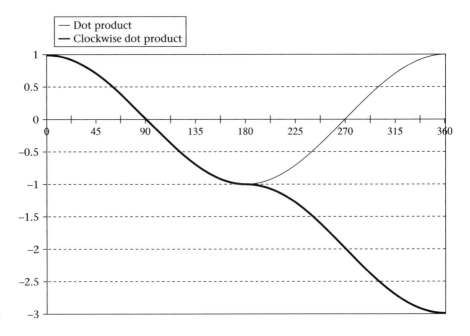

Figure 1.9
A 'clockwise' dot product.

```
    return dot;
}

void flyPolygon::order_verts()
{
    int i,j,next;
    float maxdot,f;
    flyVector centre,v0,v1;

    // find polygon center
    centre.null();
    for(i=0;i<verts.num;i++)
        centre+=verts[i];
    centre*=1.0f/verts.num;

    // find vector for first vertex
    v0=verts[0]-centre;
    v0.normalize();

    // for every other vertex
    for(i=0;i<verts.num-2;i++)
    {
        // find vertex with biggest clockwise dotproduct
        maxdot=-4.0f;
        next=-1;
        for(j=i+1;j<verts.num;j++)
        {
            v1=verts[j]-centre;
            v1.normalize();
            if((f=clockwise_dot(v0,v1,normal))>maxdot)
            {
```

```
                maxdot=f;
                next=j;
            }
        }

        // swap vertex to correct order
        flyVertex aux=verts[i+1];
        verts[i+1]=verts[next];
        verts[next]=aux;
    }
}
```

Convex volumes and pseudo-portals

The convex volumes of the BSP tree can be further exploited during the build process to provide a structure, such as a directed graph, which can be used by a path planner. Such an AI method is required by an autonomous agent navigating a level. The basic idea is to find 'pseudo-portals' that connect adjacent volumes. A pseudo-portal represents a clear path between two convex volumes. Consider Figure 1.10 which shows a very simple level divided into three convex volumes. The plane separating region A from regions B and C contains both walls and a pseudo-portal. Examples of pseudo-portals from a games level are shown in Figure 1.11 (also Colour Plate).

The problem is thus defined as: find the sub-area of such planes that form a pseudo-portal.

We can proceed as follows:

> **for** each convex volume
>> **for** each face in the convex volume
>>> **if** this face is in the same plane of any face from any other convex volume
>>>> check for 2D intersection between these two faces
>>>> **if** an intersection exists then this defines a pseudo-portal
>>>>> add to the directed graph
>>>>> continue to next face
>>> the face must be a wall and can be eliminated

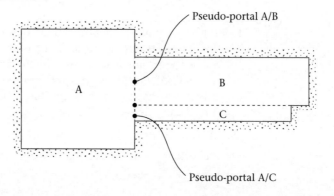

Figure 1.10
Convex volumes and pseudo-portals.

(a)

Figure 1.11
(a) Showing pseudo-portals in an open space in a level. The multiplicity of portal faces is due to the BSP grid size setting which generates convex volumes whose clear connecting faces are shown. (b) In this example the pseudo-portal planes coincide with a real portal.

(b)

Checking for a face being contained within the plane of another is reasonably straightforward. We need to consider the plane offsets and normals, bearing in mind that two planes can be coincident with opposite normals.

```
int test_coplanar(flyPolygon &p1,flyPolygon &p2)
{
   float dot=FLY_VECDOT(p1.normal,p2.normal);
   if(dot>0.999f && (float)fabs(p1.d0+p2.d0)<0.01f)
     return TRUE;
   return FALSE;
}
```

Finding the intersection polygon of two convex polygons is more difficult. The two polygons are in the same plane and we can thus project into a plane to reduce the problem to a two-dimensional one. We require the maximum area projection and this is achieved by finding which of the three normal components (x,y,z) has the greater absolute value and dropping this component.

To find the intersection in 2D we have to find:

(1) all vertices from the first polygon that are inside the second polygon;

(2) all vertices from the second polygon that are inside the first polygon;

(3) all edge intersections.

This gives an unordered set of points that is the intersection polygon vertices. The vertex ordering method of the previous section can then be applied to find the polygon itself. Certain difficulties need to be considered to make the algorithm sufficiently robust. These are:

(1) Polygons that are perfectly coincident must generate a valid polygon.

(2) Polygons that are connected by a coincident edge should not produce a degenerate polygon – the algorithm must return zero intersection.

To solve these problems we must incorporate thresholds in the containment tests. The first problem is addressed as follows. When testing if a point is inside a polygon the distance from the point to all the polygon edges must be considered. We can only accept a point for containment if its distance passes a threshold test. Also when adding vertices to the output polygon list we must check if the vertex is not already part of the list. The second problem is in effect the inverse of the first and we use the threshold tests in the opposite sense.

The edge intersection problem is similar to that of the collision detection edge intersection (Section 2.4.3) except that now the two edges are static. In this case we need to intersect two line segments (two polygon edges) in 2D. This is accomplished by the following two tests.

(1) If the product of the distance of each vertex, of one edge, to the other edge is positive then they cannot intersect. This means that the two vertices are on the same side of the (infinite) line containing the other edge.

(2) The same test but now for the other edge.

(3) If both these tests succeed then there is an intersection.

Figure 1.12 shows the three cases. (p_1, p_2) and (p_3, p_4) are two edges, each of which is an edge from one of the intersecting polygons. We can proceed as follows:

Distances from vertices to edge
$d_1 = p_2 - p_1$;
$d_2 = p_3 - p_4$;

Define lines containing the edges
Line 1: $p_1 + dist_1 * d_1$
Line 2: $p_3 + dist_2 * d_2$

Solve for $dist_1$
$dist_1 = (d_2.x*(p_1.y - p_3.y) - d_2.y*(p_1.x - p_3.x))/(d_2.y*d_1.x - d_2.x*d_1.y)$;

Find the intersection point
Intersection point: $p_1 + dist_1 * d_1$

The following code integrates these methods and consists of the following:

(1) intersection test for two polygons;

(2) containment test for vertices;

(3) edge intersection tests.

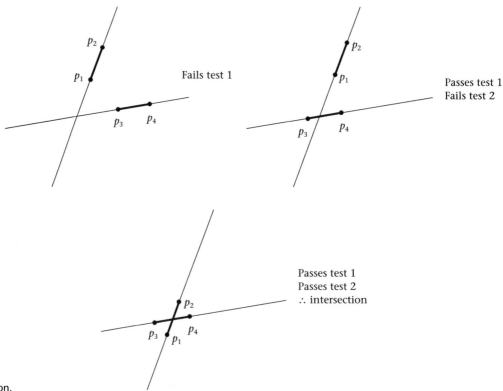

Figure 1.12
Edge intersection.

```
int flyPolygon::intersect(flyPolygon &in, flyPolygon &out)
{
    // clear output polygon
    out.verts.clear();

    // find vertices from polygon in that are inside current polygon
    build_edgeplanes();
    intersect_verts(in,out);

    // find vertices from current polygon that are inside polygon in
    in.build_edgeplanes();
    in.intersect_verts(*this,out);

    // find all intersections from edges of the current polygon
    // with edges from the in polygon
    intersect_edges(in,out);

    // return number of vertices in output polygon
    // >2 means a valid polygon
    return out.verts.num;
}
```

```
int flyPolygon::intersect_verts(const flyPolygon &in, flyPolygon &out)
{
   int i,j,k;

   // for all vertices from in polygon
   for(i=0;i<in.verts.num;i++)
   {
      // test if distance to current polygon edges is smaller then
threshold
      // (edge plane normal points inside polygon)
      for(j=0;j<edgeplanes.num;j++)
         if(edgeplanes[j].distance(in.verts[i])<-0.1f)
            break;
      // if passed all above tests, vertex is inside current polygon
      if(j==edgeplanes.num)
      {
         // test if vertex is not already in output list
         for(k=0;k<out.verts.num;k++)
            if((out.verts[k]-in.verts[i]).length2()<0.1f)
               break;
         // if not in output list, add it
         if(k==out.verts.num)
            out.verts.add(in.verts[i]);
      }
   }

   return out.verts.num;
}

int flyPolygon::intersect_edges(const flyPolygon &in, flyPolygon &out)
{
   int i,j,k,a,b;
   float f1,f2;
   flyVector p1,p2,d1,d2;

   // for every edge from current polygon
   for(i=0;i<verts.num;i++)
      // for every edge from in polygon
      for(j=0;j<in.verts.num;j++)
      {
         // test1: check if in edge vertices are on same plane
         // of current polygon edge
         f1=edgeplanes[i].distance(in.verts[j]);
         f2=edgeplanes[i].distance(in.verts[(j+1)%in.verts.num]);
         if((f1*f2)>-0.1f)
            continue;

         // test2: check if current edge vertices are on
         // same plane of in polygon edge
         f1=in.edgeplanes[j].distance(verts[i]);
         f2=in.edgeplanes[j].distance(verts[(i+1)%verts.num]);
         if((f1*f2)>-0.1f)
            continue;

         // passed test 1 and test2: intersection exists
```

```
        // compute edge vector d1
        p1=verts[i];
        d1=verts[(i+1)%verts.num]-p1;
        d1.normalize();

        // compute edge vector d2
        p2=in.verts[j];
        d2=in.verts[(j+1)%in.verts.num]-p2;
        d2.normalize();

        // project onto maximum area plane
        if (fabs(normal.x)>fabs(normal.y)) a=0; else a=1;
        if (fabs(normal[a])<fabs(normal.z)) a=2;
        if (a==0) { a=1; b=2; } else
        if (a==1) { a=0; b=2; } else { a=0; b=1; }

        // compute distance of intersection
        float dist= (d2[a]*(p1[b]-p2[b])-d2[b]*(p1[a]-p2[a]))/
                (d2[b]*d1[a]-d2[a]*d1[b]);

        // compute intersection point
        p1+=dist*d1;

        // test if vertex in not already in output list
        for(k=0;k<out.verts.num;k++)
          if((out.verts[k]-p1).length2()<0.1f)
            break;
        // if not in output list, add it
        if(k==out.verts.num)
          out.verts.add(p1);
    }

  return out.verts.num;
}
```

A simple real-time method that uses this structure for path planning is given in the next chapter.

1.2.7 Potentially Visible Set

Having built a set of convex volumes we can easily use these to define the PVS. This is just a square connectivity matrix of dimension *no. of leaves* where the binary element $(i,j) = 1$ indicates that leaf i is connected to leaf j; meaning that if we are positioned in leaf i then leaf j is potentially visible. BSP trees on their own only facilitate a visibility ordering from a leaf. This set contains all polygons in the scene. When a BSP tree is used in rendering we traverse the tree with the viewpoint to find the leaf faces clipped by the view frustum, then use the PVS connectivity matrix to take out all other leaves that are not potentially visible.

The most straightforward approach to PVS evaluation is to use some approach based on sample points. Whatever algorithm is used, PVS calculations need to consider sample points within a volume and see if any sample points in other volumes are visible. Although efficiency is not critical in the build process, PVS calculations, if not optimised, take an extremely long time. If we consider n samples/volume and m volumes, then the worst-case calculation (no volume can see any other volume) is $O((nm)^2)$. A critical design factor, then, is the construction of a set of sampling points for each convex volume.

To build the PVS we can use the pseudo-portals of the convex volumes. To do this we set up samples across the face of the test pseudo-portal and use ray intersect to see if any points on any pseudo-portal of any other volumes are visible. Consider Figure 1.13 which shows four convex volumes A, B, C and D. In the figure B is an immediate neighbour to A and thus B is visible to A. To test the visibility of C from A we construct rays from a sample point of a pseudo-portal belonging to volume A to a sample point of the pseudo-portal between B and C. In this example rays from the A/B pseudo-portal reach pseudo-portal B/C. C is thus potentially visible from A. Now the visibility of A/D is tested; any ray from A to D will collide and so D is not visible to A. Embedding this approach in a recursive structure will then, for volume A, find all the potentially visible volumes.

To sample the pseudo-portals we use a random set of sample points. For the same number of samples, a well-distributed set of random points will give a result closer to a complete deterministic solution than a set of uniformly spaced points. The number of points generated for a polygon needs to be a function of the polygon's area. Random points within a polygon are generated by calculating a random point inside the polygon bounding box and projecting it into the polygon plane. We then need to test if the point is contained within the polygon and, if not, generate a new random sample. This test needs to be

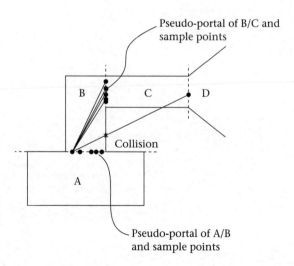

Figure 1.13
Three convex volumes A, B and C and their portals.

further elaborated to prevent points being generated coincident with a polygon edge where collision test precision errors could occur.

To prevent a combinatorial explosion the recursion needs to be carefully structured. Every leaf node needs its visibility to be computed and the same algorithm is applied independently to each one.

Main pseudo-code:

> for every leaf node
>> create list with immediate neighbours of current node
>> call recursion passing current node and the neighbours list

Recursion pseudo-code:

> create a new list with all neighbours of all leaf nodes in passed list

> for every node in the new list,
>> test its visibility against the original leaf node
>> if not visible, remove it from the new list

> if new list is not empty, recurse passing the original leaf and new list of neighbours

```
void flyEngineBuild::compute_visibility()
{
  int i,j,k;
  // set all pvs bits to not visible (0)
  memset(pvs,0,pvssize);

  // create flag array and neighbours list
  flags=new char[nleaf];
  flyArray<flyBspNodeBuild *> list;

  // for every leaf node
  for( i=0;i<nleaf;i++ )
  {
    // set node self visibility to 1 (pvs matrix diagonal)
    pvs[i*pvsrowsize+(i>>3)] =1<<(i&7);

    // clear flag array and set current leaf node
    memset(flags,0,nleaf);
    flags[i]=1;

    // for every neighbour, set it as visible and add it to the list
    for( j=0;j<leaf[i]->neighbors.num;j++ )
    {
      k=leaf[i]->neighbors[j]->leaf;
      pvs[i*pvsrowsize+(k>>3)] =1<<(k&7);
      flags[k]=1;
      list.add((flyBspNodeBuild *)leaf[i]->neighbors[j]);
    }
```

```
        // recurse computing visibility
        compute_visibility(i,list);
    }

    // free flags
    delete[] flags;
}

void flyEngineBuild::compute_visibility(int
leafnum,flyArray<flyBspNodeBuild *> &list)
{
    int i,j,k,n,l;
    flyArray<flyBspNodeBuild *> list2;

    // create new list with all neighbours from all nodes
    // in received list that have not been already used
    for( n=0;n<list.num;n++ )
    for( i=0;i<list[n]->neighbors.num;i++ )
    {
        j=list[n]->neighbors[i]->leaf;
        if (flags[j]==0)
        {
            list2.add((flyBspNodeBuild *)leaf[j]);
            flags[j]=1;
        }
    }

    // for every node in the new list
    for( i=0;i<list2.num;i++ )
    {
        // for every node in original list
        for( j=0;j<list.num;j++ )
        {
            // test for a connecting portal between the two nodes
            for( k=0;k<list[j]->neighbors.num;k++ )
                if (list[j]->neighbors[k]==list2[i])
                    break;
            if (k<list[j]->neighbors.num)
            {
                // if a portal is found, test its visibility against
                // all portals from original node
                l=list[j]->leaf;
                for( n=0;n<leaf[leafnum]->neighbors.num;n++ )
                    if (test_visibility(leafnum,n,l,k))
                        break;
                if (n<leaf[leafnum]->neighbors.num)
                    break;
            }

        }
        if (j==list.num)
        {
```

```
        // if no portals leading to new list node are visible
        // remove it from the new list as it is not used
        flags[list2[i]->leaf]=0;
        list2.remove(i--);
      }
      else
      {
        // if any portal leading to the new list node
        // set it as visible in the pvs matrix
        j=list2[i]->leaf;
        pvs[leafnum*pvsrowsize+(j>>3)]|=1<<(j&7);
      }
    }

    // if new list is not empty, recurse using the new list
    if (list2.num)
      compute_visibility(leafnum,list2);
}

int flyEngineBuild::test_visibility(int leafnum,int portalnum,int
testleaf,int testportal)
{
    // return true if portal (leafnum,portalnum) can see
    // portal (testleaf,testportal)

    // compute portal areas
    float a1=leaf[leafnum]->portals[portalnum].area();
    float a2=leaf[testleaf]->portals[testportal].area();

    // compute number of random sample points in each portal as a
function of area
    int i1,i2,j1,j2;
    j1=(int)(a1/pvsgridsize)+1;
    j2=(int)(a2/pvsgridsize)+1;

    // ray intersect all portal sample points
    flyVector v1,v2;
    for( i1=0;i1<j1;i1++ )
      for( i2=0;i2<j2;i2++ )
      {
        leaf[leafnum]->portals[portalnum].random_point(v1);
        leaf[testleaf]->portals[testportal].random_point(v2);

        // if any ray does not have a collision
        if (0==collision_test(v1,v2,FLY_TYPE_STATICMESH))
          // portals are visible to each other, return true
          return 1;
      }

    // portals are not visible, all rays collided, return false
    return 0;
}
```

Figure 1.14 shows a rendered view of a level together with two corresponding wireframes – with and without PVS.

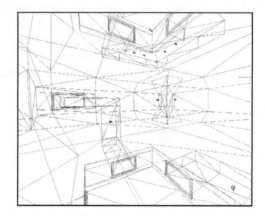

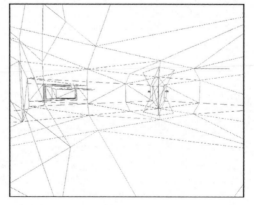

Figure 1.14
Three views of the same
room – rendered,
wireframe without PVS
and wireframe with PVS.

Light map build

The use of light maps to store pre-calculated lighting was one of the enabling technologies of 3D games. Caching the illumination in a light map means that we can use texture mapping hardware to light static levels. The light map build process is separated into three distinct phases:

(1) generating the light map coordinates;

(2) packing the light maps into large maps;

(3) illuminating the light maps by applying a reflection model.

Generating the light map coordinates

To generate the light map coordinates we proceed as follows. For every face we consider the plane that contains it and in this plane, find the bounding box for the face. A plane coincident with the face is the best strategy. We need some projection from the face in 3D space into 2D space. A coincident plane means that the projected area of the face in the light map is equal to the area of the face. Thus the calculated light is cached at the highest accuracy. The texture coordinates for the light map are then defined (Figure 1.15) as:

$$t_{cx} = \frac{v_{1x} - p_{1x}}{p_{2x} - p_{1x}}$$

$$t_{cy} = \frac{v_{1y} - p_{1y}}{p_{2y} - p_{1y}}$$

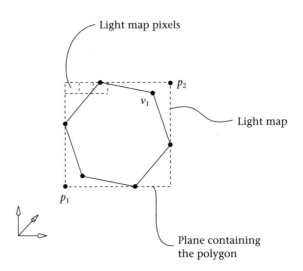

Figure 1.15
A polygon, its containing plane and light map pixels.

Light map pixels

p_2

v_1

Light map

p_1

Plane containing
the polygon

These need to be further refined because individual light maps are packed (next section) into large maps. We need to use hardware texture filtering for the light maps otherwise the light map pixel boundaries will be visible in the final rendered image. This means that we have to ensure that when a light map pixel is being filtered the hardware does not include in the filter process pixels for a neighbouring light map. This can be done by 'shrinking' the coordinates slightly so that for each light map there is a $1/2$ pixel region around the border. Thus:

$$t_c = \frac{t_c(s-1)}{s} + \frac{1}{2s}$$

where
  s is the (x or y) dimension of the light map

Light map packing

Effective light map packing into larger texture maps is an important optimisation. The strategy described generates as many light maps as there are faces and having a large number of small textures will require a lot of texture swapping when drawing. Packing many light maps into a single large texture will reduce the number of texture swaps to a minimum.

This is the classic bin-packing problem – pack the largest remaining material into the largest available space. A good algorithm is shown in Figure 1.16. It is as follows:

Figure 1.16
Visualisation of the light map packing algorithm.

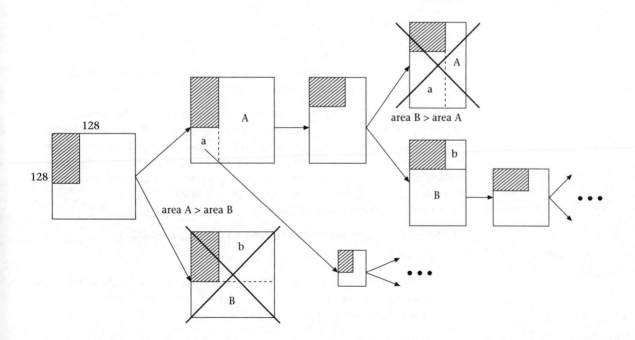

(1) Sort the light maps by area.

(2) Initialise a working area at (usually 128×128 pixels).

(3) Loop through the sorted list and place the largest available map that fits into the working area. If no light map fits into the current working area, go to step 2.

(4) The map inserted defines two remaining areas in the current working area:

> A defined by the right-hand edge of the map until the end of the area;
> B defined by the bottom side of the map until the end of the area.

(5) Recurse in the larger of the two areas A or B by calling item 3.

(6) Recurse in the smaller area of the previous recursion (area a if previous recursion was A and area b if previous recursion was B) by calling item 3.

Illuminating light maps

Illuminating the light map means applying the lighting model to cache the illumination. Light maps can accept any view-independent lighting model including radiosity. It is a method for caching the illumination and is independent of how the illumination is calculated. We must also find if the faces are in shadow and reduce the illumination. The process begins by recursing the BSP tree with every light reference coordinate to find, for each light, the faces within its sphere of influence. Then for every (face) light map we proceed as:

> **for each** pixel in the light map
>   **if** pixel is inside the polygon
>   find the pixel's world coordinates
>   apply ray intersect collision detection from pixel to light
>   **if** no intersection apply light reflection model

Shadows appear because all light maps are initialised to the ambient light. Applying the light model raises the illumination above the ambient (shadow) level. For soft shadows the light centre is randomly perturbed within a radius to define a number of light sample points. Each of these is used in a ray collision detection and a light value for the light map pixel is computed by weighting the calculated intensity by the number of collisions.

Simple light models are as follows:

(1) linear or square law attenuation based on distance;

(2) **L.N** shading together with distance attenuation.

In the engine each light can be configured with any combination of the above models. Using different light modes produces different atmospheres. The same level lit with two different maps is shown in Figure 1.17 (also Colour Plate).

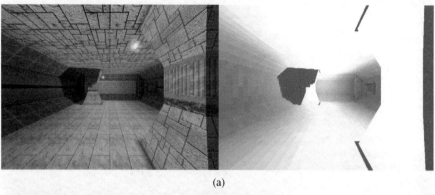

(a)

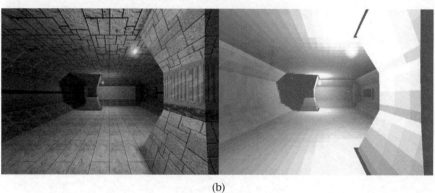

(b)

Figure 1.17
(a) Illuminating the light map – square law attenuation (texture filtering turned off to enable the light map pixels to be visualised). (b) Illuminating the light map – square law attenuation plus **L.N** (texture filtering turned off to enable the light map pixels to be visualised).

1.4   BSP management

Using BSP management in a games application is a well-established and extremely versatile method. As we have seen, it can be used both in the build process and in the game execution. During execution the BSP tree is recursed at least once for viewing and rendering. Other recursions are caused by dynamic lights which need to find the light map faces to illuminate. Collision detection makes most use of the BSP, a recursion being called for every ray intersect (Section 1.4.1). It is this generality of usage that has made the approach popular and enduring. In this section we will look at advanced extensions whose aim is to generalise the approach.

1.4.1   Generic recursion methods

We now return to BSP management to consider the best way to recurse the tree for different functions. We call this approach generic recursion. Another significant problem with BSP management is dynamic objects. Large dynamic objects can range over several leaf nodes and cause problems. For example,

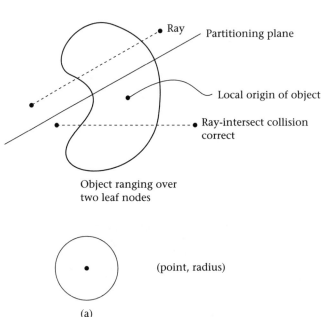

Figure 1.18
Ray intersect collision
detection and large
objects.

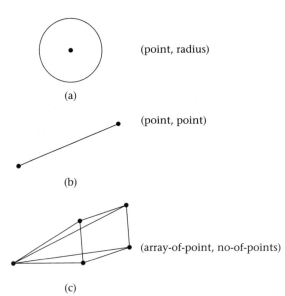

Figure 1.19
Generic recursion modes.

consider the situation in Figure 1.18. A large object is clipped by a partitioning plane and its local origin can only occupy a single partition. A collision ray wholly in the upper region and intersecting the object will not return a collision using a simple ray intersect approach. This problem also occurs with dynamic lights and drawing. The best way to deal with all the problems that are thrown up by entities appearing in more than one leaf node is to use generic recursion methods.

When recursing a BSP tree we are always asking the question: which subset of leaf nodes are contained within the space of the object? For example, in the case of collision detection we recurse the BSP tree with a ray to find the nodes that include potentially colliding objects. Now consider Figure 1.19. This shows three ways of selecting nodes from the BSP tree. The first is a sphere represented

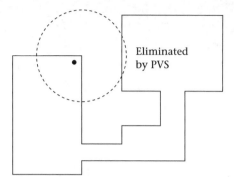

Eliminated
by PVS

Figure 1.20
Dynamic light and generic
recursion. The room that
cannot see the light is
eliminated by the PVS.

by a point and a radius. All BSP leaf nodes that the sphere clips are selected by the recursion. In the second case – a ray – two points are used to select all the leaf nodes the line segment clips. The third case is a generalisation of the second case where we pass any number of points and find all clip nodes that the represented volume clips. For example, a common represented object in this category is a view frustum.

Thus generic recursion is a method that recurses the BSP tree from the root node with selection mechanisms defined by one of the options in Figure 1.19. For every node that the mechanism selects we can test for PVS connectivity if required. This is extremely useful for render recursions with the view frustum or a sphere of influence. Figure 1.20 shows a simple level plan. A dynamic light positioned as shown with a certain radius of influence would find nodes representing two rooms. The room that cannot see the light is eliminated from its influence by the PVS.

Efficient implementation of generic recursion

Two issues arise when considering the implementation of a generic recursion method. First, the method can operate in different modes, as illustrated in Figure 1.21. This shows four of the six modes of operation which are made from three modes to which the PVS can be applied. The three basic modes are as follows:

- Recurse the BSP and select only leaf nodes clipping the specified selection object (can be sphere, line segment or list of points). Returns a list of leaf nodes.
- Recurse the BSP and select all objects included in the leaf nodes clipping the specified selection object. Returns a list of objects.
- Recurse the BSP and select all objects of a certain type included in the leaf nodes clipping the specified selection object. Returns a list of objects of the same type.

When a PVS leaf node is passed with any of these modes, the selected leaf nodes are tested for PVS occlusion before further consideration.

Figure 1.21
Generic BSP recursion:
four examples. (a) Recurse
and return only leaf
nodes clipping the
selected object, e.g.
`recurse_BSP (point,`
`radius, -1, -1).`
(b) Recurse and return
all objects in leaf
nodes clipping the
selected object, e.g.
`recurse_BSP (point,`
`radius, 0, -1).` (c) as
(b) but returns objects of
a specified type, e.g.
`recurse_BSP (point,`
`radius, object-type,`
`-1).` (d) as (c) but with
PVS, e.g. `recurse_BSP`
`(point, radius,`
`object-type,`
`current_PVS_leaf_`
`node).`

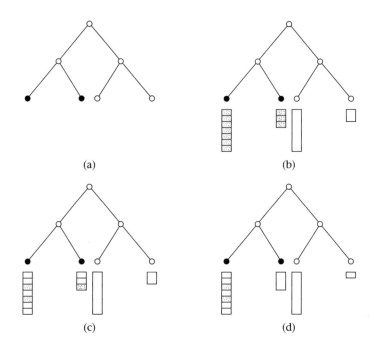

(a)   (b)

(c)   (d)

The most efficient way to implement this method is not by using a normal recursion but instead by using a simple push/pop pointer stack. This eliminates the normal overheads associated with using recursive function calls.

The following definitions are used for fast floating point tests (using integers). These exploit certain strategies inherent in the nature of the tests. They treat the bit representation of a float as if it were an integer. For example, when testing for zero, the floating point bit representation is all zeros – the same as an integer zero. When testing the sign of a float only a single bit needs testing.

```
#define  FLY_FPBITS(fp)      (*(int *)&(fp))
#define  FLY_FPABSBITS(fp)   (FP_BITS(fp)&0x7FFFFFFF)
#define  FLY_FPSIGNBIT(fp)   (FP_BITS(fp)&0x80000000)
#define  FLY_FPONEBITS       0x3F800000
```

The following definition is used to test a bit from the PVS matrix. This determines whether a node is visible from another node. The *from* parameter is the leaf node index of the origin node. The *to* parameter is the leaf node index of the node to be tested to see if it is visible from the *from* leaf node.

```
#define  FLY_PVS_TEST(from,to)  \
   (*(pvs + (from)*pvsrowsize + ((to)>>3)) & (1 << ((to) & 7)))
```

We now consider the general recursion method. A pseudo-code implementation of the recursive method for a sphere of influence is:

```
recurse_bsp( point, radius, objtype, pvsnode )
{
  clear selection list

  push(bsp root node)

  while (stack is not empty)
  {
    node = pop_node()
    if (node is leaf)
    {
      if (pvsnode no equal to -1 or PVS_TEST(pvsnode,node))
      {
        add node to slection list

        if (objtype not equal to -1)
          if (objtype equal to 0)
            add all objects in node to selection list
          else
            add all objects in node with type objtype
            to selection list
      }
    }
    else
    {
      dist = distance from point to node plane

      if (abs(dist)<radius)
      {
        push(node child 0)
        push(node child 1)
      }
      else
      {
        if (dist>0)
          push(node child 0)
        else
          push(node child 1)
      }
    }
  }
}
```

The following method is the full code that recurses the BSP tree using a sphere. The sphere is defined by the point *p* and the radius *rad*. If *elemtype* is set to −1, the recursion only selects the leaf nodes that the sphere clips. If *elemtype* is 0, all objects included in the selected leaf nodes are also returned (note that objects that may not be inside the sphere might be returned as they are inside a leaf node that is clipped by the sphere). If *elemtype* is > 0, only the objects with this type id will be selected.

```
void flyEngine::recurse_bsp(flyVector& p,float rad,int elemtype,int
pvsleaf)
{
   static flyBspNode *stack[64];
   flyBspNode *n;
   float d;
   int nstack=1;
   stack[0]=bsp;

   cur_bsprecurse++;
   nselnodes=0;
   nselobjs=0;
   while(nstack)
   {
      n=stack[--nstack];

      if (n->leaf!=-1)
      {
         if (pvsleaf==-1 || PVS_TEST(pvsleaf,n->leaf))
         {
            selnodes[nselnodes++]=n;
            if (elemtype!=-1)
            {
            flyBspObject **elem=&n->elem[0];
            for( int e=0;e<n->nelem;e++,elem++ )
               if ((elemtype==0 || (*elem)->type==elemtype) &&
                  (*elem)->lastbsprecurse!=cur_bsprecurse)
                  {
                     (*elem)->lastbsprecurse=cur_bsprecurse;
                     selobjs[nselobjs++]=(*elem);
                  }
            }
         }
      }
      else
      {
         d=n->distance(p);

         if (fabs(d)<rad)
            {
            if (FP_SIGN_BIT(d)==0)
               {
               if (n->child[1])
                  stack[nstack++]=n->child[1];
               if (n->child[0])
                  stack[nstack++]=n->child[0];
               }
            else
               {
               if (n->child[0])
                  stack[nstack++]=n->child[0];
               if (n->child[1])
                  stack[nstack++]=n->child[1];
               }
```

```
            }
        else
          if (FP_SIGN_BIT(d)==0)
          {
            if (n->child[0])
              stack[nstack++]=n->child[0];
          }
          else
          {
            if (n->child[1])
              stack[nstack++]=n->child[1];
          }
      }
    }
}
```

The expansion into the full code from the pseudo-code also includes front to back ordering.

Following is the pseudo-code for the other generic recursion methods using a line segment and list of points as selection objects:

```
recurse_bsp( point1, point2, objtype, pvsnode )
{
  clear selection list

  push(bsp root node)

  while (stack is not empty)
  {
    node = pop_node()

    if (node is leaf)
    {
      if (pvsnode not equal to -1 or PVS_TEST(pvsnode,node))
      {
        add node to selection list

        if (objtype not equal to -1)
          if (objtype equal to 0)
            add all objects in node to selection list
          else
            add all objects in node with type
            objtype to selection list
      }
    }
    else
    {
      dist1 = distance from point1 to node plane
      dist2 = distance from point2 to node plane

      if (dist1*dist2<0)
      {
```

```
          push(node child 0)
          push(node child 1)
        }
        else
        {
          if (dist1>0)
            push(node child 0)
          else
            push(node child 1)
        }
      }
    }
  }
}

recurse_bsp( points[], numpoints, objtype, pvsnode )
{
  clear selection list

  push(bsp root node)

  while (stack is not empty)
  {
    node = pop_node()

    if (node is leaf)
    {
      if (pvsnode not equal to -1 or PVS_TEST(pvsnode,node))
      {
        add node to slection list

        if (objtype not equal to -1)
          if (objtype equal to 0)
            add all objects in node to selection list
          else
            add all objects in node with type objtype
            to selection list
      }
    }
    else
    {
      dist0 = distance from points[0] to node plane

      for i = 1 to numpoints
      {
        dist = distance from points[i] to node plane
        if (dist1*dist2<0)
          break;
      }

      if (i<>numpoints)
      {
        push(node child 0)
        push(node child 1)
      }
      else
      {
```

```
          if (dist0>0)
             push(node child 0)
          else
             push(node child 1)
       }
     }
   }
}
```

Advanced static lighting – radiosity

This section needs to be read in conjunction with Appendix 1.2 which gives a basic treatment of classical radiosity theory.

In Section 1.3.3 we stated that since the build process was off-line, any lighting model could be used to assign light intensity values to light maps. Currently the highest quality lighting method available for diffuse environments is radiosity. This is used routinely in CAAD (Computer Aided Architectural Design) to construct accurate real-time walkthroughs for interiors that are lit by real lighting set-ups (as opposed to the normal computer graphics approximation of point light sources). However, the radiosity method is extremely time consuming and may add an unacceptable wait time to the build process. In this section we introduce a fast radiosity method that exploits the BSP/PVS set-up that we already have available.

The first question that should be addressed is: why use radiosity with its attendant time penalty? The answer is quality; although the difference in quality between a radiosity rendered environment and the same rendered with a simple (non-global) lighting model is small, it is precisely these small differences that the human eye is sensitive to. Because the radiosity method is a global illumination method, areas of the environment that cannot directly 'see' a light source have their reflected illumination correctly calculated, instead of being set to an (arbitrary) ambient component. Simple shadow algorithms, as we know, can only calculate the geometry of a shadow, not the value of the reflected light intensity within the shadow. The radiosity algorithm does not separate shadow calculations. Shadows 'emerge' from the algorithm – areas in shadow are no different to any other area in the environment and have their intensity set by the global nature of the method. Also, the graduation from an area in shadow to an area not in shadow is correctly rendered in the radiosity method. Simple shadow algorithms that deal only with the shadow geometry generally can only calculate hard-edged shadows. In the radiosity method lights themselves are treated no differently to other areas except that they possess a non-zero emissivity and this means that the implementation of an area light source becomes a part of the method.

The radiosity method is a world space algorithm which calculates the light intensity for every surface in the environment. The solution can then be cached in light maps. The algorithm computes a solution by dividing the environment into so-called patches, and in our games set-up it is convenient to use the light map pixels (more precisely their images in the 3D environment) as the patches.

An easy insight into the method is to imagine that we have a single patch functioning as a light source which we switch on to illuminate an initially dark environment. We can calculate all those patches in the environment that this initial patch can see, and according to a geometric relationship (known as a form factor) between the emitting patch and those it can see, we can transfer light energy to these patches. Thus after the first pass we have a number of patches that have received light and they themselves become emitters, reflecting the light they have received according to their own reflectivity coefficients. We continue this process until convergence, which is when there is no more light energy to consider. This comes about because, by definition, reflectivity coefficients are always less than one. (When a patch receives light energy it always emits less than the amount received.) In fact this explanation is just a simplification of the progressive refinement method detailed in Appendix 1.2.

Figure 1.22 (also Colour Plate) shows a radiosity solution for an extremely simple scene. The first image is rendered by considering the bare radiosity solution where the calculated radiosity value is constant across a lightmap pixel. In the second image the radiosity solution is subjected to bi-linear interpolation (Gouraud shading) which provides the final preferred solution. The images exhibit two important attributes of the radiosity method. First, the global nature of the solution is apparent. The only illumination is coming from the window; the wall that contains the window is receiving no direct illumination. It is illuminated by indirect illumination. Second, a phenomenon known as colour bleeding is apparent on the window wall. This means that the colour of the blocks 'bleeds' onto the wall which they indirectly illuminate.

Thus within such a simple iterative framework we have to include three calculations: an energy transfer calculation mediated by a form factor calculation and a method that evaluates the visibility between pairs of patches.[1] For the form factor calculation we make a (fairly unjustified) assumption that the form factor does not vary across the extent of a patch and use the formula (equation 1.1) without integrating. The correctness of this approximation depends on the size of the patches and their distance apart.

The energy transfer and form factor calculation can be implemented as:

```
emmitted_energy=E*pixel_area
form_factor=(dot1*dot2)/(2*PI*R^2)
transferred_energy=emmitted_energy*face_reflectance*factor
receiving_pixel_R += transferred_energy
receiving_pixel_E += transferred_energy
```

---

1. In the original classical radiosity algorithms of the 1980s, both the form factor calculation and the visibility problem were solved by an elegant device called a hemi-cube.

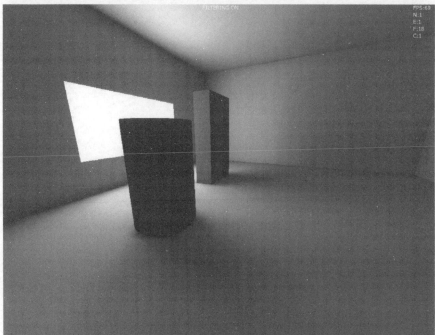

Figure 1.22
A simple environment illuminated using the radiosity method.

This is embedded in the following structure:

Inititialise all light map pixels
> R = 0 (R stores the accumulated energy for each pixel)
> E = emissive surface values (lights, windows etc.)

Calculate each light map's total energy (E pixels * area)
Calculate the total scene energy as sum of all light map totals
while total scene energy not yet emitted > threshold
> Find the light map with largest not yet emitted energy
> **for all** pixels in selected light map
>> Find pixel position and normal in scene space
>> Emit energy from pixel
>> Zeroise E for that pixel

Zeroise light map's total energy and subtract its energy from the total scene energy

When calculating those pixels that are visible from the currently emitting pixel we can invoke a PVS-based node selection and a (fast) ray intersection test (for efficiency, restricted to one ray intersect per emitter; in other words, partial visibility per pixel is not considered). This is an extremely simple implementation that suffers from high costs as the complexity of the scene increases. It is implemented using the following three methods:

```
Intensity(C) = grayscale value for color C

// main radiosity lighting
void flyEngineBuild::radiosity_lighting()
{
   int l,count=radmaxpasses;
   float f;
   printf("\n");
   while(count--)
   {
      l=find_lm(radminenergy);
      if (l==-1)
         break;

      f=Intensity(unshotenergy);
      printf("Radiosity energy left : %-12.2f (%5.1f%%)\r",
         f,100.0f-100.0f*f/starttotalenergy);

      if (((flyLightMapBuild *)lm[l])->emmit_light()==0)
         break;
   }
   printf("\n");
}

// finds light map with largest energy to emit
int flyEngineBuild::find_lm(float energy)
{
```

```
      int i,j=-1;
      flyVector v;
      float f;
      for( i=0;i<lm.num;i++ )
      {
        v=((flyLightMapBuild *)lm[i])->totalenergy;
        f=Intensity(v);
        if (f>energy)
        {
          energy=f;
          j=i;
        }
      }
      return j;
}

// emit light from all pixels in light map
int flyLightMapBuild::emmit_light()
{
   int x,y,i,j,k;
   flyVector p,n,energy;

   float fi=1.0f/sizex,fj=1.0f/sizey,fu,fv;

   flyBspNode *node;
   flyMesh *mesh;
   flyFace **face;
   float *f=emm;
   flyLightMapBuild *lmb;
   flyVector transferedenergy(0);

   fv=fj*0.5f;
   for( y=0;y<sizey;y++,fv+=fj )
   {
      fu=fi*0.5f;
      for( x=0;x<sizex;x++,fu+=fi,f[0]=f[1]=f[2]=0,f+=3,cur_emm++ )
      {
      map_point_local(fu,fv,p,n);
      energy.vec(pixelarea*f[0],pixelarea*f[1],pixelarea*f[2]);

      node=g_flyengine->find_node(p);
      if (node==0)
        continue;
      j=node->leaf;

      for( i=0;i<g_flyengine->nleaf;i++ )
      if (FLY_GLOBAL_PVS_TEST(j,i) &&
        g_flyengine->leaf[i]->elem.num &&
        g_flyengine->leaf[i]->elem[0]
          ->type==FLY_TYPE_STATICMESH)
      {
        mesh=((flyStaticMesh *)g_flyengine->leaf[i]
          ->elem[0])->objmesh;
        if (mesh)
```

```
                {
                face=mesh->faces;
                for( k=0;k<mesh->nf;k++ )
                   if (face[k]->lastupdate!=cur_emm &&
                      face[k]->lm!=-1) // lightmap radioity
                   {
                      face[k]->lastupdate=cur_emm;
                      lmb=(flyLightMapBuild *)g_flyengine
                         ->lm[face[k]->lm];
                      if (this!=lmb)
                         transferedenergy+=lmb
                         ->receive_light(p,n,energy);
                   }
                   else // vertex colour radiosity
                   if (face[k]
                      ->facetype==FLY_FACETYPE_TRIANGLE_MESH)
                   {
                      face[k]->lastupdate=cur_emm;

        transferedenergy+=tri_receive_light(face[k],p,n,energy);
                   }
                }
             }
           }
        }
     ((flyEngineBuild *)g_flyengine)->unshotenergy-=totalenergy;
     totalenergy.vec(0,0,0);

     return 1;
}

// loops all pixels in light map and
flyVector flyLightMapBuild::receive_light(const flyVector& P,const
flyVector& N,const flyVector& E,int flag)
{
   int x,y;
   float fi=1.0f/sizex,fj=1.0f/sizey,fu,fv;
   float *f=emm,*r=rad;
   flyVector p,n,dir,e;
   float l2,dot1,dot2;

   flyVector receivedenergy(0);

   ((flyEngineBuild *)g_flyengine)->unshotenergy-=totalenergy;
   fv=fj*0.5f;
   for( y=0;y<sizey;y++,fv+=fj )
   {
      fu=fi*0.5f;
      for(
x=0;x<sizex;x++,fu+=fi,receivedenergy+=flyVector(f[0]*pixelarea,f[1]*
pixelarea,f[2]*pixelarea),f+=3,r+=3 )
      {
         // map pixel to 3D point p and normal n
         map_point_local(fu,fv,p,n);
```

```
        dir=P-p;
        l2=dir.length2();
        if (l2<1.0f)
           continue;

        dir*=1.0f/(float)sqrt(l2);

        dot1=FLY_VECDOT(dir,n);
        if (dot1<=0.01f)
           continue;

        if (flag==0) // point light emit all 360 degrees
        {
           dot2=-FLY_VECDOT(dir,N);
           if (dot2<=0.01f)
              continue;

           e=(E*reflectance)*((dot1*dot2)/(l2*FLY_2PI));
        }
        else
           // surface light emit 180 degrees
           e=(E*reflectance)*(dot1/(l2*2.0f*FLY_2PI));
        if ((lmshadows&8) &&
           g_flyengine->collision_test(P-
dir,p+dir,FLY_TYPE_STATICMESH))
           continue;

        f[0]+=e.x;
        f[1]+=e.y;
        f[2]+=e.z;

        r[0]+=e.x;
        r[1]+=e.y;
        r[2]+=e.z;
     }
  }

  e.vec(receivedenergy.x-totalenergy.x,receivedenergy.y-
totalenergy.y,receivedenergy.z-totalenergy.z);
  totalenergy=receivedenergy;
  ((flyEngineBuild *)g_flyengine)->unshotenergy+=totalenergy;

  return e;
}
```

Figure 1.23 (also Colour Plate) shows a comparison between a games level rendered normally and using radiosity. The increase in quality should be apparent. Of course, in practice much of the differences between the two renderings are 'masked' by texture mapping but we return to a point that we made earlier, which is that the human eye is very sensitive to inadequacies in environmental lighting. A problem visible in both these images is the staircase edges of shadows. In classical radiosity this problem is a research area in its own right and an overview of various meshing strategies is given in [WATT00]. Basically we need to subdivide the patches in areas where there is a rapid change in

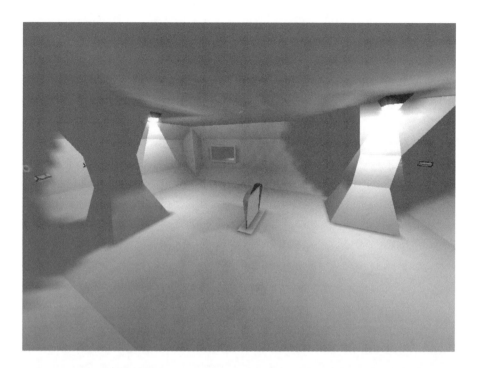

Figure 1.23
A games level rendered
with and without
radiosity.

calculated radiosity. But this is not a straightforward problem because we do not know where these areas are until we calculate a solution.

Leaving aside quality problems we now return to the efficiency consideration. Each face of type triangle mesh detail or curved Bézier surface is a list of triangles. If the curve or detail mesh is too complex, ray intersect calculations become slow because they test against each triangle. A simple solution to this problem is to enclose each face in an octree.

The octree is just a tree of bounding boxes and at each leaf we have a list of integers that represent the triangle indices representing triangles that clip the node's bounding box. The node is subdivided at the bounding box centre point (creating eight new child nodes). We start putting all faces in the root node and call a recursive subdivision method that stops based on some rule that defines if a subdivision is valid or not. The ray intersection method recurses the tree intersecting the bounding boxes and continues recursing only on the collided boxes. The box collision uses the *clip_bbox* method to find the faces that are included in the octree nodes clipped by a supplied bounding box. The subdivision is considered valid when for N faces in the parent node, none of the child nodes has more the N*0.6 faces. The faces are then split into eight regions. If at least half the faces get into different nodes we consider it good. Figure 1.24 (also Colour Plate) shows a scene with octrees built around both Bézier surfaces and triangle meshes.

The following code implements the octree algorithm.

```
//! OcTree node class
class FLY_ENGINE_API flyOcTreeNode
{
public:
   flyBoundBox bbox;          //!< Node bound box
   flyArray<int> faces;       //!< Node triangle faces
   flyOcTreeNode *nodes[8];   //!< Node childs

   //! Default constructor
   flyOcTreeNode();

   //! Default destructor
   virtual ~flyOcTreeNode();

   //! Copy constructor
   flyOcTreeNode(flyOcTreeNode& in);

   //! Split faces into child nodes if a subdivison is needed (used
   //on the octree build process)
   void build_node(int *triverts,flyVertex *verts);
};

//! OcTree class
class FLY_ENGINE_API flyOcTree
{
public:
   flyOcTreeNode *root;       //!< Root node for octree
   flyFace *face;             //!< Face from where octree was
                              //created
```

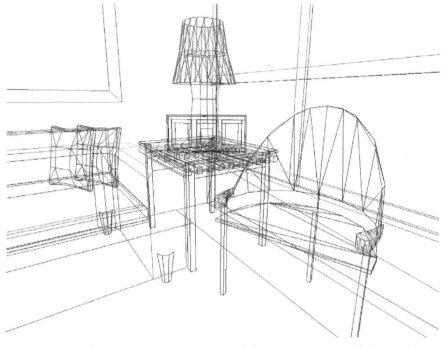

Figure 1.24
A scene with octrees built around both Bézier surface and triangle meshes.

```
    //! Default constructor
    flyOcTree();

    //! Default destructor
    virtual ~flyOcTree();

    //! Copy constructor
    flyOcTree(flyOcTree& in);

    //! Operator equal
    void operator=(flyOcTree& in);

    //! Free the tree data
    void reset();

    //! Builds the octree for the given triangle face or Bezier face
    void build_tree(flyFace *f);

    //! recurse octree and ray intersect test the triangles (just
    // bool result with no intersection info)
    int ray_intersect_test(const flyVector& ro,const flyVector&
            rd,float dist) const;

    //! recurse octree and ray intersect the triangles for the
    // closest collision
    int ray_intersect(const flyVector& ro,const flyVector&
            rd,flyVector& ip,float& dist) const;

    // Recurse octree and find all faces from nodes clipped by the
    //given bbox
    void clip_bbox(const flyBoundBox& bbox,flyArray<int>& faces) const;

    //! Draw the bbox as wireframe
    void draw();
};

// Build octree from triangles found in face f
void flyOcTree::build_tree(flyFace *f)
{
  face=f;
  root=new flyOcTreeNode;

  for( int i=0;i<f->ntriface;i++ )
        root->faces.add(i);
  root->bbox=f->bbox;

  root->build_node(f->trivert,f->vert);
}

// Split node into eight sub-nodes, separate faces belonging to each
//node and test
// if split was within threshold parameters (if not, collapse split
//and stop recursion)
```

```
void flyOcTreeNode::build_node(int *triverts,flyVertex *verts)
{
  if (faces.num<=FLY_OCTREE_MINFACES)
    return;

  int i,j;
  flyVector center=(bbox.min+bbox.max)*0.5f;

  for( i=0;i<8;i++ )
    nodes[i]=new flyOcTreeNode;

  nodes[0]->bbox.min.vec(bbox.min.x,bbox.min.y,bbox.min.z);
  nodes[0]->bbox.max.vec(center.x,center.y,center.z);

  nodes[1]->bbox.min.vec(center.x,center.y,bbox.min.z);
  nodes[1]->bbox.max.vec(bbox.max.x,bbox.max.y,center.z);

  nodes[2]->bbox.min.vec(center.x,bbox.min.y,bbox.min.z);
  nodes[2]->bbox.max.vec(bbox.max.x,center.y,center.z);

  nodes[3]->bbox.min.vec(bbox.min.x,center.y,bbox.min.z);
  nodes[3]->bbox.max.vec(center.x,bbox.max.y,center.z);

  nodes[4]->bbox.min.vec(bbox.min.x,bbox.min.y,center.z);
  nodes[4]->bbox.max.vec(center.x,center.y,bbox.max.z);

  nodes[5]->bbox.min.vec(center.x,center.y,center.z);
  nodes[5]->bbox.max.vec(bbox.max.x,bbox.max.y,bbox.max.z);

  nodes[6]->bbox.min.vec(center.x,bbox.min.y,center.z);
  nodes[6]->bbox.max.vec(bbox.max.x,center.y,bbox.max.z);

  nodes[7]->bbox.min.vec(bbox.min.x,center.y,center.z);
  nodes[7]->bbox.max.vec(center.x,bbox.max.y,bbox.max.z);

  int v;
  flyBoundBox bb;
  for( i=0;i<faces.num;i++ )
  {
    v=faces[i]*3;
    bb.reset();
    bb.add_point(verts[triverts[v]]);
    bb.add_point(verts[triverts[v+1]]);
    bb.add_point(verts[triverts[v+2]]);
    for( j=0;j<8;j++ )
      if (nodes[j]->bbox.clip_bbox(bb.min,bb.max))
        nodes[j]->faces.add(faces[i]);
  }
  for( i=0;i<8;i++ )
    if (nodes[i]->faces.num>faces.num*3/5)
      break;

  if (i<8)
  {
    for( i=0;i<8;i++ )
    {
```

```
          delete nodes[i];
          nodes[i]=0;
       }
    }
    else
    {
       faces.free();

       for( i=0;i<8;i++ )
          if (nodes[i]->faces.num==0)
          {
             delete nodes[i];
             nodes[i]=0;
          }
          else
             if (nodes[i]->faces.num>FLY_OCTREE_MINFACES)
                nodes[i]->build_node(triverts,verts);
    }
}

// Ray intersect octree faces returning true or false
// only on first intersection and with no intersection info
int   flyOcTree::ray_intersect_test(const   flyVector&   ro,const
flyVector& rd,float dist) const
{
    static flyOcTreeNode *stack[64];
    static float f1,f2;
    if (root->bbox.ray_intersect(ro,rd,f1,f2)==-1)
       return 0;

    flyOcTreeNode *n;
    int nstack=1,i;
    stack[0]=root;

    while(nstack)
    {
       n=stack[--nstack];
       if (n->faces.num==0)
       {
          for( i=0;i<8;i++ )
             if (n->nodes[i] &&
                n->nodes[i]
                ->bbox.ray_intersect(ro,rd,f1,f2)!=-1)
                stack[nstack++]=n->nodes[i];
       }
       else
          if (face->ray_intersect_tri_test(n->faces.buf,
          n->faces.num,ro,rd,dist))
             return 1;
    }

    return 0;
}

// Ray intersect octree faces returning face number (-1 on no
// intersection),
```

```
// closest intersection point (ip) and intersection point distance
(dist)
int flyOcTree::ray_intersect(const flyVector& ro,const flyVector&
rd,flyVector& ip,float& dist) const
{
  static flyOcTreeNode *stack[64];
  static float f1,f2;
  if (root->bbox.ray_intersect(ro,rd,f1,f2)==-1)
    return -1;

  flyOcTreeNode *n;
  int nstack=1;
  stack[0]=root;

  int i,min_face=-1;
  float min_dist=FLY_BIG;
  flyVector min_ip;

  while(nstack)
  {
    n=stack[--nstack];
    if (n->faces.num==0)
    {
      for( i=0;i<8;i++ )
        if (n->nodes[i] &&
          n->nodes[i]
          ->bbox.ray_intersect(ro,rd,f1,f2)!=-1)
          stack[nstack++]=n->nodes[i];
    }
    else
    {
      i=face->ray_intersect_tri(n->faces.buf,
        n->faces.num,ro,rd,ip,dist);
      if (i!=-1 && dist<min_dist)
      {
        min_dist=dist;
        min_ip=ip;
        min_face=n->faces[i];
      }
    }
  }

  ip=min_ip;
  dist=min_dist;
  return min_face;
}

// Recurse octree filling in faces array with all faces inside
// octree leaf nodes clipped by specified bound box
void flyOcTree::clip_bbox(const flyBoundBox& bbox,flyArray<int>&
faces) const
{
  static flyOcTreeNode *stack[64];

  faces.clear();
```

```
    if (bbox.clip_bbox(root->bbox.min,root->bbox.max)==0)
       return;

    flyOcTreeNode *n;
    int nstack=1,i;
    stack[0]=root;

    while(nstack)
    {
       n=stack[--nstack];
       if (n->faces.num==0)
       {
          for( i=0;i<8;i++ )
             if (n->nodes[i] &&
                bbox.clip_bbox(n->nodes[i]->bbox.min,
                   n->nodes[i]->bbox.max))
                stack[nstack++]=n->nodes[i];
       }
       else
          faces+=n->faces;
    }
}

// Draw recursing octree and draw leaf nodes' bound boxes
void flyOcTree::draw()
{
    static flyOcTreeNode *stack[64];

    flyOcTreeNode *n;
    int nstack=1,i;
    stack[0]=root;

    root->bbox.draw();

    while(nstack)
    {
       n=stack[--nstack];
       if (n->faces.num==0)
       {
          for( i=0;i<8;i++ )
             if (n->nodes[i])
                stack[nstack++]=n->nodes[i];
       }
       else
          n->bbox.draw();
    }
}
```

Appendix 1.1 Building in practice

At the end of each of the practically oriented chapters we present demonstrations of the material described in the text. This first demonstration deals with build processes.

(1) Building from an existing level

This demonstration starts from the basis that a .fmp file containing the raw geometry for the level exists. We need to activate the build process to construct the BSP, PVS and light maps. For this we use the *flyBuild* console front-end (Chapter 3). To make things as easy as possible this is controlled by a simple interface called *flyBuilder*. This calls *flyBuild* with the appropriate command line based on the options selected.

Open the *flyBuilder* tool, select the map file *ship_mp1.fmp* and make sure that the settings are as shown in Figure A1.1. This will generate a full level build, including PVS and shadows. After the build is complete the level is ready to be run. Meaningful experimentation with the parameters in the advanced option window might include:

- Changing the light map pixel size to a higher/lower value. This will generate more coarsely/finely defined shadows. (Turn off texture filtering with F8 to better observe this.)

- Selecting hard shadows will make the light map computation quicker but at the cost of lower quality shadows.

- Changing the BSP grid size will change the number of BSP sectors in the level. For a very small level this does not alter the speed of the build process significantly. However, it is an important parameter in the case of a very large

Figure A1.1
Builder tool and options.

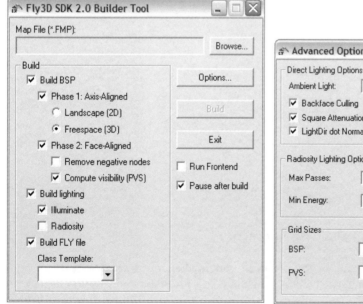

level (such as the Mars landscape *mars.fmp*). To load this level note that you must check the *landscape BSP* box.

(2) Importing an existing level into a level editor

Load 3D Studio MAX and make sure that the Fly3D plug-ins are installed. Use the 3D Studio MAX import command and select the Fly3D Map (.fmp) format. Then select any of the existing demos from the SDK data folder.

This will load all the map geometry in 3D Studio MAX and create the materials with proper texture maps and mapping coordinates. All game lights will be converted into 3D Studio MAX omni lights and all game entities placed as simple spheres with their parameters in the 3D Studio MAX object custom user parameters.

Lights will render in 3D Studio MAX very similar to their appearance in the real game. Only light colour and attenuation far distance parameters from the lights are used and 3D Studio MAX shadow maps will be sufficient to preview the ray-traced lights from the build process. When creating new lights all you should set is the mentioned parameters.

The geometry found in the map file will be loaded and separated into different objects based on the geometry type (Figure A1.2 (also Colour Plate). The following is the list of supported geometry types and their character identifier:

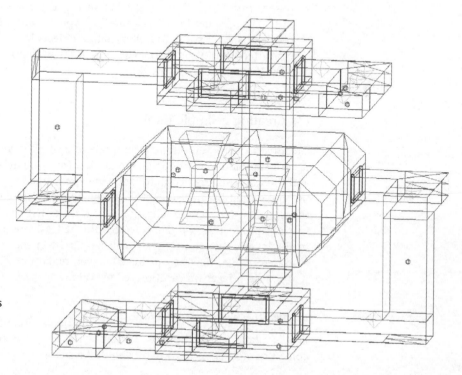

Figure A1.2
A wireframe of a level showing different geometry types:

Blue   structural polygons
Green detail polygons
Red   game entities
Purple curved surfaces
Yellow lights

- Structural polygons (*)   Objects tagged as such will be converted into a set of convex large polygons (polygons with any number of vertices). Connecting all structural polygons together must form a closed concave volume. There will be a BSP tree splitting plane for all planes defined by these faces. Structural polygons must always connect to other structural polygons by the edges only (an edge should not connect to another polygon by the surface).

- Detail polygons (&)   Objects tagged as such will be converted into a set of large polygons (polygons with any number of vertices). These polygons are free to be anywhere in the level and do not need to break the geometry they touch.

- Detail triangle mesh (^)   Each object tagged as such will be considered a triangle-based detail face. Used for modelling lamps, statues, and all small detail geometry.

- Landscape faces (#)   Objects tagged as such will be used for landscapes. They will be stored as individual triangles and processed by the build tool in a different way. At the end of the BSP build process triangles tagged as such inside the same BSP sector will be collapsed into a detail triangle mesh (type ^), allowing the vertices from faces in the same BSP sector to share its vertices.

- Bézier surface (~)   Each object tagged as such will be considered a bi-quadratic Bézier surface with any number of patches in u and v directions. Each mesh vertex will be considered a surface control point.

- Game entity ($)   Objects tagged as such will represent game entities defined in the Fly3D plug-ins. This will allow you to place, for example, the game power-ups, birthpads, and all dynamic objects in the editor and have them converted into the level script automatically with position, rotation and other user-defined properties used.

(3) Creating a simple level

Creating a new level requires the modelling of all geometry, texture mapping it with standard 3D Studio MAX materials (multi-materials are also supported) and then tagging the geometry with the appropriate type tags. The entities can be represented by any geometry (in the above example spheres are used) and the initial position and orientation of the entity will be acquired when the level is exported. In the *ship* demo we require at least one birthpad entity to exist in the level; otherwise the ship will be placed at the origin when the level is activated (which may be outside the level, making it invisible).

To build a level we can proceed as follows.

Building the level's structural faces

Draw a plan view of the level using the line tool. The plan of the model must consist of a closed polygon and should be snapped to the grid (Figure A1.3(a)).

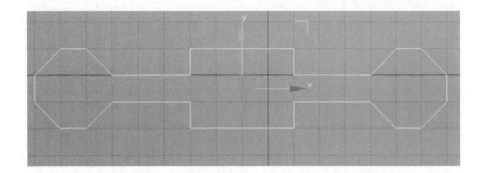

Figure A1.3(a)
Plan view of a level.

Use the *Extrude* modifier to convert the plan into a 3D model (Figure A1.3(b)).

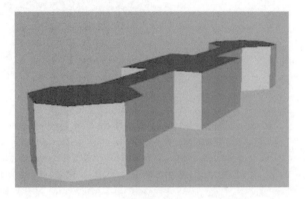

Figure A1.3(b)
Extruded view of the level.

Invert the faces' normals using the *Edit Mesh* modifier. This is done by selecting the face node in the modifier, selecting all faces from the model with a selection window and then clicking the *Invert Normals* button. This is a important step, and converts the model from a normal 3D graphics object, with outwards-facing normals, to an interior (Figure A1.3(c)).

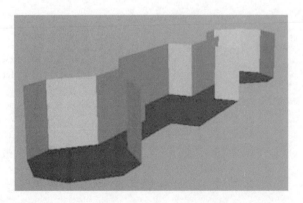

Figure A1.3(c)
Inverted extruded view of the level.

Create the texture coordinates using the *UVW Map* modifier and select box mapping. Set the length, width and height to appropriate values for your level.

Define the required materials using the standard material with bitmap difuse mapping and apply it to the model (Figure A1.3(d)). You can also apply different materials to different parts of the model.

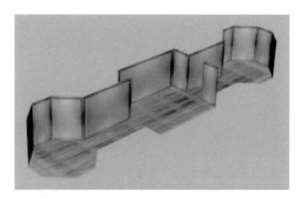

Figure A1.3(d)
Textured view of the level.

The next step is setting the created mesh as *structural*. Fly3D uses a *prefix tag system* for recognising the various types of meshes and faces. To set the mesh's faces as *structural faces*, just rename it, placing a '*' before its name. For example, a mesh named 'structure' must be renamed to '*structure'.

It is of great importance that some properties are maintained by the level model, especially when modelling more complex environments: the whole set of structural faces must define a closed concave volume. This is achieved by having two and only two faces sharing an edge, for all edges that compound the model. If these properties are kept, the BSP building routine will generate only positive (valid) leaf nodes, making it possible to use PVS culling and portals technology for path-finding.

Adding detail objects

In this step, *detail objects* will be added to the scene, making it more realistic. Typical detail objects are picture frames, pillars, tables, boxes etc. Figure A1.4 shows pillars and boxes added to the original scene.

Detail objects follow the same *prefix tag* pattern. Therefore, a '^' must be added to the beginning of the object's name, if the object is made of triangular faces, or a '&', if the object is made of faces with more than three vertices.

Special care must be taken when adding detail objects to the level. Their volumes must all be located inside the concave volume defined by the structural model. However, detail faces do not have the same limitations as structural ones: edges and vertices can be shared by any number of faces in any fashion.

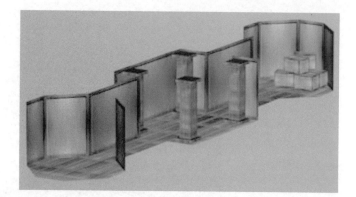

Figure A1.4
Adding detail objects to
the textured view of the
level.

It is also important to note that detail objects made of large faces (faces with more than three vertices) will have light maps applied to them for static (pre-calculated) illumination, while objects made of triangular faces will be illuminated with vertex lights technology.

Adding lights

In this step, lights will be added to the scene (Figure A1.5 (also Colour Plate)). Lights must always be of the *Omni* type, and their colour and illumination radius must be defined in the *far attenuation* submenu. Lights do not need a *prefix tag* before their names.

Figure A1.5(a)
Lighting an environment.

Figure A1.5(b)

Adding entities

The last step in building the level is inserting *entities* in it. *Entities* can be power-ups, birthpads, portals, mirrors etc. In this tutorial example, a birthpad and a power-up entity were added to the scene. The entities' names must match the names of classes that exist in a Fly3D plug-in, and they are represented by simple meshes, like boxes. Figure A1.6 (also Colour Plate) shows the birthpad and power-up entities (highlighted in red).

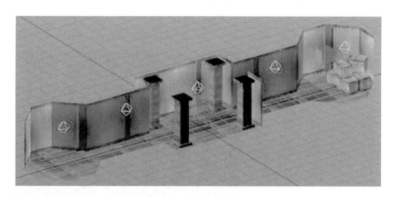

Figure A1.6
Adding entities.

Entities must have a '$' *prefix tag* before their names.

(4) Exporting a created level

To export a created level, use the 3D Studio MAX export command and select the Fly3D Map (.fmp) format (Figure A1.7). All tagged geometry will be processed and an information dialog will show the statistics for the exported level, showing the number of elements of each type.

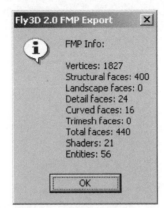

Figure A1.7
Export button showing level statistics.

(5) Modelling, exporting and building a more complex level

This section explains how to model and illuminate a complex level, build the structure, build detail objects, build curves, texturise and export it to be used as a Fly3D scene environment. 3D Studio MAX 3.x or 4.x can be used as modelling tools. The user must have basic knowledge of this software. Fly3D export/import plug-ins and curve plug-in for the corresponding MAX version must be installed through the **flyInstPlugins.exe** application.

The concept of a new level

The very first step when building a new level is to design structures and details as in an architectural project, where decisions about measurements, type of materials used, textures etc. must be made. The drawings shown in Figure A1.8 are

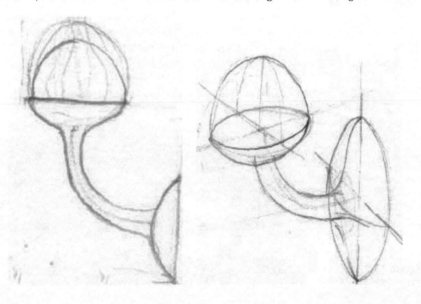

Figure A1.8(a)
Conceptual sketches of detail objects and a level.

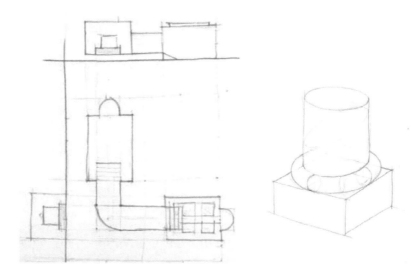

Figure A1.8(b)

conceptual sketches of an example level and detail objects, made before the construction of the environment.

Building the level's structural faces

Structural faces are the ones that define the geometry of the scene, dividing the space between 'in' and 'out' of the environment, like walls, ceilings, floors, etc. It is of great importance that some properties are maintained by the structural model, specially when modelling more complex environments: the whole set of structural faces must define a closed concave volume. This is achieved by having two and only two faces sharing a given edge, for all edges that compound the model. If these properties are kept, the BSP building routine will generate only positive (valid) leaf nodes, making it possible to use PVS culling and portals technology for path-finding.

The structure of the scene in this tutorial (Figure A1.9) was built in 3D Studio MAX, where it is important to ensure that the *Snap to Grid* option is turned on. A level's structure can also be built using AutoCAD, and then exported as a .3ds file to be imported in MAX.

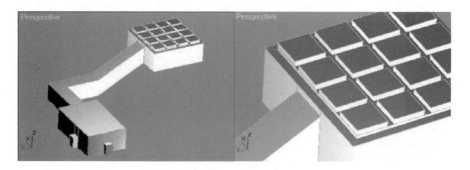

Figure A1.9
An example level.

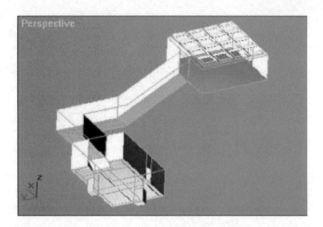

Figure A1.10
Inverting the face normals.

It is necessary to invert these faces' normals so that they are turned to inside the level, as in Figure A1.10.

The next step is to texturize the structural faces using UVW mapping. The *Planar*, *Box* or *Cylindrical* mapping templates can be used, as well as *Face Map*. To make the task of mapping the structural faces easier, the *Detach* procedure can be used to separate the faces, making it possible to map each face in a unique way.

The next step is to set the created mesh as *structural*. Fly3D uses a *prefix tag system* for recognising the various types of meshes and faces. To set the mesh's faces as *structural faces*, just rename it, placing a '*' (asterisk) character before its name. For example, a mesh named 'structure' must be renamed to '*structure'.

Adding detail objects

In this step, *detail objects* will be added to the scene, making it more realistic. Typical detail objects are picture frames, pillars, tables, boxes, stairs etc. Figure A1.11 (also Colour Plate) shows pillars and stairs added to the original scene.

Figure A1.11
Adding detail objects.

Detail objects follow the same *prefix tag* pattern. Therefore, a '^' must be added to the beginning of the object's name, if the object is made of triangular faces, or a '&', if the object is made of faces with more than three vertices.

Figure A1.12 (also Colour Plate) shows examples of a triangular detail object (on the left) and a polygonal detail object (on the right).

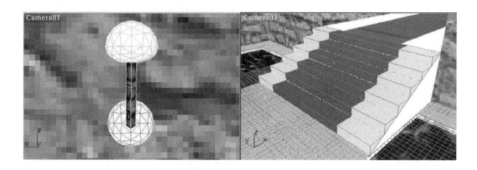

Figure A1.12
Triangles and polygonal detail objects.

Special care must be taken when adding detail objects to the level. Their volumes must be located all inside the concave volume defined by the structural model. However, detail faces do not have the same limitations of structural ones: edges and vertices can be shared by any number of faces in any fashion. It is also important to note that detail objects made of large faces (faces with more than three vertices) will have light maps applied to them for static (pre-calculated) illumination, while objects made of triangular faces will be illuminated with vertex lights technology.

Adding lights

In this step, lights will be added to the scene (Figure A1.13 (also Colour Plate)). Lights must always be of the *Omni* type, and their color and illumination radius

Figure A1.13
Adding lighting.

must be defined in the *far attenuation* submenu. Lights do not need a *prefix tag* before their names.

In the lights *Far Attenuation* submenu, the default lighting radii are set as: *Start=80* and *End=500*.

Lighting is a major feature that adds ambience and depth to a level. It is probable that the level designer will want to test several light configurations before the intended visual impressions are achieved.

(6) Modelling with curves

This section explains how to build curves in 3D Studio MAX for Fly3D. These are special types of curves, and the curve object plug-in was created specifically for making curves that integrate with Fly3D and take advantage of the engine's dynamic LOD algorithms and other optimisations.

Step 1: Creating a structure

In this step, a big box will be created and used as a structure, which will represent the level itself and will contain the curves to be exported at the end of the tutorial. A box is created in our simple example with dimensions $1000 \times 1000 \times 400$, as seen in Figure A1.14 (also Colour Plate).

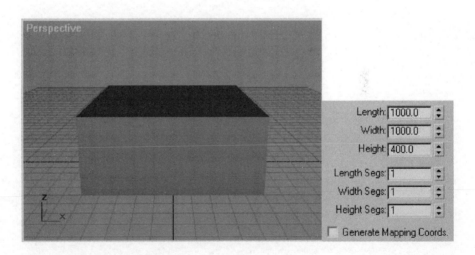

Figure A1.14
Creating a box structure.

Step 2: Inverting the normals

Now the box's normals should be inverted, making the inside space valid, and the outside, invalid (Figure A1.15 (also Colour Plate)). Also, a '*' (asterisk) character must be added to the beginning of the box's name (in our case, *structure*), so that the export plug-in will later recognise it as the level's structure.

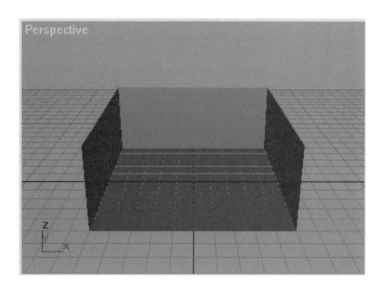

Figure A1.15
Inverting the normals.

Step 3: Mapping

In this step, the box will be texturised for a better look, which is completely optional (Figure A1.16).

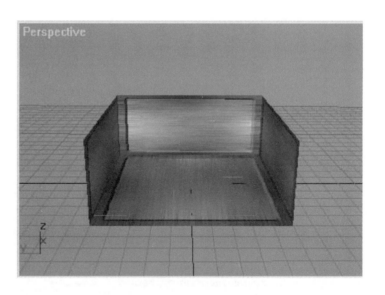

Figure A1.16
Adding texture.

Step 4: Creating curves

The Fly3D curve creation plug-in is found inside the *Create/Geometry* menu, in the *Paralelo* category.

Clicking on the *flycurve* button, various curve types will be available, such as cylinders, cones, spheres, caps etc. Also, some options are available, such as the dimensions and number of segments of the curve.

First, a cylinder will be created as a *Full* one (4 × 1 segments), positioned at the centre of the room, with dimensions set at 50 × 50 × 200 (Figure A1.17).

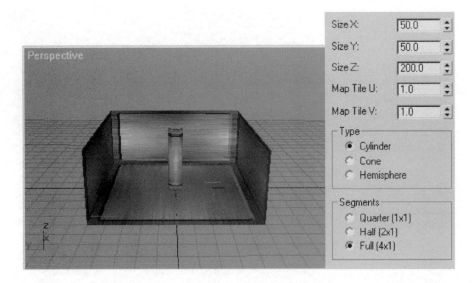

Figure A1.17
Creating a cylinder.

Now a quarter-sphere will be created, positioned anywhere in the room. A quarter-sphere is created by selecting *hemisphere* in the *type* menu, and then *Quarter* (1 × 1) in the *Segments* menu. Its dimensions will be 200 × 200 × 100, as seen in Figure A1.18.

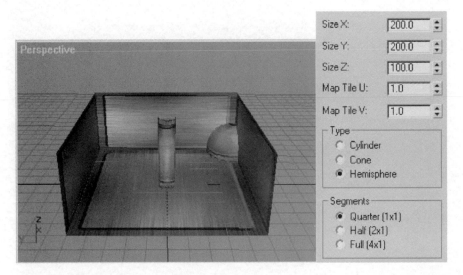

Figure A1.18
Creating a quarter-sphere.

This time, another kind of curve will be created. In the *type* menu, the *Cone* option will be selected, and a *Full* (4 × 1) cone will be created, with dimensions 50 × 50 × 100 and positioned against the wall, as seen in Figure A1.19.

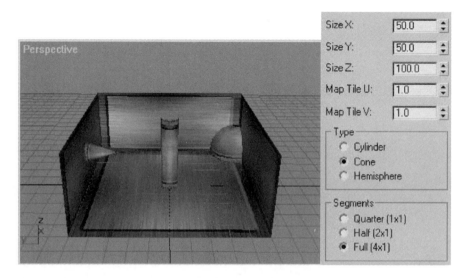

Figure A1.19
Creating a cone.

The next step is to make a capped thin half-cylinder. First, the body of a half-cylinder must be created with dimensions set to 200 × 200 × 20 (Figure A1.20).

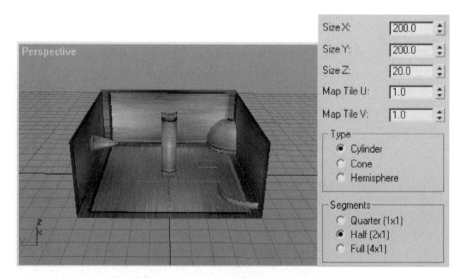

Figure A1.20
Creating a capped half-cylinder.

Now the cylinder must be cloned and placed on the same position, but this time the *Cap Up* option of the *Part* menu must be used to make a cap for the cylinder, as seen in Figure A1.21.

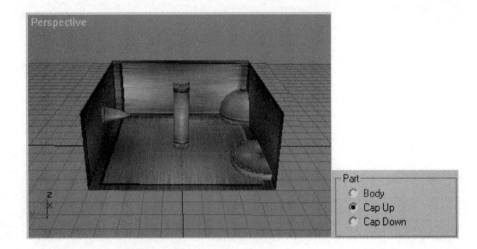

Figure A1.21
Creating a capped half-cylinder.

Step 5: Editing the curves

In this step, another cylinder will be created, and the *Edit Mesh* modifier will be applied to it afterwards, making it possible to move the curve's vetices. A *Full* (4 × 1) cylinder will be created, and the *Part* menu must be set to *Body*.

The *Edit Mesh* modifier is then applied, and the vertices are edited to make it for a curved cylinder. Note that, once the modifier is applied, the curve is no longer visible; its control points appear instead. The vertices we move are actually the curve's control points, but in Fly3D it will still be seen as a curve (Figure A1.22).

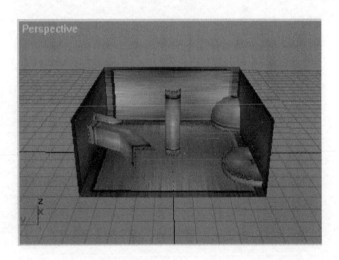

Figure A1.22
Creating a curved cylinder (connecting the left wall and the wall backfacing the view).

This last curve will be another cylinder (a quarter-cylinder, actually), but this time we will set the *Invert Normals* option to make a rounded corner. This quarter-cylinder will have dimensions of 200 × 200 × 200 (Figure A1.23).

Figure A1.23
Creating a quarter-cylinder.

Step 6: Illuminating, adding entities and exporting

In this last step, lights and a birthpad are positioned in the level (Figure A1.24 (also Colour Plate)).

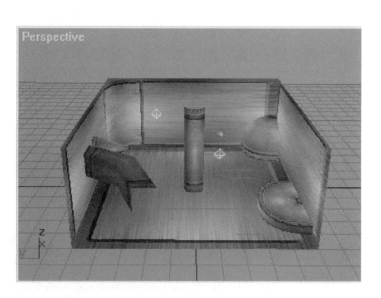

Figure A1.24
Adding lighting.

Export it as a Fly3D Map file (.fmp), build the level with flyBuilder and run one of the engine's front-ends to see the level. Some screenshots from the level in Fly3D are shown in Figure A1.25 (also Colour Plate).

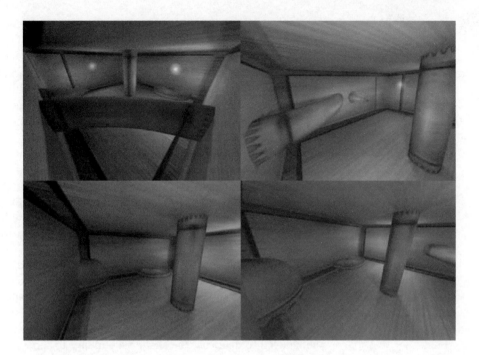

Figure A1.25
Screen shots of a
completed level.

Appendix 1.2 Basic radiosity theory

In 1984, using a method whose theory was based on the principles of radiative heat transfer, researchers at Cornell University developed the radiosity method [GORA84]. This is now known as classical radiosity and it simulates light interaction between diffuse surfaces. That is, it can only be used, in its unextended form, to render scenes that are made up in their entirety of (perfect) diffuse surfaces.

To accomplish this, every surface in a scene is divided up into elements called patches and a set of equations is set up based on the conservation of light energy. A single patch in such an environment reflects light received from every other patch in the environment. It may also emit light if it is a light source – light sources are treated like any other patch except that they have non-zero self-emission. The interaction between patches depends on their geometric relationship. That is, distance and relative orientation. Two parallel patches a short distance apart will have a high interaction. An equilibrium solution is possible if, for each patch in the environment, we calculate the interaction between it and every other patch in the environment.

One of the major contributions of the Cornell group was to invent an efficient way – the hemi-cube algorithm – for evaluating the geometric relationship between pairs of patches; in fact in the 1980s most of the innovations in radiosity methods came out of this group.

The cost of the algorithm is $O(N^2)$ where N is the number of patches into which the environment is divided. To keep processing costs down, the patches are made large and the light intensity is assumed to be constant across a patch. This immediately introduces a quality problem – if illumination discontinuities do not coincide with patch edges, artefacts occur. This size restriction is the practical reason why the algorithm can only calculate diffuse interaction, which by its nature changes slowly across a surface. Adding specular interaction to the radiosity method is expensive and is still the subject of much research. Thus we have the strange situation that the two global interaction methods – ray tracing and radiosity – are mutually exclusive as far as the phenomena that they calculate are concerned. Ray tracing cannot calculate diffuse interaction and radiosity cannot incorporate specular interaction. Despite this, the radiosity method has produced some of the most realistic images to date in computer graphics.

The radiosity method deals with shadows without further enhancement. The geometry of shadows is more or less straightforward to calculate and can be part of a ray tracing algorithm or an algorithm added on to a local reflection model renderer. However, the intensity within a shadow is properly part of diffuse interaction and can only be arbitrarily approximated by other algorithms. The radiosity method takes shadows in its stride. They drop out of the solution as intensities like any other. The only problem is that the patch size may have to be reduced to delineate the shadow boundary to some desired level of accuracy. Shadow boundaries are areas where the rate of change of diffuse light intensity is high and the normal patch size may cause visible aliasing at the shadow edge.

The radiosity method is an object space algorithm, solving for the intensity at discrete points or surface patches within an environment and not for pixels in an image plane projection.

Radiosity theory

The radiosity method is a conservation of energy or energy equilibrium approach, providing a solution for the radiosity of all surfaces within an enclosure. The energy input to the system is from those surfaces that act as emitters. In fact a light source is treated like any other surface in the algorithm except that it possesses an initial (non-zero) radiosity. The method is based on the assumption that all surfaces are perfect diffusers or ideal Lambertian surfaces.

Radiosity, B, is defined as the energy per unit area leaving a surface patch per unit time and is the sum of the emitted and the reflected energy:

$$B_i \, \mathrm{d}A_i = E_i \, \mathrm{d}A_i + \rho_i \int_j B_j F_{ji} \, \mathrm{d}A_j$$

Expressing this equation in words, we have for a single patch i:

Radiosity × area = emitted energy + reflected energy

E_i is the energy emitted from a patch. The reflected energy is given by multiplying the incident energy by ρ_i, the reflectivity of the patch. The incident energy is that energy that arrives at patch i from all other patches in the environment; that is, we integrate over the environment, for all j $(j \neq i)$, the term $B_j F_{ji} dA_j$. This is the energy leaving each patch j that arrives at patch i. F_{ji} is a constant, called a form factor, that parameterises the relationship between patch j and i.

We can use a reciprocity relationship to give:

$$F_{ij} A_i = F_{ji} A_j$$

and dividing through by dA_i gives:

$$B_i = E_i + \rho_i \int_j B_j F_{ij}$$

For a discrete environment the integral is replaced by a summation and constant radiosity is assumed over small discrete patches, giving:

$$B_i = E_i + \rho_i \sum_{j=1}^{n} B_j F_{ij}$$

Such an equation exists for each surface patch in the enclosure and the complete environment produces a set of n simultaneous equations of the form:

$$\begin{bmatrix} 1 - \rho_1 F_{11} & -\rho_1 F_{12} & \cdots & -\rho_1 F_{1n} \\ -\rho_2 F_{21} & 1 - \rho_2 F_{22} & \cdots & -\rho_2 F_{2n} \\ \vdots & \vdots & \cdots & \vdots \\ \rho_n F_{n1} & -\rho_n F_{n2} & \cdots & 1 - \rho_n F_{nn} \end{bmatrix} \begin{bmatrix} B_1 \\ B_2 \\ \vdots \\ B_n \end{bmatrix} = \begin{bmatrix} E_1 \\ E_2 \\ \vdots \\ E_n \end{bmatrix}$$

Solving this equation is the radiosity method. Out of this solution comes B_i, the radiosity for each patch. However, there are two problems left. We need a way of computing the form factors. And we need to compute a view and display the patches. To do this we need a linear interpolation method – just like Gouraud shading, otherwise the subdivision pattern – the patches themselves – will be visible.

The E_i's are non-zero only at those surfaces that provide illumination and these terms represent the input illumination to the system. The ρ_i's are known and the F_{ij}'s are a function of the geometry of the environment. The reflectivities are wavelength-dependent terms and the above equation should be regarded as a monochromatic solution; a complete solution being obtained by solving for however many colour bands are being considered. We can note at this stage that $F_{ii} = 0$ for a plane or convex surface – none of the radiation leaving the surface will strike itself. Also, from the definition of the form factor the sum of any row of form factors is unity.

Since the form factors are a function only of the geometry of the system they are computed once only. The method is bound by the time taken to calculate the form factors expressing the radiative exchange between two surface patches A_i and A_j. This depends on their relative orientation and the distance between them and is given by:

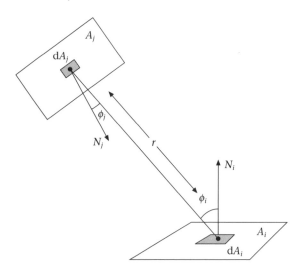

Figure A1.26
Form factor geometry for two patches i and j (after Goral *et al.* [GORA84]).

$$F_{ij} = \frac{\text{Radiative energy leaving surface } A_i \text{ that strikes } A_j \text{ directly}}{\text{Radiative energy leaving surface } A_i \text{ in all directions}}$$
$$\text{in the hemispherical space surrounding } A_i$$

It can be shown that this is given by:

$$F_{ij} = \frac{1}{A_i} \int\limits_{A_i} \int\limits_{A_j} \frac{\cos \phi_i \cos \phi_j}{\pi r^2} \, dA_j dA_i \tag{1.1}$$

where the geometric conventions are illustrated in Figure A1.26. In any practical environment A_j may be wholly or partially invisible from A_i and the integral needs to be multiplied by an occluding factor which is a binary function that depends on whether the differential area dA_i can see dA_j or not. This double integral is difficult to solve except for specific shapes.

Progressive refinement

In 1988 the Cornell team developed an approach called 'progressive refinement' [COHE88]. The original motivation for this technique was to enable a designer to see an early (but approximate) solution. In the conventional evaluation of the radiosity matrix (using for example the Gauss-Seidel method) a solution for one row provides the radiosity for a single patch i:

$$B_i = E_i + \rho_i \sum_{j=1}^{n} B_j F_{ij}$$

This is an estimate of the radiosity of patch i based on the current estimate of all other patches. This is called 'gathering'. The equation means that

Gathering: a single iteration (k) updates a single patch i by gathering contributions from all other patches.

$$B_i^{(k+1)} = E_i + R_i \sum_{j=1}^{N} F_{ij} B_j^{(k)}$$

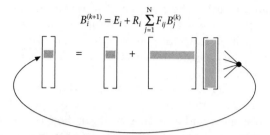

Equivalent to gathering light energy from all the patches in the scene.

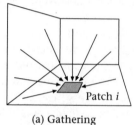

(a) Gathering

Shooting: a single step computes form factors from the shooting patch to all receiving patches and distributes (unshot) energy ΔB_i

for all j:
$$B_j^{(k+1)} = B_j^{(k)} + R_j F_{ji} \Delta B_i$$

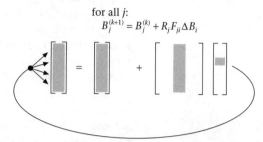

Equivalent to shooting light energy from a patch to all other patches in the scene.

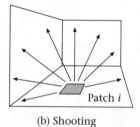

(b) Shooting

Figure A1.27
(a) Gathering and
(b) shooting in radiosity
solution strategies (based
on an illustration in
Cohen *et al.* [COHE88]).

(algorithmically) for patch i we visit every other patch in the scene and transfer the appropriate amount of light from each patch j to patch i according to the form factor. The algorithm proceeds on a row by row basis and the entire solution is updated for one step through the matrix (although the Gauss-Seidel method uses the new values as soon as they are computed). If the process is viewed dynamically, as the solution proceeds, each patch intensity is updated according to its row position in the radiosity matrix. Light is gathered from every other patch in the scene and used to update the single patch currently being considered.

The idea of the progressive refinement method is that the entire image of all patches is updated at every iteration. This is termed 'shooting', where the contribution from each patch i is distributed to all other patches. The difference between these two processes is illustrated diagramatically in Figures A1.27(a) and (b). This reordering of the algorithm is accomplished in the following way.

A single term determines the contribution to the radiosity of patch j due to that from patch i:

$$B_j \text{ due to } B_i = \rho_j B_i F_{ji}$$

This relationship can be reversed by using the reciprocity relationship:

$$B_j \text{ due to } B_i = \rho_j B_i F_{ij} A_i / A_j$$

and this is true for all patches j. This relationship can be used to determine the contribution to each patch j in the environment from the single patch i. A single radiosity (patch i) shoots light into the environment and the radiosities of all patches j are updated simultaneously. The first complete update (of all the radiosities in the environment) is obtained from 'on the fly' form factor computations. Thus an initial approximation to the complete scene can appear when only the first row of form factors has been calculated. This eliminates high start-up or pre-calculation costs.

This process is repeated until convergence is achieved. All radiosities are initially set either to zero or to their emission values. As this process is repeated for each patch i the solution is displayed and at each step the radiosities for each patch j are updated. As the solution progresses, the estimate of the radiosity at patch i becomes more and more accurate. For an iteration the environment already contains the contribution of the previous estimate of B_j and the so-called 'unshot' radiosity – the difference between the current and previous estimates – is all that is injected into the environment.

If the output from the algorithm is displayed without further elaboration, then a scene, initially dark, gradually gets lighter as the incremental radiosities are added to each patch. The 'visual convergence' of this process can be optimised by sorting the order in which the patches are processed according to the amount of energy that they are likely to radiate. This means, for example, that emitting patches, or light sources, should be treated first. This gives an early well-lit solution. The next patches to be processed are those that received most light from the light sources and so on. By using this ordering scheme, the solution proceeds in a way that approximates the propagation of light through an environment. Although this produces a better visual sequence than an unsorted process, the solution still progresses from a dark scene to a fully illuminated scene. To overcome this effect an arbitrary ambient light term is added to the intermediate radiosities. This term is used only to enhance the display and is not part of the solution. The value of the ambient term is based on the current estimate of the radiosities of all patches in the environment, and as the solution proceeds and becomes 'better lit', the ambient contribution is decreased.

Four main stages are completed for each iteration in the algorithm. These are:

(1) Find the patch with the greatest (unshot) radiosity or emitted energy.

(2) Evaluate a column of form factors, that is, the form factors from this patch to every other patch in the environment.

(3) Update the radiosity of each of the receiving patches.

(4) Reduce the temporary ambient term as a function of the sum of the differences between the current values calculated in step 3 and the previous values.

## 2

The anatomy of an advanced games system II
Real-time processes

In the previous chapter we looked at the off-line build processes necessary in a game system. In this chapter we move on to consider the real-time processes that the engine must be capable of to run a game. The topics listed below are, in our opinion, the generic real-time methods that must be incorporated in a modern games engine capable of processing the visual aspect of high complexity games. Advanced aspects of rendering, animation and other methods are covered in Chapters 4–11 and may or may not be incorporated in a system depending on the application. The bias of the chapter is the development of high optimisation in the methods; more general material on the topics is to be found in [WATT01]. All processes in this chapter use the BSP tree scene management.

The topics dealt with in this chapter are:

- **View frustum culling** is a real-time optimisation that enhances the build optimisations and enables us to select only those BSP leaf nodes which clip the view frustum.

- **Camera control** is a somewhat neglected topic but it contributes significantly to the feel and quality of an action game.

- **Collision detection and response**   Fast and accurate collision detection and response is critically important again as a dominant contributor to game feel and quality.

- **Path planning** We introduce a simple method that utilises the pseudo-portals introduced in the previous chapter. Enhanced with an A* algorithm, this real-time process can serve as a foundation for higher-level AI processes.

2.1 Viewing and the BSP

The main recursion in any game is that which selects the faces to draw. Good view frustum culling is thus critically important for scenes of high complexity where the currently visible faces may be a small proportion of the total. A basic method can proceed as follows:

(1) From the camera position, orientation, viewing angle, aspect ratio and far plane distances we generate the view frustum planes. (Five planes are used because we can ignore the clipping effect of the near plane.)

(2) The BSP is recursed, selecting all the leaf nodes that are clipped by the view frustum.

(3) The PVS is used to reduce the number of selected leaf nodes while recursing the BSP.

(4) To achieve further culling, for every face contained in each of the selected leaf nodes, we clip their face bounding box against the frustum. AABBs are used as bounding boxes throughout.

(5) All remaining faces are passed for rendering.

2.1.1 Generating the frustum planes

To compute the vertices of the frustum is straightforward and from these the view frustum planes can be generated. The following class definition is used:

```
class FLY_ENGINE_API flyFrustum
{
  public:
    flyVector verts[5];
    flyVector planes[5];
    int bboxindx[8][3];

  inline int clip_bbox(const flyBoundBox& bbox) const;
  void build(const flyVector& pos,const flyVector& X,
      const flyVector& Y,const flyVector& Z);
};
```

The planes are generated by calculating the frustum vertices and then using the three pairs of vertices as axes for calculating the plane normals.

```
void flyFrustum::build(const flyVector& pos,const flyVector& X,const
flyVector& Y,const flyVector& Z)
{
   float farplane=flyRender::s_farplane;
   float
disty=farplane*(float)tan(flyRender::s_camangle*0.5f*FLY_PIOVER180);
   float distx=disty*flyRender::s_aspect;

   verts[0]=pos;

   verts[1].x = pos.x - farplane*Z.x + distx*X.x + disty*Y.x;
   verts[1].y = pos.y - farplane*Z.y + distx*X.y + disty*Y.y;
   verts[1].z = pos.z - farplane*Z.z + distx*X.z + disty*Y.z;

   verts[2].x = pos.x - farplane*Z.x + distx*X.x - disty*Y.x;
   verts[2].y = pos.y - farplane*Z.y + distx*X.y - disty*Y.y;
   verts[2].z = pos.z - farplane*Z.z + distx*X.z - disty*Y.z;

   verts[3].x = pos.x - farplane*Z.x - distx*X.x - disty*Y.x;
   verts[3].y = pos.y - farplane*Z.y - distx*X.y - disty*Y.y;
   verts[3].z = pos.z - farplane*Z.z - distx*X.z - disty*Y.z;

   verts[4].x = pos.x - farplane*Z.x - distx*X.x + disty*Y.x;
   verts[4].y = pos.y - farplane*Z.y - distx*X.y + disty*Y.y;
   verts[4].z = pos.z - farplane*Z.z - distx*X.z + disty*Y.z;

   planes[0].cross(verts[2]-verts[1],verts[0]-verts[1]);
   planes[0].normalize();
   planes[0].w=FLY_VECDOT(verts[0],planes[0]);

   planes[1].cross(verts[3]-verts[2],verts[0]-verts[2]);
   planes[1].normalize();
   planes[1].w=FLY_VECDOT(verts[0],planes[1]);

   planes[2].cross(verts[4]-verts[3],verts[0]-verts[3]);
   planes[2].normalize();
   planes[2].w=FLY_VECDOT(verts[0],planes[2]);

   planes[3].cross(verts[1]-verts[4],verts[0]-verts[4]);
   planes[3].normalize();
   planes[3].w=FLY_VECDOT(verts[0],planes[3]);

   planes[4].cross(verts[3]-verts[1],verts[2]-verts[1]);
   planes[4].normalize();
   planes[4].w=FLY_VECDOT(verts[1],planes[4]);

   static int table[8][3]=
       { {4,5,6},{4,5,2},{4,1,6},{4,1,2},
         {0,5,6},{0,5,2},{0,1,6},{0,1,2} };
   int i,j;
   for( i=0;i<5;i++ )
   {
       j = (FLY_FPSIGNBIT(planes[i].x)>>29)|
           (FLY_FPSIGNBIT(planes[i].y)>>30)|
```

```
                        (FLY_FPSIGNBIT(planes[i].z)>>31);
            bboxindx[i][0]=table[j][0];
            bboxindx[i][1]=table[j][1];
            bboxindx[i][2]=table[j][2];
    }
}
```

An important optimisation concerns the intersection of object/scene AABBs with the view frustum. Every AABB needs to be tested to see if it is intersected by a view frustum plane. The conventional way to approach this would be, for every plane in the frustum, to check the distance to every vertex in the bounding box. If no vertices have a positive distance it means that the box is behind the plane and there is no intersection. And if any vertex has a positive distance we move to the next plane. If all planes are passed with at least one point on the positive side, then the box is clipped by the view frustum. This could be coded as:

```
int flyFrustum::clip_bbox(const flyVector& min,const flyVector& max)
const
{
  const flyVector *v=frustum_clip;
  for( int i=0;i<5;i++,v++ )
  {
    if (v->x*min.x+v->y*min.y+v->z*min.z-v->w>0)
      continue;
    if (v->x*max.x+v->y*max.y+v->z*max.z-v->w>0)
      continue;
    if (v->x*max.x+v->y*min.y+v->z*min.z-v->w>0)
      continue;
    if (v->x*min.x+v->y*max.y+v->z*min.z-v->w>0)
      continue;
    if (v->x*min.x+v->y*min.y+v->z*max.z-v->w>0)
      continue;
    if (v->x*max.x+v->y*max.y+v->z*min.z-v->w>0)
      continue;
    if (v->x*min.x+v->y*max.y+v->z*max.z-v->w>0)
      continue;
    if (v->x*max.x+v->y*min.y+v->z*max.z-v->w>0)
      continue;

    return 0;
  }

  return 1;
}
```

This can be reduced to a single rejection test per plane because of the fact that all bounding boxes are AABBs. When a frustum plane is created we can define a **single** vertex of any AABB that needs to be tested against this plane. If the

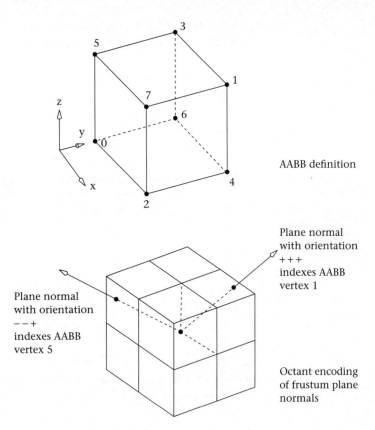

AABB definition

Plane normal
with orientation
+ + +
indexes AABB
vertex 1

Plane normal
with orientation
− − +
indexes AABB
vertex 5

Octant encoding
of frustum plane
normals

Figure 2.1
Associating a plane
(normal) with the AABB
vertex against which it
must be tested.

distance from the plane to this point is negative then all of the vertices must also be negative. To identify the required AABB test vertex for a particular frustum plane we use the plane normal and find the octant which contains it. To do this we pre-compute a vertex index per frustum plane, that is, a bit field (3 bits) representing the signs of the normal components x,y,z of the plane normal (Figure 2.1). For example:

normal (+,+,+) encodes as bits 000 = 0 decimal
normal (−,−,−) encodes as bits 111 = 7 decimal
normal (+,−,+) encodes as bits 101 = 5 decimal

The code to build the bitfield for every frustum plane is:

```
for( int i=0;i<5;i++ )
  bbox_verts[i]=
    (FLY_FPSIGNBIT(planes[i].x)>>29)|
    (FLY_FPSIGNBIT(planes[i].y)>>30)|
    (FLY_FPSIGNBIT(planes[i].z)>>31);
```

The `FLY_FPSIGNBIT` define statement accesses a float **as** an integer. It does not convert the float into an integer, instead it uses the float bits as an integer.

```
#define FLY_FPBITS(fp)    (*(int *)&(fp))
```

The correspondence thus is:

Plane normal encoding	AABB vertex to test
0	1
1	4
2	7
3	2
4	3
5	6
6	5
7	0

The following code uses the above table testing a single vertex per plane, but the switch is inefficient and we have to build a temporary vertex from the minmax definition of the AABB:

```
int flyFrustum::clip_bbox(const flyVector& min,const flyVector& max)
const
{
    flyVector v;
    for( int i=0;i<5;i++ )
    {
        switch(bbox_verts[i])
        {
        case 0: v=max;  break;
        case 1: v.vec(max.x,max.y,min.z);  break;
        case 2: v.vec(max.x,min.y,max.z);  break;
        case 3: v.vec(max.x,min.y,min.z);  break;
        case 4: v.vec(min.x,max.y,max.z);  break;
        case 5: v.vec(min.x,max.y,min.z);  break;
        case 6: v.vec(min.x,min.y,max.z);  break;
        case 7: v=min;  break;
        }

        if (FLY_VECDOT(v,planes[i])-planes[i].w<0)
            return 0;
    }
    return 1;
}
```

A far better approach is to use the following table:

Plane normal encoding	AABB vertex to test
0	4,5,6
1	4,5,2
2	4,1,6
3	4,1,2
4	0,5,6
5	0,5,2
6	0,1,6
7	0,1,2

Min	0: min.x	1: min.y	2: min.z	3: not used
Max	4: max.x	5: max.y	6: max.z	7: not used

In the first table each group of three integers selects the appropriate combination of the minmax vertices to define the required vertex. The final code is

```
int flyFrustum::clip_bbox(const flyBoundBox& bbox) const
{
    float *f=(float *)&bbox.min.x;

    for( int i=0;i<5;i++ )
        if (planes[i].x*f[bboxindx[i][0]]+
        planes[i].y*f[bboxindx[i][1]]+
        planes[i].z*f[bboxindx[i][2]]-planes[i].w<0)
        return 0;
    return 1;
}
```

Figure 2.2 (also Colour Plate) shows the effectiveness of this strategy for a reasonably complex level. The illustrations are rendered from a viewpoint directly above the operational view point. The statistics for this level are:

No. of (AABB) faces in the level   5204
No. of BSP leaf nodes clipped by frustum   1453
No. of AABBs clipping view frustum   587

Near and far planes and the view frustum

There are certain subtleties involved in view frustum parameters, particularly with respect to setting near and far view plane distances.

A common defect exhibited by many implementations is being able to see through a wall when the viewpoint becomes too close to it. This is because

(a)

Figure 2.2
(a) The Padgarden level and a view frustum. All BSP leaf nodes clipped by the view frustum are shown (1453 faces). (b) The Padgarden level with view frustum clipping. Only those faces whose AABB intersects the view frustum are selected for rendering (587 faces).

(b)

particle collision detection is being used by the view frustum (the view-point itself is the particle) and when the distance from the viewpoint to the wall becomes less than the near plane distance, objects on the other side of the wall are rendered. Another factor involved is precision in the Z-buffer: a largish distance for the near view plane is preferable to cut down on Z-buffer artefacts.

We tend always to include a viewpoint in a bounding box. This will either be a player bounding box (first-person games) or a camera bounding box (third-person games). In this way we guarantee that the viewpoint will maintain a minimum distance to all walls. This means that we can have a fixed (large) near plane distance which will not clip objects when the camera moves close to a wall. A good setting for the near plane distance is 0.5 the 'radius' of the bounding box that contains the viewpoint. By radius we mean the distance from the centre of the box to the closest side.

Consider now the far plane. This should be set dynamically to the farthest distance we are rendering in the current frame (to maintain the highest Z-buffer precision). Figure 2.3 (also Colour Plate) demonstrates the effects of far plane setting options.

2.2 Camera control

The most common camera in games is a first-person camera which simply inherits the interface-derived motion of the game player and is therefore straightforward to implement. Another type of camera is a scripted camera in which case the camera becomes an animated rigid body subject to the techniques described in Chapter 8. A topic which can be discussed in its own right is a third-person camera. More possibilities (and difficulties) arise when we come to consider a third-person camera, which is usually located above and behind the game character. We can begin by listing the constraints and requirements of such a camera:

- The camera should never be closer to a wall than the near plane.
- It should never go outside a level.
- It should translate and rotate smoothly.
- It should be able to take different motions to the character so as, for example, to smooth out discontinuities in the character motion which it might inherit.
- The camera needs to be treated for collision detection (like any other dynamic object) using a bounding box.
- The camera should be able to enter the character to take care of situations when, for example, the character is near a wall and with its back close to the wall.

We can program the behaviour of such a camera by breaking it down into the following separate parts:

(a)

Figure 2.3
(a) Correct near and far plane setting for the Padgarden level. (b) Far plane too distant, causing Z-buffer precision artefacts.

(b)

(c)

Figure 2.3 *continued*
(c) Far plane too close –
visible in the scene.
(d) Close far plane
visibility reduced by fog.

(d)

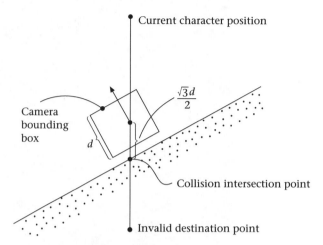

Figure 2.4
Positioning a third person camera for an invalid destination point.

(1) Find the destination point for the camera from the character's position.

(2) Check the validity of the destination point.

(3) Calculate appropriate translation motion of the camera and move it, checking for collision detection with its bounding box.

(4) At the same time, calculate the appropriate rotation motion to make the camera face the new direction.

For a current frame, the required camera destination point is calculated by using the displacement from the position that the game character has just moved to. This can be done as:

(1) Calculate the destination point.

(2) Check the validity of the destination point (it could be on the wrong side of a wall). This can be done using a ray intersect from the character local origin to the destination point (Figure 2.4).

(3) If the destination point is invalid then we need to move the camera reference point back along the line from that point so that it is positioned appropriately on the correct side of the wall. This means moving it so that its distance from the wall is:

$$\sqrt{3}\,d/2$$

where
    d is the dimension of the camera bounding box
    near plane distance $< d/2$

We now have a valid camera destination point and we now have to consider what the motion of the camera should be in moving to its new position. This has to be done carefully for the pursuing camera. Basic strategies will result in undesirable effects, like the camera motion oscillating about the character position by accelerating past the character and moving back.

The most straightforward way to compute this motion is to handle the translation and the rotation component separately. Integrated with the motion computation, we have to call the collision detection routine to see if the motion results in the camera bounding box colliding with the scene at its destination point. (This is exactly the same as the character bounding box collision detection as described in the next section.) If the camera cannot move to its destination point then the collision detection and response becomes responsible for supplying a new destination point.

For translation we could define a maximum velocity and position the camera either at the required destination point or some way towards it, depending on whether the product of the maximum velocity and the frame elapsed time is greater than or less than the distance to be travelled. Pseudo-code for this approach is:

vec = destination − character_position
normalise(vec)
if len > max_velocity*dt **then** len = max_velocity*dt
box_collision(character_position, character_position + vec.len)

This approach suffers from the disadvantage that when the maximum velocity exceeds the character velocity the camera will 'stick' to the character. Alternatively, if the character velocity becomes greater than the maximum velocity it will move away from the camera. A better approach is to define a maximum acceleration and have no limits on the velocity. When the camera reaches the destination point, infinite deceleration is applied to brake it. The code is as follows:

```
// find target position of the camera based on
// dist and height from character position
targetpos=target->pos+dist*target->Z+height*target->Y;

// collision detection to find a valid target position
if (collision_bsp(target->pos,targetpos)!=0)
  targetpos=hitip-(target->Z*(radius*(float)sqrt(3)));

// compute displacement vector for camera
displace=targetpos-pos;

// compute required velocity to cover displacment in this frame
targetvel=displace*(1.0f/dt);

// for each axis
for(i=0;i<3;i++)
{
  // compute required velocity change
  f=targetvel[i]-vel[i];
  // if current velocity and desired velocity
  // are in same direction (same sign)
  if(targetvel[i]*vel[i]>0)
  {
```

```
      // crop with maximum acceleration
      if (f>maxaccel*dt)
        f=maxaccel*dt;
      if (f<-maxaccel*dt)
        f=-maxaccel*dt;
      // change velocity
      vel[i]+=f;
    }
    else
      // braking, infinite acceleration
      vel[i]+=f;
}

// compute new destination position
newpos=pos+vel*dt;
```

For rotation we can define a maximum angular velocity. Not to do so would produce instantaneous alignment to the required view direction, resulting in non-smooth motion. Pseudo-code for this approach is similar to the translation and is:

vec = destination − character_position
normalise(vec)
angle = acos(vec_dot(required_lookdn,vec)
if (angle > max_rot_vel*dt) **then** angle = max_rot_vel*dt
rotate(angle)

rotate implies two separate components. First, we need to rotate the camera to the character look direction, the rotation being in the plane containing the two vectors that define the angle. Second, the camera needs to match the character's orientation about its look direction. Just as with the translation component, a better approach is to define a maximum rotational acceleration:

```
// find desired look direction vector
v=pos-target->pos;
v.normalize();

// compute the angular velocities in each axis
float targetrotvel[2];
targetrotvel[0]=acos(vecdot(Y,target->Y))/dt;
targetrotvel[1]=acos(vecdot(Z,v))/dt;

// for each axis
for(i=0;i<2;i++)
{
   // compute required angular velocity change
   f=targetrotvel[i]-rotvel[i];

   // if current angular velocity and desired
   // angular velocity are in same direction
   if(targetrotvel[i]*rotvel[i]>0)
   {
```

```
         // crop with maximum angular acceleration
      if(f>maxrotaccel*dt)
         f=maxrotaccel*dt;
      if(f<-maxrotaccel*dt)
         f=-maxrotaccel*dt;
      // change angular velocity
      rotvel[i]+=f;
   }
   else
      // braking, infinite angular acceleration
      rotvel[i]+=f;
}

// rotate
rotate(Y,target->Y,rotvel[0]*dt);
rotate(Z,v,rotvel[1]*dt);
```

2.3   Generic collision detection and response with BSPs

Efficient, accurate collision detection is a mandatory part of 3D games. In this section we look at methods to perform particle/scene and bounding box/ scene collision detection with BSP management. General collision detection is a complex, much-researched topic that we cover in some detail in [WATT01]. Collision detection using a BSP management scheme is reasonably straight-forward for simple cases involving particles and bounding boxes, but time has to be handled correctly – we cannot tolerate any 'lost' time. Standard game genres can function well with a simple collision response model, providing this is handled correctly. This response for particle/scene collision uses the concept of an infinitely small sphere together with a factor determining the reaction to the normal component of the incoming velocity (bump) and a factor which determines the tangential reaction (friction). This simple model is shown in Figure 2.5.

2.3.1   Collisions and BSP recursion

Conventional recursion and selection in BSPs can be optimised for collision detection. Consider Figure 2.6. This shows a collision detection from point p_1 to p_2, where p_1 and p_2 are separated by a partitioning plane. We recurse the BSP from front to back and check all objects within the node for intersection. If no intersection is found we move to the next node. The optimisation arises because we can terminate the process at the node the collision is found in. In the example, collisions will be found in the order A,B. D will not be tested.

```
collision_bsp(point1, point2)
{
   push(bsp root node)
```

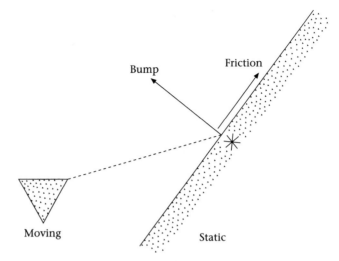

Figure 2.5
A moving object colliding
with a plane.

```
while (stack is not empty)
{
  node = pop_node()
  if (node is leaf)
  {
    ray intersect all objects in node
    return closest intersection
  }
  else
  {
    dist1 = distance from point1 to node plane
    dist2 = distance from point2 to node plane
    if (dist1*dist2<0)
    {
      if (dist1>0)
      {
        push(node child 0)
        push(node child 1)
      }
      else
      {
        push(node child 1)
        push(node child 0)
      }
    }
    else
    {
      if (dist1>0)
        push(node child 0)
```

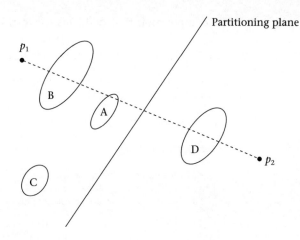

Partitioning plane

p_1

B

A

D

p_2

C

Figure 2.6
Ray intersect collision
detection and BSP nodes.

```
            else
                push(node child 1)
        }
    }
  }
}
```

In the event that we do not require the closest collision, but simply an indication that a collision has occurred, we terminate the process at the first face intersection found. This is useful in the context of lighting, for example, in generating shadows. Alternatively, if we have a homing missile tracking a player, we need to know if there are any objects in the line of sight. We need no information concerning the identity of the intervening objects.

2.3.2 Particle/Scene detection and response

We now consider the collision of a particle with a static object such as a wall. This a standard well-known procedure with many optimisations. Its simplest manifestation consists of intersecting a ray with the plane containing the polygon, then finding if the intersection is contained by the polygon. Consider Figure 2.7a. The particle is initially positioned at p_0 with velocity $\mathbf{v}_0$ and is moving to position p_1:

$$p_1 = p_0 + \mathbf{v}_0{}^*dt$$

After finding the intersection at position p_x, which is a small distance before the actual intersection point, we could find an easy solution by setting the final particle position to p_x and computing the new velocity at point p_x as follows:

$$\mathbf{v_r} = f(\mathbf{v}_0, \mathbf{N}, \text{bump\_factor}, \text{friction\_factor}) \qquad (2.1)$$

where
  $\mathbf{N}$ is the surface normal at the point of intersection
  friction_factor and bump_factor are explained in Section 2.4.4.

The computation that performs this can be implemented as:

```
compute_reflection(dir,normal,bump_factor,friction_factor,refdir)
{
    reflectdir = dir + normal*(-2.0f*vec_dot(normal,dir));
    reflectdir.normalize();

    normalfactor=vec_dot(normal,reflectdir);

    len=dir.length();

    normalvel=normal*(normalfactor*len);
    tanvel=reflectdir*len-normalvel;
    refdir=normalvel*bump_factor+tanvel*friction_factor;
}
```

The problem with this simple solution is that the time at which we position the particle at p_x is the time it would have taken to travel to position p_1 had the collision not occurred. If we use this we have effectively 'lost' time. At this

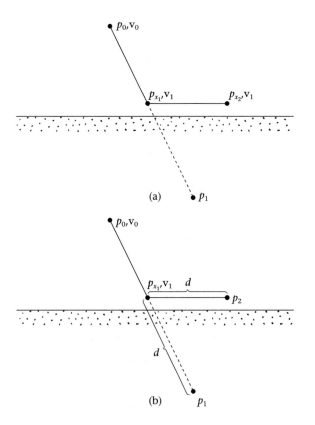

Figure 2.7
Particle collision and 'lost' time.

time the particle must have already collided, responded and moved some distance out of the collision point p_x.

To solve this inadequacy we need to enter a loop at every collision point. Consider the sequence shown in Figure 2.7b. After we find the first collision at point p_x we compute a new velocity at point p_x based on equation 2.1. Say for simplicity the bump factor is 0 and friction factor is 1. The new velocity will be parallel to the plane. We calculate distance d and use this to move the particle to position p_2. We now do exactly the same collision detection and response from p_x to p_2. Thus we must loop until no further collisions are found from one point to the other before returning the final point and velocity. This approach means that no time is lost and the particle will exhibit correct sliding motion (to within the limitations of the simple physics of the simulation model). Pseudo-code for this process is:

```
compute_collision(p0,v0,p1,v1)
{
    p=p0
    repeat
    {
        dir = p1-p
        if(dir length is 0)
            break

        normalize dir
        if (no collision from p to p1)
            break

        p0 = intersectpoint

        compute_reflection(dir,normal,bump_factor,friction_factor,refdir);

        v1 = refdir*v1

        normalize refdir
        p1 = refdir*length(p1-p0)
    }
}
```

2.4

Specialised collision detection and response

Having looked at collision detection in general, we now examine how this important function can be fully optimised for many applications. These are any applications, like FPS games, with fast-moving dynamic objects interacting with other dynamic objects and scene geometry.

It goes without saying that good collision detection is critically important in a game. What does 'good' mean? Brute-force polygon object/polygon object is too expensive and we must make some compromise for the sake of efficiency. Consider action games which are characterised by a player wandering through a complex environment which has been pre-processed – in our case into a BSP tree. Also, small projectiles fly around the environment until they collide with a static object or another dynamic object. First-person shooter games platforms can support other applications – such as immersive shopping – and it is worth developing as good a collision detection and response as we can afford.

The solution we adopt in this case is to accurately detect collisions between dynamic objects as bounding boxes and individual level or static object polygons. In a sense this is an asymmetric solution: why use a bounding volume for dynamic objects and the actual polygons for the static objects? The answer to this is that we can afford to do it because of the BSP pre-processing and it results in the most accurate model.

The dimensions of the player bounding box impact on the game play and determine where the player can go: the smallest aperture through which he can squeeze and the smallest diameter of a hole in the floor into which he will fall. A user soon picks up and subconsciously perceives the 'physical' feel of the bounding box dimension. The bounding box need not completely enclose the player. It may be better to tolerate the resulting penetration to achieve a tighter bounding volume, as we demonstrate in Appendix 2.1.

Note that the bounding box for an animated player must enclose the full extent of the animation. It obviates the efficiency advantage of a bounding volume for a dynamic player if its extent is to change from frame to frame depending on the animation state. It is also the case in multi-player games that even if different characters are of a different size, for game play fairness, all should have the same bounding box dimensions. Thus we see that the choice of bounding volume dimensions involve factors other than the geometry of the object they enclose.

Correct collision response is also extremely expensive and can only be accurately calculated as part of a dynamic simulation where the response is a complex function of (at least) the masses, the angular and linear velocity and the friction of the colliding objects. For a number of game genres a very simplified reaction model suffices, controlled by the previously discussed friction and bump factors.

Consider now the nature of the bounding box. There is a well-known and well-researched trade-off between the shape of a bounding volume, its bounding efficiency and its processing cost. It is also the case that in many demanding applications bounding volumes are arranged into hierarchies. In our case we have chosen to use AABBs (axis-aligned bounding boxes) to bound dynamic objects and to embed them in a method that very quickly checks for collisions between such a box and a BSP processed complex level.

The algorithm now described collision checks:

- an AABB enclosing a dynamic object with the complex geometry of a static level;
- an AABB enclosing a dynamic object with another dynamic object represented either by another AABB or by its actual mesh faces.

The algorithm presented is for the case of an AABB colliding with a convex polygon of any number of edges but it can be easily extended to handle other types of geometry like dynamic LOD Bézier surfaces and triangle soups. The algorithm has been implemented and tested over a huge number of level geometry configurations. The implementation in the engine already extends the concepts presented here to curved faces and other types of geometry supported by the engine. The algorithm extends previously existing algorithms like [COHE95] and [GOTT96], adding an efficient narrow phase collision detection handling and the use of a BSP tree for fast global culling.

The collision detection is accomplished by using the following basic intersection checks:

- a ray/polygon intersection check;
- a ray/AABB intersection check;
- an edge/edge intersection check.

2.4.1 AABB definition

An AABB is a common and popular choice because, by definition, the geometric attributes used in the intersection calculation do not change and can thus be precalculated for a particular dynamic object. The AABB is defined by its minimum and maximum points (6 floats). Static constants can be used for representing the AABB vertex normals (8), face normals (6), edges (12) and edge normals (12). They are all constant for any AABB with any size and are implemented as constant static members.

2.4.2 AABB class definition and static members definition

```
Class FLY_ENGINE_API flyBoundBox
{
    public:
      flyVector min,max;

    static int    facevert[6][4];
    static int    edgevert[12][2];
    static int    edgefaces[12][2];
    static float  vertnorm[8][3];
    static float  edgenorm[12][3];
    static float  facenorm[6][3];
```

```
   // gets AABB vertex position given an vertex index
inline flyVector get_vert(int ind)
   {
      switch(ind)
      {
      case 0: return min;
      case 1: return max;
      case 2: return flyVector(max.x,min.y,min.z);
      case 3: return flyVector(min.x,max.y,max.z);
      case 4: return flyVector(max.x,max.y,min.z);
      case 5: return flyVector(min.x,min.y,max.z);
      case 6: return flyVector(min.x,max.y,min.z);
      case 7: return flyVector(max.x,min.y,max.z);
      default: return flyVector(0,0,0);
      }
   };


   // get distance from the origin to one of
   // the 6 AABB face planes given a face index
   inline float get_plane_dist(int ind)
   {
      return ind>2?max[ind-3]:min[ind];
   };


   // check if two AABB intersect
   inline int clip_bbox(flyVector& bbmin, flyVector& bbmax)
   {
      if (max.x>bbmin.x && min.x<bbmax.x &&
        max.y>bbmin.y && min.y<bbmax.y &&
        max.z>bbmin.z && min.z<bbmax.z)
        return 1;
      return 0;
   }


   // checks if a point is inside a bounding box
   inline int is_inside(flyVector& p)
   {
      return p.x>min.x && p.x<max.x &&
             p.y>min.y && p.y<max.y &&
             p.z>min.z && p.z<max.z;
   }
};


int flyBoundBox::facevert[6][4]=
     { {1,7,2,4},{0,5,3,6},{1,4,6,3},
       {0,2,7,5},{1,3,5,7},{0,6,4,2} };


int flyBoundBox::edgevert[12][2]=
     { {0,6},{6,4},{4,2},{2,0},
       {1,3},{3,5},{5,7},{7,1},
       {0,5},{3,6},{4,1},{7,2}                 };
```

```
int  flyBoundBox::edgefaces[12][2]=
    {  {0,2},{4,2},{3,2},{1,2},
       {4,5},{0,5},{1,5},{3,5},
       {0,1},{0,4},{3,4},{1,3}                    };

float  flyBoundBox::vertnorm[8][3]=
    {  {-FLY_COS45,-FLY_COS45,-FLY_COS45},
       { FLY_COS45, FLY_COS45, FLY_COS45},
       { FLY_COS45,-FLY_COS45,-FLY_COS45},
       {-FLY_COS45, FLY_COS45, FLY_COS45},
       { FLY_COS45, FLY_COS45,-FLY_COS45},
       {-FLY_COS45,-FLY_COS45, FLY_COS45},
       {-FLY_COS45, FLY_COS45,-FLY_COS45},
       { FLY_COS45,-FLY_COS45, FLY_COS45}    };

float  flyBoundBox::edgenorm[12][3]=
                      { {-FLY_COS45,          0,    -FLY_COS45},
                        {         0,  FLY_COS45,    -FLY_COS45},
                        { FLY_COS45,          0,    -FLY_COS45},
                        {         0, -FLY_COS45,    -FLY_COS45},
                        {         0,  FLY_COS45,     FLY_COS45},
                        {-FLY_COS45,          0,     FLY_COS45},
                        {         0, -FLY_COS45,     FLY_COS45},
                        { FLY_COS45,          0,     FLY_COS45},
                        {-FLY_COS45, -FLY_COS45,            0},
                        {-FLY_COS45,  FLY_COS45,            0},
                        { FLY_COS45,  FLY_COS45,            0},
                        { FLY_COS45, -FLY_COS45,            0}};

float  flyBoundBox::facenorm[6][3]=
    {  {-1,0,0},
       {0,-1,0},
       {0,0,-1},
       {1,0,0},
       {0,1,0},
       {0,0,1}  };
```

Collision detection and collision response

We now extend the particle collision method described in Section 2.3.2, replacing the particle with an AABB. It is convenient first to separate the collision detection from the collision response. The main collision detection function will be called with a local AABB (minimum and maximum points relative to its origin), the current position (p_1) – the position the object reached in the previous frame – and the desired destination position (p_2) – the position the object wants to move to in the current frame (Figure 2.8).

The function will check if the supplied AABB can move from p_1 to p_2 and, if a collision is found, it will process it applying the collision response code and recurse to compute the path required by the movement.

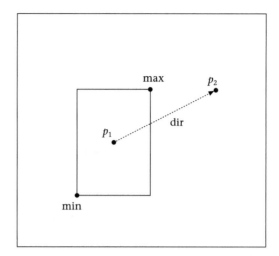

Figure 2.8
AABB defined by max and min points moving from point p_1 to p_2.

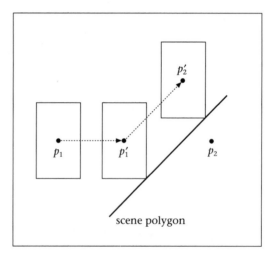

Figure 2.9
Collision detection/ response recursion. AABB was moving from p_1 to p_2. Collision detection determines the point p_1' and collision response the point p_2'. Recursion continues with the AABB colliding now from p_1' to p_2' until no collision is found between the two points.

For a simple box/face intersection as in Figure 2.9, only two loops will be required. The first collision moves the box to p_1' and computes the new destination position p_2' using the response code. Then it loops again, doing collision detection for moving from p_1' to p_2'. As no collision is found between p_1' and p_2', it will stop the loop and return p_2' as the current position for the AABB. In some cases more loops are needed, as in the case of another collision being found between p_1' and p_2'.

The pseudo-code for the main collision detection function is as follows:

Calculate the reflection vector (for the AABB as a particle) and normalise it

Calculate the collision normal (normal to the colliding plane)

normal_factor = vec_dot(collision_normal , reflect_dir)
length_left = length($p_2 - p'_1$)

v_1 = collision_normal * (normal_factor*length_left)
v_2 = reflect_dir*length_left − v_1

$p'_2 = p'_1 + v_1$*bump + v_2*friction

v_1 is a vector parallel to the collision normal and v_2 is parallel to the colliding plane.

Faking collision response with AABBs

Exact collision response between two polygonal objects is expensive. The expense comes not only from the inherent cost of the response calculation but also from the fact that to be able to initiate such a calculation we must have performed collision detection at a polygon/polygon level. And besides, we are not colliding two polygons but an AABB considered as a single entity and a polygon.

The simplest collision response model that we can implement is one that is almost a *de facto* standard, particularly in first-person shooter games. This is the particle model we introduced in Section 2.3.2 which treats the colliding object as a particle and the surface that it is colliding with as a plane. We will now look at this in more detail.

The particle is reflected from the surface, making an exit angle with respect to the normal equal to the incident angle. The behaviour can be modified and made more convincing by using a bump and friction factor. These take values in the range 0 to 1. A value of 0 for the friction factor means an infinite friction (box sticks to the collision plane) and a friction factor of 1 means no friction. A bump factor of 0 means no bump (the box will slide on collision plane) and bump factor of 1 means that the normal component of the velocity will be maintained (the box will bounce with no damping). The most popular bump/friction setting for a first-person shooter game is 0/1, which causes the player to slide along walls with which he collides. The particle is some notional centre of the player; we use this to calculate the response, but we cannot use this to move the player. The player geometry should not penetrate on collision and we must integrate the geometry of the AABB into our response calculations.

The response behaviour can be summarised as:

Bump	Friction	Effect
0	1	Object moves along the collision plane. The object's component normal to the collision plane has been destroyed. There is no resistance to the component parallel to the plane.
1	0	Object moves along the collision normal. The object's velocity component parallel to the collision plane is destroyed by infinite friction.
Non-zero	Non-zero	Objects moves along a direction between the collision normal and the colliding surface plane. The angle depends on the relative values of the two factors.
0	0	Object 'sticks' to the surface.

2.4.5   Collision detection with AABBs

The collision detection method has to find if a box defined by its minimum and maximum points, moving from point p_1 to point p_2, will collide with anything. If a collision is found we need to supply information such as the collision point and collision normal. To achieve this we will need to perform several computations, but fortunately we can cull several of them with simple dot product tests, thus facilitating real-time performance.

Consider the AABB defined by a set of 8 vertices, 12 edges and 6 faces. We then need to compute the closest collision of the following set:

(a) Collision of each of the 8 vertices of the AABB with the scene geometry. To check this we require a ray/polygon intersection method.

(b) Collision of each of the scene geometry vertices with the 6 faces of the AABB (this can be simplified with a ray/AABB optimised intersection routine).

(c) Collision of each of the 12 edges of the AABB with every other scene edge.

It looks like a lot of computation but culling allows us to reduce the computation to a minimum and we only compute the vertices and edges that could actually generate a collision. We start by creating a temporary bound box that will enclose the two (original and destination) bound boxes as in Figure 2.10.

This super AABB must then enclose the AABB of the moving object when and if it collides with a static object. The super AABB facilitates the first culling operation. We use this bounding box to recurse the BSP tree and find the BSP tree leaf nodes that intersect the temporary bounding box. For all the faces in these leaf nodes we cull their bounding boxes with the temporary bound box using the very simple and fast clip_bbox code that checks if two AABB intersect (Section 2.4.2).

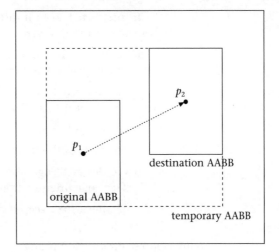

Figure 2.10
Temporary AABB that
encloses all movement.
Created by adding the
point (max+dir) and
(min+dir) to the original
AABB.

At this point we have selected only the faces that intersect the temporary bounding box and we now have to test them precisely for collision, doing the tests for (a), (b) and (c).

Further culling is applied in each of the intersection checks as follows:

(a) Collision of each of the 8 vertices of the AABB with the scene geometry: we can discard AABB vertices that have negative dot products of vertex normal and moving direction.

(b) Collision of each of the scene geometry vertices with the 6 faces of the AABB: we can discard face vertices that have positive dot products of vertex normal and moving direction.

(c) Collision of each of the 12 edges of the AABB with every other scene edge: we can discard AABB edges that have negative dot products with moving direction and also discard face edges that have positive dot products with moving direction.

The pseudo-code for the collision detection routine is:

```
create temporary bound box (original AABB plus move direction*len)

recurse bsp tree with temporary bound box

for all selected leaf nodes

    for all faces in each leaf node

        if face bound box clips temporary bound box
        {
            for each of the 8 AABB vertices
                if vec_dot(vertex normal,move direction) is positive

                    ray intersect face from vertex and move direction
```

> if intersected, keep if distance smaller than current
>
> for each of the face vertices
>
> if vec_dot(vertex normal,move direction) is negative
>   ray intersect AABB from vertex and inverted move direction
>
> if intersected, keep if distance smaller than current
>
> for each of the 12 AABB edges
>
> if vec_dot(AABB edge normal,move direction) is positive
>
> for each of the face edges
>
> if vec_dot(face edge normal,move direction) is negative
>   face edge intersect from from AABB edge and move direction
>
> if intersected, keep if distance smaller than current
>
> }
>
> return closest intersection if any

(2.4.6) **AABB vertex intersecting scene face**

This is the simplest case and a very common computation (Figure 2.11).

We have to test the bound box vertices (8) to check whether their movement in the direction (dir) will hit any of the scene face that clip the temporary bounding box. To reduce the computations required we can cull vertices from the bounding box which have the dot product of their vertex normal and move direction negative. The normal at the collision point will be defined by the collided face normal. We use a simple polygon ray intersection that functions as follows:

> check if face is backfacing the move direction (dir) by the sign of the dot product from face normal and move dir

Figure 2.11
AABB vertex colliding with scene polygon. In this case we use a standard ray/polygon collision code for rays defined by the AABB vertices and the move direction (dir).

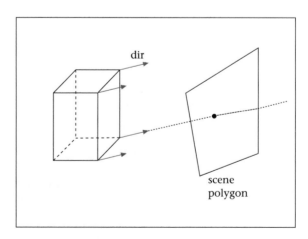

compute the intersection distance from ray defined by vertex position and move direction against the face plane

if distance is negative, return no intersection

compute intersection point using the distance

check if intersection point is inside the polygon

Ray/polygon collision detection code is:

```
// computes intersection from a ray defined by its origin (ro) and
// direction vector (rd). Returns true on a collision and the
// intersection point (ip) and collision distance (dist)

int flyFace::ray_intersect(flyVector& ro,flyVector& rd,flyVector&
ip,float& dist)
{
  // back face culling

  float x=FLY_VECDOT(normal,rd);
  if (FLY_FPSIGNBIT(x)==0)
    return 0; // no intersection

  // compute intersection distance from ray and face plane

  dist=(d0-FLY_VECDOT(normal,ro))/x;
  if (FLY_FPSIGNBIT(dist))
    return 0; // no intersection

  // compute intersection point in face plane

  ip.x=ro.x+rd.x*dist;
  ip.y=ro.y+rd.y*dist;
  ip.z=ro.z+rd.z*dist;

  // check if intersection point is inside the polygon
  // testing the dot products with the polygon edge normals

  for( int i=0;i<nvert;i++ )
    if ((ip.x-vert[i].x)*en[i].x+
       (ip.y-vert[i].y)*en[i].y+
       (ip.z-vert[i].z)*en[i].z > 0)
      return 0; // no intersection

  return 1; // intersection found
}
```

(2.4.7) ## Scene vertex intersecting AABB face

The corollary to the previous case is a scene vertex intersecting the AABB. Here we have to intersect scene vertices from faces that clip the temporary bound box with the bound box in the inverse of the move direction (Figure 2.12).

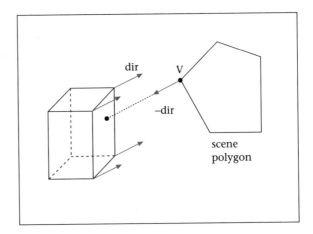

Figure 2.12
Scene polygon vertex
colliding with AABB. In
this case we use a ray/box
collision code for a ray
defined by the scene
vertex (v) and inverted
move direction (–dir).

For this computation we use a simple and optimised ray/AABB intersection routine. To cull some of the computations we can cull vertices that are not inside the temporary bound box. If a face intersects the temporary bound box it is possible that only some of the face vertices lie inside the temporary bound box.

The normal at the collision point will be the AABB face normal at the intersection.

The ray/AABB intersection is a fast algorithm described in [WATT01]. We treat each pair of parallel planes of the AABB in turn, calculating the distance along the ray to the first plane (t_{near}) and the distance to the second plane (t_{far}). The larger of t_{near} and the smaller value of t_{far} are retained between comparisons (of pairs of planes). If the larger value of t_{near} is greater than the smaller value of t_{far} the ray cannot intersect the box.

Ray/AABB collision detection code is:

```
// collide ray defined by ray origin (ro) and ray direction (rd)
// with the bounding box. Returns -1 on no collision and the face
index
// for first intersection if a collision is found together with
// the distances to the collision points (tnear and tfar)

int flyBoundBox::ray_intersect(flyVector& ro,flyVector& rd,float&
tnear,float& tfar)
{
   float t1,t2,t;
   int ret=-1;
   tnear=-FLY_BIG;
   tfar=FLY_BIG;

   int a,b;
   for( a=0;a<3;a++ )
   {
```

```
        if (rd[a]>-FLY_SMALL && rd[a]<FLY_SMALL)
          if (ro[a]<min[a] || ro[a]>max[a])
            return -1;
          else ;
        else
        {
            t1=(min[a]-ro[a])/rd[a];
            t2=(max[a]-ro[a])/rd[a];
            if (t1>t2)
            {
                t=t1; t1=t2; t2=t;
                b=3+a;
            }
            else
                b=a;
            if (t1>tnear)
            {
                tnear=t1;
                ret=b;
            }
            if (t2<tfar)
                tfar=t2;
            if (tnear>tfar || tfar<FLY_SMALL)
                return -1;
        }
    }

    if (tnear>tfar || tfar<FLY_SMALL)
      return -1;

    return ret;
}
```

AABB edge intersecting scene edge

The most complicated computation required is the intersection of the bounding
box edges (12) and all edges from scene faces which clip the temporary bounding box. As before, we can cull edges that have the dot product of their normals and move direction negative. We define the bounding box edge by two
points (p_1,p_2) and the scene edge by two other points (p_3,p_4). We then have to
find if the edge (p_1,p_2) moving in the move direction (dir) will collide the scene
edge (p_3,p_4) and return the distance along the move direction vector and intersection point.

We start by creating a plane that is made from the edge (p_1,p_2) and the move
direction vector (dir). The first test is shown in Figure 2.13.

There are three possible cases and only one can generate a collision. In the
first two cases (Figures 2.13(a) and (b)) the edge vertices (p_3,p_4) are both on the
same side of the plane and no intersection is possible. In the third case we
may have an intersection as each of the edge (p_3,p_4) vertices are on different

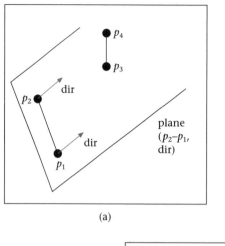
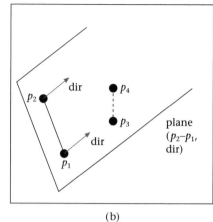

(a)

(b)

Figure 2.13
(a) No collision as p_3 and p_4 are above plane of movement defined by edge (p_1,p_2) and move direction (dir). (b) No collision as p_3 and p_4 are below plane of movement defined by edge (p_1,p_2) and move direction (dir). (c) Collision possible as p_3 and p_4 are each at a different side of the plane. A product between the distances from each edge vertex to the plane must be negative.

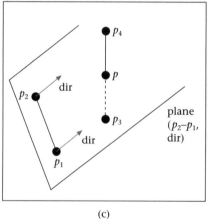

(c)

sides of the plane. If such a case (Figure 2.13(c)) is found, we compute the intersection point (p) of the edge (p_3,p_4). We then end up as in Figure 2.14 and all we have to do now is intersect the two lines defined by edge (p_1,p_2) and (p,–dir).

As the two lines are in the same plane we can use a fast 2D line/line intersection by projecting the 3D lines into the axis plane of greatest projection. If the lines intersect in this plane then they intersect in 3D space. We then test if the intersection point of the two lines lies between the edge vertices (p_1,p_2). This is done efficiently by using a simple dot product as in Figure 2.15. Figure 2.15(a) shows a situation where the intersection point is outside the edge vertices and Figure 2.15(b) shows a case where a collision is found as the intersection point is between the edge (p_1,p_2) vertices.

The normal at the collision point is defined by the cross-product of the two colliding edges. Because the edge orientation of the scene edges is not pre-defined

Figure 2.14
After we find a case like in Figure 2.13(c) we compute the intersection point p from the edge (p_3,p_4) and plane of movement. Then we compute the intersection of the two lines (p_1,p_2) and $(p,-\text{dir})$.

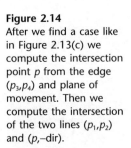

Figure 2.15
(a) No collision as intersection point (ip) from the intersection of line (p_1,p_2) and line $(p,-\text{dir})$ is not between (p_1,p_2). Dot product of $(p_1-\text{ip}).(p_2-\text{ip})$ is positive. (b) Collision is found as intersection point (ip) from the intersection of line (p_1,p_2) and line $(p,-\text{dir})$ is between (p_1,p_2). Dot product of $(p_1-\text{ip}).(p_2-\text{ip})$ is negative.

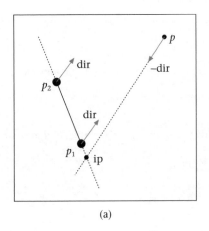

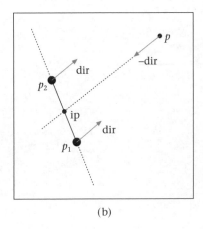

(a)

(b)

we must test for the dot product of the normal and the move direction; if it is positive we must then invert the normal (−normal.x,−normal.y,−normal.z).

The pseudo-code for the algorithm is as follows:

```
edge_edge_collision(p₁,p₂,dir,p₃,p₄,dist,ip)
{
        build plane defined by edge (p₁,p₂) and move direction (dir)
        if edge verts (p₃,p₄) is in same side of plane return false
        compute intersection point of line (p₃,p₄) and plane
        compute largest axis projection of plane
        compute line/line intersection in 2d from line (p₁,p₂) and
        line (p,−dir)
        if new intersection point is not between edge verts (p₁,p₂) return false
        return true

}
```

Edge/Edge collision detection code is:

```
// collide edge (p1,p2) moving in direction (dir) colliding
// with edge (p3,p4). Return true on a collision with
// collision distance (dist) and intersection point (ip)
int flyBoundBox::edge_collision(flyVector& p1,flyVector&
p2,flyVector& dir,flyVector& p3,flyVector& p4,float& dist,flyVector&
ip)
{
  flyVector v1=p2-p1;
  flyVector v2=p4-p3;

  // build plane based on edge (p1,p2) and move direction (dir)
  flyVector plane;
  plane.cross(v1,dir);
  plane.normalize();
  plane.w=FLY_VECDOT(plane,p1);

  // if colliding edge (p3,p4) does not cross plane return no
collision
  // same as if p3 and p4 on same side of plane return 0

  float temp=(FLY_VECDOT(plane,p3)-plane.w)*(FLY_VECDOT(plane,p4)-
plane.w);
  if (FLY_FPSIGNBIT(temp)==0)
    return 0;

  // if colliding edge (p3,p4) and plane are parallel return no
collision

  v2.normalize();
  temp=FLY_VECDOT(plane,v2);
  if(FLY_FPBITS(temp)==0)
    return 0;

  // compute intersection point of plane and colliding edge (p3,p4)

  ip=p3+v2*((plane.w-FLY_VECDOT(plane,p3))/temp);
  // find largest 2D plane projection

  FLY_FPABS(plane.x);
  FLY_FPABS(plane.y);
  FLY_FPABS(plane.z);
  int i,j;
  if (plane.x>plane.y) i=0; else i=1;
  if (plane[i]<plane.z) i=2;
  if (i==0) { i=1; j=2; } else if (i==1) { i=0; j=2; } else
{ i=0; j=1; }

  // compute distance of intersection from line (ip,-dir) to line
(p1,p2)

  dist=(v1[i]*(ip[j]-p1[j])-v1[j]*(ip[i]-p1[i]))/
    (v1[i]*dir[j]-v1[j]*dir[i]);
  if (FLY_FPSIGNBIT(dist))
    return 0;
```

```
        // compute intersection point on edge (p1,p2) line

        ip-=dist*dir;

        // check if intersection point (ip) is between edge (p1,p2)
    vertices

        temp=(p1.x-ip.x)*(p2.x-ip.x)+(p1.y-ip.y)*(p2.y-ip.y)+
    (p1.z-ip.z)*(p2.z-ip.z);
        if (FLY_FPSIGNBIT(temp))
            return 1;  // collision found!

        return 0; // no collision
    }
```

More accurate collision detection

In many applications, enclosing a character in a single AABB is of insufficient accuracy. Two examples might be a football game where we need to know the limb of the player that the ball has collided with, and a martial arts game where a combatant in a fight sequence may need to select one of a number of MoCap sequences depending on where an opponent's punch has landed. In such a set-up a hierarchy of bounding boxes can be used as shown in Figure 2.16.

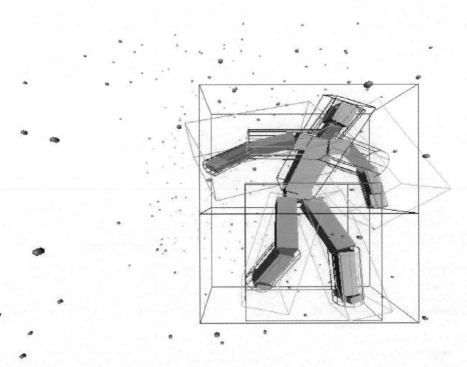

Figure 2.16
A bounding box hierarchy enclosing a character (courtesy of Dan Hawson).

This uses a variety of bounding boxes, including AABBs, OBBs (oriented bounding boxes) and cylinders.

Maintaining a collision threshold

In this final section we attend to the important practical point of floating point precision regarding collision detection. The practical import of this point is that we should never be allowed, for example, to cross through a wall or player due to floating point inaccuracies. As always in such situations, we need to maintain a threshold distance. We can describe the problem by examining a number of cases. The simplest involves moving normally towards a wall (Figure 2.17(a)). There are three possibilities:

(1) The destination point p_2 is well before the collision plane. In which case we can move to p_2 and there is no problem.

(2) p_2 is positioned well beyond the collision plane. In this case a collision is found at the collision plane and we can move to this position less a threshold ε.

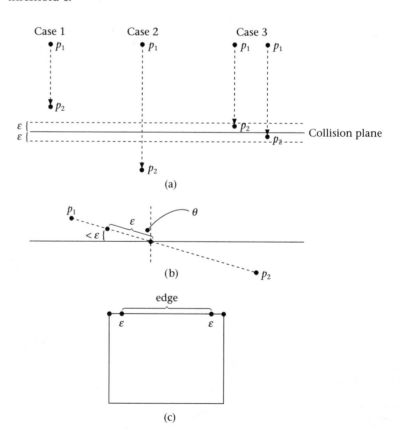

Figure 2.17
Using collision thresholds. (a) Three cases of motion normal to a wall. (b) Motion almost parallel to a wall. (c) Reducing an edge extent by 2ε.

(3) The destination point p_2 is within a distance ε of the collision plane. This is problematic as we may or may not find a collision. If a collision is found we could proceed as the previous case and there will be no problem. However, if a collision is not found and we move to the position p_2 then we will be closer to the collision plane than the threshold. To solve this problem we proceed as follows:

(i) Always add the threshold ε to the destination point. If no collision is found, move to the original destination point. However, if a collision is found we move to the intersection point and subtract the threshold in the direction of movement.

(ii) The above will suffice for objects moving normally or near normally towards a collision plane. However, if the movement is close to being parallel to the collision plane, returning the threshold from the intersection point in the direction of movement will not maintain the required threshold (Figure 2.17(b)). In this case we should return a corrected threshold based on the angle θ between the direction of movement and the collision plane normal. Thus the correct formula is:

$$p_2 = \text{intersection\_point} - \text{dir}*(\varepsilon/\text{vecdot}(\text{normal},\text{dir}))$$

where
$$\text{dir} = \text{normalise}(p_2 - p_1)$$

When considering edges a related problem occurs. If the edges are considered to be their full extent (from one vertex to the other), we could not distinguish between a vertex collision and an edge collision when two polygons are colliding and are within the threshold. This can be solved by considering the extent of an edge to be reduced by 2ε (Figure 2.17(c)).

2.5 Generic path planning

Path planning clearly depends on application. Many applications constrain the path planning problem to two dimensions. In this section we look at a generic three-dimensional method which could service many applications and runs as a real-time process.

As we described in Section 1.2.6, we derive from the convex volume a set of pseudo-portals which can enable basic navigation from a source to a destination by extracting a sequence of convex volume transversals through these portals. The simplest possible navigation just moves from one convex volume into a neighbour, which is randomly chosen from all neighbours of the current convex volume.

In the following example, we move from the centre of the current convex volume to the centre point of the pseudo-portal associated with the chosen neighbour and then to the centre of the destination convex volume. Alternatively, we could choose to move directly from portal centre to portal centre. Because we can guarantee that the volumes are convex we know that a sequence of such paths will never penetrate a wall or other static structure. This is a basis which can be overlaid with an AI application to provide application-dependent path planning.

```
int target::step(int dt)
{
    flyVector dir=targetpos-pos;
    float dist=dir.length();

    if(dist<0.1f)
    {
        find_target();
        dir=targetpos-pos;
        dist=dir.length();
    }

    if(FLY_FPBITS(dist)!=0)
        dir*=1.0f/dist;
    flyVector p=pos+dir*(maxvel*dt);
    if((p-pos).length()>dist)
        pos=targetpos;
    else
        pos=p;

    align_z(dir);

    return 1;
}

void target::find_target()
{
    if(nextnode)
    {
        targetpos=nextnode->centre;
        nextnode=0;
    }
    else
    {
        if(clipnodes.num)
        {
            int r=rand()%clipnodes[0]->neighbors.num;
            nextnode=clipnodes[0]->neighbors[r];
            targetpos=clipnodes[0]->portals[r].get_centre();
        }
    }
}
```

It is important to bear in mind that this method, if extended to produce a valid sequence through many convex volumes, will result in a path whose shape derives from the convex volume decomposition. Because these volumes do not necessarily relate to volumes of space in the level (they emerge from the

BSP granularity and the convex volume finding algorithm), the method may not produce a very direct path. Nevertheless, a valid path is produced from information constructed during the build process.

We now consider how to find a path automatically. Using an A* algorithm, we can very efficiently find a path through the portals which moves an object from a given source to a given destination in the level. We can do this by first finding the leaf nodes which contain the start and destination points, then apply the A* algorithm to find all leaf nodes we will have to cross. From the list of leaf nodes to cross we can compute a path, linear through the portal centres (or even curved using simple Bézier curves with control points at the portal centre).

Figure 2.18(a) (also Colour Plate) shows the missile, now randomly selecting a power-up anywhere in the level and computing a path (shown in red) to travel from its current position to the power-up position anywhere in the level (drawn in red). Figure 2.18(b) (also Colour Plate) shows a simple 'smoothing' process applied to the path. We test for point removal ray intersecting the first and last of each group of three vertices.

2.5.1 A* path selection

The A* algorithm, first proposed in 1968, is a classic AI algorithm that can be applied directly to finding an optimal path from a source to a destination. Although AI is outside the scope of this text, since we have included, as part of the build process, the decomposition of a level into a set of convex volumes, we will include an A* algorithm that selects an optimal path. Recall that we have available from the convex volumes potential paths from any source convex volume to any destination convex volume and the A* algorithm will find for us the least cost path from a given source to a given destination.

We can note in passing that effective AI in games is likely to be a multi-layered approach. Here we have what may comprise the two lowest layers in an AI system which control the behaviour of an agent navigating a level or game environment. At the lowest level we have a geometric decomposition – the convex volumes – that enables us to find potential paths; the next level up analyses these paths to find the best one according to some criteria. Above this level would be higher-order behaviour controllers: for example, how is the destination node selected, is there any strategy to be followed in travelling to the destination? Many other low-level considerations may be involved depending on the application. In our case collision avoidance of detail objects and other dynamic objects would have run concurrently with the agent motion. We have derived paths on the basis of (ray) visibility between convex volumes. What if the object using the path is of a size that does not permit navigation through one part of a path? Should this criterion be part of the path search algorithm; or should we let the object proceed and explore, backing up when 'stuck'?

As we have already discussed, these topics are properly part of an AI text; but we certainly consider that implementing automatic *potential* path finding,

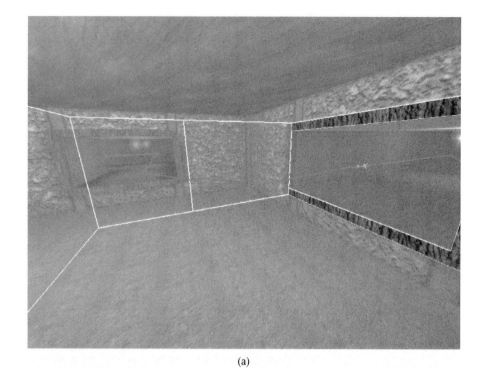

(a)

Figure 2.18
(a) Part of a path from a source convex volume to a destination volume generated using A*.
(b) The same partial path 'collapsed' by ray intersecting the first and last of each group of three vertices to remove points.

(b)

as a real-time process onto which higher-level AI can be grafted, is part of the generic real-time processes of a modern games engine.

The A* works by assigning a cost function $f(n)$ to every node in the current path or iteration. This function is:

$$f(n) = g(n) + h(n)$$

where

$g(n)$ is the cost of the path between the initial node and the current node n

$h(n)$ is a heuristic expressing the cheapest cost path from n to the destination node

In our case 'cost' will relate to distance. For example, consider we are trying to find the best route between two cities through a number of intermediate cities. For a current city, n, $g(n)$ would be the distance travelled from the start city and $h(n)$ could be the straight line distance from n to the destination city. h is known as an 'admissible heuristic' because it calculates a cost that will always be less than or equal to the cost of the best route from n to the destination. (Trivially $h(n)$ can be set to zero for all n and the algorithm then reduces to a blind search.) Under this condition the A* algorithm is guaranteed to return a minimum cost path.

The algorithm's ability to find the optimal path relies on the heuristic function $h(n)$. The higher the weight of this function in the decision of which next step to take, the lower the number of nodes that will be processed, but the higher the probability of finding a sub-optimal path. The trade-off in using A* is just about that: the more it approaches the blind (but exact) search, the more wrong nodes it will have to explore. Steve Rabin's 'A* Speed Optimizations' article [RABI01] discusses the impact of the heuristic cost on the quality of the solution and the speed of the search.

The algorithm explores all routes through the graph that encapsulates the paths connecting nodes together and it does this by preferring nodes with lowest f values. For each iteration, there are some nodes that the algorithm has already visited and others it has not. For each visited node, it may be part of already found paths from source to destination and the information at the node may need to be updated. The node only memorises the minimum cost path.

This behaviour is implemented by having the program maintain two lists – Open and Closed – for unvisited and visited nodes respectively. Both list are initialised to empty and at the first iteration, the start node is placed in the Open list and the algorithm explores the neighbouring nodes (the nodes directly connected to the start node). Such an examination of nodes adjacent to the nth node is called an expansion of n. At each iteration the algorithm removes the best node (lowest f) from the Open list and expands the node. When such an expansion includes a node n' already visited, it may be that this expansion is a path with a lower cost than any of the previously explored paths from the start node, causing the algorithm to update the node.

The following structure is the basic knowledge that the A* search needs.

```
struct a_star_node
{
   int leaf;
   float cost;
   float estimate;
   a_star_node* parent;
};
```

Each A* node is related to a convex volume in the scene. The leaf variable is an index to an external array of convex volumes, defining this relationship. The cost and estimate variables represent the $g(n)$ and $h(n)$ components of the $f(n)$ function, respectively. The parent pointer is required for A* to be able to build the path backwards from the goal node, once it is found.

The following method finds the 'best' node in a list of nodes. Typically, the best node is the one with the least estimate cost to the goal.

```
int get_best_node(flyArray<a_star_node*> list,flyBspNode*
dest,a_star_node* &node)
{
   float f,mindist=FLY_BIG;
   int best=-1;

   for(int i=0;i<list.num;i++)
      if(list[i]->leaf!=-1)
      {
         f=list[i]->cost+list[i]->estimate;
         if(f<mindist)
         {
            mindist=f;
            best=i;
            node=list[i];
         }
      }

   return best;
}

float get_cost(flyBspNode* a,flyBspNode* b)
{
   return (a->centre-b->centre).length();
}
```

A* still needs a method to find out if a given node is inside a given list, and if so, what is the index of the node in the list:

```
int is_in(flyArray<a_star_node*> list, a_star_node* node)
{
   if(node->leaf==-1)
      return -1;
```

```
       for(int i=0;i<list.num;i++)
         if(list[i]->leaf==node->leaf)
            return i;

     return -1;
}
```

Finally, the following method is the A* itself, as described above.

```
int a_star( flyBspNode* source,flyBspNode* dest,
             flyArray<a_star_node*> nodes,flyArray<flyBspNode*>& path)
{
  flyArray<a_star_node*> open,closed;
  a_star_node* node=0;
  int ind;

  nodes[source->leaf]->leaf=source->leaf;
  nodes[source->leaf]->cost=0;
  nodes[source->leaf]->estimate=get_cost(source,dest);
  nodes[source->leaf]->parent=0;
  open.add(nodes[source->leaf]);

  while(open.num)
  {
     ind=get_best_node(open,dest,node);
     open.remove(ind);

     if(g_flyengine->leaf[node->leaf]==dest)
     {
       path.add(g_flyengine->leaf[node->leaf]);
       while(node->parent)
       {
          node=node->parent;
          path.add(g_flyengine->leaf[node->leaf]);
       }

       return 1;
     }
     else
     {
      for(int i=0;i<g_flyengine->leaf[node->leaf]->neighbors.num;i++)
      {
          int neighbor_leaf=g_flyengine->leaf[node->leaf]->
          neighbors[i]->leaf;
          a_star_node* newnode=nodes[neighbor_leaf];

          if(newnode->leaf==-1)
          {
             newnode->leaf=neighbor_leaf;
             newnode->cost=get_cost(source,g_flyengine->leaf
             [neighbor_leaf]);
          }

          float newcost=node->cost+
             get_cost(g_flyengine->leaf[node->leaf],
             g_flyengine->leaf[newnode->leaf]);
```

```
                         if(((is_in(open,newnode)!=-1)||
                             (is_in(closed,newnode)!=-1))&&
                             (newcost>=newnode->cost))
                             continue;
                     else
                     {
                        newnode->parent=nodes[node->leaf];
                        newnode->cost=newcost;
                        newnode->estimate=
                           get_cost(g_flyengine->leaf[newnode->leaf],dest);

                        int j=is_in(closed,newnode);
                        if(j!=-1)
                           closed.remove(j);
                        j=is_in(open,newnode);
                        if(j!=-1)
                           open[j]=newnode;
                        else
                           open.add(newnode);
                     }

                     closed.add(node);
                  }
               }
            }

      return 0;
}
```

Appendix 2.1 Demonstrations of real-time processes

The demonstrations in this section relate to the real-time processes described in the text and consists of parameter experimentation, either by using console commands or by using the editor.

(1) View frustum culling

This demonstration enables you to visualise the effects of view frustum culling. It sets a camera to look down vertically on the scene and draws lines to visualise the view frustum. The scene is rendered with all the frustum clipped BSP leaf nodes (with or without VFC).

(1) Run any level.

(2) Press esc to reveal the console. Use the console command *set debug 4* and translate and rotate the view frustum by using the controls in the normal manner. This mode renders the subset of the scene which clips the view frustum using VFC.

(3) Use the console command *set debug 12* to turn the VFC off.

(4) F6 turns PVS on/off.

(2) Third-person camera

Figure A2.1
Third-person camera mode.

(1) Run the *ship_Mp1* demo which has the described third-person camera implemented (press z for third-person mode) (Figure A2.1 (also Colour Plate)).

(2) In the editor (or the console) you can experiment with the camera parameters. For example on the console:

```
set cam.height –100        // look from below, instead of above
set cam.dist 250           // look from far away
set cam.maxaccel 0.0002    // 'loosen' camera character coupling
```

(3) Collision detection

This demonstration enables you to become familiar with the behaviour of the collision detection methodology described in the chapter.

(1) Run the Padgarden level.

(2) Press esc to reveal the console. Use the console command *set debug 1* to visualise the AABBs of all dynamic objects including the first person. (Note that bounding boxes for animated static objects such as power-ups are enclosed in a box that encompasses their entire movement. It is more efficient to compute such bounding boxes once, rather than re-compute at every frame.)

(3) **Edge/Edge**: Try to move to similar positions as the following third-person view screen shots show. The two screen shots (Figure A2.2 (also Colour Plate)) show edge/edge collisions only and you get a good idea of the behaviour of the collision response code when forcing yourself into such situations.

(4) **Scene Vertex/AABB**: Here vertices from the yellow garden tool hit the player AABB (Figure A2.3 (also Colour Plate)). Note that the player's bounding box does not in fact bound the entire extent of the player. This is because we must decide on a static box irrespective of the animation extents and a choice

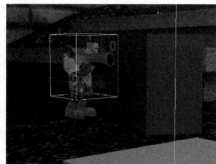

Figure A2.2
Edge/edge collision.

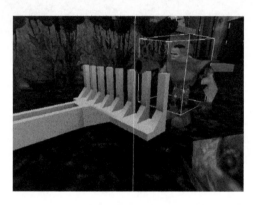

Figure A2.3
Scene vertex/AABB
collision.

must be made which trades between the tightness of the box and the accuracy of the detected collision. Thus we tolerate some penetration. There are also considerations concerning apertures etc. in the level that we may want the player to go through. In a multi-player application all players should have the same bounding box extent and therefore the same ability to reach all areas in the level.

(5) **AABB Vertex/Scene**: Here the player is inside another dynamic object (the boat) (Figure A2.4 (also Colour Plate)). In this case the player is colliding with the faces of the boat object which could itself be moving. If the boat is moving it will be an AABB which is tested for.

(6) **Player dynamics – friction and bump**: A player is dynamic object and, as we described, the collision response is determined by the current velocity, the collision normal bump and friction factors. Change the friction to zero by typing *set player.friction 0* on the console, which will cause an infinite friction and adhesion at the point of impact. The bump factor maintains the reaction along the collision normal. Setting this to 1 means that you reflect along the collision normal at the incident speed. Normal setting for a first-person shooter is friction = 1 and bump = 0. In this case you slide along the contact face until you change the direction.

Figure A2.4
AABB vertex/scene
collision.

(7) **Player mass and level gravity:** When the player jumps or falls from a high point, its mass and gravity control the subsequent motion. A jump pad by definition possesses a target point. When the jump pad is activated it will push the player so that with its current mass and gravity it reaches the target point with an appropriate motion. Set the player mass to 5 (much heavier) and note the effect. Because the player is much heavier but must be propelled to the same destination, a stronger force is required from the jump pad and the player lands more heavily.

Pseudo-portal demonstration

This demo runs a level with pseudo-portal faces superimposed. Always choosing a direction through a pseudo-portal will enable easy navigation through the level.

To view all the portals from the leaf node in which the camera centre is contained, use the following console command:

set debug 4

This can be used in any level and while you move around you will be able to see all portals from all nodes.

3

The anatomy of an advanced games system III

Software design and application programming

3.1 Types of applications

3.2 Fly3D engine architecture

Appendix 3.1 Writing a plug-in

(**Note** that this chapter should be read in conjunction with the Engine Reference Manual available on the CD-ROM.)

The aim of this chapter is to describe how the methods developed in the previous two chapters fit together into a games engine, how new functionality can be created from the games system and the other components – such as front-ends – which are necessary to embed everything in an operating system. It is also, at the same time, a description of how to use the system which we hope the reader will experiment with.

A games engine must satisfy two demands. It should enable the efficient rendering of all the static and dynamic objects together with their interaction. It should also easily facilitate new functionalities and game entities. It must implement all processes that are generic to applications that are going to be implemented. Thus all behaviours that we decide are generic – for example, collision detection, should be part of the engine. The set of all current game genres encompasses a large volume of generic processes. The question is what is the best way to implement generic behaviour and enable a game builder to interface with it. A good way to do this is to have all game-specific behaviour embedded in plug-ins and all major operating system calls in a front-end application. With this approach it is simple to add a new behaviour or feature to the software without having to recompile it. We simply construct a plug-in DLL and link it to the engine's main library. Thus a new game or application can be developed as a plug-in DLL linked to the engine and is able to use all the engine's interface classes, methods and variables.

One of the most important aspects of a good engine is efficiency. In this case the critical aspect of performance is partially addressed by keeping highly related methods and classes 'close' and accessible in the code to avoid unnecessary levels of indirection when a desired piece of data is required. On the other hand, classes and modules that need no knowledge of each other are kept separate for the sake of portability, stability and code security.

What follows then is a description of the particular software design that we have adopted for Fly3D. Like many games engines, and indeed any software project, experience gained in the development of the first version motivates the development of a second version. This chapter describes in detail the software architecture of Version 2 of Fly3D and gives the motivation for the important enhancements to Version 1 [WATT00]. Although these are somewhat specific to Fly3D, they demonstrate general principles of any games engine that admits common games applications where user-controlled action takes place in a complex navigable environment. We offer our approach, not as 'the last word in software design for games', but as an example of a state-of-the-art games SDK.

The treatment that follows generally adopts the form: motivation of the application followed by a simple example of its implementation.

3.1 Types of applications

To implement new functionality in the games system we use the following types of application:

Plug-ins
Front-ends
Utilities

3.1.1 Plug-ins

Plug-ins are dynamic link libraries, or DLLs, that implement new or specific game behaviour. As the name implies, a DLL is linked to the application at run time. Plug-in behaviours are implemented through virtual functions in the C++ classes defined in them. Each new class defined in the plug-in must be derived from the engine *flyBspObject* from where it inherits functionality and properties such as position, velocity etc.

Common plug-in characteristics

Each plug-in must implement three global methods exported in its DLLs to be recognised as a plug-in in Fly3D. These are:

```
int num_classes()
```

The method must return the number of classes implemented by the plug-in.

```
flyClassDesc *get_class_desc(int i)
```

The method must return the class description pointer for the ith implemented class.

```
int fly_message(int msg,int param,void *data)
```

This is where the plug-in processes the messages it receives from the engine or from other plug-ins.

Types of plug-ins

Each plug-in can be one of the following types:

- processing plug-ins;
- plug-ins that define a collection of objects – an object repository plug-in;
- composite plug-ins of both the above types.

An entire game can be built in a single plug-in, but any application should be divided into different modules to facilitate code reuse, maintenance and bug-catching.

Processing plug-ins

Processing plug-ins do not enumerate any classes. They implement all their functionality through the global method exported from the DLL *fly_message()*. This is called by the engine during the simulation to notify the plug-in of the initialisation of the scene, closing of the scene, and also causes the plug-ins to update their (frame) state, draw themselves in 3D and then in 2D.

Such plug-ins process the following standard messages plus any custom-defined messages.

```
FLY_MESSAGE_INITSCENE       // Initialise scene
FLY_MESSAGE_UPDATESCENE     // Update scene
FLY_MESSAGE_DRAWSCENE       // Draw scene (3D drawing)
FLY_MESSAGE_DRAWTEXT        // 2D drawing
FLY_MESSAGE_CLOSESCENE      // Close scene
FLY_MESSAGE_MPMESSAGE       // Multiplayer message
FLY_MESSAGE_MPUPDATE        // Multiplayer update
```

Plug-ins that enumerate objects

These plug-ins enumerate new game objects which are classes derived from the *flyBspObject* engine class. Each plug-in can enumerate an unlimited number of objects implementing their functionality through the virtual methods from the base class. Each object can export parameters of pre-defined types (integer, float, vector, colour, string, etc. . . .).

Composite plug-ins

Composite plug-ins enumerate objects and process messages. An entire game can be implemented in such a plug-in, but for reuse of components and the organisation of the code it is better to break up the application into separate plug-ins.

Example of a composite plug-in

The example developed in this section (see code below) is a simple dynamic object with the geometry of a box. It moves around in space and can potentially collide with level geometry.

First, every object must have the following class entities:

- object parameters (floats, integers, vector, pointers to other objects);
- constructor;
- copy constructor;
- destructor;
- custom methods;
- virtual methods.

The header file defines the new class implemented by the plug-in *observer* and its class description *observer_desc*. The *observer* object derives from the engine-based class *flyBspObject* and implements functionality through the virtual functions *init* and *step*. The *observer* is configured by five float parameters that specify its keyboard rotational velocity, mouse rotational velocity, player acceleration, maximum velocity and damping factor. Note that in the class constructor we must initialise all class parameters with their default values so that when a new object of this type is created, the object will be valid. Every object must implement a copy constructor from a reference *const* class where all object parameters are copied from the supplied object (note that the copy constructor from the base class must also be called). The object destructor must be virtual.

The object's behaviour is implemented through its virtual functions. The *clone* method must return a new instance that is exactly the same as the original object. Its implementation calls the *copy constructor* and returns. The *init* method is called once for each object, just before it is added to the simulation; here the object is subject to any required custom initialisation. In this case the object's bounding box (used for collision detection) is set up based on its *radius* parameter.

Also, for each class implemented in the plug-in, a class description class must be created. The class description must derive from the engine *flyClassDesc* class and implements very simple virtual functions:

create()	returns a new instance of this class
get_name()	returns a string with the class name
get_type()	returns an integer identifying this class

The main behaviour simulation is incorporated in the *step* method. This method receives the elapsed time (for the previous frame in mS) and updates the object's state accordingly. In this case updating the object state means moving it, based on its current velocity and force, and at the same time, applying collision detection. The exact sequence of operations implemented by the observer object is as follows:

(1) Check inputs (keys and mouse).

(2) Apply the damping factor to the current velocity vector and crop with maximum velocity.

(3) Compute the desired destination position and velocity.

(4) Apply collision detection, which returns a new position and velocity (if a collision has occurred).

The final method *get_custom_param_desc* is used to inform the engine about the object's custom parameters – in this case the five floats. For each parameter the following information has to be supplied:

• parameter name (string);

• parameter type (integer);

• parameter data pointer (void pointer).

The processing part of the plug-in is implemented by the *fly_message* global exported plug-in method. In this case we are processing two messages – 3D scene draw and 2D scene draw. The 3D scene draw renders the world as seen from the point of view of the observer. The 2D scene draw prints the current frame rate etc.

observer.h

```
enum
{
  TYPE_OBSERVER=0x199,
};

class observer : public flyBspObject
{
public:
  // object parameters
  float radius;
  float rotvel;
  float mousevel;
  float moveforce;
  float maxvel;
  float veldamp;

  // constructor
  observer() :
    radius(20),
    rotvel(0.1f),
```

```
          mousevel(0.1f),
          moveforce(0.01f),
          maxvel(0.1f),
          veldamp(0.001f)
      { type=TYPE_OBSERVER;  }

    // copy constructor
    observer(const observer&  in)  :
        flyBspObject(in),
        radius(in.radius),
        rotvel(in.rotvel),
        mousevel(in.mousevel),
        moveforce(in.moveforce),
        maxvel(in.maxvel),
        veldamp(in.veldamp)
      { }

    // destructor
    virtual ~observer()
      { }

    // custom methods
    void check_keys(int dt);

    // virtual methods
    void init();
    int step(int dt);
    int get_custom_param_desc(int i,flyParamDesc *pd);
    flyBspObject  *clone()
      { return new observer(*this); }
};

class observer_desc : public flyClassDesc
{
public:
    flyBspObject *create() { return new observer; };
    const char *get_name() { return "observer"; };
    int get_type() { return TYPE_OBSERVER; };
};
```

observer.cpp

```
#include "..\..\lib\Fly3D.h"
#include "observer.h"

observer_desc cd_observer;

__declspec( dllexport )
int num_classes()
{
    return 1;
}
```

```
__declspec( dllexport )
flyClassDesc *get_class_desc(int i)
{
  switch(i)
  {
  case 0:
     return &cd_observer;
  default: return 0;
  }
}

__declspec( dllexport )
int fly_message(int msg,int param,void *data)
{
  switch(msg)
  {
  case FLY_MESSAGE_DRAWSCENE:
     g_flyengine->set_camera(g_flyengine->cam);
     g_flyengine->draw_bsp();
     break;
  case FLY_MESSAGE_DRAWTEXT:
     {
     char str[64];
     sprintf(str,"FPS:%i ",g_flyengine->frame_rate);
     g_flyrender->draw_text( flyRender::s_screensizex-56, 0, str );
     }
     break;
  }
  return 1;
}

void observer::init()
{
  bbox.min.vec(-radius,-radius,-radius);
  bbox.max.vec(radius,radius,radius);
}

int observer::step(int dt)
{
  check_keys(dt);

  float len=vel.length();
  if (len<0.01f)
    vel.null();
  else
  {
    vel/=len;
    len-=dt*veldamp;
    if (len>maxvel)
       len=maxvel;
    if (len<0.0f)
       len=0.0f;
    vel*=len;
  }
```

```
        static flyVector p,v;
        p=pos+vel*(float)dt;
        v=vel+force*((float)dt/mass);
        box_collision(p,v);
        pos = p;
        vel = v;

        return 1;
    }

void observer::check_keys(int dt)
{
    unsigned char *keys=g_flydirectx->keys;

    if (keys[0x38])  // ALT key
        {
        if (keys[0xcb])  // left arrow
            vel-=X*(moveforce*dt);

        if (keys[0xcd])  // right arrow
            vel+=X*(moveforce*dt);

        if (keys[0xc8])  // up arrow
            vel+=Y*(moveforce*dt);

        if (keys[0xd0])  // down arrow
            vel-=Y*(moveforce*dt);

        if (keys[0x1f])  // S key
            vel-=Z*(moveforce*dt);

        if (keys[0x2d])  // X key
            vel+=Z*(moveforce*dt);
        }
    else
        {
        if (keys[0xc8])  // up arrow
            rotate(-dt*rotvel,X);

        if (keys[0xd0])  // down arrow
            rotate(dt*rotvel,X);

        if (keys[0xcb])  // left arrow
            rotate(dt*rotvel,Y);

        if (keys[0xcd])  // right arrow
            rotate(-dt*rotvel,Y);

        if (keys[0x10])  // Q key
            vel-=X*(moveforce*dt);

        if (keys[0x12])  // E key
            vel+=X*(moveforce*dt);

        if (keys[0x1f])  // S key
            vel-=Z*(moveforce*dt);
```

```
            if (keys[0x2d])  // X key
              vel+=Z*(moveforce*dt);
            }

      if (keys[0x1e])  // A key
        rotate(dt*rotvel,Z);
      if (keys[0x20])  // D key
        rotate(-dt*rotvel,Z);

      if (g_flydirectx->mouse_smooth[0]) // mouse X
        rotate(-g_flydirectx->mouse_smooth[0]*mousevel,Y);
      if (g_flydirectx->mouse_smooth[1]) // mouse Y
        rotate(g_flydirectx->mouse_smooth[1]*mousevel,X);
    }


    int observer::get_custom_param_desc(int i,flyParamDesc *pd)
    {
      if (pd!=0)
      switch(i)
      {
      case 0:
        pd->type='f';
        pd->data=&radius;
        pd->name="radius";
        break;
      case 1:
        pd->type='f';
        pd->data=&rotvel;
        pd->name="rotvel";
        break;
      case 2:
        pd->type='f';
        pd->data=&mousevel;
        pd->name="mousevel";
        break;
      case 3:
        pd->type='f';
        pd->data=&moveforce;
        pd->name="moveforce";
        break;
      case 4:
        pd->type='f';
        pd->data=&maxvel;
        pd->name="maxvel";
        break;
      case 5:
        pd->type='f';
        pd->data=&veldamp;
        pd->name="veldamp";
        break;
      }
      return 6;
    }
```

Front-ends

Front-ends are executables that provide a user interface and execute system elements within the current operating system. In this section we describe a typical set of such executables.

Examples of front-ends are as follows.

Simple front-ends (flyFrontend.exe, flyFe.exe)

These use the basic sequence of operations:

(1) initialise the main window, the 3D engine, render and other necessary components,

(2) load a level (static geometry, plug-ins, models, etc.),

(3) loop – calling the simulation for each frame (*flyEngine->step()*),

(4) finalise the engine and free the allocated resources,

and form the main game interface that enables the game to be executed. For example, *flyFrontend.exe* is the main front-end application of the engine. It consists of a rendering window, where simulation occurs, and a menu for opening .fly files. By pressing F1 while in this front-end, one can run a menu where one can choose single or multi-player modes, load a .fly file and start a simulation, or play a pre-recorded demo file. Also included in this interface are the rendering options:

> F1: Menu
> F2: Mute
> F3: Record Demo
> F4: Take Screenshot
> F5: Node-only Mode
> F6: PVS Toggle
> F7: Mip-Mapping Toggle
> F8: Texture Filtering Toggle
> F9: Multitexture Toggle
> F10: Stencil Toggle
> F11: Wireframe Toggle
> F12: Clear Background

Editor front-ends (flyEditor.exe, flyShader.exe)

These are more complex and larger applications which enable user access to the game configuration and entities while running the game. They are a useful development tool that expose the plug-in parameters for developer experimentation.

flyEditor.exe is the main editing tool in Fly3D. It consists of a tree-view, where all entities of the scene are displayed and categorised; a list-view, where parameters are shown and edited; and a rendering window, where the game or application is in action. *flyEditor.exe* allows on-the-fly parameter change visualisation, that is, you can changes a value in the list-view and see the results immediately in the rendering view. You can also load additional plug-ins to use in the game or application, add and delete entities, modify existing ones, and save a .fly file with all these configurations.

flyShader.exe is the shader effects editing tool. With it, you can load the entire shaders list (a .shr file) of a given scene, edit the effects and see the shader in action in the rendering window. You can also load a .f3d mesh object, edit its shader and see it animating. Vertex programs can be applied to the mesh, using a script file.

flyShader.exe features all the possible shader effects for a maximum of eight shader passes, with alpha channel blending, RGB generation functions, animation maps consisting of various key-frames, scrolling, rotation and scaling of textures, environment mapping, texture clamping, etc.

Front-ends in MFC (Fly3D.ocx, flyEditor.exe)

These use the Microsoft Foundation Class library integrated with the engine classes which enables the use of new Windows components. *Fly3D.ocx* is the Fly3D ActiveX Control. With it, the whole Fly3D Engine is available for in-browse applications, such as Web 3D games, 3D browsing, 3D virtual shopping, 3D presentations, etc. An HTML file with **Fly3d.ocx** inside it is built, and uses the control's commands to load .fly files and start the 3D simulation.

Console front-ends (flyServer.exe, flyBuild.exe)

These are front-ends which do not require a render and process all their input/output through a command line interface. They are used for processing data or for simulating the complete game as a server.

Code for the simplest possible front-end now follows. The sequence of operations is:

(1) Create the application window.

(2) Initialise the DirectX, render and engine.

(3) Set full screen mode.

(4) Load a sample level (in this case the Menu).

(5) Loop on simulation until the application is quit.

(6) Free all resources and close the application window.

```
#include <windows.h>
#include "..\..\lib\Fly3D.h"

char szTitle[100]="MyGame Title";
char szWindowClass[100]="MyGame";
```

```
// loads the menu level
void LoadLevel(HWND hWnd, HINSTANCE hInst)
{
   fly_init_directx(hWnd,hInst);
   fly_init_render(hWnd,hInst);
   fly_init_engine(hWnd,hInst,FLY_APPID_FLYFRONTEND);

   flyRender::s_fullscreen=1;
   g_flyrender->set_full_screen();

   g_flyengine->open_fly_file("menu.fly");
}

int WINAPI WinMain (HINSTANCE hInst, HINSTANCE hPrev, LPSTR lp, int nCmd)
{
WNDCLASS wcl;
MSG msg;

// register window class
wcl.style          = CS_HREDRAW | CS_VREDRAW;
wcl.lpfnWndProc    = (WNDPROC)WinFunc;
wcl.cbClsExtra     = 0;
wcl.cbWndExtra     = 0;
wcl.hInstance      = hInst;
wcl.hIcon          = LoadIcon(NULL, IDI_WINLOGO);
wcl.hCursor        = 0;
wcl.hbrBackground  = 0;
wcl.lpszMenuName   = NULL;
wcl.lpszClassName  = szWindowClass;
if (!RegisterClass (&wcl))
{
   MessageBox (0, "Can't register Window", "ERROR", MB_OK);
   return 0;
}

// create main window
HWND hWndMain = CreateWindowEx(0,szWindowClass,szTitle,WS_POPUP,
                0, 0,GetSystemMetrics( SM_CXSCREEN ),
                GetSystemMetrics(SM_CYSCREEN ),
                NULL,NULL,hInst,NULL );

// load the level
ShowWindow (hWndMain, SW_MAXIMIZE);
LoadLevel (hWndMain, hInst);

// main loop
while (1)
  {
   while (PeekMessage(&msg, NULL, 0, 0, PM_NOREMOVE) == TRUE)
     {
      if (GetMessage(&msg, NULL, 0, 0))
        {
         if (g_flyengine)
           if (msg.message==WM_KEYDOWN)
             g_flyengine->con.key_down(msg.wParam);
```

```
            else if (msg.message==WM_CHAR)
                g_flyengine->con.key_char(msg.wParam);

        TranslateMessage(&msg);
        DispatchMessage(&msg);
        }
      else
        return TRUE;
      }

  if (g_flyrender && g_flyengine)
    if (g_flyengine->step())
      g_flyengine->draw_frame();
  }
}

// main window message processing
LRESULT CALLBACK WinFunc (HWND hWnd, UINT mens, WPARAM wParam,
LPARAM lParam)
{
  switch (mens)
  {
  // window resize
  case WM_SIZE:
    if (g_flyrender)
      g_flyrender->resize(LOWORD(lParam),HIWORD(lParam));
    break;

  // window activation
  case WM_ACTIVATE:
    if (g_flyengine)
      if (LOWORD(wParam)==WA_INACTIVE || g_flyengine->con.mode)
        g_flyengine->noinput=1;
      else g_flyengine->noinput=0;
    break;

  // quit app
  case WM_DESTROY:
    fly_free_engine();
    fly_free_render();
    fly_free_directx();
    PostQuitMessage(0);
    break;
  }

  return DefWindowProc (hWnd, mens, wParam, lParam);
}
```

3.1.3

Utilities

Utilities are applications that are not used during the execution of the game. Normally they convert data from other formats or process internal data. They can utilise the API of Fly3D. Examples are:

- **3DSMax plug-ins for import/export (.FMP, .F3D, .K3G)**. This plug-in loads and saves data converted from 3D Studio MAX for game levels and animated objects.
- **Level converters from other game formats**. This converts geometry and texture maps from other game formats into the engine format so that other level editors can be used to create content for Fly3D.
- **Plugin Wizard for VisualC++**. This is a Microsoft Visual C++ Wizard that makes the creation of Fly3D plug-ins considerably easier by creating the skeleton plug-in codes from a set of dialog boxes.

3.2 Fly3D engine architecture

At an early stage it was decided to separate the Fly3D engine architecture into four components:

FlyMath   vectors, matrix, quaternion, vertex definitions
FlyDirectX   wrapper interface for DirectInput, DirectPlay and DirectSound
FlyRender   main interface to OpenGL and textures
FlyEngine   main interface to the engine

These are related to plug-ins, OpenGL and input devices as shown in Figure 3.1.

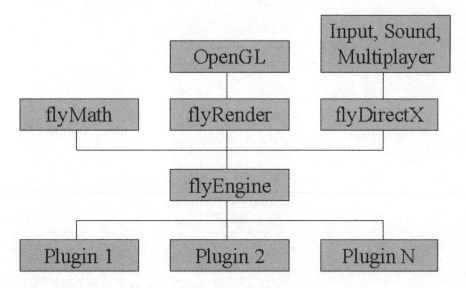

Figure 3.1
Fly3D architecture.

3.2.1 FlyMath

The FlyMath dynamic link library implements several classes and definitions relating to common 3D mathematics used in games.

```
class FLY_MATH_API flyVector; // 4 floats
class FLY_MATH_API flyQuaternion;   // 4 floats
class FLY_MATH_API flyMatrix; // 16 floats
class FLY_MATH_API flyPlane; // 5 floats
class FLY_MATH_API flyVertex; // 8 floats, 1 int
```

- The *flyVector* class implements a four-component vector (*x,y,z,w*) and includes operators such as addition, dot product, cross product, normalisation etc.
- The *flyQuaternion* class implements the common quaternion functions such as *slerp* and conversion of quaternions to and from a matrix.
- The *flyMatrix* class implements such functions as matrix multiplication, vector matrix multiplication, translation, rotation, scaling etc.
- The *flyPlane* class implements a plane based on its normal and distance to the origin. It has methods such as distance from a point to the plane etc.
- The *flyVertex* class is the class that holds all the information associated with a vertex: position, normal, texture coordinates, light map coordinates and colour.

Examples of common maths operations are:

```
flyVector v1(1); // initialize to (1,1,1,1)
flyVector v2(2,2,2); // initialize (2,2,2,0)
flyVector v3(0,1,0,1); // initialize (0,1,0,1)

flyVector v=v1+v2*v3; // v=(1,3,1,1);

float distance=(v1-v2).length();
float dotprod=FLY_VECDOT(v1,v2);

v.cross(v1,v2); // sets v to cross product of v1 and v2

flyMatrix m;
m.set_rotation(10,flyVector(0,0,1)); // set to a rotation matrix of
10 degrees around z axis

v.vec(1,2,3); // sets v to (1,2,3,0)
v.normalize(); // set v to unit length

v=v*m; // rotate vector v with matrix m
```

(3.2.2) FlyDirectX

FlyDirectX dynamic link library is an interface to those facilities of DirectX that we use. Only plug-ins and front-ends that require such features need to initialise this component. The library implements classes that deal with input, sound and multi-player gaming.

The main class of the library is the *flyDirectx* class, and a global instance of that class, *g_flydirectx*, is available. Through *g_flydirectx*, you can check for input from the keyboard or mouse, add a new sound to the simulation, access multi-player information, join and create multi-player games, and so forth.

To initialise and free this component we use the following two global methods:

```
// global DirectX initialisation method
FLY_DIRECTX_API void fly_init_directx(HWND hwnd,HINSTANCE hinst);

// global DirectX release method
FLY_DIRECTX_API void fly_free_directx();
```

After initialising this component it is available through the following global variable:

```
// global flyDirectx instance
extern FLY_DIRECTX_API flyDirectx *g_flydirectx;
```

Through the initialised global pointer we can access methods for input, sound and multi-player.

Input processing

Input processing requires the following two methods. The *get_input* method samples the input devices and stores the sampled data in the public input variables. It is called once per frame by the engine and all that is required in a plug-in is the checking of the public input variables for device information.

The input variables hold information such as which keys are currently pressed (*keys[]*), mouse position and offsets (*mouse_pos[], mouse_delta[]*), mouse down and mouse clicks (*mouse_down, mouse_click*).

```
// input methods
// get user input from input devices
void get_input();
// reset all input
void zero_input();
```

```
// input variables
unsigned char keys[256]; // keyboard keys
int mouse_pos[2];        // current mouse position in screen pixels
int mouse_delta[2];      // mouse displacement from last frame
float mouse_smooth[2];   // smoothed movement displacement
char mouse_down;         // bitfield: which mouse buttons are down
char mouse_click;        // bitfield: which mouse buttons have been
                         // clicked
```

Sound utilities

Sound processing can use the following methods.

```
// load .wav sound file
int load_wav_file(LONG cchBuffer,HPSTR pchBuffer,LPDIRECTSOUNDBUFFER
*buf,LPDIRECTSOUND3DBUFFER *buf3d);
```

loads a .wav sound file.

```
// clone an existing sound
LPDIRECTSOUNDBUFFER clone_sound(LPDIRECTSOUNDBUFFER buf);
```

clones an existing sound enabling repetition.

```
// sets position, velocity and alignment of a listener
void set_listener(const float *pos,const float *vel,const float
*Y,const float *Z);
```

The correct perception of a sound from the game user's point of view depends on his or her current position and velocity as a virtual game character.

```
// set master sound volume
void set_master_volume(int volume);
```

sets the sound volume: volume zero is maximum volume – smaller values are negative.

Multi-player processing

A full multi-player application is described in [WATT01]. Here we briefly describe the methods that enable a plug-in to access DirectPlay. Multi-player applications are best implemented using this API. It gives a single interface to the Internet and enables you to avoid low-level programming associated with setting up and handling messages.

A user application will create either a server or a client. Servers are initialised only by a server front-end. Usually an application will be creating clients. The sequence of operations required to create a client is:

(1) Call *init_multiplayer*, passing the server address to connect to.
(2) If no server address is specified, it connects to the first available server in your local network.
(3) Calling *enum_games* gives the games available in the specified server.
(4) Calling *join_game* with one of the enumerated games will enable a connection to the game.

Once a game has been joined, messages can be sent and received. Messages are sent by the *send_message* method. This method sends a message of specified length to a designated player (if no player is specified it is sent to all players).

Multi-player methods are as follows:

```
// initialise multi-player session
int init_multiplayer(const char *netaddress=0);
// destroy multiplayer session
void free_multiplayer();

// get a pointer to the list of available games
flyMPGames *enum_games(LPGUID app_guid);
// join an existing game
int join_game(LPGUID game_guid,const char *player_name,unsigned
color=0xFF808080);
// create (host) a new game
int create_game(LPGUID app_guid,const char *game_name);
// get player IP address from its DirectPlay id
char *get_player_address(DWORD dpid);

// send a message over the net
void send_message(const flyMPMsg *msg,int len,DWORD dpid=0);
// get total number of messages
int get_num_messages();
// get a message
flyMPMsg *get_message(DWORD *size);
// add a new player to the environment
int add_player(const char *name,DWORD dpid,void *data,unsigned
color=0xFF808080);
// remove a player from the environment
void *remove_player(int i);
```

3.2.3   FlyRender

The purpose of this dynamic link library is to encapsulate the OpenGL interface and enable render settings, texture management and hardware programming. It is the engine's rendering module and takes care of all operations and
data structures related to the rendering task, using OpenGL as the graphics API.
The DLL exports its main class, *flyRender*, and a global instance of that class,
g_flyrender, allowing full access to its functionality.

    To initialise and free this component we use the following two global methods:

```
// global render manager initialisation method
FLY_RENDER_API void fly_init_render(HWND hWnd,HINSTANCE hInst);
// global render manager release method
FLY_RENDER_API void fly_free_render();
```

After initialising this component it is available through the following global
variables:

```
// global flyTexCache instance
extern FLY_RENDER_API flyTexCache *g_flytexcache;
// global flyRender instance
extern FLY_RENDER_API flyRender *g_flyrender;
```

Using the texture manager may involve, for example, loading new textures dynamically, changing a complete texture map or part of it, as in, for example, light map changes due to a dynamic light. Also texture setting, such as filter options, can be specified for each texture (or for all of them). Optimisation of multi-texture hardware allows easy selection of textures for any texture units.

The following texture management methods handle these facilities:

```
// Dynamically add a new texture to the cache, passing all info
int add_tex(const char *name,int sx,int sy,int bytespixel,const
unsigned char *buf,int flags);

// Dynamically add a new texture to the cache, passing the picture
index int add_tex(int np,flyPicture **pic,int flags);

// Update the texture in the texture manager with a new pixel array
void update_tex(int pic,int sx,int sy,int bytespixel,const unsigned
char *buf);

// Update part of a texture in the texture manager.
// Only the sub-texture pixels are passed.

// If 'x' and 'y' are 0 and 'sx' and 'sy' the size of the image,
// it will work just like the update_picture function.
void update_subtex(int pic,int x,int y,int sx,int sy,int
bytespixel,const unsigned char *buf);

// Select a texture unit
inline void sel_unit(int u);

// Select a texture
inline void sel_tex(int t);

// Select a texture and unit
inline void sel_tex(int t,int u);
```

The *flyRender* class handles the initialisation and release of OpenGL, OpenGL extensions, window sizing – including full screen switching, 3D and 2D drawing and render flags such as wire frame rendering, background colour etc.

Render methods

```
// Initialise the state for every frame
void init();

// Resize the rendering window
void resize(int sx,int sy);
// Change to fullscreen mode
void set_full_screen();

// Enter drawing mode
void begin_draw();
```

```
// Leave drawing mode
void end_draw();

// Enter 2D drawing mode
void begin_draw2d();
// Leave 2D drawing mode
void end_draw2d();

// Draw text aligned to the left of the given position
void draw_text(int x,int y,const char *text,int
size=FLY_FONTS_SIZE,int n=-1);
// Draw text centralised on the given position
void draw_text_center(int x,int y,const char *text,int
size=FLY_FONTS_SIZE);
```

Render flags

```
static int s_screensizex;      // screen width in pixels
static int s_screensizey;      // screen height in pixels
static int s_fullscreen;       // fullscreen flag
static int s_clearbg;          // background clear flag
static int s_antialias;        // anti-aliasing flag
static int s_wireframe;        // wireframe flag
static int s_fog;              // fog flag
static int s_stencil;          // stencil flag
static float s_brightness;     // brightness level
static float s_ambient;        // ambient lighting level
static float s_aspect;         // screen aspect ratio
static float s_camangle;       // camera angle
static float s_nearplane;      // near rendering plane
static float s_farplane;       // far rendering plane
static float s_background[4];  // background colour
```

3.2.4   FlyEngine

The engine itself handles loading and saving of static scenes, plug-ins, dynamic objects and performs the simulation. *flyEngine* is the engine's main module and is effectively an interface between plug-ins and the back-end modules. This DLL implements several classes and useful methods that handle the per-frame update of the application state and coordinate the various plug-ins, giving each of them a chance to add their functionality to the simulation. It also includes the several off-line phases required to load a scene, initialise plug-ins and objects and start the simulation from a valid initial state.

The engine module is characterised mainly by the *flyEngine* class, which encloses the most vital data and methods of the engine, like data loading, lighting calculations and BSP recursion functions, as well as the BSP tree itself, geometry data in the form of vertices and faces and all the simulation global parameters. You can access the data and use the methods in this class via its global instance, called *g_flyengine*, available throughout the application.

The engine component is independent from the render component and an example of this independent use is the server front-end, which only uses the engine to perform all simulation and does not draw anything.

The complete list of classes included in the engine is:

```
template <class T> class FLY_ENGINE_API flyArray;
class FLY_ENGINE_API flyString;
class FLY_ENGINE_API flyBoundBox;
class FLY_ENGINE_API flyFrustum;
class FLY_ENGINE_API flyLocalSystem;
class FLY_ENGINE_API flyBaseObject;
class FLY_ENGINE_API flySound;
class FLY_ENGINE_API flyPolygon;
class FLY_ENGINE_API flyFace;
class FLY_ENGINE_API flyMesh;
class FLY_ENGINE_API flyAnimatedMesh;
class FLY_ENGINE_API flySkeletonMesh;
class FLY_ENGINE_API flyBezierCurve;
class FLY_ENGINE_API flyBezierPatch;
class FLY_ENGINE_API flyParticle;
class FLY_ENGINE_API flyBspNode;
class FLY_ENGINE_API flyBspObject;
class FLY_ENGINE_API flyStaticMesh;
class FLY_ENGINE_API flyLightMap;
class FLY_ENGINE_API flyLightMapPic;
class FLY_ENGINE_API flyLightVertex;
class FLY_ENGINE_API flyClassDesc;
class FLY_ENGINE_API flyParamDesc;
class FLY_ENGINE_API flyConsole;
class FLY_ENGINE_API flyShader;
class FLY_ENGINE_API flyShaderFunc;
class FLY_ENGINE_API flyShaderPass;
class FLY_ENGINE_API flyInputMap;
class FLY_ENGINE_API flyFile;
class FLY_ENGINE_API flyDll;
class FLY_ENGINE_API flyDllGroup;
class FLY_ENGINE_API flyEngine;
```

We now give a brief overview of each class; for full details consult the Engine Reference Manual.

```
template <class T> class FLY_ENGINE_API flyArray;
```

This template class implements a dynamic re-sizable array of any type. The array can be indexed with the standard *[ ]* operator and elements can be added to the array dynamically. A feature of the facility is that it doubles its size when a new element is added and no more space is currently available in the array. This makes for efficient reallocation. Another important feature is that the array can only grow (it can never shrink) and eventually it will grow to a required limit size. It is thus as efficient as a pre-allocated fixed size array when this limit is reached.

```
class FLY_ENGINE_API flyString;
```

This facility is similar to the previous and operates like an array of chars. Several operators are included to facilitate concatenating a string, formatting etc.

```
class FLY_ENGINE_API flyBoundBox;
```

This class implements an axis-aligned bounding box (AABB), which every object in the scene must possess. The bounding box is used in collision calculations, and for the engine's aggressive view culling as fully described in Chapter 2. This class includes all the detailed functionality required for collision detection, including, for example, *ray_intersect* which you will recall is used as part of a highly optimised AABB/polygon collision check.

```
class FLY_ENGINE_API flyFrustum;
```

This class implements a view frustum, storing its vertices and planes. A frustum building method and a fast bounding-box clipping test are also provided.

```
class FLY_ENGINE_API flyLocalSystem;
```

This class implements a local system defined by three perpendicular vectors (Figure 3.2). Methods included:

- Rotate the system by a rotation matrix.
- Rotate the system by angle 'ang' about vector 'v'.
- Rotate the system from 'v' to 'u', in the plane defined by 'v' and 'u', by a maximum angle of 'maxang' degrees.
- Align the z axis of the system with a given vector.

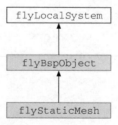

Figure 3.2
Class dependency for
flyLocalSystem.

```
class FLY_ENGINE_API flyBaseObject;
```

This class is the base class for all objects (Figure 3.3). Several other classes from the engine derive from this class. It holds the object name and a pointer to the next object in the specific object linked list.

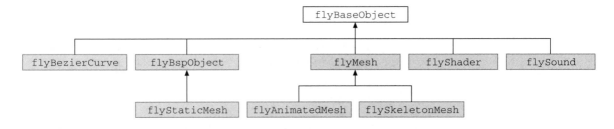

Figure 3.3
Class dependency for
flyBaseObject.

```
class FLY_ENGINE_API flySound;
```

This class implements raw sound data that can be loaded from a .wav file (Figure 3.4).

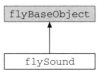

Figure 3.4
Class dependency for
flySound.

```
class FLY_ENGINE_API flyPolygon;
```

This class implements a convex polygon with any number of vertices. Methods are availabe to cut the polygon by custom-generated planes and to order its vertices.

```
class FLY_ENGINE_API flyFace;
```

This class (Figure 3.5) implements a face of any type supported by the engine, which are:

- normal faces (that is, large faces);
- Bézier patches;
- triangular surfaces;
- triangular strips;
- triangular fans.

Figure 3.5
Class dependency for
flyFace.

```
class FLY_ENGINE_API flyMesh;
```

This class (Figure 3.6) implements a 3D object polygonal mesh. Its faces may reference the local faces or the global engine BSP faces.

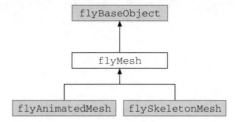

Figure 3.6
Class dependency for
flyMesh.

```
class FLY_ENGINE_API flyAnimatedMesh;
```

This class (Figure 3.7) implements key-based vertex-animated meshes, and provides built-in blending methods for multi-animation blending.

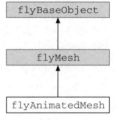

Figure 3.7
Class dependency for
flyAnimatedMesh.

```
class FLY_ENGINE_API flySkeletonMesh;
```

This class (Figure 3.8) implements animated skeleton meshes and includes methods for interpolation, animation blending and skinning.

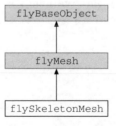

Figure 3.8
Class dependency for
flySkeletonMesh.

```
class FLY_ENGINE_API flyBezierCurve;
```

A Bézier curve is implemented by this class (Figure 3.9). The world coordinates and tangent can be evaluated at any point on the curve, and the curve can be adaptively subdivided until the curve error is less than a maximum error factor. (The curve can have any dimensionality, 2D, 3D, 4D etc.)

Figure 3.9
Class dependency for
flyBezierCurve.

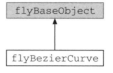

```
class FLY_ENGINE_API flyBezierPatch;
```

This class implements a bi-quadratic or bi-cubic parametric Bézier patch. The patch can have any number of segments in *u* and *v* directions. It is made of several connected cubic or quadratic Bézier patches. At run time the surface can be rendered at any level of detail by down-sampling the control point array to provide a fast LOD approach for static level data (see [WATT01] for further details on this approach). The illumination for the patch is calculated at the highest LOD and mapped onto whatever LOD is currently being rendered.

nsu is the number of patches in the *u* dir and *nsv* in the *v* dir.
npu and *npv* are the number of control points in each direction.
For quadratic patches: $nsu = (npu-2)/2$ $nsv = (npv-2)/2$
For cubic patches: $nsu = (spu-1)/2$ $nsv = (spv-1)/2$

The surface is discretised based on the subdivision level. The number of vertices in *u* and *v* directions are:

$$nvertu = (1<<levelu)*nsu+1 \qquad nvertv = (1<<levelv)*nsv+1$$

At run time, the surface can be drawn at any level of detail up to its current selected level. The *set_detail* method sets the desired level of detail. The number of vertices skipped (col/row draw loop increment) on each direction is:

$$nvertskip = (1<<nleveldrop)$$

```
class FLY_ENGINE_API flyParticle;
```

A single (invisible) particle is implemented by this class (Figure 3.10).

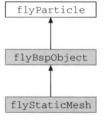

Figure 3.10
Class dependency for
flyParticle.

```
class FLY_ENGINE_API flyBspNode;
```

This class (Figure 3.11) implements a node from the bsp tree. If it has no children (child[0] = child[1] = 0), elements inside or clipping the node are stored in the *elem* dynamic array.

Figure 3.11
Class dependency for
flyBspNode.

```
class FLY_ENGINE_API flyBspObject;
```

This class (Figure 3.12) implements any object that moves and is considered as an AABB by the BSP tree.

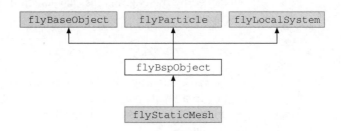

Figure 3.12
Class dependency for
flyBspObject.

```
class FLY_ENGINE_API flyStaticMesh;
```

This class (Figure 3.13) impements the group of faces that are present in a BSP leaf node.

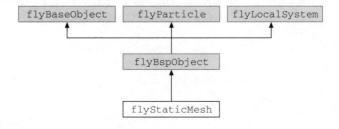

Figure 3.13
Class dependency for
flyStaticMesh.

```
class FLY_ENGINE_API flyLightMap;
```

This class implements a light map. Several faces can share the same light map and many light maps can share the same light map picture.

```
class FLY_ENGINE_API flyLightMapPic;
```

This class implements the light map texture used when drawing. This texture can have several light map pictures in it as many instances of the *flyLightMap* class will use a single *flyLightMapPic*.

```
class FLY_ENGINE_API flyLightVertex;
```

This class holds information on dynamic hardware lights. When a dynamic object receives a FLY_OBJMESSAGE_ILLUM message it adds the light parameters to this class with the *add_light* method. When rendering, it calls the *init_draw* method before drawing the mesh to get the hardware lights in place. After finishing the render it calls *end_draw* to reset the hardware lights.

```
class FLY_ENGINE_API flyClassDesc;
```

This meta-class implements a class description for plug-in management and object instantiation and referencing. Any plug-in class that wants to be recognised and referenced by the engine must have a child class from this one, with the class's description.

```
class FLY_ENGINE_API flyParamDesc;
```

This class holds information on Fly3D plug-in object parameters. Each class defined in a Fly3D plug-in (derived from *flyBspObject*) can have any number of parameters. Each parameter must have an associated *flyParamDesc* class describing its data.

```
class FLY_ENGINE_API flyConsole;
```

This class implements the console, consisting of a command line where you can execute commands. Runtime information can also be printed out on the console, and the navigation keys 'home', 'end', 'page up' and 'page down' can be used to scroll through messages.

```
class FLY_ENGINE_API flyShader;
```

This class (Figure 3.14) implements a multi-pass shader.

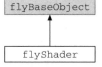

Figure 3.14
Class dependency for
flyShader.

```
class FLY_ENGINE_API flyShaderFunc;
```

This class implements a typical shader function, whose type can be: Sin, Triangle, Square, Saw-tooth, or Inverse saw-tooth.

```
class FLY_ENGINE_API flyShaderPass;
```

This class implements a shader pass. A shader consists of various shader passes.

```
class FLY_ENGINE_API flyInputMap;
```

This class maps input from the keyboard and mouse into game actions.

```
class FLY_ENGINE_API flyFile;
```

Implements a manager and interface for Fly3D scene data files (*.fly* files).

```
class FLY_ENGINE_API flyDll;
```

This class holds information for each Fly3D plug-in DLL, including the number of classes implemented in the DLL, and the pointers to the DLL exported functions.

```
class FLY_ENGINE_API flyDllGroup;
```

This class implements a group of Fly3D plug-in DLLs. Each plug-in DLL can enumerate any number of *flyBspObject* classes.

```
class FLY_ENGINE_API flyEngine;
```

The methods available in the *flyEngine* class make up the main interface with the engine functionality.

To initialise and free the engine we use the following two global methods:

```
// global engine initialisation method
FLY_ENGINE_API void fly_init_engine(HWND hWnd,HINSTANCE hInst,int
appid=FLY_APPID_NONE);
// global engine release method
FLY_ENGINE_API void fly_free_engine();
```

After initialising this component it is available through the following global variable:

```
// global flyEngine instance
extern FLY_ENGINE_API flyEngine *g_flyengine;
```

Loading and saving

Loading begins with the configuration file which is set up by the user, with the *flyConfig* tool, enabling the configuration of machine-specific settings.

```
// Load Fly3D configuration file (Fly3D.ini)
int load_ini();
// Save Fly3D configuration file (Fly3D.ini)
int save_ini();
```

The next sequence of operations involves the loading of a complete scene: static geometry, BSP tree, PVS, light maps, texture maps, plug-ins, dynamic objects (and all their resources such as sounds, 3D meshes etc.). These are contained in a *.fly* file which is a script (text file) that includes all references for these resources. Saving involves only the retention of this text file.

```
// Open a .fly file
int open_fly_file(const char *file);
// Close a .fly file
void close_fly_file();
// Save to a .fly file
int save_fly_file(const char *file);
```

Any dynamic loading during gameplay uses the following methods. A resource is requested by filename and a pointer to the requested resource is returned. If the resource is already loaded then the pointer to the already existing object is returned.

```
// Load a picture to the texture cache or return
// its index if already loaded
int get_picture(const char *file,int droplevel=0);
// Load a shader file
int load_shaders(const char *file);
// Get a mesh object
flyMesh *get_model_object(const char *name);
// Get a sound object
flySound *get_sound_object(const char *name);
// Get a bezier curve
flyBezierCurve *get_bezier_curve(const char *name);
```

Scene updating

Scene updating is activated by the following:

```
// Update scene for elapsed time from last frame
int step();
// Update scene for elapsed time dt in milliseconds
void step(int dt);
```

This is the main loop of the simulation which performs the following sequence of operations:

(1) Query the DirectX interface to sample the user input devices.

```
// get input
if (noinput)
  g_flydirectx->zero_input();
else g_flydirectx->get_input();
```

(2) All light maps that were changed in the previous frame due to a dynamic light are restored to their original values computed during the build process.

```
for( i=0;i<lmchanged.num;i++ )
{
  map=lm[lmchanged[i]];
  map->load(lmpic[map->pic]);
```

```
g_flytexcache->update_subtex(
  map->pic+lmbase,map->offsetx,map->offsety,
  map->sizex,map->sizey,3,map->bmp);
}
```

(3) All fog maps that were changed in the previous frame are cleared. Fog maps change because of the influence of the fog volumes. The view frustum may intersect a fog volume as it moves. Then either the player is inside the fog volume or is looking through it, in which case the fog map pixels need to be updated.

```
for( i=0;i<fmchanged.num;i++ )
{
  map=fm[fmchanged[i]];
  memset(map->bmp,0,map->bytesxy);
  g_flytexcache->update_subtex(
    map->pic+fmbase,map->offsetx,map->offsety,
    map->sizex,map->sizey,4,map->bmp);
}
```

(4) If running in a client machine, at this point the elapsed time from the last update of the player's state is checked. If this time is greater than a pre-defined network update interval (determined by the network connection speed), a message is sent to all plug-ins informing them to send messages with their current updated states.

```
// if in client multiplayer mode
if (g_flydirectx->mpmode==FLY_MP_CLIENT)
  {
  // update client objects to server at slower intervals
  static int last_mp_update=0;
  if (cur_time-last_mp_update>mpdelay)
    {
    last_mp_update=cur_time;
    dll.send_message(FLY_MESSAGE_MPUPDATE,0,0);
    }
  }
```

(5) Now all (active) dynamic objects are processed as:

> **for** every active object
>> Call the object's virtual step function
>> **if** the object step function returns true **then**
>>> Remove from the BSP tree and add it again recalculating all the nodes the object in its new position clips
>> **else**
>>> the object did not move (do nothing)
>> **if** the object life < 0 **then**
>>> remove object from the BSP and destroy it

(6) All light maps that have been changed by an object step function (dynamic lights) are updated to the texture manager.

```
for( i=0;i<lmchanged.num;i++ )
  {
```

```
map=lm[lmchanged[i]];
g_flytexcache->update_subtex(
    map->pic+lmbase,map->offsetx,map->offsety,
    map->sizex,map->sizey,3,map->bmp);
}
```

(7) Similarly, all fog maps that have been changed are updated to the texture manager.

```
for( i=0;i<fmchanged.num;i++ )
    {
    map=fm[fmchanged[i]];
    g_flytexcache->update_subtex(
        map->pic+fmbase,map->offsetx,map->offsety,
        map->sizex,map->sizey,4,map->bmp);
    }
```

(8) The *FLYM_UPDATESCENE* message is sent to all loaded plug-ins. This causes the plug-ins to update their state and render their layers if required.

```
// step all running plug-ins
dll.send_message(FLY_MESSAGE_UPDATESCENE,dt,0);
```

(9) If running on a server or a client machine, *check_multiplayer* is called to process the multi-player messages. This queries the available messages in the message queue. If the message is a system message (player joined, player quit etc.) this is processed. A game application message is passed on to the plug-ins through the plug-in *fly_message* exported function. The plug-ins will respond (or not) to the message according to the application.

```
// if in multiplayer, check multiplayer messages
if (g_flydirectx->mpmode!=FLY_MP_NOMP)
    check_multiplayer();
```

Scene drawing

Activation of *draw_frame* causes all drawing operations to be performed. In this, 'drawing' means performing the geometric operations on the scene data and rendering. At least one *draw_bsp* will be called, which causes all the (BSP) selected faces to be passed to *draw_faces* which is the method in which rendering occurs. *draw_faces* uses shader technology and sorts the faces into the best order for minimising state changes (Chapter 5).

```
// Send drawing messages to all objects and draw
// everything in the current frame
void draw_frame();
// Sets the current camera to the given object
void set_camera(flyBspObject *d);
// Draw all scene elements viewed from the current camera
void draw_bsp();
// Draw the given faces
void draw_faces(int nfd,flyFace **fd,flyVertex *v,int sort=1);
```

draw_bsp may be called many times for a frame. For example, multiple viewports may be active, each requiring their own BSP recursion. Also, individual mesh objects will call *draw_faces* for rendering themselves using shaders.

Collision detection

Collision detection (Chapter 2) is activated either for a particle or for an AABB. For a particle we use:

```
// Collision detection from p1 to p2, computes the closest collision
int collision_bsp(const flyVector& p1,const flyVector& p2,int
elemtype=0);
```

This returns information about the closest intersection from *p*1 to *p*2. If the method returns true then the collision information such as the collision normal etc. will be available in the following engine public variables:

```
// ray intersection data
flyBspObject *hitobj;      // current hit object
flyMesh *hitmesh;          // current hit mesh
int    hitface,            // current hit face
       hitsubface,         // current hit subface
       hitshader;          // current hit face shader
flyVector    hitip,        // last collision intersection point
       hitnormal;          // last collision hit normal
float hitdist;             // last collision hit distance
```

Alternatively, the following method returns on the first collision found between *p*1 and *p*2, but no information on the collision is made available.

```
// Collision detection from p1 to p2, returns when finds the first
// collision
int collision_test(const flyVector& p1,const flyVector& p2,int
elemtype=0);
```

This is faster than the first method and is used when we only need to know whether a collision has occurred or not. We can also restrict the collision to certain game element types using the parameter *elemtype* (if 0 all element types are checked).

AABB collision detection is located in the *flyBoundBox* class and *flyBspObject* class.

Generic recursions of BSP tree

Generic recursion implements efficient recursion based on a stack as fully described in Chapter 1. This is utilised as follows:

```
// Recurse the BSP selecting nodes and objects clipped by the
// sphere centred at p with radius rad
void recurse_bsp(const flyVector& p,float rad,int elemtype,int
pvsleaf=-1);

// Recurse the BSP selecting nodes and objects between p1 and p2
void recurse_bsp(const flyVector& p1,const flyVector& p2,int
elemtype,int pvsleaf=-1);

// Recurse the BSP selecting nodes and objects clipped by the
// volume defined by the array of points p
void recurse_bsp(const flyVector *p,int np,int elemtype,int
pvsleaf=-1);

// Recurse the BSP selecting nodes and objects clipped by the box
// defined by min and max
void recurse_bsp_box(const flyVector& min,const flyVector& max,int
elemtype,int pvsleaf=-1);
```

All selections can be restricted to a certain object type and use the PVS for node clipping.

Plug-in messages

Plug-ins are groups of objects and there are two types of messages used for communication between them – object messages and plug-in messages. Object messages are processed in the *message* method from the *flyBspObject* virtual function. Plug-in messages are processed in the DLL exported *fly_message* function. Messages are sent to objects by activating a generic BSP recursion:

```
// Recurse the BSP sending messages to all selected objects
void send_bsp_message(const flyVector& p,float rad,int msg,int
param,void *data,int elemtype=0,int pvsleaf=-1);

// Send a message to all plugin DLLs
int send_message(int msg,int param,void *data) const;
```

The *send_message* function sends the message to all plug-in DLLs in the current scene calling the *fly_message* exported function of all DLLs. The *send_bsp_message* sends a message to all *flyBspObject* derived classes included in the specified sphere of influence.

Stock and active objects

During the simulation process, many objects can be inserted in the scene; for example, when a shooter-game player fires his gun, a projectile must be added to the game, with its starting position and velocity given by the position of the gun and by characteristics of that projectile. Once it hits a surface (an enemy or a wall), the projectile must be removed from the game, and perhaps an explosion object is inserted on the spot where the projectile collided. And of course, multiple copies of the same object (say, the gun's projectile) could exist in the simulation at the same time. Therefore, all adding and removing of objects must be handled in such a way that each copy of a given object has its own parameter values, and is controlled independently of the other copies. Also, when a copy of the object is inserted in the simulation, it must retain the original values for that type of object, that is, the previously inserted objects cannot change the original values.

This coherence is achieved by always maintaining a **stock** object, which has the original properties and parameter values for that kind of object. Then, to add a new copy of that object into the simulation, the engine uses the **clone** function to make a copy of the **stock** object, and then inserts that copy into the environment. The added copy of the object is called an **active** object, as the act of inserting an object is called **activation**. This way, several **active** copies of the same object will each have their own parameter values changing over time, and the original **stock** object will remain unchanged, so that further **activation** of new copies of the object can occur by making a **clone** of the **stock** object.

All objects defined in a *.fly* file are loaded into the stock objects linked list when a *open_fly_file* command is executed. When saving a *.fly* file, all object properties in the stock objects linked list are saved to the file.

Any stock object can be activated (cloned and added to the BSP) using the following command from the flyEngine class:

```
// Activate an object from the stock
void activate(flyBspObject *d);

// Add an object to the BSP tree
void add_to_bsp(flyBspObject *obj);
```

This will add the object to the end of the active object linked list and also add it to the BSP tree. All objects in the active object linked list will have their *step* function called for every frame and may be selected for drawing if they are in the current view frustum and not culled by the PVS.

Scene querying

To query the scene for objects, we can acquire an object pointer by name, or loop through the objects for a certain type. We can also query objects from the stock object list or from the active object list.

```
// Get the stock object with the given name
flyBspObject *get_stock_object(const char *name) const;
// Get an active object with the given name
flyBspObject *get_active_object(const char *name) const;
// Get the stock object immediately after 'o' in the respective
array
```

```
flyBspObject *get_next_stock_object(flyBspObject *o,int type=0) const;
// Get the active object immediately after 'o' in the respective
array
flyBspObject *get_next_active_object(flyBspObject *o,int type=0) const;
```

Object parameter setting and querying

Every object parameter in the engine can be represented as a string. Given an object name and parameter name, the string containing the parameter value can be queried or we can pass the parameter value from a current string. Also, global engine parameters can be queried and set in the same manner.

```
// Set an object's parameter value
int set_obj_param(const char *objname,const char *param,const char
*value);
// Get an object's parameter value
int get_obj_param(const char *objname,const char *param,flyString&
value) const;
// Set a global parameter value
int set_global_param(const char *name,const char *value);
// Get the value of a non-scene dependant global parameter
int get_global_param_desc1(int i,flyParamDesc *pd);
// Get the value of a scene dependant global parameter
int get_global_param_desc2(int i,flyParamDesc *pd);
```

Miscellaneous methods

We complete this section by listing a few miscellaneous methods. The first prints out a text string on the console with standard *printf* C++ formatting.

```
// Print a string out on the console
void console_printf(const char *fmt, ...);
```

The next two methods are used for mapping input controls – keys and mouse buttons. An input can be queried by a name – say *walk_forward*, and will return a handle. This handle can then be used in the *check_input_map*, passing the handle for checking the current state of the input. The *flyConfig* utility can be used to assign keys and mouse buttons to the string game actions.

```
// Get a input map
int get_input_map(const char *name);
// Checks the given input map for input
int check_input_map(int i);
```

The final method recurses the BSP tree to find the node containing a specified point.

```
// Recurse the BSP and return the node where the point p is located
flyBspNode *find_node(const flyVector& p) const;
```

Appendix 3.1 Writing a plug-in

1. Introduction

This programming tutorial intends to introduce Fly3D plug-in development to users. It serves as a good example of a simple plug-in that uses some of the engine's functionalities and shows typical techniques for working with Fly3D.

The steps include installation of the necessary tools, a simplistic starting plug-in and the incremental enhancement of this simple module, making it more complex and complete.

The tutorial requires intermediate skill in C++, as well as basic knowledge of Visual C++ 6.0.

2. Installing Fly3D, 3DSMax plug-ins and Visual C++ Wizard

Fly3D installation is as follows: run the installation executable and follow the instructions on choosing the installation folder, etc.

After copying all the files, *flyConfig.exe* will run automatically (Figure A3.1), for the user to choose a graphics renderer, set some rendering options, configure profile and keyboard mappings, and much more. For the renderer, an accelerated mode should be selected.

After configurations are saved and *flyConfig.exe* is closed, the plug-in installation program (*flyInstPlugins.exe*) will also run automatically (Figure A3.2). This software lets the user install Fly3D import and export plug-ins for 3D Studio MAX 3.x or 4.x and the Visual C++ Plugin Wizard. For the installation of the MAX plug-ins, the correct 3DSMax version and installation path must be selected. For the Plugin Wizard, just the Visual C++ path is needed.

After installing everything, the user may be prompted about rebooting the system, which must be done for the installation proccess to be finally complete.

3. Creating a Fly3D plug-in with the Visual C++ Wizard, implementing two classes: camera and object

In this step, a new Fly3D plug-in will be created from scratch, using the Visual C++ Plugin Wizard.

First of all, Visual C++ must be run. In the 'File' menu, the 'New' sub-menu will open a window for choosing the kind of document to be created. Fly3D Plugin Wizard should be enumerated in the 'Projects' tab. It must be selected, a name must be given to the new project (in this case, 'Tutorial 1') and a folder must be chosen for the project to be saved in. If Fly3D Plugin Wizard is not included in the list, the plug-in installation program can be run again for the proper installation of the Wizard. *flyInstPlugins.exe* can be found inside the 'util' folder in the Fly3D installation directory. Refer back to **step 2** for more info on installing the Plugin Wizard.

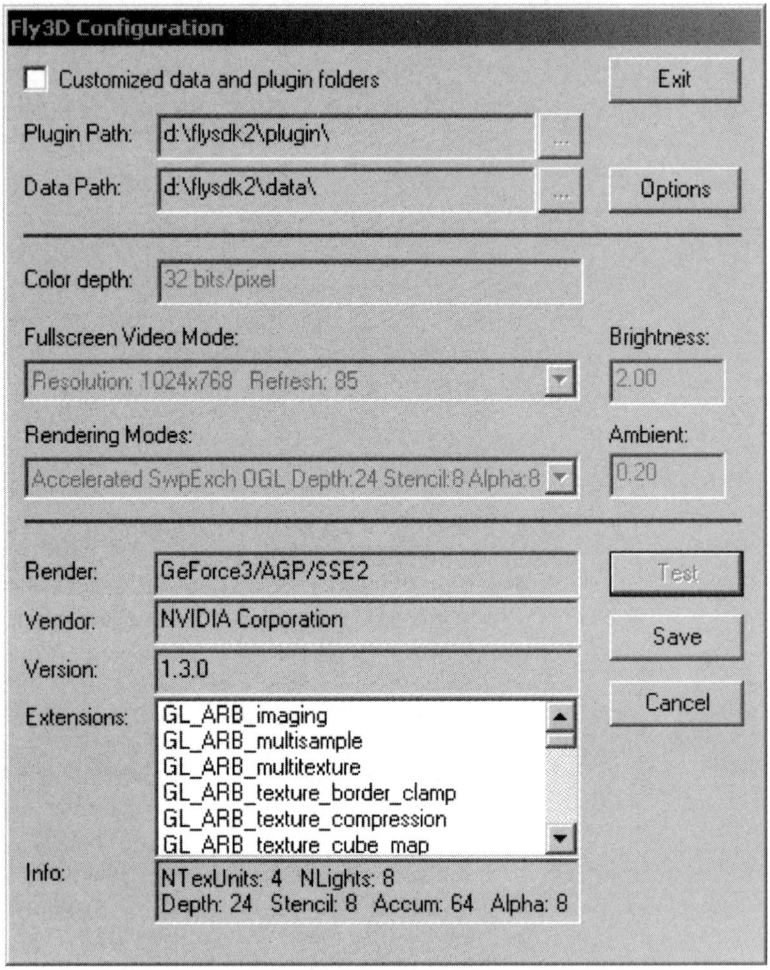

Figure A3.1
Fly3D Configuration.

Figure A3.2
Fly3D Plugins Installation.

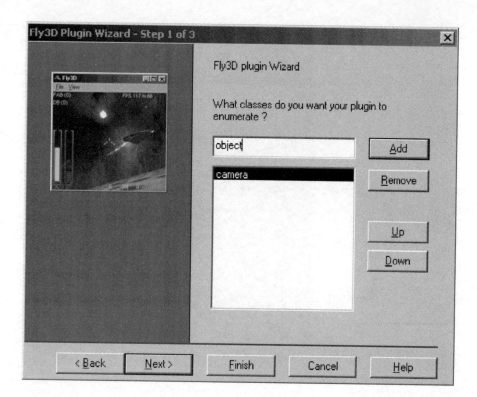

Figure A3.3
Fly3D Plugin Wizard –
Step 1.

In the first step of the Plugin Wizard (Figure A3.3), the classes must be named and added to the plug-in. In this tutorial, two classes will be created: 'object' and 'camera'.

In the second step (Figure A3.4), all parameters exported by the classes in the plug-in must be enumerated: their name, type and default value must be specified. Every parameter must be of one of the Fly3D pre-defined types, enumerated in the corresponding combo-box.

In our tutorial, the 'camera' class will have 2 parameters: 'mousevel' (a float-ing point number that defines the velocity of mouse-look) and 'movevel' (another floating point defining the velocity of camera movement). The 'object' class will have only 1 parameter, 'objmesh', of type 'f3d static mesh', that will be the triangular mesh of the object.

4. Creating a .fly file with flyEditor including the new plug-in

Now that the plug-in has been successfully created, this step consists of creating a new .fly file and including the plug-in in it using the *flyEditor* front-end.

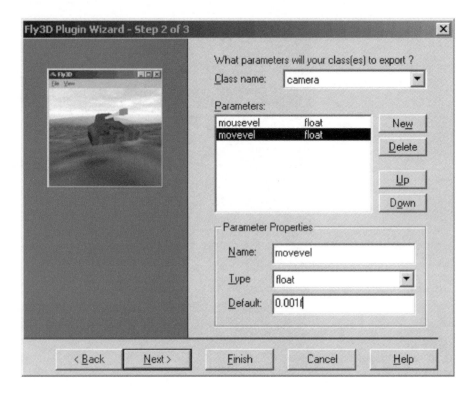

Figure A3.4
Fly3D Plugin Wizard –
Step 2.

First of all, *flyEditor.exe* must be run (Figure A3.5). It is located in the Fly3D installation folder. In the 'File' menu, the 'Save' sub-menu option must be used to save a new .fly file. Saving is necessary for loading a BSP file to the scene.

After saving the .fly file, a BSP must be loaded. This is achieved by editing the 'bspfile' parameter in the 'Global' group (select the 'Global' item in the tree-view on the left, then look for the 'bspfile' in the list-view in the centre).

Now, the DLL generated by the 'Tutorial1' plug-in must be inserted in the .fly file. The plug-in must be compiled and its resulting DLL file copied to the 'plugin' folder in the Fly3D installation path. Then it can be inserted in the .fly file by right-clicking on the 'Plugins' item in the tree-view on the left, and selecting 'Insert'. A dialog box will appear and the DLL file must be chosen. The final look of the file in *flyEditor* will be like Figure A3.6.

The third and last step of the wizard consists simply of selecting the Fly3D installation path.

After all this, Fly3D Plugin Wizard must have created 3 files in your project: 'Tutorial1.h', 'Tutorial1.cpp' and 'Tutorial1.def'. The header file now contains all the information enumerated in the steps 1 and 2 of the Plugin Wizard: the classes and their parameters.

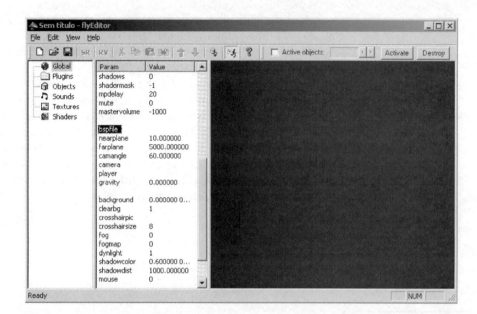

Figure A3.5
flyEditor.

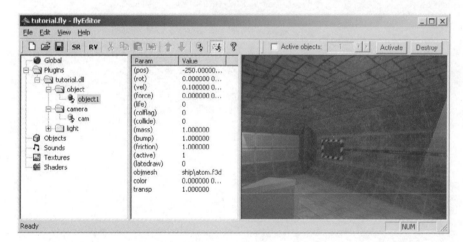

Figure A3.6
flyEditor and game.

5. Processing the engine's global messages

Among many global methods created by the Plugin Wizard in the tutorial's .cpp file, one deserves special attention: the *fly_message* function. This function is used by the engine to notify the plug-ins of events like scene initialisation, between-frames update time, draw time, scene closing, etc. Any plug-in that wishes to respond to these events must implement the response in this function.

During the simulation, Fly3D engine sends the *FLY_MESSAGE_UPDATESCENE* and *FLY_MESSAGE_DRAWSCENE* messages to the plug-ins whenever it is time to update the state or to draw between frames. Typically, one of the plug-ins must receive and respond to the *FLY_MESSAGE_DRAWSCENE* message, drawing a view of the simulation from some point, or nothing will be drawn (or seen).

In this tutorial example, the *FLY_MESSAGE_INITSCENE* message does not need to be implemented, as the plug-in has nothing to do upon scene initialisation; the same occurs with the *FLY_MESSAGE_UPDATESCENE, FLY_MESSAGE_DRAWTEXT* and *FLY_MESSAGE_CLOSESCENE* messages. The only message that must be implemented by the plug-in is the *FLY_MESSAGE_DRAWSCENE* message, where it must set the engine's camera to the desired camera object, and tell the engine to draw the scene from that camera. The code for the *fly_message* function that implements this is as follows:

```
__declspec( dllexport )
int fly_message(int msg,int param,void *data)
{
   switch(msg)
   {
     case FLY_MESSAGE_INITSCENE:
     break;
     case FLY_MESSAGE_UPDATESCENE:
     break;
     case FLY_MESSAGE_DRAWSCENE:
     {
        g_flyengine->set_camera(g_flyengine->cam);
        g_flyengine->draw_bsp();
     }
     break;
     case FLY_MESSAGE_DRAWTEXT:
     break;
     case FLY_MESSAGE_CLOSESCENE:
     break;
   }

   return 1;
}
```

6. Implementing the object's methods

In this step, the object class's methods will be implemented. These methods are, basically, the virtual functions inherited from the *flyBspObject* class.

Init

```
void object::init()
```

This is the object's initialisation funtion. For our small example, it just has to initialise the object's axis-aligned bounding box (every Fly3D entity must have one). And since the object has a mesh asociated with it, the object's AABB should be the mesh's. Then we have the following code for the **init** function:

```
void object::init()
{
   if(objmesh)
     bbox=objmesh->bbox;
}
```

Refer to **step 8** for a small addition to the object's **init** method.

Step

```
int object::step(int dt)
```

This is the per-frame update function. Every entity must update its state in this function, as it will be called once per frame during the simulation. In this example, the object will just stay still (for now). So, there is no need to implement anything in this function: just returning a valid value (1, for the object is still alive) will do. Refer to **step 9** and **step 11** for modifications in the object's **step** function.

```
int object::step(int dt)
{
   return 1;
}
```

Draw

```
void object::draw()
```

This is the drawing function. It must be used to draw the object using OpenGL calls. In this tutorial example, a simple draw is implemented: the object is translated to its position in 3D space (given by the pos variable), rotated to its current orientation (given by the mat variable), and its mesh is drawn. The code is as follows:

```
void object::draw()
{
   if(objmesh)
   {
     glPushMatrix();
     glTranslatef(pos.x,pos.y,pos.z);
     glMultMatrixf((float *)&mat);
     objmesh->draw();
     glPopMatrix();
   }
}
```

Message

```
int object::message(const flyVector& p,float rad,int msg,int
param,void *data)
```

This is the message receiving function. It must test the value of the `msg` parameter, treating the known message types. For now, this example's simple object will not receive any messages, returning the value 1 as an indication of normal function termination. Refer to **step 11**, which adds a message treatment in the object's **message** function.

```
int object::message(const flyVector& p,float rad,int msg,int
param,void *data)
{
   return 1;
}
```

Get custom parameters description

```
int object::get_custom_param_desc(int i,flyParamDesc *pd)
```

This is a function used by the front-ends to obtain information regarding the plug-ins' classes' exported variables. It should always return the total number of exported variables in the class (in this case, 1), and switch the `i` parameter, filling the pd *flyParamDesc* instance with the desired `type`, `data` pointer and `name`. `type` must be a character representing one of Fly3D default parameter types (described in the `class_typeid.txt` document located in the 'util' folder inside Fly3D directory); `data` must be a pointer to the variable itself; `name` must be a string with the parameter's friendly name, to be used by the front-ends. The code is as follows:

```
int object::get_custom_param_desc(int i,flyParamDesc *pd)
{
   if (pd!=0)
     switch(i)
     {
       case 0:
          pd->type='m';
          pd->data=&objmesh;
          pd->name="objmesh";
       break;
     }

   return 1;
}
```

Refer to **step 8** for an addition to the object's *get_custom_param_desc* method.

7. Implementing the camera's methods

In this step, the camera class's methods will be implemented. These methods are, basically, the virtual functions inherited from the *flyBspObject* class.

Init

```
void camera::init()
```

This is the camera's initialisation funtion. As with the object class, all we have to do is initialise the camera's axis-aligned bounding box. But since the camera does not have a mesh associated with it, an AABB must be created. In the following code, the camera's AABB is initialised with side 50:

```
void camera::init()
{
    bbox.min.vec(-25,-25,-25);
    bbox.max.vec(25,25,25);
}
```

Step

```
int camera::step(int dt)
```

This is the per-frame update function. The camera must test for input and update its position (move dt milliseconds) in this method. In this example, the camera will move like this: the left mouse button will act as an accelerator (when pressed, the camera will move forward), and the mouse axes will be used for rotation (pitching and yawing). The following code can be divided into three parts:

(1) The mouse_down variable of the *flyDirectX* class is accessed, and a test is made using the constant value *FLY_MOUSE_L* to check if the left mouse button has been pressed since the last frame; if the test succeeds, the camera's velocity must be increased by a value that depends on the direction the camera is facing (Z negative), the move velocity and the elapsed time since the last frame (dt); if the test fails, the velocity of the camera must be nullified.

(2) The mouse axes are tested through the mouse_smooth variable in *flyDirectX* (for smooth mouse movement). Note that this variable is an array of two positions, corresponding to the X and Y mouse axes, respectively. If a test succeeds, the camera must be rotated over the other axis, by a value given by the mouse movement velocity and the displacement of the mouse pointer position since the last frame. The negation in the Y-axis rotation refers to inverted mouse rotation.

(3) The camera must move. This part of the code is explained in **step 9**, as the camera's movement and collision avoidance works the same way as the object's.

```
int camera::step(int dt)
{
  if (g_flydirectx->mouse_down&FLY_MOUSE_L)
    vel=Z*movevel*(float)(-dt);
  else
    vel.null();

  if (g_flydirectx->mouse_smooth[0]) // mouse X
    rotate(-g_flydirectx->mouse_smooth[0]*mousevel,Y);

  if (g_flydirectx->mouse_smooth[1]) // mouse Y
    rotate(g_flydirectx->mouse_smooth[1]*mousevel,X);

  flyVector p,v;
  p=pos+vel*(float)dt;
  v=vel+force*((float)dt/mass);
  box_collision(p,v);
  pos = p;
  vel = v;

  return 1;
}
```

Draw

```
void camera::draw()
```

This is the drawing function. Since the camera will not appear in the simulation, no drawing needs to be made here, and the method is left blank.

Message

```
int camera::message(const flyVector& p,float rad,int msg,int
param,void *data)
```

This is the message receiving function. Just like the object, the camera will not receive any messages, and this method must just return 1 for normal termination.

```
int camera::message(const flyVector& p,float rad,int msg,int
param,void *data)
{
  return 1;
}
```

Get custom parameters description

```
int camera::get_custom_param_desc(int i,flyParamDesc *pd)
```

This is a function used by the front-ends to obtain information regarding the plug-ins' classes' exported variables. It is similar to the object's methods of the

same name, and a complete explanation can be found in the **last step**. The
code is as follows:

```
int camera::get_custom_param_desc(int i,flyParamDesc *pd)
{
  if (pd!=0)
    switch(i)
    {
      case 0:
        pd->type='f';
        pd->data=&movevel;
        pd->name="movevel";
      break;
      case 1:
        pd->type='f';
        pd->data=&mousevel;
        pd->name="mousevel";
      break;
    }
  return 2;
}
```

8. Adding new member variables to the plug-in classes

In this step, the addition of members to existing classes in the plug-in will be
exemplified. A new variable will be added to the 'object' class: the mesh colour.

Firstly, the variable must be added to the 'object' class definition in the .h
file. The following line should be inserted:

```
flyVector color;
```

The *flyVector* class defines a four-component vector of floating point numbers.
Our colour will be represented by the **x**, **y** and **z** components of the vector,
while the **w** component will be used to represent transparency (0..1, 0 for fully
transparent, 1 for fully opaque).

For these values to be exported and edited in the front-ends, the variables
must be enumerated in the *get_custom_param_desc* method. The code for this
method, after these additions, is as follows:

```
int object::get_custom_param_desc(int i,flyParamDesc *pd)
{
  if (pd!=0)
    switch(i)
    {
      case 0:
        pd->type='m';
        pd->data=&objmesh;
        pd->name="objmesh";
```

```
            break;
            case 1:
               pd->type='c';
               pd->data=&color;
               pd->name="color";
            break;
            case 2:
               pd->type='f';
               pd->data=&color.w;
               pd->name="transp";
            break;
        }

    return 3;
}
```

Note that the `'c'` data type represents colours; *flyEditor* will open a colour browsing dialog box upon editing this type of parameter. For the transparency variable, a standard floating point editing box will be used.

Now that the mesh colour can be edited outside the plug-in, it must be assigned to the object's mesh colour. The *flyMesh* class has a colour member variable to which the colour parameter of the object will be set. This will be done in the object's **init** method, as seen below:

```
void object::init()
{
    if(objmesh)
    {
        bbox=objmesh->bbox;
        objmesh->color=color;
    }
}
```

9. Adding movement and collision detection to the object class

This step exemplifies movement simulation and collision detection for the 'object' class. The object will move with constant acceleration and bounce from walls, and its velocity vector will be represented by the variable `vel`, inherited from *flyParticle* (through *flyBspObject*). Collision will be handled by the `box_collision` method inherited from *flyBspObject*, which implements collision detection and response for the object's axis-aligned bounding box.

The code is structured as follows: firstly, the object's position and velocity are updated: position depends on velocity and time, and velocity depends on force, mass and time. Then, the `box_collision` method is called, and it handles collision detection and bouncing automatically (bouncing depends on the object's `bump` and `friction` parameters, inherited from *flyBspObject*), updating the position and velocity parameters passed to it. Finally, these values must be assigned to the object's original position and velocity. All this is inserted in the object's **step** method:

```
int object::step(int dt)
{
   flyVector p,v;
   p=pos+vel*(float)dt;
   v=vel+force*((float)dt/mass);
   box_collision(p,v);
   pos = p;
   vel = v;

   return 1;
}
```

10. Adding a new class to the plug-in: light

In this step, a new class will be added to the tutorial plug-in. And since the next step is about adding lighting to the simulation, the new class will be a light source.

Firstly, a new type must be added to those enumerated at the top of the .h file. It will be called *TYPE_LIGHT*. Every class in the plug-in must have a corresponding type. The enumeration should now look like this:

```
enum
{
   TYPE_OBJECT=100000,
   TYPE_CAMERA,
   TYPE_LIGHT,
};
```

Now for the definition of the **light** class. Like all other classes that exist in the scene, it must derive from the *flyBspObject* class. The **light** class will have two member variables, color and illumradius, representing the colour and the light radius of the light, respectively. Also, a constructor and a copy-constructor must be created. The constructor must assign initial values to the member variables and set the type variable (inherited from *flyBspObject*) to the constant defined before; the copy-constructor must call *flyBspObject*'s copy-constructor, and assign the member variables to the values given by the source object that is being copied. All the *flyBspObject* pure virtual functions must also be implemented, and the entire definition of the **light** class should look like this:

```
class light : public flyBspObject
{
public:
   flyVector color;
   float illumradius;
```

```
light()  :
  color(1),
  illumradius(100)
{ type=TYPE_LIGHT;  }

light(const light& in)  :
  flyBspObject(in),
  color(in.color),
  illumradius(in.illumradius)
{  }

virtual ~light()
{  }

void init();
int step(int dt);
void draw();
int get_custom_param_desc(int i,flyParamDesc *pd);

flyBspObject *clone()
{ return new light(*this);  }
};
```

Another important step is to create a description class for the new **light** class. Description classes allow external modules to see what classes exist in the plug-in and what members they export. All description classes are alike, so **light**'s description class will be similar to **camera**'s or **object**'s:

```
class light_desc : public flyClassDesc
{
public:
  flyBspObject *create() { return new light; };
  const char *get_name() { return "light"; };
  int get_type() { return TYPE_LIGHT; };
};
```

In the above class, the `create` method must return a new instance of the described class; the `get_name` method must return a string containing the friendly name of the class; and the `get_type` method must return the type that defines that class.

Now that the description class is created, the plug-in's exported methods must be modified to include the new **light** class. Two methods must be modified: the `num_classes` method, which must return the total number of classes in the plug-in, and the `get_class_desc`, which must return a pointer to a description class for each class in the plug-in. They should look like this:

```
__declspec( dllexport )
int num_classes()
{
  return 3;
}
```

```
__declspec( dllexport )
flyClassDesc *get_class_desc(int i)
{
   switch(i)
   {
     case 0:
        return &cd_object;
     case 1:
        return &cd_camera;
     case 2:
        return &cd_light;
   }

   return 0;
}
```

Finally, the **light** class methods must be implemented. They are quite simple: the **init** method must create an axis-aligned bounding box for the light; the **step** and **draw** methods will do nothing (for now); the *get_custom_param_desc* method must enumerate the two member variables in the class. They should be implemented as follows:

```
void light::init()
{
   bbox.max.vec(-10,-10,-10);
   bbox.min.vec(10,10,10);
}

int light::step(int dt)
{
   return 0;
}

void light::draw()
{

}

int light::get_custom_param_desc(int i,flyParamDesc *pd)
{
   if (pd!=0)
     switch(i)
     {
       case 0:
          pd->type='c';
          pd->data=&color;
          pd->name="color";
       break;
       case 1:
          pd->type='f';
          pd->data=&illumradius;
          pd->name="illumradius";
```

```
            break;
        }

    return 2;
}
```

The next step is about adding lighting and shadows to the simulation, and will use the newly created **light** class to represent light.

11. Adding dynamic lighting and dynamic shadows to the object

For the last step of the tutorial, lighting and shadowing will be implemented for the **object** class, so that the object's mesh is lit and casts shadows.

Firstly, a *flyLightVertex* member variable must be added to the **object** class. *flyLightVertex* is a class from inside Fly3D engine, which implements an array of dynamic lights. It should be declared in the **object** class definition like this:

```
flyLightVertex dynlights;
```

Now the object must search the environment around it, looking for light sources that will light it. This is done in the object's **step** function through the engine method *recurse_bsp*:

```
int object::step(int dt)
{
    flyVector p,v;
    p=pos+vel*(float)dt;
    v=vel+force*((float)dt/mass);
    box_collision(p,v);
    pos = p;
    vel = v;

    g_flyengine->recurse_bsp(pos,2048,TYPE_LIGHT);
    for(int i=0;i<g_flyengine->selobjs.num;i++ )
    {
        light *l=(light *)g_flyengine->selobjs[i];

        if (g_flyengine->collision_test(pos,l-
>pos,FLY_TYPE_STATICMESH)==0)
            dynlights.add_light(l->pos,l->color,l->illumradius);
    }

    return 1;
}
```

Note that the *collision_test* call tests if there is a wall (*FLY_TYPE_STATICMESH*) between the light and the object.

Now that the object can already find light sources around it, it must be lit by them. This is done in the object's **draw** function, using the *flyLightVertex* method init_draw:

```
void object::draw()
{
  if(objmesh)
  {
    dynlights.init_draw(this);

    glPushMatrix();
    glTranslatef(pos.x,pos.y,pos.z);
    glMultMatrixf((float *)&mat);
    objmesh->draw();
    glPopMatrix();

    glDisable(GL_LIGHTING);
  }
}
```

The two lines of code added above are enough for the object to be lit by the dynamic lights stored in the `dynlights` variable. As a last task, shadow casting will now be implemented in the **object** class. It will be done through overriding the *flyBspObject* virtual function *draw_shadow*:

```
void object::draw_shadow()
{
  int i=dynlights.get_closest(pos);
  if (i!=-1)
  {
    glPushMatrix();
    glTranslatef(pos.x,pos.y,pos.z);
    glMultMatrixf((float *)&mat);
    flyVector v=dynlights.pos[i]-pos;
    v.normalize();
    objmesh->draw_shadow_volume(v*mat_t);
    glPopMatrix();
  }
}
```

The `get_closest` method finds the closest light in the array; the `draw_shadow_volume` method draws a shadow of the mesh in a given position and orientation.

Finally, a note concerning the object searching for lights around it. There is another way of determining which lights will apply to which objects: the lights themselves could send messages to every object within the sphere defined by their position and radius. This option suits better in a situation where the number of lights is less than the number of objects to be lit. If this is not the case, the way it was implemented in this tutorial will do, with the objects themselves looking for light sources around them.

Real-time rendering

Rendering in this text has been divided into two chapters, one mainly theoretical (this chapter) and one mainly practical (Chapter 5). The development of the latest hardware, which enables the GPU to be programmed, is a specialised topic in its own right and because of this we think it better to separate the theory from the practice, although it is the case that the selection of the theoretical techniques described in this chapter is very much influenced by the hardware model. As we shall see, the emphasis is on achieving quality by real-time per-pixel shading and this relies on texture mapping hardware extensions. Thus rendering theory in this chapter is approached very much from the point of view of map implementable techniques.

4.1 Introduction

At the time of writing (2002), we appear to be on the edge of an era where many advanced rendering techniques, previously only practical in off-line applications, are now implementable in interactive applications. This is due to the massive graphics processing power now available in consumer hardware.

Much of this is embedded in the shift of rendering techniques from the CPU onto programmable GPUs. We deal with this important new development in some detail in Chapter 5. That these developments have come about is due in no small part to the demands of the games industry and this chapter looks at how the theory behind rendering techniques can now be incorporated into games applications.

One of the enabling technologies of 3D computer games in the 1990s was the use of pre-calculated lighting in the form of light maps. This enabled the use of complex and thus interesting levels through which a shooter could wander and encounter opponents. Light maps, however, suffer from the limitation that, as a pre-calculation technique, they can only light static objects. Shading of dynamic objects was limited in that era to, say, Gouraud shading and/or some other simple device like a moving object 'picking up' the ambient light as it moved. In this chapter we will look at the various ways in which recent hardware developments can be used to shade dynamic objects efficiently. We are particularly interested in what is sometimes called per-pixel shading, which means that a separate shading calculation can be applied to each pixel – as in, for example, the Phong specular term. The term is used to distinguish the method from per-vertex shading where a shading calculation is made only at a vertex and then hardware interpolation is used to derive pixel intensities (Gouraud shading).

We should note in passing that in the recent history of off-line rendering much research has been devoted to global illumination methods such as ray tracing, radiosity and general solutions to the rendering equation. This research was, and still is, motivated by the assertion that in the pursuit of photo-realism, a solution to the global illumination problem must be found. (As is well known, all current solutions to global illumination are outside the capability of consumer hardware, at least for real-time rendering.) However, it is the case that the high quality shading attained in Pixar movie productions in the 1990s relied solely on the shader technology of RenderMan – an API which does not implement global illumination – and it is this high quality of local reflection model technology that we examine in the chapter from the point of view of interactive rates. We should also remember that many phenomena, which are strictly a consequence of global illumination, can be approximated by cheaper mechanisms that can be incorporated in real-time applications. Environment mapping and shadow algorithms are good examples of this and we can be certain that such devices will continue to be used for some time until a feasible pure solution to global illumination is reached.

The motivation for the use of advanced rendering techniques is, of course, image quality. Image quality has often been crudely discussed in terms of geometric complexity which in itself has been interpreted as number of polygons/object. This argument has led to an equally crude assumption that the quality problem will be solved by more and more powerful hardware. That polygon count is only one factor in image quality can be seen by examining the evolution of Pixar's productions *Toy Story* (1995) and *Toy Story 2* (1999). In comparing these two productions, Pixar re-rendered frames from both movies on the same contemporary hardware. An average taken over all frames showed a ratio of 5:1 in processing time for the later movie. However, *Toy Story2* had only doubled its predecessor's complexity in terms of polygons/frame . . .

4.2   Vertices, pixels and maps

New hardware, as we examine in detail in Chapter 5, gives a programmer control over vertex processing and pixel processing on the GPU. These facilities are also known as vertex shaders and pixel shaders by the DX8 API and by the hardware manufacturer NVIDIA, presumably because they are mostly intended to be used for lighting a vertex or a pixel. As is well known, the perceived quality of a shaded surface is strongly dependent on whether we implement a vertex shading model (such as Gouraud shading) and then have the GPU interpolate values from the vertices, or whether we implement a model which requires evaluation for each pixel (such as Phong shading or bump mapping). (Although we can note that for Phong shading there may be little difference in quality between a vertex model and a pixel model providing the object mesh is of sufficiently high polygonal resolution.) Thus most of the increased quality available in real-time rendering emerges from a programmer having access to per-pixel functionality. It should be mentioned immediately that this does not imply that we have access to independent pixel functionality. The functionality revolves around the exploitation of new texture mapping and addressing facilities and in this respect the developments can be seen as an evolution of the use of maps for rendering – a device that has a long history in graphics and games.

The original motivation of texture maps was storing diffuse reflection coefficients and in this form they are sometimes known more aptly as colour maps, the act of texture mapping simply modulating the colour over the surface of an object. The success of texture mapping and the expansion of hardware facilities has led to new forms of information being stored in maps. Normal maps, and maps which store the information in a BRDF (see Section 4.4), are good examples of this. In this section we will look at texture mapping in its historical context, then move on to new implementations whose novelty derives either from new mapping techniques, new hardware or a combination of both.

4.2.1   Basic per-pixel shading

We begin by briefly reviewing Phong's empirical model – the foundation stone of modern rendering technology. This is a local reflection model so-called because it considers only the interaction between the object being shaded and the light source. (Local reflection models are distinguished from global reflection models which simulate all light interaction, including object/object interaction.

Although local reflection models give high quality shading for an object, they cannot be used to calculate vital global phenomena, the most important of which is shadows.)

The model can be written as:

reflected light = ambient + diffuse + specular

or

$$I = I_a + I_l(k_d(\mathbf{N.L}) + k_s(\mathbf{R.V})^n)$$

where

I_a is an arbitrary constant representing ambient light
I_l is the light source intensity
$\mathbf{N}$ is the surface normal at the point of interest
$\mathbf{L}$ is the light direction vector or the vector from the point of interest to the point light source
$\mathbf{R}$ is the mirror reflection direction with respect to $\mathbf{L}$
$\mathbf{V}$ is the view vector
k_d is the diffuse reflection coefficient 'carrying' the colour of the object
k_s is the specular reflection coefficient set to the colour of the light source
n is the shininess index

Note that unless we are shading solely by distance from a so-called positional light, we ignore light attenuation due to distance. Also, we can factor I_l into the reflection coefficients. If we consider diffuse illumination only and remove the light source to infinity (the light source is then termed a directional source as opposed to a point source), the lighting reduces to a function of the surface normal only:

$$I_{\text{diffuse}} = f(\mathbf{N})$$

And this is the foundation equation of light maps in games. It means that we can pre-calculate light maps for static objects in games where only the view-point changes. We simply pre-calculate shading using this equation, providing there is no relative motion between the light source(s) and the static objects. In certain circumstances pre-calculated light maps can be updated in real time to enable, for example, the effect of explosions to be 'painted' on nearby static objects. Such implementations are fully discussed in [WATT01].

A simplifying modification due to Blinn [BLIN77] replaced the term $(\mathbf{R.V})$ with the term $(\mathbf{N.H})$, where $\mathbf{H}$, the halfway vector, is given by:

$$\mathbf{H} = \mathbf{L} + \mathbf{V}$$

Again, if we remove the light source to infinity, we have:

$$I_{\text{specular}} = f(\mathbf{N,V})$$

The diffuse component is thus view independent and can be pre-calculated and cached in light maps. The specular component is a function only of the surface normal and the view vector. For dynamic objects and specular lighting we can use normal maps with dot product texture blending (Section 4.2.4) or pre-filtered environment maps (Section 4.5.1) to calculate:

$$I = f(\mathbf{N}, \mathbf{V})$$

in real time.

Implicit in any implementation of these equations is a so-called self-shadowing evaluation:

$$I_{\text{diffuse}} = (k_d \ \text{max\_of}(0, \mathbf{N.L}))$$
$$I_{\text{specular}} = (k_s \ \text{max\_of}(0, \mathbf{N.H})^n)$$

where $(\mathbf{L.N})$ and $(\mathbf{N.H})$ are clamped to zero if negative

When shading bump maps two normals are involved – the per-pixel normal of the unpeturbed surface, $\mathbf{N}$, and the perturbed normal $\mathbf{N'}$ and both self-shadowing evaluations should be made:

$$I_{\text{diffuse}} = I_l(k_d \ *s*\text{max\_of}(0, \mathbf{N'.L}))$$
$$I_{\text{specular}} = I_l(k_s \ *s*\text{max\_of}(0, \mathbf{N'.H})^n)$$

$$\text{where } s = \begin{cases} 1, \mathbf{L.N} > 0 \\ 0, \mathbf{L.N} \le 0 \end{cases}$$

Otherwise it may be that a perturbed pixel facet can see the light source even if it is part of a surface that cannot. Kilgard [KILG99] points out that using a step function to represent the self-shadowing term can lead to temporal aliasing artefacts in the form of popping and suggests that this term be transformed into a ramp as:

$$\begin{cases} 1 & (\mathbf{L.N}) > c \\ \dfrac{1}{c}(\mathbf{L.N}) & 0 < (\mathbf{L.N}) \le c \\ 0 & (\mathbf{L.N}) \le 0 \end{cases}$$

where a suggested value of c is 0.125.

Having reduced the basic Phong shading model to a function only of $\mathbf{N}$ and $\mathbf{V}$ there are various ways in which this can be implemented using texture mapping on hardware. The most direct method is to use a normal map to represent $\mathbf{N}$, as we describe in Section 4.2.4.

(4.2.2) Shading and coordinate spaces

An important issue in real-time rendering is that of the coordinate space in which the lighting calculation is carried out. This is of no theoretical import – we simply have to have all the contributors to the lighting equation defined in the *same* coordinate space – the practical consequence is, as always, efficiency.

For per-vertex lighting it is common (in OpenGL, for example) to perform the calculations in eye space, in which case the object normals must be trans-

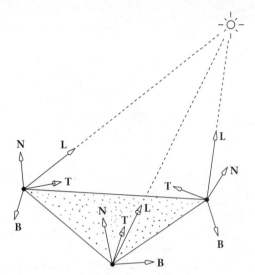

Figure 4.1
Tangent space is formed by the vertex normal **N** and two vectors **B** and **T** lying in the tangent plane. It is local to each vertex, and local to each pixel.

formed into eye space. To transform normals we must use the transpose of the inverse of the matrix used to transform the geometry. In OpenGL this is done by using the inverse-transpose of the model-view matrix.

$$\mathbf{N}_{eye} = (\mathbf{M}^{-1})^{T}\,\mathbf{N}_{obj}$$

Alternatively we can calculate in object space. It does not matter which space is used – the answer will be the same.

In the case of per-pixel lighting we apply a shading equation at every pixel. In many applications we have, or derive, per-pixel normals from a map. Effectively these normals are in a coordinate system that is local to a pixel; or more precisely local to a coordinate system at a point on the object which projects onto the pixel. It would be convenient if we could calculate the lighting in this system. We can transform the eye and light vectors at the vertices of the object and interpolate to obtain per pixel values (Figure 4.1). The pixel normal is then fetched from a texture map.

Thus we need to calculate an orthonormal basis at each vertex **TBN**, where

    N is the vertex normal
    T is the tangent vector
    B = **T** × **N** is the so-called bi-normal

Then the light vector is transformed into this space, known as surface local space,[1] by using the matrix

$$\begin{bmatrix} \mathbf{T}_x & \mathbf{T}_y & \mathbf{T}_z \\ \mathbf{B}_x & \mathbf{B}_y & \mathbf{B}_z \\ \mathbf{N}_x & \mathbf{N}_y & \mathbf{N}_z \end{bmatrix}$$

---

1. This space is also known as tangent space or texture tangent space.

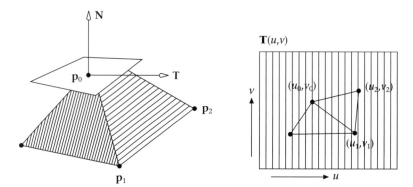

Figure 4.2
Finding the tangent
vector at a vertex.

For a polygonal object, given a vertex normal **N**, the tangent lies in a plane normal to this vector. To choose a consistent direction for the tangents over the surface of the object we can use the texture map parameterisation and choose the direction that always points along one of the coordinate axes of the texture map (Figure 4.2). This is calculated as follows:

For each vertex, for each triangle that contributes to the vertex:

$$\mathbf{v}_0 = \mathbf{p}_1 - \mathbf{p}_0$$
$$\mathbf{v}_1 = \mathbf{p}_2 - \mathbf{p}_0$$
$$\Delta u_0 = u_1 - u_0$$
$$\Delta u_1 = u_2 - u_0$$
$$\mathbf{T} = \Delta u_0 \mathbf{v}_1 - \Delta u_1 \mathbf{v}_0$$

where
  (u_0, v_0), (u_1, v_1) and (u_2, v_2) are the texture coordinates associated with
  $\mathbf{p}_0$, $\mathbf{p}_1$ and $\mathbf{p}_2$

averaging the vector **T** results in a vector lying in the tangent plane.

If the object has a general parametric description $O(u,v)$ then we have the concept of a tangent plane defined by the vectors:

$$\frac{\partial O}{\partial u} \text{ and } \frac{\partial O}{\partial u}$$

and the normal as:

$$\frac{\partial O}{\partial u} \times \frac{\partial O}{\partial u}$$

(4.2.3) The 25-year reign of interpolative shading and colour maps

Ever since the invention of interpolative shading in the 1970s, texture maps have been used to add detail and hence 'visual interest' to a surface. This established culture has been incorporated in graphics hardware and has been heavily exploited and extended (light maps) by the games industry. Indeed it may be the case that without texture mapping hardware the games industry might not have developed into the buoyant culture that it is today.

The use of the term texture maps is, of course, a misnomer and a better term would have been colour maps. The ubiquity of colour/texture maps and their treatment as a separate entity to light/object interaction has resulted perhaps in the suppression of the obvious physical attribute possessed by most real textures, which is that they are viewing angle and illuminating angle dependent. You cannot simulate a brick texture by using a photograph of a brick wall. (Exactly the same thing has happened with shadows. They have been separated from light/object interaction in interpolative shaders, when in fact they are a consequence of global illumination interactions.) In fact there is now a publicly available database (www.cs.columbia.edu/CAVE/curet) which consists of BTFs (bidirectional texture functions) which are texture maps as functions of viewing and illumination directions. These have been generated from physical measurements on real surfaces and the database consists of 14,000 images. Using BTFs, classic texture mapping can be used to 'correctly' simulate texture as a function of viewing and illumination angle and thus incorporate self-shadowing. The problem here is the explosion of data in the BTFs. Dana *et al.* [DANA99] use 205 maps for each texture and evaluate a BTF for the required viewing and illumination angle by interpolation amongst the maps in this database. This would obviously cause texture management problems in real-time applications.

Lighting, maps and games technology – some history

One of the enabling software technologies in 3D games was light maps. A light map caches reflected light on all (static) surfaces in a scene due to all light sources. As a viewer moves around a scene the view-independent object shading is obtained from the light map. The two significant advantages of the light map are that it enables lighting to be pre-calculated and for view-independent lighting – diffuse – the light map texels can be large. In other words the light map caches low-frequency reflected light and it is view independent.

This general approach has evolved, with multi-texture hardware and texture blending modes providing additional flexibility. For example, a technique which appears to have been pioneered by Quake3 developers extends light maps to include high frequency detail. This is just an approximation to the BTP technique described in the previous section – it uses just four maps/surfaces instead of 205. It is a crude but efficient approximation to bump mapping. It calculates a series of high frequency light maps that cache the light reflected from the surface detail into a number of different view directions. Ideally we would want to cache the reflected light from all directions but this can be restricted, without loss of generality, to say four viewing directions with the view vector at an elevation of 45° in each case. Now the three-dimensionality of the detail must be apparent as the viewer moves around with respect to the surface, and this is achieved by calculating the dot product between the current viewing direction and each of the 45° pre-calculation view vectors and using the resulting values as a blend factor for the four maps. Thus in a multi-texture pipeline all that has to be done dynamically as the camera moves is to calculate the viewing direction/bump map angle dot products and use these to blend the bump maps.

The current state of the conventional mapping art can be summarised as follows:

Lighting phenomenon	Map name	View dependent/ view independent (parameter modulated/cached)	Pre-calculated or updated
object colour	texture	independent k_d	pre-modelled
object texture	bump	dependent (N)	pre-modelled
object diffuse reflection	light	independent (L.N)	pre-calculated
static object shadows	light	independent	pre-calculated
fog	fog	dependent	pre-calculated
moving lights	light	independent	update light map by constraining light's influence
object specular reflection	specular map gloss map	dependent	pre-calculated
object/environment specular reflection	environment	dependent	pre-calculated

A general lighting equation in terms of map blending may then be written as:

C = fog*(texture map*(light map) + specular map + environment map)

where for simplicity we can constrain blending to the operators + and *.

In the event that the previous bump mapping approximation is used, the light map term expands to:

((((light map * bump1)*bump2)*bump3)*bump4)

Here the light map/texture map operator is * and this darkens or lightens the texture map appropriate to the result of the lighting calculations cached in the light map. Specular maps, on the other hand, are added to the current result. That this should be is easily seen by referring to the Phong local reflection model where the diffuse and specular components are added together. The diffuse component is:

$k_d(\mathbf{L.N})$

Here k_d, the diffuse reflection coefficient, is equivalent to the texture map and (**L.N**) is of course the reflected intensity cached in the light map. The specular term is replaced in its entirety by a specular map which is indexed by the reflected view vector.

In the above equations there is a hierarchy implied by the parentheses. Obviously fog should be factored with the result of all previous operations since it can affect all of the image. Other options are not so clear cut and may require experimentation. For example, adding the light specular map to the product of the light and texture map:

(texture map*light map) + specular map

may cause the specular detail to be too bright (appearing emissive) in regions which are also in shadow. In which event

(texture map + specular map)*light map

may be a better option. This problem originates from the fact that we may be using the light map to cache direct reflection and shadows. The normal Phong method adds shadow areas onto the image **after** the full equation has been applied.

Scalar representations

A scalar representation of a 3D model is the encoding of geometric variations in a 2D map. The most familiar example of this form is bump mapping where a low resolution mesh is enhanced with a map containing high resolution detail. The methods we describe follow this pattern, differing in the form of the representation and the origin of the low resolution mesh.

Scalar representations of a polygon mesh emerged out of the realisation of the vast redundancy inherent in a triangle mesh. First, there is the connectivity information which must be set up in an object data structure, and second, it is the case that representing geometry with vertex triples is redundant. Traditional geometry compression (see, for example [DEER95]) has operated on vertex positions using, for example, coarse quantisation and delta encoding of the vertices. In addition, tri-stripping, to address the connectivity redundancy in adjacent triangles, has also been a popular resource. With scalar representation schemes the original mesh is replaced with a low resolution or base mesh together with a low amplitude scalar displacement map. The potential advantages of this approach are particularly reflected in compression possibilities.

Differential geometry tells us that we should be able to represent geometry with a single scalar value. The scalar takes the form of a displacement, along the surface normal, from the tangent plane to the surface. At first this seems a contradiction. Certainly we can have a displacement map to describe the geometric variation across the surface, but we still need a description of the surface that we are displacing from. This apparent contradiction is solved by the device, which, in its most general terms, means that we store a low resolution representation for the surface together with a displacement map, consisting of scalars, which contains the high resolution detail.

Bump maps

Bump maps are 2D patterns – procedurally generated or painted – which modulate the surface of an object with high frequency detail. In this section we will look at a deeper interpretation of bump maps. First some background detail.

The key idea of bump maps is that small-scale geometric surface variation over a surface can be **encoded** by a single scalar function – a height field – of two variables. If we were going to take a vertex-based representation down to the same fine level of detail then, of course, we need three scalars for each point. However, this implies that we need a parameterisation for the surface that enables us to map from some 3D object space to a 2D parametric space.

Consider first displacement mapping. In a terrain model the parameterisation may be a regular grid and the object – the terrain – is just a height field. In general we have the concept of an object being modulated by high frequency detail by displacing a point on the surface of an object by some small amount. In the terrain example the object is a plane and the mapping between the height field and the object is one to one. If the object was a sphere – a planet – then we can still encode the terrain as a height map $H(u,v)$. Points (x,y,z) on the surface of a sphere can be mapped into (u,v) space using the conventional latitude/longitude mapping:

$$v = \text{latitude}/\pi = \arccos(-z)/\pi$$

$$u = \text{longitude}/2\pi = \begin{cases} \arccos\left(\dfrac{x}{\sin(\text{latitude})}\right)\Big/2\pi & y \geq 0 \\[2mm] 2\pi - \arccos\left(\dfrac{x}{\sin(\text{latitude})}\right)\Big/2\pi & y < 0 \end{cases}$$

Then for a point $\mathbf{P}$ on the surface of the sphere we move it to $\mathbf{P}'$ along its surface normal as:

$$\mathbf{P}' = \mathbf{P} + H(u,v)\mathbf{N}_p$$

Displacement mapping would solve all our problems except that computationally it is no better in cost terms than conventionally modelling the geometry at the required fine level of detail. Using a standard renderer, the displacement would have to be applied to the object at the start of the pipeline.

The great breakthrough with bump mapping was that it had the effect of displacement mapping but could be applied at the same stage, and in the same way, in rendering as colour mapping. Bump mapping rotates the surface normal associated with a pixel in such a way that the shading equation makes the surface look as if it had been displaced by a scalar height field $B(u,v)$.

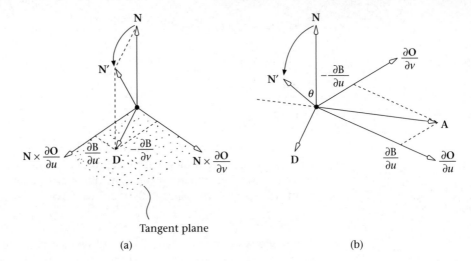

Figure 4.3
Bump maps can be represented as offset vectors or notations. (a) **D** is an offset vector in the tangent plane. (b) **N** rotates angle θ about axis **A**.

The variations in bump mapping algorithms relate to the way in which the perturbations are encoded in the bump map, which in turn depends on coordinate space considerations. The classic method [BLIN78] uses an offset vector to perturb the normal:

$$\mathbf{N}' = \mathbf{N} + \mathbf{D}$$

where **D** is an offset vector lying in the tangent plane of the surface (Figure 4.3a)

$$\mathbf{D} = \frac{\dfrac{\partial B}{\partial u}\left(\mathbf{N} \times \dfrac{\partial \mathbf{O}}{\partial \mathbf{v}}\right) - \dfrac{\partial B}{\partial v}\left(\mathbf{N} \times \dfrac{\partial \mathbf{O}}{\partial \mathbf{u}}\right)}{|\mathbf{N}|}$$

the bump map is then either $B(u,v)$ or we pre-calculate and cache $\mathbf{D}(u,v)$. If we pre-calculate **D** then the map is tied to the object geometry. $B(u,v)$ on the other hand can be shared amongst object surfaces but at the expense of performing the above calculation.

Normal maps

Another method is to store the perturbation as a vector rotation (Figure 4.3b):

$$\frac{\mathbf{N}'}{|\mathbf{N}'|} = \mathbf{N}\,R(u,v)$$

where **R** is a 3×3 rotation matrix $\begin{bmatrix} r_{00} & r_{01} & r_{02} \\ r_{10} & r_{11} & r_{12} \\ r_{20} & r_{21} & r_{22} \end{bmatrix}$

In this interpretation **N** is rotated about an axis **A** that lies in the tangent plane. Since **N** and **N**′ lie in the same plane the axis of rotation is given by:

$$\mathbf{N} \times \mathbf{N}' = \mathbf{N} \times \mathbf{D} = |\mathbf{N}| \left(\frac{\partial B}{\partial v} \frac{\partial O}{\partial u} - \frac{\partial B}{\partial u} \frac{\partial O}{\partial v} \right) = |\mathbf{N}|\mathbf{A}$$

where $\mathbf{A}$ is the axis of rotation:

It can be shown that:

$$\tan \theta = \frac{|\mathbf{N}|}{|\mathbf{D}|} = \frac{|\mathbf{N}|}{|\mathbf{A}|}$$

The obvious objection to this method – nine scalars per (u,v) – can be ameliorated by using tangent or surface local space. The normal map is already in this space and we can transform the light direction vector.

In this space $\mathbf{N}$ becomes $[0,0,1]$ and we have

$$\mathbf{N}' = [r_{02} \quad r_{12} \quad r_{22}]$$

The obvious question is what is the difference between a normal map and a bump map? One answer is nothing; both encode variations in the surface normal as a texture map. Bump maps have usually serviced applications where the required texture is set up by an artist using a paint package – we are not usually trying to exactly imitate precise variations in the surface geometry but to imitate the look of the material. Normal maps, on the other hand, are used to store precise geometric variations. What we can thus achieve with normal maps is a decoupling of surface detail from mesh geometry. We can render a complex object using a low resolution mesh and have the detail rendered using a texture map operation, as Figure 4.4 illustrates. Here the surface detail remains at the 'same' resolution in the sense that the same map is used, while the polygonal resolution degrades.

Figure 4.4
A normal map used to render a model at different levels of detail. The levels of detail contain 7809, 3905, 1951, 975, and 488 triangles, respectively (from nearest to farthest)

From Cohen, J. Olano, M. and Manocha, D. (1998) Appearance-preserving simplification, *Proceedings SIGGRAPH 98*, pp. 115–22 © 1998, ACM, Inc. Reprinted by permission.

Thus the concept of rendering with normal maps involves considering a surface as consisting of:

- positional information as a low or variable resolution polygon mesh;
- surface detail information as a high resolution normal map.

The practical problem with normal maps is their generation and this is the reason why they are less familiar than the ubiquitous bump maps, which can be created interactively or procedurally and need only to imitate surface displacement, not to model it exactly. To create a normal map for a polygon mesh object we need the following ingredients:

(1) a high resolution polygonal model;

(2) a simplified version of (1) together with a parameterisation that can be used to enable the normal map to be used as a conventional texture for rendering;

(3) a method that in some way invokes a geometric comparison between (1) and (2) to derive the 'lost' normals across the faces of the large polygons. Methods that address this problem are described in the next section and in Sections 6.4 and 6.5.3.

A particularly straightforward approach in this category is described in detail in [WATT01]. (Here high resolution light maps are used as the detail but the principle is exactly the same.) This is to use Bézier quadrics as the underlying geometry, calculate a light map off-line, then downsample the quadric mesh geometry according to the desired LOD during rendering. Whatever LOD is selected, we texture map with the light map obtained from the original high resolution curved surface.

Maps and silhouette edge processing

The approaches described in the previous section – texture mapping a low resolution base mesh with surface detail – ignores the silhouette edge problem. On average there are $\sqrt{n}$ edges contained in a silhouette edge (where n is the number of faces in the object). Here the low resolution geometry becomes visible. The visual quality of the silhouette edge is important since it gives visual clues to the shape of the object. Also, the effort of using high quality shading models is somewhat diminished by crude silhouette edges. These factors motivated Sander *et al.* [SAND00] in a method they call silhouette clipping. This approach involves extracting a silhouette edge from the high resolution model and rendering into the stencil or alpha buffer to create a mask which then clips the low resolution rendering. Their work addresses the two obvious requirements of such an approach.

First, since the rendered image of the coarse mesh is going to be clipped by the silhouette edge of the original mesh, the coarse mesh M^0 must contain the original mesh M^n. Sander *et al.* develop a structure they term progressive hulls and, as the name suggests, this is an adaptation of progressive meshes (Chapter 6). An outer progressive hull, defined as:

$$\bar{M}^n \subseteq \ldots \subseteq \bar{M}^0$$

is obtained by adapting the progressive mesh simplification procedure so that all geometry in $\bar{M}^{k+1}$ is contained within $\bar{M}^k$. This means that the surface must remain unchanged or move outwards.[2]

The second requirement of the method is the extraction of the silhouette edge of M^n in real time. This is accomplished by ordering the edges into a hierarchy. A silhouette edge is defined as one whose adjacent faces are front and back facing respectively. A tree is organised as face clusters where each node contains a cluster of faces, which for a region of space, are all completely front facing or back facing. Traversal of this tree enables runtime extraction of the (external) silhouette edge.

Displaced subdivision surfaces

This work [LEE00] unifies subdivision surfaces and displacement maps. Displacement maps have been around for as long as texture maps but their main use has been in high-end rendering systems because of the expense of adding high frequency detail as a geometry perturbation. Their real-time utility has been in animation applications, such as water surface, where analytic scripting of changes in the map is straightforward because of the 2D parameterisation.

The base mesh or subdivision surface control mesh is derived using the classic edge collapse transformation ordered by the QEM (see Chapter 6). Candidate edge collapses in the simplification process are further restricted as follows. The idea is that as the surface is simplified, the space of the normals to the subdivision products is locally similar to the corresponding space of the normals to the original mesh. This ensures that the smooth domain surface – the eventual result of the simplification process – is able to express the original mesh accurately by scalar displacement along its normals.

The base representation in a displaced subdivision surface is a control net which generates a limit surface using loop[3] subdivision and a displacement map which perturbs points on the limit surface along the surface normal to the limit surface. The end result, which uses the displacement map to move points out from the smooth domain surface, is called a DSS.

---

2. A similar procedure can be used to define an inner progressive hull:

$$\bar{M}^0 \subseteq \ldots \subseteq \bar{M}^n$$

and the two together bound the original mesh from both sides (reminiscent of the simplification envelopes method [COHE98]).

3. Loop subdivision is an **approximating** scheme for triangular meshes (Catmull-Clark is an approximating scheme for quad meshes), as opposed to an **interpolating** scheme. In an interpolating scheme points in the control net are also points on the limit surface, but the quality of the limit surface is generally lower than that of an approximating scheme.

The immediate advantage here is that detail is represented by a single scalar or a scalar map as opposed to a vector map. This is an optimal representation – a surface is a height/scalar field on some domain surface (just as a terrain can be represented as a height field on a 2D regular array). This makes it ideal for applications requiring high compression. The displacement maps can be pre-filtered using mip-mapping, which contrasts with filtering normal maps which is not straightforward. Also, there is an 'easy' parameterisation between the control mesh and the displacement map. If the scheme was used for per-pixel shading, we need to calculate the normal to the displaced surface. Although this can be computed quickly from the subdivision surface, it still needs adjacency information. If we pre-calculate the normal maps then we lose the scalar and filtering advantages and the approach reduces to a normal map generation method for very high resolution surfaces. It is not clear at this stage if the method has any advantages over the 'rendering' method for normal map generation.

The pre-processing phase is as follows:

(1) A control mesh is obtained from the original high resolution mesh by using a variation of an edge collapse algorithm.

(2) A limit surface is generated. This will be a smoothed version of the original surface.

(3) The displacement map is generated by sampling the limit surface and casting rays, along the direction of the surface normal, from these sample point onto the original surface.

The derivation of the required normal is straightforward. We have:

$$\mathbf{s} = \mathbf{p} + D\mathbf{N}$$

where
 $\mathbf{s}$ is the point on the displaced surface
 $\mathbf{p}$ is the corresponding point on the limit surface
 $\mathbf{N}$ is the normal at $\mathbf{p}$
 D is the displacement scalar

$\mathbf{N}$ is obtained from

$$\mathbf{N} = \frac{\partial \mathbf{p}}{\partial u} \times \frac{\partial \mathbf{p}}{\partial v}$$

where the partials are easily computed using first derivative masks on the subdivision surface. The calculation of $\mathbf{N}_s$, the normal at the point s on the displaced surface, is given by the cross-product of the tangent vector in the displacement surface

$$\mathbf{N}_s = \frac{\partial \mathbf{s}}{\partial u} \times \frac{\partial \mathbf{s}}{\partial v}$$

$$\frac{\partial \mathbf{s}}{\partial u} = \frac{\partial \mathbf{p}}{\partial u} + \frac{\partial D}{\partial u}\mathbf{N} + \frac{\partial D}{\partial u}\frac{\partial \mathbf{N}}{\partial u}$$

Figure 4.5
Displaced subdivision surfaces (DSS): the first image is the control mesh; the second – the domain surface – is generated from the first by Loop subdivision; the third – the DSS – is generated from the second by using the displacement map

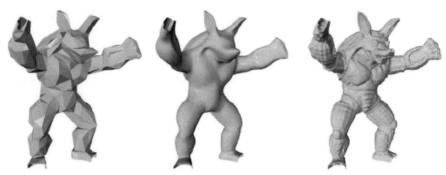

From Lee, A., Moreton, H. and Hoppe, H. (2000) Displaced subdivision surfaces, *Proceedings SIGGRAPH 00*, pp. 85–94 © 2000, ACM, Inc. Reprinted by permission.

with a similar expression for the other tangent. As in bump mapping, the final term (which contains second derivatives) can be ignored for small displacements. Figure 4.5 gives an overview of the scheme. The method bears some similarity to the MAPS scheme described in Section 6.5.3.

4.3 Factorisation methods

We now look at how the power of texture map hardware can be harnessed to provide more elaborate functions. This is generally made possible by factorising the models and storing pre-calculated shading component values in two-dimensional texture maps. Subsequent hardware interpolation of the values in the texture map is equivalent to vector interpolation without re-normalisation (sometimes called fast Phong shading). Thus such methods are subject to the restriction that the values obtained per pixel are not exactly equal to those which would be obtained by applying the model at each pixel. The approach can be used with any shading model that can be implemented as one or more two-dimensional lookup tables, including the basic Phong model. The models used as examples of this technique are the Cook–Torrance model and the Banks anisotropic model.

4.3.1 Per-pixel shading using factorised shading models – isotropic models

Two years after the appearance of Phong's work in 1975, J. Blinn [BLIN77] published a paper describing how a physically based specular component could be used in computer graphics. In 1982 Cook and Torrance [COOK82] extended this model to account for the spectral composition of highlights – their dependency on material type and the angle of incidence of the light. These advances have a subtle effect on the size and colour of a highlight compared to that obtained from the Phong model. The model still retains the separation of the reflected light into a diffuse and specular component and the new work concentrated mostly on the specular component, the diffuse component being calculated in the same way as before. The model is most successful in rendering shiny metallic-like surfaces, and through the colour variation in the specular high-light being able, for example, to render similar-coloured metals differently.

The problem of highlight shape is quite subtle. A highlight is just the image of a light source or sources reflected in the object. Unless the object surface is planar, this image is distorted by the object, and as the direction of the incoming light changes, it falls on a different part of the object and its shape changes. Therefore we have a highlight image whose overall shape depends on the curvature of the object surface over the area struck by the incident light and the viewing direction, which determines how much of the highlight is visible from the viewing direction. These are the geometric factors that determine the shape of the patches of bright light that we see on the surface of an object and are easily calculated by using the Phong model.

The physical factors which determine the highlight image are the dependence of its intensity and colour on the angle of incoming light with respect to a tangent plane at the point on the surface under consideration. This identifies the nature of the material to us and enables us, for example, to distinguish between metallic and non-metallic objects.

What is meant by a physical simulation in the context of light reflection is that we attempt to model the micro-geometry of the surface that causes the light to reflect, rather than simply imitating the behaviour, as we do in the Phong model, with an empirical term.

This early simulation of specular highlights has four interacting components, and is based on a physical microfacet model consisting of symmetric V-shaped grooves occurring around an average surface (Figure 4.6(a)). We now briefly describe each of these components in turn. (A more comprehensive description and rendered examples are to be found in [WATT00].)

(1) A statistical distribution is set up for the orientation of the microfacets and this gives a term D for the light emerging in a particular (viewing) direction. A simple Gaussian can be used:

$$D = k \exp[-(\delta/m)^2]$$

where δ is the angle of the microfacet with respect to the normal of the (mean) surface, that is the angle between $\mathbf{N}$ and $\mathbf{H}$, and m is the standard deviation of the distribution. Evaluating the distribution at this angle simply returns the number of microfacets with this orientation, that is, the number of microfacets that can contribute to light emerging in the viewing direction. Two reflection lobes for $m = 0.2$ and 0.6 are shown in Figure 4.6(b).

Using microfacets to simulate the dependence of light reflection on surface roughness makes two enabling assumptions:

(a) It is assumed that the microfacets, although physically small, are large with respect to the wavelength of light.

(b) The diameter of the incident beam is large enough to intersect a number of microfacets that is sufficient to result in representative behaviour of the reflected light.

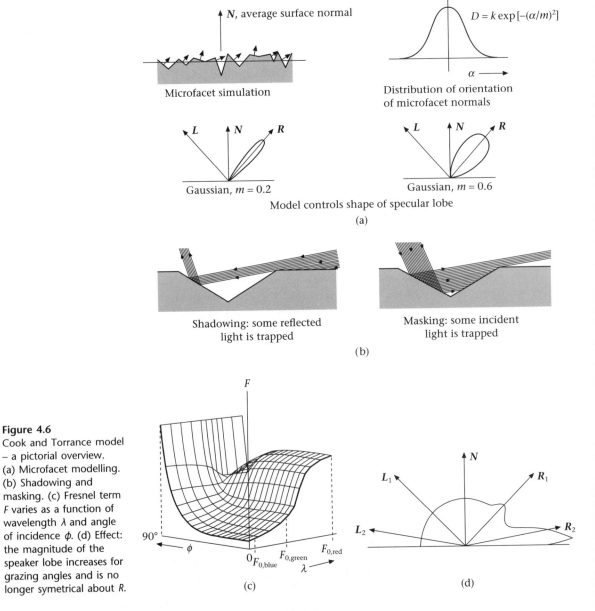

Figure 4.6
Cook and Torrance model – a pictorial overview. (a) Microfacet modelling. (b) Shadowing and masking. (c) Fresnel term F varies as a function of wavelength λ and angle of incidence ϕ. (d) Effect: the magnitude of the speaker lobe increases for grazing angles and is no longer symetrical about R.

N, average surface normal

Microfacet simulation

$D = k \exp[-(\alpha/m)^2]$

Distribution of orientation of microfacet normals

Gaussian, $m = 0.2$

Gaussian, $m = 0.6$

Model controls shape of specular lobe

(a)

Shadowing: some reflected light is trapped

Masking: some incident light is trapped

(b)

(c)

(d)

Thus this factor controls the extent to which the specular lobe bulges.

(2) Where the viewing vector or the light orientation vector begins to approach the mean surface, interference effects occur. These are called shadowing and masking. Masking occurs when some reflected light is trapped by the sides of the microfacets and shadowing when incident light is intercepted, as can be seen from Figure 4.6(b).

A detailed derivation of the dependence of this factor on **L**, **V** and **H** was given by Blinn in [BLIN77]. For masking:

$$G_m = 2(\mathbf{N.H})(\mathbf{N.V})/\mathbf{V.H}$$

For shadowing the situation is geometrically identical with the role of the vectors **L** and **V** interchanged. For shadowing we have:

$$G_s = 2(\mathbf{N.H})(\mathbf{N.L})/\mathbf{V.H}$$

The value of G that must be used is the minimum of G_s and G_m. Thus:

$$G = \text{min\_of} \{1, G_s, G_m\}$$

(3) Another pure geometric term is implemented to account for the glare at low angles of incidence. As the viewing angle and incidence angle approach grazing the specular reflection increases greatly. As the angle between the view vector and the mean surface normal is increased towards 90 degrees, an observer sees more and more microfacets and this is accounted for by a term:

$$1/\mathbf{N.V}$$

that is, the increase in area of the microfacets seen by a viewer is inversely proportional to the angle between the viewing direction and the surface normal. If there is incident light at a low angle then more of this light is reflected towards the viewer than if the viewer was intercepting light from an angle of incidence close to normal. This effect is countered by the shadowing effect which also comes into play as the viewing orientation approaches the mean surface orientation.

(4) The next term to consider is the Fresnel term F. This term concerns the amount of light that is reflected as opposed to being absorbed – a factor that depends on the material type considered as a perfect mirror surface, which our individual microfacets are. In other words, we now consider behaviour for a perfect planar surface, having previously modelled the entire surface as a set of such microfacets which individually behave as perfect mirrors. This factor determines the strength of the reflected lobe as a function of incidence angle and wavelength (Figure 4.6(c)). The wavelength dependence accounts for subtle colour effects in the specular highlight.

$$F = \frac{1}{2}\left\{\frac{\sin^2(\phi - \theta)}{\sin^2(\phi + \theta)} + \frac{\tan^2(\phi - \theta)}{\tan^2(\phi + \theta)}\right\}$$

where:

ϕ is the angle of incidence
θ is the angle of refraction
$\sin \theta = \sin \phi / \mu$
where μ is the refractive index of the material

These angles are shown in Figure 4.7. F is minimum, that is, most light is absorbed when $\phi = 0$ or normal incidence. No light is absorbed by the

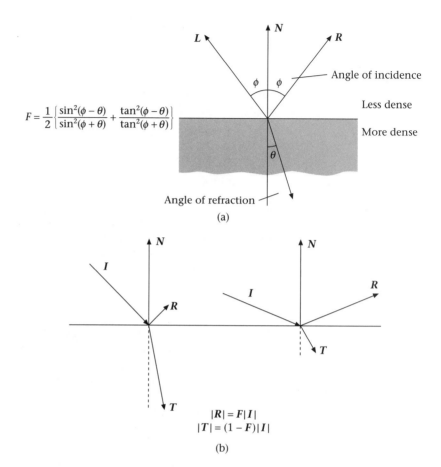

$$F = \frac{1}{2} \left\{ \frac{\sin^2(\phi - \theta)}{\sin^2(\phi + \theta)} + \frac{\tan^2(\phi - \theta)}{\tan^2(\phi + \theta)} \right\}$$

$$|R| = F|I|$$
$$|T| = (1 - F)|I|$$

Figure 4.7
The Fresnel equation.
(a) Angles in the Fresnel
equation. (b) Two
examples showing the
behaviours of the
equation.

surface and F is equal to unity for $\phi = \pi/2$. The wavelength dependent property of F comes from the fact that μ is a function of wavelength.

The practical effect of this term is to account for subtle changes in colour of the specular highlight as a function of angle of incidence. For any material, when the light is incident at an angle nearly parallel to the surface, the colour of the highlight approaches that of the light source. For other angles the colour depends on both the angle of incidence and the material.

The effect of this term is to cause the reflected intensity to increase as the angle of incidence increases (just as did the previous term $1/\mathbf{N}.\mathbf{V}$) – less light is absorbed by the material and more is reflected. (A more subtle effect is that the peak of the specular lobe shifts away from the perfect mirror direction as the angle of incidence increases.)

The overall effect of the model is shown in Figure 4.6(d), which shows two distinctly different shaped/sized specular lobes. In the Phong model the specular lobe always has the same magnitude and shape.

Thus putting the above four factors together the specular term now becomes:

specular component $= DGF/(\mathbf{N.V})$

where D is the micro-geometry term
  G is the shadowing/masking term
  F is the Fresnel term
  $(\mathbf{N.V})$ is the glare effect term

the direction of the incoming light and controls subtle second-order effects concerning the shape and the colour of the highlight. This effect is important when trying to simulate the difference between, say, shiny plastic and metals. Gold, for example, exhibits yellow highlights when illuminated with white light and the highlight only tends to white when the light grazes the surface.

The specular term is separately calculated and combined with a uniform diffuse term to provide a bi-directional reflectivity distribution function or BRDF:

$$\text{BRDF} = sR_s + dR_d \quad \text{where } s + d = 1$$

This term emphasises that the light reflected in any particular direction (in computer graphics we are mostly interested in light reflected along the viewing direction $\mathbf{V}$) is a function, not only of this direction, but also of the direction of the incoming light. A BRDF is can be written as:

$$\text{BRDF} = f(\theta_{in}, \phi_{in}, \theta_{ref}, \phi_{ref}) = f(\mathbf{L}, \mathbf{V})$$

(see Figure 4.11) and many models used in computer graphics differ amongst themselves according to which of these dependencies are simulated. A more comprehensive treatment is given in Section 4.3.2.

Metals are simulated, usually with $d = 0$ and $s = 1$, and shiny plastics with $d = 0.9$ and $s = 0.1$. Note that if d is set to zero for metals the specular term controls the colour of the object over its entire surface. Compare this with the Phong reflection model where the colour of the object is always controlled by the diffuse component. The Phong model, because of this, is incapable of producing metallic-looking surfaces and all surface objects rendered using Phong have a distinct plastic look. A selection of different materials using this model with the same lighting conditions is shown in Figure 4.8 (also Colour Plate). From this can be seen the wide variation in the nature of the specular highlight.

Thus for a given $\mathbf{L}$ and $\mathbf{V}$, the reflectance is given by the Fresnel factor for that angle of incidence multiplied by the proportion of microfacets that have their normal vector oriented as $\mathbf{H} = \mathbf{L} + \mathbf{V}$. Each of these microfacets contributes to the reflected light if the outgoing light is not shadowed and the incoming light is not masked. Thus this product is scaled by the shadowing and masking term and inversely by $\mathbf{N.V}$. (Ashikhmin et al. [ASHI00] point out that the shadowing and masking term is problematic with microfacet-based models. This is because many possible surface geometries – causing different shadowing and masking behaviour – will be consistent with $D(\alpha)$.)

Cast and machined aluminium

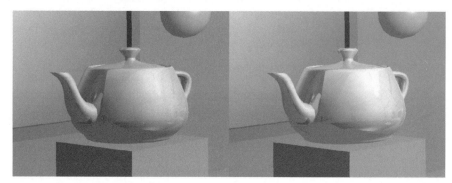

Burnished gold and polished gold

Copper and bronze

Figure 4.8
Different materials rendered with the same lighting conditions. In the case of the polished materials the model was used as a local component in a ray tracer.

To implement the Cook and Torrance model using texture hardware we first look at the dependencies of the contributing terms. F, the Fresnel term, for fixed n, depends only on the angle of incidence $\mathbf{L}.\mathbf{H} = \mathbf{H}.\mathbf{V}$. D depends on the angle δ, or equivalently $\cos \delta$. The shadowing and masking term is a function of four dot products, but simpler functions can reduce this to two – $\mathbf{L}.\mathbf{N}$ and $\mathbf{N}.\mathbf{V}$ [HEID99], giving for a point or directional light source:

$$R_s = \frac{F(\cos\phi)D(\cos\delta)G(\cos\alpha,\cos\beta)}{\pi\cos\beta}$$

where

$$\cos\varphi = \mathbf{L.H} = \mathbf{H.V}$$
$$\cos\delta = \mathbf{N.H}$$
$$\cos\alpha = \mathbf{L.N}$$
$$\cos\beta = \mathbf{N.V}$$

This is then factored into two expressions each stored in a 2D texture:

$$F(\cos\phi)D(\cos\delta) \text{ and } \frac{G(\cos\alpha,\cos\beta)}{\pi\cos\beta}$$

where for constant **L** and **V** this operation can be set up as a single rendering pass with multi-texture or two passes, as we discuss in Chapter 5. The texture matrices[4] are set as:

$$\begin{bmatrix} 0 & 0 & 0 & \cos\theta \\ H_x & H_y & H_z & 0 \\ 0 & 0 & 0 & 0 \\ 0 & 0 & 0 & 1 \end{bmatrix} \begin{bmatrix} N_X \\ N_Y \\ N_Z \\ 1 \end{bmatrix} = \begin{bmatrix} \cos\theta \\ \cos\delta \\ 0 \\ 1 \end{bmatrix}$$

and

$$\begin{bmatrix} L_x & L_y & L_z & 0 \\ H_x & H_y & H_z & 0 \\ 0 & 0 & 0 & 0 \\ 0 & 0 & 0 & 1 \end{bmatrix} \begin{bmatrix} N_X \\ N_Y \\ N_Z \\ 1 \end{bmatrix} = \begin{bmatrix} \cos\alpha \\ \cos\beta \\ 0 \\ 1 \end{bmatrix} \tag{4.1}$$

4.3.2 Per-pixel shading using factorised shading models – anisotropic models

The previous section described an isotropic shading model where we considered a single angle describing the angle of incidence. This is the elevation angle that the incoming light makes with the surface normal. Anisotropic behaviour occurs when the reflected light depends on this angle and also the azimuth angle of the incoming light. Anisotropic BRDFs abound; hair and brushed metal are two materials with anisotropic BRDFs that have received much attention in computer graphics. Thus an anisotropic BRDF is one that varies as we rotate about

---

4. Texture matrices in OpenGL can be used to operate on texture coordinates (scale translate etc.) before they are applied.

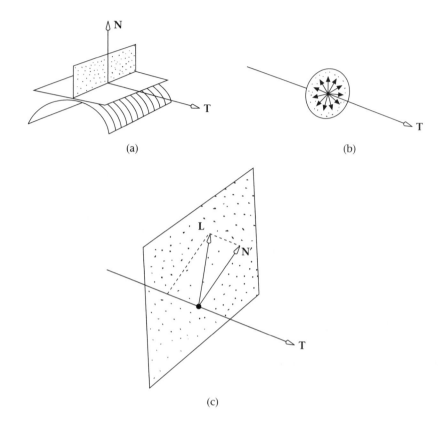

Figure 4.9
Anisotropic reflection.
(a) Surface 'grain' defines
T and a normal plane
at each vertex. (b) An
isolated fibre can have
any surface normal **N**.
(c) Diffuse component:
choose **N'** that makes
maximum dot product
with **L**.

the normal. When **L** and **V** align with the 'grain' of the material the reflection maximises and a highlight characteristic of the material is perceived.

A remarkably simple but effective anisotropic shading model was introduced by Banks in 1994 [BANK94]. Essentially this uses the Phong model but substitutes vectors particular to the anisotropic geometric model. The easiest way to consider the model is that the surface is made up of fibres – like the coloured satin covering a Christmas ball. This gives the concept of a fibre as a very thin, long cylinder. The model is defined per vertex (Figure 4.9) with a tangent vector which aligns with the grain of the material; the entire model being defined by a vector field. This defines a normal plane or space allowing for a choice of normal vectors **N**. The assumption is that the most significant light reflection is from the normal **N'**, the one which makes the maximum dot product with the light vector **L**. We can then use this normal in the Phong reflection model to obtain:

$$I = I_a + I_l(\mathbf{N.L})(k_d(\mathbf{N'.L} + k_s(\mathbf{N'.H})^n)$$

Thus the reflected intensity is a function of the two angles that **L** and **V** make with the tangent plane. This means that it can be implemented using a pre-calculated two-dimensional texture indexed by the tangent **T** and using the same texture matrix as in Equation 4.1.

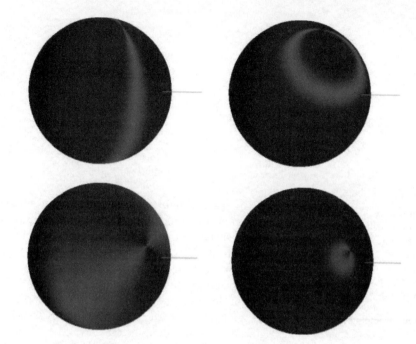

Figure 4.10
The Banks anisotropic shading model for a sphere. The green line shows the direction of the light. The grain changes from longitude alignment to latitude alignment horizontally (view remains the same) and vertically the view changes (images generated using a program written by Heidrich at http://www9.informatik.uni-erlangen.de/eng/research/rendering/anisotropic/).

Figure 4.10 (also Colour Plate) shows a sphere rendered using this model. The grain of the material is alternatively aligned with lines of longitude and latitude.

4.4 BRDFs and real materials

This section is effectively a generalisation of the previous two sections which developed particular models that dealt with certain aspects of light–object interaction. Light–object interaction for a particular surface and material is characterised completely by its BRDF. We will begin by explaining exactly what a BRDF is, then look at ways in which it can be simulated in real time.

A BRDF (bi-directional reflectance distribution function) quantifies the behaviour of light at a point of interest $\mathbf{x}$ on the surface of an object. This term emphasises that the light reflected in any particular direction (in computer graphics we are mostly interested in light reflected along the viewing direction $\mathbf{V}$) is a function, not only of this direction, but also of the direction of the incoming light. A BRDF can be written as:

$$\text{BRDF} = f(\theta_{in}, \phi_{in}, \theta_{ref}, \phi_{ref})$$

and many reflection models in computer graphics differ amongst themselves according to which of these dependencies are simulated. Figure 4.11 shows these angles together with a BRDF computed for a particular set of angles. The rendered BRDF function shows the magnitude of the reflected light (in any outgoing direction) for an infinitely thin beam of light incident in the direction

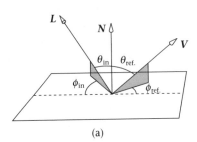

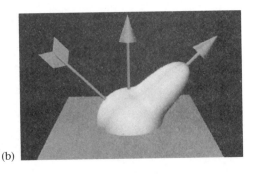

(a)   (b)

Figure 4.11
Bi-directional reflectivity function. (a) A BRDF relates light incident in direction *L* to light reflected along direction *V* as a function of the angles θ_{in}, ϕ_{in}, θ_{ref}, ϕ_{ref}. (b) An example of a BRDF.

shown. In practice light may be incident on a surface point from more than one direction and the total reflected light would be obtained by summing a separate BRDF for each incoming light beam. This particular simulated, as opposed to measured, BRDF was constructed using a standard Phong model.

In real surfaces the BRDF would be a function of six variables, the other two being the position of the point of interest, x, on the surface and the wavelength of the light. In computer graphics we normally consider homogeneous materials – no dependency on x, and we tend to ignore wavelength dependency (although as Figure 4.12 clearly demonstrates, wavelength dependency is important).

A precise definition of the BRDF now follows. It is the ratio of differential reflected radiance in direction ω_{ref} to the differential irradiance from the incident direction:

$$f_r(\omega_{in} \rightarrow \omega_{ref}) = \frac{L_{ref}(\omega_{ref})}{L_{in}(\omega)\cos\theta_{in}\,d\omega_{in}}$$

where

ω_{in} is a differential angle around the incoming direction
ω_{ref} is a differential angle around the outgoing direction
θ_{in} the angle between the incoming direction and the surface normal

This definition is then used in the reflectance equation:

$$L_{ref}(\omega_{ref}) = \int_\Omega f_r(\omega_{in} \rightarrow \omega_{ref})L_{in}(\omega_{in})\cos\theta_{in}d\omega_{in}$$

where $f_r(\omega_{in} \rightarrow \omega_{ref})$ is the BRDF

which integrates the product of the BRDF with the incoming light in all directions over the hemisphere centred at the point of interest to give the reflected radiance at that point.

Note that the angles ω_{in} and ω_{out} are with respect to the local TBN frame (Section 4.2.2) and for BRDF rendering we need to define a local frame for each vertex. This contrasts with rendering using simple models such as Phong where vectors **L**, **V** and **N** are used, and this is because in BRDF terms the Phong model only depends on the θ component of ω.

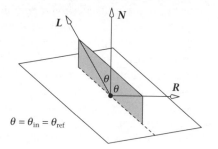

Plane containing *L* and *R* the mirror direction

(a)

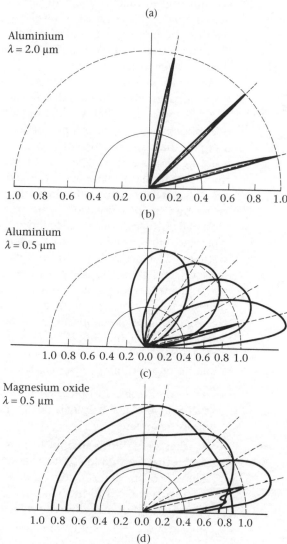

(b)

(c)

(d)

Figure 4.12
BRDF cross-section for different materials and wavelengths (after an illustration by He *et al.* (1991)).

For many years computer graphics has worked with simple, highly constrained BRDFs such as that shown in Figure 4.11 – the Phong model. Figure 4.12 gives an idea of the difference between such computer graphics models and what actually happens in practice. The illustrations are cross-sections of the BRDF in the plane containing $\mathbf{L}$ and $\mathbf{R}$, the mirror direction for different angles of θ, the angle of incidence (and reflection). In particular, note the great variation in the shape of the reflection lobes as a function of the wavelength of the incident light, the angle of incidence and the material. In the case of aluminium we see that it can behave like either a mirror surface or a directional diffuse surface depending on the wavelength of the incident light. When we also take into account that in practice incident light is never monochromatic (and we thus need a separate BRDF for each wavelength of light that we are considering), we see that the behaviour of reflected light is a far more complex phenomenon than we can model by using simple approximations like the Phong model at three wavelengths.

An important distinction that has to be made is between isotropic and anisotropic surfaces. An isotropic surface exhibits a BRDF whose shape depends only on $(\theta_{in}, \theta_{ref}, \phi_{ref} - \phi_{in})$. That is, if the surface is rotated about the normal the BRDF does not change. An anisotropic surface is, for example, brushed aluminium or a surface that retains coherent patterns from a milling machine. In the case of a brushed surface the magnitude of the specular lobe depends on the angle the incoming light makes with the grain of the surface. This is precisely the behaviour we simulated with the Banks anisotropic model in Section 4.3.2.

Another complication that occurs in reality is the nature of the atmosphere. Most BRDFs used in local reflection models are constrained to apply to light reflected from opaque materials in a vacuum. We mostly do not consider any scattering of reflected light in an atmosphere (in the same way that we do not consider light scattered by an atmosphere before it reaches the object). The reason for this is, of course, simplicity and the subsequent reduction of light-intensity calculations to simple comparisons between vectors categorising surface shapes, light directions and viewing direction.

We might imagine that if we have a BRDF for a material, the light–object interaction is solved. However, a number of problems remain to this day, despite a quarter of a century of research. Some of these are:

- If we want to use real BRDFs, where do we get the data from? Some data is available for some materials in the metallurgical literature but this is by no means complete.

- At what scale do we attempt to represent a BRDF? What is the area of the region that we should consider receives incident light? Should this be large enough so that the statistical model is consistent over the surface? Should it be large enough to include surface imperfections such as scratches? This is very much an unaddressed problem.

- How do we simulate BRDFs in computer graphics? This final point accounts for most variation amongst models. In particular, the distinction between empirical and physically based models is often made. An empirical model is one that imitates light–object interaction. For example, in the Phong model a simple mathematical function is used to represent the specular lobe. In the Cook and Torrance model a statistical distribution represents the surface geometry and this is termed a physically based model. It is interesting to note that there is no general agreement on the visual efficacy of empirical vs physically based models. Often a better result can be obtained by carefully tuning the parameters of an empirical model than by using a physically based model.

4.5 Per-pixel shading using BRDFs

The approach we describe in the following sections decomposes the BRDF so that the information in the function can be represented in 2D texture maps and a multi-pass/multi-texture algorithm employed to render the surface.

We first look at the special case of 'Phong-like' BRDFs and see how they can be implemented using conventional environment maps. Then we take a more general look at BRDFs and how any arbitrary function can be decomposed or compressed in such a way that it can be mapped to 2D textures.

4.5.1 Implementing BRDFs: pre-filtering environment maps

In this section we will look at environment map methods which enable us to simulate materials, other than perfect mirrors,[5] by using the convenient, hardware-supported method of environment maps. This then enables us, for example, to perform diffuse and Phong shading by indexing into a map. We also remind ourselves that as well as being an empirical model, Phong shading is unrealistic because it is a local model and only reflects images of light sources. We can remove this restriction by calculating an environment map for specular reflection that includes reflections of other objects as well as light sources. We do this by pre-filtering[6] the 'perfect' environment map. Effectively the environment surrounding a point becomes an infinity of light sources, and for that point we pre-calculate and cache the interaction of all these light sources with the point. Before we begin we should remind ourselves that all environment map technology suffers from two limitations as far as realism is concerned. First,

---

5. Traditionally, environment maps have been used to render perfect reflections of environment detail on the surface of a shiny object.

6. The term pre-filtering in this context is somewhat confusing. It is used both to describe the process of transforming a perfect environment map into one that simulates a practical surface, and to produce mip maps for anti-aliasing. This is because both of these operations are produced by a filtering or convolution operation.

the reflections are only geometrically correct as a function of the size of the object. The environment map caches incoming light from the environment at a single point and only if the object is infinitely small – it is reduced to a point – is the reflection image correct. Second, although it can implement light reflected from the environment – other objects, self-reflection cannot appear and if the object is not convex this is clearly wrong.

We begin by revisiting the general idea of environment maps and developing a model that includes the BRDF of a material. We remind ourselves that an environment map is a capture, for a point $\mathbf{x}$ in 3 space, of all the light rays incident on that point. For an object positioned at a reference point, which is small with respect to its environment, we can write:

light reflected in the viewing direction $\mathbf{V}$ = incoming light in direction $\mathbf{R}_v$

where $\mathbf{R}_v$ is the reflected view vector with respect to a point $\mathbf{p}$ on the surface of the object

$$\mathbf{R}_v = 2(\mathbf{N}.\mathbf{V})\mathbf{N} - \mathbf{V}$$

where $\mathbf{N}$ is the normal to the surface at $\mathbf{p}$.

This is the model used in conventional environment mapping and simulates a perfect mirror surface. To simulate the effect of a practical surface that is homogeneous in terms of its BRDF, we can use the reflectance equation:

$$L_{\mathrm{ref}}(\omega_{\mathrm{ref}}) = \int_{\Omega} f_r(\omega_{\mathrm{in}} \to \omega_{\mathrm{ref}}) L_{\mathrm{in}}(\omega_{\mathrm{in}}) \cos \theta_{\mathrm{in}} \, d\omega_{\mathrm{in}}$$

where $f_r(\omega_{\mathrm{in}} \to \omega_{\mathrm{ref}})$ is the bi-directional reflectivity function or BRDF.

The domain of integration of the integral is the hemisphere centred on the point of interest and we can see that the integral is effectively weighting the light from all incoming directions with the BRDF – a filtering operation. This equation suggests that a brute force pre-filtering method consists of: for each pixel in a target environment map we perform an integration involving all the source map pixels – an N^2 operation, where N is the number of pixels in the map.

We can consider the $L_{\mathrm{in}}(\omega_{\mathrm{in}})$ term to be the unfiltered environment map and the LHS of the equation, $L_{\mathrm{ref}}(\omega_{\mathrm{ref}})$, the filtered or target environment map. Thus instead of an environment map storing, for a point on the surface of the object, the incoming radiance, it stores the outgoing radiance. It is in effect the environment convolved with the BRDF.

A useful way to perform this pre-filtering was first suggested by Miller and Hoffman in 1984 [MILL84] and this is to compute separately a diffuse and a Phong specular map. This splits the BRDF into a hemisphere (the BRDF of a perfect diffuser) and a single specular lobe. Having two such maps enables a series of effects by using a blending or mixing factor. The Phong model is suitable for simple pre-filtering because its specular lobe is constant for all $\mathbf{R}_v$ and it is radially symmetric about $\mathbf{R}_v$. A simple visualisation of the pre-filtering process is shown in Figure 4.13. Here we consider a source environment map

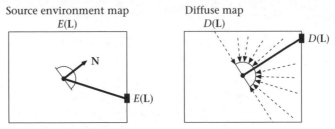

Diffuse map – for each **N** calculate and sum all
the contributions in the direction **N**

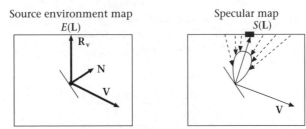

Figure 4.13
Pre-filtering an
environment map.

Specular map – for each (**R**$_v$,**N**) calculate and sum all
the contributions within the specular lobe

$E(\mathbf{L})$ and two target maps $D(\mathbf{L})$ and $S(\mathbf{L})$. The diffuse map $D(\mathbf{L})$ caches the summation of all incoming light rays that contribute to the hemisphere given by **N**. The specular map $S(\mathbf{L})$ caches the contribution of all incoming light rays around direction $\mathbf{R}_v$ which contribute to the specular refection along the view direction **V**.

For a perfectly diffuse surface the BRDF reduces to k_d – the diffuse reflection coefficient in the Phong reflection model and the reflectance equation can be written using the 'standard' computer graphics vectors as:

$$L_{\text{diffuse}}(\mathbf{N}) = k_d \int_{\Omega} L_{\text{in}}(\mathbf{L})(\mathbf{N}.\mathbf{L})\,d\omega(\mathbf{L})$$

the only remaining dependency being the surface normal.

The Phong model expresses the specular term as:

$k_s(\mathbf{R}.\mathbf{V})^n$ or equivalently $k_s(\mathbf{R}_v.\mathbf{L})^n$

where

R is the reflected light vector
V is the view vector
$\mathbf{R}_v$ is the reflected view vector
L is the light direction vector
k_s is the specular reflection coefficient
n is the shininess exponent

and the reflectance equation for the specular map then becomes:

$$L_{\text{specular}}(\mathbf{R}_v) = k_s \int_\Omega (\mathbf{R}_v.\mathbf{L})^n L_{\text{in}}(\mathbf{L})(\mathbf{N}.\mathbf{L})\,d\omega(\mathbf{L})$$

For the diffuse map, for each value of $\mathbf{N}$ we sum over all values of $\mathbf{L}$ the area-weighted dot product or Lambertian term. This results in a very blurred version of the original map which simulates diffuse–diffuse interaction between an object and the scene. In the case of the specular map the operation again produces a blurred version of the original map where the extent of the blurriness is determined by the index n. It is of course important to realise that this is not a general approach to implementing BRDFs. It only applies to Phong-like BRDFs with specular lobes that are rotationally symmetric about $\mathbf{R}_v$ and whose shape is not a function of the angle $(\mathbf{R}_v.\mathbf{N})$.

The reflected intensity at a surface point is thus:

$$k_d D(\mathbf{N}) + k_s S(\mathbf{R}_v)$$

The specular contribution can be further weighted with an approximate Fresnel term giving:

$$(1 - F)k_d D(\mathbf{N}) + F k_s S(\mathbf{R}_v)$$

Using this expression means, for example, that for a high refractive index (glass) the specular term dominates for grazing angles whereas for metal the specular term is high for all angles.

In a game application involving a dynamic object, we need to re-calculate the environment map and pre-filter it as the object moves through a scene. We now consider the implications of this.

First, note that because the diffuse map is such low resolution it would not be necessary to create a new diffuse map every frame. Second, we note that the pre-filtering operation, if carried out as suggested by the simple interpretation in the previous section, is extremely expensive and unsuitable for real-time application.

For fast real-time pre-filtering Heidrich [HEID00] suggests a solution that uses texture hardware. A pre-condition of the method is an environment map representation that maps a shift-invariant filter kernel on the hemisphere to a shift-invariant circular kernel in texture space. (The Phong model has a shift-invariant filter kernel – a constant radially symmetric specular lobe. However, if a cube map is used the mapping of this kernel into texture space is not invariant.) If such a mapping is available then the OpenGL imaging subset – which supports shift-invariant two-dimensional filters – can be used.

Heidrich points out that parabolic maps (Section 4.6.3) exhibit this property approximately and demonstrates that the distortion depends on the radius of the kernel and its distance from the sphere centre. However, the size of the kernel varies also with distance to the centre of the map – the mapping is not shift invariant and the suggested solution is to generate two pre-filtered environment maps and blend between them during rendering as a function of the distance from the centre of the map.

4.6

Environment map parameterisations

To use environment maps we need a parameterisation. The common approaches are cubic and spherical, both supported by hardware. The disadvantage of the cubic approach is that six maps are required and seams can be visible if mip-mapping is applied individually to each map. Spherical maps suffer from highly non-uniform sampling of the environment and are only suitable for viewing directions equal to the direction from which the map was created. In other words, a new map has to be created as the viewing direction changes. A recent innovation, the dual paraboloid map, appears to overcome the disadvantages of both these 'traditional' parameterisations.

4.6.1

Environment map parameterisations: cubic map

Cubic mapping is popular because the maps can easily be constructed using a conventional rendering system. The environment map is in practice six maps that form the surfaces of a cube (Figure 4.14). To generate a cubic map a viewpoint

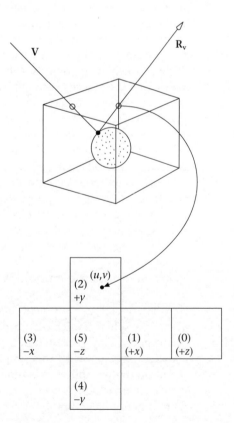

Figure 4.14
Cubic environment mapping or cube mapping.

is fixed at the centre of the object to receive the environment map, and six perspective views of the scene are rendered from that point.

With environment maps we need to determine the mapping from the three-dimensional view vector into one of the two-dimensional maps. If we consider that the reflected view vector is in the same coordinate frame as the environment map cube, for a normalised reflection vector $\mathbf{R}_v$:

(1) Find the face it intersects – the map number. This involves considering the components of $\mathbf{R}_v$ with the largest magnitude and its sign.

(2) Map the components into (u,v) coordinates. For example, if z is the largest component and negative then face 5 (Figure 4.15 (also Colour Plate)) is intersected. The texture coordinates are then given by

$$u = x/z$$
$$v = y/z$$

Figure 4.15 shows an example of cube mapping in a game environment. The teapot is cube-mapped both with a simple six-colour map and the level environment itself. Note that the individual maps do not 'fold up' into a cube as you might expect. That is, if the component images are folded into a cube interior as suggested by their layout they will not join correctly. This is a consequence of the simple formula used above which requires relative orientations of the component images as shown in the figure.

Currently it is still too expensive and slow to use a cube map in a game environment for dynamic objects – the six views would have to be rendered every frame from the object's current position. However, we could economise by constructing a new cube map, say, five times a second or only after the object has moved a certain distance. Also, dynamic texture technology (pbuffer) could be used, as we describe in the next chapter.

One of the applications of cubic environment maps (or indeed any environment map method) that became popular in the 1980s is to 'matte' an animated computer graphics object into a real environment. In that case the environment map is constructed from photographs of a real environment and the (specular) computer graphics object can be matted into the scene, and appears to be part of it as it moves and reflects its surroundings.

4.6.2 Environment map parameterisations: spherical map

The first use of environment mapping was by Blinn and Newell [BLIN76] wherein a sphere rather than a cube was the basis of the method used. The environment map consisted of a latitude–longitude projection (Section 4.2.4). The main problem with this simple technique is the singularities at the poles.

An alternative sphere mapping form (supported in OpenGL) consists of a circular map which is the orthographic projection of the reflection of the environment as seen in the surface of a perfect mirror, vanishingly small sphere.

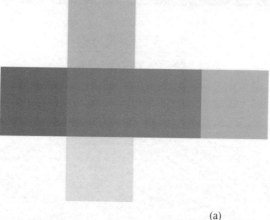

Figure 4.15
(a) Showing a cube-mapped object where the map is made up of six constant colours.

(a)

Such a map is shown from the point of view of its construction in Figure 4.16(a). Although the map caches the incident illumination at the reference point by using an orthographic projection, it can be used to generate, to within the accuracy of the process, a normal perspective projection.

To index into the map we reflect the view vector R_v as before. We then calculate H, the halfway vector between the reference view direction V_0 and R_v (Figure 4.16(b)). H defines a normal and thus a point on the virtual sphere – corresponding to a point on the map – which stores the radiance information

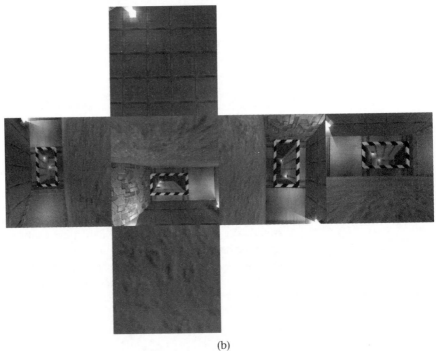

Figure 4.15 *continued*
(b) The same cube-mapped object which is now reflecting the environment in which it is placed.

(b)

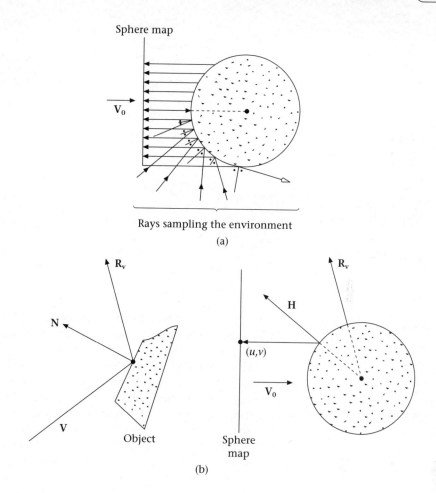

Figure 4.16
Spherical environment
map. (a) Constructing a
sphere map by reflecting
a parallel bundle of rays
into the environment.
(b) Accessing the map:
calculate $\mathbf{R_v}$, calculate $\mathbf{H}$
and u,v.

for the direction $\mathbf{V}$. Assuming the reference view direction $\mathbf{V_0}$ corresponds to the negative z axis in eye or view space, the texture coordinates are simply the x and y components of the normalised $\mathbf{H}$ vector, and these are computed in hardware.

The map could be generated by ray casting a parallel bundle or rays from the map texels, reflecting these from the virtual sphere and assigning the point in the environment hit by the reflected ray to the texel. A more practical generation method is given below.

The details are as follows:

$$\mathbf{H} = \frac{-\mathbf{V_0} + \mathbf{R_v}}{\|-\mathbf{V_0} + \mathbf{R_v}\|} = \frac{(0,0,1) + \mathbf{R_v}}{\|(0,0,1) + \mathbf{R_v}\|}$$

The required (u,v) coordinates for the sphere map are then given by the x and y components of the normalised $\mathbf{H}$ vector scaled and biased by $^1/_2$ to convert the range from $[-1,1]$ to $[0,1]$. Thus:

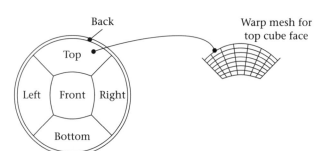

Figure 4.17
Warping a cube map to a sphere map.

$$u = \frac{R_x}{2p} + \frac{1}{2}$$

$$u = \frac{R_y}{2p} + \frac{1}{2}$$

where

$$p = (R_x^2 + R_y^2 + (R_z + 1)^2)^{\frac{1}{2}}$$

There are two connected problems associated with this parameterisation. As Figure 4.16(a) demonstrates, the rate at which the method samples the environment varies extensively. As we move out from the centre of the map – which is a circle – the sampling rate increases substantially and those parts of the environment in front of the viewer are concentrated into a small annulus corresponding to the tangential areas of the virtual sphere. The borders of the map, corresponding in our ray tracing model to rays tangential to the sphere, all terminate on the same point in front of the viewer and the border consists of identical pixels. Thus the method is only suitable for viewing direction equal to or close to the reference direction from which the map was constructed.

A practical method for generating a spherical map is to warp the contents of a cubic map [BLYT00]. The relationship between the cubic map faces and a sphere map is shown in Figure 4.17. This can use texture mapping for hardware acceleration. We can consider the process as the reverse of generation by ray tracing. Each texel (s,t) on the cubic map is considered as the destination of a reflection vector originated by a (reference) view vector reflecting from the virtual sphere and corresponding to a sphere map texel (u,v). Blythe suggests a technique in which a warp mesh is pre-calculated. Full details are given in [BLYT00].

Environment map parameterisations: dual paraboloid map

Dual paraboloid maps were first proposed by Heidrich and Siedel [HEID98] and they appear to overcome the two significant problems with the sphere map – view dependence and artefacts (see next section). The dual paraboloid map has better sampling characteristics than the sphere map and does not suffer from the

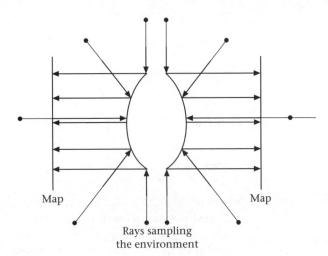

Map   Map

Rays sampling
the environment

Figure 4.18
Dual paraboloid mapping.

tangential singularity. Its disadvantage is that two maps are required instead of one, implying that four maps would be required to support combinations of diffuse and specular shading.

The principle behind the parabolic map is familiar nowadays in its manifestation as a satellite dish. Parallel incoming rays are focused into a single point. In dual paraboloid mapping we use the convex side of the parabola (Figure 4.18). Parallel rays from the texture map are spread outwards from the focal point to sample the environment far more evenly than the sphere map. An image seen by an orthographic camera along the negative z axis is given by:

$$I(x,y) = \frac{1}{2} - \frac{1}{2}(x^2 + y^2), \quad x^2 + y^2 \le 1 \qquad (4.2)$$

The key to its advantage is that fact that the sampling rays all emerge from a single point compared to the assumption in the case of the sphere map that the sphere has to be vanishingly small. Since the map is view independent we consider the origin of the object and the map to be the world coordinate origin and the viewing direction for the map generation to be the negative z axis.

Following the treatment in [BLYT00] we have the reflection vector in world space:

$$\mathbf{R}_{v0} = \mathbf{M}^{-1}\mathbf{R}_v$$

where:

$\mathbf{R}_v$ is, as usual, the reflected view vector
$\mathbf{M}$ is the model-view matrix

The map – front or back – which needs to be accessed is given by the z component of this vector; that is, whether it faces towards or away from the viewpoint. $\mathbf{R}_{v0}$ is the reflection vector of a vector $\mathbf{D}_0 = (0,0,1)$ at some point $\mathbf{x}$ on the paraboloid; that is:

$$\mathbf{R}_{v0} = 2(\mathbf{N}_0.\mathbf{D}_0)\mathbf{N}_0 - \mathbf{D}_0$$

where $\mathbf{N}_0$ is the paraboloid normal at point x given by:

$$\mathbf{N}_0 = \frac{1}{(x^2 + y^2 + 1)^{\frac{1}{2}}}\begin{bmatrix} x \\ y \\ 1 \end{bmatrix}$$

Combining these two equations yields:

$$\mathbf{D}_0 + \mathbf{R}_0 = \begin{bmatrix} k.x \\ k.y \\ k \end{bmatrix}$$

for some value k, so that finally a division of this vector by its z component will yield the desired texture coordinates.

Heidrich and Siedel point out that with the exception of the calculation of $\mathbf{R}_v$ and the final division, all operations are linear. If the final division is implemented as a perspective divide then the transformations can be concatenated into a single texture matrix:

$$\begin{bmatrix} u \\ v \\ 1 \\ 1 \end{bmatrix} = \mathbf{TPS(M_1)}^{-1}\begin{bmatrix} R_{Vx} \\ R_{Vy} \\ R_{Vz} \\ 1 \end{bmatrix}$$

where

$$\mathbf{T} = \begin{bmatrix} \frac{1}{2} & 0 & 0 & \frac{1}{2} \\ 0 & \frac{1}{2} & 0 & \frac{1}{2} \\ 0 & 0 & 1 & 0 \\ 0 & 0 & 0 & 1 \end{bmatrix}$$

is the matrix that scales and biases the 2D coordinate in the range $[-1,1]$ to $[0,1]$

$$\mathbf{P} = \begin{bmatrix} 1 & 0 & 0 & 0 \\ 0 & 1 & 0 & 0 \\ 0 & 0 & 1 & 0 \\ 0 & 0 & 1 & 0 \end{bmatrix}$$

is the projective transform effecting the divide by z

$$\mathbf{S} = \begin{bmatrix} -1 & 0 & 0 & D_{0x} \\ 0 & -1 & 0 & D_{0y} \\ 0 & 0 & 1 & D_{0z} \\ 0 & 0 & 0 & 1 \end{bmatrix}$$

subtracts $\mathbf{R}_0$ from $\mathbf{D}_0$. $\mathbf{M}_1^{-1}$ is the inverse of the linear part of the (affine) model-view matrix. Thus we plug $\mathbf{R}_v$ into the transformation and it outputs a

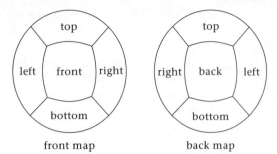

Figure 4.19
Cubic/dual paraboloid
map correspondence.

2D texture coordinate for the front or back map depending on the orientation of D_0.

A dual paraboloid map can be constructed similarly to a sphere map – by warping the contents of a cube map as shown in Figure 4.19. Full details on how to do this are given in [BLYT00].

Figure 4.19 emphasises that each map contains an incomplete copy of the environment and there is overlapping information. However, within the overlap, for the same environment information, one map will exhibit a better sampling rate than the other.

Since we have two basic environment maps we need a method for combining them. Each map mostly contains detail that does not appear in the other map but there is overlap and this occurs in the regions outside a central circle. Consider the circle

$$x^2 + y^2 \leq 1$$

where (x,y) are the coordinates in equation 4.2

Complete environmental information is contained within this circle in each map. This suggests the following combination procedure. The above transformations ensure that if a reflection vector maps within the circle of one map it will fall outside the circle in the other. We can therefore encode the alpha channel of texels inside the circle in each map with one and zero outside. For a two-pass approach we first bind to the front texture, enable alpha testing and construct a texture matrix with $D_0 = (0,0,-1)$. The second pass follows with D_0 set to $(0,0,1)$.

4.6.4   Environment maps – comparative points

As we have already discussed, geometric inaccuracies are associated with all environment map parameterisations due to the assumption that the object being mapped is vanishingly small. This is the least objectionable of environment map inaccuracies because as viewers we generally have no accurate notion of what exactly the shape of scene reflections in the mapped object should be. Another problem arises as a consequence of the uneven sampling by the different methods of the environment. The sphere map sampling approaches zero as the direction approaches the viewing direction but becomes very large as the direction becomes tangential.

More problematic are disturbances that arise from the nature of the parameterisation and/or the use of hardware for texture interpolation. Uneven sampling in all parameterisations causes the environment map to be in the form of a warped mesh rather than a regular mesh, as Figure 4.17 clearly shows. However, texture interpolation hardware assumes that linear interpolation of texture coordinates is appropriate. In the case of sphere mapping this can lead to another noticeable artefact – sparkling at the silhouette edge of the mapped object. This is because triangle coordinates may be interpolated within the circle of the sphere map instead of wrapping through the sphere boundary.

With the advent of cube map hardware the additional complexity of six maps becomes transparent to the user and a single texture application is all that is required. This results in an easy to construct and use facility which is view independent. Sphere maps are view dependent, as we have seen, and although dual paraboloid maps are view independent they are far more difficult to construct than cube maps and two texture applications are required.

Cube maps and vector normalisation

Cube maps can be used to implement vector normalisation calculations used in interpolatory shading where a normalisation operation is required per pixel. The concept is quite simple. In the conventional environment map application we index into the map using a reflected view vector. The result is a triple – an RGB colour. There is no reason why we cannot return a normalised version of the indexing vector. The environment map then becomes a lookup table indexed by a vector that returns its normalised value.

To construct the vector normalisation texture map values we use the same inverse mapping as described in Section 4.6.3. Each (u,v) texel position has the appropriate face index added to define the vector that would have indexed into this position on the cube map. This vector is then normalised and stored in the texture map. In the operation phase all vectors of the same orientation but different magnitude will index into this position. A detail is that normalised vectors lie in the range $[-1,1]$ but texture map values take values in the range $[0,1]$. Thus a range compression transformation has to be applied when the normalisation values are pre-calculated and the reverse transformation applied when the map is accessed.

This is useful, for example, in real-time shading where the halfway vector:

$$\mathbf{H} = \frac{\mathbf{L} + \mathbf{V}}{\|\mathbf{L} + \mathbf{V}\|}$$

can be normalised using the cube map and per-pixel specular shading applied as $\mathbf{L}$ and/or $\mathbf{V}$ changes.

Implementing BRDFs: separable approximations

In the previous section we looked at the simple case of implementing a Phong local reflection model by separating it into two component environment maps or cube maps. In this section we look at BRDFs in a more general light based on reports by Kautz and McCool [KAUT99] and Wynn [WYNN00].

Factorisation methods (Section 4.3) factorised parametric BRDFs or shading models analytically defined in terms of **L** and **V** so that they could be pre-calculated and stored in texture maps. In this section we look at how any arbitrary BRDF – data from physical measurements, for example, can be reduced from a four-dimensional function to 2 two-dimensional functions and thus are also implementable in texture hardware.

The first question we need to ask is: how is the BRDF to be modelled? There has been much research in this area and we will confine ourselves to answering the question by giving a few representative examples. The first obvious source is measured data and a public database.[7] Data is collected using a gonioreflectometer which mechanically varies the position of a small light source and a spectral sensor to sample over the hemisphere. Second, we can generate a BRDF by assuming a particular physical model for the surface and pre-calculating the value of the BRDF for all possible incoming and outgoing directions using a light–surface interaction algorithm like, for example, ray tracing. An early example of this approach is given by Cabral in [CABR87]. In this work a surface was represented by an array of triangular microfacets whose orientation was set by perturbing the vertices with a bump map. This approach is sometimes referred to as virtual gonioreflectometry.

Assuming therefore that we have a set of samples representing a BRDF, we proceed as follows. We consider a BRDF as a set of samples arranged in the form of a table or matrix, with each row representing a fixed outgoing direction ω_{ref} and each column representing a fixed incoming direction ω_{in}. Each element in

---

7. **Columbia-Utrecht Reflectance and Texture Database**
This is the same database as described in Section 4.2.3. In fact it contains both BRDFs and BTFs. See [DANA99] for a precise description of the difference between these two functions. The database contains:

(1) BRDF (bidirectional reflectance distribution function) database with reflectance measurements for over 60 different samples, each observed with over 200 different combinations of viewing and illumination directions.

(2) BRDF parameter database with fitting parameters from two recent BRDF models: the Oren-Nayar model and the Koenderink *et al.* representation. These BRDF parameters can be directly used for both image analysis and image synthesis.

(3) BTF (bidirectional texture function) database with image textures from over 60 different samples, each observed with over 200 different combinations of viewing and illumination directions.

the matrix is a single sample $\text{BRDF}(\theta_{in}, \phi_{in}, \theta_{ref}, \phi_{ref})$. For n^4 samples of a BRDF, the first row of n^2 elements of the matrix would contain:

$$\text{BRDF}((\theta_{in,0}, \phi_{in,0}, \theta_{ref,0}, \phi_{ref,0}) \quad \text{BRDF}((\theta_{in,0}, \phi_{in,1}, \theta_{ref,0}, \phi_{ref,0}) \quad \text{BRDF}((\theta_{in,1}, \phi_{in,0}, \theta_{ref,0}, \phi_{ref,0})$$
$$\ldots \text{BRDF}((\theta_{in,n}, \phi_{in,n}, \theta_{ref,0}, \phi_{ref,0})$$

Note that for any reasonable sampling resolution this is a hopelessly large number for current hardware. (For example, a relatively low resolution of 64^4 ($\times$ 3bytes) samples would result in a four-dimensional lookup table of 50 MB.)

The goal of the process is to represent the BRDF as a separable decomposition where it becomes the sum of products of lower-dimensional functions G_k and H_k:

$$\text{BRDF}(\theta_{in}, \phi_{in}, \theta_{ref}, \phi_{ref}) \approx \sum_{k=1}^{N} G_k(\theta_{in}, \phi_{in}) H_k(\theta_{ref}, \phi_{ref})$$

In particular, we are interested in decompositions where N has a low value and, if possible, we would like a representation where $N = 1$:

$$\text{BRDF}(\theta_{in}, \phi_{in}, \theta_{ref}, \phi_{ref}) \approx G_k(\theta_{in}, \phi_{in}) H_k(\theta_{ref}, \phi_{ref})$$

Although any BRDF can be represented faithfully, if enough terms are used, we are interested in single term decomposition. It turns out that providing a 'good' parameterisation is used this is indeed possible and we can thus use texture hardware for real-time rendering using arbitrary BRDFs.

The two main constraints of the method are:

(1) A parameterisation must be chosen that results in a good decomposition; so that the approximation:

$$\text{BRDF}(\theta_{in}, \phi_{in}, \theta_{ref}, \phi_{ref}) \approx G_k(\theta_{in}, \phi_{in}) H_k(\theta_{ref}, \phi_{ref})$$

is valid. Kautz *et al.* point out that the spherical parameterisation works well for many, but not all, BRDFs and a better one is the Gram-Schmidt Half-angle Difference vector parameterisation.

(2) The parameterisation must be consistent with hardware linear interpolation of 2D texture maps.

The overall approach is therefore a pre-processing phase where the BRDF is sampled or generated and then decomposed into 2×2D texture maps.

The conventional decomposition approach is singular value decomposition or SVD. Kautz *et al.* [KAUT99] point out that although this produces optimal approximations, it is very expensive in time and space, and they suggest a simpler technique called normalised decomposition or ND. They state that, for most cases, a single term ND is as good as using a single term SVD as far as the visual effect is concerned. We define the ND as:

For each row R of a BRDF matrix as described above, compute the p norm:

$$G_1(\omega_{in}) = \sum_{j=1}^{n^2} |\text{BRDF}|^p (\omega_{in,j}, \omega_{ref,R})^{\frac{1}{p}}$$

For each column C of the BRDF matrix compute the average of:

$$H_1(\omega_{ref}) = \frac{1}{n} \sum_{j=1}^{n^2} \frac{\text{BRDF}(\omega_{in,C}\omega_{ref,j})}{G_1(\omega_{in})}$$

that is, each column value is normalised by its corresponding row norm.

We now look at the parameterisation issue. Up to now we have used the standard parameterisation – spherical coordinates – where $(\theta_{in}, \phi_{in}) \times (\theta_{ref}, \phi_{ref})$ specifies an incident and reflected direction relative to the local surface frame. This is not compatible with normal hardware linear interpolation of 2D maps, but interpolation artefacts are reduced if cube maps are used. Since the BRDF is only defined over the hemisphere of incoming directions, only the upper half (+z) of the cube map needs to be used. To map the G and H functions into cube maps is straightforward (see Section 4.6.1), providing the spherical coordinates (θ_t, ϕ_t) corresponding to a texel has a BRDF sample. Otherwise some procedure, like bi-linear interpolation, has to be employed.

An important issue is that of dynamic range. BRDFs can take very high values and leaving these unmodified degrades the quality of the separation. Thus all values have to be clamped to a pre-determined maximum. We have:

$$\text{BRDF} = \delta \hat{G} \hat{H}$$

where δ is a floating point scaling value and $\hat{G}$ and $\hat{H}$ ($\in [0,1]$) are G_1 and H_1 divided by their maximum values

This raises another problem for real-time implementation, which is that we cannot scale by an arbitrary float during texture combining, and Wynn [WYNN00] suggests the following:

$$\text{BRDF} = D\frac{S}{D}\hat{G}\hat{H} = D\left(\sqrt{\frac{\delta}{D}}\hat{G}\right)\left(\sqrt{\frac{\delta}{D}}\hat{H}\right)$$
$$= D\hat{g}\hat{h}$$

where
$\quad D$ is the minimum of (1,2,4) such that $\delta < D$ or $D = 4$ if $\delta > D$

Assuming BRDF data and the pre-process that computes G and H, our reflectance equation becomes:

$$L_{ref}(\omega_{ref}) = \int_{\Omega} DG_1(\omega_{in})H_1(\omega_{ref})L_{in}(\omega_{in})\cos\theta_{in}\,d\omega_{in}$$

Examples are shown in Figure 4.20 (also Colour Plate).

Polished gold and anisotropic gold

Figure 4.20
Different materials
rendered with the same
lighting using separable
approximations
(illustration produced
using a program
downloadable from
www.nvidia.com).

Polished bronze

Figure 4.20 *continued*   Orange peel

Shading languages and shaders

Previous sections have looked at various rendering methods – different ways of shading a surface. The final topic in this chapter is shaders. This attends to providing the tools that enable different rendering components to be combined to achieve a desired effect. 'Shader' is a sloppily used jargon word that has many different manifestations and it is of recent interest to us in computer games because of new hardware developments. Currently it means possibly three different, but connected, aspects of rendering:

(1) It originally meant (and still does mean) a module (written in a C-type language) in the RenderMan API which enables high-level control over rendering components. Here the term refers to a specific code module – a surface or light shader. These specify how a surface is to be shaded in terms of its materials and reflection model parameters (surface shader) and how the intensity and colour of a light source is evaluated (light shader) for use by the surface shader. As with any specialised high-level language, the aim is to enable the programmer to write and experiment with direct rendering possibilities in an easier manner than implementing such effects in a general-purpose HLL. This aspect is described in the succeeding sections.

(2) Recently in games technology it has been used to refer to use of multi-pass/multi-texture facilities on fixed-function graphics hardware. The specification of render states and texture maps for a multi-pass or multi-texture render of an object is known as a shader. Here, instead of writing a code module we can experiment with effects using a shader editor, the final output of which becomes the shader for an object or object part. This usage is described in the first part of Chapter 5.

(3) More recently in games technology, hardware manufacturers have adopted the terms Vertex Shader and Pixel Shader to describe new hardware functionality for programmable GPUs. Here we write low-level code that utilises the graphics hardware. This aspect is described in Chapter 5.

Recent research [PROU01] concentrates on uniting aspects (1) and (3) where instead of controlling the functionality of programmable GPUs by writing in assembly code, high-level RenderMan-type languages and the associated compilers can be used. This addresses the current unfortunate situation where the availablity of programmable GPUs comes at the cost of programming in an assembly code particular to each manufacturer.

Although such a strategy is currently locked into research institutions, it is likely that a shading language for programmable graphics hardware will emerge in OpenGL 2.0 (and DirectX). After all, the goal of such standards is to provide hardware-independent access to graphics processors. However, with the advent of programmable GPUs, OpenGL is simply becoming more cumbersome, with sets of specialised (manufacturer) extensions.

4.8.1   Shading languages: a brief history

Using a renderer with very basic facilities is a simple matter involving no more than a selection of options – Gouraud or Phong shading, shadows or no shadows etc. For a renderer that offers a number of different reflection models, texture maps, texture map blending, transparency, etc. a 'shading language' is a better approach for controlling these options.

The idea was first floated by Cook in [COOK84] and was eventually developed into the design of RenderMan [PIXA88], [UPST89]. We can do no better here then reproduce a quote from [UPST89]. On the importance of a shading language, Upstill states:

There is an alternative, based on giving the user more access to the shading system itself, rather than its external interface. The critical thing is to give users access to the useful parts of the system without burdening then with irrelevant details. . . . By writing an appropriate shader in the shading language, a programmer can extend old shading models or implement entirely new ones, light sources can be defined with any radiant distribution, and new and novel surface properties can be introduced easily. Any parameter to these processes can be set up with a constant value, a value that varies smoothly over a surface, or one modulated arbitrarily by a surface map.

Cook's approach to a shading language involved eliminating 'fixed' reflection equations, such as the Phong model with its linear combination of terms involving dot products, and allowed a user to specify the components in a shading operation and the way in which these components combine. This approach allowed for both the specification of existing shading methodologies and an experimental testbed where new combinations could be experimented with. Cook

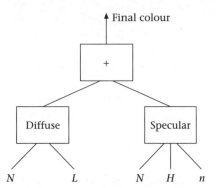

Figure 4.21
The Phong reflection model represented as a shade tree.

separated the shading process into the conceptually independent tasks of light source specification, surface reflectance, and atmospheric effects.

Specification of the surface reflectance proved to be the most flexible and powerful. This is done using a shade tree which organises the shading operations into a tree structure. The idea of using a tree is to facilitate the combination of several effects at a given surface point into the overall process. Let us assume that the root node of the tree is at the top and the leaves are at the bottom. Values pertinent to the shading process (Cook terms them 'appearance parameters') are generated at the leaves of the tree. These values are then passed upwards and and are manipulated at nodes. A node takes one or more of these values and combines them together to produce a single value which in turn is passed upwards. Finally, arriving at the top of the tree, the output is the value passed by the root node which is the final shaded colour value for that surface.

For example, breaking down the operation of Phong shading into a shade tree gives us a specular node and a diffuse node. The inputs to the diffuse node are the surface normal and a light vector producing an intensity value. A specular node takes three values, the surface normal, the eye position, and the surface roughness, and outputs a specular component. A standard Phong reflection model can then be represented as a tree (Figure 4.21).

Cook's idea was extended by Perlin in [PERL85] who constructed a shading language embedded in an environment called a Pixel Stream Editor or PSE. The PSE allows for more general flow of control structures than those provided by the original shade tree. The language supports conditional and looping control structures, function definitions and logical operators. One of the consequences of the use of such a system is that it enables the rendering process to be broken down into intermediate images or stages, where each stage is a single pass through the PSE.

(4.8.2) RenderMan shading language

The ideas discussed in the previous section were eventually generalised into a complete shading language in RenderMan [PIXA88],[UPST89],[HANR90]. As is well known, Pixar have successfully used RenderMan to make highly successful feature films such as *Toy Story* and *A Bug's Life*. The high quality of these productions attests to the success of this approach; and it is useful to bear in mind that RenderMan does not incorporate any global illumination models – the use of which is normally associated with high quality rendering.

Among the motivations for RenderMan, Hanrahan discusses the following points. The language should allow 'tricks' to be incorporated, providing a testbed for experimentation with different effects. For example, many effects in shading are acheived by various combinations of texture with local reflection models. This fact should be recognised and facilities for developing such tricks incorporated in the language. This supports the notion of shaders as procedures or modules.

The goals of the language are quoted in [HANR90] as:

(1) To develop an abstract shading model based on ray optics that is suitable for both global and local illumination models. It should also be abstract in the sense of being independent of a specific algorithm or implementation in either hardware or software.

(2) To define the interface between the rendering program and the shading modules. All the information that might logically be available to a built-in shading module should be made available to the user of the shading language.

(3) To provide a high-level language that is easy to use. It should have features – point and colour types and operators, integration statements, built-in functions – that allow shading calculations to be expressed naturally and succintly.

The language enables procedures called shaders to be written. These simulate local processes and can be used either singly or together – several types of shaders being used to contribute to the final image. Shader types are distinguished by the inputs they use and the kind of output they produce. The three major types of shaders are:

(1) Light source shaders: such a shader calculates the colour of light emitted from a light source. They take as input the position of a light source and the direction of a surface point from the light. They output the colour of the light striking that surface point. Typically, light sources may possess a frequency spectrum, an intensity, a directional dependency and a distance related fall-off.

(2) Surface reflectance shaders: these implement a local reflection model and compute the light reflected in a particular direction by summing over the incoming light and considering the reflective properties of the surface. They make no assumption about the source of the incoming light distribution, which can either come direct from a light source or be secondary reflected light from another object.

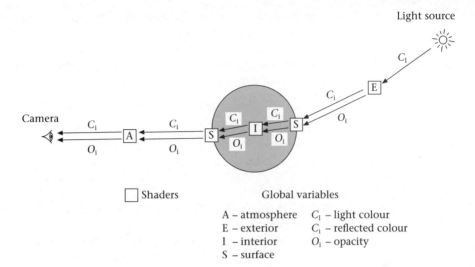

Light source

Camera

Figure 4.22
RenderMan dataflow
model of shaders.

☐ Shaders

Global variables

A – atmosphere C_l – light colour
E – exterior C_i – reflected colour
I – interior O_i – opacity
S – surface

(3) Volume shaders: these implement the effect of light passing through a volume of space. This can be a volume exterior to the object, in which case the shader is an atmospheric shader, or it may be a volume interior to the object.

A representation of the way in which these entities fit together is shown in Figure 4.22.

The following is an example of a (pre-defined) RenderMan surface shader taken from [UPST89]:

```
surface
plastic(
    float Ks          = .5,
          Kd          = .5,
          Ka          = 1,
          Roughness = .1,
    color specularcolor = 1)
{

point Nf = faceforward(N,l);

Oi = Os;
Ci = Os *(Cs * (Ka*ambient() +Kd*diffuse(Nf)
    + specularcolor*Ks*specular(Nf, -l, roughness)));
}
```

This is the code for one of RenderMan's standard or pre-defined shaders and it implements standard Phong shading. A familiarity with the Phong reflection model (Section 4.2.1) should illuminate most of the code. Pre-defined global variables are used to communicate information or results from one shader module to another. Ci represents the output from a shader and Cs its current surface colour, or reflectivity coefficients, that is bound to the object. The reflected light from a point is Ci and this will normally be an expression involving the incoming light and Cs. In its simplest form this will be:

$Ci = Os * Cs *$ (an implementation of a reflection model)

Os is the opacity of the surface where a completely opaque surface will have its opacity set to one. An opacity Oi is associated with the light ray and normal surface shaders will contain the assignment

$Oi = Os$

Associating an opacity with a light ray is a confusing concept but it generalises transparency.

Further examples of more elaborate shaders are given in [UPST89]. From this it can be seen that the language is superficially similar to C. A shader is defined by preceding its definition with one of the shading language keywords: light, displacement, surface or volume.

Shading languages for real-time rendering

As we shall see in the next chapter, complex effects are now implementable on programmable GPUs. At the same time, low-level programming of the GPU is less than straightforward. In addition, new hardware manufacturers are likely to develop new functionality and there is clearly a need for shading language that can be compiled to a number of GPUs.[8]

In recently reported work, Proudfoot *et al.* [PROU01] address exactly this problem. They enable shaders to be written in a high-level language that is somewhat similar to RenderMan. (Chapter 5 details one of the the programming models for the GPU for which this language was designed and it may need to be referred to when reading this section.)

Although the conventional *raison d'être* of high-level languages is to free users from low-level machine-dependent complexities, in the case of programmable GPUs there is an extra complication – the programmable hardware exists at different stages in the graphics pipeline. A feature of their system is the concept of different computation frequencies. This reflects the hardware architecture, where some computations are performed either in the CPU, vertex programming hardware or pixel programming hardware. Specifically, Proudfoot *et al.* support four computation frequencies:

---

8. Coping with different hardware platforms, be they consoles or PC GPUs, consumes massive manpower in the games industry.

- **constant** – expressions that are evaluated once at compile time and are not evaluated by the programmable pipeline;
- **per-primitive** – computations that occur once per group of primitives;
- **per-vertex** and **per fragment** – map onto the per-vertex and per-pixel part of the hardware.

It is the compiler's responsibility to infer the computation frequency from the user program. The language enables programmers to mix these computations within a single shader, thus freeing the user from having to write separate code for each of the hardware stages (or even having to know that the computations occur at different frequencies on different hardware components). This is done by having the compiler front-end separate the program into the three types of computation and invoke separate compiler back-ends for each computation group and for different architecture within each group.[9]

As in RenderMan, the system supports the two common shader types: surface shaders and light shaders. Surface shaders return an RGBA colour to be composited with the frame buffer. Light shaders calculate the intensity and colour of the light that is used by the surface shader. In this shading language a linear integrate operator evaluates a 'per light' expression for every light source and sums the results. For example:

```
surface float4
lightmodel_diffuse(float4 ka, float4 kd, )
{
   perlight float NdotL = max(0, dot(N.L);
   return ka * Ca + integrate(kd * NdotL *Cl);
}
```

performs diffuse shading due to all active light sources.

The following examples of surface shaders will give some insight into the philosophy and syntax of the language. These are intended merely to give a flavour of the approach; full details are given in [PROU01]. All the examples were generated by the excellent system available from the Stanford Real-Time Programmable Shading Project (www.grahics.stanford.edu).

Figure 4.23 (also Colour Plate) shows the simplest possible shader. It exposes the standard Phong shading parameters as constants and uses the lightmodel() method to evaluate the colour at each pixel, integrating all available or active lights.

---

9. Their current implementation consists of two different CPU back-ends, three vertex back-ends and two pixel or fragment back-ends.

Figure 4.23
The simplest surface
shader – Phong shading.
Created using software
from the Stanford Real-
Time Programmable
Shading Project (www.
graphics.stanford.edu).

```
surface float4
lightmodel (float4 a, float4 d, float4 s, float4 e, float sh)
{
   perlight float diffuse = dot(N,L);
   perlight float specular = pow(max(dot(N,H),0),sh);
   perlight float4 fr = d * max(diffuse, 0) +
                        s * select(diffuse > 0, specular, 0);
   return a * Ca + integrate(fr * Cl) + e;
}

constant float4 Ma = { 0.35, 0.35, 0.35, 1.00 };
constant float4 Md = { 0.50, 0.50, 0.50, 1.00 };
constant float4 Ms = { 1.00, 1.00, 1.00, 1.00 };
constant float4 Me = { 0.00, 0.00, 0.00, 0.00 };
constant float Msh = 300;

surface shader float4
default ()
{
   return lightmodel(Ma, Md, Ms, Me, Msh);
}
```

```
constant  float4  Ma  =  {  0.35,  0.25,  0.25,  1.00  };
constant  float4  Md  =  {  0.70,  0.70,  0.70,  1.00  };
constant  float4  Ms  =  {  0.00,  0.00,  1.00,  1.00  };
constant  float4  Me  =  {  0.00,  0.00,  0.00,  0.00  };
constant  float   Msh =  50;

surface  shader  float4
default  ()
{
    return  lightmodel(Ma,  Md,  Ms,  Me,  Msh);
}
```

Figure 4.24
Variations on Figure 4.23.
Created using software
from the Stanford Real-
Time Programmable
Shading Project (www.
graphics.stanford.edu).

The second example (Figure 4.24 (also Colour Plate)) shows a simple variation where the ambient and specular colours have been changed, together with
the specular factor.

Figure 4.25 (also Colour Plate) shows a mix of two different materials, one
glossy and one diffuse. The diffuse material is used as the base or background
material and the glossy material is added to the base material only where the
supplied texture map is white (the texture map acts as a black and white mask).
The final colour is a calculated using a compositing expression which adds the
base material (computed using a diffuse model) to the glossy material multiplied by the texture map colour. Thus black texture pixels will not be rendered glossy as they are multiplied by 0 (glossy only shows where the texture
is white).

```
surface shader float4
glossy_moons (texref gloss, float4 uv)
{
    float4 base_a = { 0.1, 0.1, 0.1, 1.00 };
    float4 base_d = { 0.70, 0.40, 0.10, 1.00 };
    float4 base_s = { 0.07, 0.04, 0.01, 1.00 };
    float4 base_e = { 0.00, 0.00, 0.00, 1.00 };
    float base_sh = 15;

    float4 gloss_a = { 0.07, 0.04, 0.01, 1.00 };
    float4 gloss_d = { 0.07, 0.04, 0.01, 1.00 };
    float4 gloss_s = { 1.00, 0.90, 0.60, 1.00 };
    float4 gloss_e = { 0.00, 0.00, 0.00, 1.00 };
    float gloss_sh = 25;

    float4 Cbase = lightmodel(base_a, base_d, base_s, base_e, base_sh);
    float4 Cgloss = lightmodel(gloss_a, gloss_d, gloss_s, gloss_e,
gloss_sh);

    float4 uv_gloss = invert(scale(.335,.335,1)) * uv;
    return Cbase + Cgloss * texture(gloss, uv_gloss);
}
```

Figure 4.25
Mixing glossy and matte materials. Created using software from the Stanford Real-Time Programmable Shading Project (www.graphics.stanford.edu).

In Figure 4.26 (also Colour Plate), the effect is inverted and the glossy effect is applied to the pixels where the texture map is black (0). The white (1) areas of the texture map are mapped with the simple diffuse. The result is that the crescent moons are rendered diffuse and the background glossy. This is achieved by inverting the texture colour and using it as the multiplying factor for the glossy material.

```
surface shader float4
glossy_moons (texref gloss, float4 uv)
{
   float4 base_a = { 0.1, 0.1, 0.1, 1.00 };
   float4 base_d = { 0.70, 0.40, 0.10, 1.00 };
   float4 base_s = { 0.07, 0.04, 0.01, 1.00 };
   float4 base_e = { 0.00, 0.00, 0.00, 1.00 };
   float base_sh = 15;

   float4 gloss_a = { 0.07, 0.04, 0.01, 1.00 };
   float4 gloss_d = { 0.07, 0.04, 0.01, 1.00 };
   float4 gloss_s = { 1.00, 0.90, 0.60, 1.00 };
   float4 gloss_e = { 0.00, 0.00, 0.00, 1.00 };
   float gloss_sh = 25;

   float4 Cbase = lightmodel(base_a, base_d, base_s, base_e, base_sh);
   float4 Cgloss = lightmodel(gloss_a, gloss_d, gloss_s, gloss_e,
gloss_sh);

   float4 uv_gloss = invert(scale(.335,.335,1)) * uv;

   float4 col = texture(gloss, uv_gloss);
   float4 invcol = { 1, 1, 1, 0 } - col;

   return Cgloss*invcol + Cbase*col;
}
```

```
surface float4
lightmodel_cartoon (texref cartoon, float4 a, float4 d)
{
    perlight float fr = max(dot(N,L),0);
    // clamp upper end to avoid texture border color
    float4 uv = { min(integrate(fr) + 0.2, 0.75), 0, 0, 1 };
    return a * Ca + d * texture(cartoon, uv);
}

surface shader float4
cartoontest (texref cartoon)
{
    return lightmodel_cartoon(cartoon, {.4, .4, .8, 1}, {.4, .4, .8,
1});
}
```

Figure 4.27
Cartoon rendering.
Created using software
from the Stanford Real-
Time Programmable
Shading Project (www.
graphics.stanford.edu).

The next example (Figure 4.27 (also Colour Plate)) shows a simple form of cartoon rendering (see Chapter 5 for a more advanced form of cartoon rendering). It uses the dot product of the light direction and surface normal (**N** dot **L**) to index a 1D texture map which contains only two distinct colours.

```
surface float4
lightmodel_cartoon (texref cartoon, float4 a, float4 d)
{
    perlight float fr = max(dot(N,L),0);
    // clamp upper end to avoid texture border color
    float4 uv = { min(integrate(fr)+0.4, 0.75), 0, 0, 1 };
    return a * Ca + d * texture(cartoon, uv);
}

surface shader float4
cartoontest (texref cartoon)
{
    return lightmodel_cartoon(cartoon, {.4, .4, .8, 1}, {.4, .4, .8,
1});
}
```

Figure 4.28
Cartoon rendering variation. Created using software from the Stanford Real-Time Programmable Shading Project (www. graphics.stanford.edu).

Altering the threshold factors in Figure 4.28 (also Colour Plate) will make the light/dark area ratio change.

Figure 4.29
Bump mapping. Created
using software from
the Stanford Real-
Time Programmable
Shading Project (www.
graphics.stanford.edu).

```
surface shader float4
bumpdifftest (texref bumps, float4 uv)
{
    perlight float3 Lt = { dot(T,L), dot(B,L), dot(N,L) };
    return integrate(Cl * bumpdiff(bumps, uv, Lt));
}
```

Figure 4.29 (also Colour Plate) is a standard bump example. It integrates all available lights and computes the bump colour based on the dot products of (**T,L**), (**B,L**) and (**N,L**).

Figure 4.30
Inverting the bumps
in Figure 4.29. Created
using software from
the Stanford Real-
Time Programmable
Shading Project (www.
graphics.stanford.edu).

```
surface shader float4
bumpdifftest (texref bumps, float4 uv)
{
    perlight float3 Lt = { dot(T,L), dot(B,L), dot(N,L) } * {-1,-1,1};
    return integrate(Cl * bumpdiff(bumps, uv, Lt));
}
```

In Figure 4.30 (also Colour Plate) the bump effect is inverted by negating the **T** dot **L** and **B** dot **L**. This gives the effect of holes in the teapot.

5 Real-time rendering – practice

This chapter is about the practice of programming GPUs and divides into two parts:

(1) Programming a fixed function GPU. At first sight a contradiction, fragment functionality on a fixed function GPU is enabled by multi-pass rendering and multi-texture, where render states and texture maps are altered for each pass. Although this approach will eventually die with the march of hardware, it is currently very popular and surprisingly effective.

(2) Writing code for a programmable GPU. Here, within certain constraints, a programmer has access to functionality exposed in the vertex processing and fragment processing part of the graphics pipeline.

It is the case that the use of both of these approaches is likely to diminish in the future. The first will go as fixed function GPUs are replaced by programmable ones and the second with the adoption of hardware-independent shading languages as we discussed in the previous chapter. However, regardless of their possible demise, they do represent the current practice.

Some familiarity with the OpenGL rendering architecture is assumed in this chapter. An excellent reference is [BLYT00].

5.1 Basic shaders

A shader in the context of a fixed function GPU is an entity that is bound to an object or part of it. Its utility is usually exposed through an editor and its real function is to enable artists to design and easily experiment with texture map combinations and animations. As we discussed in the previous chapter, the term shader has a more general meaning, but this restricted usage has been heavily exploited by the games industry. In essence it conforms exactly to Cook's shade trees (Section 4.8.1), where the operations are restricted to texture maps and blending operators. Implemented as described in this chapter, shaders effectively offer a high-level interface to a fixed function GPU.

Basic shaders can be easily implemented by using a combination of multi-pass rendering and multi-texture facilities. A rudimentary multi-pass approach would involve drawing a polygon with the appropriate rendering states for the desired material. This process may be repeated several times, changing the state settings between each invocation as required. Each such operation is called a shader pass and the final render is built up in the frame buffer. With multi-texture hardware we can concatenate several passes into a single multi-texture pass. (However, the use of multi-texture hardware does not give a muti-plicative speed-up according to the number of texture units available. This is because we are replacing n state settings and n render operations with n state settings followed by a single render operation. We are only economising on the rasterisation.)

5.1.1 Render states

The render state is a structure which holds all the information on the settings which are going to be active for the following render operations. Some common examples are as follows:

- geometry flags: wireframe/filled, flat shaded/smooth shaded, one/two-sided rendering, back-face culling/front-face culling;
- geometry transformations: scaling, translation, rotation, perspective etc.;
- material flags: diffuse colour, specular colour, transparency;
- lighting configuration: number of lights, position, colour, attenuation;
- texture mapping: which texture maps, transformations in texture space;
- Z-buffer options: z test ($<, \leq, =, \geq, >$, always, never), enable/disable Z-buffer writes;

- blending options: how the current draw operation is to be mixed with information in the frame buffer (replace, add, subtract etc.).

There is an important practical/efficiency consideration involved in state settings. This is that the number of state changes must be minimised. We must remember that each polygon can have a different shader and each shader can have many passes. To minimise the number of changes we need to sort the faces by shader. Then we can set the state for the first pass of the first shader and draw all faces that need this shader. We then set the second pass of the first shader and re-draw all faces that use this shader. We only move to the next shader after we complete all the passes of the current shader. In this way we have set each state structure only once – no structure is duplicated, and we make the smallest number of shader changes possible per frame.

5.1.2 Shader sorting

The sorting is accomplished as follows. When recursing the BSP tree for a draw: at each leaf node that we find inside the view frustum (and not culled by the PVS), we add its face pointer to an array that stores the faces which should be drawn in the current frame. We then sort this array of face pointers by shader, putting all faces that share the same shader together.

Drawing is accomplished as follows:

```
For each face group
    Set shader state
    For each shader pass
        Set shader pass state
        Draw all faces from this face group
        Restore shader pass state
    Next shader pass
    Restore shader state
Next face group
```

Note that there is a difference between the operation *set shader state* and *set shader pass state*. A shader will possess some global settings that are common to all passes. The states that are unique to a pass are set by *set shader pass state*.

Another consideration to note is that we are drawing the same geometry over and over again. This implies the use of pre-compiled vertex arrays for speed-up. All transformations and clipping are performed once for the faces and stored in the 3D card local memory, speeding up subsequent draws of the same geometry.

Yet another consideration is the light maps. All the faces that share the same shader do not necessarily share the same light map. If we do not take this into consideration there may be too many light map switches. Thus we must also minimise the light map texture changes by making a composite sorting key using both the shader and light map texture.

A simple sort of shaders would progress as follows. For each face, loop all other faces and move the faces with the same shader to a position next to the current one:

```
for( i=0;i<nfaces;i++ )
  for( j=i+1;j<nfaces;j++ )
    if (sortkey[i]==sortkey[j])
    {
        swap(faces[j],faces[i+1])
                    i++;
    }
```

This can be speeded up by using a version of the Dutch flag sort algorithm: if the current key is the same as the first key, move it to the front; if the current key is the same as the last key, move it to the end. This will sort two times faster. This is a good sort as the number of faces using the same key is large (we have a lot of faces, but very few different keys).

To extend the process for shaders and light maps we need to sort the faces into groups using the same shader, and inside each group sort them by the light map texture. This can be accomplished by doing two sorts, like the above, one after the other. One uses just the shader key and the other uses the shader and light map texture composite key:

```
sortkey = (shader<<16) | lightmappic
```

The sortkey is a 32-bit integer (the first 16 bits have the shader identity and the last 16 bits have the light map texture identity).

This approach is optimal as the first sort will group all faces using the same shader, and then the next sort will just group faces with same light map texture without affecting the shader groups.

The final sort code is:

```
fd is the array of faces to be drawn
nfd is the number of face pointers in fd array

// sort faces by shader (sortkey&0xffff0000)
p1=0;
p2=nfd-1;
while(p1<p2)
{
  s1=fd[p1]->sortkey&0xffff0000;
  s2=fd[p2]->sortkey&0xffff0000;
  if (s1==s2)
    s2=-2;
  for( i=p1+1;i<p2;i++ )
    if (s1==(fd[i]->sortkey&0xffff0000))
    { // swap with begining
      f=fd[i];
```

```
          fd[i]=fd[++p1];
          fd[p1]=f;
        }
        else
        if (s2==(fd[i]->sortkey&0xffff0000))
        { // swap with end
          f=fd[i];
          fd[i--]=fd[--p2];
          fd[p2]=f;
        }
    p1++;
    if (s2!=-2)
      p2--;
}

// sort faces by composite key
// (sortkey=(shader<<16)|lightmappic)
p1=0;
p2=nfd-1;
while(p1<p2)
{
  s1=fd[p1]->sortkey;
  s2=fd[p2]->sortkey;
  if (s1==s2)
    s2=-2;
  for( i=p1+1;i<p2;i++ )
    if (s1==fd[i]->sortkey)
    { // swap with begining
      f=fd[i];
      fd[i]=fd[++p1];
      fd[p1]=f;
    }
    else
    if (s2==fd[i]->sortkey)
    { // swap with end
      f=fd[i];
      fd[i--]=fd[--p2];
      fd[p2]=f;
    }
  p1++;
  if (s2!=-2)
    p2--;
}
```

5.1.3   Shader class implementation

A simple shader class definition is as follows:

```
class FLY3D_API flyShaderPass
{
```

```
public:
    int flags;
    int tex;
    int blendsrc;
    int blenddst;

    int depthfunc;
    int alphafunc;
    float alphafuncref;

    int rgbgen;
    flyShaderFunc rgbgen_func;

    int tcmod;
    float tcmod_rotate;
    float tcmod_scale[2];
    float tcmod_scroll[2];
    flyShaderFunc tcmod_stretch_func;

    float anim_fps;
    int anim_numframes;
    int anim_frames[MAX_SHADER_ANIMFRAMES];

    void load(flyFile *fp,char *section,int i);
    void save (FILE *fp,int i);
    void set_state_1();
    void set_state_2();
};

class FLY3D_API flyShader
{
    int curpass;

public:
    int flags;
    int npass;
    flyShaderPass pass[MAX_SHADER_PASSES];

    int set_state(int cp);
    int restore_state();
    void load(flyFile *fp,char *section);
    void save(char *filename,int i);
};
```

5.2   Render states

We now look in detail at the render states and other options that are available to us in constructing a shader implementation. These are divided into two main categories: global settings which are active through all passes and settings which are local to a pass.

(5.2.1)

Global settings

Global parameter	Description
no culling	turns back-face culling on and off (used mostly for transparent objects)
depth writing	turns Z-buffer writing on and off (used mostly for transparent and special effect objects)
colliding	this is a game-dependent parameter (see below)
transparent	if a shader is found with a transparent flag set it has to be rendered later than opaque shaders
sky	used for skybox and panorama projections. Nothing collides with the sky-tagged faces. Any projectile will disappear when it crosses the sky

Game-dependent parameters can be extremely useful incorporated in shaders. For example, damage values can be gained from lava or fire shaders. The object that has been rendered with such a shader can now possess the ability to cause damage. In the case of a player walk we could cause the floor to emit appropriate sounds at each footstep.

(5.2.2)

Local settings

Local parameter	Description
depth function	compare function for drawing pixels depending on their z value ($<, \leq, =, >, \geq$, never, always)
colour	always white, vertex colour from mesh, a function that generates the colour (see separate table)
blend	how the current pass blends with the previous pass: replace (no blend), add (1,1), multiply (DestColor,0), Alpha Transparency (SrcAlpha, 1-SrcAlpha).
alpha test	render pixels based on the outcome of an alpha test. This compares the pixel alpha with a reference value [0,1] using the following relational operators: $<, \leq, =, >, \geq$
light map/ texture map	the pass uses a pre-defined light map from the BSP or the user must select a texture map
animation map	selects several textures and a frame rate. The textures are swapped at the specified frame rate (used for fire, explosions etc.)
texture coordinate modifier	see separate table
environment mapping	modifies texture coordinates based on viewpoint (chrome mapping)
texture clamp	tile the texture or not

The texture coordinate modifiers change the texture coordinate of the objects as some function of time. This effectively animates the texture maps. For example, it is commonly used to simulate moving water surfaces such as a stream or ripples moving outwards from a disturbance.

Texture coordinate modifier	Description
scale	scale factor in u and v for the texture mapping (not animated over time)
rotate	rotates the texture map (degrees/sec). The rotation is based on the centre of (u,v,w) space
scroll	translates the texture map as a function of time (units/sec). A value of 1 means that the texture translates its entire space each second
stretch	stretch is a function that defines the scaling of the texture over time (commonly used for pulsing radial effects)

Functions in the above definitions are periodic functions of a single variable. Commonly used functions are sine waves, triangular waves and sawtooth waves. A single period is defined by five parameters which particularise the following equation:

$$y = \text{offset} + \text{amplitude}*\text{func}((\text{time} + \text{phase})*\text{frequency})$$

examples of which are shown in Appendix 5.1.

Function parameter	Description
type	sin, square, triangle, saw-tooth or inverse saw-tooth
offset	the DC level of the waveform. If this is 0 the waveform oscillates about equal negative and positive values
amplitude	the half amplitude value of the function
phase	the lead or lag of the waveform. This has a value 0 to 1 corresponding to the length of the period. A value of -0.25 applied to a sine wave changes it to a cosine. A value of 0.5 applied to any type inverts the waveform
frequency	the rate of repetition of a complete period (Hertz)

Code for generating the periodic functions is straightforward and now follows:

```
#define SHADER_FUNC_SIN                1
#define SHADER_FUNC_TRIANGLE           2
#define SHADER_FUNC_SQUARE             3
#define SHADER_FUNC_SAWTOOTH           4
#define SHADER_FUNC_INVERSESAWTOOTH    5
```

```
class FLY3D_API shader_func
{
  public:
    int type;
    float args[4]; /* offset, amplitude, phase, frequency */

  float eval();
  {
    float x, y;

    /* Evaluate a number of time based periodic functions */
    /* y = args[0] + args[1] * func( (time + arg[2]) * arg[3] ) */

    x = (flyengine->cur_time_float + args[2]) * args[3];
    x -= (int)x;

    switch (type)
    {
    case SHADER_FUNC_SIN:
      y = (float)sin(x * 6.2831853071795864769252866766559f);
      break;

    case SHADER_FUNC_TRIANGLE:
      if (x < 0.5f)
        y = 4.0f * x - 1.0f;
      else
        y = -4.0f * x + 3.0f;
      break;

    case SHADER_FUNC_SQUARE:
      if (x < 0.5f)
        y = 1.0f;
      else
        y = -1.0f;
      break;

    case SHADER_FUNC_SAWTOOTH:
      y = x;
      break;

    case SHADER_FUNC_INVERSESAWTOOTH:
      y = 1.0f - x;
      break;
    }

    return y * args[1] + args[0];
  }
};
```

Code for state setting is inevitably tied to the engine and OpenGL. However, a number of points need to be made. In particular, multi-texture facilities need to be handled. Processing the first pass consists of setting the global parameters and evaluating the number of texture units available for multi-texture. After the first pass is processed we restore the settings (as we do in between all passes).

Consider first the pseudo-code process for rendering without multi-texture:

for each pass i
set the state for pass i
draw the object
restore the state for pass i

If multi-texture facilities are available this is modified to:

i = 0
while i < no of passes
        set the state for pass i
        draw the object
        restore the state for pass i
        increment i based on the number of texture units used

The code now presented is for the simpler of these two processes (full code for multi-texture can be found on the CD-ROM). The set state function first checks for pass 0 and if so it sets the global states. It then initialises the settings for the current pass that are not related to texture mapping (depth function, blend, and colour). If the pass is a light map we return, otherwise we need to set the configurations for texture mapping.

```
int shader::set_state(int cp)
{
  curpass=cp;

  shader_pass *p=&pass[curpass];

  if (curpass==0)
  {
  if (flags & SHADER_NOCULL)
    glDisable(GL_CULL_FACE);
  else
    glEnable(GL_CULL_FACE);

  if (flags & SHADER_NODEPTHWRITE)
    glDepthMask(GL_FALSE);
  else
    glDepthMask(GL_TRUE);
  }

  p->set_state_1();

  if (p->flags & SHADER_LIGHTMAP)
    return 1;

  p->set_state_2();

  return 0;
}
```

```
int shader::restore_state()
{
   shader_pass *p=&pass[curpass];

   if (p->rgbgen == SHADER_GEN_VERTEX)
      glDisableClientState(GL_COLOR_ARRAY);

   if (p->flags & SHADER_LIGHTMAP)
      {
      if (curpass==0 && npass>1 &&
         flyengine->multitexture && ntextureunits>1)
         {
         tc->sel_unit(1);
         tc->sel_tex(-1);
         if (p[1].flags & SHADER_TCMOD)
            glPopMatrix();
         if (p[1].flags & SHADER_TCGEN_ENV)
            {
            glDisable(GL_TEXTURE_GEN_S);
            glDisable(GL_TEXTURE_GEN_T);
            }
         tc->sel_unit(0);
         return 2;
         }
      return 1;
      }
   if (p->flags & SHADER_TCMOD)
      glPopMatrix();
   if (p->flags & SHADER_TCGEN_ENV)
      {
      glDisable(GL_TEXTURE_GEN_S);
      glDisable(GL_TEXTURE_GEN_T);
      }
   return 1;
}

void shader_pass::set_state_1()
{
   glDepthFunc(depthfunc);

   if (flags & SHADER_BLEND)
      {
      glEnable(GL_BLEND);
      glBlendFunc(blendsrc, blenddst);
      }
   else
      glDisable(GL_BLEND);

   if (rgbgen == SHADER_GEN_IDENTITY)
      glColor4f(1.0f, 1.0f, 1.0f, 1.0f);
   else
   if (rgbgen == SHADER_GEN_WAVE)
      {
      float rgb = rgbgen_func.eval();
      glColor4f(rgb, rgb, rgb, 1.0f);
      }
```

```
         else
         if (rgbgen == SHADER_GEN_VERTEX)
           glEnableClientState(GL_COLOR_ARRAY);
         else
         if (rgbgen == SHADER_GEN_DEFAULT)
           glColor4fv(&flyengine->shadercolor.x);
     }

    void shader_pass::set_state_2()
    {
       if (flags & SHADER_ALPHAFUNC)
          {
          glEnable(GL_ALPHA_TEST);
          glAlphaFunc(alphafunc, alphafuncref);
          }
       else
          glDisable(GL_ALPHA_TEST);

       if ((flags & SHADER_ANIMMAP) && anim_numframes>0)
          tc->sel_tex(anim_frames[(int)(anim_fps*flyengine-
    >cur_time_float)%anim_numframes]);
       else tc->sel_tex(tex);

       if (flags & SHADER_TEXCLAMP)
          {
          glTexParameteri(GL_TEXTURE_2D,GL_TEXTURE_WRAP_S,GL_CLAMP);
          glTexParameteri(GL_TEXTURE_2D,GL_TEXTURE_WRAP_T,GL_CLAMP);
          }
       else
          {
          glTexParameteri(GL_TEXTURE_2D,GL_TEXTURE_WRAP_S,GL_REPEAT);
          glTexParameteri(GL_TEXTURE_2D,GL_TEXTURE_WRAP_T,GL_REPEAT);
          }

       if (flags & SHADER_TCGEN_ENV)
          {
          glEnable(GL_TEXTURE_GEN_S);
          glEnable(GL_TEXTURE_GEN_T);
          }

       if (flags & SHADER_TCMOD)
          {
          glPushMatrix();

          glTranslatef(0.5f, 0.5f, 0.0f);

          if (tcmod & SHADER_TCMOD_ROTATE)
             glRotatef(tcmod_rotate * flyengine->cur_time_float, 0.0f,
    0.0f, 1.0f);

          if (tcmod & SHADER_TCMOD_SCALE)
             glScalef(tcmod_scale[0], tcmod_scale[1], 1.0f);

          if (tcmod & SHADER_TCMOD_STRETCH)
             {
             float y = tcmod_stretch_func.eval();
```

```
                      glScalef(1.0f/y, 1.0f/y, 1.0f);
                      }

                if (tcmod & SHADER_TCMOD_SCROLL)
                   glTranslatef(
                      tcmod_scroll[0] * flyengine->cur_time_float,
                      tcmod_scroll[1] * flyengine->cur_time_float, 0.0);

                glTranslatef(-0.5f, -0.5f, 0.0f);
                }
          }
```

5.3   Shader examples

In games design, basic shaders are commonly used to conveniently implement a number of effects. They are used to design composite textures, the structure being identical to the texture tree described in Section 4.8.1. Texture coordinate animation can be implemented which can be used to imitate water surface disturbance, lava flow etc. We now introduce a number of examples which will illustrate the utility of basic shaders.

The vast majority of shaders used in a game implement the common light map/texture map combination. The following examples are intended to demonstrate more complex possibilities that use more elaborate combination operators and animation. Clearly the construction of original and innovative shaders depends predominantly on the creative skills of an artist.

5.3.1   Environment and chrome mapping effects – glass, metal and chrome

All these effects use the standard texture coordinate generation routines for spherical environment mapping. A simple chrome texture map (Figure 5.1) is used for all examples that function well for either metal or glass. The map itself consists of lines which are random, blurred and curved. The image is dark because of the use of special blending modes (usually additive) and this prevents unwanted saturation.

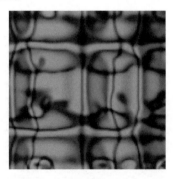

Figure 5.1
Chrome texture.

Figure 5.2
A glass and metal table using chrome texture for both materials.

'Clean' metallic surfaces can be generated using a single pass of the above texture map set to spherical environment mapping (no special blending is required).

Glass effects can be generated by the same map but this time using an additive blend mode (1,1).

Chrome textures require two passes, one for the surface texture with no blend and another one with the chrome texture and multiplicative/add blend mode (DestColor,1).

Figure 5.2 (also Colour Plate) shows a glass and metal table which uses this effect. Changing the viewpoint gives a convincing feeling of real glass. Obvious limitations of the still images tend to be diminished in a real-time walk-through. (One of the potential non-game applications of a games engine is Computer Aided Architectural Design (CAAD). Until recently the rendering quality of games engines would not have sufficed for such an application. Now the quality that can be obtained with shaders means that CAAD applications can be served.)

(5.3.2)

Moving illuminated billboards

A moving billboard effect (Figure 5.3) on a wall can easily be generated, as the figure shows.

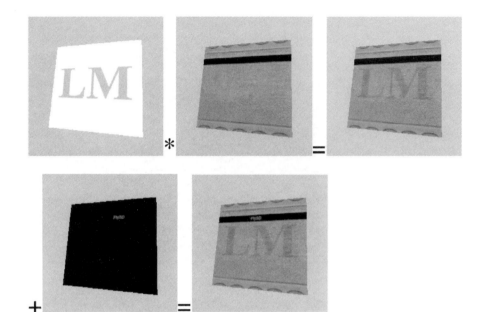

Figure 5.3
Generating a moving
illuminated billboard.

The first operation combines two passes: conventional light map/texture map combination which is multiplicative (DestColor,0). Added to this is an illuminated billboard which is a simple texture on a black background scrolling horizontally at a rate of .2 units/sec. This is blended additively (1,1).

5.3.3 Simple grating effect

Grating effects are common in games. The idea is that the grating itself is a light map plus a texture map representing the grate object. Through the gaps is revealed either an animated texture map or other scene geometry. The first example considers the simpler case of an animated texture map.

The first two images in Figure 5.4 (also Colour Plate) are scrolling texture maps moving with different speed and directions. They combine additively to simulate the effect of a wind-perturbed water surface or an 'energy field'. A light-mapped grating is combined using alpha (SrcAlpha, 1-SrcAlpha) to give the final effect shown in Figure 5.5 (also Colour Plate).

5.3.4 Advanced grating effect

If game geometry is to be seen through the grating, this requires more elaborate combination operations. We begin with the grate object as an unlit texture map (Figure 5.6(a)).

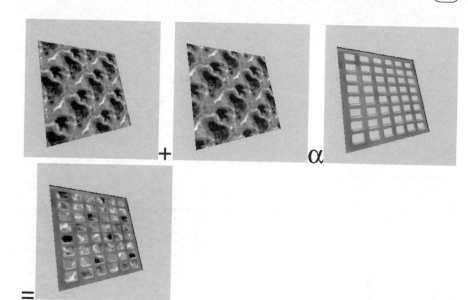

Figure 5.4
Generating a grating effect.

Figure 5.5
The final effect with volumetric fog added.

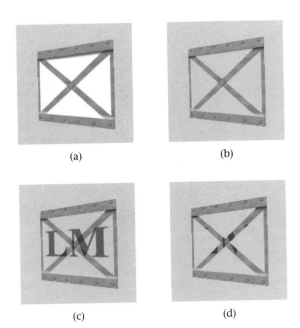

(a)

(b)

(c)

(d)

Figure 5.6
Operations required for grating effects wherein game objects are to be seen through the grating. (a) The grate object as an unlit texture map. (b) Z-buffer must be unchanged at transparent pixels. (c) Adding a light map also illuminates transparent pixels. (d) Setting Z-buffer test to *equal*.

Setting the blend for alpha transparency (SrcAlpha,1-SrcAlpha) will allow us to see though the texture map. However, this will not discard the fully transparent pixels and the Z-buffer will be 'contaminated' by them. This problem is solved by using an alpha test that rejects fragments on a per-pixel basis, leaving the Z-buffer unchanged at the fully transparent pixels. Multiplying by the light map to illuminate the grating will also illuminate the transparent pixels. This problem is solved by setting the Z-buffer test to *equal*. As the previous pass rejected pixels with the alpha test, the rejected pixels will not write to the Z-buffer, making the respective z tests fail.

Figure 5.7 (also Colour Plate) shows examples of gratings in practice.

5.3.5 A 'monitor' effect

This example is the most complex one in terms of the number of passes (5). The desired effect is that of a monitor showing a background of white noise, superimposed on which is a horizontal scrolling red line. Finally text is superimposed on this.

We begin with a random noise texture (to simulate the white noise). This is set to scroll very fast. To this is added a vertically scrolling red line with additive blending (1,1), as shown in Figure 5.8 (also Colour Plate).

A frame alpha texture is then added (Figure 5.9 (also Colour Plate)) to the current combination, replacing pixels only where the alpha value is not zero (SrcAlpha, 1-SrcAlpha).

Figure 5.7
Examples of gratings in
practice.

Figure 5.8
Random or white noise with a scrolling red line superimposed.

Figure 5.9
Addition of a frame texture.

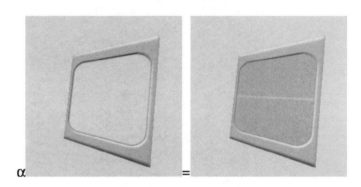

Figure 5.10
Applying a light map (multiplicative blend).

A light map is then applied (Figure 5.10 (also Colour Plate)) with a multiplicative blend (DestColor,0).

Finally a chrome texture is applied (Figure 5.11 (also Colour Plate)) as a spherical environment mapping using a multiply/add blend (DestColor,1).

This final pass can be moved up to occur before the alpha pass so that only the glass on the monitor screen is chrome mapped (Figure 5.12 (also Colour Plate)).

This final effect is shown incorporated into a level in Figure 5.13 (also Colour Plate).

*+ =

Figure 5.11
The final effect achieved by applying the chrome texture.

Figure 5.12
Restricting the chrome mapping to the glass.

Figure 5.13
The monitor effect incorporated into a level.

5.4   Real-time rendering in hardware

In the second part of the chapter we develop programming methods for basic real-time rendering on hardware. These will exploit the programmability of the GPU. Recently hardware has been developed that enables a wholesale shift of advanced rendering techniques from the host to the graphics hardware. And so at the time of writing (2002), practical coverage of real-time rendering has to assume particular graphics hardware. This is a somewhat unfortunate state of affairs, particularly given the rate at which hardware evolves. Although the latest GPUs are powerful and flexible, they have to be programmed through an assembly language interface which, of course, varies across vendors. However, there is some light on the horizon with the development of high-level shading languages and associated compiler technology which will enable different GPUs to be targeted (see, for example, [PROU01] and Chapter 4). We have thus chosen to base the chapter on NVIDIA's GeForce unit, programmed by their custom assembly language. Despite the specificity, there are general principles that can be extracted from a reading of the chapter and the examples have been incorporated into the engine.

We will cover two main topics:

- vertex programs which operate upon a vertex stream;
- 'fixed' pixel programs which apply the same pixel-level operations (such as dot products).

The description of the GeForce program model follows that of [PROU01] and also the comprehensive documentation available at www.nvidia.com.

Modern hardware now has (or shortly will have) the capacity to render all game geometry – static and dynamic objects – in real time, obviating the need to have pre-calculated lighting in the form of light maps. Unifying dynamic objects' and static objects' lighting is the ideal goal for a game engine. This will allow equal illumination quality and characteristics for both types of objects and all lights will be able to change position, colour and radius dynamically. Instead of storing light maps associated with static geometry, we can store normal maps using the same representational structure. This facilitates, for example, perfect bump maps and other special effects on static geometry and will usher in a new increase in rendering quality.

5.4.1   Vertex programming

Within certain limits, mainly constant storage constraints, vertex programming can be used to perform any desired operation on vertices considered as independent entities. Thus advanced lighting effects and operations that alter geometry, such as perturbation of a water surface and skinning, are implementable. Note, however, that when a vertex program is used for lighting – to implement

Phong shading efficiently for a dynamic object, for example, the mesh must have a fairly high resolution (because the lighting is only calculated at the vertices). However, many vertex programs are used in conjunction with fixed per-pixel programming (see below) and this requirement then becomes less severe. Vertex programs in games can be applied to both static objects and dynamic objects through the convenience of a shader model.

Vertex programming gives a programmer access to GPU functionality, which as we have studied in the first half of this chapter, has consisted of fixed function units with settable modes of operation. The vertex processing hardware replaces the transform and lighting unit of recent hardware and operates solely on vertices – no topological information is supplied to the unit. The vertex program is thus responsible for transform and other effects which can be implemented by the application at this stage. Other complex operations in the graphics pipeline remain fixed function, including video memory access, texture management, polygon management etc. If vertex programming is not enabled then the GPU reverts to a complete fixed function GPU with a transform and lighting unit. It is also possible to switch between vertex programming and fixed function processing and also to switch between different vertex programs. If conventional transform and lighting is all that is required then it is more efficient to use the fixed function hardware. This facility also enables backwards compatibility.

A vertex program[1] (also known as a vertex shader) is an assembly code module that operates on one vertex at a time. Program operations follow conventional assembly code programming conventions for a register–register processor and consist of functional operations on entities stored in the register. The format of a two-register instruction is:

   OPCODE   destination reg,   source reg1,   source reg2;

A program model for a vertex program is shown in Figure 5.14. The current vertex attributes are available to the program, which writes to the output attribute registers. A constant memory holds data from the CPU that is constant for a frame. There is a register file for temporary results.

What now follows is an overview of how to write a vertex program and how to integrate it into a games engine. Since the processing model is register–register, we begin with a brief description of the register set.

Input attribute registers

These are 16 read-only quad-float registers that contain the data or attributes for a vertex. Such components as:

---

1. We use the term vertex program consistently throughout and reserve the term shader for the model introduced at the beginning of the chapter and the usage in Chapter 4. In our system a shader can have a vertex program as one of its passes. Also, it is the case that the term shader applied to a vertex program implies that the only function of the program is to light the vertex. But geometric operations on the vertex are also possible.

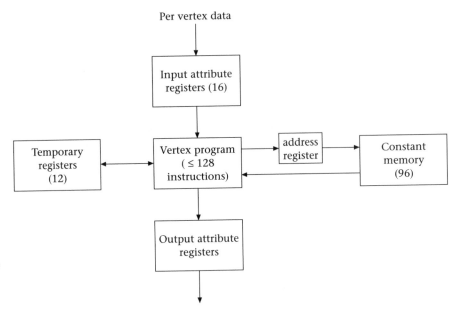

Figure 5.14
Vertex program model
(arrows indicate read-only,
write-only or read-write
with respect to the
program).

position (x,y,z,w)
texture coordinate (u,v,w,q)
colour (r,g,b,a)

associated with a vertex will be contained in these registers. The vertex program operates on this data, storing the results in write-only attribute registers. Each vertex provokes the execution of the vertex program and a program cannot generate new vertices. The results of a vertex program depend only on the instructions executed, the data in the input attribute registers and the data in the constant memory. The vertex program cannot generate persistent data that is available to the next vertex in the stream. Additionally, no branching or looping instructions are available. Every instruction in the program executes exactly once for each vertex that the program processes.

Constant memory

Constant memory, consisting of 96 quad-floats, is also read-only and its purpose is to store persistent data, or data that changes per frame, which will be used by the vertex program. This can be, for example, material properties, for use in Phong shading, light direction vectors etc. Although this memory is read-only to the vertex program, an application can write frame-changing data that may emerge from the game application.

Temporary registers

Temporary registers provide the working memory for the vertex program and are read/write. There are 12 of these, again quad-floats.

Output attribute registers

Output attribute registers contain the results of the vertex program and match the input attribute registers in capacity. From this point vertices are further processed by the remainder of the GPU. The first output register contains the vertex's clip space position and every vertex program must write a value to this register.

Address register

In addition to the above, an additional write-only temporary register – the address register – stores a scalar. This is used as an indirect address operator for the constant memory.

Vertex programming practice

The current nature of vertex programming is that of conventional assembly code programming with the constraints that looping and branching are not possible. Each instruction executes in a single tick and the performance of the program is thus directly proportional to the number of instructions that it contains. Programs are thus optimised by ensuring that there are no redundant instructions and this can be achieved by fully exploiting the vector nature of the functions and by the source data 'swizzle' function (see below). The instruction set rationale is based on the fact that the same instructions are used by the fixed function hardware and by a statistical analysis of use of these functions in fixed hardware [LIND01].

The information given in this section is intended as an informal introduction to vertex programming and should be sufficient to enable understanding of the examples. A detailed list of instructions together with a list of mnemonic names for attribute registers etc. is given in Appendix 5.2.

All vertex programs must obey the following constraints:

- The program must write to the o[HPOS] register the clip space position of the vertex.
- It must contain no more than 128 instructions.
- Each instruction may not source more than one constant register.
- Each instruction may not source more than one vertex attribute register.

The simplest possible vertex program is the single instruction:

```
MOV  o[HPOS], v[OPOS];
```

which copies the contents of the first input register (object space position) to the first output register (clip space position).

An instruction can use modifiers on its input and output arguments. The modifier for the output registers is a write mask enabling component selection and that of the input register is a component swizzle with optional negation. A swizzle means that any component (x,y,z,w) may appear and/or be replicated in another component position. For example:

.xxxx   replicates the x component in all positions
.wzyx   reverses the order of the components.

There are $4^4 = 256$ permutations possible, all of which are legal. Swizzling is useful, for example, for efficient calculation of cross-products, as we demonstrate shortly.

The instruction set consists of simple arithmetic operations such as **MOV**, **MUL**, **ADD** and **MAD** together with more complex instruction such as **LIT** which performs Phong shading.

LIT is a complex function that is best defined in pseudo-code as:

output.x = 1.0   //will contain the ambient
                           // component
output.y = max(**N.L**, 0.0)   //diffuse component
output.z = 0.0   //will contain the specular
                           // component
if (**N.L** > 0.0 **and** n = 0.0) **then** output.z = 1.0
else if(**N.L** > 0.0 **and** **N.H** > 0.0) **then** output.z = $(\mathbf{N.H})^n$
output.w = 1.0

LIT assumes that the x component of the source vector contains **N.L**, the y component contains **N.H** and the z component contains the specular index n. After executing **LIT** the separate components need to be combined using **MAD**s.

Another instruction associated with lighting is **DST** which constructs an attenuation 'vector'. The purpose of this instruction is that the vector can be used in a dot product operation to produce attenuation factors such as:

$$k_0 + k_1{*}d + k_2{*}d{*}d = (k_0,k_1,k_2) \cdot (1,d,d{*}d)$$

DST takes as input:

$(n/a,d{*}d,d{*}d,n/a)$ and $(n/a,1/d,1/d,n/a)$

and returns:

$(1,d,d{*}d,1/d)$

Dot product instructions can be used to effect vertex transformations. For example, to transform a vertex into clip space we can use the four-component dot product instruction:

```
DP4   o[HPOS].x,   c[0],   v[OPOS];
DP4   o[HPOS].y,   c[1],   v[OPOS];
DP4   o[HPOS].z,   c[2],   v[OPOS];
DP4   o[HPOS].w,   c[3],   v[OPOS];
```

and this assumes that the concatenation of the model-view matrix and the projection matrix is already stored in c[0] to c[3].

A cross-product R0 = R1 × R2 can be implemented using **MUL** and **MAD** as:

```
MUL  R0,   R1.zxyw,   R2.yzxw;
MAD  R0,   R1.yzxw,   R2.zxyw,   -R0;
```

where R0, R1 and R2 are temporary registers.

The following code performs the frequently required normalisation of a vector. It normalises a vector held in R0:

```
DP3  R0.w,    R0,    R0;
RSQ  R0.w,    R0.w;
MUL  R0.xyz,  R0,    R0.w;
```

The first instruction **DP3** performs a three-term dot product, the second, **RSQ**, a reciprocal square root and the third performs the normalisation.

To keep the overall hardware design simple, branching and looping, as we have already mentioned, are not possible. However, the effect of an if-then-else statement is implementable. Consider:

if <condition> **then** x **else** y

This can be implemented as

```
compute x
compute y
use SLT or SGE to generate a condition result (0 or 1)
x = x* condition result
y = y* condition result
```

Another common requirement in a vertex program is sine/cosine functions. These are commonly used in games to perturb, say, water surfaces where we assume that a good approximation to a wind-perturbed surface is to simply displace the z axis according to a combination of harmonic components.

Sine and cosine can be efficiently calculated by a Taylor series expansion truncated after four terms:

$$\sin(x) = x - \frac{x^3}{3!} + \frac{x^5}{5!} - \frac{x^7}{7!}$$

$$\cos(x) = 1 - \frac{x^2}{2!} + \frac{x^4}{4!} - \frac{x^6}{6!}$$

where $(-\pi \le x \le \pi)$

The algorithm for this is:

(1) set up $\left(1, -\frac{1}{3!}, \frac{1}{5!} - \frac{1}{7!}\right)$

(2) set up $\left(1, -\dfrac{1}{2!}, \dfrac{1}{4!}, -\dfrac{1}{6!}\right)$

(3) convert x $(0 \le x \le 2\pi)$ to $(-\pi \le x \le \pi)$

(4) generate the vector (x, x^3, x^5, x^7)

(5) generate the vector (x, x^2, x^4, x^6)

(6) calculate the dot product $\sin(x) = \left(1, -\dfrac{1}{3!}, \dfrac{1}{5!}, -\dfrac{1}{7!}\right) \cdot (x, x^3, x^5, x^7)$

(7) calculate the dot product $\cos(x) = \left(1, -\dfrac{1}{2!}, \dfrac{1}{4!}, -\dfrac{1}{6!}\right) \cdot (x, x^2, x^4, x^6)$

The code for this calculation, using the appropriate constant register settings (see below), is:

```
# scalar r0.x = cos(r1.x), r0.y = sin(r1.x)
MAD R0.x,  R1.x,  c[21].w,  c[21].y;    # bring argument into
                                        # -pi, .., +pi range

EXP R0.y,  R0.x;
MAD R0.x,  R0.y,  c[21].z,  -c[21].x;
DST R2.xy, R0.x,  R0.x;                 # generate
                                        # 1, (r0.x)^2, .. (r0.x)^6

MUL R2.z,  R2.y,  R2.y;
MUL R2.w,  R2.y,  R2.z;
MUL R0,    R2,    R0.x;                  # generate
                                        # r0.x, (r0.x)^3, .., (r0.x)^7
DP4 R0.y,  R0,    c[23];                 # compute sin(r0.x)
```

Basic vertex programs for lighting

The following is a complete vertex program that performs standard transform and lighting for a point light source. Remember that the vertex program replaces transform and lighting hardware and thus itself is responsible for this function. A vertex program is enclosed between:

!! VP1.0 and END

which is explained in the next section.

The first group of instructions transforms the vertex into eye space. Here the lighting calculations are made. This assumes that the model-view matrix is loaded into the constant registers c[4] to c[7].

To load parameters into the constant memory it is convenient to use the OpenGL tracking utility. The OpenGL implementation maintains matrices and their inverse and this should be exploited to the full. In this case the model-view matrix can be loaded into c[4] to c[7] with:

```
glTrackMatrixNV(GL_VERTEX_PROGRAM_NV, 4, GL_MODELVIEW,
    GL_INDENTITY_NV);
```

The next group of instructions calculates the normalised light direction vector for the point light source. This is followed by the calculation of the vertex normal in eye space which assumes the existence of the inverse transpose of the model-view matrix in c[8] to c[11] loaded by:

```
glTrackMatrixNV(GL_VERTEX_PROGRAM_NV, 8, GL_MODELVIEW,
    GL_INVERSE_TRANSPOSE_NV);
```

It is then possible to compute the dot product **N.L** followed by the multiplication by the diffuse reflection or material coefficients.

```
!!VP1.0
# standard transform diffuse lighting

# compute eye space vertex position
DP4 R0.x, c[4], v[OPOS];
DP4 R0.y, c[5], v[OPOS];
DP4 R0.z, c[6], v[OPOS];

# computes normalised light direction
ADD R0.xyz, c[30], -R0;
DP3 R0.w, R0, R0;
RSQ R0.w, R0.w;
MUL R0.xyz, R0, R0.w;

# computes normal in eye space
DP4 R1.x, c[8], v[NRML];
DP4 R1.y, c[9], v[NRML];
DP4 R1.z, c[10], v[NRML];

# compute N dot L and crop [0-1]
DP3 R2, R0, R1;
MAX R2, R2, c[20].x;

# set output colour to product light_colour*(N dot L)
MUL o[COL0], R2, c[31];

# set output texture co-ordinate
MOV o[TEX0], v[TEX0];

# set output vertex position in clip space
DP4 o[HPOS].x, c[0], v[OPOS];
DP4 o[HPOS].y, c[1], v[OPOS];
DP4 o[HPOS].z, c[2], v[OPOS];
DP4 o[HPOS].w, c[3], v[OPOS];

END
```

The next vertex program implements full Phong shading using the opcode **LIT**. This operates with the standard approximation which is to assume, for the lighting calculation, that the light and viewpoint are positioned at infinity, making the definition of the Blinn halfway vector, **H**, a constant for each frame.

```
!!VP1.0
# transform and Phong lighting

# compute eye space vertex position
DP4 R0.x, c[4], v[OPOS];
DP4 R0.y, c[5], v[OPOS];
DP4 R0.z, c[6], v[OPOS];

# computes normalised light direction
ADD R0.xyz, c[30], -R0;
DP3 R0.w, R0, R0;
RSQ R0.w, R0.w;
MUL R0.xyz, R0, R0.w;

# computes normal in eye space
DP4 R1.x, c[8], v[NRML];
DP4 R1.y, c[9], v[NRML];
DP4 R1.z, c[10], v[NRML];

# compute N dot L
DP3 R2.x, R0, R1;
DP3 R2.y, c[34], R1;
MOV R2.w, c[34].w;
LIT R3, R2;

# set output colour to ambient + diffuse*(L.N) + (H.N)^n
MAD R4, R3.y, v[COL0], R3.z;
ADD o[COL0], R4, c[35];

# set output texture co-ordinate
MOV o[TEX0], v[TEX0];

# set output vertex position in clip space
DP4 o[HPOS].x, c[0], v[OPOS];
DP4 o[HPOS].y, c[1], v[OPOS];
DP4 o[HPOS].z, c[2], v[OPOS];
DP4 o[HPOS].w, c[3], v[OPOS];

END
```

Integrating vertex programs into multi-pass shaders

The vertex programs are integrated into the engine via the shader structure. This is now extended from a utility that controls fixed function hardware and a shader can now access or possess a vertex program. Thus we can still use the multi-pass shader structure, but now a pass can have a vertex program.

The Fly3D shader editor allows the selection of a vertex program text file (.vp) for each shader pass. When a shader is loaded, the vertex program file is loaded and compiled. Each shader pass vertex program is also associated with a custom-defined shader function. At run time, when the shader is selected for drawing, the function is evaluated and passed to the program by a constant register.

Figure P.1
Showing the engine being used for non-game applications.

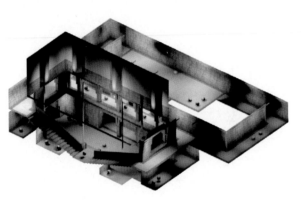

Figure 1.1
A view of an entire games level

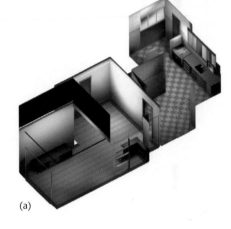

(a)

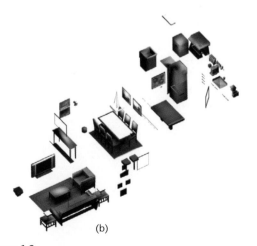

(b)

(c)

Figure 1.2
(a) Structural elements in a CAAD application used as BSP splitting planes.
(b) Detail elements in a CAAD application. (c) The entire apartment scene showing both structural and detail elements.

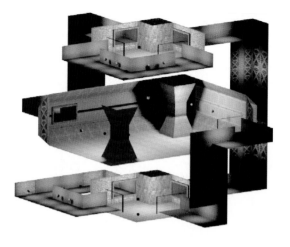

(a)

Figure 1.6
A level modelled so as to produce no negative nodes.

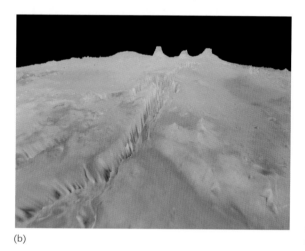

(b)

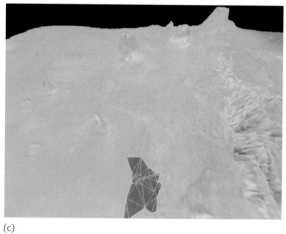

(c)

Figure 1.7
(a) A complex landscape – part of the Martian surface. (b) A closer view showing the high level of detail. (c) The contents of a single BSP sector.

Figure 1.11
(a) Showing pseudo-portals in an open space in a level. The multiplicity of portal faces is due to the BSP grid size setting which generates convex volumes whose clear connecting faces are shown. (b) In this example the pseudo-portal planes coincide with a real portal.

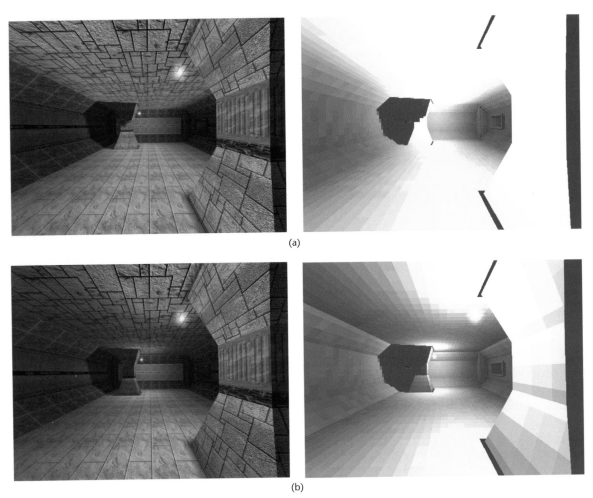

(a)

(b)

Figure 1.17
(a) Illuminating the light map – square law attenuation (texture filtering turned off to enable the light map pixels to be visualised). (b) Illuminating the light map – square law attenuation plus **L.N** (texture filtering turned off to enable the light map pixels to be visualised).

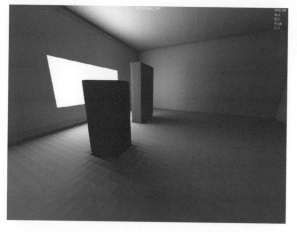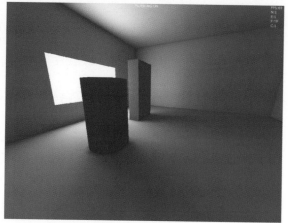

Figure 1.22
A simple environment illuminated using the radiosity method.

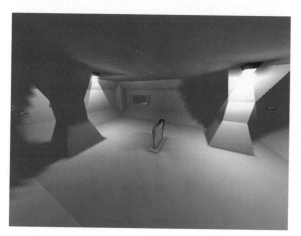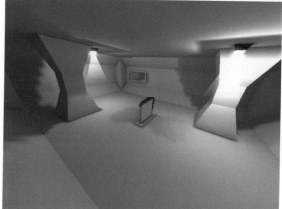

Figure 1.23
A games level rendered with and without radiosity.

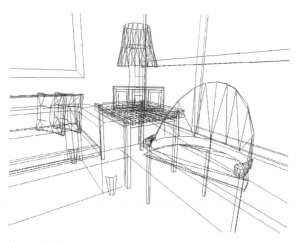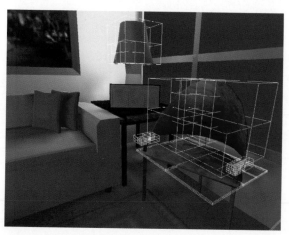

Figure 1.24
A scene with octrees built around both Bézier surface and triangle meshes.

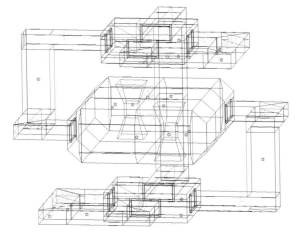

Figure A1.2
A wireframe of a level showing different geometry types:
Blue   structural polygons
Green   detail polygons
Red   game entities
Purple   curved surfaces
Yellow   lights

Figure A1.5(a)
Lighting an environment.

Figure A1.5(b)
Lighting an environment.

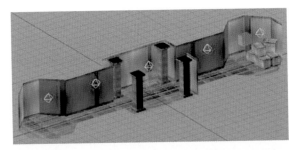

Figure A1.6
Adding entities.

Figure A1.11
Adding detail objects.

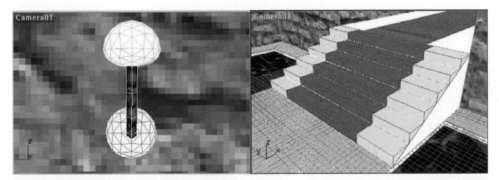

Figure A1.12
Triangles and polygonal detail objects.

Figure A1.13
Adding lighting.

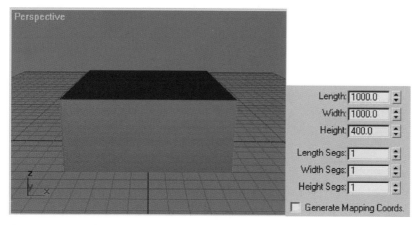

Figure A1.14
Creating a box structure.

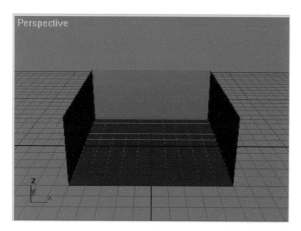

Figure A1.15
Inverting the normals.

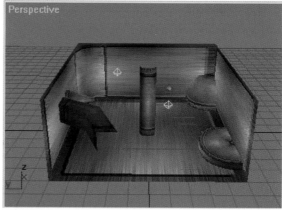

Figure A1.24
Adding lighting.

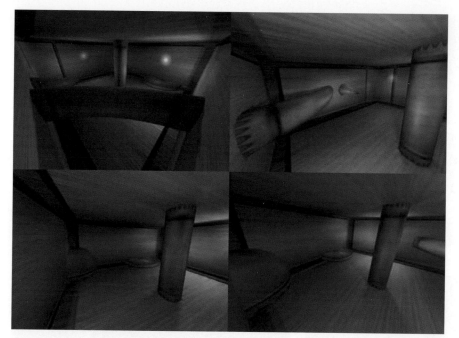

Figure A1.25
Screen shots of a completed level.

(a)

(b)

Figure 2.2
(a) The Padgarden level and a view frustum. All BSP leaf nodes clipped by the view frustum are shown (1453 faces). (b) The Padgarden level with view frustum clipping. Only those faces whose AABB intersects the view frustum are selected for rendering (587 faces).

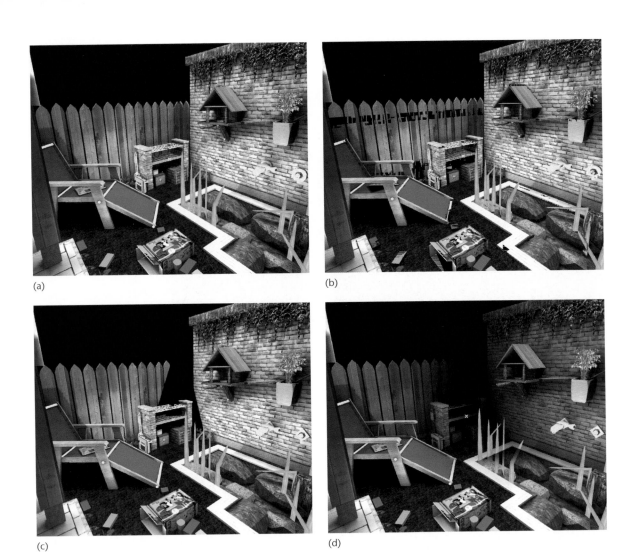

Figure 2.3
(a) Correct near and far plane setting for the Padgarden level. (b) Far plane too distant, causing Z-buffer precision artefacts.
(c) Far plane too close – visible in the scene. (d) Close far plane visibility reduced by fog.

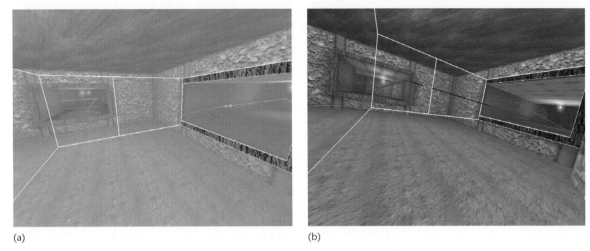

(a)   (b)

Figure 2.18
(a) Part of a path from a source convex volume to a destination volume generated using A*. (b) The same partial path 'collapsed' by ray intersecting the first and last of each group of three vertices to remove points.

Figure A2.1
Third-person camera mode.

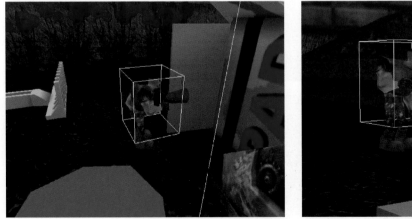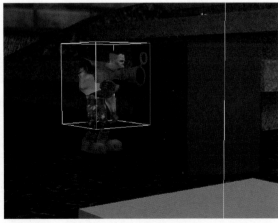

Figure A2.2
Edge/edge collision.

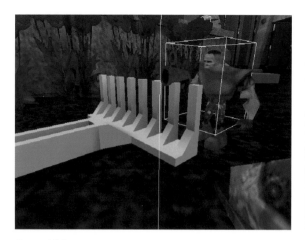

Figure A2.3
Scene vertex/AABB collision.

Figure A2.4
AABB vertex/scene collision.

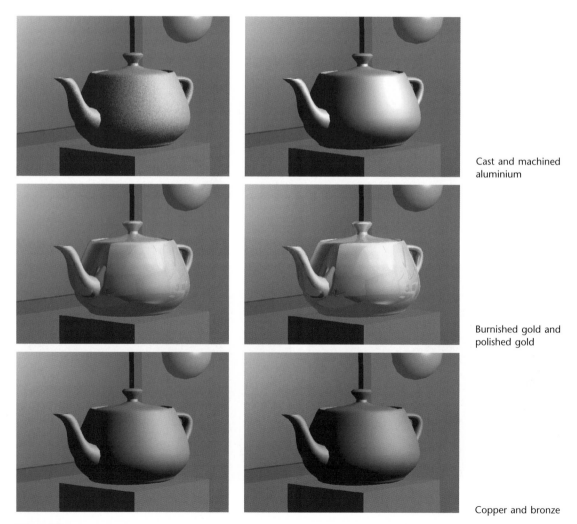

Cast and machined
aluminium

Burnished gold and
polished gold

Copper and bronze

Figure 4.8
Different materials rendered with the same lighting conditions. In the case of the polished materials the model was used as a local component in a ray tracer.

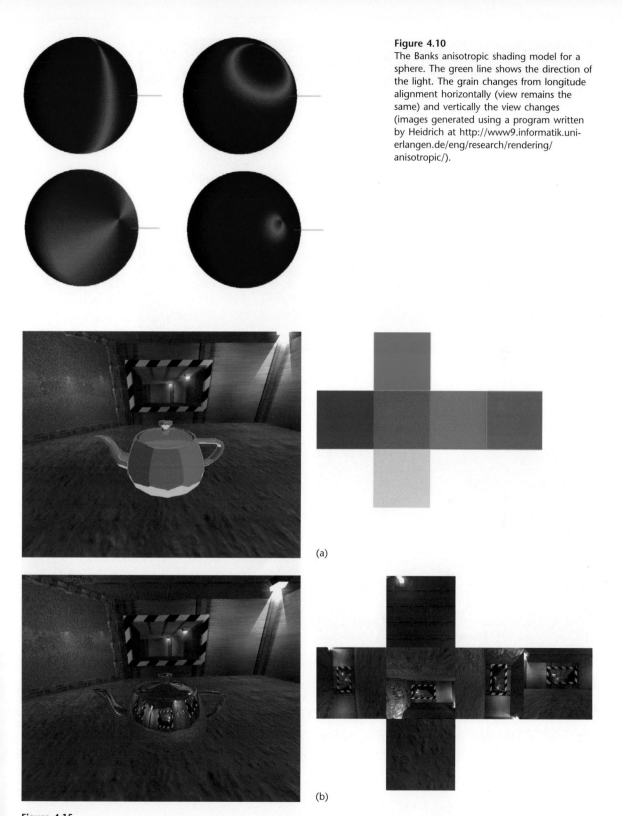

Figure 4.10
The Banks anisotropic shading model for a sphere. The green line shows the direction of the light. The grain changes from longitude alignment horizontally (view remains the same) and vertically the view changes (images generated using a program written by Heidrich at http://www9.informatik.uni-erlangen.de/eng/research/rendering/anisotropic/).

(a)

(b)

Figure 4.15
(a) Showing a cube-mapped object where the map is made up of six constant colours. (b) The same cube-mapped object which is now reflecting the environment in which it is placed.

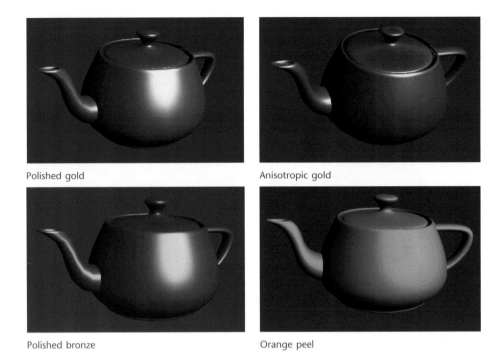

Polished gold

Anisotropic gold

Polished bronze

Orange peel

Figure 4.20
Different materials rendered with the same lighting using separable approximations (illustration produced using a program downloadable from www.nvidia.com).

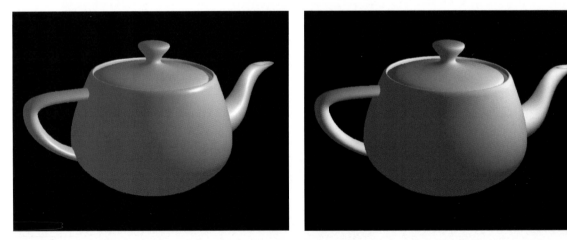

Figure 4.23
The simplest surface shader – Phong shading.

Figure 4.24
Variations on Figure 4.23.

Figures 4.23 to 4.30 created using software from the Stanford Real-Time Programmable Shading Project (www.graphics.stanford.edu).

Figure 4.25
Mixing glossy and matte materials.

Figure 4.26
Reversing the materials in Figure 4.25.

Figure 4.27
Cartoon rendering.

Figure 4.28
Cartoon rendering variation.

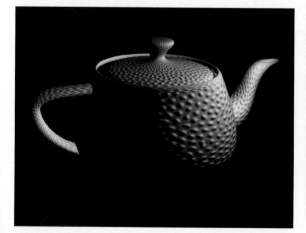

Figure 4.29
Bump mapping.

Figure 4.30
Inverting the bumps in Figure 4.29.

Figure 5.2
A glass and metal table using chrome texture for both materials.

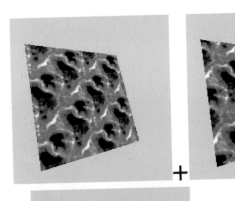

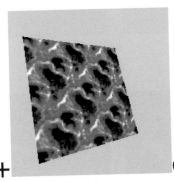

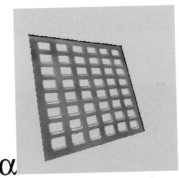

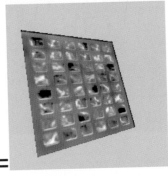

Figure 5.4
Generating a grating effect.

Figure 5.5
The final effect with volumetric fog added.

Figure 5.7
Examples of gratings in practice.

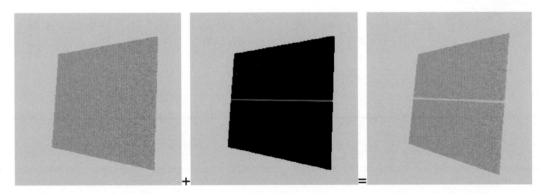

Figure 5.8
Random or white noise with a scrolling red line superimposed.

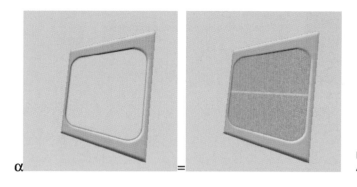

α   =

Figure 5.9
Addition of a frame texture.

*   =

Figure 5.10
Applying a light map (multiplicative blend).

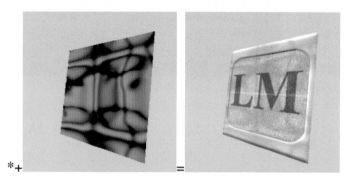

*+   =

Figure 5.11
The final effect achieved by applying the chrome texture.

Figure 5.12
Restricting the chrome mapping to the glass.

Figure 5.13
The monitor effect incorporated into a level.

Figure 5.17
The padgarden level with the water surface gently undulating according to the wave vertex program (apparent in the image in the duck and boat water level). Difficult to demonstrate with a static image, this effect imparts a good atmosphere when animated.

Figure 5.15
A three-colour cartoon rendering vertex program. The black colour comes from the inflated object and the two shades of blue represent the coarse **N.L** shades.

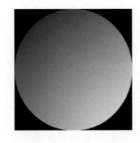

Figure 5.20
The quad map used to render a sphere – the colour represents the normal direction.

Figure 5.21
The quad map in the game engine lit by a nearby light. The second image with the alpha test eliminated showing the quad background.

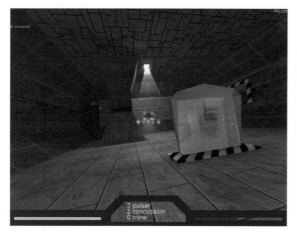
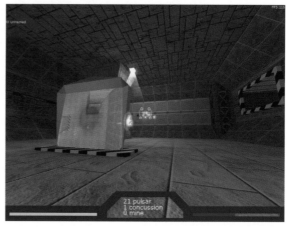

Figure 5.22
Two views of a mode 1 portal image. The portal image remains fixed as the player moves and is generated from a viewpoint positioned on the light immediately behind and above the portal/mirror object. The rear of the portal object appears in the image. Normally the portal target would be in a different room.

Figure 5.24
Portal mode 2 (mirror mode) showing the reflection of the player.

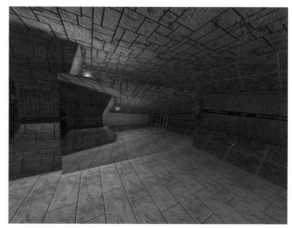

Figure 5.25
The projection of a subdivided portal/mirror object.

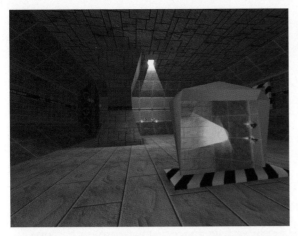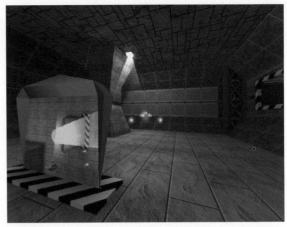

Figure 5.26
In this image the portal target is again the light above and behind the portal/mirror object. The portal camera orientation relative to the portal target is the same as the normal camera relative to the portal. Thus as the player moves around the portal/mirror object different areas of the target are seen. This compares with mode 1 where the view is always the same.

Figure 5.27
The afterburner effect.

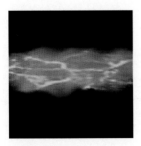

Figure 5.31
The texture map used.

Figure 5.32
The final effect.

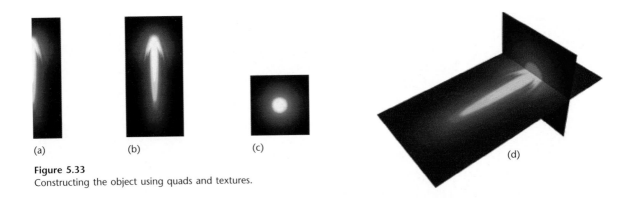

(a)   (b)   (c)   (d)

Figure 5.33
Constructing the object using quads and textures.

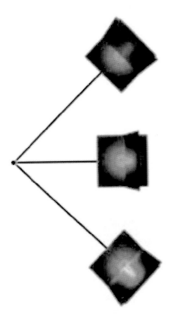

Figure 5.35
The pulsar object positioned
orthogonal to the viewer.

Figure 5.36
Pulsar objects in a game level.

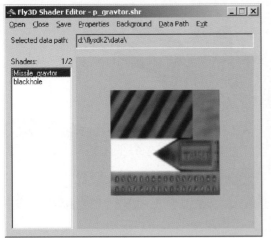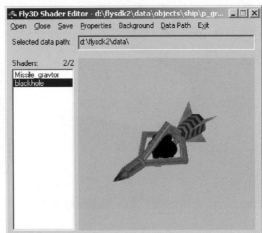

Figure A5.1
Two shaders for a missile.

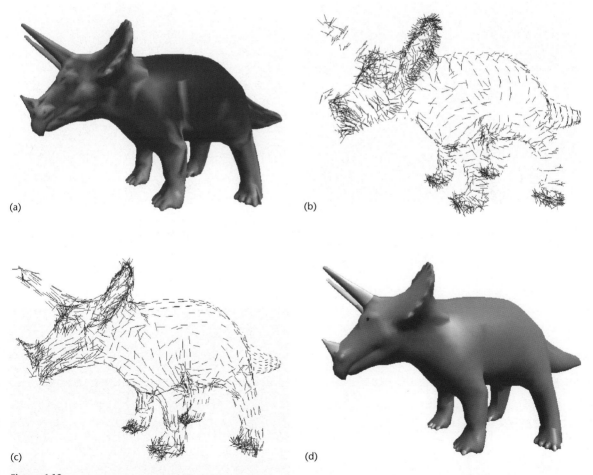

(a)

(b)

(c)

(d)

Figure 6.19
Example of discrete differential geometry operators on triceratops mesh. (a) Mean curvature ($\frac{1}{2}(\kappa_1 + \kappa_2)$) rendering. (b) Normalised maximum principle curvature (κ_1) direction vector field. (c) Normalised minimum principle curvature (κ_2) direction vector field. (d) Mesh conventionally rendered (courtesy of Mark Eastlick).

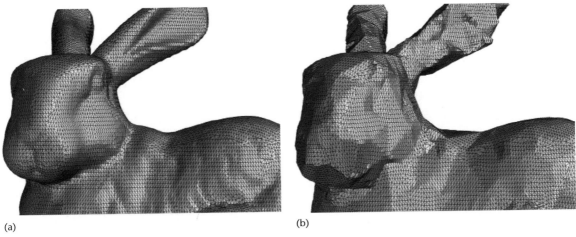

(a)   (b)

Figure 6.23
(a) Original mesh (a low resolution version of the Stanford Bunny). (b) Base mesh and vertex parameterisation.

Figure 7.2
Two views of a simple flocking population in a games level (courtesy of F. Paganelli and M. Mustapic, Universidad de Buenos Aires).

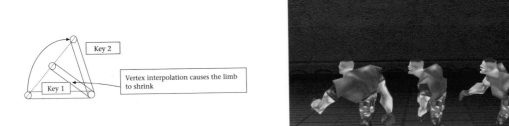

Figure 7.4
Distortion due to vertex interpolation (compare with Figure 7.7).

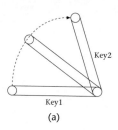

(a)

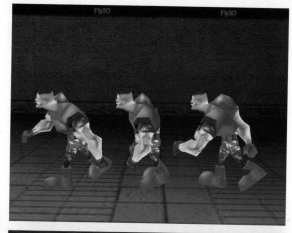

(b)

(c)

Figure 7.7
Showing the advantage of skeleton animation over vertex animation for eliminating geometric distortion of the skin layer. (a) Interpolating rotation removes vertex interpolation distortion. (b) Key interpolation for the entire figure (compare with Figure 7.4). (c) Showing the skeleton used.

Figure 7.8
Quaternion interpolation for the skeleton plus translation and orientation of the root node controlled by a Bézier curve.

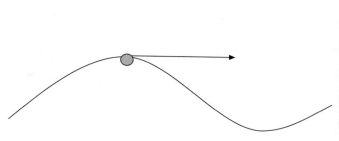

Figure 7.12
Controlling the position and orientation of a character's root node from a Bézier curve.

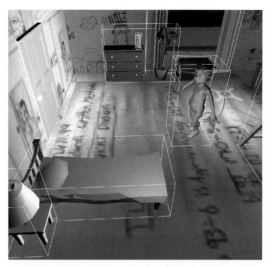 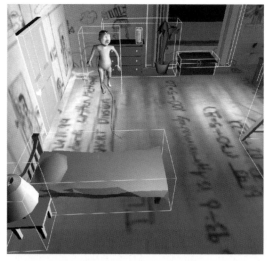

Figure 7.14
Two walks from different positions to the *in* point of the 'lie down' animation. Each path ends at the same point and the character is in the same pose at that point so that the lie down animation blends successfully with the walk animation (courtesy of Kelseus.com).

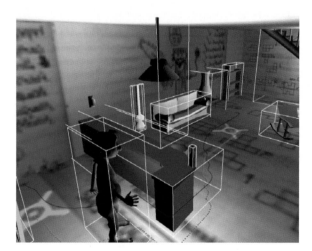

Figure 7.16
Moving from red position to blue position avoiding the bar. In this case the objects are encased in AABBs (courtesy of Kelseus.com).

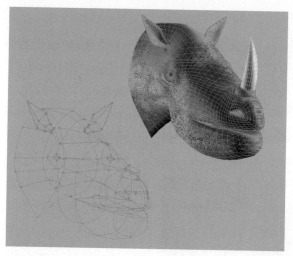

Figure 8.1
Modelling with spline cages in 3D Studio MAX.

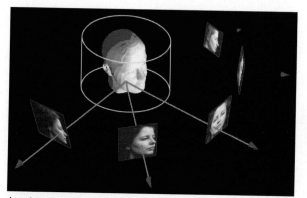

A point **p** may appear in more than one image

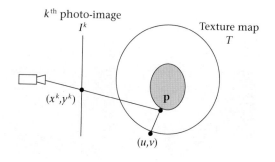

k^{th} photo-image
I^k

Texture map
T

(x^k, y^k)

p

(u, v)

Figure 9.4
Constructing a 'cylindrical' texture map
(courtesy of F. Pighin).

Composited texture map T

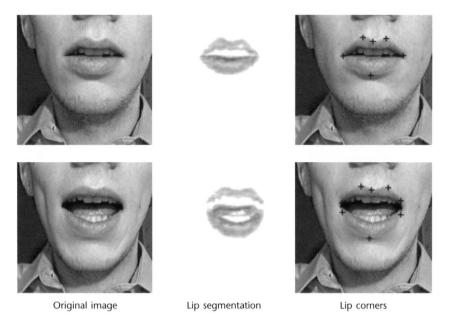

| Original image | Lip segmentation | Lip corners |

Figure 9.6
Image processing operations on the lips (courtesy of James Edge, University of Sheffield).

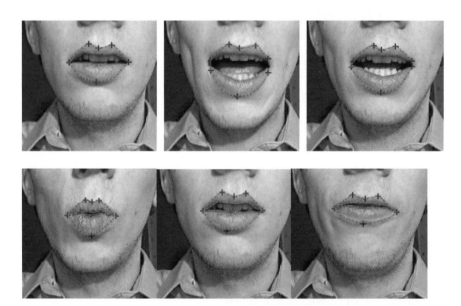

Figure 9.7
Lip tracking using snakes. Top row outer lip contour. Bottom row inner lip contour
(courtesy of James Edge, University of Sheffield).

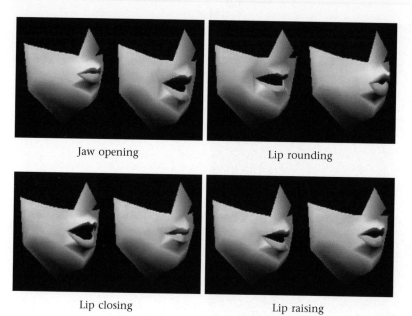

Jaw opening   Lip rounding

Lip closing   Lip raising

Figure 9.9
Extreme variations of articulatory parameters in MOTHER (courtesy of L. Reveret [REVE00]).

Figure 9.14
The baby from Pixar's 1988 production *Tin Toy* (© Pixar Animation Studios).

Figure A9.1
Two frames from a pseudo-muscle
model implementation in Fly3D
(courtesy of Emmanuel Tanguy,
University of Sheffield).

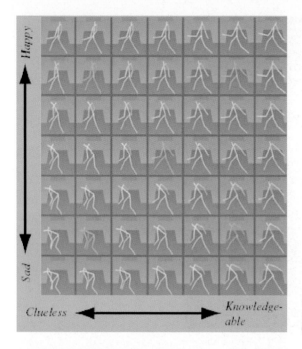

Figure 10.8
Deriving a continuous space of motion from verb examples
(green = examples) (courtesy of C. Rose).

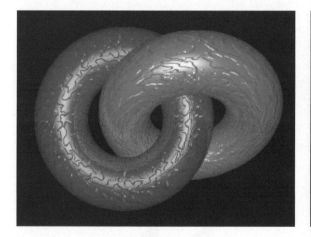

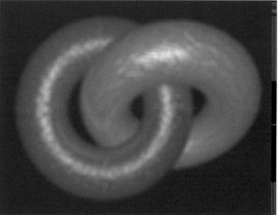

Figure 10.13
Two classic image processing filtering operations: low pass
filtering which blurs because it removes high frequency
components; and high pass filtering which emphasises detail
by removing slow changing variations (low frequency
components).

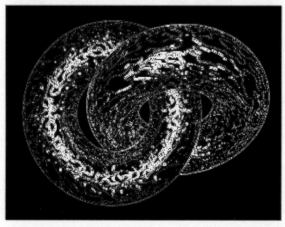

Figure 10.22
Problems with generic character/object interaction. If the same animation script is used to pick up similar large objects, then character/object penetration (visible in the image) should be handled. Alternatively a different script is required for each object (courtesy of Kelseus.com).

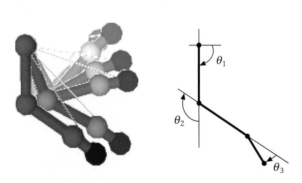

Figure 11.8
A differential IK solution for a three-link structure using joint angle constraints (courtesy of Michael Meredith).

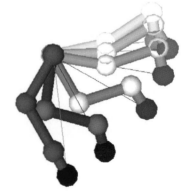

Figure 11.9
The three-link structure with all joint constraints removed. Compare with previous solution.

The following code loads and compiles a vertex program:

```
str=g_flyengine->flysdkdatapath+"programs\\"+programfile;
flyFile vpfile;
if (vpfile.open(str))
{
   char *buf=new char[vpfile.len+1];
   memcpy(buf,vpfile.buf,vpfile.len);
   buf[vpfile.len]=0;

   glGenProgramsNV(1,&vpid);
   glBindProgramNV(GL_VERTEX_PROGRAM_NV,vpid);

   nvparse(buf);

   delete buf;
   vpfile.close();
}
```

First the program file is loaded into a char string. Then the program id is generated and bound. The actual compiling is performed by the *nvparse* call, which uses the NVIDIA parser[2] to compile vertex program assembly code.

The following code from the shader *set_pass* selects and enables the vertex program:

```
if (vpid!=-1)
{
   glBindProgramNV(GL_VERTEX_PROGRAM_NV, vpid);
   glEnable(GL_VERTEX_PROGRAM_NV);
   float f=vpfunc.eval();
   glProgramParameter4fNV(GL_VERTEX_PROGRAM_NV, 16,f,f,f,0);
}
```

The program function is also evaluated and stored in a program constant.

Constant program parameter setting

To some extent the setting of the constant registers is application dependent. For example, in implementing a skinning operation as a vertex program the

---

2. NVParse is an OpenGL tool that simplifies the programming of vertex and pixel computations on NVIDIA GPUs. It is a library that can be used in conjunction with native OpenGL calls to:

- simplify the process of configuring texture shaders;
- simplify the process of configuring register combiners;
- load vertex programs (with improved error reporting).

In addition, NVParse provides limited support for standard Microsoft DirectX 8.0 Vertex Shaders and Pixel Shaders.

registers would be set up to contain the bone matrices. However, for general applications it is good practice to set these always to contain information that is likely to be used by most vertex programs.

The following represents a simple and reasonably general choice for a single light source application:

Constant register	Contents
0–3	Concatenated modelview and projection matrix
4–7	modelview matrix
8–11	Inverse transpose of modelview matrix
12–15	Inverse of modelview matrix
20	(0,0.5,1,2) – general constants which can be swizzled and replicated
21	Sin/Cos helper constants
22	Cos Taylor series coefficients
23	Sin Taylor series coefficients
24	Program function arguments
25	Program function (f,f,f,0)
26	Time (t,t,t,0)
30	Light position in eye coordinates
31	Light colour
32	Light attenuation
33	**L** light vector
34	**H** halfway vector
35	Ambient colour

This is set up by the following:

```
glTrackMatrixNV(GL_VERTEX_PROGRAM_NV,  0,  GL_MODELVIEW_PROJECTION_NV,
GL_IDENTITY_NV);
glTrackMatrixNV(GL_VERTEX_PROGRAM_NV,  4,  GL_MODELVIEW,
GL_IDENTITY_NV);
glTrackMatrixNV(GL_VERTEX_PROGRAM_NV,  8,  GL_MODELVIEW,
GL_INVERSE_TRANSPOSE_NV);
glTrackMatrixNV(GL_VERTEX_PROGRAM_NV,  12,  GL_MODELVIEW,
GL_INVERSE_NV);

glProgramParameter4fNV(GL_VERTEX_PROGRAM_NV, 20, 0,  0.5f,  1,2);
glProgramParameter4fNV( GL_VERTEX_PROGRAM_NV, 21,  PI,  0.5f,
2.0f*PI,1.0f/(2.0f*PI));
glProgramParameter4fNV( GL_VERTEX_PROGRAM_NV, 22,  1.0f, -
0.5f,1.0f/24.0f,-1.0f/720.0f);
glProgramParameter4fNV( GL_VERTEX_PROGRAM_NV, 23,  1.0f, -
1.0f/6.0f,1.0f/120.0f,  -1.0f/5040.0f);

float f=vpfunc.eval();
glProgramParameter4fNV(GL_VERTEX_PROGRAM_NV,24,
   vpfunc.args[0],vpfunc.args[1],vpfunc.args[2],vpfunc.args[3]);
```

```
float f=shader->pass->vpfunc.eval();
glProgramParameter4fNV(GL_VERTEX_PROGRAM_NV, 25,f,f,f,0);

glProgramParameter4fNV(GL_VERTEX_PROGRAM_NV,26,
    cur_time_float,cur_time_float,cur_time_float,0);

glProgramParameter4fNV(GL_VERTEX_PROGRAM_NV,
    30,lightpos[0].x,lightpos[1].y,lightpos[2],0);
glProgramParameter4fNV(GL_VERTEX_PROGRAM_NV,31,
    lightcolor[0],lightcolor[1],lightcolor[2],0);
glProgramParameter4fNV(GL_VERTEX_PROGRAM_NV,32,
    lightatten[0],lightatten[1],lightatten[2],0);

glProgramParameter4fNV(GL_VERTEX_PROGRAM_NV, 33,L.x,L.y,L.z,0 );
H=(L+Z)*0.5f;
H.normalize();
glProgramParameter4fNV(GL_VERTEX_PROGRAM_NV, 34,H.x,H.y,H.z,32 );

glProgramParameter4fNV(GL_VERTEX_PROGRAM_NV,
35,ambient.x,ambient.y,ambient.z,0 );
```

We will now demonstrate examples that implement functionality beyond that of standard transform and lighting. We begin with a vertex program for cartoon rendering. It is convenient to split this task into two programs. These can then be implemented as separate passes in the shader. The first accesses a one-dimensional lookup table which replaces the lighting calculation. Transformations etc. are as before. **N.L** is set to the *u* texture coordinate which accesses the one-dimensional lookup table/texture map. The *v* texture coordinate is set to zero. This results in the stylised colouring that replaces the diffuse lighting calculation. Note that the program is almost the same as the previous one except for the addition of the instruction which sets **L.N** to the *u* texture coordinate.

```
!!VP1.0
# cartoon lighting

# compute eye space vertex position
DP4 R0.x,  c[4],  v[OPOS];
DP4 R0.y,  c[5],  v[OPOS];
DP4 R0.z,  c[6],  v[OPOS];

# computes normalised light direction
ADD R0.xyz, c[30], -R0;
DP3 R0.w,  R0,  R0;
RSQ R0.w,  R0.w;
MUL R0.xyz, R0,  R0.w;

# computes normal in eye space
DP4 R1.x,  c[8],  v[NRML];
DP4 R1.y,  c[9],  v[NRML];
DP4 R1.z,  c[10], v[NRML];
```

```
# compute N dot L and crop [0-1]
DP3 R2, R0, R1;
MAX R2, R2, c[20].x;

# set output u texture co-ordinate to (L dot N)
MOV o[TEX0].x, R2.x;

# set output v texture co-ordinate to 0
MOV o[TEX0].y, c[20].x;

# set output colour to input vertex colour
MOV o[COL0], v[COL0];

# set output vertx position in clip space
DP4 o[HPOS].x, c[0], v[OPOS];
DP4 o[HPOS].y, c[1], v[OPOS];
DP4 o[HPOS].z, c[2], v[OPOS];
DP4 o[HPOS].w, c[3], v[OPOS];

END
```

The next vertex program performs the second cartoon lighting function – the emphasis of (external) silhouette edges. This can be done efficiently by the following simple manipulations. First we render the object in black with front-face culling enabled. Also the object is 'inflated' – that is, it is expanded slightly by moving the vertices along the direction of their vertex normals. The object is then drawn normal size, with the previously developed cartoon lighting, with back-face culling enabled. A feature of this demonstration is that the silhouette edge width is animated. This is done by passing the shader function into constant register c[16] as explained in the subsection 'Integrating vertex programs into multi-pass shaders' and is an example of a changing parameter value used by the vertex program.

```
!!VP1.0
# cartoon silhouette edge enhancement

MOV R0,v[OPOS];
MOV R1,v[NRML];
MAD R0,R1,c[25],R0;

DP4 o[HPOS].x, c[0], R0;
DP4 o[HPOS].y, c[1], R0;
DP4 o[HPOS].z, c[2], R0;
DP4 o[HPOS].w, c[3], R0;

MOV o[COL0], c[20].x;
MOV o[TEX0], c[20].x;

END
```

Figure 5.15 (also Colour Plate) shows an object rendered using this code. For a dynamic object this stylisation is very effective in giving a user a feel for the interaction between the object and the lights it is interacting with. The

Figure 5.15
A three-colour cartoon
rendering vertex program.
The black colour comes
from the inflated object
and the two shades of
blue represent the coarse
N.L shades.

underlying polygonal resolution is apparent in this image, again emphasising
that if a vertex program is used on its own for rendering then the mesh must
be of a reasonably high resolution.

There is an additional practical problem in this particular example concerning the action of hardware texture filtering. We require texture filtering to apply
to all of the game objects which are not cartoon rendered. However, texture
filtering should not diminish the hard-edge stylisation of cartoon rendered objects
but we still want the colour transition edges to be anti-aliased. This can be
achieved by ensuring that the one-dimensional texture map is large (say 256
texels) and blending from region to region over a few texels (Figure 5.16). To
prevent texture filtering between the first and last texture pixels we need to set
the texture clamp to the 1D texture map.

Figure 5.16
A (256 × 1) texel texture
map used in the cartoon
rendering.

Another obvious and useful vertex program application is the perturbation of
a surface, such as a water surface (Figure 5.17 (also Colour Plate)). Here we perturb the z axis of the surface according to a harmonic function. The following
simple formula is used for a travelling wave:

$$f(\text{pos}) = x + y \sin(z + w(\text{time} + \text{pos}))$$

where
    x is an offset
    y is the sine wave amplitude
    z is the sine wave phase
    w is the frequency

Figure 5.17
The padgarden level with the water surface gently undulating according to the wave vertex program (apparent in the image in the duck and boat water level). Difficult to demonstrate with a static image, this effect imparts a good atmosphere when animated.

From this is computed

```
Vpos.z += f(Vpos.x).f(Vpos.y)
```

modulating the height of the surface with two waves.

```
!!VP1.0

MOV  R1, v[OPOS];
ADD  R1, R1, c[26].x;                  # add time
MAD  R1, R1, c[24].w, c[24].z;         # multiply rate and add phase

# scalar r0.x = cos(r1.x), r0.y = sin(r1.x)
MAD  R0.x, R1.x, c[21].w, c[21].y;     # bring argument into
                                       # -pi, .., +pi range

EXP  R0.y, R0.x;
MAD  R0.x, R0.y, c[21].z, -c[21].x;
DST  R2.xy, R0.x, R0.x;                # generate
                                       # 1, (r0.x)^2, .. (r0.x)^6

MUL  R2.z, R2.y, R2.y;
MUL  R2.w, R2.y, R2.z;
MUL  R0, R2, R0.x;                     # generate
                                       # r0.x, (r0.x)^3, .., (r0.x)^7
                                       # compute sin(r0.x)
DP4  R0.y, R0, c[23];                  # compute sin(r0.x)
DP4  R0.x, R2, c[22];                  # compute cos(r0.x)
```

```
# apply amplitude and offset
MAD R4.x, R0.x, c[24].y, c[24].x;

# scalar r0.x = cos(r1.y), r0.y = sin(r1.y)
MAD R0.x, R1.y, c[21].w, c[21].y;   # bring argument
                                    #into -pi, .., +pi range
EXP R0.y, R0.x;
MAD R0.x, R0.y, c[21].z, -c[21].x;
DST R2.xy, R0.x, R0.x;              # generate
                                    #1, (r0.x)^2, .. (r0.x)^6

MUL R2.z, R2.y, R2.y;
MUL R2.w, R2.y, R2.z;
MUL R0, R2, R0.x;                   # generate
                                    # r0.x, (r0.x)^3, .., (r0.x)^7
DP4 R0.y, R0, c[23];               # compute sin(r0.x)
DP4 R0.x, R2, c[22];               # compute cos(r0.x)

# apply amplitude and offset
MAD R4.y, R0.x, c[24].y, c[24].x;

# multiply cos(x)*cos(y)
MUL R0.x, R4.x, R4.y;

# move R1 r0.x along normal direction
MOV R1, v[OPOS];
MAD R1.xyz, v[NRML], R0.x, R1;

# set output registers
DP4 o[HPOS].x, R1, c[0];
DP4 o[HPOS].y, R1, c[1];
DP4 o[HPOS].z, R1, c[2];
DP4 o[HPOS].w, R1, c[3];
MOV o[COL0], v[COL0];
MOV o[TEX0], v[TEX0];

END
```

5.4.2   Pixel programming

Pixel programming (also known as pixel shaders) is something of a misnomer. Currently no consumer hardware supports full pixel programming, which would mean treating each pixel as a separate entity (just like vertex programming). Despite this, facilities exist with exposed functionality which will apply functionality at the pixel level in a limited way. For example, we can 'combine' two texture maps using a dot product as a combination operator. Thus an individual computation is applied to each and the same generic function to all pixels. This approach is also known as texture blending.

Currently pixel programming means an architecture like that shown in Figure 5.18, which shows four texture shaders supplying input to eight register combiners. The texture shader architecture enhances normal texture lookup and, as we shall see, enables such operations as dependent addressing, where the results of one texture lookup can be used to address a subsequent texture.

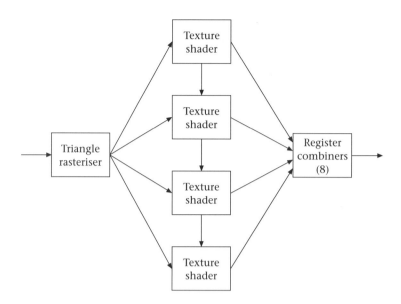

Figure 5.18
NVIDIA's pixel
programming architecture.

Pixel programming using register combiners

Register combiners are so called because they combine, in some way, RGBα vectors – texture maps – stored in input registers. The functionality of NVIDIA's architecture is summarised in the following list (a complete description is given in Appendix 5.3).

- Any four input registers, called A, B, C and D, can be combined as:

  A <op> B
  C <op> D
  AB + CD

  where <op> is:

dot product	A.B
multiply	AB

  with certain restrictions on combinations as explained in Appendix 5.3

  In addition to these operations, the following mux operation is available:

  mux(AB,CD) = (Spare0[alpha] $\geq$ $\frac{1}{2}$)? AB:CD

  The input registers contain enabled textures, primary (diffuse) and secondary (specular) colours as well as two constant colours and two spares.
- Computations use a signed numeric range [–1,1].
- RGB and alpha are processed separately.

- A final combiner stage combines final register values into an RGB and alpha for each fragment.
- Current hardware (GeForce3) supports eight general combiners and one final combiner.

Register combiner practicals

In this section we look at programming practice of the register combiners using *nvparse* which enables a user programming model that uses high-level language type assignment statements. This is very much a subset of all the information required for a complete treatment of register combiners. The idea is to present the general principles involved in the programming model.

Figure 5.19 shows a data flow diagram for the hardware. This implies that the information flow through a register combiner program uses the general combiners in order, outputting their results into the register set and eventually into the final combiner. Mnemonic names recognised by *nvparse* are given in Table 5.1.

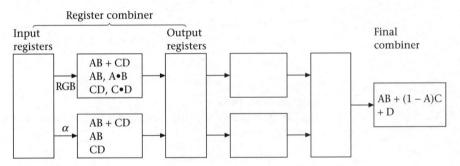

Figure 5.19
Data flow and register combiners.

Table 5.1 Mnemonic names for registers recognised by *nvparse*

Register	Name	Read	Write
Diffuse colour	col0	yes	yes
Specular colour	col1	yes	yes
Texture 0 colour	tex0	yes	yes
Texture 1 colour	tex1	yes	yes
Texture 2 colour	tex2	yes	yes
Texture 3 colour	tex3	yes	yes
Spare 0	spare0	yes	yes
Spare 1	spare1	yes	yes
Constant colour 0	const0	yes	no
Constant colour 1	const1	yes	no
Fog colour and factor	fog	RGB only	no
Zero	zero	yes	no
Discard	discard	no	yes

Each combiner to be used is preset to a particular state which is some pattern of the three function outputs:

A <op> B
C <op> D
AB + CD

RGB functions using dot products must discard the third result and a combiner RGB function can thus have only the following patterns:

dot-dot-discard
This calculates A.B and C.D and is set up using the *nvparse* mnemonics as:

spare0 = expand(col0) · expand(tex0)
spare1 = expand(col1) · expand(tex1)

dot-mult-discard
This calculates A.B and CD and is set up using the *nvparse* mnemonics as:

spare0 = expand(col0) · expand(tex0)
spare1 = col1 * tex1

mult-dot-discard
This calculates AB and C.D and is set up using the *nvparse* mnemonics as:

spare0 = col0 * tex0
spare1 = expand(col1) · expand(tex1)

mult-mult-mux
This calculates AB, CD and mux(AB,CD) and is set up using the *nvparse* mnemonics as:

discard = col0 * tex0
discard = col1 * tex1
spare1 = mux()

mult-mult-sum
This calculates AB, CD and (AB + CD) and is set up using the *nvparse* mnemonics as:

discard = col0 * tex0
discard = col1 * tex1
spare1 = sum()

The final combiner RGB function is hard-coded to compute:

A * B + (1 − A) * C + D

for any given registers A, B, C and D. In *nvparse*, the RGB final equation can be written in many different ways:

Trivial assignment:

```
out.rgb = tex0;
```

Product:

```
out.rgb = tex0 * final_product;
```

Sum:

```
out.rgb = tex0 + final_product;
```

Linear interpolation (A*B + (1 – A)*C):

```
out.rgb = lerp(fog.a, const0, color_sum);
```

Linear interpolation and sum:

```
out.rgb = lerp(fog.a, const0, color_sum) + const1;
```

Register combiner example: per-pixel diffuse shading using normal maps

This example implements ambient and diffuse shading of a dynamic object using the dot product operator in the register combiners. The dynamic objects are spheres, represented by a single normal map, bouncing around a level (as particles). This representation is shown in Figure 5.20 (also Colour Plate) where the colour represents the normal direction. The spheres are lit by the closest light and rendering takes place using ambient light if no light source is in range. When a sphere becomes sufficiently close to a light, per-pixel shading of the diffuse contribution is invoked.

The spheres are rendered as a single quad billboard and do not spin. The quad must always be aligned with the camera/view vector by definition and so the view vector and the quad plane form a local coordinate system for the sphere. **L** is calculated (and normalised) relative to the system as the sphere moves around. The rendering takes place in a single pass using a single combiner. The following remarkably simple code implements the register combiner settings needed.

```
!!RC1.0
{
    rgb
    {
    spare0 = expand(col0) . expand(tex0);
    }
}
out.rgb = spare0 * const1 + const0;
out.a = tex0;
```

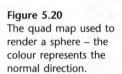

Figure 5.20
The quad map used to render a sphere – the colour represents the normal direction.

The details are:

(1) The first statement sets up the rgb part of the first stage and expands the vector **L** (passed as a colour), expands vector **N** (passed as a texture map) and computes the dot product **L.N**.

(2) The final combiner rgb part is set to add in the ambient contribution (passed in constant 0) and multiply **L.N** by the diffuse colour (passed as constant 1).

(3) The final combiner alpha part is set to the normal map texture alpha. This is used with an alpha test to eliminate the part of the quad that does not contain sphere normals.

Figure 5.21 (also Colour Plate) shows this effect incorporated into a game level. The second image reveals the actual quad by eliminating the alpha test.

To compile a register combiner program we load the program from a .rc file and generate a new OpenGL compiled list. The program is parsed into the compiled list for fast subsequent selection.

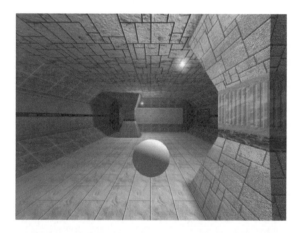

Figure 5.21
The quad map in the game engine lit by a nearby light. The second image with the alpha test eliminated showing the quad background.

```
flyString str=g_flyengine->flysdkdatapath+"programs\\"+file;
flyFile rcfile;
if (rcfile.open(str))
  {
  char *buf=new char[rcfile.len+1];
  memcpy(buf,rcfile.buf,rcfile.len);
  buf[rcfile.len]=0;

  rclist=glGenLists(1);
  glNewList(rclist,GL_COMPILE);
  nvparse(buf);
  glEndList();

  delete buf;
  rcfile.close();
  }
```

The following code from the shader *set_pass* calls the compiled list to set all register combiners' parameters and enables the register combiners' extension:

```
if (rclist)
  {
  glCallList(rclist);
  glEnable(GL_REGISTER_COMBINERS_NV);
  }
```

5.4.4   Texture address programming

Termed texture shaders by NVIDIA, this is the second per-pixel facility exposed to the programmer (Figure 5.18). The functionality of normal texture lookup is enhanced to include the following:

- **Dependent**: This uses the output of a previous texture read to bias the current stage's (u,v) for a 2D fetch, or uses the output of a previous texture read directly as (u,v) for a 2D fetch.
- **Dot product**: This functionality compute a single high-precision floating point scalar from the dot product of the stage's texture coordinate (u,v,w) as a vector and a vector derived from the results of a previous shader stage. This can be used for shading calculations, just as we did with the register combiners. (In fact, being able to implement the same functionality in different stages of the architecture is a confusing aspect of the architecture from the point of view of a programmer.)

5.4.5   Texture address programming – Phong mapping

This method again uses a normal map for an object and assumes a constant **L** and **H**. The steps are as follows:

(1) Use the dot product functionality to compute **N.L**.

(2) Repeat this process to compute **N.H**.

(3) Use the results of the previous two steps as texture coordinates:

$$u = \mathbf{N.L} \quad v = \mathbf{N.H}$$

to index into a texture map, known as a Phong map, that contains pre-calculated values for **N.L** and **N.H**. This may appear something of a redundancy – we compute **N.L** and **N.H** into texture coordinates, then use these to look up **N.L** and **N.H**; but we need to bear in mind that the only functionality we have is to set up and use a texture map to produce a per-pixel result. This point emphasises the difference between this technology and a full pixel program technology.

(4) The exponentiation can be implemented in a register combiner.

Vertex and pixel programming and multi-pass shaders

As we implied in Section 5.4.1, it is convenient to incorporate vertex and pixel programming into a shader structure. The cartoon method, for example, uses two passes to build up the image and each shader pass uses a different vertex program. There are, however, certain implications or contradictions if a multi-pass approach is required. These are:

- We cannot routinely use multi-texture to collapse all types of shader passes, as was suggested in Section 5.1. If two passes use different vertex or pixel programs then they cannot be collapsed.

- If multi-texture is not used then a register combiner program can only use a single texture source, which imposes a limit on the register combiner functionality.

A strategy is to use multi-texture collapse only for static structures, using light maps and a multiplicative blend, and have vertex and pixel programs operating with no multi-texture. Thus each pass now can have associated with it a single texture map, a vertex program and a register combiner program. The single texture restriction could be resolved, but at the cost of no backwards compatibility, by allowing each shader pass to have more than one texture selection as required.

5.5 Dynamic textures

Dynamic textures are texture maps that are generated within each frame. This implies that the generation and transfer into texture memory should be localised within the GPU. There are three ways to do this. The texture image can be written into the framebuffer, prior to this being used to generate the new frame, then transferred into texture memory. This works well on most modern GPUs. There are certain disadvantages in using the framebuffer for this purpose: the resolution is determined by the window resolution and we may require a different pixel format (for example, depth may not be required).

Alternatively, the pbuffer (NVIDIA's pixel buffer) can be used. With a pbuffer the dimensions and bit properties are independent of the current display mode. Using a pbuffer is straight forward and involves rendering to it, then copying the contents to texture or alternatively binding the pbuffer as texture. The texture is then used in the same way as a static texture.

Finally we can render into the backbuffer, then copy from this buffer into the system memory and from there into the texture memory. This is the slowest method but does not require any hardware support and enables alterations to be made in the system memory.

There are many applications of dynamic textures. An obvious one that we will study is dynamic reflection. By this we mean either reflections in a static mirror or a moving object reflecting the environment as it travels through a level. Other applications are dynamic procedural texture generation such as flame and applications that can exploit real-time image processing effects.

Consider now a simple and obvious application of dynamic textures: mirrors and portals. What we mean by a portal in this context is a glass window in a level through which may be viewed activity in an adjacent level. You will recall from Chapter 1 that BSP processing is localised to a single level and thus cannot implement views into neighbouring levels. Portals can be implemented by a variation of the mirror algorithm; mirrors can be considered portals through which we see the reflected scene content.

We can consider three possible portal 'modes'. The first mode is equivalent to a security camera and given a viewpoint and view direction in the level, the portal image is rendered and applied as a texture map to the portal polygon as a whole. Figure 5.22 (also Colour Plate) shows two views of a mode 1 portal.

The portal image remains fixed as the player moves and is generated from a viewpoint positioned on the light immediately behind and above the portal/mirror object. Thus the image consists of the floor of the level together with part of the rear of the portal/mirror object.

The second mode is the mirror mode. Figure 5.23 shows in principle the two steps required to generate mirror reflections. We render the scene from the reflected viewpoint, then render the scene normally, texture mapping the reflected view into the mirror object. When generating the reflected image we must place a clip plane coincident with the mirror plane so that no objects behind the mirror (in between the reflected viewpoint and the mirror) appear in the rendered reflected image. Figure 5.24 (also Colour Plate) shows the portal/mirror object displaying the reflection of the player.

Figure 5.22
Two views of a mode 1 portal image. The portal image remains fixed as the player moves and is generated from a viewpoint positioned on the light immediately behind and above the portal/mirror object. The rear of the portal object appears in the image. Normally the portal target would be in a different room.

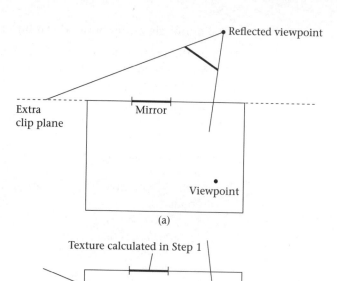

(a)

Figure 5.23
Rendering mirror reflections. (a) Step 1: render scene from reflected viewpoint into a texture map. (b) Step 2: render the scene normally.

Figure 5.24
Portal mode 2 (mirror mode) showing the reflection of the player.

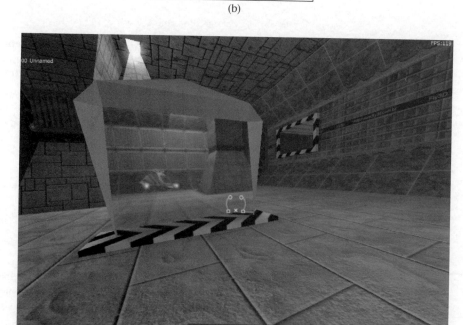

The mirror algorithm breaks down into five steps which are as follows:[3]

(1) Find the camera point 'inside' the mirror. This is done by moving the current viewpoint twice the distance to the mirror in the direction of the mirror plane normal:

```
plane.normal=Z;
   plane.d0=FLY_VECDOT(pos,Z);
   camobj.pos-=2.0f*plane.distance(camobj.pos)*Z;
```

(2) Now find the mirror camera look (Z) direction reflecting the original camera look direction. This involves projecting the camera Z (look dir) into mirror axis (X,Y,Z), inverting the sign of Z and rebuilding the vector from its components.

```
v.x=FLY_VECDOT(X,camobj.Z);
v.y=FLY_VECDOT(Y,camobj.Z);
v.z=FLY_VECDOT(Z,camobj.Z);
v.z=-v.z;
camobj.Z=X*v.x+Y*v.y+Z*v.z;
```

(3) Find the mirror camera X and Y axis by applying the same process to the Y vector and computing X with the cross-product of Y and Z:

```
v.x=FLY_VECDOT(X,camobj.Y);
v.y=FLY_VECDOT(Y,camobj.Y);
v.z=FLY_VECDOT(Z,camobj.Y);
v.z=-v.z;
camobj.Y=X*v.x+Y*v.y+Z*v.z;
camobj.X.cross(camobj.Y,camobj.Z);
```

(4) Project the mirror vertices in screen space to compute the mirror texture coordinates. The rendered image cannot be applied as a whole to the mirror; it is normally larger than that required to fill the mirror. Only when the camera is close to the mirror is the complete rendered image used. Calculating the bounding box of the mirror texture coordinates will give the area in the image requiring rendering and transferring to texture memory.

```
for( i=0;i<4;i++ )
{
  gluProject(
    mirror_verts[i].x,mirror_verts[i].y,mirror_verts[i].z,
    g_flyengine->cam_model_mat,
    g_flyengine->cam_proj_mat,
    g_flyengine->cam_viewport,
    &dx,&dy,&dz);
```

---

3. It is, of course, easy in principle to generate a correct mirror reflection using the basic two-pass algorithm (Figure 5.23). The first pass renders the reflected scene into the frame-buffer. The second pass renders the scene as normal but does not overwrite the mirror area. In each pass we are rendering 3D objects, rather than a mixture of 3D objects and a 2D reflection image. But this requires some masking facility, such as a stencil buffer, for the second pass and currently stencil buffers are not universally available on GPUs.

Figure 5.25
The projection of a subdivided portal/mirror object.

```
    mirror_texcoord[i][0]=(float)dx/g_flyengine->cam_viewport[2];
    mirror_texcoord[i][1]=(float)dy/g_flyengine->cam_viewport[3];
}
```

(5) Draw the mirror polygon with the rendered texture.

Because the image rendered for the mirror is a perspective projection we cannot map it directly into a single quad representing the mirror. Texture interpolation treats the quad as a normal computer graphics object which is to receive a texture map. However, we have to 'force' the texture interpolation into a sampling pattern that corresponds to the non-linearity of the projected portal vertices. Figure 5.25 (also Colour Plate) shows a visualisation of the problem. The inner image is a sheet of glass placed within the level. Within that sheet the green dots are the portal vertices subdivided. Thus we need a portal or mirror subdivided into several vertices. This has the additional benefit that the subdivision can be used to implement a dynamic LOD system for the mirrors and portals. The further away you are from the mirror, the fewer vertices are used.

The third possible portal mode operates like the mirror but instead of calculating the target camera position it can be pre-defined anywhere in the level. This mode means that a virtual camera placed elsewhere in the level takes its orientation from the player orientation. Figure 5.26 (also Colour Plate) shows the idea. In this mode a player is usually allowed to fly into the portal object and be teleported to the portal target.

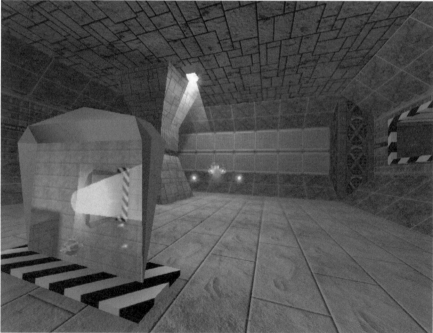

Figure 5.26
In this image the portal target is again the light above and behind the portal/mirror object. The portal camera orientation relative to the portal target is the same as the normal camera relative to the portal. Thus as the player moves around the portal/mirror object different areas of the target are seen. This compares with mode 1 where the view is always the same.

5.6

Effects

No chapter on practical rendering techniques in games would be complete without some mention of 'effects'. These are generally built using a combination of standard rendering methods combined with 'tricks'. In particular, many effects use billboards – two-dimensional texture mapped entities in a variety of different guises. Much of the apparent visual complexity in games derives from such techniques and we complete the chapter by giving typical examples.

5.6.1

The afterburner

Figure 5.27 (also Colour Plate) shows two views of the afterburner effect.

The faces that comprise the effect are drawn from point P_0 (the ship's turbine) to P_n, where n is the number of points generated during the time the afterburner key remained pressed (Figure 5.28). The textures (see below) are applied on the faces, and are wrapped until the afterburner stops, always followed by a fading effect.

Three textures are used to produce the effect. The halo texture (Figure 5.29a) remains at P_0, and is always aligned orthogonally to the observer. The texture is mapped on a face whose colour is set by the ship's variable *spritelight colour*, and the result of this mapping is that the two colours (the face's and the

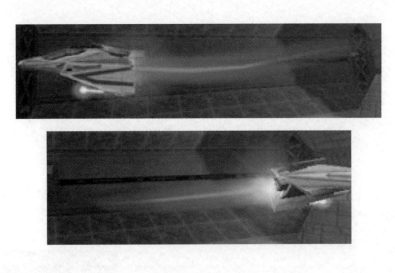

Figure 5.27
The afterburner effect.

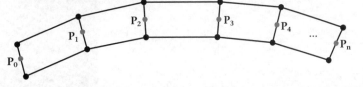

Figure 5.28
Quads are generated along the ship's path for as long as the afterburner key is pressed.

Figure 5.29
Textures used for the
afterburner. (a) Halo.
(b) Alpha channel.
(c) RGB channels.

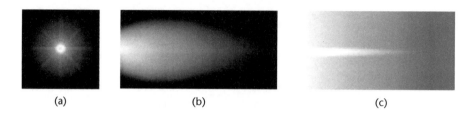

(a)   (b)   (c)

texture's) are multiplied. The texture colour is also modified by the speed of the ship, to further enhance the sense of movement. When the ship stops, the texture becomes almost invisible. The second texture (Figure 5.29(b)) is the alpha channel and the final one (Figure 5.29(c)) is the RGB texture map.

5.6.2

The gravator

This effect consists of concentric spheres (Figure 5.30) that constantly decrease in radius. When they reach 1/3 of their original size, they revert to the initial size. The spheres are texture mapped with a scrolling texture (Figure 5.31 (also Colour Plate)). A particle system emits points to which rays from the centre of the sphere are joined. The ray objects are flat polygons (billboards) which are texture mapped. Figure 5.32 (also Colour Plate) shows the final effect.

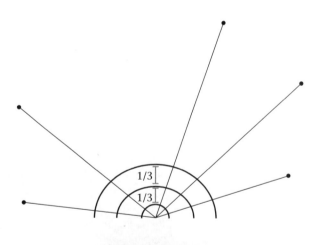

Figure 5.30
Construction of object.

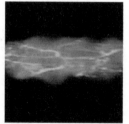

Figure 5.31
The texture map used.

Figure 5.32
The final effect.

5.6.3

The pulsar

The final effect, which uses billboards in combination, can be used as a missile trail or as an entity in its own right. The object shown in Figure 5.33(d) (also Colour Plate) was built from two cross-sectional planes that are maintained orthogonal to each other. To a certain extent this solves the two-dimensional problem that is common to all billboards. First, half of a longitudinal cross-section was painted and reflected to produce a full cross-section (Figure 5.33(a) and (b) (also Colour Plate)). A line of pixels in this image was then rotated to produce the other cross-section (Figure 5.33(c) (also Colour Plate)). This object is blended into the frame buffer, with the fire added to the current frame buffer and with the black background having no effect.

The key to making the object appear three-dimensional is to rotate it about its current position so that the longitudinal cross-section is normal to the plane containing the camera point, the current position of the fire object and the vector joining them. The spatial relationship of the camera point and direction and the current position of the fire and its direction is constantly changing as

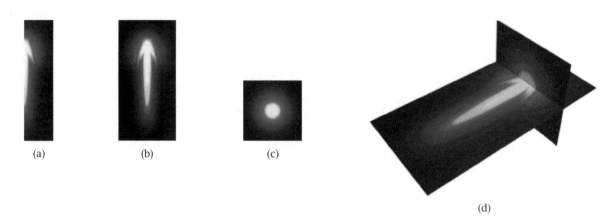

(a)   (b)   (c)

(d)

Figure 5.33
Constructing the object
using quads and textures.

we assume in general that the vessel that fired the weapon can immediately change direction before the fire has struck home.

This orientation of the billboard is calculated as follows. First we evaluate $\mathbf{V}$ (Figure 5.34)

$$\mathbf{V} = \mathbf{C_p} - \mathbf{M_p}$$

the vector containing the current positions of both the camera and the fire object. Then $\mathbf{X}$ is a vector normal to $\mathbf{V}$ and $\mathbf{M_z}$ given as:

$$\mathbf{X} = \mathbf{V} \times \mathbf{M_z}$$

where $\mathbf{M_z}$ is the direction of fire (the missile Z axis).

We embed the longitudinal cross-section in the plane containing $\mathbf{X}$ and $\mathbf{M_z}$. This then ensures that, irrespective of the constantly changing spatial relationship between the fire and the viewer, the viewer always sees the billboard cross-sections oriented exactly as if they were the cross-section of a three-dimensional object representing the fire.

Figure 5.35 (also Colour Plate) shows the pulsar shot object always orthogonal to the observer; Figure 5.36 (also Colour Plate) shows the final effect.

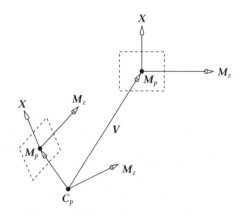

Figure 5.34
Positioning the missile
billboard wrt to $\mathbf{C_p}$ for
two positions $\mathbf{M_p}$.

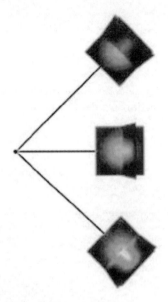

Figure 5.35
The pulsar object positioned orthogonal to the viewer.

Figure 5.36
Pulsar objects in a game level.

Appendix 5.1 Using and experimenting with shaders

The shader editor

The effective use of shaders requires the use of a shader editor and in this section we demonstrate the facilities and structure of such a utility. The main window visualises the loaded shaders either as a two-dimensional map or a mapped object. Each shader file can store several shaders, each of which can have up to eight passes.

Figure A5.1 (also Colour Plate) shows a shader file with two shaders for a *gravator* missile.

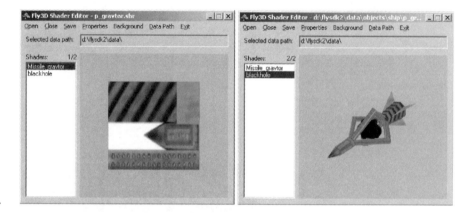

Figure A5.1
Two shaders for a missile.

Selecting the 'Properties' menu will bring a new window with the selected shader passes shown, allowing modifications to be made. Passes can be displayed singly or in any combination by checking each pass checkbox. All possible shader options can be changed in the shader properties window. Figure A5.2 shows the monitor shader and its parameters.

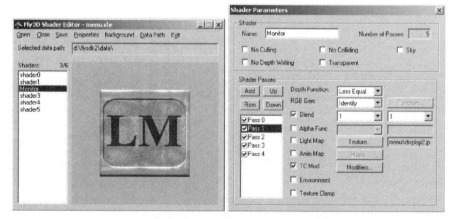

Figure A5.2
The monitor shader.
(a) The monitor shader showing all 5 passes and the render states for pass 1.

(a)

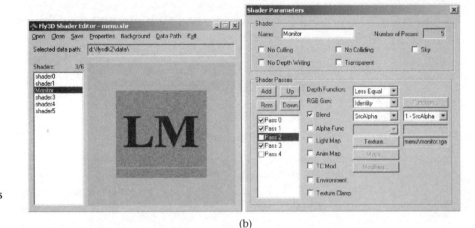

Figure A5.2 *continued*
(b) The monitor shader
showing showing passes
0, 1 and 3.

(b)

In the shader parameters window, you can add/remove passes and change
their order, moving them up or down in the list.

For the monitor red-line pass we need to use the texture coordinate modifier
and this is implemented in a separate window (Figure A5.3). In this example
we need to translate the texture in the vertical direction.

Figure A5.3
Scrolling a texture
vertically.

Periodic functions are edited by another window and used for modulating
colours and to define scaling. Figure A5.4 shows the missile *blue ball* that blinks
twice a second, ranging its opacity from half to full opacity back and forth.
Functions can be sin, triangle, square and saw-tooth. Four floats define the function range based on offset, amplitude, phase and rate.

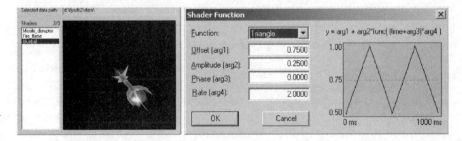

Figure A5.4
Setting the parameters for
periodic functions.

Appendix 5.2 Vertex programming for NVIDIA GeForce3

This appendix gives the detail required to support Section 5.4. Comprehensive documentation on vertex programming is to be found at http://developer.nvidia.com/

The instruction set

The instruction set consists 17 register–register instructions. Each instruction operates on four-component source registers, and generates a result for a single destination register. Instructions that require a scalar input (RCP, RSQ, EXP, LOG), must have a modifier ('.x', '.y', '.z' or '.w') indicating which individual component of the four-component register should be used as the scalar input. Instructions that generate a replicated scalar output compute a single scalar result but copy that result to all four components of the register (unless output register masking is applied).

Instruction	Parameters	Action
NOP		do nothing
MOV	dest, src	move
MUL	dest, src1, src2	component multiply
ADD	dest, src1, src2	component add
MAD	dest, src1, src2, src3	component multiply *src1* by *src2* and add *src3* – into dest
RSQ	dest, src	reciprocal square root of *src* dest.x = dest.y = dest.z = dest.w = 1/sqrt(src)
DP3	dest, src1, src2	3-component dot product
DP4	dest, src1, src2	4-component dot product
DST	dest, src1, src2	calculates an attenuation vector (see main text)
LIT	dest, src	calculates Phong lighting (see main text)
MIN	dest, src1, src2	component-wise min operation dest.x = (src1.x<src2.x) ? src0.x : src1.x etc.
MAX	dest, src1, src2	component-wise max operation dest.x = (src1.x>=src2.x) ? src0.x : src1.x etc.

SLT	dest, src1, src2	dest.x = (src1.x < src2.x) ? 1 : 0 etc.
SGE	dest, src1, src2	dest.x = (src1.x >= src2.x) ? 1 : 0 etc.

EXP	dest, src.w	dest.x = 2 ** (int)src.w
		dest.y = fractional part (src.w)
		dest.z = 2 ** src.w
		dest.w = 1.0

LOGT	dest, src.w dest.	x = exponent((int)src.w)
		dest.y = mantissa(src.w)
		dest.z = log2(src.w)
		dest.w = 1.0

RCP	dest, src.w dest.	x = dest.y = dest.z = dest.w = 1 / src

Vertex attribute registers

There are a total of 16 vertex attribute registers. Each of these registers holds 'per-vertex data' and may be referred to using a numerical or mnemonic name.

Vertex attribute register name	Mnemonic name	Mnemonic meaning
v[0]	v[OPOS]	object position
v[1]	v[WGHT]	vertex weight
v[2]	v[NRML]	vertex normal
v[3]	v[COL0]	primary colour
v[4]	v[COL1]	secondary colour
v[5]	v[FOGC]	fog coordinate
v[6]	--	--
v[7]	--	--
v[8]	v[TEX0]	texture coordinate 0
v[9]	v[TEX1]	texture coordinate 1
v[10]	v[TEX2]	texture coordinate 2
v[11]	v[TEX3]	texture coordinate 3
v[12]	v[TEX4]	texture coordinate 4
v[13]	v[TEX5]	texture coordinate 5
v[14]	v[TEX6]	texture coordinate 6
v[15]	v[TEX7]	texture coordinate 7

Vertex result registers

There are 15 vertex result registers whose output goes to the setup and rasterisation hardware.

Vertex result register name	Component	Description interpretation
o[HPOS]	Homogeneous clip space position	(x,y,z,w)
o[COL0]	Primary colour (front-facing)	(r,g,b,a)
o[COL1]	Secondary colour (front-facing)	(r,g,b,a)
o[BFC0]	Back-facing primary colour	(r,g,b,a)
o[BFC1]	Back-facing secondary colour	(r,g,b,a)
o[FOGC]	Fog coordinate	(f,*,*,*)
o[PSIZ]	Point size	(p,*,*,*)
o[TEX0]	Texture coordinate set 0	(s,t,r,q)
o[TEX1]	Texture coordinate set 1	(s,t,r,q)
o[TEX2]	Texture coordinate set 2	(s,t,r,q)
o[TEX3]	Texture coordinate set 3	(s,t,r,q)
o[TEX4]	Texture coordinate set 4	(s,t,r,q)
o[TEX5]	Texture coordinate set 5	(s,t,r,q)
o[TEX6]	Texture coordinate set 6	(s,t,r,q)
o[TEX7]	Texture coordinate set 7	(s,t,r,q)

Temporary registers

There are a total of 12 temporary registers. Each of these registers is referred to by the name 'Rn' where n is an integer in [0, 11]. These registers are both **read-able** and **write-able**. These registers are initialised to (0,0,0,0) at each vertex program invocation.

Address register

The register A0.x is the 'address register'. This register is a **write-only** register and only allows the 'x' component to be written to (i.e. 'MOV A0.x, R0;'). This register (with the '.x' modifier) may be used as an index to a constant register. This register is initialised to (0,0,0,0) at each vertex program invocation.

Constant registers

The constant registers are used to access constant data, which is stored in the constant memory space. Typically, this is data that does not change on a per-vertex basis. There are 96 constant registers, each of which is referred to by the name 'c[n]' where n is an integer in [0, 95]. Alternatively, data that is stored in the constant memory space may be accessed using the address register (i.e.

'MOV R0, c[A0.x];'). When used in a normal vertex program, these registers are **read-only**. When used in a vertex state program, these registers are both **readable** and **write-able**. Any given instruction may access only a single constant register. However, when reading from a constant register, a single instruction may use the same constant register for multiple source registers (i.e. 'ADD R0, c[5], c[5];').

Appendix 5.3 NVIDIA register combiner operation

This appendix expands Section 5.4.3 and gives more detail on the register combiner operation. A particularly readable resource on register combiners is [KILG99].

The combiner data flow (for two general combiners and a final combiner) is shown in Figure 5.19. Data flows sequentially from the input through General Combiner 0 which becomes the input either for General Combiner 1 (if used) or the Final Combiner.

The input registers containing varying parameters are the interpolated diffuse and specular colours (primary and secondary), filtered texels from enabled texture units and the fog factor (alpha). Two spare registers are used as scratch registers and four constant registers contain the RGB fog colour, two RGBα colour constants and the value zero. The constant registers can be read from, but not written to, by combiner operations. The fog colour and two constants can be initially specified by the application.

Figure A5.5(a) shows the data flow through two general combiners' architecture and emphasises the separate processing of RGB and alpha. Each general combiner can output three RGB values and three alpha values. Thus with two general combiners, up to 12 results/fragment can be generated, including four dot products.

As can be deduced from Figure A5.5(b), the four variables A, B, C and D are assigned to registers and one of eight input mappings is performed. Three output values are computed, scaled and biased, clamped to [–1,1] and written to an output register.

In addition to the operations:

AB + CD
AB
CD
A•B
C•D

the following mux operation is available:

mux(AB,CD) = (Spare0[alpha] $\geq$ $^1/_2$)? AB:CD

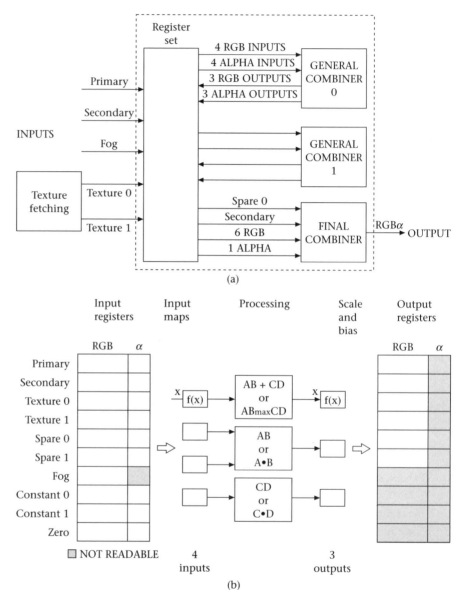

Figure A5.5
NVIDIA's register combiners' architecture. (a) Complete register combiner architecture of two general and one final combiner. (b) General combiner operation for RGB portion of the combiner.

The input assignments, input mapping, processing options, output scale and bias are configured by the application prior to rendering. The final combiner computes a single RGBα output as shown in Figure A5.5(a). The final combiner always computes:

$$AB + (1 − A)C + D$$

6 Geometry processing

6.1 Introduction

Geometry processing is the name we have given to a set of algorithmic and analytical techniques that have emerged in the last decade to deal with very high polygon count objects. Given that the development of shading models began 30 years ago it has been a long time coming and, of course, has been primarily motivated by the demand for the real-time rendering of very complex objects.

Although it may have been assumed that advances in hardware will have successfully dealt with the demands from real-time applications, this has proved not to have been so. There are many reasons for this. For example, it is certainly the case in non-game applications that the increase in model complexity always seems to be ahead of current hardware. CAD models and VR applications consisting of objects made up of millions of triangles are not uncommon. Such complexity is currently greater than that used in the games industry, but it is likely that in the future the games industry will also create a demand for scenes far more complex than currently used. Although triangle rates are nowadays vast, bandwidth and memory problems have persisted. In particular, the transmission of 3D content over the Internet requires carefully considered progressive transmission. A notorious problem in the games industry

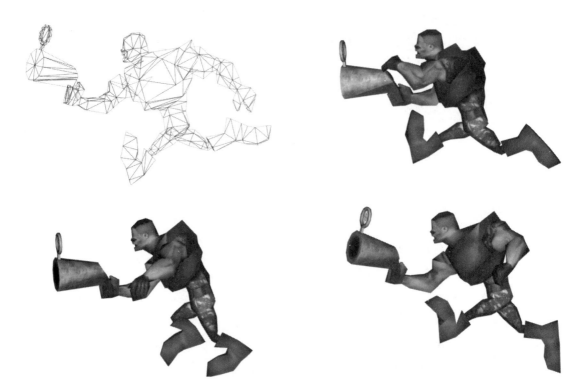

Figure 6.1
An example of manual
animation of a character
(courtesy of Consequência
Animação).

is scalability where the performance difference between new and older platforms
needs to be handled. There may be a vast difference between the triangle rate
of a new and an older system.

Why do we use polygonal representations? Certainly their 'status', in the past,
has been uncertain. Many renderers have been constructed to process bi-cubic
parametric meshes. Perhaps the most famous of these is REYES [COOK87] where
model patches are 'diced' into micropolygons approximately $^{1}/_{2}$ pixel wide. Despite
this and much research in the 1980s into alternative representations, the polygon mesh has survived to become the *de facto* standard in the games industry
and in most general-purpose 3D graphics applications.

In the games industry early processing constraints – now being rapidly
removed – motivated the use of careful artist-constructed models; either single
models or a small LOD set. Here the only way in which visual quality could
be optimised with low polygon count models was to use artists to do this. A
typical example of such an object is shown in Figure 6.1 where creative use of
texture maps and a low polygon count gives an archetypal games character.
The obvious evolution of such characters is both an increase in their complexity
and development of new genres which demand that a number of detailed
characters be rendered in a frame.

The aim of this chapter is to look at the many and varied approaches to the
representation of polygon meshes. Such methods find their main applications

in LOD rendering, progressive transmission and multi-resolution editing of meshes. Another important advantage of multi-resolution representations, which have a simple low resolution base mesh, is that it considerably simplifies kinematic and dynamic computation.[1]

The high variation of the approaches described in this chapter is a consequence of the fact that there is no 'natural' multi-resolution representation for a triangle mesh. We can consider a triangle mesh to consist of two parts: the connectivity which can be considered a planar graph, and the vertex position information. If we consider two arbitrary triangle meshes then we cannot compare them directly because their connectivity graphs are different. This contrasts with information signals, where a regularly sampled function of a single variable can be decomposed into, for example, wavelets. For a surface, unless there is an underlying parameterisation, like the Bézier patch representation, no analytical or 'natural' multi-resolution method is available.

The explosion of research in this field in the 1990s means that there is a large body of published work available. A single chapter cannot therefore be a comprehensive review of this topic. What we have tried to do is to extract the general principles and give a taxonomy of the subject together with representative examples. A potentially important bridge between the piecewise linear nature of the polygon mesh and the techniques of differential geometry is examined at some length and some background information on differential geometry is given at the end of the chapter.

We should point out that nowadays the term polygon mesh means a mesh of triangles. Although triangles are the primitive for which increasingly powerful hardware renderers are designed, they also possess a strong topological advantage. This is that they can represent surfaces of arbitrary shape and topology, unlike, for example, bi-cubic parametric patches whose 'four-sidedness' imposes restrictions.

Finally we note that there are two connected applications of simplification algorithms. First, the obvious LOD application where we generate a spectrum of models such as a progressive mesh and render the one appropriate to current viewing conditions. The second application is a variation of the first and involves the derivation of a low resolution base mesh whose geometry is rendered together with a map (for example, a normal map) which, ignoring the silhouette edge, restores the detail 'lost' in the simplification. This is really a rendering method and is mainly covered in Chapter 4, although certain aspects are described in this chapter.

Before we begin we should examine some general considerations and motivating factors that relate to meshes and their simplification.

---

1. This is precisely the philosophy of skeleton animation (Chapter 7). Here we can consider that we have as two-level representation. The base level is the skeleton and the skin forms the second level which is rendered.

6.2   Motivating factors and definitions

6.2.1   Off-line and real-time phases

Like building scene management and pre-calculated lighting schemes in games, mesh simplification algorithms operate with a (usually) long off-line analysis phase. This phase simplifies the mesh and builds a multi-resolution structure – the best possible according to some criteria. The trade-off in this phase is the quality of the simplification from one level in the mesh M^k to the next coarse level M^{k-1}. If we consider a simple local algorithm that removes one vertex at a time, selecting which vertex to remove by examining the effect of removing every vertex at every level, then this approach will have complexity $O(n!)$ for an original mesh M^n. Such cost may be inconvenient in many applications. The real-time phase, which by definition we expect to operate in real time, means deciding what resolution mesh, M^k, we want to render and then building or extracting this mesh from the multi-resolution representation.

6.2.2   Topology considerations

Algorithms either preserve or modify the topology of a mesh. And applications may allow or disallow topological modifications. The topology of an object is categorised by its *genus* – the number of holes in the object. For example, the genus of objects like spheres and cubes, which have no holes, is zero. The genus of a toroid or doughnut-like object is 1. A cup and a teapot are objects with genus 1.

Topology-preserving algorithms preserve the genus of an object and consequently cannot achieve as high a simplification as topology-modifying algorithms. By definition, topology-modifying algorithms will produce multi-resolution representations which will exhibit popping when they are rendered, as holes disappear or re-emerge. A simple example of a topology-modifying sequence is shown in Figure 6.13.

A triangle mesh is a 2D manifold if its local topology is everywhere equivalent to a disc. That is, if we examine any vertex on the surface we see a connected ring of triangles – the one-ring neighbourhood. A mesh with manifold topology means that exactly two triangles share an edge. In addition, boundary edges must have exactly one face incident on them and the neighbourhood of a vertex must consist of a ring of faces. Manifold meshes with no borders (closed surfaces) conform to the famous Euler equation:

$$F - E + V = 2 - G$$

where
$\quad$ F is the number of faces
$\quad$ E is the number of edges
$\quad$ G is the genus number
$\quad$ V is the number of vertices

The importance of this property is that such meshes are straightforward to simplify and it is the application of algorithms to meshes that preserve this property that we study in this chapter. Simplification algorithms need special heuristics to deal with non-manifold meshes.

Discrete vs continuous simplification

Until recently, most games applications used multiple discrete versions of a mesh with largish jumps in the polygon count from level to level. These would be created off-line and painstakingly optimised by an artist. The application stores all levels and an appropriate one is selected at run time. The two obvious disadvantages of this approach are that the data structure requires more memory than that needed for the high resolution mesh and the creation costs. Because the levels are usually fairly well separated in polygon count, popping will occur unless handled by some device like blending which possesses the obvious disadvantage that two levels have to be rendered simultaneously.

In a continuous[2] structure a single *spectrum* is created during the off-line phase. This is most often encoded as a base mesh M^0 plus the information required to perform a reverse simplification at run time. At run time a level is selected according to some criteria, built and rendered.

The popular example of this model is the progressive mesh or PM (Section 6.5.1) which has the important property that memory requirements for the structure are generally no more than what would be required for the original mesh M^n. Also, in the PM approach a process called *geomorphing* effects a pseudo-continuous transition in the reverse simplification process.

The simplest example of a geomorphing approach is given by considering a fine to coarse transition by collapsing a single edge into a vertex:

$$M^k \rightarrow M^{k-1}$$

An iterative contraction algorithm will have yielded for every edge collapse (Figure 6.2(a)) the vertices $(\mathbf{v}_1, \mathbf{v}_2)$ that form the edge and the position of the new vertex $\mathbf{v}$. Over a few frames we can animate $\mathbf{v}_1$ and $\mathbf{v}_2$ towards $\mathbf{v}$. The edge will then shrink rather than disappearing suddenly. An obvious drawback of this simple example is that we have to render M^k when we actually require M^{k-1}.

A progressive mesh structure could be formulated as a continuous spectrum where the change from M^k to M^{k-1} was a single edge collapse or alternatively a discrete set of LOD models could be built where the inter-level change comprised n edge collapse operations.

---

2. The term continuous needs some qualification. The simplification process removes edges or vertices one at a time, causing the mesh at each level to change shape. Thus the structure is still in a sense discrete.

(6.2.4)

Intra-object resolution variation[3]

If we consider a single level in a spectrum, the polygonal resolution tends to be the same all over the surface. Such models do not function well for large objects that extend over a large distance. The classic example is, of course, terrain when viewing is from a low angle towards the horizon. The terrain object can project onto most if not all of the view surface and we require the level of detail to vary *within* the model according to distance from the viewpoint. Several approaches are possible and most exploit the topological restriction of terrain based on a height field, which means that a regular parameterisation in 2D space exists. Many use quadtrees or triangle bintrees (for example, [DUCH97]) to effect the required adaptive subdivision. Real-time reconstruction then builds an object from the subdivided structure, truncating each tree branch according to a screen space error bound. Such approaches have a 20–30-year history, having been pioneered by the flight simulator industry. Much less work has been done on applying equivalent approaches to general polyhedra (but see Section 6.5.3 for an extension of progressive meshes).

(6.2.5)

Symetry/reversibility

Asymmetric in processing time, many if not most approaches are symmetric in the sense that the reverse of the simplification process results in exact copies of the off-line simplification phase. An important exception class to this is discussed in Section 6.5.3.

(6.2.6)

Local simplification operations

The set of common local simplification operations are shown in Figure 6.2. These are the atomic operations that, in a simplification algorithm, remove a single entity from mesh M^k to make mesh M^{k-1}. Most algorithms operate by repeatedly using just one of these operations, the most popular being the edge collapse. Local simplification operations are categorised as follows:

(a) **Edge collapse**. This simple and popular operation is the foundation of many approaches. It collapses an edge into a single vertex. The main reason for its popularity is its simplicity. Another reason is that a continuous scheme can be incorporated in both the simplification process (to find the best position of the new vertex) and in the reverse simplification where a re-constructed edge can grow continuously in time (geomorphing). Allowing a choice for the position of the new or *unified* vertex means that the

---

3. This is sometimes called view-dependent simplification (a somewhat confusing term since all multi-resolution rendering is controlled by some form of view dependence).

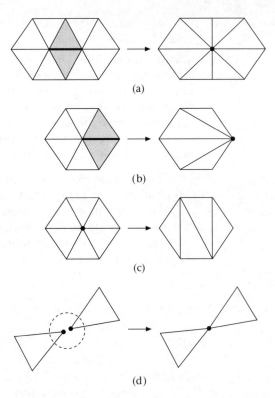

Figure 6.2
Local operations used
in mesh simplification.
(a) Edge collapse.
(b) Half-edge collapse.
(c) Vertex removal and
re-triangulation. (d) Vertex
merge or cluster.

space formed by the collapsed triangles and their neighbours can be re-triangulated in an infinity of ways. Note that the position of the unified vertex does not have to lie on the removed edge.

(b) **Half-edge collapse**. Strictly a subset of the previous operation, we collapse an edge onto one of its vertices (in fact the method is sometimes known as subset placement). In this approach each vertex can be removed in one of six ways on average (corresponding to a mean vertex degree of 6). Thus an advantage of the operation is that the search space for the best option is linear in the degree of the vertex.

(c) **Vertex removal and re-triangulation**. In this operation a vertex is removed and the resulting 'space' is re-triangulated. A disadvantage of the scheme is that the resulting triangles in M^{k-1} tend towards being equilateral. This does not make economical use of the vertices, especially for aggressively simplified meshes. In this operation the search space dimension for an n-triangle neighbourhood is the $(n-2)$th catalan number; that is, 14, 42 and 132 for 6, 7 and 8 neighbours respectively.

Re-triangulation is distinctly non-trivial and a classic problem in computational geometry. However, as we shall see, the generality of re-triangulation enables us to incorporate differential geometry metrics into the computation. These can lead to higher quality simplifications at low vertex counts.

(d) **Vertex cluster**. This is an operation that considers the position of the vertices rather than their connectivity – nearby vertices are merged. The importance of this approach derives from the fact that it can be applied to arbitrary meshes whereas the previous approaches will only work on manifolds. The simplest approach to finding which vertices to merge is to uniformly divide the object bounding box [ROSS93] and consider as candidates for merging those vertices that are located within a single cell.

From the above we can note that methods that use re-triangulation or half-edge collapse result in levels in M^{k-1} whose vertices are subsets of the next finer level M^k and so on. Methods which use edge collapse, on the other hand, allow vertices to move – a vertex in M^{k-1} can travel along the removed edge in M^k. Pure edge collapse preserves topology. If arbitrary vertices, not connected by edges, are allowed to contract, the topology is not preserved.

6.3 Ordering or error criteria

The other vital component of a simplification algorithm, and one that is critical to the quality of the simplification, is a process which determines the order in which mesh entities are removed. Whatever level M^k we wish to render at run time, we want to ensure that that this is the highest quality possible. We do this in general by subjecting each potential vertex operation in M^k to a metric that operates on M^k and the proposed M^{k-1}. The metric is then used to select a particular vertex for removal. Such metrics vary enormously between methods and we will give a few representative approaches. Most of the research effort in simplification algorithms has concentrated on this aspect.

6.3.1 Ordering criteria – similarity of appearance

The most direct way to measure the quality of a simplification operation is to use a standard image metric to evaluate the difference between M^k and M^{k-1}. The rendered image is what is finally viewed by a user and it is the quality of this that we should thus consider.

We can easily define a difference metric between two images as:

$$E = \frac{1}{n^2} \sum_u \sum_v \| M_R^k(u,v) - M_R^{k-1}(u,v) \|^2$$

where

$M_R^k(u,v)$ and $M_R^{k-1}(u,v)$ are the rendered versions of M^k and M^{k-1}

n is the number of pixels

This straightforward approach conceals a number of difficulties. For the method to be effective we need to evaluate E over a representative sample of viewpoints, but this will make for an extremely expensive off-line phase.

Lindstrom and Turk [LIND00] take this approach in a recent report. They found that the method yielded simplifications of high geometric fidelity and state that the advantages of the method over geometric approaches are attention to silhouette edge quality, extreme simplification of hidden portions of a model, attention to shading interpolation effect and simplification that is sensitive to the texture content. They use an edge collapse scheme wherein edge collapses are ordered according to the smallest visual difference. The above expression is summated over a set of sample viewpoints. These are distributed uniformly over a sphere surrounding the test object and correspond to the vertices of a regular dodecahedron (resulting in 20 images). The sphere is double the radius of the minimum bounding sphere of the test object.

The authors address the image generation cost by setting up a unique scheme that makes incremental changes to the existing rendered image to produce the next iteration. To do this for a candidate edge collapse the new triangles, T^{k-1}, in the one-ring neighbourhood of the new vertex need to be rendered and replace the existing rendered triangles T^k in the same neighbourhood. This process then has to be repeated for all sample views. But since on average $|T^k| = 10$, an algorithm that rendered the new triangles only would be ideal. Lindstrom and Turk refer to this as an *unrendering* problem, where the set T^k is 'unrendered' (to reveal any parts of the surface that they were previously obscuring) before rendering T^{k-1}. They accomplish this by exploiting the screen space locality of the edge collapse and maintaining a triangle bucket for each pixel row and column. This then enables the following algorithm that replaces the set T^k with T^{k-1}:

(1) Clear the rectangular region R in screen space in which these two sets are contained.

(2) Render all triangles in R (both visible and occluded) *except* those to be unrendered.

(3) Render the set T^{k-1}.

Ordering criteria – local volume preservation

A direct geometric approach for vertex removal and re-triangulation measures the difference in volume between M^k and M^{k-1}. That is the local volume change for a vertex removal candidate which is the difference in volume of the meshes over the one-ring neighbourhood of the vertex which is a candidate for removal (Figure 6.3). From the figure it can be seen that the volume change E_i is the polyhedron formed by the upper surface with its peak at the vertex i and the lower surface formed by the re-triangulation. In this particular example we can consider E_i to be made up of four tetrahedra, making the volume of the polyhedron:

Figure 6.3
Example of error
polyhedron E_i. (a) Focus
vertex neighbourhood.
(b) Vertex neighbourhood
re-triangulation.
(c) Resulting error
polyhedron.

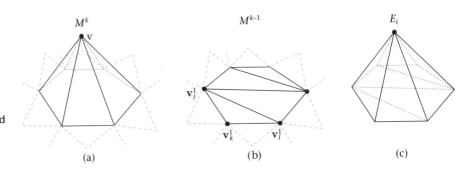

(a)   (b)   (c)

$$\sum_{i=1}^{4} \frac{1}{6} \begin{vmatrix} \mathbf{v}_x & \mathbf{v}_y & \mathbf{v}_z & 1 \\ \mathbf{v}_{jx}^i & \mathbf{v}_{jy}^i & \mathbf{v}_{jz}^i & 1 \\ \mathbf{v}_{kx}^i & \mathbf{v}_{ky}^i & \mathbf{v}_{kz}^i & 1 \\ \mathbf{v}_{lx}^i & \mathbf{v}_{ly}^i & \mathbf{v}_{lz}^i & 1 \end{vmatrix}$$

The same approach can be used for the edge removal method. Here a new vertex is created by collapsing an edge and Lindstrom and Turk [LIND00] describe an analytical approach that finds the best position for that vertex. They note that in the case of an edge collapse the tetrahedral volumes 'swept out' by the change can be categorised positive or negative. For example, in Figure 6.4 the new vertex $\mathbf{v}$ has moved below the plane containing the new triangle and the tetrahedron is categorised as negative. To make the volume change zero the sum of the signed tetrahedral volume contributions can be equated to zero. This results in a linear equality that constrains the solution for the position of $\mathbf{v}$ to

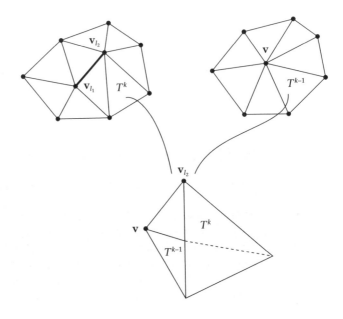

Figure 6.4
Using an error volume for
edge removal.

be a plane. Further optimisation within this plane is achieved by minimising the unsigned volume of each tetrahedron.

Ordering criteria – quadric error metric

Originally developed for a vertex clustering algorithm, the quadric error metric (QEM) [GARL97] can also be used with other simplification operators such as edge collapse. The error introduced by a candidate vertex-merge operation is calculated by summing the QEMs of the vertices being merged and that sum becomes the QEM of the new vertex.

Garland motivates his QEM with an insightful 2D analogy which we describe here. Figure 6.5(a) shows an edge $(\mathbf{v}_i,\mathbf{v}_j)$ which is a candidate for collapse. We require the optimum position for the resulting single vertex. To do this, lines are associated with each vertex:

$$L_i = \{A,C\}$$
$$L_j = \{B,C\}$$

These lines are the edges incident on the vertices i and j. The edge is collapsed and we define a new vertex $\mathbf{v}$. The lines associated with the new vertex is the set

$$L = L_i \cup L_j = \{A,B,C\}$$

The position of the vertex $\mathbf{v}$ is chosen to minimise the sum of the squared distances to all the lines in L. This is as shown in the figure, at the centre of the triangle formed by A, B and C. Figure 6.5(b) shows a series of concentric ellipses surrounding $\mathbf{v}$. These represent the iso-contours:

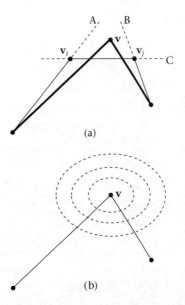

(a)

(b)

Figure 6.5
2D analogue of the QEM. The ellipses are iso-cost contours for the position of **v** (after an illustration in [GARL99]).

$$E(\mathbf{v}) = \varepsilon$$

In 3D we associate vertices with planes and the error iso-contours are quadrics, hence the name. Each vertex is now assigned a set of planes formed by the faces incident at the vertex.

We will now develop the QEM using a treatment given in [HOPP99]. The error metric between a point $\mathbf{p}$ and a face is defined to be the squared distance between the point and the plane containing the face. Call this $Q^f(\mathbf{v})$. We then define an error metric between a point and a vertex $\mathbf{v}$ as:

$$Q^{v}(\mathbf{v}) = \sum_{\substack{\text{faces} \\ \text{that meet at } \mathbf{v}}} \text{area}(f) Q^f(\mathbf{v})$$

That is, the weighted sum of the metrics associated with each of the faces that meet at the vertex $\mathbf{v}$. After an edge collapse:

$$(\mathbf{v}_1, \mathbf{v}_2) \rightarrow \mathbf{v}$$

vertex $\mathbf{v}$ is assigned the position which minimises:

$$\mathbf{Q}^{v}(\mathbf{v}) = Q^{v_1}(\mathbf{v}) + Q^{v_2}(\mathbf{v})$$

That is, for a number of candidate edges, the edge which has the lowest $Q^v(\mathbf{p})$ is chosen.

We now define $Q^f(\mathbf{v})$ for a face with vertices $\mathbf{v}_1, \mathbf{v}_2, \mathbf{v}_3$.

$$Q^f(\mathbf{p}) = (\mathbf{n}^T\mathbf{p} + d)^2$$

where

$\mathbf{n}$ is the face normal $\dfrac{(\mathbf{v}_2 - \mathbf{v}_1) \times (\mathbf{v}_3 - \mathbf{v}_1)}{\|(\mathbf{v}_2 - \mathbf{v}_1) \times (\mathbf{v}_3 - \mathbf{v}_1)\|}$

$d = -\mathbf{n}^T\mathbf{v}_1$

Thus

$$Q^f(\mathbf{v}) = \mathbf{v}^T(\mathbf{n}\mathbf{n}^T)\mathbf{v} + 2d\mathbf{n}^T\mathbf{v} + d^2$$
$$= \mathbf{v}^T(\mathbf{A})\mathbf{v} + 2\mathbf{b}^T\mathbf{v} + c$$

is a quadratic, where:

$\mathbf{A}$ is a symteric 3×3 matrix
$\mathbf{b}$ is a column vector
c is a scalar

Thus the best vertex $\mathbf{v}$ and its position $\mathbf{v}$ is found from

$$2\mathbf{A}\mathbf{v} + 2\mathbf{b} = 0$$

by solving

$$\mathbf{A}\mathbf{v}_{\text{min}} = -\mathbf{b}$$

One of the main advantages of the QEM is its efficiency. There is exactly one quadric associated with each vertex and this requires 10 components (6 for $\mathbf{A}$, 3 for $\mathbf{b}$ and 1 for c).

Ordering criteria – simplification envelopes

In work reported in 1996 Cohen *et al.* [COHE96] construct *simplification envelopes* between which the original surface is contained. Similar to offset surfaces, these are constructed to deviate by no more than a pre-specified tolerance ε above and below the original surface. The error criterion during simplification then reduces to checking if the modified triangles intersect either of the surfaces. A simplified mesh is then guaranteed to be within ε of the original surface. This approach is topology preserving and guarantees a surface which nowhere deviates from the user-supplied tolerance.

The off-line phase consists of the construction of the simplification envelopes followed by the simplification process. Construction of the envelopes is in principle straightforward. We simply need to move each vertex in a positive and negative direction along the vertex normal (Figure 6.6(a)). This construction for a single triangle is called the fundamental prism. The only problem is that self-intersection can occur and this must be prevented. Self-intersection can occur for the positive offset surface in concave areas of the original surface and in convex areas for the negative surface. Cohen *et al.* prevent this happening by allowing ε to decrease where necessary (Figure 6.6(b)). A condition to prevent self-intersection is that a vertex cannot be displaced outside the Voronoi region of the edge to which it belongs. Remarking that Voronoi region determination in 3D is extremely expensive, Cohen *et al.* adopt an iterative solution, starting with an envelope equal to the original surface,

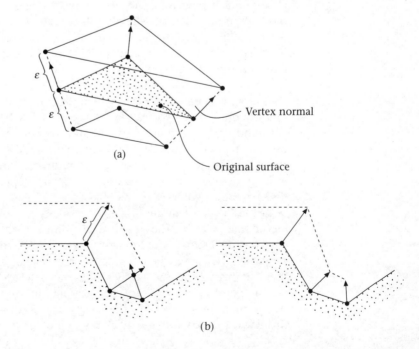

Figure 6.6
Simplification envelopes.
(a) Simplification
envelopes. (b) Self-
intersection; reducing ε to
prevent self-intersection.

and, for each step, moving envelope vertices some fraction of ε and testing to see if adjacent triangles intersect.

During the simplification phase a new candidate triangle is tested against the envelope surfaces. Since the triangle vertices are a subset of the original surface vertices, the vertices must lie within the two envelopes and the validity test for the candidate becomes an intersection test with the two envelopes. These tests can be made efficient by embedding the triangles in a spatial partitioning scheme.

6.4 Simplification and attributes

Many, if not most, object models possess vertex attributes and a parameterisation. The most common attribute is colour derived from a texture map via vertex (u,v) coordinates. In games design this texture map parameterisation is usually set up interactively by an artist. In this section we consider what happens to this parameterisation as the model is simplified. In general, if we are constructing a spectrum of models then we need the texture map coordinates for each of these. In the event that we move the vertices in a simplification process we need to calculate new texture map coordinates.

As we cover in Section 6.5.1, another important approach to simplification is to use a base mesh in conjunction with the detail map that represents the information in M^n. In this case we would want to terminate the simplification at some level where the silhouette edge problem was not too severe. If we use this approach then we need only derive a single parameterisation of the base mesh. Cignoni *et al.* [CIGN98] do this directly by sampling from the base mesh. After simplification, the faces of the base mesh are regularly sampled, at some pre-determined resolution across each face. For each sample point the nearest point on the original surface is found and its attribute (texture, normal or displacement map value) determined.

A more elaborate approach, which deals with attributes in the context of a multi-resolution representation, is taken in [COHE98]. Here the application is to find new texture map coordinates for a normal map that is going to be used to represent surface detail when the model is rendered. Distortion in the mapping at various levels in the multi-resolution structure may thus be more noticeable than distortions in a colour mapping (since the normal map represents the geometry of the object).

Just as the downsampling of the mesh proceeds according to an error metric that measures the surface deviation between M^k and M^{k-1}, so should the deviation in texture coordinates also be minimised. We may consider that a simple edge collapse where the new vertex is taken as the midpoint of the edge that has been collapsed implies that the new texture coordinate should be the midpoint of the coordinates corresponding to the collapsed edge vertices (Figure 6.7). In other words, the mesh simplification geometry pre-determines the new texture coordinate calculation but other considerations come into play.

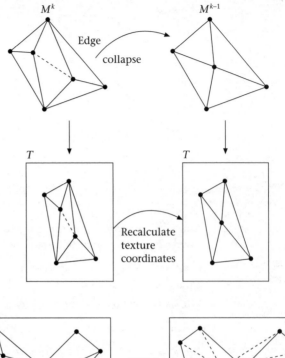

Figure 6.7
Calculating new texture coordinates after an edge collapse.

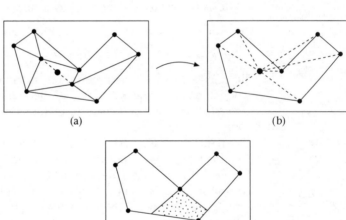

Figure 6.8
Invalid texture coordinates and an allowable region. (a) New texture coordinates. (b) Showing the invalidity of new coordinates. (c) Convex kernel of M^k.

Consider Figure 6.8 which shows a texture space midpoint as an invalid choice for a new vertex. This is because the new triangles in M^{k-1} (dotted lines) will receive texture that is outside the boundary of their parents in M^k. Also, two triangles are now overlapping in texture space. It can be shown that the new texture coordinate must lie in the shaded region (Figure 6.8(c)) formed by the convex kernel of M^k to ensure that the triangles in M^{k-1} receive exactly the same region in texture space as the corresponding simplified region in M^k.

Thus, given that a new texture coordinate must satisfy constraints, we need a texture deviation measure that enables the best choice within a constraint

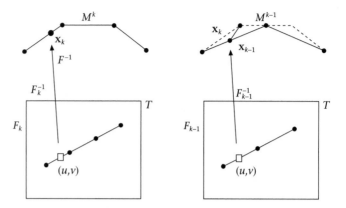

Figure 6.9
Measuring texture deviation.

region. This is done by comparing the point $\mathbf{x}_k$ in mesh M^k with the point $\mathbf{x}_{k-1}$ that shares the same texture coordinate (u,v) (Figure 6.9). That is:

$$C(\mathbf{x}_k) = F_k^{-1}(T(u,v)) \qquad \text{and} \quad C(\mathbf{x}_{k-1}) = F_{k-1}^{-1}(T(u,v))$$

where

C is the value of T received by $\mathbf{x}$ under mapping F_k

Then the distance between these points is given by

$$D(u,v) = |F_k^{-1}(T(u,v)) - F_{k-1}^{-1}(T(u,v))|$$

This is effectively a surface deviation metric that uses the texture parameterisation and is just a quantification of the well-established manual process where an artist distorts a world space to texture space mapping by pulling a 2D grid around in texture space.

Garland and Heckbert [GARL98] extend the QEM to solve this problem. They treat each vertex position with its corresponding RGB texture value as a single point in 6D space and formulate an extended version of the QEM. Their motivation for this is, first, that there is a correlation between attributes; and second, the position of the unified vertex in the QEM method does not have to lie on the removed edge (so attributes cannot necessarily be linearly interpolated). Given that texture is linearly interpolated over a triangle, the three six-dimensional triangle vertices lie in a 2D plane in 6D space. The extended QEM measures the squared distance from a point to this plane.

6.4.1 Simplification and game texture

Texture deviation can be catastrophic in games systems where *composite* texture maps are routinely used for objects. To ease the hardware texture management problem different maps are composited into a single map. Any deviation in the simplification algorithm can then cause a vertex to receive coordinates relating to a completely different texture map rather than a distortion of the same map.

Another problem with composite texture maps relates to texture seams. For normal rendering vertices that lie on a texture seam it is conventional to 'split' these and treat them as separate vertices; each one associated with a different face and texture. If such duplication is input to a simplification algorithm they may be collapsed differently and open up a hole in the mesh. The best solution is to mark edges that belong to texture seams and disallow their collapse.

6.4.2 Simplification and skinned models

In the above, our discussion has centred on standard polygonal objects. In modern games, however, a common complex object is a game character whose vertices are associated with one or more skeleton bones via a weighting factor. The neutral pose of such a character, conveniently used for modelling and texture mapping, may not be the best representation for input to a simplification algorithm because it will not be typical of the shapes adopted by the character when it receives its animation during the game execution. A better approach is to use a number of sample poses from an animation sequence and compute average values for edge collapse metrics. Another problem arises when considering vertices bound to more than one bone. When an edge is collapsed, whose vertices are tied to different bones, a new association needs calculating for the new vertex.

6.4.3 Algorithm frameworks

The simplest possible framework that can be employed in a simplification algorithm is a greedy algorithm. For any level M^k we apply an error criterion E_i (Section 6.3) to evaluate the cost of a local simplification operation and construct a priority queue ordered by decreasing error. For re-triangulation or hole filling, this process might be to generate, and evaluate the effect of, all possible combinations of triangles. Removing the vertex from the top of the list gives us M^{k-1} and overall ensures that we remove those entities, which according to the error metric, result in the least difference, first. For the next iteration we need to re-calculate E_i for all vertices whose incident triangles have changed as a result of the operation and update their position in the queue.

The effect of removing a vertex can be measured against the neighbourhood or against the geometry of the original mesh (categorised as local or global algorithms respectively). Global approaches can be used in conjunction with guaranteed error bounds.

6.4.4 Re-triangulation for vertex removal algorithms

An algorithm based on a simple edge collapse operator does not give us the freedom to re-triangulate if the new vertex is to lie on the removed edge. Vertex

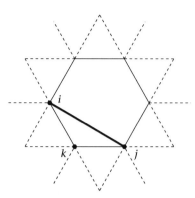

Figure 6.10
Edge $\{i,j\}$ is defined as an
ear edge.

removal algorithms, on the other hand, present the problem of how to re-triangulate the hole caused by the removed vertex. We will look at two common techniques, the first operating in three-dimensional space, the second in two-dimensional space.

Minimum weight triangulation in 3D

Re-triangulation can be carried out either in two dimensions by projecting vertices onto a plane, or in three dimensions. Although two-dimensional methods are popular we can easily avoid certain 3D to 2D projection constraints and work directly in three dimensions providing we can determine that a proposed triangle does not result in a topology change. This validity check can be done in linear time by using the notion of consistent triangle orientation. We try to find a point which is in each of the half spaces defined by the triangles and their normals, before and after the re-triangulation. If such a point exists there has been no topology change.

A common algorithm for re-triangulation is the Euclidean minimum weight triangulation or MWT [BARE94]. A fast but approximate version of this proceeds as follows. We first define an *ear* edge $e = \{i,j\}$ as any edge that partitions an n-vertex polygon along edge e into a triangle $\{i,j,k\}$ and a $n{-}1$ vertex polygon (Figure 6.10); in other words, an edge spanning consecutive vertex triples. Each ear edge e is assigned a weight $w(e)$ which is an objective function to be minimised over all for the given polygon. For example, w can be set as:

$$w(e) = |\mathbf{v}_i - \mathbf{v}_j|$$

and the algorithm then reduces to an approximation of the MWT. The algorithm can be structured as a simple greedy approach which incrementally adds the current ear edge of lowest weight $w(e)$ to derive a polygon with one fewer vertices until all that remains of the re-triangulation working area is a single triangle. This algorithm is adapted in the case study in Section 6.5.2 to admit the use of differential geometry.

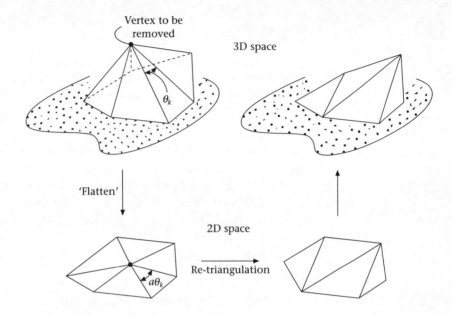

Figure 6.11
Map the star of the vertex to be removed into a plane using the conformal mapping z^a. Remove the vertex and re-triangulate in the plane.

Re-triangulation in 2D

This approach is used in the simplification phase of the MAPS algorithm in Section 6.5.3. Its motivation is that if the problem can be mapped into 2-space then the re-triangulation is straightforward and a number of established algorithms (for example, a Delaunay triangulation) can be used. A simple example of the process is shown in Figure 6.11.

Consider the one-ring neighbourhood or star of a vertex being removed. We wish to 'flatten' this structure into a plane. To do this we use the conformal mapping $w = z^a$ described in Appendix 6.1. We consider each of the vertices to which the vertex to be removed connects, which then define a set of edges. These define edges in the z plane as:

$$r_k \exp(i\theta_k)$$

where

r_k is the length of each edge
θ_k is the angle between two consecutive edges in the ring

The required mapping is then given by:

$$r_k^a \exp(i\theta_k a)$$

where

$$a = \frac{2\pi}{\sum \theta_k}$$

Note that, as shown in Figure 6.11, θ_k are the angles between consecutive edges in 3-space.

Case studies

In this section we will study three complete simplification algorithms or approaches. We have chosen these to illustrate how the various ingredients of a simplification algorithm fit together and to introduce certain potentially useful differential geometry definitions:

(1) Progressive meshes – this well-established method is based on edge collapse and has been enhanced for view-dependent selective refinement.

(2) Using differential geometry – in this method we introduce the use of differential geometry parameters to assist in the re-triangulation phase of a simplification approach based on vertex removal.

(3) Re-meshing – this is a recent approach which falls into the general category of simplification algorithms. It uses subdivision of the base mesh to generate a mesh to render.

Case Study 1 – Progressive mesh technology

We now look at a typical application that uses the above techniques. Perhaps the most popular[4] edge collapse algorithm is Hoppe's progressive meshes (Figure 6.12). Hoppe [HOPP96] realised that to store all the information in an analysis involving edge collapses it was better to store the base mesh M^0 and reconstruction information, rather than the original mesh M^n together with the analysis information. Storing M^n and edge collapse information results in a structure much larger than the original mesh; storing the base mesh M^0 and reconstruction information results in a structure (generally) smaller than M^n. The technique relies on the edge collapse being invertible, and the reverse of an edge collapse operation is a vertex split. The reconstruction information required between levels is thus:

• the vertex being split;

• the positions of the new vertices;

• the triangles to introduce into the mesh.

An important aspect of the progressive mesh idea is that the overall approach is not restricted necessarily to edge collapse/vertex split operations, but it can be used as a structure for any analysis/synthesis method whose local operation is invertible.

The simplification algorithm Hoppe employed encapsulates mesh fidelity as an energy function to be minimised. A mesh M is optimised with respect to a set of points X which are the vertices of the mesh M^n together (optionally) with points randomly sampled from its faces. (Although this is a lengthy process it is,

---

4. Progressive mesh technology is available in the D3DX library of DirectX 8.0

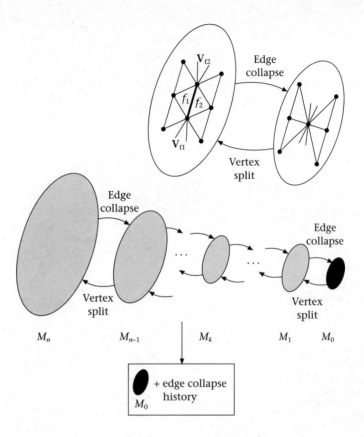

Figure 6.12
A schematic representation of Hoppe's progressive mesh method.

of course, executed once only as an off-line pre-process.) The energy function to be minimised is:

$$E(M) = E_{\text{dist}}(M) + E_{\text{spring}}(M)$$

where

$$E_{\text{dist}} = \sum_i d^2(x_i, M)$$

is the sum of the squared distances from the points x to the mesh – when a vertex is removed this term will tend to increase

$$E_{\text{spring}}(M) = \sum \kappa \| \mathbf{v}_j - \mathbf{v}_k \|^2$$

is a spring energy term that assists the optimisation. It is equivalent to placing on each edge a spring of rest length zero and spring constant κ

Hoppe orders the optimisation by placing all (legal) edge collapse transformations into a priority queue, where the priority of each transformation is its estimated energy cost ΔE. In each iteration, the transformation at the front of the queue (lowest ΔE) is performed and the priorities of the edges in the neighbourhood of this transformation are recomputed. An edge collapse transformation

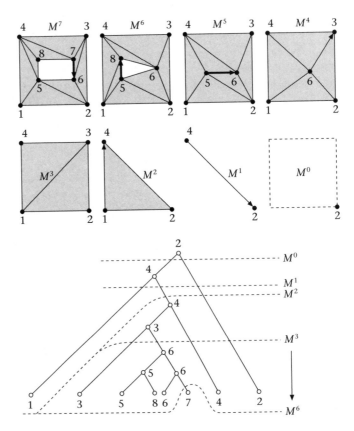

Figure 6.13
A simple (topology modifying) example and its vertex tree (after an illustration by Garland [GARL99]).

is only legal if it does not change the topology of the mesh. For example, if V_{f1} and V_{f2} are boundary vertices, the edge $\{V_{f1}, V_{f2}\}$ must be a boundary edge – it cannot be an internal edge connecting two boundary points.

In a later work [HOPP97] Hoppe describes how to extend progressive meshes so that the polygonal resolution can vary according to view-dependent criteria. He terms this *selective refinement*. Like many terrain algorithms, the common approach is to descend a tree building a subtree that is determined by some screen space criterion. The tree used with polygonal models is called a **merge tree** or **vertex hierarchy**.

The tree (which unless M^0 is a single vertex is in fact a forest) is built bottom up at the same time as an iterative contraction algorithm of a progressive mesh method using say edge collapses. Leaves of the tree represent M^n and the roots M^0. Because the edge collapse operation converts two vertices into a single one, the tree is binary. A vertex tree for a simple example is shown in Figure 6.13.

Normally the reconstruction phase of a progressive mesh reconstructs models that are identical to the models in the analysis phase. Also, the models appear in exact reverse order to the order in the analysis phase. We can visualise the process of tree growing by considering a single instant in the simplification process. At this stage the vertex tree will have grown to form a subset of the final

Figure 6.14
Notation for the pre-
conditions for a vertex
split and edge collapse
operation in Hoppe's
selective refinement of
progressive meshes.

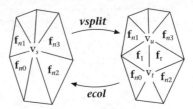

tree. As the simplification process continues, a 'wave front' of edge collapses moves down from the root to grow the final tree. If we consider the process in reverse, we have the vertex tree shrinking with the wave front moving in the opposite direction. The reverse process is generated by using the history of the simplification process – the conventional progressive mesh usage.

The idea of selective refinement is that we do not have to reverse the generation process – we can generate any valid subset of the vertex tree to correspond to some screen dependent criteria, say. We can thus generate a model whose polygonal resolution overall varies to meet the criteria. The model generated will not, in general, correspond to any mesh generated in the simplification processes and the runtime phase has to consider performing edge collapse as well as vertex splits to meet the criteria.

Prior to rendering a frame the algorithm examines all active vertices and for each vertex either it splits it, collapses it or leaves it alone. An active vertex is one that exists in the mesh just rendered. Because both vertex splits and edge collapse are being performed in an order which in general is different to the simplification process order, the relevant dependencies in the hierarchy must exist for either operation to be possible. Hoppe represents these as pre-conditions (Figure 6.14):

A vertex split is legal iff:

(1) v_s is an active vertex;

(2) the faces $\{f_{n0}, f_{n1}, f_{n2}, f_{n3}\}$ are active faces.

An edge collapse is legal iff:

(1) v_t and v_u are both active vertices;

(2) the faces adjacent to f_l and f_r, $\{f_{n0}, f_{n1}, f_{n2}, f_{n3}\}$, are active faces.

Hoppe uses three factors as the criteria which determine whether a node should be refined. The effect of these is shown in Figure 6.15.

- **View frustum** Here the motivation is to coarsen the mesh outside the view frustum, thus reducing the graphics load. (In Chapter 2 we introduce an efficient method for view frustum culling for dynamic objects but this, of course, retains the objects' polygonal resolution outside the frustum for objects that intersect the view frustum.) In this approach a bounding sphere, centred on the current vertex and with a radius that encapsulates the region of all its descendants, is used. If the bounding sphere is completely outside the view frustum the vertex is not refined.

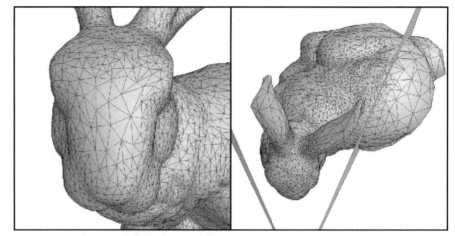

From Hoppe, H., View-dependent refinement of progressive meshes, *Proceedings SIGGRAPH 97*, pp. 189–98 © 1997, ACM, Inc. Reprinted by permission.

Figure 6.15
Hoppe's view-dependent refinement. The image on the left is the rendered view and that on the right is a 'view of the view' showing the position of the view frustum

- **Surface orientation**   A similar approach is applied to back-facing surfaces, again to reduce the graphics load. This time a bounding cone of surface normal (on the Gaussian map) is constructed for a vertex and its dependants. This can be used in conjunction with the viewpoint to determine if the vertex lies in a back-facing region.

- **Screen space geometric error**   This is a screen space error metric, variations of which are common amongst LOD criteria. In this case the mesh is refined until the distance between the refined mesh and the original mesh is less than a screen space tolerance.

6.5.2   Case Study 2 – Using differential geometry

Previous sections have described techniques that operate on the geometry of a triangular mesh expressed as vertex positions and connectivity. However, we should remember that a triangular mesh is usually an approximation to a smooth surface, or at least one which is locally smooth. This concept leads us to examine the utility of basic differential geometry approaches. To use differential geometry we need a parameterisation.

Now, given that triangular meshes do not possess a parameterisation, the question is: can we construct one? There are many different ways of doing this – each of which will produce different results. We could, of course, interpolate and convert a mesh into a net of bi-cubic parametric patches by using a surface interpolation procedure. That is, we fit such a surface through the vertex points. In principle, a straightforward approach to surface interpolation is a difficult problem. (One approach – scattered data interpolation – is given in Chapter 8.) Before we examine parameterisation schemes we need to ask what

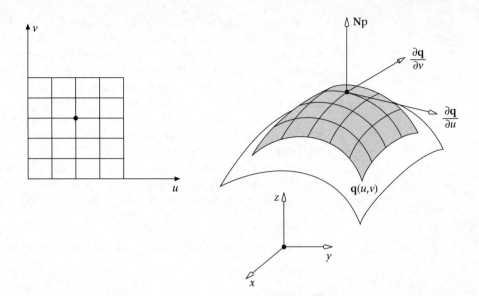

Figure 6.16
A surface parameterised in (u,v).

the utility of such an approach is. The general answer is that it enables us to use mathematical tools and operations that would otherwise be impossible or difficult to apply to a triangular mesh.

Unless we have access to a texture map parameterisation (as we use in Section 6.5.3), our representation is without a parametrisation. The only common natural parameterisation of an object in computer graphics is the bi-cubic parametric representation which is defined as a mesh of patches, where a single patch – Bézier, for example, is defined as:

$$\mathbf{q}(u,v) = \sum_{i=0}^{3} \sum_{j=0}^{3} \mathbf{p}_{ij} B_i(u) B_j(v)$$

where

$\mathbf{q}$ is a point on the surface of the object
$\mathbf{p}_{ij}$ are a set of 16 fixed points known as control points
B are the Bézier basis functions

A surface parameterisation means that we can inject a (u,v) value into the equation which returns an (x,y,z) value for the position on the surface specified by the parameters (u,v) (Figure 6.16). Such a parameterisation solves many problems in computer graphics. For example, texture mapping is very easy. Also, we can use differential geometry on the surface – we can calculate derivatives at any point (u,v).

A quadric neighbourhood parameterisation for differential geometry operators

(This section needs to be read in conjunction with Appendix 6.1, Mathematical background – basic differential geometry, at the end of the chapter.)

In Section 6.3.2 we saw how we could use a simple local volume preservation error criterion in a mesh simplification procedure. In this section we look at how we can construct a quadratic surface over the neighbourhood. Approximating triangular meshes in this manner is well established. The approach is yet another variation on interpolation methods and makes the usual assumption that the vertices of the piecewise linear surface are samples of the 'real' surface. In which case we can fit a quadric surface through these points and the result will better approximate the real surface. We then have access to differential geometry and can calculate such metrics as surface curvature for each neighbourhood vertex $\mathbf{v}$. Access to such information can lead to more intelligent re-triangulation strategies, as we shall see.

We define a bi-quadratic polynomial as:

$$f(u,v) = \lambda_1 u^2 + \lambda_2 v^2 + \lambda_3 u + \lambda_4 uv + \lambda_5 v \tag{6.1}$$

We compare this equation with a second-order Taylor series:

$$f(u,v) = f_u(0,0,)u + f_v(0,0)v + \tfrac{1}{2}(f_{uu}(0,0)u^2 + 2f_{uv}(0,0)uv + f_{vv}(0,0)v^2)$$

to derive:

$$\lambda_1 = 2f_{uu}(0,0)$$
$$\lambda_2 = 2f_{vv}(0,0)$$
$$\lambda_3 = f_u(0,0)$$
$$\lambda_4 = f_{uv}(0,0)$$
$$\lambda_5 = f_v(0,0)$$

To solve for λ we can construct a local parameterisation for the neighbourhood. The local coordinate system is given by the basis vectors $\mathbf{e}_1, \mathbf{e}_2, \mathbf{e}_3$, where $\mathbf{e}_1$ is the vertex normal. We project the vertices into the $\mathbf{e}_2, \mathbf{e}_3$ plane to give the (u,v) vertex correspondence and the heights of the vertices to this plane give f (Figure 6.17). Thus the vertex positions are interpreted locally as a height field:

$$\mathbf{x}(u,v) = f(u,v)\mathbf{e}_1 + u\mathbf{e}_2 + v\mathbf{e}_3 \tag{6.2}$$

Equation 6.1 can then be solved using a variation of Newton's method for non-linear systems [PRES01]. An example of the process is shown in Figure 6.18. The edges in the neighbourhood map to quadratic curves and the triangles map two quadratic patches. This surface has second-order differentiability (C^2 as opposed to the original piecewise mesh (C^0). The above partial derivatives for the triangle mesh can then be determined.

Figure 6.17
Example of vertex neighbourhood parameterisation. (a) Vertex neighbourhood in local frame. (b) Orthogonal projection of neighbourhood onto plane $\mathbf{e}_2 \wedge \mathbf{e}_3$. (c) Projection defines projected points $u\mathbf{e}_2 + v\mathbf{e}_3$ = (u,v) and corresponding $f(u,v)$ values.

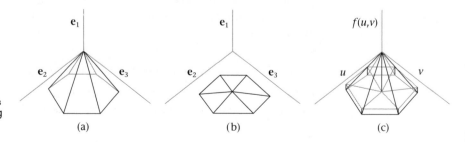

Figure 6.18
An example of vertex neighbourhood parameterisation and C^2 least-squares surface.
(a) Vertex neighbourhood.
(b) Parameterisation domain formed by planar vertex neighbourhood orthogonal projection.
(c) C^2 least-squares approximation of parameterisation
(courtesy of Mark Eastlick).

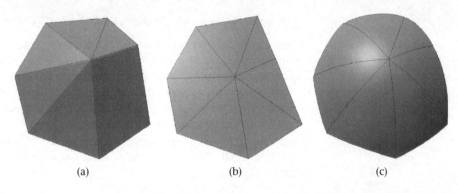

(a) (b) (c)

Using Equation 6.2 we have the first and second partial derivatives for the surface in the neighbourhood of $\mathbf{x}_i$ as:

$$\mathbf{x}_u(0,0) = f_u(0,0)\mathbf{e}_1 + \mathbf{e}_2 = \lambda_3\mathbf{e}_1 + \mathbf{e}_2$$
$$\mathbf{x}_u(0,0) = f_v(0,0)\mathbf{e}_1 + \mathbf{e}_3 = \lambda_5\mathbf{e}_1 + \mathbf{e}_3$$
$$\mathbf{x}_{uu}(0,0) = f_{uu}(0,0)\mathbf{e}_1 \quad = {}^1\!/_2\lambda_1\mathbf{e}_1$$
$$\mathbf{x}_{uv}(0,0) = f_{uv}(0,0)\mathbf{e}_1 \quad = \lambda_4\mathbf{e}_1$$
$$\mathbf{x}_{vv}(0,0) = f_{vv}(0,0)\mathbf{e}_1 \quad = {}^1\!/_2\lambda_2\mathbf{e}_1$$

and this is the result we require – the first and second partial derivatives of the surface in the neighbourhood of $\mathbf{v}$.

Using these derivatives we can easily define various differential geometry metrics (Appendix 6.1) at each mesh vertex. For example, Figure 6.19 (also Colour Plate) shows a rendered object colour coded with mean curvature.

Figure 6.19
Example of discrete differential geometry operators on triceratops mesh. (a) Mean curvature $({}^1\!/_2(\kappa_1 + \kappa_2))$ rendering. (b) Normalised maximum principle curvature (κ_1) direction vector field. (c) Normalised minimum principle curvature (κ_2) direction vector field. (d) Mesh conventionally rendered (courtesy of Mark Eastlick).

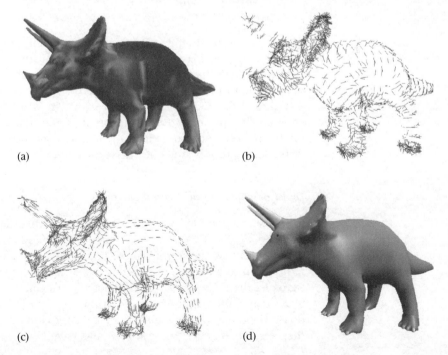

(a) (b)

(c) (d)

Using differential geometry in re-triangulation

In this section we look at a method [EAST01] that uses vertex removal followed by re-triangulation. The idea is to base the re-triangulation on the magnitudes and directions of the second partial derivatives as defined in the previous section. Providing these derivatives are accurate, this approach has the potential of producing high quality simplifications at low vertex counts. Lack of quality in simplification algorithms tends to become apparent as the number of vertices becomes very low. The re-triangulation structure of Section 6.4.4 can easily be adapted to use differential geometry parameters by defining $w(e)$ (Section 6.4.4) as follows:

$$w(e) = \kappa_d^k |(\mathbf{v}_i - \mathbf{v}_j) \wedge \mathbf{d}_\kappa| + (1 - \kappa_d^k)|\mathbf{v}_i - \mathbf{v}_j|$$

$$\kappa_d^k = \begin{cases} \dfrac{||\kappa_1^k| - |\kappa_2^k||}{\kappa_{max}} & \textbf{if } ||\kappa_1^k| - |\kappa_2^k|| < \kappa_{max} \\ \textbf{else } 1 \end{cases}$$

$$\mathbf{d}_\kappa = \frac{\mathbf{d}_\kappa}{|\mathbf{d}_\kappa|} \quad (\kappa = \kappa_2^k)$$

where
  κ_1^k and κ_2^k are the principal curvatures of vertex k
  κ_d^k is the relative curvature between the two principal directions of curvature
  κ_{max} $(0 \Leftarrow \kappa_{max} \Leftarrow 1)$ is a factor that controls the sensitivity of the curvature adaptation
  $\mathbf{d}$ = direction of κ_2

For regions of the mesh that are strongly curved in one direction this enhancement forces the triangulation edges to align with the direction of *minimum* curvature. Note that the principal curvatures are not re-calculated as the simplification proceeds. They are calculated once only before the mesh is changed.

Figure 6.20 compares this approach with an MWT algorithm. The difference between the two algorithms is apparent in the limbs. The triangles using the differential geometry-based re-triangulation align themselves with the long axis of the leg – precisely the effect that we want.

Direct derivation of differential operators

In a recent report Desbrun *et al.* [DESB00] describe the derivation of formulae that operate directly on a triangle mesh. The significant advantage of such an approach is that the formulae can be directly applied to the mesh geometry, rather than to a derived or interpolated surface as in the previous section. For example, there are established methods for calculating the normal at a vertex by averaging the weighted normal of the contributing faces. They authors state that if the initial triangle mesh is a good approximation to the original surface, their results approach those that would have been obtained by operating on

(a)

(b)

(c)

(d)

(e)

(f)

Figure 6.20
Example of curvature- and MWT-based simplifications of cow mesh. (a) Curvature-based simplification (50% reduction, 1453 vertices). (b) MWT-based simplification (50% reduction, 1453 vertices). (c) Curvature-based simplification (25% reduction, 729 vertices). (d) MWT-based simplification (25% reduction, 729 vertices). (e) Curvature-based simplification (12% reduction, 354 vertices). (f) MWT-based simplification (12% reduction, 354 vertices) (courtesy of Mark Eastlick).

the smooth surface. They motivate the work using the concept of spatial averages in the region around a vertex $\mathbf{v}$.

They consider first the Laplace-Beltrami operator which maps a point $\mathbf{p}$ to the vector $\mathbf{K}(\mathbf{p})$, the mean normal curvature:

$$\mathbf{K}(\mathbf{p}) = 2\kappa_p \mathbf{N}_p = \lim_{A \to 0} \frac{\nabla A}{A}$$

where
κ_p is the mean curvature
A is the infinitesimal area around $\mathbf{p}$
∇A is the gradient at $\mathbf{p}$

(Note the similarity between expressing the mean normal curvature as a limit and the limit expression for Gaussian curvature.)

Case Study 3 – Re-meshing algorithms – MAPS

In this section we look at a new class of techniques that process polygon meshes, called re-meshing algorithms [ECK95], [KOBB98] and [LEE98]. These algorithms are so called because they convert an existing triangle mesh of arbitrary connectivity, which may have been derived from hardware (such as a 3D digitiser device) or output from modelling software, into one that has subdivision connectivity. We will describe a particular algorithm in this category called MAPS (Multi-resolution Adaptive Parameterisation of Surfaces) [LEE98], chosen because it is typical and has been used in other applications. Here the main aim of the method is to construct a parameterisation for a two-manifold model where one does not exist. Such a parameterisation is required, for example, for normal map rendering (Chapter 4). A mesh with subdivision connectivity is one that closely approximates the original mesh, but which has been obtained by subdividing a base mesh and moving the vertices of the resulting piecewise regular mesh so that the whole approximates, as closely as possible, the original mesh. Thus a mesh with arbitrary connectivity is transformed into a mesh with subdivision or semi-regular connectivity. The immediate advantage that accrues from such a process is the availability of multi-resolution techniques, which can be performed more robustly on such a representation. In particular, wavelet techniques can be employed.

At this stage it may useful to make a simple comparison between such approaches and PM technology (Figure 6.21). A PM simplifies a mesh storing the difference information between levels which is needed to reconstruct the mesh. This reconstruction from the base mesh is simply the reverse of the simplification process and ends up, if taken to its limit, with an exact copy of the start mesh. A re-meshing algorithm, such as MAPS [LEE98], re-meshes the base mesh by using a subdivision algorithm and perturbing the vertices of the resulting mesh by re-sampling the original geometry. The re-sampling of the original geometry reduces to a 'point in triangle location' problem due to the parameterisation. The limit of the subdivision phase, which can function as an LOD, is a mesh with subdivision connectivity that closely approximates, but is not identical to, the original mesh. Thus the re-meshing phase functions as an LOD as the subdivision can be terminated at any point and the object rendered.

The main emphasis of the MAPS algorithm is the construction of a smooth parameterisation of the original mesh over the base domain mesh. This, put simply, means that the positions of the original vertices are expressed with respect to the base domain triangles. Such a parameterisation can be used, as we shall see, for a variety of applications. These include 3D morphing, multi-resolution editing adaptive simplification, and transmission as well as LOD rendering.

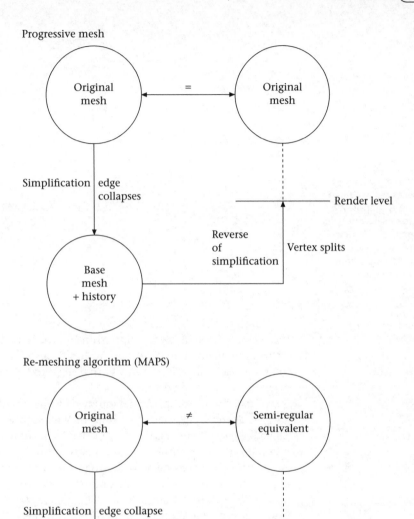

Figure 6.21
A schematic diagram comparing a progressive mesh with a re-meshing algorithm.

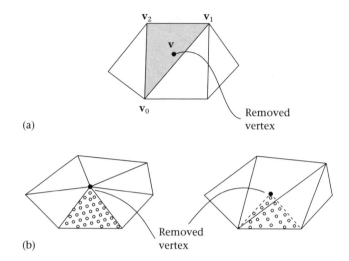

Figure 6.22
Re-parameterising
vertices removed in a
previous simplification.
(a) Removed vertex is
contained by a new
triangle. (b) New
triangle results from
re-triangulation.

Although Lee *et al.* were not the first researchers to adopt this approach (see, for example [ECK95]), their algorithm has the benefit of being simple[5] and easier to implement than most approaches. It also has the advantage that feature lines, or 'real' edges, in the model that need to be preserved as such in the base domain can be catered for.

Overall, the algorithm divides into two distinct phases – the simplification phase and the re-meshing phase. Lee *et al.* in [LEE98] use vertex removal, whereas in [LEE00] edge collapse mediated by Garland's quadratic error metric (Section 6.3.3) is employed. When either operation is performed we have to re-triangulate. This is done in 2-space using a constrained Delauney triangulation or CDT. CDT is a special case of DT which constrains the boundary edges (of the hole) to be part of the solution triangulation. The general DT is a unique or deterministic triangulation that simultaneously optimises several quality measures concerning the triangulation, such as, for example, the minimum angle.

As we describe in Section 6.4.4, re-triangulation takes place in 2-space through the use of the conformal map z^a (Appendix 6.1) to map the neighbourhood of the removed vertex into the plane. Now as we stated, the aim of the process is to obtain a parameterisation of the original vertices over the base domain. This is done by propagating a parameterisation down through the intermediate meshes that are formed between the original mesh and the base domain mesh as the simplification process proceeds.

Let us now consider what we mean by propagating the parameterisation. Consider the removal of a vertex **v** (Figure 6.22(a)). The removed vertex is now contained by a new triangle (shaded) formed by the re-triangulation process.

---

5. A simplified version of MAPS together with code skeletons is given in [LEE00].

We express this by forming the barycentric coordinates of $\mathbf{v}$ with respect to the shaded triangle (see Appendix 6.1 for a definition of barycentric coordinates). That is, we compute the quadruple (α,β,γ,T). where (α,β,γ) are the barycentric coordinates of $\mathbf{v}$ with respect to the triangle T, the triangle that $\mathbf{v}$ is now associated with.

As well as considering the vertex just removed, we also have to consider all the points parameterised in previous simplifications which have barycentric coordinates with respect to triangles that have now been removed. These need to be re-parameterised with respect to the new triangles that they are now contained by. In this manner the parameterisation of all the original vertices is propagated down through the simplification levels. Eventually we end up with the base domain where all the original vertices are parameterised on the base domain triangles. Effectively the vertices are flattened onto the planes of the base domain faces, and at the end of the process we have:

(1) a low resolution or base domain triangle mesh;

(2) a quadruple (α,β,γ,T) for every original vertex identifying the triangle in the base domain that contains it and its barycentric coordinates for that triangle;

(3) the original vertex (x,y,z) coordinates of each vertex.

A visualisation of this is shown in Figure 6.23 (also Colour Plate).

To re-mesh to any (subdivision) level we proceed as follows. We invoke a simple quadrisection subdivision on the base domain mesh triangles. This produces subdivision vertices lying in the planes of the base domain triangles. The vertices now need to be pulled into a new position so that they lie on the surface of the original model. The first step in this process is to find the original mesh triangle in the flattened base domain mesh that contains the vertex $\mathbf{v}_s$. Note that $\mathbf{v}_s$ is already contained in the plane of a base domain triangle and finding the flattened mesh triangle is a 2-space problem. A suitable algorithm to use is described in [GUIB85]. This is a 'walking' method that starts at a random edge and then moves one edge at a time in the general direction of $\mathbf{v}_s$.[6] Once the containing triangle is found, we find the barycentric coordinates (α,β,γ) of $\mathbf{v}_s$ with respect to it. To re-sample the original geometry and thus position $\mathbf{v}_s$ on the original surface, we use:

$$\mathbf{v} = \alpha\mathbf{v}_a + \beta\mathbf{v}_b + \gamma\mathbf{v}_c$$

where

$\mathbf{v}_a$, $\mathbf{v}_b$, and $\mathbf{v}_c$ are the original vertices corresponding to the vertices of the flattened triangle lying in the base domain triangle

---

6. Note that the simplest and most efficient implementation of this algorithm presupposes a data structure where an edge in the mesh is directional and contains pointers to its origin vertex, its destination vertex, the previous edge from its destination vertex and the next edge from its origin vertex; the three edges forming a triangle.

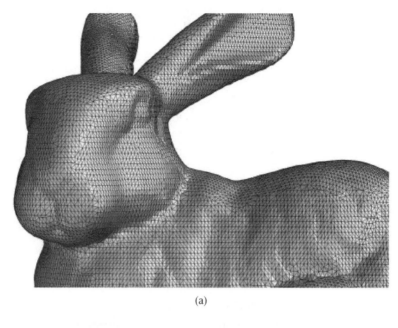

(a)

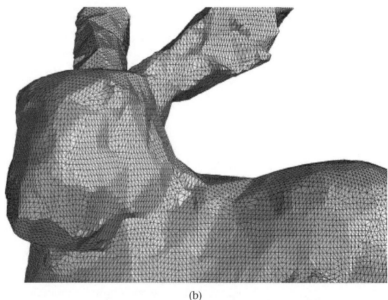

(b)

Figure 6.23
(a) Original mesh (a low resolution version of the Stanford Bunny). (b) Base mesh and vertex parameterisation.

Lee *et al.* invoke another mandatory process in the re-meshing phase. The necessity for this comes from the fact that the parameterisation, although smooth within each base domain triangle, is not globally smooth across the base triangles. To cure this they use a smoothing technique based on Loop subdivision.

Appendix 6.1 Mathematical background

(1) Basic differential geometry

The aim of this section is to introduce differential geometry concepts that enable us to quantify the behaviour of a surface in the region of a point **p**. We do this in the most general terms, by calculating how rapidly the surface departs from the tangent plane at **p** – hence the term differential geometry. This is done by measuring the rate of change of the unit normal vector field in the region of **p** and this is known as the linear map dN.

We begin by introducing some curvature definitions for a surface. We will eventually see how these can be calculated.

Normal curvature

Normal curvature $\kappa^N(\theta)$ in the direction $\mathbf{e}_\theta$ is the curvature of the curve C which lies in the surface and is contained by a plane containing $\mathbf{e}_\theta$ and **N** (Figure 6.24). κ_1 and κ_2 are the extremum values of all the normal curvatures at point **p** and lie in the orthogonal directions $\mathbf{e}_1$ and $\mathbf{e}_2$. They are known as the maximum normal curvature and the minimum normal curvature

Mean curvature

The mean curvature is the average of all normal curvatures or $^1/_2$ the sum of the principal curvatures:

$$^1/_2(\kappa_1 + \kappa_2)$$

Gaussian curvature

The Gaussian curvature is defined as:

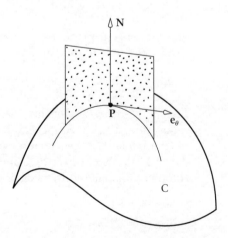

Figure 6.24
Normal curvature $\kappa^N(\theta)$ is the curvature of the curve in the plane containing **N** and $\mathbf{e}_\theta$.

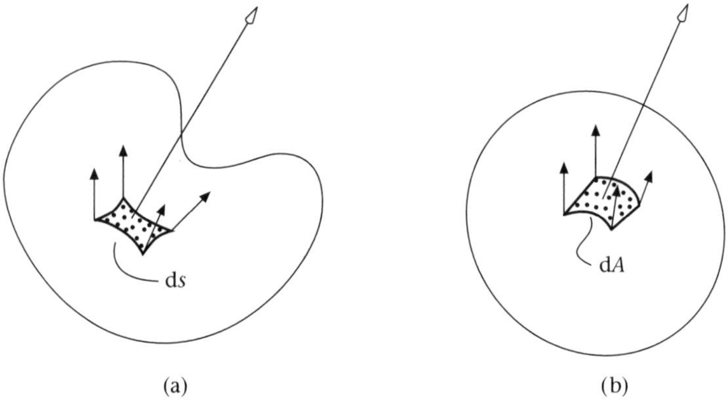

Figure 6.25
Definitions used by
Gaussian curvature.
(a) Surface *s*.
(b) Gauss map.

$$\kappa_G = \lim_{s \to 0} \frac{A}{s} = \frac{dA}{ds} = \kappa_1 \kappa_2 = |dN_p|$$

where

 s is the infinitesimal area on the surface

 A is its Gauss map

 dN_p is called the linear map, a differential we shall derive later

The Gauss map (Figure 6.25(b)) is the map of the vector normals of *s* on the surface of a unit sphere – a normal on the surface becomes a point on the sphere. Thus the Gaussian curvature of a planar patch is zero because its map is a single point, whereas that of a sphere is unity.

We define a surface with parameterisation $\mathbf{x}(u,v)$ as (Figure 6.16):

$$\mathbf{x}(u,v) = (x(u,v),\ y(u,v),\ z(u,v))$$

and if the surface is differentiable we can define:

$$\frac{\partial \mathbf{x}}{\partial u} = \mathbf{x}_u \quad \text{and} \quad \frac{\partial \mathbf{x}}{\partial v} = \mathbf{x}_v$$

and the tangent plane that contains these vectors. The tangent plane is specified by the unit normal at $\mathbf{x}$ as:

$$\mathbf{N}(u,v) = \frac{\mathbf{x}_u \times \mathbf{x}_v}{|\mathbf{x}_u \times \mathbf{x}_v|}$$

Just as we expresses the first derivative as a plane, the second derivative is a quadric – a so-called *osculating paraboloid* (Figure 6.26). If a surface is twice differentiable (C^2) then such a paraboloid exists. Refer to Figure 6.26(b). If we define $\mathbf{x}'$ as a point near to $\mathbf{x}$ and the point $\mathbf{q}$ to be the intersection of a line through $\mathbf{x}'$ parallel to the axis of the parabola and further define:

$$d = |\mathbf{x} - \mathbf{x}'|$$

$$h = |\mathbf{q} - \mathbf{x}'|$$

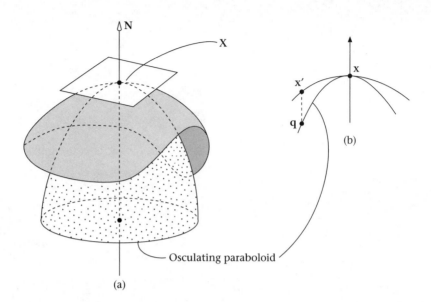

Figure 6.26
The osculating paraboloid
of a point **X** on a surface.

then the paraboloid is said to be an osculating paraboloid if:

$$h/d^2 \to 0 \quad \text{as } \mathbf{x}' \to \mathbf{x}$$

If we introduce a coordinate system with the (u,v) plane coincident with the tangent plane, then for a small neighbourhood around x we can represent the surface as:

$$z = f(u,v)$$

The tangent plane is given by:

$$z = uf_u(0,0) + vf_v(0,0)$$

and the Taylor series expansion of the function in this neighbourhood is:

$$f(u,v) = f_u(0,0)u + f_v(0,0)v + \tfrac{1}{2}(f_{uu}(0,0)u^2 + f_{uv}(0,0)uv + f_{vv}(0,0)^2)$$

This discussion leads us to the simple and intuitively obvious conclusion that for a sufficiently small neighbourhood of x the surface to a first approximation is given by a plane and to a second approximation by an osculating paraboloid. Depending on the shape of the surface, the osculating paraboloid can take one of the four forms:

- elliptic point – the osculating paraboloid is elliptical;
- hyperbolic point – the osculating paraboloid is a hyperbola;
- parabolic point – the osculating paraboloid is a parabolic cylinder;
- planar point – the osculating paraboloid degenerates into a plane.

The first three of these are shown in Figure 6.27. Thus as we drop the tangent plane downwards from x in the negative normal direction the plane will

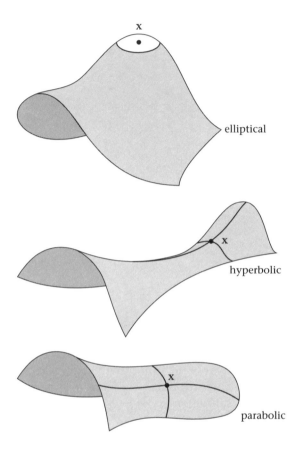

Figure 6.27
Elliptical, hyperbolic and
parabolic parts. The shape
of the surface at the point
is an elliptical, hyperbolic
or parabolic osculating
paraboloid.

intersect elliptical, hyperbolic or straight lines in the osculating paraboloid. This is the same as saying that we will intersect the same cross-sections in the surface in a very small neighbourhood around **x**. In other words, the osculating paraboloid becomes the surface in the limit.

Now what all this is leading to is the quantification of the curvature of a surface. Before we move on to this, we can make some observations on the categorisations just referred to. We assume that the curvature at a point on a surface is given by a maximum normal curvature κ_1 and a minimum normal curvature κ_2 – the principal curvatures at **p**. These are associated with surface curves whose directions at **p** are given by the principal directions which are orthogonal. Now we can further describe our categories as:

- elliptic point – κ_1 and κ_2 have the same sign and the ellipse becomes a circle for $\kappa_1 = \kappa_2$. In this case every direction is a principal direction and the point is said to be umbilic. (All points on a sphere and a plane are umbilical.)

- hyperbolic point – κ_1 and κ_2 have opposite signs.

- parabolic point – one of the principal curvatures is zero.

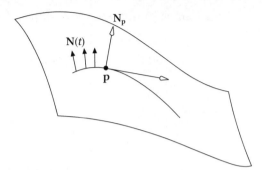

Figure 6.28
The rate of change of the normal vector to a single curve lying in a surface.

We now come to derive the expression which calculates the curvature of a surface. To calculate the curvature of a curve we look at the rate of change of the normal vector to the curve. Similarly, for a surface we can look at the variation of the normals in the region around **p**. To do this, consider all curves C lying in the surface of interest and passing through point **p** (Figure 6.28). Each curve is expressed as a parametric curve lying in the surface as:

$$c(t) = x(u(t), v(t))$$

where
$$c(0) = p$$

The tangent vector to this curve is given by:

$$\dot{c}(t) = x_u \dot{u} + x_v \dot{v}$$

and this measures the rate of change of the normal vectors to the surface which are restricted to this curve and so we can write:

$$dN(\dot{c}) = N_u \dot{u} + N_v \dot{v}$$

N_u and N_v lie in the tangent plane to the surface and so we can write:

$$N_u = a_{11} x_u + a_{21} x_v$$
$$N_v = a_{12} x_u + a_{22} x_v$$

and

$$dN(\dot{c}) = (a_{11}\dot{u} + a_{12}\dot{v})x_u + (a_{21}\dot{u} + a_{22}\dot{v})x_v$$

hence in the basis (x_u, x_v) dN is given by the matrix a_{ij}.

dN_p is the differential of the Gauss map. Its determinant is the Gaussian curvature κ and the negative half of the trace of dN_p is the mean curvature H at **p**. Returning again to our surface categorisations we can write:

surface is elliptic at **p** if $|dN_p| > 0$
surface is hyperbolic at **p** if $|dN_p| < 0$
surface is parabolic at **p** if $|dN_p| = 0$
surface is planar at **p** if $dN_p = 0$

It can be shown (see, for example, [DOCA76]) that:

$$a_{11} = \frac{fF - eG}{EG - f^2} \qquad a_{12} = \frac{gF - fG}{EG - f^2}$$

$$a_{21} = \frac{eF - fE}{EG - f^2} \qquad a_{22} = \frac{fF - gE}{EG - f^2}$$

where

$$e = \mathbf{x}_{uu}.\mathbf{N}_p \quad f = \mathbf{x}_{uv}.\mathbf{N}_p \quad g = \mathbf{x}_{vv}.\mathbf{N}_p$$
$$E = \mathbf{x}_u.\mathbf{x}_u \quad F = \mathbf{x}_u.\mathbf{x}_v \quad G = \mathbf{x}_v.\mathbf{x}_v$$

The eigenvalues of $d\mathbf{N}_p$ give us the required curvature definitions:

mean curvature $\qquad H = \dfrac{1}{2} \dfrac{eG - 2fF + gE}{EG - F^2}$

Gaussian curvature $\qquad \kappa_G = \dfrac{eg - f^2}{EG - F^2}$

principal curvatures $\qquad \kappa_i = H \pm \sqrt{H^2 - K}$

The eigenvectors of $d\mathbf{N}_p \mathbf{e}_1$ and $\mathbf{e}_2$ give the directions of the principal curvature.

Example

Consider a torus generated by sweeping a circle of radius r about an axis at distance a from the axis. This can be parameterised (Figure 6.29) as:

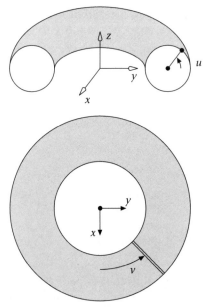

Figure 6.29
Parameterisation for a
torus.

$$\mathbf{x}(u,v) = ((r \cos u + a) \cos v, (r \cos u + a) \sin v, r \sin u)$$

$$\mathbf{x}(u,v) = ((r\cos u + a)\cos v,\ (r\cos u + a)\sin v,\ r\sin u)$$
$$0 \le u \le 2\pi \quad 0 \le uv \le 2\pi$$

From this we have:

$$\mathbf{x}_u = (-r\sin u \cos v,\ -r\sin u \sin v,\ r\cos u)$$
$$\mathbf{x}_v = (-(a + r\cos u)\sin v,\ (a + r\cos u)\cos v,\ 0)$$
$$\mathbf{x}_{uu} = (-r\cos u \cos v,\ -r\cos u \sin v,\ -r\sin u)$$
$$\mathbf{x}_{uv} = (r\sin u \sin v,\ -r\sin u \cos v,\ 0)$$
$$\mathbf{x}_{vv} = (-(a + r\cos u)\cos v,\ -(a + r\cos u)\sin v,\ 0)$$

Thus

$$E = r^2 \quad F = 0 \quad G = (a + r\cos u)^2$$

etc.

(2) Conformal mapping z^a

The conformal mapping z^a is defined as:

$$f(z) = w = z^a$$

Both z and w are complex numbers:

$$z = x + iy \quad w = u + iv$$

For example, consider the mapping:

$$w = z^2$$

we have:

$$w = x^2 - y^2 + i2xy$$

or

$$u = x^2 - y^2 \quad v = 2xy$$

In polar coordinates we have:

$$z = r\exp(i\theta)$$
$$w = z^2 = r^2\exp(2i\theta)$$

and this, for example, maps the first quadrant of the z-plane $0 \le \theta \le \pi/2$, $r \ge 0$ onto the entire half of the w plane, each point in the transformed region corresponding to a single point in the original region. Circles of radius r in the w plane are transformed into circles of radius r^2 in the w plane.

Now consider:

$$w = z^a$$

This maps an angular region:

$$0 \le \theta \le 2\pi/a, \; r \ge 0$$

into the entire w plane.

It is this mapping, or a piecewise linear version of it, that we use in Section 6.4.4.

(3) Barycentric coordinates

Barycentric coordinates (α, β, γ) express the position of a point $\mathbf{p}$, lying in the plane of a triangle, with respect to its three vertices p_1, p_2 and p_3:

$$\mathbf{p} = \alpha p_1 + \beta p_2 + \gamma p_3$$
$$\alpha + \beta + \gamma = 1$$

This can be interpreted as the relative weights of the three areas:

$$\alpha = \frac{\Delta p p_0 p_1}{\Delta p_0 p_1 p_2} \quad \beta = \frac{\Delta p p_1 p_2}{\Delta p_0 p_1 p_2} \quad \gamma = \frac{\Delta p p_2 p_0}{\Delta p_0 p_1 p_2}$$

In our application, since p, p_0, p_1 and p_2 are all known, we can determine α, β and γ.

Appendix 6.2 Demonstration

ProgMesh.exe is a rendering program that contains a simple edge collapse algorithm as detailed in [WATT01]. Import a suitable model (for example, *kagaroo*.3ds). Click on *detail level* icon and operate the slider in the window to cause edge collapses. Note how eventually the model breaks up – there is no topological checking in this algorithm.

Edge collapse can be accomplished either by using a simple heuristic approach or by a more rigorous method that measures the difference between a particular approximation and a sample of the original mesh (as we have detailed in the chapter). A simple metric that can be used to order the edges for collapse is:

$$\frac{|V_{f1} - V_{f2}|}{|\mathbf{N}_{f1} \cdot \mathbf{N}_{f2}|}$$

that is, the length of the edge divided by the dot product of the vertex normals. On its own this metric will work quite well, but if it is continually applied the mesh will suddenly begin to 'collapse' and a more considered approach to edge selection is mandatory.

7   Character animation

7.1   Introduction

That convincing character animation is possible using 3D computer graphics technology is undeniable. We can look at full-length productions such as Pixar's *Toy Story* and immediately verify that this statement is true. In such productions it is a solved problem. However, the situation for character animation in games is very different. We have to generate the animation in real time on consumer equipment. Situations demanded by the game logic have to generate a continuous animation sequence on the fly; these may be required to control an autonomous character interacting with other characters, the game environment and the player interaction. In motion picture computer graphics a single sequence is carefully produced and tuned in advance. Although we can see some of the difficulties of achieving high quality rendering in real time diminishing rapidly, the latter problem, which is sometimes called non-linear animation, is much more difficult to solve.

Character animation in games is a problem that is usually perceived as a multi-level problem or hierarchy. Out of this we can divide the task into sub-problems which at the time of writing (2002) consist of the following distinct levels.

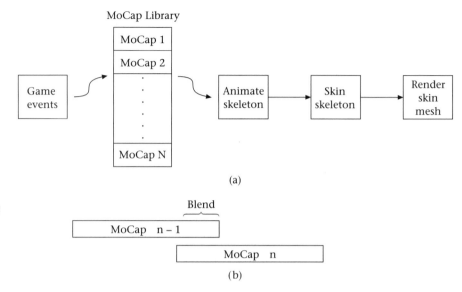

Figure 7.1
Character animation and MoCap. (a) Conventional character animation using a MoCap library. (b) A 'continuous' sequence is generated by blend joining selected MoCap sequences.

Low-level geometry control

At the lowest level the animation must generate triangles that are sent to the GPU for rendering. In the recent past, a character would have been modelled with a low-level polygon count (Figure 7.1) and animation generated from key frames by vertex morphing. For reasons that will become apparent in this chapter, the current model is to have a skeleton representation which admits the animation. This is then 'associated' with a skin which provides the material to be rendered. Thus character global motion (translation and orientation) and pose (joint angles) is applied to a skeleton and a skin 'follows' the skeleton motion. The method of association between the skeleton and the skin defines the shape-changing animation required for the skin. In this chapter we look at basic skinning and in Chapter 8 we study more elaborate approaches to what is essentially shape-changing animation.

Specialised shape-changing animation

The basic skinning approach has many disadvantages and problems. This has led to the emergence or more specialised techniques that control the skin deformation. These may be independent of the general skeleton motion and have their own animation script. The best example of this is facial animation for visual speech, which we cover in Chapter 9.

Motion control of skeletons

The most popular form of animation script for a skeleton is MoCap (Chapter 10). This has the irresistible advantage that it provides convincing animation that is (more or less) easily captured. It is also by definition self-limiting – we cannot invoke any animation in the game that has not been pre-recorded. Along with basic motion control we require methods that enable blending from one sequence to another. This is the common games model. We store a vocabulary of motion scripts, the game logic selects the current required one and we phase the current animation out and blend the next one in (Figure 7.1). In this chapter we look at how motion scripts are applied to a skeleton; more advanced aspects of MoCap are studied in Chapter 10.

Apart from the obvious sequence blending requirement, there are other demands that we make on MoCap. These are mostly to do with adaptation. If we require a character to pick up any one of a set of objects in a game environment then do we MoCap for each object or try to adapt the captured sequences to cope with different manifestations of a general motion such as 'grasp an object'?

It is the case that MoCap is not the only method for controlling an articulated structure. Rigid body simulation using dynamics has met with some success in computer games and it is also possible, but difficult, to use dynamic simulation for articulated figures. Convincingly animating a virtual human is difficult whatever means are employed and it is easy to see why using dynamic simulation is extremely difficult. Even motion as basic as the much-studied walk cycle is demanding. It consists of joints rotating, the hips moving up and down and swinging from side to side, and forward motion must occur in such a way that balance is maintained. In dynamic simulation this motion must be effected by applying time-varying torque functions to the joints and calculating their accelerations as a function of the applied force and restraining forces and the moment of inertia of the limbs.

It is unlikely in the immediate future that dynamic simulation of virtual humans will replace fine-tuned kinematic techniques (including motion capture) as the means of achieving realistic animation. On their own they are not necessarily able to produce higher quality animation than that provided by a skilled animator or a motion capture actor. However, it may become the best tool in the use of high-level behaviour functions which will presumably be used in animation in the future. Kinematic techniques are pre-scripted or recorded and by definition limit all animation to whatever is pre-calculated. If environments are to be controlled by a higher-level process which may demand 'unseen' action by the human agent(s) then behaviour functions are one way in which this goal could be achieved. The behaviour function may be specified by some language, and the underlying processes, which, at the lowest level, feature a complete dynamic simulation of a human figure, act as interpreters which eventually produce the desired action. 'X should run in a circular path towards Y with his hands outstretched' might be an example of a requirement produced by a process controlling the interaction between agents. The *raison d'être*, then, of dynamic simulation of virtual humans is not only the development of high quality motion but also the implementation of a model of general motion. The virtual human should be able to undergo any action capable by a real human being. We consider that dynamic simulation of a character is outside the scope of this text – it is currently not used, as far as the authors are aware, in games applications.

Low-level animation organisation

We could consider the previous sections as dealing with the animation of a single character moving from one position to another in an unconstrained environment. In a games application there are various aspects to attend to in organising the precise nature of the animation:

- Path planning is probably the most well worked out aspect: given that a character is to move from a source to a destination, what is the precise path to follow? In a game environment with complex level structures this is a non-trivial problem. What should be the nature of the path? In general we would prefer a 'natural' path – curves – rather than one that was made up of right-angled turns. A path can then be used as the global translation for the skeleton – we simply apply the path to the root node of the skeleton.

- A character needs to be imbued with an obstacle avoidance capability, usually involving collision detection and some 'going round the obstacle' strategy.

- A character needs to interact with objects. It needs to turn a handle to open a door. It needs to pick up an object. Character/object interaction implies organisation and/or adaptation of animation. Because objects are inanimate we assume that character/object interaction should fit into this level rather than the next one up.

High-level control

This aspect is concerned with the production of a high-level script specifying what a character is to do and how it should interact with other characters. This might be termed a decision layer or an AI layer. Inevitably application dependent, it may in a team game be some decision like:

- Keep the ball.
- Pass the ball to the closest team mate.
- Pass the ball to a medium distance player.
- Pass the ball to a team mate far away.

Because this aspect is properly the domain of AI, we consider it outside of the range of this text. The book by Funge [FUNG99] is a good index into this emerging field as well as being an excellent study in its own right.

An example of a simple, but highly effective, form of high-level control is the flocking model first proposed by Reynolds [REYN87]. This behaviour, which has been used in many different applications (stampeding herds, for example), is implemented using simple 'social' rules/strategies, which in order of precedence are:

- Collision avoidance: avoid collision with nearby flock mates.
- Velocity matching: attempt to match velocity with nearby flock mates.
- Flock centring: attempt to stay close to nearby flock mates.
- Wander randomly.

Figure 7.2 (also Colour Plate) shows a flocking simulation implemented in Fly3D. Although in this case the flock members are not virtual humans, the same algorithm can be adapted to simulate movement in a group of humans. The final rule – wander aimlessly – can be changed to simulate motion in a particular direction.

7.2

Vertex animation and blending

We begin our study of low-level control by considering how we might animate a character mesh. To begin with, we discuss the disadvantages of vertex animation or morphing.

Vertex animation produced from keyframes is the simplest model for animating a character mesh. Keyframes are built in modelling software and linear interpolation is applied to produce the in-between frames. This implies that for every keyframe we have to store the position of all vertices. For an application with many keys of a complex character there is a high memory demand. In games we normally have many different pre-recorded sequences for even a single character. A more serious problem is deformation of the mesh. We must bear in mind that the character is an articulated structure (not a rigid body) and linear interpolation of the vertex will not necessarily maintain the relative dimensions of the polygons and the in-between frames will in effect distort the limbs. This problem is minimised if the keys are close together, for example in a walk cycle. But this approach in general is not a good solution because it simply results in more keys and increases the memory problem.

The deformation problem is particularly bad when blending between two animations. Consider Figure 7.3 which represents the interpolation scheme that would be required to blend between two sequences such as, say, a forward and backward walk cycle. We consider, with respect to Figure 7.3, three modes. The extreme modes, backward and forward walking, present no problems. At time t_1 the character starts walking forward and a walk animation loops, interpolating between the keys. At time t_2 an application signal indicates that the character is to walk backwards. This causes three simultaneous interpolations

Figure 7.2
Two views of a simple
flocking population in a
games level (courtesy
of F. Paganelli and
M. Mustapic, Universidad
de Buenos Aires).

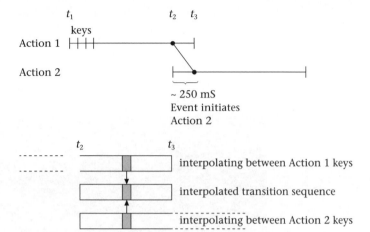

Figure 7.3
Three interpolations are
active when blending two
keyframed sequences.

to take place until time t_3. In the time interval $t_3 - t_2$, which may be as small as 250 msecs, both the forward and backward walks are interpolating their keys, and at the same time we have to interpolate the results of these to blend between the walks. Time t_2 is initiated by the user or player and can occur at any time in the forward walk cycle. In general there will a large difference between the mesh state (forward walk) and the state of the backward walk. Thus the blending interpolation will generate a large amount of deformation.[1]

Although it is obvious that geometric deformation will occur when blending different animation sequences, what is less obvious is that bad deformation also occurs within a sequence. Figure 7.4 (also Colour Plate) illustrates this effect both for a simple outstretched rotating limb and for the whole figure. Effectively the volume of the character shrinks – an extremely undesirable effect.

Another major problem that occurs with vertex animation is due to the fact that there is no structure. There is no acknowledgement of the fact that the character is an articulated structure. This makes it difficult to build interaction with scene objects. Where is the character's hand? What is its orientation? The character cannot be referenced in any convenient manner.

Despite all of these problems its an easy and fast method of animation and this is the reason for its enduring popularity. There are many contexts where it is sufficient, but for articulated structures it should only be used in simple applications.

---

1. Note that it is precisely this form of deformation which is 'tolerated' in 2D morphing in films. The morphing process in image space produces a set of in-between frames that consist of 2D images which represent (usually) gross distortions of the 3D objects they represent. Tolerating the distortion enables a morph between two objects of different shape. In the case of interpolating keyframes of the same object in 3-space, which exhibit a large difference, we obtain unwanted distortion.

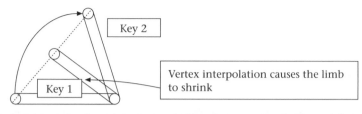

Key 2

Key 1

Vertex interpolation causes the limb to shrink

Figure 7.4
Distortion due to vertex interpolation (compare with Figure 7.7).

Controlling keyframe animation

Keyframe animation is most conveniently implemented in the following manner. The simplest type of keyframe animation is linear. Whether this will suffice, or whether we should use, say, spline interpolation [WATT92] depends on the application and crucially on the distance between keys. The greater the difference between keys, the more the need for cubic spline interpolation.

To control keyframe animation we can set up a structure that will hold any number of animations (each with any number of keys) that will be referenced by an integer index. Then we can have methods for setting the current mesh from the animations and keys available. We will need to set the current mesh from a single key of an animation; or from a single animation interpolating between two keys; or from two animation sequences.

The engine class *flyAnimatedMesh* includes all above features and can hold any number of animations. The following methods are used to set the current mesh from the available animations:

```
set_state(int anim, int key)
```

sets the current mesh from the animation and key specified. No interpolation is performed and a simple copy of the key vertices is made.

```
set_state(int anim, float key)
```

sets the current mesh from a specified animation and a float key (from 0 to 1). We find the two closest integer keys to the float key and interpolate them to generate the final result.

```
set_state(int anim1, float key1, int anim2, float key2, float factor)
```

sets the current mesh by interpolating two animations with a float key (as method above). It then interpolates the results with the specified factor (0 to 1). This allows smooth blending of two animation sequences.

The set state code is as follows:

```
void flyAnimatedMesh::set_state(int anim, int key)
{
   int i,j=animkeyspos[anim]*nv + key;
   for( i=0;i<nv;i++ )
   {
      localvert[i].x=key_verts[j+i].x;
      localvert[i].y=key_verts[j+i].y;
      localvert[i].z=key_verts[j+i].z;
   }
}

void flyAnimatedMesh::set_state(int anim, float key_factor)
{
   int i,j,k;
   float s;
   vertex *v0;
   flyVector *v1,*v2;

   j=(int)(key_factor*animkeys[anim]);
   if (j==animkeys[anim])
      { j=0; key_factor=0.0f; }
   s=1.0f/animkeys[anim];
   key_factor=(key_factor-j*s)/s;

   v1=&key_verts[(animkeyspos[anim]+j)*nv];
   if (j==animkeys[anim]-1)
      k=0;
   else k=j+1;
   v2=&key_verts[(animkeyspos[anim]+k)*nv];

   v0=localvert;
   s=1.0f-key_factor;
```

```
      for( i=0;i<nv;i++)
      {
        v0->x = v1->x*s  + v2->x*key_factor;
        v0->y = v1->y*s  + v2->y*key_factor;
        v0->z = v1->z*s  + v2->z*key_factor;
        v0++;  v1++;  v2++;
      }
}

void flyAnimatedMesh::set_state(int anim1, float key_factor1, int
anim2, float key_factor2, float blend)
{
  int i,j,k;
  float s,t,w;
  vertex *v0;
  flyVector *v1,*v2,*v3,*v4;

  j=(int)(key_factor1*animkeys[anim1]);
  if (j==animkeys[anim1])
     { j=0;  key_factor1=0.0f; }
  s=1.0f/animkeys[anim1];
  key_factor1=(key_factor1-j*s)/s;

  v1=&key_verts[(animkeyspos[anim1]+j)*nv];
  if (j==animkeys[anim1]-1)
     k=0;
  else k=j+1;
  v2=&key_verts[(animkeyspos[anim1]+k)*nv];

  j=(int)(key_factor2*animkeys[anim2]);
  if (j==animkeys[anim2])
     { j=0;  key_factor2=0.0f; }
  s=1.0f/animkeys[anim2];
  key_factor2=(key_factor2-j*s)/s;

  v3=&key_verts[(animkeyspos[anim2]+j)*nv];
  if (j==animkeys[anim2]-1)
     k=0;
  else k=j+1;
  v4=&key_verts[(animkeyspos[anim2]+k)*nv];

  v0 = localvert;
  s=1.0f-key_factor1;
  t=1.0f-key_factor2;
  w=1.0f-blend;
  for( i=0;i<nv;i++ )
  {
    v0->x=(v1->x*s+v2->x*key_factor1)*w+
          (v3->x*t+v4->x*key_factor2)*blend;
    v0->y=(v1->y*s+v2->y*key_factor1)*w+
          (v3->y*t+v4->y*key_factor2)*blend;
    v0->z=(v1->z*s+v2->z*key_factor1)*w+
          (v3->z*t+v4->z*key_factor2)*blend;
    v0++;  v1++;  v2++;  v3++;  v4++;
  }
}
```

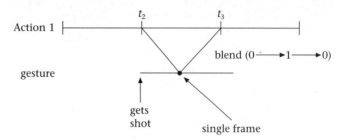

Figure 7.5
Interpolating a single
frame reaction gesture.

We now consider how to control or organise the animation sequences required. An animation controller should store the current animation index, its start time, the next animation index and the next animation start time. Usually the next animation will be −1 (no animation) and all the controller will do is loop the current animation based on its start time. When a next animation is set (with its start time), due to, for example, an interface event, the controller will use the last *set_state* method to blend between the two animations. When the blend is complete the *next* animation will become the *current* animation and the *next* is set to −1.

This simple controller blends two animations; but a more elaborate structure can easily be built which implements a modifier to the current animation. For example, consider a walking character that receives a shot. We may want to superimpose on the walk the 'I am wounded' gesture. The interpolation scheme that accomplishes this consists of two interpolations (Figure 7.5). At time t_2 a shot is received and immediately we start to superimpose the wounded gesture on the current animation. This is done by using a factor which goes from 0 to 1 then back to 0 again in the interval t_2 to t_3. After t_3 the normal animation continues. This requires a method that blends the current mesh with a single key from another animation.

```
void flyAnimatedMesh::set_state_blendcur(int anim, int key, float
blend)
{
   flyVertex *v0=localvert;
   flyVector *v1=&key_verts[(animkeyspos[anim]+key)*nv];
   float f=1-blend;
   for( int i=0;i<nv;i++ )
   {
      v0->x = v0->x*f + v1->x*blend;
      v0->y = v0->y*f + v1->y*blend;
      v0->z = v0->z*f + v1->z*blend;
      v0++; v1++;
   }
}
```

This will also modify an animation that is currently a blend between two sequences. We can also use an animation sequence as a modifier, rather than using a single frame requiring a more complex *set_state_blendcur* method.

The controller code is as follows:

```
#define ANIM_FRAME_TIME 33

int  i1,i2,j1,j2;
float  f1,f2,f3;

i1=objmesh->animkeys[cur_anim]*ANIM_FRAME_TIME;
j1=g_flyengine->cur_time-cur_anim_time;
f1=(j1%i1)/(float)i1;

if (next_anim==-1)
   objmesh->set_state(cur_anim,f1);
else
{
   i2=objmesh->animkeys[next_anim]*ANIM_FRAME_TIME;
   j2=g_flyengine->cur_time-next_anim_time;
   f2=(j2%i2)/(float)i2;

   if (j2>next_anim_dur)
   {
      cur_anim=next_anim;
      cur_anim_time=next_anim_time;
      next_anim=-1;
      objmesh->set_state(cur_anim,f2);
   }
   else
   {
      f3=(float)j2/next_anim_dur;
      objmesh->set_state(cur_anim,f1,next_anim,f2,f3);
   }
}

if (mod_anim!=-1)
{
   i1=objmesh->animkeys[mod_anim]*ANIM_FRAME_TIME;
   j1=g_flyengine->cur_time-mod_anim_time;
   if (j1>mod_anim_dur)
      mod_anim=-1;
   else
   {
      f1=1.0f-(float)abs(j1*2-mod_anim_dur)/mod_anim_dur;
      objmesh->set_state_blendcur(
         mod_anim,objmesh->animkeys[mod_anim]-1,f1);
   }
}
```

7.3 Skeleton animation

The geometric defects of vertex animation enumerated in the previous section can be overcome, at the cost of a substantial increase in complexity, by using skeleton or bone animation. (Here, of course, we mean algorithmic complexity – complexity in terms of the data required to specify the animation is substantially reduced.) Skeleton animation, as the name implies, means using an articulated structure as the framework that admits the animation control; then attaching a mesh to the skeleton which then facilitates rendering. In games, characters are carefully crafted by artists using tools that enable them to attach a mesh (or skin) to the skeleton by associating each vertex with one or a number of bones. In other applications we may see the procedural generation of skins, but like level design, the role of artist is important in building the 'look' of characters.

With skeleton animation only the animation control for the skeleton need be stored, and as the number of nodes in the skeleton is much less than the number of vertices in the mesh, this will make the memory requirement much less (albeit that the information required for a skeleton node is 4× that required for a vertex). In addition, many different meshes can share the same animations by using the same skeletons. Skeletons also admit the use of IK (Chapter 11). The issue of separation of the mesh and the animation, which skeleton animation facilitates, is of crucial importance in almost all contexts in which figure animation is used.

Consider first the skeleton structure. There are several options possible. The simplest way to store the structure is: for each node set up a matrix representing the rotation and translation from the origin. Note that this method does not explicitly link the nodes together, nor does it reflect the fact that the skeleton is a hierarchy. If each bone is specified by a position and orientation then there needs to be constraints that keep the bones joined together. All of these constraints need to be applied when any motion is applied.

Now consider the conventional tree structure, which does set up an explicit hierarchy. Each child node possesses a single matrix which represents its rotation and translation (or offset) from its parent node. Global positioning and orientation are applied to the root node (usually the hip) and all other motion is specified relative to the root node.

Thus the hierarchy is the preferred option. A simple skeleton hierarchy is shown in Figure 7.6.

Another motivation of the hierarchical structure is that we can apply joint limits easily to prevent unfeasible motion – elbow bending in the wrong direction, for example.

All skin vertices must be transformed into the world system for rendering and the required matrix is formed by concatenating the **TR**s from the root node to the bone with which the vertex is associated. For example, to map a vertex **v** in the hand into the root node we use:

$$\mathbf{v}_w = \mathbf{M}_{hand} \, \mathbf{v} \tag{7.1}$$
$$= [\mathbf{T}_{waist}\mathbf{R}_{waist}\mathbf{T}_{stomach}\mathbf{R}_{stomach}\mathbf{T}_{chest}\mathbf{R}_{chest}\mathbf{T}_{upper\text{-}arm}\mathbf{R}_{upper\text{-}arm}\mathbf{T}_{forearm}\mathbf{R}_{forearm}\mathbf{T}_{hand}\mathbf{R}_{hand}] \, \mathbf{v}$$

All translations in the skeleton hierarchy remain constant throughout the animation and simply specify the length of the bone linking the joints. The animation data consists therefore of an **R** matrix for each bone.

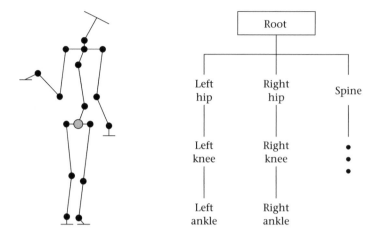

Figure 7.6
The conventional skeleton hierarchy representation used in skeleton animation.

Figure 7.7 (also Colour Plate) uses the same character that was used to produce Figure 7.4 (vertex animation). However, this time the character is skeleton animated and then skinned. We can see from this that the interpolation of rotation eliminates the gross distortion in vertex animation. Also shown in the figure is the simple skeleton used. Skeletons used in current games tend to be of this order of complexity. Note that there is no bone for the feet or hands. This, of course, means that the feet cannot rotate with respect to the ankle and the hand with respect to the wrist.

A skeleton hierarchy can be set up in a single data structure as:

```
flyMatrix skeleton_node[num_bones];
int parent_node[num_bones];
```

where the skeleton is the array of matrices *skeleton_node* (one for each bone) storing the transformation of the node relating its parent. The *parent_node* array includes the index for the parent node of each bone (where –1 means the root node). The advantage of this structure is that the parent node array is fixed and the key frames for the skeleton is stored as simple matrix arrays.

Figure 7.7
Showing the advantage of skeleton animation over vertex animation for eliminating geometric distortion of the skin layer. (a) Interpolating rotation removes vertex interpolation distortion.

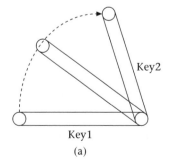

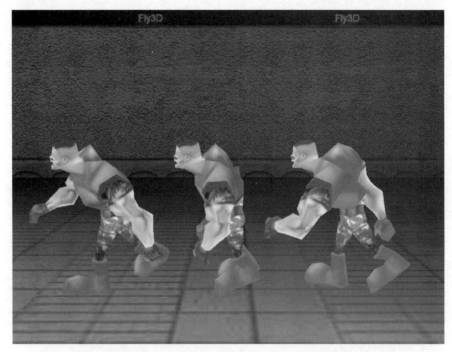

(b)

Figure 7.7 *continued*
(b) Key interpolation
for the entire figure
(compare with Figure
7.4). (c) Showing the
skeleton used.

(c)

Consider now the way in which vertices are positioned with respect to the skeleton. Each vertex is associated explicitly with at least one bone. When a vertex is assigned to a single skeleton node it is called a rigid or hard vertex. In practice, a vertex can be associated with many bones. Each association consists of the bone index, a weighting factor (0 to 1) and a displacement vector. The displacement vector is the vector from the bone to the vertex and the weighting factors for a single vertex should summate to 1. To compute the position of a vertex from its associated bones we use the product:

$$\sum_{i=0}^{n} \mathbf{M}_i \mathbf{d}_i w_i$$

where

$\mathbf{M}_i$ is the (global) matrix for bone i

$\mathbf{d}_i$ is the displacement vector from the vertex to the ith bone attachment

w_i is the weight of this attachment

n is the number of attachments

This is the basic model for skinning or enveloping a skeleton. It is simple but exhibits certain problems. These are discussed fully in Chapter 8 together with more generalised models.

The following code implements this scheme to generate all vertices from a skeleton:

```
// build the vertices based on current skeleton
void flySkeletonMesh::build_verts()
{
   int p=0;
   int i,j;
   for( i=0;i<nv;i++ )
   {
   verts[i].null();
   for( j=0;j<nvweights[i];j++,p++ )
     verts[i] += (m[vindex[p]]*vweight[p])*vweight[p].w;
   }
}
```

(Note that in the above code we have used operator overloading for the matrix vector multiplication.) This simple code generates all vertices for the mesh based on the current skeleton position. They can now be passed for rendering in the frame.

We now consider how to blend skeletons. Once the details of this are solved we can then use the same blending controller as for vertex animation, prior to calling the method that generates the vertices, providing we continue to use linear interpolation.

Interpolation in the case of vertex animation was simple linear between two positions. Now we have to decide how to interpolate between two matrices that represent rotation and translation. This is easily done in the absence of any scaling component in the matrix.

At this stage we should consider the different roles of translation and rotation. For a static figure the translation component in a matrix remains constant and simply specifies the distance of a node from its parent; in other words, the length of a limb. All movements of an arm or leg are due to rotations about a joint. In the event that this remains constant, the translation component remains constant. Note that for a real figure this is not entirely accurate; spines, for example, flex, causing the overall length effectively to change. To model this accurately we would need to imitate the structure of the spine, breaking it up into vertebrae segments. For a walking or running figure the root node translates and it is this component that is interpolated.

We can now proceed to interpolate by linearly interpolating the translation component and using quaternion interpolation (*slerp*) to interpolate the rotation (see Appendix 7.1). The following code interpolates between two matrices that do not possess any scaling component. (Note that if scaling was included we would have to adopt a procedure called an affine split that separates the rotational and scaling component.)

```
void flyMatrix::slerp(flyMatrix& m1,flyMatrix& m2,float t)
{
    flyQuaternion q1(m1),q2(m2),qt;
    qt.lerp(q1,q2,t);
    qt.get_mat(*this);
    m[3][0]=m1.m[3][0]*(1-t)+m2.m[3][0]*t;
    m[3][1]=m1.m[3][1]*(1-t)+m2.m[3][1]*t;
    m[3][2]=m1.m[3][2]*(1-t)+m2.m[3][2]*t;
}
```

Of particular note is the very low code complexity of the two methods responsible for interpolation and skinning. In the above code the constructor of the quaternion executes the conversion of a rotation matrix to a quaternion, the *slerp* method from the quaternion class interpolates two quaternions and the *get_mat* method transforms a quaternion back into a rotation matrix. This is followed by the linear interpolation of the translation. To speed up the computation the quaternions representing the rotation for each key of each skeleton node could be pre-calculated. The interpolation should take place in local coordinate space (the matrix relates to the parent node) rather than global coordinate space where the matrix would relate to the origin, which is the root node.

Figure 7.8 (also Colour Plate) shows a character animated using this scheme. *Slerp* is controlling the interpolation of the bones of the skeleton and the figure is walking along a Bézier path from which is derived a translation and orientation for the root node.

7.3.1 The role of IK in interpolation

IK in current games is used mostly in simple manifestations: controlling the player's direction of gaze, aiming guns etc. By simple we mean that the IK is only applied to an entity such as an arm. More complex structures are too difficult

Figure 7.8
Quaternion interpolation for the skeleton plus translation and orientation of the root node controlled by a Bézier curve.

and costly to solve in real time and in many instances a hybrid approach obtains. For example, consider gaze. Here a character can only move his head around, following an object, to within the rotational limit of the neck. When this is reached a body rotation movement must be invoked. A similar approach must be used in the case of a (third person) character aiming a gun towards a specific target. The body is rotated so that the arm comes into a viable sector in space from which IK can tune the orientation of the entire arm.

'In place' animation, where a walk cycle is animated with the root node never changing position (as if the character was walking on an exercise machine), is a simple and convenient way of obtaining a flexible user-controlled walk path. The control simply translates and rotates the root node as the animation loops. However, this raises a problem with synchronising the speed of the animation with the speed of the user control. Attempts to do this usually result in the character executing a sliding motion with its feet. (In fact in a real walk cycle the forward motion of the hips is not constant but varies over the walk cycle and the type of walk.) In first-person shooter games this effect is sometimes ameliorated by the speed at which the character moves. But as the forward motion of a character becomes slower this undesirable effect is highly noticeable. The ideal method of moving a human figure, at a certain speed over a certain path, under user control in a game, is to calculate the correct animation in real time. This implies the judicious use of IK, which is fully discussed in Chapter 11.

Thus we see that the current role of IK is that of a module that switches in and out of 'normal' animation control, and is applied to part of the articulated structure. It is not, nor will it be in the immediate future, a method that has control over the entire structure in an entire animation sequence.

⟨**7.4**⟩ **Low-level animation management**

As we have seen, simple character animation in games, regardless of genre, uses a mix of (usually pre-recorded or pre-scripted) sequences that blend together to form a continuous character motion. In this section we will examine how we can implement a simple scheme for the low-level organisation of animation sequences. This will involve a simple study of a character, under user control, who travels through an environment interacting with objects, which causes different animation sequences to be invoked. This is effectively an object-oriented approach to the task. We will also try to match the orientation of the character in the last frame of a sequence $n - 1$ to its required orientation in the first frame of the sequence n so that we do not have to rely on the crude technique of blending between the two sequences.

Consider first that a way of generating complete sequences is to have animation sequences for a character's interaction with objects. We categorise these sequences into three parts, *in*, *out* and *idle*. The *in* and *out* are fixed length sequences and the *idle* sequence is so named because it can be of any length. These sequences are linked with, say, a *walk* animation that takes the character from object to object. An *idle* animation state signifies some persistent action or pose of the character which may be sitting or standing still. Animation in this state may consist of the character looking around while standing still. The *in* animation is animation that takes the character into the idle state. The *idle* state repeats some sequence continuously until the character has to change state, at which point an *out* animation is played.

We now illustrate this concept with a simple scenario (Figure 7.9). This is a character, under user or AI control, who is walking through the environment and interacting with the objects in the scene.

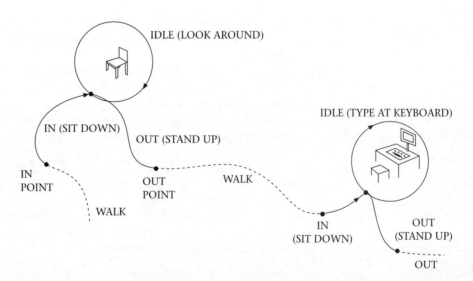

Figure 7.9
A simple approach to low-level management of animation sequences.

Each object possesses an *in/idle/out* animation. In this scenario we have three objects and a character with animations as follows:

chair

in	sit down motion
idle	relaxing and looking around
out	get up from chair

computer terminal

in	sit down motion
idle	type at keyboard
out	get up from terminal

ground

in	no motion – skip to next state
idle	standing up and looking around
out	no motion – skip to next state

character
only possesses a **transition** state which is a *walk* sequence

All animation sequences are pre-calculated/pre-captured. The character's *walk* animation is also pre-calculated but the orientation and translation for the root node are calculated on the fly as the game progresses. The character is to walk to the chair, sit down for a rest period, get up and walk to the computer terminal and start typing. The total sequence is generated by concatenating 'packs' of *in/idle/out* sequences. Between each sequence the character walks from the last frame of the *out* animation of the previous pack to the first frame of the *in* sequence of the next pack. Associated with each *in* sequence will be a position, relative to the object that the character is going to react with, and an orientation. This position and orientation are to match the first frame of the *in* sequence and it is the responsibility of the path generator to end a walk to an object in the correct position and orientation. Similarly, the end of the *out* sequence gives a position and orientation for the start of the next walk.

Refer again to Figure 7.9. Consider that the player is in the *idle* animation of the chair – he is sitting down, looking around. An event occurs that requires the player to operate the computer terminal. The *next pack* buffer is set to contain the computer terminal pack. The initialisation of the *next pack* buffer causes the player to change state and the *out* animation of the chair pack plays. The character then has to find a path from the last frame of the *out* animation of the chair pack to the first frame of the *in* animation of the computer terminal path and walks to change objects. The scheme can be considered as a series of state transition diagrams. Four states are possible: *in*, *idle*, *out* and *walk* (Figure 7.10).

This structure is clearly only appropriate for a restricted set of applications but it does correctly handle connecting animation sequences together without having to rely on the 'fix' of blending.

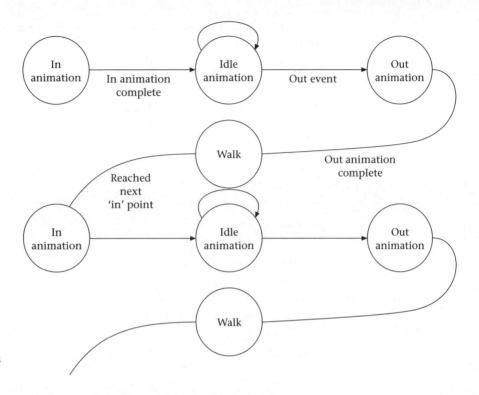

Figure 7.10
State transition diagrams for a set of sequences.

7.4.1

Path planning for walks

Starting at the lowest level, we can consider generating a path between two points each with an associated orientation required for the animation 'join'. A path can be generated for the walk using a Bézier curve. We simply need to ensure that the direction tangent for the last frame of the *out* animation matches the direction tangent for the first frame of the *walk* animation. This can be implemented in a simple case as follows (Figure 7.11).

The start of the walk and the end of the walk define the end control points p_0 and p_3. These are the *out* and *in* points of the object animation. p_1 needs to

Figure 7.11
Generating a Bézier path using the orientations at the end of sequence $n - 1$ and the start of sequence n.

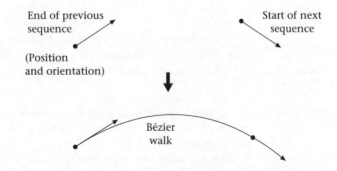

be positioned on the tangent vector that specifies the direction of the last frame of the *out* sequence and p_2 is similarly positioned on the negative of the tangent vector for the first frame of the *in* sequence.

The question is: where do we position the points on the tangent vector? Too close to the end control points will make a turn that is too fast and the character will rotate very quickly. Making the point too far away will generate too leisurely and long a walk. A simple distance value is 0.5 (say) of the distance between p_0 and p_3. This can be implemented as follows:

```
// build walk path with a single bezier segment
bezier_curve build_curve_1seg(
    vector& out_pos,vector& out_dir,vector& in_pos,vector& in_dir)
{
    bezier_curve walk_path;
    walk_path.set_dim(2);

    vector v=out_pos-in_pos;
    v.z=0;
    path_dist=v.length()/3.0f;

    walk_path.add_point(&out_pos.x);

    v=out_pos+out_dir*path_dist;
    walk_path.add_point(&v.x);

    v=in_pos-in_dir*path_dist;
    walk_path.add_point(&v.x);

    walk_path.add_point(&in_pos.x);

    return walk_path;
}
```

Once we have calculated a Bézier path, we derive the translation and orientation for the root node of the character directly from the curve parameters[2] as shown in Figure 7.12 (also Colour Plate).

The foregoing analysis applies to single-segment Bézier curves and this will not suffice in many cases. Difficult cases arise when the tangent vectors are collinear. In these cases we need to add Bézier segments to achieve a reasonable path. Figure 7.13 shows cases where two or three segments give acceptable solutions.

To implement a scheme that deals with these special cases we need to determine which of the four cases has occurred: forth–forth, forth–back, back–forth or back–back. This can be done efficiently using two dot products:

---

2. Note that for translation, equal intervals in the curve parameter do not give equal intervals along the curve – the arclength distance. This will be a problem or not depending on the application and the speed at which the character is to translate along the curve. A simple solution to arclength parameterisation is given in [WATT00].

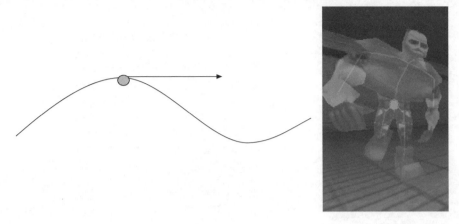

Figure 7.12
Controlling the position and orientation of a character's root node from a Bézier curve.

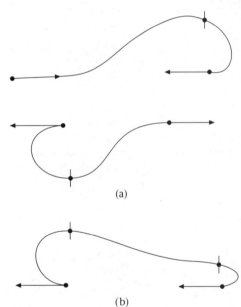

Figure 7.13
In-line tangent vectors using extra Bézier segments to obtain a reasonable path when the tangent vectors are collinear. (a) One extra Bézier segment. (b) Two extra Bézier segments.

```
// analyse the path
int analyse_path(
   vector& out_pos,vector& out_dir,vector& in_pos,vector& in_dir)
{
   verctor v=in_pos-out_pos;
   float dot1=vec_dot(out_dir,in_dir);
   float dot2=vec_dot(out_dir,v);

   if(dot1>0)
     if(dot2>0)
        return PATHCONFIG_FORTH_FORTH;
     else
        return PATHCONFIG_BACK_BACK;
```

```
    else
       if(dot2>0)
          return PATHCONFIG_FORTH_BACK;
       else
          return PATHCONFIG_BACK_FORTH;

    // unreachable
    return -1;
}
```

The following code builds a path for any case:

```
// build walk path with up to three bezier segments
bezier_curve build_curve_3seg(
   vector& out_pos,vector& out_dir,vector& in_pos,vector& in_dir)
{
   bezier_curve walk_path;
   walk_path.set_dim(2);

   // calculate 1/3 of the distance
   vector v=pos-in_pos;
   v.z=0;
   path_dist=v.length()/4.0f;

   // add the control points
   walk_path.add_point(&out_pos.x);

   v=out_pos+out_dir*path_dist;
   walk_path.add_point(&v.x);

   vector v1=out_dir*path_dist,v2;
   v2.x=v1.y;
   v2.y=v1.x;
   v1.z=v2.z=0;

   vector v3=in_dir*path_dist,v4;
   v4.x=v3.y;
   v4.y=v3.x;
   v3.z=v4.z=0;

   int i=analyse_path();

   switch(i)
   {
      case PATHCONFIG_FORTH_BACK       :
      {
         v.cross(v3,v1);
         if(v.z<0)
            v4.negate();

         v=in_pos+v3+v4;
         walk_path.add_point(&v.x);

         v=in_pos+v4;
         walk_path.add_point(&v.x);
```

```
      v=in_pos-v3+v4;
      walk_path.add_point(&v.x);
    }
  break;
  case  PATHCONFIG_BACK_FORTH        :
  {
    v.cross(v3,v1);
    if(v.z<0)
      v2.negate();

    v=out_pos+v1+v2;
    walk_path.add_point(&v.x);

    v=out_pos+v2;
    walk_path.add_point(&v.x);

    v=out_pos-v1+v2;
    walk_path.add_point(&v.x);
  }
  break;
  case  PATHCONFIG_BACK_BACK         :
  {
    v.cross(v3,v1);
    if(v.z<0)
    {
      v2.negate();
      v4.negate();
    }

    v=out_pos+v1+v2;
    walk_path.add_point(&v.x);

    v=out_pos+v2;
    walk_path.add_point(&v.x);

    v=out_pos-v1+v2;
    walk_path.add_point(&v.x);

    v=in_pos+v3+v4;
    walk_path.add_point(&v.x);

    v=in_pos+v4;
    walk_path.add_point(&v.x);

    v=in_pos-v3+v4;
    walk_path.add_point(&v.x);
  }
}

v=in_pos-in_dir*path_dist;
walk_path.add_point(&v.x);

walk_path.add_point(&in_pos.x);

return  walk_path
}
```

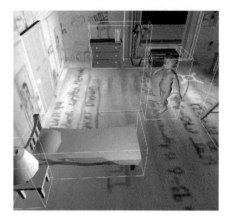 

Figure 7.14
Two walks from different positions to the *in* point of the 'lie down' animation. Each path ends at the same point and the character is in the same pose at that point so that the lie down animation blends successfully with the walk animation (courtesy of Kelseus.com).

7.4.2 Skeleton animation and object-oriented animation control

We now consider how this scheme integrates with skeleton animation. Because we are using skeleton animation we can use a generic skeleton animation sequence as the *in/idle/out* pack at each object and then map any character mesh onto this animation. This means that players represented by different meshes will be able to interact with the objects.

Consider again the path construction of the previous section. We need to find from the *out* and *in* animations the position and direction for the last and first frames respectively. With skeleton animation this is straightforward because it is already included in the animation data. (Note that for vertex animation this would have to be separately specified; it is not part of the animation data.)

The information we require is the root node matrix for the last key (*out*) and first key (*in*). The translation component in the matrix gives us the position and the rotation component decides the direction. Each column in the 3×3 rotational component of the matrix represents one component of the current rotation. We need to select either the *x* or *y* component depending on how the application has been set up. Figure 7.14 (also Colour Plate) shows the scheme in operation.

Finally note that in this simple scheme we are only matching the orientation of the character over two animation sequences. The pose of the skeleton – the actual position of the limbs – is not considered. (This is a topic we will return to in Chapter 12.) Thus we are assuming that each animation finishes and starts with a similar pose.

7.4.3 Simple obstacle avoidance

This scheme admits a simple pre-calculation scheme for path planning. If we first consider that there are no obstacles in the way then *n* paths can be pre-built

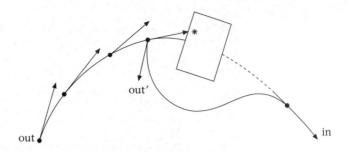

Figure 7.15
Obstacle avoidance by
using ray-intersect
collision detection. Rays
take the direction of the
tangent vector to the
proposed curve at equal
arclength sample points.

for *n* objects using the Bézier scheme of the previous section. At run time the
player walks on these paths.

If there are obstacles then there are two possibilities. First, if the character is
under user control it is simple to enhance the path generation so that the user
avoids the collision by breaking up the path into segments which together form
a clear path. If the character is controlled by game AI then we need some form
of path planning for obstacle avoidance to take place in real time.

In such applications we can proceed as follows. Ray intersect collision detection is activated at equal intervals (parametric or arclength) on the proposed
curve. The direction of the ray is defined by tangent vectors to the proposed
path. If no collision is found at every sample point then the path is clear. If a
collision is found then the player can turn 90 degrees (say) from the collision
face normal and construct a new Bézier path (Figure 7.15) using a new *out*
vector and the same *in* vector. This process can continue recursively until either
we find a path or we exceed a pre-set number of attempts limit, in which case
we conclude that there is no path possible. The problem with this method is
that it results in a series of discontinuities. These can be removed by using the
same process but looking ahead and instead of following a path through the
recursion, wait until a successful path is found and then construct a continuous intermediate segment. This will result in a three-segment curve where the
extent of the intermediate curve can be prevented from penetrating the object
by the collision point found during the recursion. Figure 7.16 (also Colour Plate)
is an example of this simple scheme in operation. Here the objects are encased in
AABBs and it is the bounding volumes that are tested for collision (Chapter 2).

Using bounding volumes for obstacle avoidance in a character usually
suffices in most cases. Note, however, that there are many applications where
an AABB enclosed character is not of sufficient accuracy. (This point is discussed
in Chapter 2.)

Generalised path planning

We are now in a position to integrate this material with the geometric path
planning scheme detailed in Chapter 2. Path planning now generalises to the
following sequence:

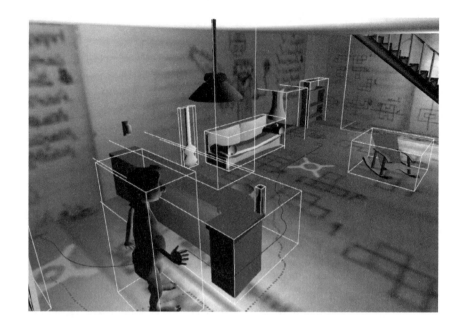

Figure 7.16
Moving from red position to blue position avoiding the bar. In this case the objects are encased in AABBs (courtesy of Kelseus.com).

(1) Use the pseudo-portal scheme described in Chapter 2 to create a graph of potential paths through the level. This is a build process.

(2) For a required walk sequence between two objects we use A* to find a path through the portals (also described in Chapter 2).

(3) Use the Bézier scheme described above to generate a curve path that passes through the nodes selected by (2).

(4) Collision avoidance against objects contained in nodes selected in (2).

This approach can be integrated with the Bézier path planning scheme. Figure 7.17 shows an *out* point in one room and an *in* point in another with a third room connecting the source and destination. The connecting portals define intermediate normals defined as shown and the complete path is formed from three segments, the centre point of each door forming the join points for the segments.

Appendix 7.1 Using quaternions to represent rotation

A useful introductory notion concerning quaternions is to consider them as an operator, like a matrix, that changes one vector into another, but where the infinite choice of matrix elements is removed. Instead of specifying the nine elements of a matrix we define four real numbers. We begin by looking at angular displacement of a vector rotating a vector by θ about an axis $\mathbf{n}$.

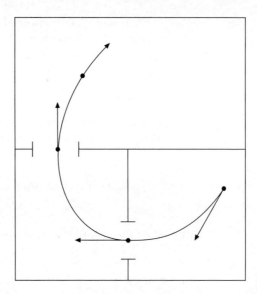

Figure 7.17
Constructing a multi-segment Bézier path through portals.

We define rotation as an angular displacement given by $(\theta, \mathbf{n})$ of an amount θ about an axis $\mathbf{n}$. That is, instead of specifying rotation as $R(\theta_1, \theta_2, \theta_3)$ we write $R(\theta, \mathbf{n})$. Consider the angular displacement acting on a vector $\mathbf{r}$ taking it to position $R\mathbf{r}$ as shown in Figure 7.18.

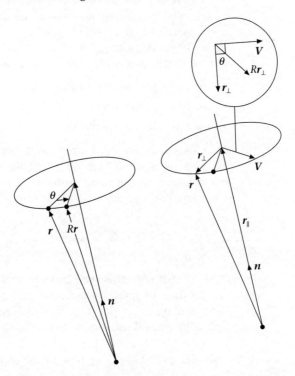

Figure 7.18
Angular displacement $(\theta, \mathbf{n})$ of $\mathbf{r}$.

The problem can be decomposed by resolving **r** into components parallel to **n**, which by definition remains unchanged after rotation, and perpendicular to **n** in the plane passing through **r** and R**r**.

$$\mathbf{r}_{\parallel} = (\mathbf{n.r})\mathbf{n}$$

$$\mathbf{r}_{\perp} = \mathbf{r} - (\mathbf{n.r})\mathbf{n}$$

$\mathbf{r}_{\perp}$ is rotated into position R$\mathbf{r}_{\perp}$. We construct a vector perpendicular to $\mathbf{r}_{\perp}$ and lying in the plane. In order to evaluate this rotation, we write:

$$\mathbf{V} = \mathbf{n} \times \mathbf{r}_{\perp} = \mathbf{n} \times \mathbf{r}$$

where $\times$ specifies the cross product

so

$$\mathrm{R}\mathbf{r}_{\perp} = (\mathrm{Cos}\,\theta)\mathbf{r}_{\perp} + (\mathrm{Sin}\,\theta)\mathbf{V}$$

hence

$$
\begin{aligned}
\mathrm{R}\mathbf{r} &= \mathrm{R}_{\parallel} + \mathrm{R}\mathbf{r}_{\perp} \\
&= \mathrm{R}_{\parallel} + (\mathrm{Cos}\,\theta)\mathbf{r}_{\perp} + (\mathrm{Sin}\,\theta)\mathbf{V} \\
&= (\mathbf{n.r})\mathbf{n} + \mathrm{Cos}\,\theta(\mathbf{r} - (\mathbf{n.r})\mathbf{n}) + (\mathrm{Sin}\,\theta)\mathbf{n} \times \mathbf{r} \\
&= (\mathrm{Cos}\,\theta)\mathbf{r} + (1 - \mathrm{Cos}\,\theta)\mathbf{n}(\mathbf{n.r}) + (\mathrm{Sin}\,\theta)\mathbf{n} \times \mathbf{r} \quad\quad\quad (7.2)
\end{aligned}
$$

We will now show that rotating the vector **r** by the angular displacement can be achieved by a quaternion transformation. That is, we apply a quaternion like a matrix to change a vector.

We begin by noting that to effect such an operation we only need four real numbers (this compares with the nine elements in a matrix). We require:

- the change of length of the vector;
- the plane of the rotation (which can be defined by two angles from two axes);
- the angle of the rotation.

In other words, we need a representation that only possesses the four degrees of freedom required according to Euler's theorem. For this we will use **unit** quaternions. As the name implies, quaternions are 'four-vectors' and can be considered as a generalisation of complex numbers with s as the real or scalar part and x,y,z as the imaginary part:

$$
\begin{aligned}
q &= s + x\mathbf{i} + y\mathbf{j} + z\mathbf{k} \\
&= (s,\mathbf{v})
\end{aligned}
$$

Here we can note their similarity to a two-dimensional complex number that can be used to specify a point or vector in two-dimensional space. A quaternion can specify a point in four-dimensional space and, if $s = 0$, a point or vector in three-dimensional space. In this context they are used to represent a vector plus rotation. **i**, **j**, and **k** are unit quaternions and are equivalent to unit vectors in a vector system; however, they obey different combination rules:

$$\mathbf{i}^2 = \mathbf{j}^2 = \mathbf{k}^2 = \mathbf{ijk} = -1, \ \mathbf{ij} = \mathbf{k}, \ \mathbf{ji} = -\mathbf{k}$$

Using these we can derive addition and multiplication rules, each of which yields a quaternion:

- addition:

$$q + q' = (s + s', \ \mathbf{v} + \mathbf{v}')$$

- multiplication:

$$qq' = (ss' - \mathbf{v}.\mathbf{v}', \ \mathbf{v} \times \mathbf{v}' + s\mathbf{v}' + s'\mathbf{v})$$

The conjugate of the quaternion

$$q = (s, \mathbf{v})$$

is

$$\bar{q} = (s, -\mathbf{v})$$

and the product of the quaternion with its conjugate defines its magnitude

$$q\bar{q} = s^2 + |\mathbf{v}^2| = q^2$$

If

$$|q| = 1$$

then q is called a unit quaternion. The set of all unit quaternions forms a unit sphere in four-dimensional space and unit quaternions play an important part in specifying general rotations.

It can be shown that if

$$q = (s, \mathbf{v})$$

then there exists a $\mathbf{v}'$ and a $\theta \in [-\pi, \pi]$ such that

$$q = (\cos \theta, \ \mathbf{v}' \sin \theta)$$

and if q is a unit quaternion then

$$q = (\cos \theta, \ \sin \theta \, \mathbf{n}) \tag{7.3}$$

where $|\mathbf{n}| = 1$.

We now consider operating on a vector $\mathbf{r}$ in Figure 7.18 by using quaternions. $\mathbf{r}$ is defined as the quaternion $p = (0, \mathbf{r})$ and we define the operation as:

$$R_p(p) = qpq^{-1}$$

That is, it is proposed to rotate the vector $\mathbf{r}$ by expressing it as a quaternion, multiplying it on the left by q and on the right by q^{-1}. This guarantees that the result will be a quaternion of the form $(0, \mathbf{v})$, in other words a vector. q is defined to be a unit quaternion $(s, \mathbf{v})$. It is easily shown that:

$$R_p(p) = (0, (s^2 - \mathbf{v}.\mathbf{v})\mathbf{r} + 2\mathbf{v}(\mathbf{v}.\mathbf{r}) + 2s(\mathbf{v} \times \mathbf{r}))$$

Using proposition 7.3 and substituting into equation 7.2 gives

$$Rq(p) = (0,(Cos^2\theta - Sin^2\theta)\mathbf{r} + 2 Sin^2\theta\mathbf{n}(\mathbf{n}.\mathbf{r}) + 2 Cos\theta Sin\theta(\mathbf{n} \times \mathbf{r}))$$
$$= (0,\mathbf{r} Cos 2\theta + (1 - Cos 2\theta)\mathbf{n}(\mathbf{n}.\mathbf{r}) + Sin 2\theta(\mathbf{n} \times \mathbf{r}))$$

Now compare this with equation 7.2. You will notice that aside from a factor of 2 appearing in the angle they are identical in form. What can we conclude from this? The act of rotating a vector $\mathbf{r}$ by an angular displacement $(\theta,\mathbf{n})$ is the same as taking this angular displacement, 'lifting' it into quaternion space, by representing it as the unit quaternion

$$(Cos(\theta/2), Sin(\theta/2)\mathbf{n})$$

and performing the operation $q()q^{-1}$ on the quaternion $(0,\mathbf{r})$. We could therefore parametrise orientation in terms of the four parameters

$$Cos(\theta/2), Sin(\theta/2)\mathbf{n}_x, Sin(\theta/2)\mathbf{n}_y, Sin(\theta/2)\mathbf{n}_z$$

using quaternion algebra to manipulate the components.

Let us now consider an example to see how this works in practice. Figure 7.19 shows two paths of a character rotating about the local origin between two keys. Using Euler angles, the first image interpolates an x rotation or roll to achieve the in-betweens; the second interpolates both a y and z rotation. The resulting in-between sequences are completely different, the first producing a direct rotation and the second a twisting and rotating motion. One of the reasons for using quaternions is to avoid such difficulties.

The first single xroll of π is represented by the quaternion

$$(Cos(\pi/2), Sin(\pi/2) (1,0,0)) = (0,(1,0,0))$$

Similarly a yroll of π and a zroll of π are given by $(0,(0,1,0))$ and $(0,(0,0,1))$ respectively. Now the effect of a yroll of π followed by a zroll of π can be represented by the single quaternion formed by multiplying these two quaternions together:

$$(0,(0,1,0)) (0,(0,0,1)) = (0,(0,1,0) \times (0,0,1))$$
$$= (0,(1,0,0))$$

which is identically the single xroll of π.

We conclude this section by noting that quaternions are used exclusively to represent orientation – they can be used to represent translation but combining rotation and translation into a scheme analogous to homogeneous coordinates is not straightforward.

Interpolating quaternions

Given the superiority of quaternion parameterisation over Euler angle parameterisation, this section covers the issue of interpolating rotation in quaternion space. Consider an animator sitting at a workstation and interactively setting up a sequence of key orientations by whatever method is appropriate. This is usually done with the principal rotation operations, but now the restrictions

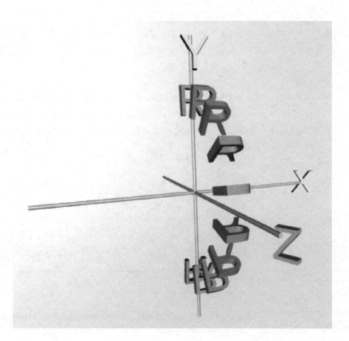

Figure 7.19
Two different paths
between the same
keys result from the
interpolation choice
of Euler angles.

that were placed on the animator when using Euler angles, namely using a fixed number of principal rotations in a fixed order for each key, can be removed. In general, each key will be represented as a single rotation matrix. This sequence of matrices will then be converted into a sequence of quaternions. Interpolation between key quaternions is performed and this produces a sequence of in-between quaternions, which are then converted back into rotation matrices. The matrices are then applied to the object. The fact that a quaternion interpolation is being used is transparent to the animator.

Moving in and out of quaternion space

The implementation of such a scheme requires us to move into and out of quaternion space, that is, to go from a general rotation matrix to a quaternion and vice versa. Now to rotate a vector p with the quaternion q we use the operation

$$q(0,p)q^{-1}$$

where q is the quaternion:

$$(\mathrm{Cos}(\theta/2), \mathrm{Sin}(\theta/2)\mathbf{n}) = (s,(x,y,z))$$

It can be shown that this is exactly equivalent to applying the following rotation matrix to the vector:

$$\mathbf{M} = \begin{bmatrix} 1 - 2(y^2 + z^2) & 2xy - 2sz & 2sy + 2xz & 0 \\ 2xy + 2sz & 1 - 2(x^2 + z^2) & -2sx + 2yz & 0 \\ -2sy + 2xz & 2sx + 2yz & 1 - 2(x^2 + y^2) & 0 \\ 0 & 0 & 0 & 1 \end{bmatrix}$$

By these means then, we can move from quaternion space to rotation matrices.

The inverse mapping, from a rotation matrix to a quaternion, is as follows. All that is required is to convert a general rotation matrix:

$$\begin{bmatrix} M_{00} & M_{01} & M_{02} & M_{03} \\ M_{10} & M_{11} & M_{12} & M_{13} \\ M_{20} & M_{21} & M_{22} & M_{23} \\ M_{30} & M_{31} & M_{32} & M_{33} \end{bmatrix}$$

where $M_{03} = M_{13} = M_{23} = M_{30} = M_{31} = M_{32} = 0$ and $M_{33} = 1$, into the matrix format directly above. Given a general rotation matrix, the first thing to do is to examine the sum of its diagonal components M_{ii}, which is:

$$4 - 4(x^2 + y^2 + z^2)$$

Since the quaternion corresponding to the rotation matrix is of unit magnitude we have:

$$s^2 + x^2 + y^2 + z^2 = 1$$

and

$$4 - 4(x^2 + y^2 + z^2) = 4 - 4(1 - s^2) = 4s^2$$

Thus for a 4×4 homogeneous matrix we have:

$$s = \pm\frac{1}{2}\sqrt{M_{00} + M_{11} + M_{22} + M_{33}}$$

and

$$x = \frac{M_{21} - M_{12}}{4s}$$

$$y = \frac{M_{02} - M_{20}}{4s}$$

$$z = \frac{M_{10} - M_{01}}{4s}$$

Spherical linear interpolation (slerp)

Having outlined our scheme we now discuss how to interpolate in quaternion space. Since a rotation maps onto a quaternion of unit magnitude, the entire group of rotations maps onto the surface of the four-dimensional unit hypersphere in quaternion space. Curves interpolating through key orientations should therefore lie on the surface of this sphere. Consider the simplest case of interpolating between just two key quaternions. A naive, straightforward linear interpolation between the two keys results in a motion that speeds up in the middle. An analogy of this process in a two-dimensional plane is shown in Figure 7.20, which shows that the path on the surface of the sphere yielded by linear interpolation gives unequal angles and causes a speed-up in angular velocity.

This is because we are not moving along the surface of the hypersphere but cutting across it. In order to ensure a steady rotation we must employ spherical linear interpolation (or *slerp*), where we move along an arc of the geodesic that passes through the two keys.

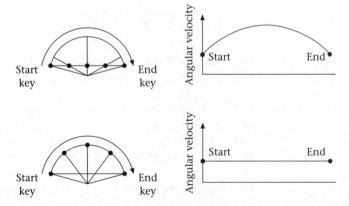

Figure 7.20
A two-dimensional analogy showing the difference between simple linear interpolation and simple spherical linear interpolation (slerp).

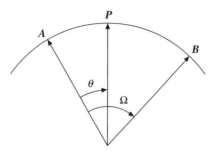

Figure 7.21
Spherical linear
interpolation.

The formula for spherical linear interpolation is easy to derive geometrically. Consider the two-dimensional case of two vectors **A** and **B** separated by angle Ω and vector **P** which makes an angle θ with **A** as shown in Figure 7.21. **P** is derived from spherical interpolation between **A** and **B** and we write

$$\mathbf{P} = \alpha\mathbf{A} + \beta\mathbf{B}$$

Trivially we can solve for α and β given

$$|\mathbf{P}| = 1$$
$$\mathbf{A}.\mathbf{B} = \text{Cos }\Omega$$
$$\mathbf{A}.\mathbf{P} = \text{Cos }\theta$$

to give

$$\mathbf{P} = \mathbf{A}\frac{\sin(\Omega - \theta)}{\sin \Omega} + \mathbf{B}\frac{\sin \theta}{\sin \Omega}$$

Spherical linear interpolation between two unit quaternions $q1$ and $q2$, where

$$q1.q2 = \cos \Omega$$

is obtained by generalising the above to four dimensions and replacing θ by Ω where $u \in [0,1]$. We write

$$\text{slerp}(q_1, q_2, u) = q_1\frac{\sin(1 - u)\Omega}{\sin \Omega} + q_2\frac{\sin \Omega u}{\sin \Omega}$$

Now given any two key quaternions, p and q, there exists two possible arcs along which one can move, corresponding to alternative starting directions on the geodesic that connects them. One of them goes around the long way and this is the one that we wish to avoid. Naively one might assume that this reduces to either spherically interpolating between p and q by the angle Ω, where

$$p.q = \cos \Omega$$

or interpolating in the opposite direction by the angle $2\pi - \Omega$. This, however, will not produce the desired effect. The reason for this is that the topology of the hypersphere of orientation is not just a straightforward extension of the three-dimensional Euclidean sphere. To appreciate this, it is sufficient to consider the fact that every rotation has two representations in quaternion space,

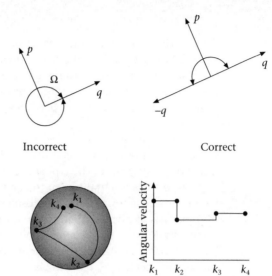

Figure 7.22
Shortest arc determination on quaternion hypersphere.

Incorrect $\qquad$ Correct

Figure 7.23
A three-dimensional analogy of using slerp to interpolate between four keys.

namely q and $-q$; that is, the effect of q and $-q$ is the same. That this is so is due to the fact that algebraically the operator $q()q^{-1}$ has exactly the same effect as $(-q)()(-q)^{-1}$. Thus points diametrically opposed represent the same rotation. Because of this topological oddity care must be taken when determining the shortest arc. A strategy that works is to choose either interpolating between the quaternion pairs p and q or the pair p and $-q$. Given two key orientations p and q, find the magnitude of their difference, that is $(p-q).(p-q)$, and compare this to the magnitude of the difference when the second key is negated, that is $(p+q).(p+q)$. If the former is smaller then we are already moving along the smallest arc and nothing needs to be done. If, however, the second is smallest, then we replace q by $-q$ and proceed. These considerations are shown schematically in Figure 7.22.

So far we have described the spherical equivalent of linear interpolation between two key orientations, and, just as was the case for linear interpolation, spherical linear interpolation between more than two key orientations will produce jerky, sharply changing motion across the keys. The situation is summarised in Figure 7.23 as a three-dimensional analogy which shows that the curve on the surface of the sphere is not continuous through the keys. Also shown in this figure is the angular velocity which is not constant and discontinuous at the keys. The angular velocity can be made constant across all frames by assigning to each interval between keys a number of frames proportional to the magnitude of the interval. That is, we calculate the magnitude of the angle θ between a pair of keys q_t and q_{t+1} as:

$$\cos \theta = q_i.q_{i+1}$$

where the inner product of two quaternions $q = (s,\mathbf{v})$ and $q' = (s',\mathbf{v}')$ is defined as:

$$q.q' = ss' + \mathbf{v}.\mathbf{v}'$$

Curing the path continuity is more difficult. What is required for higher-order continuity is the spherical equivalent of the cubic spline. Unfortunately, because we are now working on the surface of a four-dimensional hyper-sphere, the problem is far more complex than constructing splines in three-dimensional Euclidean space. [DUFF86], [CABR85] and [SHOE87] have all tackled this problem.

Finally, we mention a potential difficulty when applying quaternions. Quaternion interpolation is indiscriminate in that it does not prefer any one direction to any other. Interpolating between two keys produces a move that depends on the orientations of the keys and nothing else. This is inconvenient when choreographing the virtual camera. Normally when moving a camera the film plane is always required to be upright – this is usually specified by an 'up' vector. By its very nature, the notion of a preferred direction cannot easily be built into the quaternion representation and if it is used in this context the camera up vector may have to be reset or some other fix employed. (Roll of the camera is, of course, used in certain contexts.)

Appendix 7.2 Implementing quaternions

The following code is the class definition for a quaternion:

```
class FLY3D_MATH_API flyQuaternion
{
public:
  float x,y,z,w;

  // empty constructor
  flyQuaternion() {};
  // constructor from angle and axis
  flyQuaternion(float angle, flyVector &axis);
  // constructor from a rotation matrix
  flyQuaternion(flyMatrix &mat);

  // normalize quaternion
  void normalize();
  // get current quaternion axis and rotation
  void get_rotate(float &angle, flyVector &axis);
  // spherical linear interpolation
  void slerp(flyQuaternion& q1,flyQuaternion& q2,float t);
  // transform the quaternion into matrix
  void get_mat(flyMatrix &mat);

  // quaternion add operator
  flyQuaternion operator +(flyQuaternion &q)
  // quaternion multiply operator
  flyQuaternion operator *(flyQuaternion &q);
};
```

This code builds a quaternion from a specified axis and angle to rotate about the axis.

```
flyQuaternion(float angle, flyVector &axis)
{
  float f=(float)sin(angle*PiOver180*0.5f);
  x=axis.x*f;
  y=axis.y*f;
  z=axis.z*f;
  w=(float)cos(angle*PiOver180*0.5f);
};
```

The following code builds a quaternion from a 3×3 rotation matrix. In this way we transform into quaternion space to enable slerp.

```
flyQuaternion::flyQuaternion(flyMatrix &mat)
{
  float tr,s,q[4];
  int i,j,k;

  int nxt[3] = {1, 2, 0};

  tr = mat.m[0][0] + mat.m[1][1] + mat.m[2][2];

  // check the diagonal
  if (tr > 0.0)
  {
    s = (float)sqrt(tr + 1.0f);
    w = s/2.0f;
    s = 0.5f/s;
    x = (mat.m[1][2] - mat.m[2][1]) * s;
    y = (mat.m[2][0] - mat.m[0][2]) * s;
    z = (mat.m[0][1] - mat.m[1][0]) * s;
  }
  else
  {
    // diagonal is negative
    i = 0;
    if (mat.m[1][1] > mat.m[0][0]) i = 1;
    if (mat.m[2][2] > mat.m[i][i]) i = 2;
    j = nxt[i];
    k = nxt[j];

    s=(float)sqrt((mat.m[i][i]-(mat.m[j][j] + mat.m[k][k])) + 1.0);

    q[i]=s*0.5f;

    if(s!=0.0f) s = 0.5f/s;

    q[3] = (mat.m[j][k] - mat.m[k][j]) * s;
    q[j] = (mat.m[i][j] + mat.m[j][i]) * s;
    q[k] = (mat.m[i][k] + mat.m[k][i]) * s;
```

```
      x = q[0];
      y = q[1];
      z = q[2];
      w = q[3];
   }
}
```

The following code normalises a quaternion, making its magnitude unit length.

```
void flyQuaternion::normalize()
{
   float  factor  =  1.0f/(float)sqrt(x*x+y*y+z*z+w*w);

   x*=factor;
   y*=factor;
   z*=factor;
   w*=factor;
}
```

The following code returns the current quaternion axis and rotation about it.

```
void flyQuaternion::get_rotate(float &angle, flyVector &axis)
{
   angle=(float)acos(w)*2*PiUnder180;

   float  f=(float)sin(angle*PiOver180*0.5f);

   axis.x=x/f;
   axis.y=x/f;
   axis.z=x/f;
}
```

The following code interpolates between two quaternions and returns a quaternion representing a rotation between the two given quaternions. The t parameter must be in the range [0–1].

```
void flyQuaternion::slerp(flyQuaternion& q1,flyQuaternion& q2,float t)
{
   float v;       // complement to t
   float o;       // complement to v (t)
   float theta;   // angle between q1 & q2
   float sin_t;   // sin(theta)
   float cos_t;   // cos(theta)
   float phi;     // spins added to theta
   int flip;      // flag for negating q2

   cos_t = q1[0] * q2[0] + q1[1] * q2[1] + q1[2] * q2[2] + q1[3]
* q2[3];

   if (cos_t < 0.0)
```

```
{
    cos_t = -cos_t;
    flip = 1;
}
else
    flip = 0;

if (1.0 - cos_t < 1e-6)
{
  v = 1.0f - t;
    o = t;
}
else
{
  theta = (float)acos(cos_t);
  phi = theta;
  sin_t = (float)sin(theta);
  v = (float)sin(theta - t * phi) / sin_t;
  o = (float)sin(t * phi) / sin_t;
}
if (flip) o = -o;

x = v * q1[0] + o * q2[0];
y = v * q1[1] + o * q2[1];
z = v * q1[2] + o * q2[2];
w = v * q1[3] + o * q2[3];
}
```

The following code transforms the quaternion into a 3×3 rotation matrix.

```
void flyQuaternion::get_mat(flyMatrix &mat)
{
  float wx, wy, wz, xx, yy, yz, xy, xz, zz, x2, y2, z2;

  // calculate coefficients
  x2 = x + x;
  y2 = y + y;
  z2 = z + z;
  xx = x * x2;
  xy = x * y2;
  xz = x * z2;
  yy = y * y2;
  yz = y * z2;
  zz = z * z2;
  wx = w * x2;
  wy = w * y2;
  wz = w * z2;

  mat.m[0][0] = 1.0f-(yy+zz);
  mat.m[1][0] = xy - wz;
  mat.m[2][0] = xz + wy;
  mat.m[3][0] = 0.0;
```

```
    mat.m[0][1] = xy + wz;
    mat.m[1][1] = 1.0f-(xx + zz);
    mat.m[2][1] = yz - wx;
    mat.m[3][1] = 0.0;

    mat.m[0][2] = xz - wy;
    mat.m[1][2] = yz + wx;
    mat.m[2][2] = 1.0f - (xx + yy);
    mat.m[3][2] = 0.0;

    mat.m[0][3] = 0;
    mat.m[1][3] = 0;
    mat.m[2][3] = 0;
    mat.m[3][3] = 1;
}
```

The following code multiplies two quaternions.

```
flyQuaternion flyQuaternion::operator *(flyQuaternion &q)
{
    float A, B, C, D, E, F, G, H;
    flyQuaternion res;

    A = (q.w + q.x)*(w + x);
    B = (q.z - q.y)*(y - z);
    C = (q.w - q.x)*(y + z);
    D = (q.y + q.z)*(w - x);
    E = (q.x + q.z)*(x + y);
    F = (q.x - q.z)*(x - y);
    G = (q.w + q.y)*(w - z);
    H = (q.w - q.y)*(w + z);

    res.w = B + (-E - F + G + H) /2;
    res.x = A - (E + F + G + H)/2;
    res.y = C + (E - F + G - H)/2;
    res.z = D + (E - F - G + H)/2;

    return res;
}
```

The following code adds two quaternions.

```
flyQuaternion operator +(flyQuaternion &q)
{
    flyQuaternion res;
    res.x=x+q.x;
    res.y=y+q.y;
    res.z=z+q.z;
    res.w=w+q.w;
    return res;
};
```

Appendix 7.3 Efficiency consideration in character animation (optimising for SIMD Pentium3 intructions)

Animating characters is one of the most CPU-intensive operations in games. The task of interpolating between animation keys for a very smooth animation play and also blending between different animations requires a lot of CPU work. Because this is usually a fixed computation applied to each vertex from the character model, we can use SIMD Pentium3 instructions to speed up the computation needed with instructions that operate in parallel for x, y and z vertices components. In this appendix we look at how we can make a major gain in efficiency over the code in the main text of the chapter by using the SIMD Pentium3 instructions.

Aligned memory allocation

The SIMD Pentium3 instructions all need aligned data (the x component of the vector must be aligned so that its address modulo 16 is equal to 0). We can only make sure data is properly aligned using special allocation routines that allocate and free 128-bit aligned memory. You must also make sure the your structure size modulo 16 is always 0 so that each array item will be properly aligned.

```
void *aligned_alloc(int n)
{
   char *data=new char[n+20];
   unsigned t=(unsigned)data+4;
   t=((t&0xf)==0?0:16-(t&0xf));
   *((unsigned *)&data[t])=t;
   return &data[t+4];
}

void aligned_free(void *data)
{
   if (data==0)
     return;
   int t=*(((unsigned *)data)-1);
   char *d=(char *)data;
   d-=t+4;
   delete d;
}
```

For unaligned arrays:

```
flyVector *vecs=new flyVector[nvec];
flyMatrix *mats=new flyMarix[nmat];
flyVertex *verts=new flyVertex[nvert];
```

```
delete[] vecs;
delete[] mats;
delete[] verts;
```

For aligned arrays:

```
flyVector *vecs=(flyVector *)aligned_alloc(sizeof(flyVector)*nvec);
flyMatrix *mats=(flyMarix *)aligned_alloc(sizeof(flyMarix)*nmat);
flyVertex *verts=(flyVertex *)aligned_alloc(sizeof(flyVertex*nvert);
```

```
aligned_free(vecs);
aligned_free(mats);
aligned_free(verts);
```

Vertex mesh animation key interpolation

Interpolates the mesh vertices for a float key in the animation (linearly interpolates between two keys).

```
void flyAnimatedMesh::set_state(int anim, float key_factor)
{
    int i,j,k;
    float s;
    flyVertex *v0;
    flyVector *v1,*v2;

    // compute local key factor between the two
    // animation keys to be interpolated (key_factor)
    j=(int)(key_factor*animkeys[anim]);
    if (j==animkeys[anim])
      { j=0; key_factor=0.0f; }
    s=1.0f/animkeys[anim];
    key_factor=(key_factor-j*s)/s;

    // find vertex pointers for the two
    // animation keys to be interpolated (v1 and v2)
    v1=&key_verts[(animkeyspos[anim]+j)*nv];
    if (j==animkeys[anim]-1)
      k=0;
    else k=j+1;
    v2=&key_verts[(animkeyspos[anim]+k)*nv];

    v0=localvert;// output vertex array

    s=1.0f-key_factor; // compute 1-factors

#ifdef INTEL_SIMD
    if (g_processor_features&_CPU_FEATURE_SSE && g_flyengine->sse)
    {
      flyVector f1(s);
      flyVector f2(key_factor);
      i=nv*0x40;
```

```
            __asm
            {
              // xmm2=(s,s,s,s)
              // xmm3=(key_factor,key_factor,key_factor,key_factor)
              movups xmm2,f1
              movups xmm3,f2

              // init loop registers (ebx->flyVector, ecx->flyVertex)
              mov ebx,0
              mov ecx,0
            L1:
              // xmm0=v1[ebx]
              mov eax,v1
              movaps xmm0,[eax+ebx]

              // xmm0=v2[i]
              mov eax,v2
              movaps xmm1,[eax+ebx]

              // interpolate position to xmm0
              mulps xmm0,xmm2
              mulps xmm1,xmm3
              addps xmm0,xmm1

              // v0[i]=xmm0
              mov eax,v0
              movaps [eax+ecx],xmm0

              // increment loop registers
              add ebx,0x10
              add ecx,0x40

              // loop until all vertices are processed
              cmp ecx, i
              jl L1
            }
          }
          else
#endif
        for( i=0;i<nv;i++)
        {
          v0->x = v1->x*s + v2->x*key_factor;
          v0->y = v1->y*s + v2->y*key_factor;
          v0->z = v1->z*s + v2->z*key_factor;
          v0++; v1++; v2++;
        }
```

Vertex mesh animation blending interpolation

Interpolates the mesh vertices between two float keys for two different animations (linearly interpolates between two keys of animation one, linearly interpolates between two keys of animation two and then linearly interpolates between the two results for the final key (three linear interpolations).

```
void flyAnimatedMesh::set_state(int anim1, float key_factor1, int
anim2, float key_factor2, float blend)
{
  int i,j,k;
  float s,t,w;
  flyVertex *v0;
  flyVector *v1,*v2,*v3,*v4;

  // compute local key factor between the first
  // animation keys to be interpolated (key_factor1)
  j=(int)(key_factor1*animkeys[anim1]);
  if (j==animkeys[anim1])
    { j=0; key_factor1=0.0f; }
  s=1.0f/animkeys[anim1];
  key_factor1=(key_factor1-j*s)/s;

  // find vertex pointers on the first animation for
  // the two keys to be interpolated (v1 and v2)
  v1=&key_verts[(animkeyspos[anim1]+j)*nv];
  if (j==animkeys[anim1]-1)
    k=0;
  else k=j+1;
  v2=&key_verts[(animkeyspos[anim1]+k)*nv];

  // compute local key factor between the second
  // animation keys to be interpolated (key_factor2)
  j=(int)(key_factor2*animkeys[anim2]);
  if (j==animkeys[anim2])
    { j=0; key_factor2=0.0f; }
  s=1.0f/animkeys[anim2];
  key_factor2=(key_factor2-j*s)/s;

  // find vertex pointers on the second animation for
  // the two keys to be interpolated (v3 and v4)
  v3=&key_verts[(animkeyspos[anim2]+j)*nv];
  if (j==animkeys[anim2]-1)
    k=0;
  else k=j+1;
  v4=&key_verts[(animkeyspos[anim2]+k)*nv];

  v0 = localvert; // output vertex array

  s=1.0f-key_factor1; // compute 1-factors
  t=1.0f-key_factor2;
  w=1.0f-blend;

#ifdef INTEL_SIMD
  if (g_processor_features&_CPU_FEATURE_SSE && g_flyengine->sse)
  {
    flyVector f1(s);
    flyVector f2(key_factor1);
    flyVector f3(t);
    flyVector f4(key_factor2);
    flyVector f5(w);
```

```
flyVector f6(blend);
i=nv*0x40;


__asm
{
  // xmm2=(s,s,s,s)
  // xmm3=(key_factor1,key_factor1,key_factor1,key_factor1)
  // xmm2=(t,t,t,t)
  // xmm3=(key_factor2,key_factor2,key_factor2,key_factor2)
  movups xmm4,f1
  movups xmm5,f2
  movups xmm6,f3
  movups xmm7,f4

  // init loop registers (ebx->flyVector, ecx->flyVertex)
  mov ebx,0
  mov ecx,0
L1:
  // xmm0=v1[i]
  mov eax,v1
  movaps xmm0,[eax+ebx]

  // xmm1=v2[i]
  mov eax,v2
  movaps xmm1,[eax+ebx]

  // interpolate first anim to xmm0
  mulps xmm0,xmm4
  mulps xmm1,xmm5
  addps xmm0,xmm1

  // xmm2=v3[i]
  mov eax,v3
  movaps xmm2,[eax+ebx]

  // xmm3=v4[i]
  mov eax,v4
  movaps xmm3,[eax+ebx]

  // interpolate second anim to xmm2
  mulps xmm2,xmm6
  mulps xmm3,xmm7
  addps xmm2,xmm3

  // blend the two anims to xmm0
  movups xmm1,f5
  movups xmm3,f6
  mulps xmm0,xmm1
  mulps xmm2,xmm3
  addps xmm0,xmm2

  // v0[i]=xmm0
  mov eax,v0
  movaps [eax+ecx],xmm0
```

```
                    // increment loop registers
                    add ebx,0x10
                    add ecx,0x40

                    // loop until all vertices are processed
                    cmp  ecx, i
                    jl L1
            }
        }
        else
#endif
        for( i=0;i<nv;i++ )
        {
                v0->x=(v1->x*s+v2->x*key_factor1)*w+
                       (v3->x*t+v4->x*key_factor2)*blend;
                v0->y=(v1->y*s+v2->y*key_factor1)*w+
                       (v3->y*t+v4->y*key_factor2)*blend;
                v0->z=(v1->z*s+v2->z*key_factor1)*w+
                       (v3->z*t+v4->z*key_factor2)*blend;
                v0++;  v1++;  v2++;  v3++;  v4++;
        }
}
```

Skeleton mesh vertex computation

At the end of a skeleton animation interpolation (using quaternions) we have to generate the vertices' positions based on the skeleton bone matrices and the vertex weight and displace vector (each vertex might be influenced by several bone matrices).

```
void flySkeletonMesh::build_mesh()
{
    int  i,j;
    int  p=0;
#ifdef INTEL_SIMD
    if (g_processor_features&_CPU_FEATURE_SSE && g_flyengine->sse)
    {
        flyVertex *v1=localvert;
        flyVector *v2=vweight;
        flyMatrix *m1=m;
        int *i1=vindex;
        flyVector f1(0);

        // for all vertices
        for( i=0;i<nv;i++ )
        {
            j=nvweights[i];
            __asm
            {
                // xmm0=(0,0,0,0)
                movups xmm0,f1
```

```
        // ebx=&vindex[p]
        mov ebx,p
        add ebx,i1

        // initialize loop register
        mov ecx,0
L1:
        // compute matrix memory pos
        // for vindex[p]
        mov eax,[ebx]
        sal eax,0x6
        add eax,m1

        // load matrix m[vindex[p]] into xmm4-7
        movaps xmm4,[eax]
        movaps xmm5,[eax+16]
        movaps xmm6,[eax+32]
        movaps xmm7,[eax+48]

        // xmm3=v2
        mov eax,v2
        movaps xmm3,[eax]

        // multiply first matrix line
        // and accumulate into xmm0
        movaps xmm1,xmm3
        shufps xmm1,xmm1,0x00
        mulps xmm1,xmm4
        addps xmm0,xmm1

        // multiply second matrix line
        // and accumulate into xmm0
        movaps xmm1,xmm3
        shufps xmm1,xmm1,0x55
        mulps xmm1,xmm5
        addps xmm0,xmm1

        // multiply third matrix line
        // and accumulate into xmm0
        movaps xmm1,xmm3
        shufps xmm1,xmm1,0xAA
        mulps xmm1,xmm6
        addps xmm0,xmm1

        // multiply fouth matrix line
        // and accumulate into xmm0
        movaps xmm1,xmm3
        shufps xmm1,xmm1,0xFF
        mulps xmm1,xmm7
        addps xmm0,xmm1

        // increment loop registers
        add v2,0x10
        add ebx,0x4
```

```
                   // loop until all matrices influencing
                   // this vertex are processed
                   inc ecx
                   cmp ecx,j
                   jl L1

                   // v1=xmm0, v1++
                   mov eax,v1
                   movaps [eax],xmm0
                   add v1,0x40

                   // store current p
                   sub ebx,i1
                   mov p,ebx
                 }
               }
           }
           else
    #endif
         for( i=0;i<nv;i++ )
         {
            localvert[i].null();
            for( j=0;j<nvweights[i];j++,p++ )
              // vertex = (matrix * vector) * float
              localvert[i] += (m[vindex[p]]*vweight[p])*vweight[p].w;
         }
    }
```

8 Animating shape – methods

8.1 Introduction

Animating shape change, originally termed soft object animation in computer graphics, is one of the most enduring and difficult problems of computer animation. Its inherent difficulty is best thought of as being due to the enduring conflict between the representational complexity and the ease of animation. For realism and efficient rendering, we prefer triangle meshes with large numbers of triangles. In embracing such a low-level and complex representational scheme we make shape animation extremely difficult. A low-level model would have us adjusting the position of all the vertices as a function of time. As always in animation, we seek a higher level of control – that is obvious. We seek to reduce the complexity of the entity we have to control for the animation. It is also obvious that our representational method influences the ease or otherwise of the animation. In this chapter we will look at various generic approaches to the animation of shape; in the next chapter we will examine one of the major application demands of this type of animation – animating facial expressions and visual speech.

Like articulated structure animation, for facial animation we can use motion capture and this is precisely the mainstream method currently used in games. It suffers, however, from the inherent drawback of MoCap which is that only pre-recorded animations can be activated in real time. This eliminates what will be the major application of facial animation – visual speech driven from a text generator. We do not know in advance what sentences are going to be constructed by a text generator.

Before we begin, perhaps we should address an obvious question that often occurs: why is it not possible to use conventional vertex animation to produce soft object animation by keyframing poses? Well, the answer is that it is possible and it is an oft-employed method. However, it is unlikely to be sustained as a preferred general model. Consider again the example of facial animation. If we have two poses representing two facial expressions then we can produce an in-between sequence by interpolation. However, it is unlikely that such a sequence will accurately imitate the sequence that would be produced in reality. This would imply that every point on the face moved at the same rate using the same interpolant between the two poses. Given the nature of the dynamics of facial expressions and their complexity and subtlety, this is hardly likely.

In this chapter we will look at the main technologies that are used to deform or change the shape of objects. Most of these can be considered two-level models. At the bottom level is a detailed model that is finally rendered – the triangle or polygon mesh; above that is a 'framework' that encloses the detailed model and admits the deformation control. The key point about the framework level is that it is manipulable or controllable by an editor or scripting mechanism. Usually the detailed model can contain an arbitrary number of vertices and editing the framework level deforms the detailed model in some way that appears natural or is understood by the editor. The classic FFD method is a good example of this notion and Sederburg in [SEDE86] uses the following analogy:

A good physical analogy for FFD is to consider a parallelepiped of clear, flexible plastic in which is embedded an object, or several objects, which we wish to deform. The object is imagined to be flexible, so that it deforms along with the plastic that surrounds it.

Here the flexible plastic is the framework level. An artist or animator works with the plastic and the embedded mesh objects, of arbitrary complexity, are deformed in an expected manner along with the plastic in which they are inescapably anchored.

Another model to which many deformation methods are effectively equivalent is the conventional skinning summation (Chapter 7 and Section 8.6.2 of this chapter). Here the equation:

$$\mathbf{x}'_i = \sum_{i=0}^{n} \mathbf{M}_i \mathbf{d}_i w_i$$

is moving a vertex $\mathbf{x}_i$ to a new position $\mathbf{x}'_i$ by summing over a number of bones to which it is connected. In conventional skinning the w_i are set by an animator;

in the FFD method they are analytically defined. The equation emphasises that eventually, at the lowest level, we move a vertex according to its relationship to a higher-level framework which, in the case of skinning, happens to be the skeleton.

Most current shape animation methods conform to a two-level hierarchy. The upper level – the deformer model – accepts an animation or motion shape script which then automatically controls the lower level – the object vertices. From this two-level paradigm we have two expectations:

(1) An entity in the deformer level corresponds to many entities (vertices) in the object.

(2) Deformer entities possess a structure or coherence such that the desired shape change in the object can be easily scripted.

In terms of these two requirements the common models are:

(1) **Spline cages** Currently an off-line sculpting technique, the deformer level consists of a wire frame of B-splines with which an artist interacts. Those then can 'spawn' a low-level model by converting the cage into patches and subdividing.

(2) **Bones** or **skinning** Discussed in Chapter 7 as well as this chapter, the deformer is a simplified human skeleton which accepts joint animation. Skin vertices are associated with bones (usually more than one), and weights to each attachment control the relative influence that a bone has on a vertex.

(3) **FFDs** Here the deformer structure is a 3D array of control points that control a tri-cubic Bézier patch or volume. The vertices in the object are bound to the control points and move with the patch as it is deformed by the control points. At the lowest level the method reduces to being equivalent to the bone model – vertices are associated via weights to moving points.

(4) **Pseudo-muscle** models (Chapter 9) In this approach muscle models controlled by high-level parameters are bound to object vertices. An animation script controls the parameters which contract the muscle which in its turn pulls the vertices with which it is associated.

(5) **Wires** The deforming structure is a 3D parametric space curve which the animation script controls by moving its control points. Such curves can be bound to object vertices and the difference between their current position and their initial position is used to pull vertices around in their pre-defined field of influence.

(6) **Wrappers** Here the deforming structure is a low resolution version of the structure itself. This approach, like bones, corresponds exactly to our two-level model.

Deforming technology spans both off-line and real-time applications. In sculpting an object, which subsequently never changes shape after the design is satisfactory, an artist will use a modelling tool. Alternatively, an artist may sculpt a series of keyframe poses which are interpolated in real time as a game is played. We are eventually interested in using such techniques in real time. In particular, we would want the animation to be driven by game events, so that instead of an animation re-playing deformations pre-sculpted by an artist, game events cause the deformation technique to operate on the low-level model. Consider the elbow joint problem. Here, as we shall see, we can enclose the joint in an FFD. A game event – elbow bend – would then apply a simple bending script to the FFD which pulled all the skin vertices into the appropriate configuration. A more complex example is visual speech where we wish to control jaw and mouth motion to conform to the speech being emitted by a speech synthesiser. Low-level speech units (visemes) then cause the face to deform in an appropriate manner.

In what follows we will first introduce established deformation techniques, making no distinction between techniques that are currently used off-line for sculpting purposes only and those that have migrated into real-time applications. In both cases the requirements of the method are identical – we need a framework level controllable either manually by an artist or automatically by game logic. That is, we describe methods where the interactive or modeling mode can be automated and controlled in real time by the game. Following that, we will look at games applications, the two most important being skin deformation under skeleton control and facial animation. Since there is much more involved in facial animation than the geometric deformation model, we will deal with it in a separate chapter.

8.2 Spline cages

We begin with this method because it is commonly used in off-line sculpting or modelling software, although like all such methods it could admit an animation script. The high-level framework is an orthogonal net of B-splines which are understood to form the boundary edges of a net of bi-cubic parametric patches – the low-level representation (Figure 8.1 (also Colour Plate)).

The artist works with the splines, individually adjusting them until the desired shape represented by the patch mesh is achieved. Unlike the other two techniques described in this chapter, the deformer model is actually embedded in the low-level model – the patch mesh – that it controls. However, the patch mesh is able to be subdivided to any level and to a certain extent this potential ameliorates the disadvantage. The aesthetic interface that this technique offers to the artist – the artist has to think of the patch surface as he or she pulls the cage around – seems to be successful and popular. For example, an artist can begin building a face, by describing a closed curve that forms a profile cross-section through the head. Building spline curves interactively is now second nature to a 3D artist and the programming technology to convert a mesh of curves, which form patch boundaries, into a patch mesh for rendering and further manipulation is straightforward (see, for example, [WATT92]).

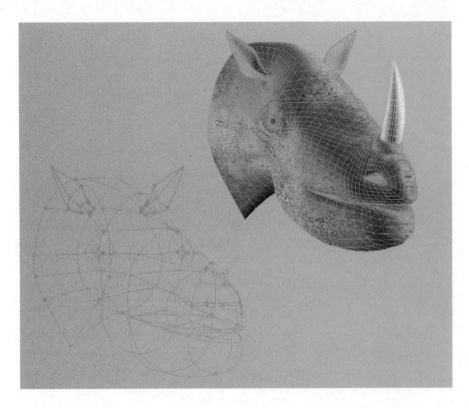

Figure 8.1
Modelling with spline
cages in 3D Studio MAX.

The spline cage model is essentially a method for creating and controlling the shape of a patch mesh. Over the years many techniques have been examined that layer a framework on the low-level control of patch meshes, which means controlling the position of control points as a function of time. Although many of these appeared promising, the spline cage model appears to be the only one that has migrated into mainstream usage. In Chapter 9 we look at another technique – hierarchical B-splines applied to facial animation. This is effectively a multi-layer technique, as the name implies.

8.3 Free form deformation (FFD)

Although Bézier himself had suggested extending bi-cubic parametric patches to be functions of three or more parameters, the first use of this technology in computer graphics is attributed to Sederburg [SEDE86] who coined the term Free Form Deformation or FFD. Sedeburg's breakthrough was to realise that an object model of any representation, say, for example, a triangular mesh, could be 'embedded' in the space of a parametric patch and be deformed in an 'expected' manner as the patch was deformed by control point motion.

We can define a tri-cubic Bézier patch as:

$$\mathbf{Q}(u,v,w) = \sum_{i=0}^{3} \sum_{j=0}^{3} \sum_{k=0}^{3} \mathbf{P}_{ijk} B_i(u) B_j(v) B_k(w) \tag{8.1}$$

where

$\mathbf{P}_{ijk}$ are a lattice of $4 \times 4 \times 4$ control points

$B_i(u) = B_j(v) = B_k(w)$ are the Bézier basis functions:

$B_0(u) = (1 - u)^3$

$B_1(u) = 3u(1 - u)^2$

$B_2(u) = 3u^2(1 - u)$

$B_3(u) = u^3$

This entity is the volumetric equivalent of a planar patch – where the 16 control points lie in the plane of the patch. Now if we move points in the lattice we deform the volume. The FFD model of surface deformation is a three-step method:

(1) We 'embed' a polygon mesh object in the tri-cubic volume. To do this we express the vertex coordinates in lattice space. If $\mathbf{x}$ is the vertex posituion we have:

$\mathbf{x} = \mathbf{x}_0 + u\mathbf{u} + v\mathbf{v} + w\mathbf{w}$

$u = \mathbf{u}.(\mathbf{x} - \mathbf{x}_0)$

$v = \mathbf{v}.(\mathbf{x} - \mathbf{x}_0)$

$w = \mathbf{w}.(\mathbf{x} - \mathbf{x}_0)$

where

$\mathbf{x}_0$ defines the origin of $\mathbf{uvw}$ space.

(2) The lattice is deformed by moving the control points, pulling each vertex $\mathbf{x}$ to a new position $\mathbf{x}'$.

(3) The value of $\mathbf{x}'$ is obtained by evaluating equation 8.1 with the (u,v,w) coordinates of $\mathbf{x}$ and the new control point positions.

The particular advantage of FFDs is that the number of lattice points can be, and generally is, much lower than the number of object points. Effectively an FFD acts as a device that accepts linear transformations on its control points and transmits these to the vertices of the object to be deformed. Although FFDs provide an elegant shape deformation model, they do have disadvantages. There is a relationship between the complexity of the deformation required and the difficulty of achieving this by deforming an FFD lattice. Thus the method copes well with skin deformation at a hinge or elbow-type joint, but for highly complex deformations we need a dense control lattice and it may be easier to move the vertices under control of a bone model. It is also the case that there is generally no relationship between the rectangular nature of the control point array and the surface to be deformed. This point is addressed by the method of SOFFDs in Section 8.6.1 and to a limited extent by the method of the next section (EFFDs).

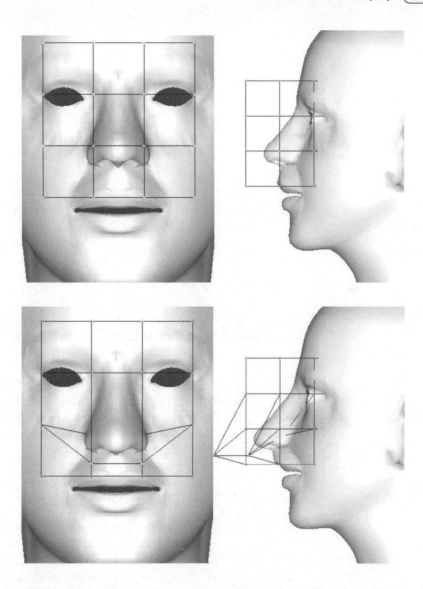

Figure 8.2
A FFD applied to the nose region of a face mesh (courtesy of James Edge, University of Sheffield).

In Figure 8.2 an FFD is set to enclose part of a face. The 64-point lattice is then deformed as shown with the resulting deformation in the mesh.

Although FFDs are extremely popular in modelling, their real-time control use, where game logic would be invoking the shape animation, requires careful consideration. Of course we can easily store deformation motion, set up in advance by an artist, but this somewhat diminishes the generality of the method. We can invoke continuous real-time control of potentially useful deformation motion by applying scripting curves to the lattice. This approach is fully described in [WATT92]. For example, to bend the lattice continuously about an axis we can use two control functions – a lattice space control which

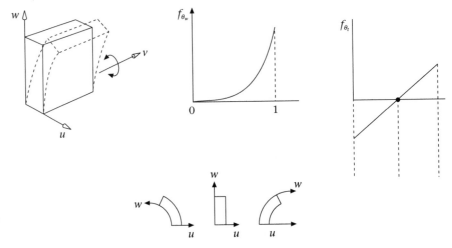

Figure 8.3
Scripting the animation of
lattice points in an FFD.

controls the shape of the bend f_{θ_w} and a time control f_{θ_t} which controls the animation of the deformation motion. In Figure 8.3 the expression:

$$\theta = \theta_0 f_{\theta_w}(w) f_{\theta_t}(t)$$

causes the lattice to bend, as shown in the figure, about the w axis.

FFD deformations are easiest to consider when the lattice encloses the entire object – in other words, global deformations. As Figure 8.2 demonstrates, they can be applied locally but depending on the application it may be that the method described in Section 8.2 is more appropriate.

8.4   Extended free form deformations (EFFDs)

A development of the FFD by Coquillart [COQU90] was introduced to overcome the deformation constraints imposed by the parallelepiped shape of the lattice. This was called an Extended FFD or EFFD and consisted of sets of FFDs of volumes joined together in a particular configuration. Figure 8.4 shows an example of a cylinder configuration constructed from six 'elementary' FFD volumes. As the figure shows, the two end faces of the row of FFDs are joined together, then all the u axes are made coincident. This cylindrical unit is now completely defined by the position of the control points. For example, all control points that lie on the u axis satisfying $u = 0$ and $w = 0$ are made coincident, as are all control points satisfying $u = 1$ and $w = 0$.

Once the required volume is constructed it can be used in the same manner as a conventional FFD. The contributing elements to an EFFD are just deformed FFDs but now there is no longer a simple relationship between $\mathbf{x}$ – a point in the object, and the lattice points. To find the (u,v,w) coordinates of $\mathbf{x}$ we must now proceed as follows:

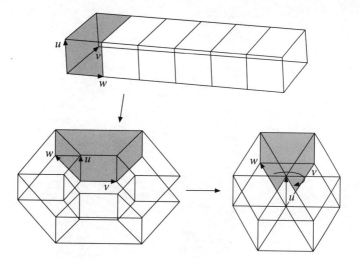

Figure 8.4
Construction of a
cylindrical EFFD.

(1) Find the unit which contains **x**.

(2) Solve

$$\mathbf{x} = \mathbf{Q}(u,v,w) = \sum_{i=0}^{3} \sum_{j=0}^{3} \sum_{k=0}^{3} \mathbf{P}_{ijk} B_i(u) B_j(v) B_k(w)$$

by Newton iteration where $\mathbf{P}_{ijk}$ are the positions of the control points in the EFFD configuration.

In Figure 8.5 the face is now subject to an initial EFFD. In this illustration this is set up by interactively deforming an FFD, then solving by Newton iteration for the correspondence between the mesh vertices and the lattice points. Now as the EFFD is deformed the resulting motion of the mesh vertices is a function of the non-parallelepiped shape of the EFFD.

8.5 Curve deformers – Wires

The next two techniques are more recent and derive a deformation by using a type of implicit function and a domain of influence together with the relative motion of a *deformer* (curve or a surface) with respect to a reference object. *Wires* [SING98] is a modelling tool implemented in Alias Wavefront's *Maya* modelling and animation software. The method bears something in common with the B-spline cage idea in that a cage of wires can be set up to surround a surface – in the manner of a sculptor's armature. It is also similar in conception to some methods in CAGD where sets of control points are controlled by a curve near the surface – a least squares metric being used to associate the control points with the curve. As the curve is moved the control points move and the surface is deformed. Wires can act either singularly or in a group to influence some region of the object. Like an FFD the method does not assume any underlying representation – it moves points which could be control points for a parametric

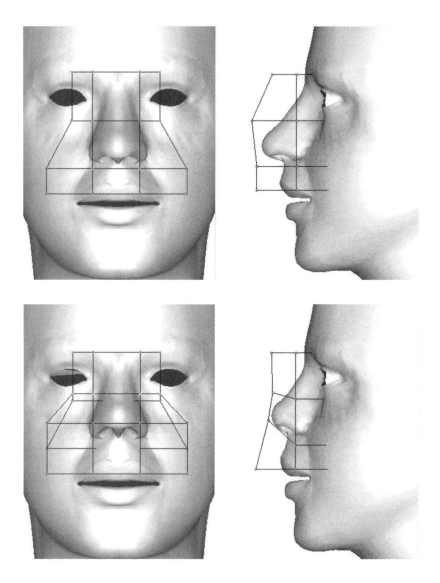

Figure 8.5
An EFFD deforming the nose region (compare with Figure 8.2) (courtesy of James Edge, University of Sheffield).

surface or vertices of a polygon mesh. The other similarity between this method and the FFD is that an initial binding – using a reference curve – is made between the object and the wire. The motion between the initial curve and the wire curve then controls the deformation (just as the motion between the initial FFD or EFFD and the deformed FFD controls the deformation of the object embedded in the lattice).

A wire is defined as a tuple (W,R,s,r,f) where:

W and R are free-form parametric space curves – W is the wire curve and R is a reference curve. Initially W and R are coincident

s is a scalar that controls radial scaling around the curve

r is a radius of influence around the curve

f is a density or field function. This is a monotonically decreasing function with

$$f(0) = 1, \ f(x) = 0 \text{ for } x \geq 1$$

When a wire is bound to an object a volume of influence is determined. Points within this region are influenced according to the density function f as:

$$F(\mathbf{x},R) = f\left(\frac{\|\mathbf{x} - R(u_{min})\|}{r}\right)$$

where

u_{min} is the value of the parameter u which minimises the distance between R and $\mathbf{x}$

When the W is moved, the difference between W and R, together with s, is used to influence the object points $\mathbf{x}$. Object points that are initially on the reference curve R move exactly with W whereas objects outside the offset volume do not move at all. $F(\mathbf{x},R)$ controls the attenuation of the movement of points smoothly between these two extremes. The deformation within the field of influence of R is separated into three components – scale, rotation and translation. We consider how a point $\mathbf{x}$ moves to $\mathbf{x}^{def}$ with reference to Figure 8.6. In the figure point $R(\mathbf{x}_R)$ is the nearest point on R to $\mathbf{x}$, $W(\mathbf{x}_R)$ is the corresponding point on W.

Uniform scale – $\mathbf{x}$ moves to $\mathbf{x}_s$ as:

$$\mathbf{x}_s = \mathbf{x} + (\mathbf{x} - R(\mathbf{x}_R))(1 + (s - 1)F(\mathbf{x},R))$$

Rotation – angle θ is defined as the angle between the tangent vectors $W'(\mathbf{x}_R)$ and $R'(\mathbf{x}_R)$. This is applied to $\mathbf{x}_s$ which is rotated $\theta F(\mathbf{x},R)$ about the axis $W'(\mathbf{x}_R) \times R'(\mathbf{x}_R)$ about point $R(\mathbf{x}_R)$ resulting in the point $\mathbf{x}_r$

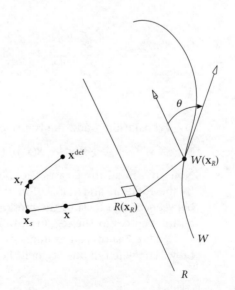

Figure 8.6
Notation used in Wires.

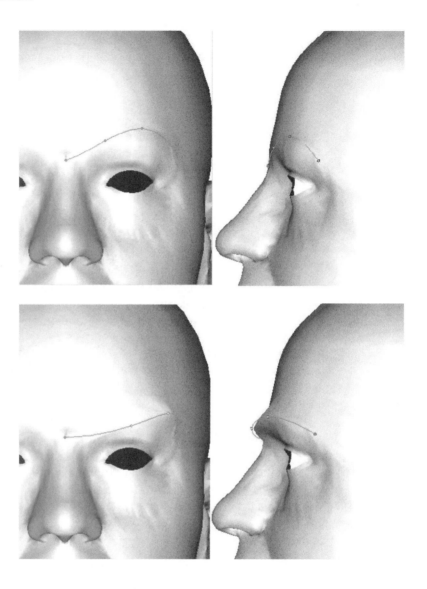

Figure 8.7
A wire (formed from a single segment Bézier curve) being used to deform the eyebrow region of a face (courtesy of James Edge, University of Sheffield).

Translation – add the translation to give $\mathbf{x}^{\mathrm{def}}$

$$\mathbf{x}^{\mathrm{def}} = \mathbf{x}_r + (W(\mathbf{x}_R) - R(\mathbf{x}_R))F(\mathbf{x},R)$$

Note that in all three cases the motion is modulated by the density function. In the rotation and translation the motion is a function of some difference between W and R. Thus the motion of W with respect to R induces motion in all the vertices in the region of influence of the wire.

Figure 8.7 shows an example of a wire used to control the raising of an eyebrow. The wire is a one-segment Bézier curve and the off-line or set-up consists simply of associating the four control points with the face mesh. In real time we can easily have a selection of eyebrow movements/expression controls which have been pre-set to cause the appropriate mesh deformation. Alternatively, we could have continuous lifting control invoked by one or more parameters. We see from this example that *wires* is ideally suited to local or detailed deformations, although it can also be used in the same way as B-spline cage as we have already noted.

8.6 Skinning revisited

8.6.1 Surface-oriented free-form deformations (SOFFDs)

This technique [SING00] is also implemented in the modelling and animation system *Maya* (wherein they are termed wrap deformers) and can be used as a general deformation technique, although the authors emphasise its utility in automating the skinning of characters. The technique relates to both the previous method *wires* in that the deformation motion is controlled by the relationship between a reference (control) surface, originally bound to the object to be deformed, and a movable surface. In this sense it extends the *wires* approach from 3D space curves to a surface. Comparing it with an FFD we say that it emphasises deformation based on surfaces – whereas the FFD is based on a volume.[1] The motivation for this is that we end up with a deforming control – in this case a surface – which visually correlates with the underlying object to be deformed. This contrasts with a conventional FFD where the deforming entity is a lattice of control points. This means that it is clearer how to move the deforming structure to effect the desired change in the deformed structure. Another advantage over the FFD is that the equivalent of the control points can be arbitrarily distributed, making it easy to introduce local control where required.

In SOFDDs the deformer is a triple $\{D,R,local\}$ where:

D is the *driver* surface

R is the reference surface originally bound to and registered with the object surface

local is a scalar

A reference surface R will usually be a low resolution scaled version of the object mesh and originally R and D are coincident. D is then moved and the deviation between R and D controls the deformation of the object. The parameter *local* controls the locality of the deformation. The registration phase of the process calculates influence weights based on a distance metric which controls, along

---

1. A consequence of the volume nature of the FFD is that we have to control all the points in the lattice as if the object we were deforming was a volume rather than a surface.

with the R–D deviation, the deformation of object points by a control element. A control element on R is a triangular facet and the function:

$$f(d,local) = \frac{1}{1 + d^{local}}$$

is calculated for each point on the object surface, where d is the closest distance from the object point to a face of R. For each point x and each control element k a weight:

$$w_k^x = f(d_k^x, local)$$

is determined so that each x has associated with it a weight vector. In practice the number of control elements associated with each object point will be small.

The faces of R – the control elements also define, for each face, a face coordinate system derived from two edges and their cross-product and in addition to calculating the influence weights the registration phase computes the coordinates of the undeformed objects points x in this local face coordinate system.

The deformation phase proceeds with faces in D changing shape, position and orientation and maps each object point x to x^{def}. The points moves such that its local position in the face coordinate space of D remains the same as D moves. This is achieved as follows. The world space position of x^{def} deformed by face element k is given by:

$$x_k^{def} = x_k^R M_k^D$$

where
$\quad x_k^R$ is the local coordinates of x in R
$\quad M_k^D$ is the transformation matrix for face k of the driver

x^{def}, the deformed position of x taking into account the n faces it is associated with, is then:

$$x^{def} = \sum_{k=1}^{n} w_k^x x_k^{def}$$

A simple example using spheres is shown in Figure 8.8.

The use of this method in a skinning algorithm is straightforward. The driving surface D is bound to the skeleton – rather than the skin of the object. D then controls the animation of the skin as the skeleton is animated. In this context D is a low resolution version of the skin and an artist is faced with the task of associating D, which will bear a close resemblance to the skin surface but is low resolution, with the skeleton instead of the skin.

8.6.2

Skeleton skinning refinements

We now return to the skeleton skinning topic of Chapter 7 and look at why the basic model described there falls down and how to overcome this. (Much

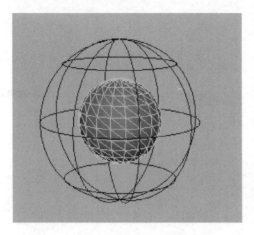 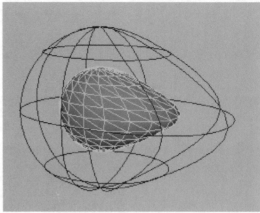

Figure 8.8
A simple example of
SOFFDs using initially
two concentric spheres.

of the material described in this section is based on a treatment in [WEBE00].)
We begin by reminding ourselves of the basic model, which is reproduced here
for convenience. To compute the position of a vertex from its associated bones
we use the product:

$$\mathbf{x}'_i = \sum_{i=0}^{n} \mathbf{M}_i \mathbf{d}_i w_i \qquad (8.2)$$

where

$\mathbf{M}_i$ is the (global) matrix for bone i
$\mathbf{d}_i$ is the displacement vector between the vertex and the ith
w_i is the weight of this attachment
n is the number of attachments

We now look at how to generalise this model and fix the artefacts produced by
it. Also, we will use it as a kind of conceptual benchmark against which we can
examine what more elaborate models do.

Consider first how the model can be used to implement skin deformation
around a joint when it rotates. For example, we can consider an approximation of the elbow as a hinge joint (1 DOF). When an elbow bends the skin folds
on the acute side and stretches on the other side. If skin vertices at the joint
region are associated with only one bone then it is obvious that an unsatisfactory deformation occurs (Figure 8.9(a)). In Figure 8.9(b) the centre vertices are
attached to each bone. Within the summation each of these vertices is split
into two under the transformation for each bone. The summation then averages these. In the figure the resulting position for the centre vertices will lie on
a straight line joining the split components. In general then, skin behaviour
will be satisfactory on the obtuse side of such a joint and will shrink on the
acute side (Figure 8.9(c)).

Another serious effect comes as a consequence of rotating one bone about
the common axis joining two extended bones. For example, rotating the forearm

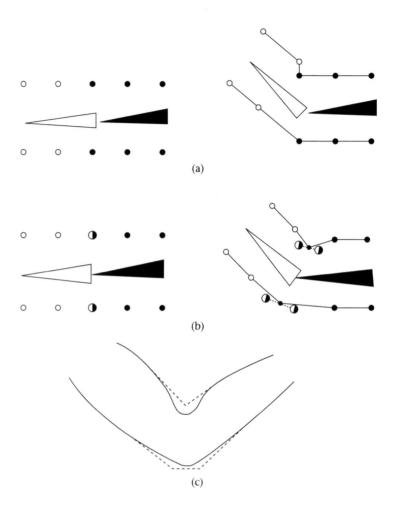

Figure 8.9
Skin behaviour at an
elbow joint. (a) Each
vertex attached to one
bone. (b) Two centre
vertices attached to both
bones. (c) Skin behaviour
satisfactory on 'obtuse'
side of joint, shrinking
occurs on acute side
(partially based on an
illustration in [WEBE00]).

(a)

(b)

(c)

with respect to the upper arm. As Figure 8.10 demonstrates, this will result in a total collapse for a rotation of 180 degrees. Such visual inconsistencies are characteristic of a simple skinning scheme. An important observation is that the extent of the problem is a function of joint angle. The undesirable practical consequence is that animators cannot directly manipulate the deformation and indeed may be unsure if continuing to manipulate the weights w_i will result in any improvement.

A distinct advantage of the scheme is that the bones can be abstractions – they need not relate to physical bones. Effects such as the bulging of the biceps due to elbow bending can be animated by secondary bones which pick up their animation from the primary bones. This idea can also be used to refine joint behaviour, as Figure 8.11 demonstrates. Here a subsidiary link structure controls the vertices in the vicinity of the joint and is animated as a consequence of the main joint animation. Abstract bones are used for facial animation. Facial

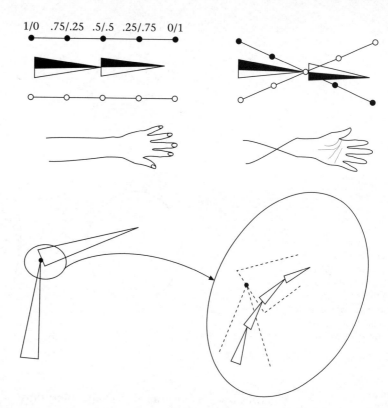

Figure 8.10
Problems with large joint angles (based on an illustration in [WEBE00]).

Figure 8.11
Using subsidiary bones to control skin deformation in a joint region.

motion is not, in reality, motivated by bones (except for the jaw) but by muscles. To animate the face using bones these can be placed so that they hinge about an appropriate axis to effect the desired control. The outer tip of the bones must move such that they do not project outside the skin layer of the face (Figure 8.12).

Finally, consider why there are problems with this scheme. All of the problems emerge from the fact that we are trying to choreograph the deformation of a polygon mesh model by moving the vertices individually and without regard to the context in which they are embedded. We can apply fixes and 'relate' vertices by tying them to more than one bone. This helps, but all such fixes are context dependent and somewhat unsatisfactory. What we need is a better way of pulling vertices around.

A more general approach is to combine skinning with shape blending or interpolation, which is the subject of the next section. This is something of a contradiction in that the motivation for skeleton animation is precisely to avoid the low-level approach of shape interpolation. However, it seems that a compromise may well be the best strategy. One of the main problems in skinning algorithms is the gap between an interface – offered to an artist to adjust the skin weights – and the resulting deformation effects that occur during the skeleton animation.

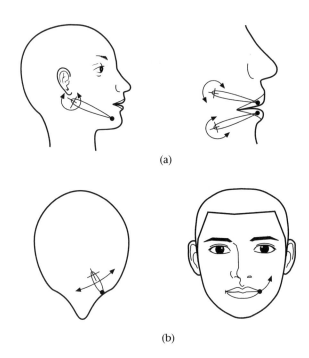

(a)

Figure 8.12
Bones are pure
abstractions if used in
facial animation. (a) Bones
for facial animation are
abstractions (i.e. no basis
in anatomy). (b) Bones for
facial animation should
track curvature of skull.

(b)

8.6.3

Combining skinning and shape blending

As we have seen, a significant disadvantage of the previous technique is that
unwanted deformations have to be corrected for by the inconvenient and
indirect method of adjusting the vertex-bone attachment weights. Sloan *et al.*
[SLOA00] term this approach transform blending, noting equation 8.2, for a
two-bone attachment, to emphasise this as:

$$\mathbf{x} = \alpha M_1^\theta \mathbf{x}_0 + (1 - \alpha) M_0 \mathbf{x}_0$$

where now we are considering two bones with 1 DOF (elbow joint) and

> where
> $\alpha \in [0,1]$ is the weighting for bone 1 and $(1 - \alpha)$ for bone 0 ($\alpha = w$ in
> equation 8.2)
>
> M_0 is the global matrix for bone 0
>
> $\theta \in [0,1]$ is the joint angle, w.r.t bone 0, mapped into the range $[0,1]$
>
> M_1^θ is the global transform for bone 1 at angle θ

They suggest generalising this process so that it becomes a combination of transform and shape blending. To do this they proceed as follows. The two poses
(for bent and straight arm) are sculpted as keys with $\mathbf{x}^1$ as a vertex in the bent
arm and $\mathbf{x}_0$ the corresponding vertex in the straight arm (outstretched). The

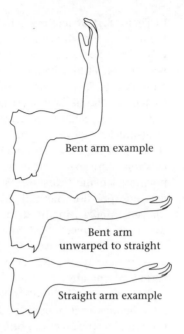

Bent arm example

Bent arm
unwarped to straight

Straight arm example

Figure 8.13
Arms used in shape and
transform blending
(after an illustration in
[SLOA00].

keys can also include other desired effects such as muscle bulging. Consider a
bent arm sculpted with a muscle bulge. This can be unwarped to a straight pose.
That is, we arrive at a distorted or bulging arm in the rest position as:

$$\mathbf{x}_0^1 = (\alpha \mathbf{M}_1^{\theta=1}\mathbf{x}_0^1 + (1 - \alpha)\mathbf{M}_0)^{-1}\mathbf{x}^1$$

which follows from

$$\mathbf{x}^1 = \alpha \mathbf{M}_1^{\theta=1}\mathbf{x}_0^1 + (1 - \alpha)\mathbf{M}_0\mathbf{x}_0^1$$

This is the arm (Figure 8.13) which is distorted in the rest or straight position
such that if it were used in transform blending it would produce the required
(wanted and unwanted) deformation in the bent position. What we now do is
to perform a geometric blend with the new (distorted) arm in the rest position
with the original arm in the rest position (shape blend) giving:

$$\mathbf{x}_\theta' = \theta \mathbf{x}_0^1 + (1 - \theta)\mathbf{x}_0 \tag{8.3}$$

This is then followed by a transform blend giving the final result:

$$\mathbf{x}_\theta = (\alpha \mathbf{M}_1^\theta + (1 - \alpha)\mathbf{M}_0)(\theta \mathbf{x}_0^1 + (1 - \theta)\mathbf{x}_0), \quad \alpha, \theta \in [0,1]$$

In practice, it is likely that a number of shapes or keys would be scuplted for
this context. In which case all forms are untransformed to the rest position and
equation 8.3 is replaced by a multi-way shape blend.

Lewis *et al.* [LEWI00] term the approach described in Section 8.6.1 skeleton
subspace deformation or SSD because the required skin deformations lie in the
skeleton subspace. The extreme example of this is the cross-over effect shown

in Figure 8.10 where the skin collapses at the elbow joint due to a twisting of the lower arm with respect to the upper arm. They suggest a new approach called Pose Space Deformation or PSD which facilitates keyframe interpolation between skeleton-driven deformations which have been directly sculpted by the animator. In SSD the animator has to tediously adjust weights by trial and error to achieve the desired deformation. Pose space is either the space of the joint state of the skeleton or a more abstract space, for example the state of the UIs (smile, raise-eyebrow in facial animation etc.) that produced the pose of the skeleton or bones. Alternatively, pose space can be a combination of both these controls. Pose space acts as an interpolation domain and a scattered data interpolation scheme (Appendix 8.1) is used to interpolate in-betweens. A scattered data interpolation method recognises that the deformations may be sculpted at uneven intervals in the deformation space. The mapping from pose space to the mesh or object local coordinate frame then produces the required (interpolated) skin deformation. Lewis *et al.* report that the approach is efficient enough for real-time synthesis, being only marginally more expensive than shape or vertex interpolation.

The process of using PSD divides into a number of steps as follows. First, the artist defines a set of poses and sculpts or models the skin for each pose. A pose is defined as the state or configuration of the pose controls – joint angles or UI manipulators – with respect to the rest pose. Pose space is, in general, a multi-dimensional space where the dimensionality is a function of the number of joints and their degree of freedom. In this n-dimensional space a pose is a single point. Each of these points in pose space is associated with a set of deformed vertices and these are determined and expressed as delta values with respect to the rest configuration. Thus a point **p** moves under skeleton key poses as:

$$\mathbf{p}' = \mathbf{p} + \boldsymbol{\delta} \tag{8.4}$$

Scattered data interpolation is essentially a two-phase process – the sculpted keys enable the set of weights w_i to be determined for these keys, as we detail in Appendix 8.1. To synthesise the skin deformation for an arbitrary pose, the required pose is placed in pose space and equation 8.4 is applied to find the new vertex values. A separate interpolation is performed for each vertex.

Appendix 8.1 Scattered data interpolation using radial basis functions

We wish to approximate a function $f(\mathbf{x})$ by $s(\mathbf{x})$ given the set of values (the keys)

$(f_1, \ldots, f_N)$

at the distinct points

$\{\mathbf{x}_1, \ldots, \mathbf{x}_N\} \in \Re^d$

where d is the dimensionality of the pose space.

We choose $s(\mathbf{x})$ to be of the form:

$$s(\mathbf{x}) = p(\mathbf{x}) + \sum_{i=1}^{N} w_i \phi(|\mathbf{x} - \mathbf{x_i}|), \; \mathbf{x} \in \Re^d$$

where

    p is a low degree polynomial (or is not present – as in our application)
    $|\mathbf{x} - \mathbf{x_i}|$ is the Euclidean norm or distance between $\mathbf{x}$ and $\mathbf{x_i}$
    w_i is a real-valued weighting
    ϕ is a radially symmetric basis function

The equation is thus a linear combination of non-linear functions of distance from the key poses. It is solved to give us the set of weights w_i we require to find $s(\mathbf{x})$, the arbitrary pose, as a weighted linear combination of the key poses.

Common choices for ϕ include:

- the thin plate spline $\phi(r) = r^2 \log(r)$
- the Gaussian $\phi(r) = \exp(-cr^2)$

As we have implied, radial basis functions are effective for interpolating scattered data and in particular they place little or no restriction (depending on the choice of ϕ) on the location of the supplied points.

Introducing the following vectors and matrices

$$\mathbf{w} = (w_1, \ldots, w_i)$$
$$\mathbf{f} = (f_1, \ldots, f_n)^T$$
$$\mathbf{G} = \mathbf{G}_{ij} = \phi(|\mathbf{x_i} - \mathbf{x_j}|), \; i,j = 1, \ldots N$$

then the set of unknown weight parameters is given by

$$\mathbf{w} = (\mathbf{G}^T\mathbf{G})^{-1}\mathbf{G}^T\mathbf{f}$$

9 Elements of advanced character animation

Within 5 years virtual humans will have individual personalities, emotional states and live conversations. They will have roles, gender, culture and situation awareness. They will have reactive, proactive and decision-making behaviours for action execution. But to do these things, they will need individualized perceptions of context. They will have to understand language so real humans can communicate with them as if they were real . . .

Norman Badler 1999 [BADL99]

9.1 Introduction – an anthropomorphic interface for games

In this chapter we will look both at the present and the future. Clearly character animation will evolve, with synthetic humans becoming more and more realistic. This evolution will involve a multiplicity of enabling technologies, animating shape, visual speech, computer vision, NLP, AI etc. We will concentrate on facial animation and tracking as one vital aspect of this development and study the current technology and its potential. We begin by overviewing the general area.

Facial animation, and in particular visual speech, is a long-awaited milestone in HCI from which many applications will derive. In computer games we should consider it as the output part of a new interactive modality that will enable players to interact with a game through the use of spoken high-level commands. It is clear that the degree of interactivity possible through speech, rather than direct low level of control through a keyboard, will be increased greatly. Speech input can reinforce the relationship between player and game character, making the character more believable in its role as a simulated human/alien/whatever. Speech input can also convey abstract notions. Consider the difference between 'run towards the door on the left' and 'try to reach the door, but conserve your ammunition'.

An obvious qualification in considering the use of such systems in games is that there is always going to exist a compromise between the implied AI functionality and playability. Direct control of a player, where the current play is to pick up a weapon and shoot the monster before you are killed, is more exciting than issuing the command 'pick up the weapon and shoot the monster'. In the latter case the player becomes a passive spectator.

It is useful to look at the total potential requirements of a game that would have such facilities. In this way we can see the role of facial animation in the context of the whole and gain some understanding of the current state of the art. Speech recognition, natural language processing and facial animation (comprising visual speech and expression control) would form part of an I/O layer between the game and the player. It is fairly obvious what the functional requirements of such a layer would be (Figure 9.1). What is currently less obvious is the organisation and functionality of the architecture to the right of this layer, which we will loosely refer to as the game AI. If anthropomorphic interface modalities are to be fully exploited, this will require development beyond the immediate capabilities of, for example, Natural Language Processing (NLP). The obvious prophecy is a continuum of interaction modalities from replacing keyboard/mouse interaction with spoken commands to full interaction between a live participant and synthetic characters.

Certain applications already exist that use part of this interface. For example, MoCap software is now able to animate a synthetic character in real time as the data is being collected. In this context the MoCap data collection is functioning as a computer vision facility which produces a graphics output. This is just another version of what is generally known as performance animation where actors control the animation of synthetic characters in real time. Simple database query systems operating with speech recognition and outputting to a synthetic talking head also exist.

The general task of the architecture to the right of the interface layer is to convert a semantic representation output by the NLP processor into a (low level) animation script for the graphics engine. It is easy to see why this is not straightforward – even if the NLP problem is solved. An action involving interaction with the environment, such as 'run towards the door on the right', requires a call to a path planning module to avoid obstacles. A door may possess a handle that has to be grasped and turned – an object for which there is no explicit linguistic representation. The agent may possess a personality that determines exactly how the run will be executed. Very quickly we see that path planning generalises into a far more involved action planning and that the task of controlling the game engine from a semantic interpretation of a user command may be as difficult a task as the NLP.

Although good (expensive) speech recognition technology is currently available, NLP aspects are generally still a research problem. The NLP problem, put simply, is to extract the meaning or semantic from the recognised sentence. The difficulty is a function of the nature of the command. Direct imperative commands – 'run towards the door . . .' – can be interpreted more easily than 'try to reach the door but conserve your ammunition'. The latter types express general rules that may not relate directly to the current situation. Instead they express abstract generic knowledge. The semantic interpretation has to be guided by the game environment, and extracting intention concerning direct actions is less involved than interpreting abstractions in terms of the game environment. Many current games could be controlled using fairly simple NLP technology; for example, with multi-keyword spotting, template-based finite state systems could map the input into game engine control. However, as genres evolve it is likely that more and more demands will be placed on NLP.

We can make the general comment that in many games instructions are going to be limited to the domain game environment and that in most cases this model will constrain the syntactic and semantic ambiguity of natural language sufficient for reliable disambiguation.[1] Recent work on NLP for games [CAVA99] uses DOOM spoilers as a working corpus.

9.2   Converting linguistic representations into animation – examples

In Figure 9.1 we loosely referred to the module beneath an anthropomorphic interface layer as game AI because, to exploit such systems, applications will have to possess a facility that can only be described as AI. Irrespective of application, the general task that all such modules will be required to perform is to convert linguistic representation into non-linear animation sequences.

The approaches to this problem usually adopt a multi-level architecture first suggested for the control of robots by Brooks in 1989 [BROO89]. Recent examples applied to animation are IMPROV [PERL96] and work being carried out at the University of Pennsylvania for the *Jack* virtual human called PAR architecture [BIND00]. Other work at MIT considers the totality of conversation

---

1. The minefield of syntactic/semantic disambiguation is trivially illustrated by a classic example: Concorde flies like an arrow; fruit flies like a banana.

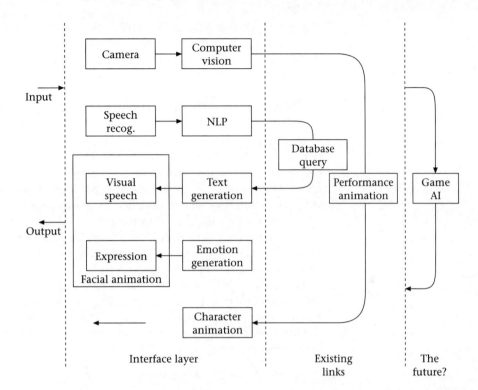

Figure 9.1
An anthropomorphic
interface layer.

– the fact that conversation between humans involves speech and facial and other gestures.

All of these systems are hierarchical or multi-level in organisation and exhibit the following general functionalities to a greater or lesser extent:

- **Low-level control** At its lowest level virtual human activity is separated into procedural actions (head turning, right arm waving etc.) which operate directly on the skeleton control of the model. These are authored as changes over time that affect particular DOFs – that is, conventional animation control.

- **Activity synthesis – within and between actors** We recognise that human body movement can be described as set of different low-level actions that take place in sequence and/or in parallel. Thus structures need to set up and control these. We need:
  - scheduling (activation/deactivation) of actions;
  - facilitating the continuation of actions in parallel by resolving conflicts between actions that access the same DOF;
  - blending between actions; in particular, avoiding self-collision;
  - coordinating actors – avoiding collisions etc.

- **High-level behavioural control** The top of the hierarchy is some kind of behavioural controller which accepts input from an NLP module as 'understood' high-level commands.

The net result is sometimes referred to as non-linear animation – the animation is put together as a function of pre-set persistent rules (agent personality), player commands, interaction with other agents and the game environment.

IMPROV (Media Research Laboratory, New York University)

This system bears some resemblance to early high-level animation scripting languages. (These languages never gained wide adoption as it became clear that off-line animation production preferred artists to interact directly with low-level controls.) Its motivation was to integrate low-level motion control with behaviour and enable designers to translate a story board directly into a behaviour script. Its interest in the context of an anthropomorphic interface layer is that it uses an English-like scripting language, although the original emphasis was on off-line design of a 'game that includes multi-actor coordination and user directed runtime control'.

In IMPROV Perlin employs a Behaviour Engine, which he analogises with 'the mind' outputting to an Animation Engine – 'the body'. The Animation Engine accepts descriptions of actions such as 'walk' and operates on the geometry.

Low-level animation is conventionally authored by grouping DOF control into action modules. For example:

```
define ACTION "talk gesture"
{
R_UP_ARM   25:55   0        -35:65     {N0 0 N0}
R_LO_ARM   55:95   0        0          {N1 0 0}
R_HAND     -40:25  75:-25   120        {N1 N2 0}
}
```

Each line refers to a single DOF <pitch roll yaw><coherent noise functions of frequency f, 2f, 4f>. At each time step the coherent noise functions control the progress of the joint angles.

The designer explicitly indicates how higher-level activities are 'composited' or how conflicts for parallel activities are resolved. This is done by grouping actions into prioritised categories and prioritising actions within a group. For example:

global/persistent – higher priority

```
GROUP       stances
   ACTION       stand
   ACTION       walk
GROUP       gestures
   ACTION       no_waving
   ACTION       wave_left
   ACTION       wave_right
```

```
GROUP          momentary
    ACTION          no_scratching
    ACTION          scratch_head_left
```

local/transitory – lower priority

Actions which access the same DOFs are placed in the same group. A selected action in a group causes the weight of the action to change from zero to one while at the same time other actions in the group change their weights smoothly to zero. At any time step a weighted sum is taken of the contribution of each action to each DOF.

Actions continually control the movements of the actor's body and these derive from higher level scripts such as:

```
define SCRIPT   "greeting"
{
    {"enter"}
    {wait 4 seconds}
    {"turn to camera"}
    {wait 1 second}
    {"wave" for 2 seconds
     "talk" for 6 seconds}
    {wait 3 seconds}
    {"sit"}
    {wait 5 seconds}
    {"bow" towards "camera"}
    {wait 2 seconds}
    {leave}
    }
```

Thus scripts are used to trigger actions to control the animation. They are also used to modify the actor's properties and thus his behaviour:

```
define SCRIPT "eat dinner"

    {"eat"}
    {set my "appetite" to 0}
```

Decision rules can be defined and invoked in a script:

```
    {choose from {"tom" "dick" "harry"} based on "who is interesting"}
```

```
define DECISION-RULE "who is interesting"

    factor {his/her "charisma"}          influence 0.8
    factor{his/her "intelligence"}       influence 0.2
```

Finally, real-time user interaction is facilitated by making the interface layer a scriptable element.

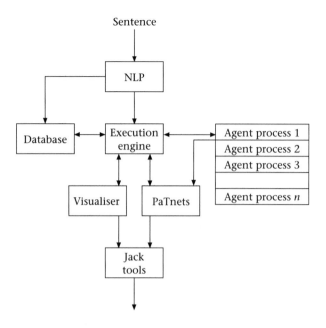

Figure 9.2
Starting at the highest
level a linguistic processor
maps the components of
a spoken instruction into
the parameters or
variables of a PAR.

(9.2.2)

PAR architecture (Center for Human Modeling and Simulation, University of Pennsylvania)

The second example we consider is closer to the games model and is work being carried out at the University of Pennsylvania [BIND00]. It is similar to IMPROV in that it is also a three-level abstraction. Motion Generators drive graphical models, activity synthesis is organised by Parallel Transition Networks and high-level representation is through Parameterised Action Representation (PAR).

Starting at the highest level, a linguistic processor maps the components of a spoken instruction into the parameters or variables of a PAR (Figure 9.2). One of the main functions of this process is to supply detail missing in the English specification. For example, a command like 'Walk to the door and turn the handle slowly' contains no information on how to grasp the handle and in which direction to turn it. The PAR representation also includes applicability, preparatory and terminating conditions. In the above example we also require the number of steps the agent needs to take to reach the door, which in turn depends on the agent's size and start location etc. The PAR representation is linked directly to the Parallel Transition Networks (PaTnets).

A reported investigation scenario is a military training simulation. The player/trainee has control (through persistent commands or standing orders) of a group of soldiers guarding an entrance. These alter the behaviour of the soldiers as they check the identity of a car driver who has approached the entrance. The soldiers are to take the driver into custody under gunpoint if the identity matches any of the entities on a list of spies. The trainee refines the soldiers' behaviour so that observed errors do not recur. For example, the soldier should take cover when threatening an intruder with his gun otherwise he gets shot and the trainee issues a persistent command: 'when you draw your weapon at the driver take cover . . .'

9.2.3   Embodied conversational interface agents (MIT Media Laboratory)

The previous examples have been concerned with setting up situations where agents have varying degrees of autonomy and respond in various ways to spoken commands. The work described in this section, carried out at the MIT Media laboratory [CASS00] and [CASS01], looks beyond setting up scenarios where agents respond to orders from human players and looks instead at how we can build agents that converse in a human-like manner. In other words, the agent becomes immersed in the scenario – at least as far as conversational interaction is concerned. This implies shaping the dialogue by a conversational structure that includes non-spoken interaction:

Communicative functions	Communicative behaviour
Initiation and termination	
React to new person	Short glance at other
Break away from conversation	Glance around
Farewell	Look at other, head nod, wave
Turn-taking	
Give turn	Look, raise eyebrows (followed by silence)
Want turn	Raise hands into gesture space
Take turn	Glance away, start talking
Feedback	
Request feedback	Look at other, raise eyebrows
Give feedback	Look at other, nod head

A sample interaction

Rea is an embodied conversational agent whose domain of expertise is real estate and she has access to a database of available condominiums and houses for sale in Boston. She can display pictures of those properties and of their various rooms, and point out and discuss their salient features. The following is an excerpt from an actual interaction:

> *Mike approaches the projection screen. Rea is currently turned side on and is gazing idly about. As Mike moves within range of the two cameras mounted above the screen, Rea turns to face him and starts the conversation:*
> REA> Hello. How can I help you?
> MIKE> I'm looking to buy a place near MIT.
> *Rea nods, indicating that she is following.*
> REA> I have a house to show you.

A picture of a house appears on-screen behind Rea who blinks and looks at the house and then at Mike.

REA> It's in Somerville.

MIKE> Tell me about it.

Rea looks up and away while she plans what to say.

REA> It's big.

Rea makes an expansive gesture with her hands.

Mike brings his hands up as if he is about to speak and so Rea does not continue; instead waiting for him to speak.

MIKE> Tell me more about it

REA> Sure thing. It has a nice garden.

Rea sketches a curved gesture with her hands indicating that the garden extends along two sides of the house.

MIKE> How far is it?

REA> It is five minutes to the Porter Square T station.

*Rea makes it clear that it is five minutes **on foot** from the T station by making a walking gesture with her fingers.*

MIKE> How big is the house?

REA> It has four bedrooms, three bathrooms . . .

Mike interrupts Rea who stops speaking immediately.

MIKE> Wait. Tell me, where is the master bedroom?

REA> I'm sorry, I didn't catch that. What did you ask me?

MIKE> Where is the master bedroom?

REA> It's upstairs.

Rea points up.

MIKE> Where is the master bathroom?

REA> It's next to the bedroom.

Rea brings her hands together to indicate the relationship between the bedroom and the bathroom.

And the house tour continues.

The architecture of the system is shown in Figure 9.3 which conforms to the general structure shown in Figure 9.1.

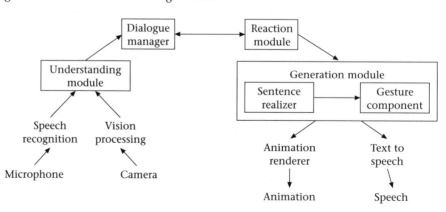

Figure 9.3
The system architecture of REA.

Conclusions for games

- As far as computer games are concerned, we can conclude that we are close to having the tools that will integrate an anthropomorphic interface with a game application.

- The examples demonstrate the (eternal) use of hierarchies as a complexity reduction mechanism and in particular a consensus that a three-level structure consisting of some form of:
  - high-level specification of behaviour;
  - synthesis – a process that controls the integration of procedural animations within an agent and the interaction of agents as the action evolves;
  - low-level motion control;

  is a good way to deal with the complexity.

Most emphasis has been on input, NLP and body/object animation control. There seem to be little work at the moment in linking existing facial animation tools into the output side of such systems. Clearly the believability of human-like agents will depend as much on the quality of the facial animation/speech as their body movement.

9.3 Facial animation, visual speech and tracking

For the remainder of the chapter we will concentrate on what will probably be one of the most important elements in an anthropomorphic interface: facial animation for visual speech and facial tracking as an aid to speech recognition and emotion recognition.

Facial animation is very much an unsolved problem in computer graphics. The reasons for this are fairly obvious and we start by considering why believable facial animation is so difficult. We can say that facial animation and associated body gestures fall into five categories:

(1) simple global movement of the head;

(2) simple movement of the eyes;

(3) complex simultaneous deformation of different parts of the face to form expressions;

(4) speech – complex deformation/movement of the lips, jaws and tongue;

(5) appropriate gestures particularly of, but not restricted to, arms and hands that accompany speech.

From this categorisation we can identify the difficulties. These are:

- **Integration** Expressive visual speech involves all of these movements and a believable model has to integrate them into a whole driven by appropriate parameters.

- **Identity/Uniqueness** A second difficulty arises from the uniqueness of faces. Ideally we would like an underlying deformation model which admitted different 'masks'. Currently the most common manifestation of this approach is (photographic) texture mapping onto a generic polygon mesh. The mesh vertices are then animated. The identity problem is absent from, or does not concern us to the same extent in, other aspects of human animation (body and fabric for instance).

- **Rendering quality** The detail of expressions (wrinkles etc.) is difficult to render convincingly using standard geometric and shading models. At a finer level of detail rendering of skin texture is also not currently accomplished to high quality. And in the absence of convincing photo-realistic quality we have sometimes resorted to cartoon-like characters.

In games, pre-designed artist-originated sequences predominate. It is still the case that skilled artists produce more convincing, less awkward sequences than parameter-driven/procedural animation. (A parallel perhaps with the situation in body animation where animator-derived or motion-capture-derived animation produces more natural motion than inverse kinematics, for example.)

On the other hand, in graphics research most progressive work seems to have been carried out in the decade 1985–95. Since then the field has been somewhat static. The ultimate goal of much research is to produce a high-level parametrically controlled model that admits any general identity and integrates the five factors enumerated above. In other words, a model that can be scripted at a high level – 'utter the following sentence angrily . . .'.

Facial tracking is a computer vision methodology which has potential importance in games. It is effectively the opposite of facial animation. Instead of driving 3D deformation of a face model we would like to be able, through a camera, to 'read' or track the 3D motion of a real face in real time. This section is worthy of study, not only because it gives examples of real-time computer vision approaches to the human face, but because the most popular approaches are analysis by synthesis. In general this means that a 3D model is stored within the application, animated and compared with the real video. The parameters of the stored model form a search space wherein we try to find a match with the video. Thus facial animation and computer vision are linked in these applications.

There are applications of this technology in future games. For example, the game AI could read the facial expression/emotion of the player. Human beings do not communicate by speech alone – speech is always accompanied by expression. Another obvious application is as an aid to speech recognition.

Facial tracking could be used to derive an animation script for a computer graphics head. Here the games application might be to include a high quality animation of the player in, say, a multi-player game environment.

Models for controlling, rendering and tracking facial meshes

We now overview the main control methods that have been investigated. This is followed by a description of examples of each category. Depending on the method used, the model representation may determine the deformation control method, but subject to that reservation we can identify a number of distinct approaches.

From an animator's point of view the issues are: what are the control parameters and how do they relate to motion of the face model, how are they manipulated and how convincingly to they deform the mesh and are they adequate and appropriate?

3D morphing of key frames

The standard approach – this method can supply high quality animation, particularly if used in conjunction with image-based rendering technology. Automatic morphing implies the modelling requirement that there is a generic mesh which is adjusted to fit a particular head. The complexity of such approaches resides in the modelling and capture phase. Morphing between keys is straightforward.

However, it is unlikely that such a simple approach to generating facial animation is correct. By this we mean that the in-between frames produced by interpolation will not correspond to the reality when a face transforms between two expressions. If it was correct then this would imply that all points in the face move from one position to another with the same motion. However, the real question is not if it is correct but if it is sufficiently correct to produce visually convincing animation. Another problem with morphing approaches is that the animation is produced from basic ingredients which are themselves finished frames – this may not be a powerful foundation for the production of novel animation.

Image-based methods and tracking

Image or model-based methods can be used for both animation and tracking. Much recent research in facial animation is involved with model-based tracking of video sequences. This means using the geometric information from a computer graphics model, together with the 2D pixel motion in a video sequence, to infer from the 2D motion in the video sequence the 3D motion of the real head. There are a number of motivations for this interest:

- Its effect is equivalent to conventional motion capture which is difficult to employ effectively for subtle facial deformations.

- Capturing the motion of facial expressions/visual speech is presumably a more correct approach than sampling or capturing static facial poses and then creating animation by interpolation and blending.

- It has potential in computer vision: for example, emotion recognition and the ultimate design interface – performance-driven animation.

- It can be used in very low bandwidth systems to transmit animation data, as has been recognised by the MPEG4 standard.

Parameterisation

The goal of this approach is to somehow extract a small set of parameters which characterise the deformation motion of the mesh. Lip motion during speech in particular is susceptible to this approach. Having a small number of representative parameters should simplify the production of novel animation. Parameterisation emerged naturally from the limitations of the keyframe approach and its first use in facial animation is usually attributed to Parke [PARK82]. Parke combined facial shape parameters and expression parameters both connected directly to mesh vertices. Examples of expression control include: eyelid opening, eyebrow arch, eyebrow separation, jaw rotation, mouth width, mouth expression, upper lip position, mouth corner position and eye gaze. The goal of this work was a model that admitted any particular face and any expression by specifying the appropriate parameter value set. A much-quoted scheme for the parametric specification of facial expressions is FACS (Facial Action Coding System [EKMA73]). Although not originally intended for computer animation, it has been used in many investigations. The scheme is based on Action Units (for example, upper-lip raiser, lip-corner depressor etc.). Forty-six of these are defined and they are based on the activity of facial muscles. A set of these may combine to produce a single facial movement. More recent work on parameterisation finds parameter sets directly by analysis of observations of facial motion.

Pseudo-muscle or vector muscle models

One of the most enduring models in recent years was introduced by Waters in 1987 [WATE87]. The idea here was to layer control on a polygon mesh that had some basis in reality – muscle control. Waters used two types of muscle abstraction – linear muscles that pull and sphincter muscles that squeeze. These are attached to the space of the mesh at a single point (that is, they are not necessarily attached to a mesh point) and they have a directional specification. Thus the muscle control is independent of specific face topology. The control parameters of this model are based on FACS.

Patch technology

This is the classic computer graphics method for deforming a mesh model. In the FFD paradigm the model is surrounded by a Bézier hyperpatch and moving, the control points of the hyperpatch deforms the mesh. Because of the complexity of the required deformations the face surface has to be enclosed in a number of Bézier volumes. As patch technology is being used, the (large) total number of control points admits hierarchical control. Alternatively, we can use hierarchical B-splines.

Physically based models

To try to overcome the limitations of the vector-based muscle model, Terzopolous and Waters [TERZ93] introduced a muscle model whose structure was closer to the biological reality and whose control was physically based. This was a complex tri-layer model of synthetic tissue where each layer is modelled by a spring mass model. The layers represent cutaneous tissue, subcutaneous tissue and muscle. Spring stiffnesses in each layer are set to reflect the different tissue properties. Facial topology is set up by building elements and the reported investigation quotes 960 elements, making a total of 6500 springs. This complex and expensive model does not seem to have produced imagery that is substantially superior to less complex models.

We will now deal with these categories in some detail, omitting 3D morphing of keyframes (which does not require any special methods beyond those already covered in Chapter 7) and physically based models (because of their uncertain relevance).

9.4.1 Image-based modelling, rendering and tracking

The next two methods use image-based[2] modelling technology to capture the fine dynamic detail in animated facial expressions. The first extracts information from photographs and the second from video sequences. They combine the philosophy of motion capture with image-based rendering and suffer from the disadvantage (like MoCap) that novel animation must be created from pre-recorded information. (Image-based technology for visual realism in visual speech is by no means a new idea, but most of the work is firmly rooted in image space and only one view of the synthesised visual speech is possible. Presumably most games applications would require a 3D model that admitted any head and camera pose.)

Morphing and image-based modelling: 3D morphing from photographs

3D morphing, using photographs, is an attractive and cheap solution to one of the enduring problems of facial animation – the believability of facial expressions. Perception of facial expressions is a deep-rooted instinct in human beings and convincing animation of facial expressions is consequently an

---

2. Image-based modelling and rendering means using information captured by a 2D imaging device in 3D rendering space. Its motivation is to save the very large modelling costs that would otherwise pertain in such applications as interactive exploration of complex environments like city centres.

extremely difficult task using conventional 3D graphics technology. An obvious (partial) solution is to use image-based tools. This bypasses most of the difficulties at the cost of some manual intervention and constraints. The general idea is to use 3D morphing of a generic head model which has been textured with 2D photographic imagery.

One of the most successful illusions created by post-processing video or film footage is 2D morphing. Wild distortions which track between two morph targets are obtained at full image resolution. In computer graphics we can employ 3D morphing because we have access to the 3D geometry and the high quality of photographic imagery can be retained by using them as texture maps in 3D space.

The idea was first proposed by Kurihara *et al.* in 1991 [KURI91]. A more elaborate version, which in particular attended to the texture blending problem, is Pighin *et al.* [PIGH98]. It is the latter version we describe here.

Morphing and image-based modelling: model fitting

The 3D morphing technique relies on a generic head model – a polygon mesh – that is 'tuned' to a particular photographed head and particular expressions of that head. Morphing between facial expressions is then straightforward – no specification of source/target correspondence is required – since the captured expressions are texture mapped onto the same generic mesh, albeit deformed to fit different expressions. Effectively the method is using 2D morphing techniques in 3D space – the 2D morphing plane is deformed onto a 3D mesh. The price paid for the quality of the resulting morphs is manual intervention in the pre-process.

For each captured expression a number of views are photographed (4 or 5). A subset of the mesh vertices are selected and (manually) associated with points in each of the captured images. This enables pose recovery of the camera where, for each image, a rotation matrix and translation vector are obtained. This is done by iteration initialised from the approximate camera position (front view, side view etc.) and the known 3D shape of the head. The iteration improves the pose estimation to minimise the difference between the observed and predicted feature point positions. The 3D position of the feature points for the real head are then known and the mesh is deformed to fit these. The remaining mesh vertices are then deformed to fit the real face by a procedure called scattered data interpolation using radial basis functions (Appendix 8.1). This calculates the displacement for the remaining vertices from the displacements and positions of the already deformed vertices. This process effectively interpolates a smooth vector-valued function from the set of known displacements which controls the movement of the remaining vertices. The process is equivalent to surface interpolation of the already deformed points.

Morphing and image-based modelling: texture compositing

The next process involves the extraction of a single texture map from the photographs. This is done by projecting each of the photographic images onto

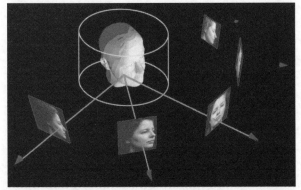

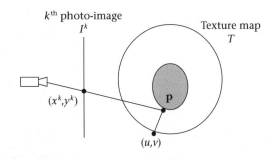

A point **p** may appear in more than one image

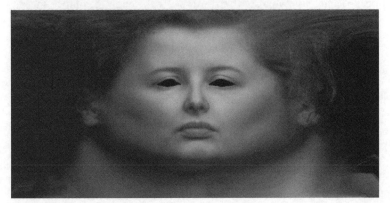

Composited texture map T

Figure 9.4
Constructing a 'cylindrical' texture map (courtesy of F. Pighin).

a virtual cylinder surrounding the head (Figure 9.4 (also Colour Plate)), which then becomes the texture map.

Because each point **p** will be imaged in more than one photograph, the map has to be constructed by compositing the contributions from the component images according to a weighting function w^k:

$$T(\mathbf{p} \rightarrow u,v) = \frac{\sum_k w^k(\mathbf{p})I^k(x^k,y^k)}{\sum_k w^k(\mathbf{p})}$$

where I^k is the kth photograph and (x^k,y^k) is the point in the photo corresponding to **p**

w is evaluated as:

- **Self-occlusion** $w^k(\mathbf{p})$ is zero unless **p** is front facing with respect to the kth image and is visible in it. This is a necessary consideration for objects that exhibit concavities.

- **Smoothness** $w^k(\mathbf{p})$ should vary smoothly so as to ensure a blend that does not exhibit seams.

- **Positional certainty** This is the dot product between the surface normal at $\mathbf{p}$ and the vector from $\mathbf{p}$ to (x^k, y^k). The 'correctness' of a texture map that is derived from a photograph is a function of this angle.

- **View similarity** Used in view-dependent compositing, it means that $w^k(\mathbf{p})$ depends on the angle between the direction of the projection of $\mathbf{p}$ onto the kth image and its direction of projection in the rendered view. However, this factor is not entirely satisfactory as it implies that we are retaining the lighting of the capture environment.

Texture compositing can be done either as a pre-process (view-independent texture mapping) or as a multi-pass during rendering for view-dependent texture mapping. Each pass weights the result with the view similarity factor. View-dependent texture mapping results in higher quality rendering.

As mentioned before, generating animation sequences by morphing between expressions is straightforward because of the correspondence between vertices in the generic mesh. In effect, the standard problem of facial animation – controlling the deformation of a polygon mesh – is solved by a combination of automatic recovery of the 3D position of selected points on a real face, surface interpolation, which fixes the displacement of the remaining points, and manual intervention, which initially sets the correspondence between certain points in the photographic images and points in the mesh. The advantages of the technique derive from the photo-realism and its obvious disadvantage is that animations are always morphs between pre-recorded expressions.

The model extends to visual speech, where the (large number of) captured expressions are the required visemes.

Tracking methods

3D model-based tracking

Model-based tracking methods, sometimes called video cloning, attempt to track video sequences by using a pre-defined 3D model of the head that appears in the video sequence. Their goal is to extract from a 2D image sequence mesh deformation information. They could be viewed as an elaboration of motion capture but whereas standard motion capture technology tracks the motion of isolated points, model-based tracking attempts to gain the motion of *every* point in the mesh. Their obvious advantage is that if they are successful then they can capture the subtleties of the dynamics of facial expressions.

The most obvious way to achieve 3D model-based tracking is by some form of 'analysis by synthesis' approach. Although the detail of such algorithms can be complex, the idea is simple. For each frame in the sequence we set up an initial estimation for the mesh vertex positions, render the model and compare it with the video image. We then search for a solution where the difference between the synthetic rendered version and the video image is minimised to within some threshold.

Pighin *et al.* [PIGH99] use the image-based model of the previous method as the model which is used as the object in the analysis by synthesis comparison. The presumption is that any video frame can be matched by a linear combination of these pre-recorded expressions. Effectively the current video frame is matched by finding a 3D morphing of the pre-recorded models.

This is done by associating with each expression model a weight W_e and searching the space of all expressions weighted by constrained values of W_e until a solution is found. The comparison image is rendered as a multi-pass and the final image is built up by blending the components as:

$$I_{\text{final}} = \sum_e W_e I_e$$

where I_e is the rendering of the eth expression model

The search space for the weight parameters W_e is constrained by the fact that weights must sum to one. A complete set of parameters, $\mathbf{P}$, also has to include a translation and rotation for the head. An iterative optimisation procedure uses the following error function of the discrepancy between the video frame and the rendered image:

$$E(\mathbf{P}) = \frac{1}{2} \| I_{\text{video}} - I_{\text{final}}(\mathbf{P}) \|^2 + D(\mathbf{P})$$

where $D(\mathbf{P})$ is a penalty function

To reduce matching problems due to colour differences that arise from the use of photographic cameras, video cameras and rendered imagery, both the rendered image and the video image were band-pass filtered. The assumption that the video image can be simulated by a rendered image clearly depends on retaining the original lighting in the texture maps or imitating the original lighting when rendering. The direct application of this process is high quality performance-driven animation and the use of the extracted parameters to animate a different face model.

In this section we have studied a tracking method that relied on detailed *a priori* knowledge of the particular face to be tracked. The search space for a match consisted of a set of pre-recorded samples of expressions of the face being tracked. Clearly, tracking any unseen face is a much more formidable problem but in game applications, where in general a single player will be communicating with a game, we have a similar situation. It is likely then that a game could tolerate a training phase where the face of the player was 'registered' with the tracking program. But such a learning phase would have to be considerably simpler than the one described here.

In the next section we examine a simpler tracking problem, which would admit a simpler learning phase – lip tracking.

Lip tracking

A simpler approach than that of the previous section is to concentrate solely on lip tracking. Lip tracking can be used as an important cue for speech recognition as well as a data collection method for visual speech. Lip tracking algorithms divide neatly into two categories – two-dimensional and three-dimensional. Two-dimensional algorithms, by definition, rely on little or no relative motion between the camera and the head. If relative head–camera motion occurs, then with a two-dimensional algorithm, changes in lip shape will occur due to this motion alone, and the algorithm will then have the onerous task of distinguishing between lip shape change due to head motion and actual lip shape motion. If the zero relative motion constraint is not realistic then a three-dimensional algorithm needs to be used. Here, as in the previous section, the three-dimensional pose becomes part of the algorithm and lip change due to pose variation can be eliminated.

Two-dimensional lip tracking

Two-dimensional lip tracking is usually a two-stage process. The first phase consists of conventional image processing which segments the lip information out of the image. This is followed by an algorithm which tracks the lip motion.

To segment the lip information in a colour image is relatively straightforward if the segmentation is carried in the appropriate colour space. We assume that the magenta/red colour of the lips can be used to identify lip pixels in the input image. This is done by first transforming the RGB pixels in the input image into a colour space where changes in hue form one of the coordinates. RGB colour space forms a cube and a convenient hue-based space is the HSV space – a single hexcone. In the HSV model varying H corresponds to selecting a colour. Decreasing S (desaturating the colour) corresponds to adding white. Decreasing V (devaluating the colour) corresponds to adding black. The derivation of the transform between RGB and HSV space is easily understood by considering a geometric interpretation of the hexcone. If the RGB cube is projected along its main diagonal onto a plane normal to that diagonal, then a hexagonal disc results.

The following correspondence is then established between the six RGB vertices and the six points of the hexcone in the HSV model (Figure 9.5(a) and (b)).

RGB		HSV
(100)	red	(0,1,1)
(110)	yellow	(60,1,1)
(010)	green	(120,1,1)
(011)	cyan	(180,1,1)
(001)	blue	(240,1,1)
(101)	magenta	(300,1,1)

where H is measured in degrees. The following code converts an RGB triple to an HSV triple.

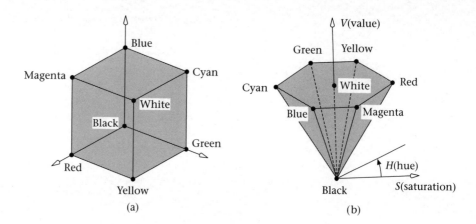

Figure 9.5
Colour spaces and
segmentation. (a) RGB
space. (b) HSV space.
(c) Lip pixels in HSV space.

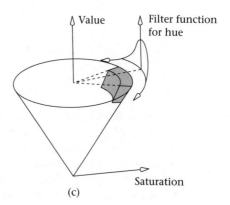

```
struct HSVTRIPLE
{
   FLOAT hsvHue;
   BYTE hsvSaturation;
   BYTE hsvValue;
};
HSVTRIPLE RGBToHSV(RGBTRIPLE rgb)
{
   HSVTRIPLE rtn;

   BYTE max = max(rgb.rgbtRed, max(rgb.rgbtGreen, rgb.rgbtBlue));
   BYTE min = min(rgb.rgbtRed, min(rgb.rgbtGreen, rgb.rgbtBlue));
   BYTE delta = max-min;

   rtn.hsvValue = max;
      //value is the maximum rgb value

   if(rtn.hsvValue)
      //if value is 0 colour is black and saturation
      //is 0 also
```

```
{ rtn.hsvSaturation = BYTE((float(delta)/max)*255); }
else
{ rtn.hsvSaturation = 0; }

if(rtn.hsvSaturation)
   //if saturation is 0 colour is grayscale
   //(black->white) and hue is undefined
{
   if(rgb.rgbtRed==max)
   { rtn.hsvHue = float(rgb.rgbtGreen-rgb.rgbtBlue)/delta; }
   else if(rgb.rgbtGreen==max)
   { rtn.hsvHue = 2+float(rgb.rgbtBlue-rgb.rgbtRed)/delta; }
   else if(rgb.rgbtBlue==max)
   { rtn.hsvHue = 4+float(rgb.rgbtRed-rgb.rgbtGreen)/delta; }

   rtn.hsvHue *= 60;
   if(rtn.hsvHue<0)
   { rtn.hsvHue +=360; }
}
else
{ rtn.hsvHue = FLT_MAX; }

return rtn;
}
```

Once a the colour value of a pixel is transformed into HSV space we decide on a median colour for the lips in the image and then set a region in this space that corresponds to lip pixels. In other words, RGB values of pixels that fall outside this region are set to zero. This is shown in Figure 9.5c, where for clarity the hexcone has been represented as a cone. The diagram also shows another elaboration to this simple scheme which implants a filter or drop-off for the hue values. The bias towards high saturation and high value discriminates against non-lip skin and shadows respectively. A drop-off can also be built into these coordinates so that a three-dimensional filtering operation is implemented. This is just a simple example which actually works quite well – the image processing literature will reveal a multitude of segmentation algorithms.

This colour space segmentation is shown in operation in Figure 9.6 (also Colour Plate). Once the lips have been segmented it is straightforward to find certain feature points, as shown in the figure. These are then used in the next stage – tracking lip motion.

The most popular method for tracking the motion of lips after they have been segmented is to use active contour models, or snakes, first proposed by Kass *et al.* in 1987 [KASS87]. Active contours are energy minimising curves, with extent in two spatial variables, where the curves themselves are B-splines or some other basis function. The curves dynamically match or track image contours that have a pre-set property, and are ideally suited to this application where a shape, of which we have some *a priori* knowledge, is continually changing.

Snakes need to be initialised in some way. That is, an approximate starting shape and position near to the desired contour have to be supplied to the

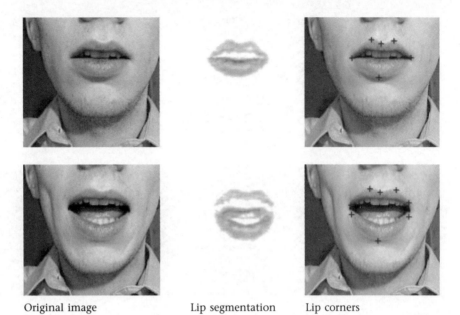

Figure 9.6
Image processing operations on the lips (courtesy of James Edge, University of Sheffield).

Original image   Lip segmentation   Lip corners

algorithm. These may originate interactively from a user, be supplied by some higher-level process or from a previous snake process. In this case lip features detected in the previous stage are used, as shown in Figure 9.7 (also Colour Plate).

When using active contour models with an image the energy to be minimised is a weighted sum of a term that originates from the current state of the deformation of the snake $Q(u)$. We have:

$$E_{\text{total}} = \int_0^1 E_{\text{internal}} Q(u) \mathrm{d}u + E_{\text{external}} Q(u) \mathrm{d}u$$

The overall energy term E_{total} thus depends both on the shape of the snake and the value of the image function along its path. The internal spline energy consists of an elasticity and rigidity term:

$$E_{\text{internal}} = w_1 \left| \frac{\mathrm{d}Q}{\mathrm{d}u} \right|^2 + w_2 \left| \frac{\mathrm{d}^2Q}{\mathrm{d}u} \right|^2$$

where w_1 and w_2 are respectively elasticity and stiffness constants. The implication of this term is that when the snake fits a contour then by definition this will be some kind of coherent structure such as an edge. A snake modelled to fit such an image structure will exhibit a lower internal energy than one that exhibits many random excursions along its path.

The external term is derived from interaction between image information and $Q(u)$. For example, if we define:

$$E_{\text{external}} = -|\nabla I(\mathbf{x})|$$

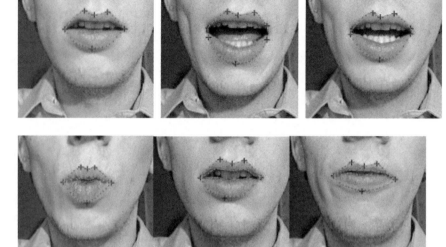

Figure 9.7
Lip tracking using snakes.
Top row outer lip
contour. Bottom row
inner lip contour (courtesy
of James Edge, University
of Sheffield).

then the curve is attracted to the local maximum of the gradient, that is, edges. Note that the term is negative and the curve moves towards areas of high gradient to minimise the sum of the two energy terms. Other image constraints can be applied. For example, lines can be used as attractors; the area enclosed by the curve can be constrained, forcing the curve to enclose homogeneous regions only. Constraints may exist between multiple snakes – Kass *et al.* describe a stereo snake where a pair of snakes operate in a stereo image pair.

Figure 9.7 shows the method in operation. In this case both the outer and inner lip contours are tracked.

Three-dimensional lip tracking

Three-dimensional lip tracking can be accomplished using the same analysis by synthesis approach described in the subsection on 3D model-based tracking. The lip model described in the next section has been used in exactly this way.

9.4.3   Parameterisation

A good example of the use of parameterisation in facial animation and tracking is given in [REVE98]. Here the idea is to derive a set of high-level parameters that can be used to best represent lip motion for visual speech (of French). The 3D model used is shown in Figure 9.8 and is a surface which interpolates 30 control points. The control points are divided into three groups of 10 points which form contour curves. Lip motion occurs as the control points are moved to new positions defining a new surface.

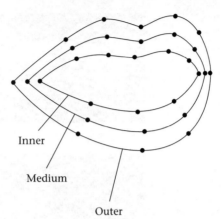

Figure 9.8
Three contour curves
defined by 30 control
points.

Each lip shape is thus described by a 90-component vector or, equivalently, a single point in 90-dimensional space. A large training set is obtained which is categorised into one of 10 lip shapes according to the utterance that motivated them (rounded vowels, non-rounded vowels, fricatives etc.). Principal component analysis (PCA) is then applied to the data for each shape set to determine three articulatory parameters.

PCA (or the Karhune–Loeve transform) is a method that finds a linear transformation in N-dimensional space so that the underlying properties of the data are most clearly represented along the coordinate axes. The data is considered to be a multivariate probability distribution. If we consider just three dimensions (instead of 90) the method finds the ellipsoid that best encloses the points and returns its axes. The principal axis of the ellipsoid is the axis along which the data exhibits maximum variance. PCA is thus used to transform interdependent coordinates into significant independent or uncorrelated ones.

The principal axes of the data are found by finding the origin – the centre of gravity – of the data and calculating a dispersion matrix whose elements are:

$$M_{ij} = \frac{1}{N} \sum_{p=1}^{N} (\mathbf{x}_i - \bar{\mathbf{x}}_i)(\mathbf{x}_j - \bar{\mathbf{x}}_j)$$

where
N is the number of points in the data
$\mathbf{x}_i$ is the ith component of data point $\mathbf{x}$

The eigenvectors give the principal axes and their eigenvalues give the variances associated with that component. The first component has the largest percentage of the total variance and each subsequent component contains the maximum variance for any axes orthogonal to the previous component. We can express the percentage of the total variance in each component by dividing the eigenvalues by their sum.

In their analysis on the 10 key shapes Reveret *et al.* [REVE00] found that the first three components of the PCA analysis accounted for 94 per cent of the

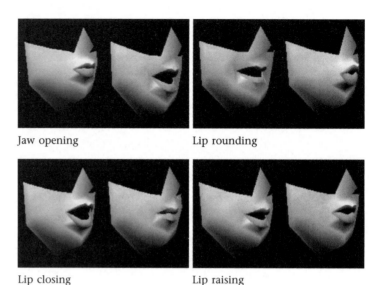

Jaw opening   Lip rounding

Lip closing   Lip raising

Figure 9.9
Extreme variations of
articulatory parameters in
MOTHER (courtesy of
L. Reveret [REVE00]).

total variance. These components are variations in lip shape along the principal component axes and are interpreted as:

First component (75%) is a rounding gesture carrying protrusion.
Second component (12%) is the motion of the lower lip.
Third component (7%) is the motion of the upper lip.

Thus the PCA analysis suggests that any lip shape should be parameterised using these three parameters as animation parameters for the model to represent lip motion in speech production. Any linear combination of these three parameters results in any lip shape in the space of the collected data.

This work was extended to six parameters to include both lip and jaw motion as reported in [REVE00]. The system developed was called Mother (Morphable Talking Head for Enhanced Reality). Reveret *et al.* found that this analysis showed that 97.7 per cent of the total variance could be accounted for by six parameters. These parameters are called articulatory parameters, some of which are shown in Figure 9.9 (also Colour Plate).

Once the best parameters have been found their 'goodness' is tested by an analysis to synthesis tracking method (identical in principle to that of Pighin *et al.*) [PIGH99] on video footage. (The same speaker is used for the video.) The six parameters are used as predictors and the polygon mesh model rendered. The difference between the rendered and video image is then used to optimise the parameter values. The difference function (between the rendered and video image) is an indication of the efficacy of the parameters as motion predictors. Tracking errors were in the order of 5 per cent. The work is an experimental verification that visual speech can be successfully parameterised (for the jaw and lips) by using only six articulatory parameters and a low resolution model.

Pseudo-muscle models

As stated in the overview, this is a popular model that was first reported in 1987 [WATE87]. The apparent attraction of the model is the fact that it is an abstraction that is based on an approximation to the facial muscles that control the deformation. The muscle models can be perceived as a specialised form of FFD. They are attached to the space of the polygon mesh (not necessarily to vertices). In a typical implementation [EDGE01] the mesh consists of 878 polygons whose vertices are controlled by 25 muscle functions together with jaw rotation. Two pseudo-muscles are simulated – linear (24) and sphincter (1) The sphincter muscle is based on the Obicularis Oris, a muscle which surrounds the lips. The contraction of this muscle corresponds to the rounding of the lips as in 'book' or 'bought'.

Linear muscles are related to the mesh by two points and a direction. The points are classified as an attachment point (v_1: equivalent to a real muscle attached to a bone) and an insertion point (p_s: equivalent to a real muscle attached to the skin). The contraction is then characterised by movement of the skin towards the attachment point (Figure 9.10). Maximum displacement occurs at the insertion point and there is zero displacement at the attachment point. The field deformation, the displacement of a point $\mathbf{p}$, within an angular sector centred on the attachment point is given by:

$$\mathbf{p}' = \mathbf{p} + akr \frac{\mathbf{p} - \mathbf{v}_1}{|\mathbf{p} - \mathbf{v}_1|}$$

we define $a = \cos(a2)$ and $D = |\mathbf{p} - \mathbf{v}_1|$, then r is given by:

$$r = \begin{cases} \cos\left(\dfrac{1 - D}{R_s}\right) & \text{for } \mathbf{p} \text{ inside sector } (\mathbf{v}_1 \, \mathbf{p}_n \, \mathbf{p}_m) \\[2ex] \cos\left(\dfrac{D - R_s}{R_f - R_s}\right) & \text{for } \mathbf{p} \text{ inside sector } (\mathbf{p}_n \, \mathbf{p}_r \, \mathbf{p}_s \, \mathbf{p}_m) \end{cases}$$

where k controls the strength of the muscle or scale of the deformation motion and the other variables are defined in Figure 9.10

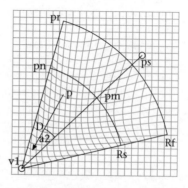

Figure 9.10
Parameters in the linear muscle model. The grid shows a contraction.

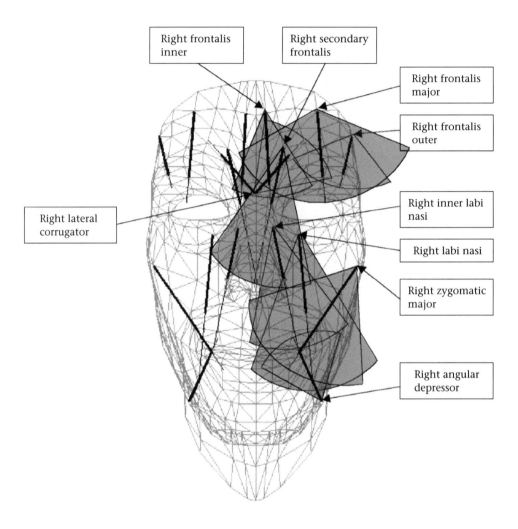

Figure 9.11
Showing the placement of
18 linear muscle models
in a mesh space (courtesy
of Steve Maddock).

Figure 9.11 shows the disposition of 18 linear muscles with respect to a face mesh. A pre-processing loop through the vertex list can label those vertices that are within the field of influence of a particular muscle.

A sphincter muscle can be simulated using a parametric ellipsoid, where vertices within the field of influence of the model are pulled towards the centre point of the ellipse. The magnitude of the displacement is a function of distance of the vertex to the centre of the ellipse. However, we need to shield the central area from muscular contractions to prevent vertices from piling up at the centre of the ellipse (Figure 9.12). Also, in reality, protrusion increases towards the centre of the such muscles and we can use the inverse of the displacement coefficient, d, to push the mesh vertices forward.

For the sphincter muscle simulation we have:

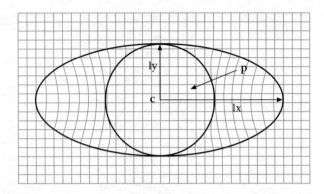

Figure 9.12
Parameters in the
sphincter muscle mode.
Grid shows a contraction.

$$\mathbf{p}' = \mathbf{p} + dk \frac{\mathbf{p} - \mathbf{c}}{|\mathbf{p} - \mathbf{c}|} \qquad d = \begin{cases} fg \text{ for } |\mathbf{p} - \mathbf{c}| > l_y \\ 0 \text{ for } |\mathbf{p} - \mathbf{c}| \le l_y \end{cases}$$

$$f = 1 - \frac{\sqrt{l_y^2 p_x^2 + l_x^2 p_y^2}}{l_x l_y} \qquad g = \frac{|\mathbf{p} - \mathbf{c}|}{l_x}$$

Another muscle model which can be implemented is a sheet. In this case the region of influence is a rectangle and the space deforms uniformly as fibres pulling parallel to the edges of the rectangle, rather than towards a single point. An example of a real sheet muscle is the lateral frontalis, one of the forehead muscles which raises the outer portion of the eyebrows.

Using these two models (linear and sphincter) plus jaw rotation, control of deformation of the facial mesh is then reduced to the manipulation of a few muscle parameters. Note also that the approach is independent of the representational method used for the mesh. Figure 9.13 shows the six so-called primary or universal expressions produced using this model.

The problem with this pseudo-muscle model is that it only simulates real facial muscles very approximately. In the case of the linear muscles it is not the case that skin is pulled towards a single attachment in a conical field of influence centred on the point of attachment. Clearly pseudo-muscle models could be made closer to realism by more elaborate modelling. For example, we could have pre-scripted FFDs more carefully tuned to simulate the action of muscle fibres. It is not clear at the moment whether this will result in greater realism. It may be that this is the best we can do with a single abstraction controlling a polygon mesh. Even if muscles are simulated more realistically we are still left with the fact that the model whose deformation is controlled is a polygon mesh.

9.4.5

Patch technology

Even a good control method may result in visual problems due to the inherent difficulty of deforming a polygon mesh. Whatever the high-level control method

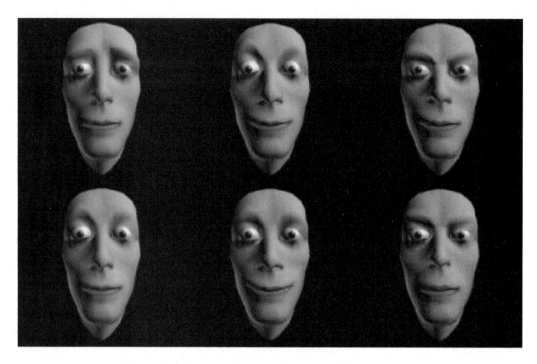

Figure 9.13
'Universal' expressions: sadness, surprise, contempt, fear, happiness, anger produced by the vector muscle model (courtesy of James Edge, University of Sheffield).

used, deforming a polygon mesh can always result in geometric configurations that produce visual defects when rendering. The only way to overcome this is to increase the polygon mesh resolution which then increases the control problem. Using bi-cubic parametric patches is the classic solution to this problem. Although a patch mesh generates a large number of control points, we would expect to have many fewer patches than polygons to achieve the same rendering quality. The need for a high-level control abstraction is just as vital in patch meshes as it is in polygon meshes. Three examples are now described – patch meshes with a pseudo-muscle control layer, hierarchical B-spline and FFDs in the context of visual speech. (FFDs are fully described – including a simple face deformation example – in Chapter 8.)

Patch meshes + pseudo-muscle control

This is the approach developed by Pixar [REEV90], who reputedly have the motto: 'never use polygons for anything that isn't flat'. It was used originally in *Tin Toy* – the short that preceded *Toy Story*.

This production was much lauded at the time (Academy Award 1988). The baby's face was given a slightly sinister appearance (Figure 9.14 (also Colour Plate)). This seems to originate from the somewhat unusual motion of the folds/wrinkles in the skin as they animate. For the baby's face in *Tin Toy* Pixar used a mesh of over 2568 Catmull-Rom patches controlled by vector/pseudo-muscle models (43 linear and 4 sphincter).

Figure 9.14
The baby from Pixar's
1988 production *Tin Toy*
(© Pixar Animation
Studios).

Perhaps this motivated the simpler face models in *Toy Story*. This production only had fleeting glimpses of virtual human characters with facial animation of a quality less than you might have expected given the convincing quality of the toy characters.

Hierarchical B-splines

Given a bi-cubic parametric patch, the straightforward way to achieve local detail shape changes that are not possible with the original control points is to subdivide the patch (thereby multiplying the number control points by a factor of almost 4). This process can continue until there are a sufficient number of control points such that moving a single point effects the desired shape change. Hierarchical B-splines [FORS88] are an economical method of achieving the same end. Patches are layered with sub-patches in the area of the surface that is to have the detail shape change. The number of control points that the sub-patches have is appropriate to the desired change. Changes to a sub-patch take place without affecting the integrity of the patch in which they are embedded. A simple visualisation of this concept is shown in Figure 9.15.

The complete structure forms a hierarchy, the surface being represented by a set of overlays at different levels of refinement. Apart from admitting detailed changes without massive explosion in the number of control points, because the structure is effectively multi-resolution it facilitates editing and modelling at any level in the hierarchy (Figure 9.16).

Muscle models are used to move the control points and skin bulging due to muscle contraction is easily incorporated into this scheme. Another novel

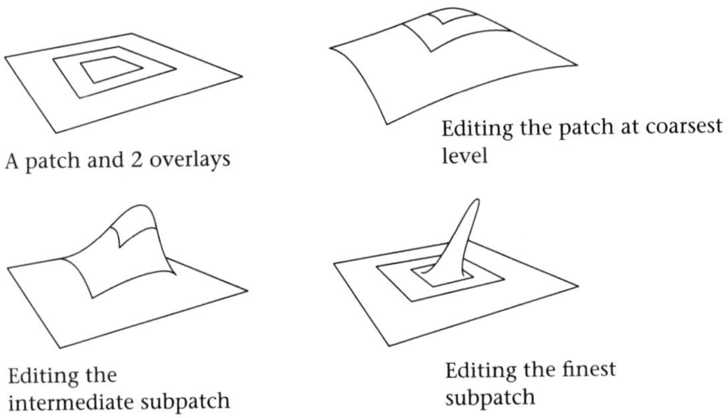

A patch and 2 overlays

Editing the patch at coarsest level

Editing the intermediate subpatch

Editing the finest subpatch

Figure 9.15
Hierarchical B-splines – a patch and two overlays.

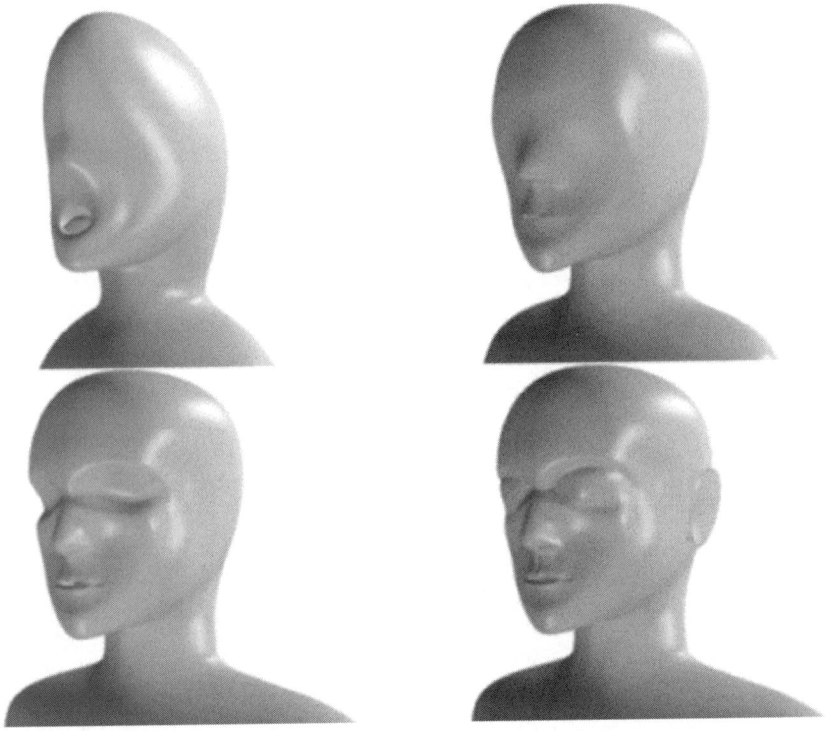

Figure 9.16
A face built as a B-spline hierarchy (courtesy of D. Forsey).

aspect of this scheme is that the muscle models are inserted within and between levels in the hiearchy.

FFDs and facial animation

The basis of the work reported in [TAO99] is the classic FFD (Free Form Deformation) method of computer graphics modelling technology described fully

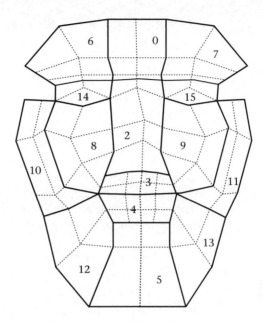

Figure 9.17
16 FFD volumes enclosing different parts of the head (after an illustration in [TAO99]).

in Chapter 8. Tao *et al.* enclose a face model in 16 Bézier volumes (Figure 9.17). Each mesh of the face is then associated with a particular Bézier volume and assigned (u,v,w) values. These are, of course, EFFDs (Chapter 8), and using a connected set of them implies that they must possess the same number of control points along the boundary.

The six universal expressions and 23 visemes are then set up interactively by deforming the model control points and (presumably) observing real images. This is clearly a labour-intensive modelling task but it has the advantage that the polygon mesh can be at any resolution (the major advantage of the FFD deformation model); the grid resolution of the Bézier volumes can be coarse in comparison.

The total deformation of the mesh for a particular facial expression i can then be written in matrix form as:

$$\mathbf{V}_i = \mathbf{BD}_i$$

where

$\mathbf{V}_i$ contains the displacement for each mesh point

$\mathbf{D}_i$ is the set of vectors each of which controls the displacement of the control points for the associated Bézier volume

$\mathbf{B}$ is a matrix containing the Bézier basis functions

Then at any instant the (non-rigid) motion of the face can be represented as:

$$\mathbf{V} = \mathbf{B}[\mathbf{D}_0, \mathbf{D}_1, \ldots \mathbf{D}_n][p_0, p_1, \ldots p_n]^T = \mathbf{BDP} = \mathbf{LP}$$

where p_i is the intensity of the expression $\mathbf{D}_i$

Including the rigid motion **R** and **T**, we can write the total motion as

$$\mathbf{R}(\mathbf{V}_0 + \mathbf{LP}) + \mathbf{T}$$

where $\mathbf{V}_0$ is the neutral mesh

Such a formalisation then gives a basis for a model-based motion tracking from video method. Unlike the method used by Pighin *et al.* [PIGH99], this approach does not rely on matching video with imagery rendered from the 3D model. Instead the 2D interframe motion of selected feature points in the video sequence is determined. The mesh is deformed in 3D to provide identical screen coordinates for the corresponding mesh points. The interframe video motion vectors are found by template matching, where the window of pixels in frame n that surrounds a feature point is searched for in frame $n + 1$. The calculated mesh point motion vectors are defined as

$$d\mathbf{V}_{2d} = \frac{\partial(\mathbf{M}(\mathbf{R}(\mathbf{V}_0 + \mathbf{LP}) + \mathbf{T}))}{\partial(\mathbf{T},\mathbf{W},\mathbf{P})}\Big|_{\mathbf{T}_n,\mathbf{W}_n,\mathbf{P}_n} \begin{bmatrix} d\mathbf{T} \\ d\mathbf{W} \\ d\mathbf{P} \end{bmatrix}$$

where

    T and **W** (the three angles of the rotation matrix **R**) represent the rigid motion of the 3D model

    P represents the non-rigid or deformation motion of the 3D model

    M is the projection matrix of the video camera

The LHS of this equation is tracked from video and the unknown variables which are to be estimated are:

$$\begin{bmatrix} d\mathbf{T} \\ d\mathbf{W} \\ d\mathbf{P} \end{bmatrix}$$

These are then added to the solution for the previous frame $\mathbf{T}_n$, $\mathbf{W}_n$ and $\mathbf{P}_n$ to give $\mathbf{T}_{n+1}$, $\mathbf{W}_{n+1}$ and $\mathbf{P}_{n+1}$. Many more 2D motion vectors are collected than unknown parameter values – an overconstrained system – and an efficient inversion (least squares estimator) can then be used.

9.5 Visual speech

As we discussed earlier, visual speech is a long-awaited milestone in HCI and its coming will undoubtedly have implications for computer games. Because of its importance, visual speech is an intensively studied area, both in the speech recognition community and in HCI areas. We will in this section look only at the simple (and crudest) approach, which is to morph between captured visemes.

The assumption in using visemes as a basic unit is that concatenating them will produce a believable animation sequence to accompany the speech. The animation is then scripted or driven by converting text into visemes. This is undoubtedly insufficient to produce high quality visual speech. It is apparent that there should be lessons for visual speech in the evolution of concatenative speech synthesis. If a small set of units – phonemes – is used in speech synthesis systems then the resulting speech sounds artificial or hyper-articulated. Speech synthesis technology has moved towards storing much larger vocabularies of longer units – even words – to overcome this problem. This, of course, moves the approach to the problem back towards the MoCap philosophy where long sequences are pre-recorded. Perhaps in the immediate future the best approach is somewhere between the two extremes of simply recording, or manually tuning, a one-to-one correspondence between animation and sound to be used in a game and viseme morphing. The point is that morphing between longer units produces better quality.

The idea of studying such a basic implementation is to give an appreciation of the difficulties of visual speech. Visual speech is a difficult area for much the same reasons that facial animation in general is difficult. We are used to observing lip motion at the same time as listening to a speaker and this (presumably) makes us extremely sensitive to deficiencies in visual speech. The best confirmation of the importance of visual speech is the McGurk effect where it is shown that vision in fact changes acoustic perception. In this classic experiment the listener is presented with a synthesised voice saying 'ba'. The same sound is then made with an artificial face making the lip shape for 'va'. The listener when observing the face hears 'va' despite the acoustic signal being 'ba'. The experiment demonstrates priority of the visual information over the auditory for this sound.

Visemes can be considered as the basic unit of visual speech and can be described as the extreme lip shapes that correspond to basic auditory speech units. Visemes form a minimally distinct set representing the sounds in a language (Figure 9.18). To drive visual speech from text, a sentence is broken into a sequence of phonemes for each of which we have an equivalent viseme. We then need some method for interpolating the visemes.

A well-known problem in visual speech is the coarticulation effect. Coarticulation refers to changes in the audio signal for a particular sound which are a function of what sounds have come before and what sounds are going to follow. The apparent importance of this phenomenon means that using phonemes, in the form of independent discrete units, as a basis for driving visual speech cannot be correct. In fact, one of the main factors in recent

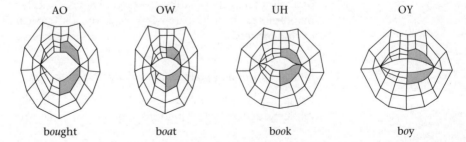

Figure 9.18
Examples of visemes.

improvements in speech synthesiser quality derives from the fact that coarticulation effects have been synthesised.

The extent of the time window over which coarticulation effects can occur can be up to 5 phonemes before (backward coarticulation) and after (forward coarticulation) the current one. Forward coarticulation often occurs when a series of consonants is followed by a vowel. Coarticulation effects have, of course, a visual as well as an auditory context. Different sounds for the same phoneme implies different lip shapes. A good example is the rounding of the lips at the beginning of the word 'stew'.

9.5.1 Morphing visemes

Dominance functions

A straightforward model for morphing phoneme target values with coarticulation taken into account was suggested by Cohen *et al.* [COHE93]. Blending functions, called dominance functions, are associated with each phoneme. The dominance functions are negative exponentials such as:

$$D_{sp} = \alpha_{sp} \exp(-\theta_{sp} |\tau|^c)$$

This means that the dominance of the phoneme duration falls off exponentially as the time distance τ from the centre of the segment. This factor is raised to the power c and modulated by a rate parameter θ_{sp}. α_{sp} controls the magnitude of the exponentials for a phoneme duration. τ is computed as:

$$\tau = t_{Csp} + t_{0sp} - t$$

where

t_{Csp} is the centre of the segment
t_{0sp} is the offset from the centre of the segment

A dominance function is required for every parameter of every phoneme and the idea is that coarticulation effects can be modelled combining the target values by a factor which is the sum of the dominant functions that are currently active. Figure 9.19 shows a simple example where the individual dominance functions are configured to show zero coarticulation compared with the influence of the second segment moving forward.

In effect the dominance functions are simultaneously accounting for coarticulation and interpolating the target values. Speech synthesis then consists of mapping text into six parameter trajectories. Coarticulation is modelled as part of this process.

Muscle control and phoneme morphing

Using the Waters muscle model for visemes implies controlling 12 of the implemented muscle functions together with jaw rotation. These can be set

1 **Dominance Functions**

segment 1   segment 2

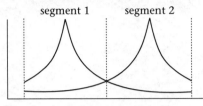

No coarticulation

Interpolating viseme targets

segment 1   segment 2

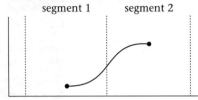

Figure 9.19
Dominance functions.
The first row shows no
coarticulation effect and
the second shows the
influence of the second
segment moving forward.

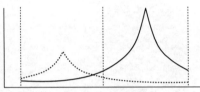

Segment 2 comes forward

Table 9.1

Muscle simulated	Shape motion
Obicularis oris (sphincter)	Increases lip rounding, reduces lip width, increases lip protrusion
Risorius (left/right linear)	Increases lip width
Depressor labii (left/right linear)	Lowers bottom lip
Labii superioris (left/right linear)	Raises upper lip
Zygomatic major (left/right linear)	Raises the lip corners
Triangularis (left/right linear)	Lowers the lip corner
Jaw rotation	Mouth openness

up interactively with the known correlation between the muscle models and
the lip shapes. Predominant lip shape muscle interaction is summarised in
Table 9.1.

Visual speech is then produced by interpolating between visemes using a sinusoid function to simulate the fluidity of muscular contraction.

Muscle control and expression – viseme interaction

Most of the work on visual speech has concentrated on animating the lips and
jaw. Conversely, the photo-realistic work described in Section 9.4.1 (on morphing facial expression) did not implement speech. Clearly, expressive visual
speech requires animation of the entire face. As well as emotional content,
normal speech is accompanied by visual cues such as eyebrow raising and blink-
ing. The muscle model admits a simple mechanism for blending expression

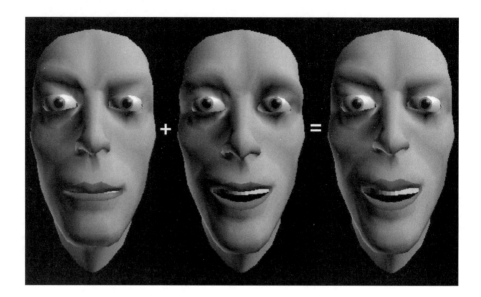

Figure 9.20
Blending the expression 'anger' with the viseme /aa/ (courtesy of James Edge, University of Sheffield).

and lip movement (Figure 9.20). However, this presupposes that mixing facial expressions with visemes when both have been captured independently is correct. This may not be the case. Consider angry speech. Extreme anger may produce snarling lip movements which do not appear when we mix silent captured anger with emotionless captured speech.

9.6 Facial animation and MPEG-4

The main goal of MPEG-4 is the support of new functionalities and in particular the standardisation of the modelling of an audiovisual scene. An important part of this scenario is the integration of synthetic and natural content. Computer games will form part of a long list of novel applications: virtual talking humans, advanced interpersonal communications systems, teleshopping, multimedia broadcasting etc. An important plank in the synthetic content part of MPEG-4 is a standardisation of facial animation, which is intended to support real or fictitious humans.

The muscle-based abstraction, which is independent of geometry representation and which has been subject to much investigation in computer graphics, is used by the MPEG-4 standard. MPEG-4, as far as facial animation is concerned, admits an analysis–description–synthesis approach. A model is analysed at the source, and this process generates animation information in the form of FAP (Facial Animation Parameters) sequences. These are transmitted over a low bandwidth channel and used to render a mesh at the receiver. Either the source and receiver both possess the same mesh geometry, in which case this information must be transmitted in a set-up phase, or the animation parameters can be used to render a different mesh at the receiver.

The other data used by facial animation in MPEG-4 are FDPs (Facial Definition Parameters). These allow the source to configure a face model at the receiver or alter an existing model. The FAP interpolation table (FIT) enables the source to define interpolation rules for the FAPs. This facility enables the source to send a subset of active FAPs, the remainder being interpolated from this subset. For example, the face can be assumed symmetrical and this feature exploited; the top-inner-lip FAPs can be sent and these used to determine the top-outer-lip motion etc. In each of these cases we would tolerate a reduction in quality to achieve data reduction.

Sixty-eight FAPs are defined, based on the study of minimal facial actions. Two are high-level parameters, visemes and expressions, which possess multiple sub-parameters, and the others are low-level 1D measurements describing the motion of facial features on the jaw, lips, eyes, mouth nose, cheek, ears etc. The motion of each FAP is relative to a neutral face.

9.7 Rendering issues

For video cloning and related applications, the popular photo-texture map is a good alternative. However, it suffers from two significant drawbacks. First, the light/face interaction is that of the data capture environment. Changing the pose of the rendered head should reflect the light/interaction of the rendered scene. Although this can be ameliorated by view-dependent texture mapping, this is at best an approximation. Second, if we want to model a novel head we cannot use a photo-texture.

Diffuse light is usually modelled on Lambert's Cosine Law which assumes that reflected light is isotropic and proportional in intensity to the cosine of the angle of incidence. Surface simulations of diffuse light are not possible because diffuse reflection originates from light that actually enters the material. This component is absorbed and scattered within the reflecting material. The wavelength-dependent absorption accounts for the colour of the material – incident white light is in effect filtered by the material. It is the multiple scattering within the material that causes the emerging light to be (approximately) isotropic. Thus a physical simulation of diffuse reflection would have to be based on subsurface scattering.

The Hanrahan and Krueger [HANR93] model is a physically based model for diffuse reflection that the authors claim is particularly appropriate for layered materials appearing in nature, such as biological tissues (skin, leaves etc.) and inorganic substances like snow and sand. The outcome of the model is, of course, anisotropy – reflecting the fact that very few real materials exhibit isotropic diffuse behaviour.

Hanrahan *et al.* address the problem by modelling the skin as two layers: the outer layer has tissue and pigment particles containing melanin which

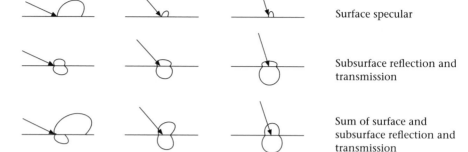

Figure 9.21
Showing the light object interaction required to successfully render skin (after an illustration in [HANR93]).

selectively absorbs light producing a brownish appearance; the inner blood and tissue layer absorbs green and blue and is assumed to cause isotropic scattering.

The reflected light forms a point on the surface which is specified as

$$L_r = L_{rs} + L_{rv}$$

where L_{rs} is the reflected light due to surface scattering – imperfect specular reflection – and L_{rv} is the reflected light that is due to subsurface scattering

The algorithm that determines the subsurface scattering is based on a 1D transport model solved using a Monte Carlo approach.

The effect is shown, for a simple case, in Figure 9.21. The first row shows high/low specular reflection as a function of angle of incidence. The behaviour of reflected light is dominated by surface scattering or specular reflection when the angle of incidence is high and by subsurface scattering when the angle of incidence is low. The second row shows reflection lobes due to subsurface scattering and it can be seen that materials can exhibit backward, isotropic or forward scattering behaviour. (The bottom lobes do not, of course, contribute to L_r but are never the less important when considering materials that are made up of multiple layers and thin translucent materials that are back lit.) The third row shows that the combination of L_{rs} and L_{rv} will generally result in non-isotropic behaviour which exhibits the following general attributes:

- reflection increases as material layer thickness increases due to increased subsurface scattering,
- subsurface scattering can be backward, isotropic or forward, and
- reflection from subsurface scattering tends to produce functions that are flattened on top of the lobe compared with the (idealised) hemisphere of Lambert's law.

Such factors result in the subtle differences between the model and Lambert's law. This successfully makes rendered skin look like real skin.

9.8   Conclusions and problems

9.8.1   Parameterisation vs photo-realism

The motivation for a high-level parameterisation as a method for controlling a facial mesh is the desire to use this abstraction to produce novel animation sequences. The search for a higher-level abstraction that will control a generic mesh has up to now only been partially successful. Perhaps this is due to the fact that the reality defies a parameterisation. Subtle changes in facial expressions are difficult to reduce to a few parameters. Model-based tracking has in general produced better quality animation but suffers for the same inherent disadvantage as motion capture. However, in the form of video cloning there is presumably potential for games applications.

9.8.2   Mesh representation

Without a doubt most work has been carried out using polygon meshes. With the notable exception of Pixar, patch representations have been avoided. This reflects the situation in mainstream computer graphics where the polygon mesh has reigned supreme for a quarter of a century and patch representations are relegated to specialist areas. Of course, visual inadequacies in a polygon mesh model can always be overcome by increasing the polygonal resolution, but this also increases the difficulty of the control problem.

Compared to a patch mesh which deforms in a smooth/predictable manner, any deformation of a polygon mesh causes the mesh to depart from its modelled polygon resolution and may cause visual defects. A patch mesh can easily admit skin bulging due to muscle contraction; this may not be the case with a polygon mesh.

9.8.3   Rendering of skin

Quality rendering of skin is an unsolved problem for real-time applications.

9.8.4   Much facial animation looks better with no sound

The main difficulty in visual speech is producing convincing novel sentences from a finite set of samples (visemes, for example) where the audio appears to a viewer to fit the animation naturally. Some animation looks more convincing when the sound is turned off – there is a conflict between what we see and what we hear. Presumably we are extremely sensitive to any discrepancy in modelling coarticulation. Driving an animation from text in such a way that perceptual synchronicity occurs is possibly a bigger problem than photo-realism in the animation. Text synthesis and graphics are more or less solved problems – it is combining them that is difficult.

9.8.5 Emotion and speech

Expressive speech will be vital in many applications – computer games, for example. Lip shapes for a sentence must vary between emotionless speech and, say, angry speech (otherwise the audio would not sound different). It cannot therefore be correct, as far as lip shape is concerned, to model emotion in speech by blending static expressions with static neutral visemes in producing expressive animation.

Appendix 9.1 A pseudo-muscle model implementation

This demonstration contains a facial animation which uses the muscle model method. The animation is interpolating continuously between three expressions.

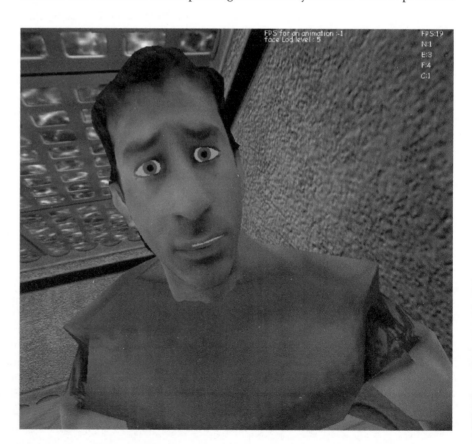

Figure A9.1
Two frames from a pseudo-muscle model implementation in Fly3D (courtesy of Emmanuel Tanguy, University of Sheffield).

Figure A9.1 *continued*

To see these more clearly, turn off the body animation by running the demo in the editor, selecting *anim_face/animface1* and setting *body_anim* (in the parameter window) to zero. This demo also contains an LOD facility whereby fewer muscles are active as a function of the view distance. Figure A9.1 (also Colour Plate) shows two frames from the animation.

10 Animating characters with motion capture

10.1   Introduction

Although the first uses of MoCap are to be found in the TV and film industry, the games industry was the first to embrace the technology as a routine method for animating human-like characters. Now the games industry accounts for 85–90 per cent of the total usage and almost all games that employ such characters use MoCap to drive the animation. The reason for this is simple: the quality of the animation is usually better than that produced by an animator and the production costs of the animation scripts tend to be lower.

The quality and convenience of MoCap is convincing. Consider Figure 10.1. Although the figure is a simple stick skeleton the resulting animation from MoCap data exhibits complex and expressive motion.

This 'ghost' sequence shows sets of superimposed frames at equal sampling intervals. Providing the motion is sampled sufficiently, the technology captures all the subtlety of the human performance. Examine the illustration; here is easily seen (right-hand leg) the deceleration in the motion. Using keyframe

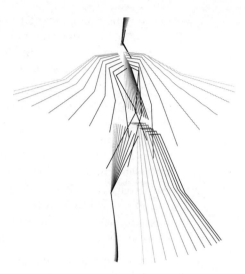

Figure 10.1
MoCap data applied to a stick figure skeleton.

animation from two keys positioned at the start and end of the ghost frames would not result in the correct motion. To imitate such a sequence using a keyframe system, the animator must position the keys appropriately so that the required accelerations and decelerations are present in the final sequence. It is precisely the difficulty and cost of accomplishing this that motivates the use of MoCap data.

MoCap technology is now well established and in this chapter we will concentrate, not on the data collection technology and low-level processing, but on techniques that address the disadvantages of MoCap. Low-level post-processing of raw MoCap data is, of course, extremely important and demands much effort. The operations are mainly 'clean-ups' and involve noise removal, filling in gaps caused by a marker going out of view for a period and eliminating confusion when two markers become coincident in a view. Another important low-level processing operation is converting the data – which specifies the position of markers as a function of time – into joint rotation form suitable for driving a skeleton hierarchy.

Current use of MoCap in the games industry consists of storing a vocabulary of sequences in the game and blending and adapting these in real time as the game progresses (Figure 7.1). Time-consuming and complex operations, such as re-targeting (using MoCap data on a figure of different scale to the figure from which the MoCap was recorded), are at the moment performed off-line. This situation is likely to change as the technology develops, with more complexity moving into the real-time domain. In a recent report Shin *et al.* [SHIN01] handle both the low-level pre-processing operations and the re-targeting operation in real time. Their application is computer puppetry, by definition a real-time application. Here the movements of a performer are mapped to an animated character and a prototype system has been used successfully to create a virtual character for a children's TV programme as well as a virtual news reporter. Computer puppetry may find applications in the future in multi-player applications; but for now the lesson that all conventional MoCap processing can be done in real time has significance for the games industry.

The two main drawbacks of MoCap technology are:

(1) We can only activate pre-recorded scripts in a game. An obvious statement, but one that needs emphasis. Although a large number of sequences are stored and selected in real time according to game logic, this is still an inherently limiting process. We would like to have facilities so that MoCap sequences continually adapt themselves to the developing game, altering themselves and producing new sequences from existing material.

(2) MoCap data is only 'valid' for a virtual character who possesses the same scale as the real human from whom the data was recorded. When we try to use the data on a character of different scale, we encounter problems. This is known as the re-targeting problem.

There are many other subtle problems in the technology. A quality consideration, which has meant less take-up from the film industry (c.f. the games industry), derives from the fact that sampling the motion of points on the surface of the skin of a character does not lead to a completely accurate script with which to animate a skeleton composed of rigid links. Currently the aesthetic demands in character animation are lower for games than for film and this has favoured the wholesale take-up of MoCap technology in games.

The motivation for dealing with MoCap in a text which purports to deal with real-time aspects of game technology is that many of the manipulation techniques developed for MoCap data can be applied at interactive rates; and many are by definition techniques that are applied as the game is executing. Ideally, we would like a human-like game character to have his motion characteristics altered according to events as the game develops. The simplest manipulation may be just to speed up or slow down the action. Alternatively, we may want the character to react by becoming angry or tired and that characteristic is reflected in the way he walks or runs. We would like to generate such motions in real time by altering in some way the existing MoCap data, perhaps, for example, by interpolation between or blending existing sequences.

Such an approach is exemplified by the work of Rose *et al.* [ROSE98], a flavour of which is given by Figure 10.8. The figure shows a sampling of the walk along the two emotional axes: happiness (vertical) and knowledge (horizontal). Each box specifies a motion sequence. The green boxes are example motions and the yellow ones are interpolations and extrapolations. Rose *et al.* point out that while only a finite number of (yellow) motion sequences are indicated, there is a continuous range of synthesised motions available from their method.

Another common requirement is to alter the motion so that a constraint is satisfied. Motion data may have been acquired for a character picking up an object. What if the object a character has to pick up in the game is larger or in a different relative position? Consider, for example, a football game. The goalkeeper character may be animated by a MoCap vocabulary of saves: 'dive

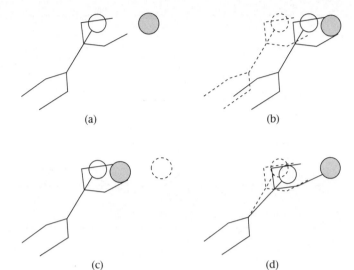

Figure 10.2
Goalkeeper possibilities.
(a) No modification.
(b) Figure translation.
(c) Ball translation.
(d) IK modification. In first-generation games (b) or (c) was usually implemented.

downwards to the ground', 'dive upwards to the corner'. So that the goalkeeper reaches the ball, the game may simply 'teleport' or translate the motion (Figure 10.2). A more correct approach would be to use inverse kinematics, altering the pose of the goalkeeper in the motion sequence so that he strives to reach the ball. And, of course, such situations depend on the demands of the game logic. It may be that we *require* the goalkeeper to catch the ball but there is no MoCap sequence – even with IK adaptation – that will position his hands at the ball position. We may then have to use a teleport. Alternatively, we have to cover all possible ball positions and trajectories with an (adaptable) MoCap sequence.

First-generation 3D computer games that use motion capture build a motion script vocabulary of around 200 sequences. A game event selects a particular sequence for a character, blends out the currently playing sequence and blends in the new sequence. Real-time motion processing tools would vastly expand this vocabulary; alternatively, it could cut down on the number of captures required for a game.

10.2   Motion data

We consider motion data to be a set of functions of single variables of time, $f_i(t)$, one for each DOF in the hierarchy. These are applied to the joints of a simple skeleton like the one we introduced in Chapter 7. Each joint exhibits one to three DOFs and we use a separate motion function for each of these. The number of DOFs for a computer graphics character is of the order of 40–50 compared with greater than 250 DOFs for the skeleton of a real human being. Originally these will be discrete functions but may be converted into, for example, (continuous) B-spline curves by interpolation:

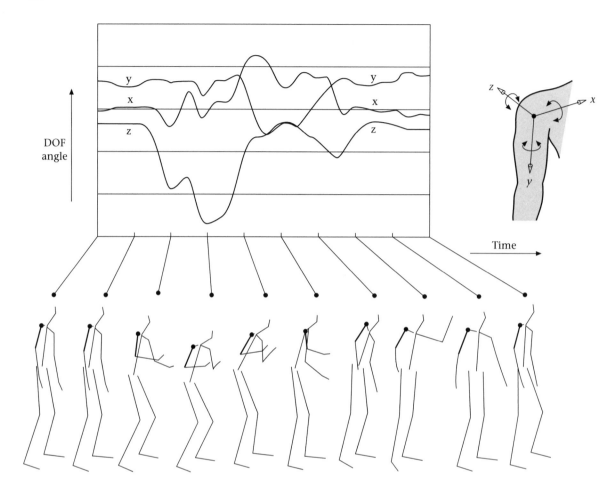

Figure 10.3
Three DOF curves for the upper arm in a ball catch (and throw) transient (courtesy of Michael Meredith).

$$f_i(t) = \sum_{j=0}^{no\_of\_CPs} \mathbf{p}_j B_j(t)$$

Each curve is then represented by its control points.

An example of three $f(t)$s controlling the joint angles of the upper arm of a character catching a ball are shown in Figure 10.3. In this figure the three curves that control the three DOFs of the right upper arm with respect to the shoulder joint are shown. Also shown is the coordinate system for the joint. The stick figures below the curves show in bold the movement of the scripted link. The motion is of a goalkeeper catching a ball, then throwing it. The figure is an example of aperiodic or transient motion – the motion begins and ends in a short period of time.

Motion curves specify rotation about the three local coordinate axes of a joint and are relative to a 'rest' pose. We can note the following characteristics of the curves shown in the figure. First, this is a transient action; the link moves as the catch action progresses, then returns to approximately the same orientation it had at the beginning of the sequence. This contrasts with cyclic actions like walking (see Figure 10.9) which continually repeat. Second, we see that the Y rotation transient is out of phase with (negative peak occurs before) the X and Z transients which are approximately in phase. Thirdly, there appears to be a relationship between the behaviour of the angle functions and the extent of the crouch posture. Superimposed on the main transients are other smaller transients. Such subtleties of natural body motion are clearly difficult to animate manually and one supposes that fine detail like phase differences in transients contributes greatly to the perceived reality of the motion. An animator can only build such subtlety by labourious trial and error coupled with experience.

10.3 Skeletons and MoCap – BVH format

When first collected raw, MoCap data is 'translational'; it contains, for each marker, the position of that point as a function of time. This has to be converted into a form that will drive the rotation of joints in a skeleton hierarchy, as we described in the previous section. This form depends on the organisation of the hierarchy. In this section we look at a common and typical data format/skeleton representation, the BVH format (Biovision Hierarchical Data). The motivation for using such a skeleton was given in Chapter 7, and whether we are using keyframe animation or MoCap data these advantages still pertain.

The following is the hierarchy specification or header for a BVH file. The indentation convention specifies the hierarchy. Each child node specifies a constant offset from its parent. When a character is activated, translation and rotation are applied to the root node (the hips) and rotation only to all other nodes. We would use exactly the same structure for keyframes. The only difference is that we would have much less data – just the rotations for each key pose – instead of rotations that have been sampled by MoCap equipment at (say) 30 times per second.

ROOT Hips

```
{
  OFFSET 0.00  0.00  0.00
  CHANNELS 6 Xposition Yposition Zposition Zrotation Xrotation Yrotation
  JOINT LeftHip
  {
    OFFSET 3.430000  0.000000  0.000000
    CHANNELS 3 Zrotation Xrotation Yrotation
    JOINT LeftKnee
    {
      OFFSET 0.000000  -18.469999  0.000000
      CHANNELS 3 Zrotation Xrotation Yrotation
      JOINT LeftAnkle
      {
```

```
          OFFSET 0.000000  -17.950001  0.000000
          CHANNELS 3 Zrotation Xrotation Yrotation
          End Site
          {
            OFFSET 0.000000  -3.119996  0.000000
          }
        }
      }
    }

JOINT RightHip
  {
    OFFSET -3.430000  0.000000  0.000000
    CHANNELS 3 Zrotation Xrotation Yrotation
    JOINT RightKnee
    {
      OFFSET 0.000000  -18.809999  0.000000
      CHANNELS 3 Zrotation Xrotation Yrotation
      JOINT RightAnkle
      {
        OFFSET 0.000000  -17.570000  0.000000
        CHANNELS 3 Zrotation Xrotation Yrotation
        End Site
        {
          OFFSET 0.000000  -3.250000  0.000000
        }
      }
    }
  }

JOINT Chest
  {
    OFFSET 0.000000  4.570000  0.000000
    CHANNELS 3 Zrotation Xrotation Yrotation
    JOINT LeftCollar
    {
      OFFSET 1.060000  15.330000  1.760000
      CHANNELS 3 Zrotation Xrotation Yrotation
      JOINT LeftShoulder
      {
        OFFSET 5.810000  0.000000  0.000000
        CHANNELS 3 Zrotation Xrotation Yrotation
        JOINT LeftElbow
        {
          OFFSET 0.000000  -12.080000  0.000000
          CHANNELS 3 Zrotation Xrotation Yrotation
          JOINT LeftWrist
          {
            OFFSET 0.000000  -9.820000  0.000000
            CHANNELS 3 Zrotation Xrotation Yrotation
            End Site
            {
              OFFSET 0.000000  -7.369996  0.000000
            }
```

```
            }
          }
        }
      }
    JOINT RightCollar
    {
      OFFSET -1.060000  15.330000  1.760000
      CHANNELS 3 Zrotation Xrotation Yrotation
      JOINT RightShoulder
      {
        OFFSET -6.060000  0.000000  0.000000
        CHANNELS 3 Zrotation Xrotation Yrotation
        JOINT RightElbow
        {
          OFFSET 0.000000  -11.900000  0.000000
          CHANNELS 3 Zrotation Xrotation Yrotation
          JOINT RightWrist
          {
            OFFSET 0.000000  -9.520000  0.000000
            CHANNELS 3 Zrotation Xrotation Yrotation
            End Site
            {
              OFFSET 0.000000  -7.140012  0.000000
            }
          }
        }
      }
    }
    JOINT Neck
    {
      OFFSET 0.000000  17.620001  0.000000
      CHANNELS 3 Zrotation Xrotation Yrotation
      JOINT Head
      {
        OFFSET 0.000000  5.190000  0.000000
        CHANNELS 3 Zrotation Xrotation Yrotation
        End Site
        {
          OFFSET 0.000000  4.140008  0.000000
        }
      }
    }
  }
}
```

10.4 Basic manipulation of motion data

We will now look at simple, basic ways in which we can alter MoCap data. By 'basic' we mean algorithms that operate on the data directly and do not require the intervention of mathematical models, such as interpolation or signal processing techniques. In games we are primarily interested in performing these operations in real time – we wish to alter the character's motion as a function of mood and also to navigate through an environment. As with any operation that changes MoCap data, there is always a limit to how far we can go before the integrity or naturalness of the original data becomes compromised. If an editing operation produces unnatural motion then this implies that we should be using a new sequence. The motivation for altering MoCap sequences is to enrich the database available to the game and thus enrich the visual experience of the player.

(10.4.1)

Speeding up and slowing down motion

If we require a character to run more quickly or slowly we can speed up or slow down the motion by operating on the MoCap data. Easy in principle, this simple operation needs to be handled with some care.

Consider speeding up the motion. Here we transform the data as:

$$f' = f(kt) \quad \text{where } k \text{ is a constant}$$

This means that we convert data that possesses n samples/unit time into m samples/unit time ($m < n$). We apply this transformation to all motion curves equally to produce a uniform speed-up of the entire motion. However, if we re-sample the data at lower and lower sampling frequencies we will encounter the aliasing problem. Frequency components that should be doubled or trebled in frequency may have their frequency reduced or the component may be zeroised. The effect is that the motion may actually slow down instead of speeding up. Thus to prevent this happening we must first determine what the limit of our speed-up is going to be and then apply an anti-aliasing filter prior to re-sampling. This removes the high frequency content in the data which cannot be correctly sampled by the new sampling frequency. We go into more detail on this in Section 10.6.

So if we decide that the minimum re-sampling rate that we are going to use is m, implying a speed-up by a factor of m/n, the motion data should be passed through a low-pass filter with a cut-off frequency of $2m$. Of course, if content exists above this frequency it is destroyed, and although the overall effect of this simple operation is to speed up the motion, it, by necessity, also destroys high frequency content. We can see this intuitively from the fact that lowering the sample rate must destroy information. We are representing the data with fewer samples. We return to this point in Section 10.6.

Slowing down motion conversely implies re-sampling the data at a higher sampling frequency. But the data has already been sampled when captured. To increase the original sampling frequency, we need to interpolate and convert the discrete representation into a curve (Section 10.5) so that an estimate of the value of $f(t)$ can be obtained between the samples.

Note that we also need interpolation, in general, to speed up the motion unless the speed-up factor n/m is an integer.

Blending and time warping

The most common blending operation with motion data occurs when we wish to provide a transition sequence between two different motions – a walk into a run, for example. We can do this most simply by 'fading out' the first sequence while 'fading in' the other. We introduced this simple idea in the context of keyframed animation in Chapter 7.

For all DOFs i

$$f_{Ti}(t) = \alpha(t_\alpha)f_{Mi}(t) + (1 - \alpha(t_\alpha))f_{Ni}(t)$$

where

T is the transition sequence, M and N are the two sequences being blended
$\alpha(t_\alpha)$ varies from 0 to 1 over the transition period

If the curves are represented by B-spline control points then we have:

for all DOFs i

$$d_{ij} = \alpha b_{ij} + (1 - \alpha)c_{ij} \quad 0 \leq \alpha \leq 1$$

where

b_{ij} and c_{ij} are the control points of the two sequences being blended

Blending is a technique that has no theoretical validity, which means that if we blend a run and a walk to produce a transition it is unlikely that the transition motion will match a real transition. However, it works reasonably well providing the motions are 'aligned' and similar. Similar means that for best results they are different manifestations of the same action – walking, say. Aligned means that key poses – a foot on the ground, say – must be made to occur in both sequences at the same time. This involves time warping, which is non-uniform re-sampling. We stretch and compress the samples of one of the motions so that the key poses in this motion sequence match the time that they occur in the other. Then we blend. In effect this is a generalisation of speeding up and slowing down the motion. Now we are varying the time from instant to instant according to the required alignment. Figure 10.4 shows an example. In this case we require poses k_1, k_2, and k_3 to occur at times t_1, t_2 and t_3 to match, say, keys in another sequence.

(Recall also that in Chapter 7 we introduced a scheme where we explicitly posed the character so that the pose at the end of one sequence matched the

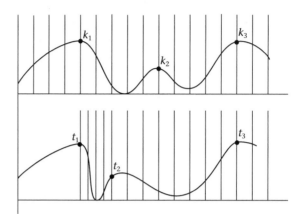

Figure 10.4
Time warping compresses and expands the samples. In the examples we required poses k_1, k_2 and k_3 to occur at time t_1, t_2 and t_3.

pose at the beginning of the next. However, in that case we only attended to the orientation of the character and not the entire pose of the limbs.)

Now we mentioned in the previous section that there are problems whenever we re-sample information at a lower rate than the original sampling frequency. This consideration also applies here.

Time warping between two sequences can be used to produce different motions without blending. Consider two walking motions – a brisk walk and a slow drunken walk. Time warping the drunken walk to align with the brisk walk gives us a drunken walk at the brisk pace. Warping the other way gives us a brisk walk at the drunken pace.

Blending or interpolating between two sequences to produce a new sequence, sometimes called multi-target interpolation, is also employed. Here we may interpolate between a brisk and tired walk sequence to produce a sequence that has characteristics of both.

10.4.3 Aligning motion sequences

We now consider time warping in more detail. Although above we considered the sampling interval varying – compressing and expanding, we said nothing about how we control this process – how we know where to compress and expand time. To time-warp we have to find the alignment. An automatic time-warping algorithm has to find the best combination of compression and expansion of time so that one sequence aligns with another. As we shall see, this is an expensive process and therefore an off-line approach. Before we begin we should point out that it may be impossible to find a suitable time warp. With many complex motions, dance movements and gymnastics, for example, it may impossible or inappropriate to find alignments and attempting to blend inappropriate sequences will in general result in unfeasible motion.

Bruderlin and Williams [BRUD95] adopt a geometric approach, noting that the problem is related to the triangulation of contour data.[1] For a given pair of sequences each of n samples, the algorithm tries various correspondences of the n points on vertices of sequence A connecting to the n vertices of sequence B and selects the best. The cost of each correspondence is measured by calculating the 'amount of work' it takes to deform one signal into the other by stretching and compressing in the sense of the previous figure. (Note that in Figure 10.4 we visualised the problem by showing compressed time intervals but in any practical method the time intervals remain constant and we have the situation where either there is a correspondence between two signals or many samples in one map into a single sample in the other.) The cost function is the sum of local stretching and bending. Bending is a function of the difference in the angle between corresponding vertex triples in each signal (Figure 10.5(a)). Stretching is defined as a function of the distance between corresponding vertex duples. The cost is minimised over the entire sequence and a vertex correspondence is then available. In the example shown in the figure, either there is one-to-one correspondence, two samples in A correspond to one in B, or two samples in B correspond to one in A. This is then used in the second phase of the algorithm which warps either A into B or vice versa. If B is being warped into A (denoted by B_w) and there are multiple samples of B corresponding to a single sample A_i, then the warped B is given by the mean of these samples. If, on the other hand, one sample of B corresponds to multiple samples of A, then we need to find new point by interpolation given by spline interpolation through the B sample. Bruderlin and Williams categorise these cases as follows (from B's point of view):

substitution 1:1 correspondence of consecutive samples
deletion multiple samples of B map to multiple samples of A
insertion a single sample of B maps to multiple samples of A

To calculate a warped version of B (B mapping to A) we have

substitution if the correspondence is $A_i = B_i$ then $B_i^{warp} = B_j$
deletion means that A_i corresponds to $(B_j, B_{j+1}, \ldots, B_{j+k})$ in which case $B_i^{warp} = \text{average\_of}(B_j, B_{j+1}, \ldots, B_{j+k})$
insertion means that $(A_i, A_{i+1}, \ldots, A_{i+k})$ correspond to B_j in which case we need to find $B_i^{warp}, B_{i+1}^{warp}, \ldots, B_{i+k}^{warp}$. This is done by extrapolating a B-spline through the original value B_j

---

1. This is the problem of converting data from a device like a laser ranger or a medical imaging device into a triangulated computer graphics object. The raw data consists of a set of closed contours in parallel planes representing cross-sections through the (real) object. The problem is to join the samples on the contours with straight lines to triangulate the space between them, and thereby triangulate the complete space. Closed contours are converted into a triangulated object. This must be done in a way that produces a computer graphics surface that is as close as possible to the surface that the contours represent.

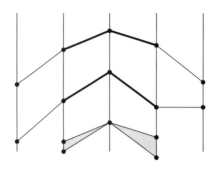
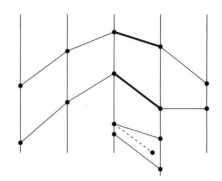

Bend – proportional to difference in
angles subtended by 3 adjacent vertices

Stretch – proportional to the
difference in length

(a)

Figure 10.5
Time warp algorithm
based on stretching and
bending cost. (a) Cost
function terms. (b)
Correspondence after
applying the cost
function (based
on an illustration in
[BRUD95]).

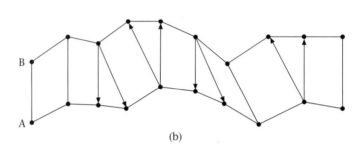

(b)

(10.4.4)

Motion warping

Motion warping or motion displacement mapping means making local adjust-
ments to the amplitude of the motion data signals. The aim is to make adjust-
ments while at the same time preserving the global characteristics of the data.
Say, for example, we have a walking motion and want the character to bend
to walk through a low doorway. We may have a key pose for the instant the
character crosses the threshold and use this to alter (displace) the walk motion
data. We can define this operation simply as:

$$f'(t) = f(t) + d(t)$$

where
   $d(t)$ is the required displacement

In this expression the required amplitude displacement is explicitly defined as
a separate function – the so-called displacement map. This is a convenience that
enables us to add the required displacement $d(t)$ into the original motion $f(t)$
over a number of frames. Simply inserting a new pose that lives for a single

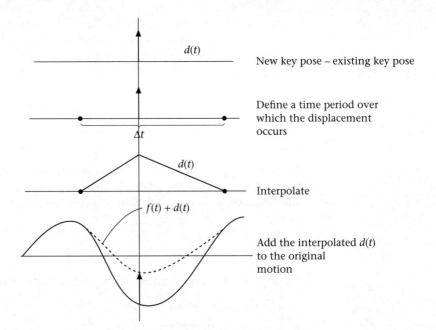

$d(t)$ — New key pose – existing key pose

Define a time period over which the displacement occurs

Δt

$d(t)$ — Interpolate

$f(t) + d(t)$

Add the interpolated $d(t)$ to the original motion

Figure 10.6
Displacement mapping.

frame will cause a discontinuity in the motion. $d(t)$ can be found by subtract-ing the new required pose from the original pose. In the simplest case, for a single new key pose $d(t)$ will be a single value (Figure 10.6). This can be added to $f(t)$ over some time period, Δt, by interpolation, linear, say, which 'expands' $d(t)$ so that it is now non-zero over the time range Δt. Thus separating the dis-placement map enables us to define the rate at which it is merged with $f(t)$. (Note that this method is just a generalisation of the single frame 'reaction ges-ture' elaboration used in Section 10.2.)

The implication of this approach for real-time low-level motion control is that when planning the motion of a character animated by MoCap, we have to look ahead, predict an interaction with an object or obstacle, pick up the appropriate displacement maps from the object and compose the new motion curves for the frames where the character is approaching, but has not reached the object. Associating a displacement map with an object gives us a natural structure to calculate how, for example, a standard walk motion is to be altered as the character encounters various obstacles.

10.5 Interpolation in MoCap

Interpolation is used in many different contexts in MoCap. It can be used as a data reduction technique – converting a motion sequence into a set of B-spline control points by fitting a curve through the data. In this case we interpolate within a single motion sequence. Alternatively, as we shall see, it can be used to expand the vocabulary of motion sequences by interpolating between them. We introduced this idea in Section 10.4.1, but there employed a simple linear mixing or blending using a single parameter. In this section we will generalise this idea.

(10.5.1) B-spline representation

Typical of approaches that use B-spline representation for motion sequences is that of Sudarsky and House [SUDA98]. They use non-uniform B-splines and the interpolation yields the standard B-spline representation:

$$f_i(t) = \sum_{j=0}^{\text{no\_of\_CPs}} \mathbf{p}_j B_j(t)$$

An appropriate knot vector is chosen according to the heuristics:

- add knots in regions of high curvature;
- avoid knots in regions of noise;
- use multiple knots to represent discontinuities in the data.

A least squares method is used to find the set of control points $\mathbf{p}$ by minimising

$$\sum_{j=0}^{n} (M(t_j) - f(t_j))^2$$

where
$n + 1$ is the number of samples in the sequence

This can be enhanced by a noise reduction strategy:

$$\sum_{j=0}^{n} \frac{1}{w_j + 1}(M(t_j) - f(t_j))^2$$

where
w_j is a weight that represents the deviation between $f(t_j)$ and the average local value

The least squares solution is found by solving the linear system

$$\mathbf{Ap} = \mathbf{f}$$

An alternative approach [LEE99] to achieving good quality interpolation is to use uniform B-splines in a multi-resolution framework (see also Section 10.7.2 for a treatment of multi-resolution representations in the context of signal processing). However, the main motivation in this work was to use the multi-resolution representation to find an efficient solution to the motion re-targeting or motion fitting problem. (We deal with this aspect in Section 10.8; in this section we will concentrate solely on the representation.)

A multi-resolution representation is a coarse to fine (or fine to coarse) hierarchy that can be accessed at any level to give an approximation to the original data or curve to within some degree of accuracy. In other words, we consider a motion curve to be a series of incrementally refined motions starting with a coarse approximation f_0 and ending with the exact sequence f_h. f_0 is the coarsest level and f_1 the next finest:

$$x(t) = f_0(t) + f_1(t) +, \ldots, + f_h(t)$$

where

$$f_1(t) = f_0(t) + d_1(t)$$
$$f_2(t) = f_1(t) + d_2(t)$$

Alternatively, we can write:

$$x(t) = (\ldots ((f_0(t) + d_1(t)) + d_2(t)) +, \ldots, + d_h(t))$$

and evaluate or select any desired level k by:

$$f_k(t) = (\ldots ((f_0(t) + d_1(t)) + d_2(t)) +, \ldots, + d_k(t))$$

Thus a motion sequence is represented by $h + 1$ levels, in this case cubic B_spline functions defined over uniform knot sequences. The knot sequences themselves define a hierarchy, doubling their density from level to level. If the knot vector τ_k has $n + 3$ control points on it, then τ_{k+1} has $2n + 3$. This effectively controls the fineness of the approximation f_k at any level k. The interpolation begins by finding f_0 using least squares as before. This will be a coarse (or smooth) approximation. In general, at each data point there will be a deviation:

$$D_j(t) = x(t) - f_j(t)$$

These deviations then become the function to be interpolated by f_k and so on.

As far as the quality of the interpolation is concerned, it eliminates the main disadvantage of single-level B-spline interpolation. This is that the choice of the knot vector is critical. If the knot spacing is too coarse then there will be a deviation between the B-spline curve and the data; too large and it oscillates between data points.

10.5.2   Motion blending – verbs and adverbs

Much motion blending is as we have described; it involves blending between two sequences. In a general extension of this method Rose *et al.* [ROSE98] describe a method where they take a number of examples of a 'verb' and interpolate to obtain a continuous space of motions derived from the example verb. Consider

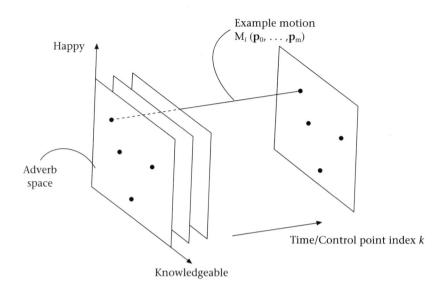

Figure 10.7
Data organisation for one
DOF of one verb.

Figure 10.7 (in conjunction with Figure 10.8 (also Colour Plate)). This shows the overall data organisation for a single DOF for a verb such as a walk action.

A single example of a motion $(\mathbf{p}_0, \ldots, \mathbf{p}_m)$ is then a sequence of B-spline control points:

$$M(t) = \sum_{j=0}^{\text{no\_of\_CPs}} \mathbf{p}_j B_j(t)$$

The control point in each plane specifies the value of the DOF for that key time. The plane is 'adverb' space – in the example the two axes are signified as happy and knowledgeable. In other words, the verb is parameterised by adverbs – in this case two.

The off-line or set-up phase of the system involves manual examination of a number of motion sequences which are then placed according to their perceived characteristics in the appropriate position in the adverb plane. A requirement of the method is that all the examples for a verb must be structurally similar (for example, all examples of a walk must start off on the same foot and have the same number of steps). Another requirement is that the examples must be time warped so that key times for similar poses occur at the same generic time. This then enables the example control points $\mathbf{p}_j$ to be placed in the same adverb plane. Thus a plane contains all the examples from structurally similar parts of the motion M.

Once the examples have been categorised according to their motion quality (their 2D position in adverb space), a scattered data interpolation method (see Appendix 8.1) is used to find a continuous function that interpolates the examples $\mathbf{p}_j$ for each plane. Such interpolation methods are chosen because they

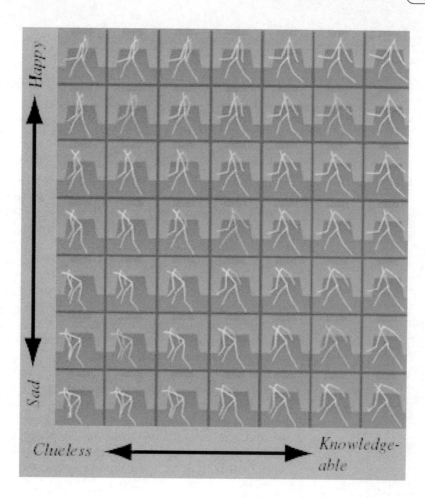

Figure 10.8
Deriving a continuous space of motion from verb examples (green = examples) (courtesy of C. Rose).

perform well on sparse data over many dimensions. Thus adverb space now defines a continuous set of control points.

The intent of the system is to perform the interpolation in real time from the adverb categorised examples; game events invoking a particular adverb. The goal is to enable adverbs to vary continuously according to the demand from the game logic.

Kinematic constraints are enforced at key times using IK (see Chapter 11 and Section 10.8.2). A pose is determined at a key time from the captive verb interpolation which it is assumed places the end effector close to the key time constraint point. This is then modified by a fast IK solver.

In a later report [SLOA01] this approach is extended to shape interpolation as described in Chapter 8. Here an adverb becomes an adjective and such words as male/female, old/young are used to characterise the variation in shape motion.

10.6   Classic signal processing and MoCap

A knowledge of Fourier theory and the signal processing operations which derive from it is extremely useful for a good overall understanding of MoCap processing. There are two fundamental reasons for this. The first is that it enables us to deal correctly with sampled data. The basis of this is Claude Shannon's 1947 sampling theorem. This elegant and prophetic theorem is fundamental to all signal processing, whatever the application. In an era when almost all analogue information signals – speech, music, vision, industrial control signals etc. – are sampled and processed digitally, Shannon's theorem tells us precisely what the minimum sampling rate should be for a signal so that no information loss is incurred. It is the case that raw data – the original motion – will have been sampled 'correctly' when it is collected, but, as we have seen, many simple MoCap processing operations involve re-sampling the data. Attending to correct sampling constraints enables us to carry out time-warping operations, for example, without engendering problems.

The second motivation of Fourier theory gives us a way of decomposing MoCap functions into (frequency) components. Operating separately on these components enables us to retain the overall basic character of, say, a walk, and add 'snap' or 'briskness' by scaling a high frequency component. (This is exactly what we do with audio systems when we use an equalising filter control or just the tone controls – we alter the character of the music by exaggerating or diminishing the influence of certain frequency bands.)

While the first motivation is undoubtedly important, the utility or even the correctness of applying signal processing techniques to MoCap data is more debatable and is an issue that we return to in Section 10.7. However, there has been a large amount of work done using signal processing operations and one must conclude that it works in the reported contexts.

10.6.1   Fourier theory

The motivation of all linear transforms in science and engineering is to facilitate the solution of a problem that may be difficult to solve on the untransformed data. With the Fourier transform many powerful operations are possible and we say that the data has been transformed into the Fourier domain. The number of fields in which the Fourier transform is a vital tool is surprisingly large and it has been used to manipulate MoCap data ever since the emergence of the technology.

Fourier theory is conventionally introduced by considering continuous functions which are also periodic. A periodic function is simply one that repeats an exact copy of itself sequentially in time. Such functions are decomposed into harmonics by the Fourier series. Much MoCap data – running and walking cycles, for example – is approximately periodic. Figure 10.9 shows the three DOFs for the femur in a run cycle.

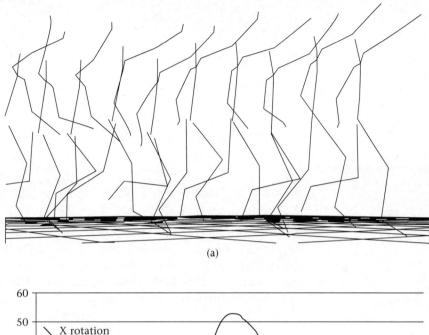

(a)

(b)

Figure 10.9
(a) 50 frames of a character running and waving – stepped every 5 frames. (b) Motion curves of the 3 DOFs of the running character's left femur (courtesy of Michael Meredith).

The near periodicity is apparent. Also apparent are small variations that take the data out of perfect periodicity. These are extremely important because they individualise human motion. Perfectly periodic MoCap data would give an avatar a robot-like feel. This concept of near periodicity is related to Perlin's work ([PERL95] and Section 9.2.1) where he models expressive motion as a base motion plus noise. The perturbation due to a noise function results in more human-like limb movement.

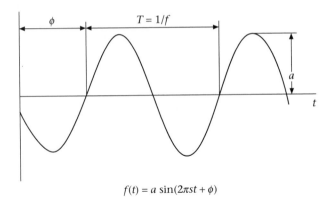

Figure 10.10
A sine wave is specified by the three parameters, amplitude a, frequency f and phase ϕ.

$$f(t) = a \sin(2\pi st + \phi)$$

Near periodic data is, of course, the practical norm in cyclic MoCap sequences, but we will begin by looking at the simpler case of perfectly periodic data. The reason for this is that we can more easily visualise the nature of the transform – what it does to the original data. Periodic data is transformed by the Fourier series which is defined as:

$$f(t) = a_0 + \sum_{i=1}^{n} a_i \sin(i*2\pi st + \phi_i) \tag{10.1}$$

In words, this says that any periodic signal can be decomposed into a set of sinusoids i having some amplitude a_i and a phase relationship ϕ_i.

A sine wave (Figure 10.10):

$$f(t) = a \sin(2\pi st + \phi)$$

is specified by three parameters: amplitude a, frequency s, and phase φ.

In Equation 10.1 the sinusoid $i = 1$ has the same frequency or period as the function $f(t)$ and is known as the fundamental. The second harmonic – given by the sinusoid $i = 2$ – is twice the frequency of the fundamental. ϕ_i specifies the phase of a harmonic – its horizontal shift in time. Alternatively, we can say that we can synthesise any periodic waveform by summing a set of sinusoids – its Fourier components. These all have different amplitudes and phases.

An intuitive idea of the significance of this series or decomposition can be gained by looking at a standard example. Consider Figure 10.11 which shows a perfect periodic signal – a square wave – and the sum of the Fourier series of the wave for values of $i = 1, 3$ and 5 (in this example there are only odd harmonics). We can make the following observations from the figure:

- The frequency of the fundamental and $f(t)$ are the same.

- As we increase i and include more and more terms in the summation, the series begins to approximate $f(t)$ to a better and better extent. The sides of the wave become more and more vertical and the oscillations at the top of each excursion decrease in value.

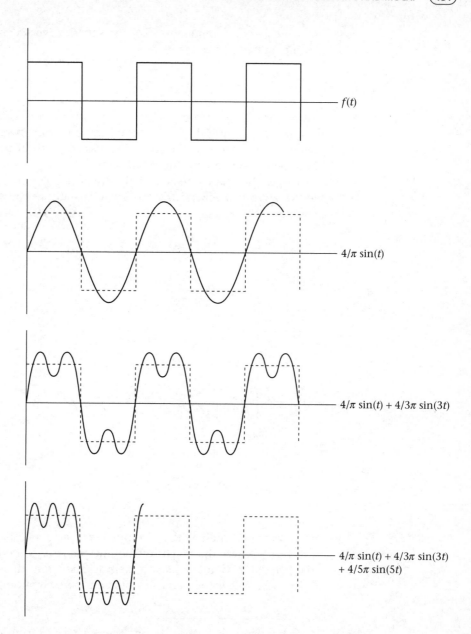

$f(t)$

$4/\pi \sin(t)$

$4/\pi \sin(t) + 4/3\pi \sin(3t)$

$4/\pi \sin(t) + 4/3\pi \sin(3t)$
$+ 4/5\pi \sin(5t)$

Figure 10.11
The first three terms in
the Fourier series for a
periodic square wave.

- a_0 – known as the DC or average component – is zero because the average of $f(t)$ in this case is zero.

Not apparent in the figure is the fact that in this case the series contains an infinite number of terms or components. This is a consequence of the sides of the square wave being vertical. In practice, there is no physical system that can change its state in zero time and therefore no data which can have infinitely high frequency components.[2] For the square wave the amplitudes of the harmonics are given by:

$$a_i = 4/\pi i \qquad i \text{ is odd}$$
$$\quad = 0 \qquad\quad i \text{ is even}$$

That is, the amplitude of the odd harmonics decreases rapidly with increasing frequency. In physical systems this means that most energy in the signal is contained in the low frequency components. The high frequency components are low energy and contain the detail – the fast changes – in the signal.

To get the relative values of the frequency components a_i we proceed as follows. We first rewrite the series equivalently as the sum of sinusoids and cosinusoids:

$$a_0 + \sum_{i=1}^{n} a_i \sin(i*2\pi st + \phi_i) = a_0 + \sum_{i=1}^{n} a_i \sin i*2\pi st + b_i \cos i*2\pi st$$

then:

$$a_0 = \frac{1}{T} \int_{-\frac{1}{2}T}^{\frac{1}{2}T} f(t)dt$$

$$a_n = \frac{2}{T} \int_{-\frac{1}{2}T}^{\frac{1}{2}T} f(t)\sin 2\pi st dt$$

$$b_n = \frac{2}{T} \int_{-\frac{1}{2}T}^{\frac{1}{2}T} f(t)\cos 2\pi st dt$$

Now we can represent the resulting series as a so-called line spectrum (Figure 10.12) where the height of the lines represents the relative amplitudes of the frequency components and their distance from the origin represents their frequency. This is the frequency domain representation.

---

2. In fact the problem of aliasing in computer graphics rendering derives from the fact that there is no limit to the frequency components in that data which we sample by calculating a value at each pixel. In this case the data is a mathematical model or is mathematically defined. This is why in texture mapping if we super-sample and average we do not get rid of aliasing artefacts but simply move their effect into higher and higher frequencies. MoCap data is, however, real data derived from a physical system and it does not contain infinitely high frequency components. Thus we say that real data is always band limited; in a real system there is always an upper and lower frequency limit.

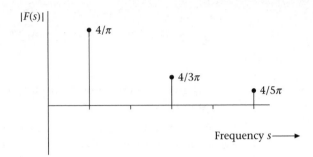

Figure 10.12
Line spectrum for the
periodic square wave.

Let us now return to MoCap which, as we discussed, was approximately periodic in many cases, and look at the significance of this. In MoCap we have high and low frequency components. A cyclic action like a walk will contain a range of frequency components that, to some extent, will reflect the nature of, or the character of, the walk. A brisk military march will contain higher frequency components than a slow drunken stagger. (It is also the case that a military march will tend to be more periodic than a drunken stagger.)

Often high frequency components are transient. Consider a walk where the walker suddenly punches the air. Transient frequency components, higher than those in the steady walk, will suddenly be introduced and will disappear. The punch motion only lasts for the duration of the punch, but within that time window we can identify high and low frequency components in the data.

Return to Figure 10.12, which shows a simple frequency spectrum. If we transform data into a frequency spectrum data, then operate separately on its frequency components, then transform the data back into the time domain, we have the classic filtering operation in the Fourier domain. This enables us to operate separately on the frequency components, thus changing the 'character' of the signal in ways that we will come to. We have:

$f(t) \rightarrow F(s)$ the series of sinusoids
$F(f) \rightarrow F'(s)$ by operating on the sinusoids (scaling them)
$f'(t) \leftarrow F'(s)$ the filtered sinusoids are summated to give the processed $f'(t)$

It is this model that we will now study.

(10.6.2)

Fourier theory and aperiodic data

Now, as we have discussed, real data differs from the square wave example in two important respects. We now have to consider data that is discrete (sampled) and either nearly periodic or aperiodic. We will deal with these two issues separately and consider first aperiodic data. All information-carrying signals are aperiodic and MoCap is no exception. Such functions are transformed by the Fourier integral transform pair:

$$F(s) = \int_{\infty}^{\infty} f(t)\, e^{-i2\pi st}\, dt \qquad f(t) = \int_{\infty}^{\infty} F(s)\, e^{i2\pi st}\, ds$$

where

i is the complex number operator (not the sinusoid index as in the Fourier series definition)

This means that the Fourier transform is a function of a complex number. Since most simple processing operations operate on the magnitude of $F(s)$ we will henceforth ignore this aspect. Interested readers can consult [BRACE 65].

The first transform – the forward transform – takes us into the Fourier domain and the second takes us back from the Fourier domain to the time domain. Figure 10.14b shows the Fourier transform of a window of a continuous function $f(t)$ compared to that of a periodic function. We can note the following:

- The frequency spectrum is now continuous.
- The frequency spectrum exhibits a maximum and minimum cut-off frequency. We say the signal is band limited. All practical systems are band limited and the cut-off frequencies are a function of the system itself.
- The frequency spectrum has a negative mirror image. This is a consequence of the mathematical definition which we shall henceforth ignore.

The most common operation carried out in the Fourier domain is (multiplicative) filtering. This means scaling each frequency component. We define a filter function $H(s)$ and we have:

$$f(t) \rightarrow F(s)$$
$$F'(s) = F(s)H(s)$$
$$f'(t) \leftarrow F'(s)$$

The most common filters are low pass, high pass and band pass. These are ideal filters which pass some frequencies and eliminate others – we select certain frequency components in the data and eliminate unwanted ones. Doing this will change, in some way, the character of the motion driven by filtered data compared to that of the original data.

This process is easy to understand using an image example. We can make more sense of the image operations because images contain contain, unlike MoCap data, immediately recognisable structures. Shown in Figure 10.13 (also Colour Plate) are two fundamental filtering operations – low pass and high pass.

The low pass filter has the effect of blurring the image because it eliminates sharp changes, in other words edges where the image intensity changes quickly. Conversely a high pass filter eliminates low frequencies – the slow changes of intensity within the image. This emphasises edges and makes uniform those areas where the image changes slowly.

We will eventually look at how these operations affect MoCap data; now we must study another complication – that fact that MoCap data is discrete.

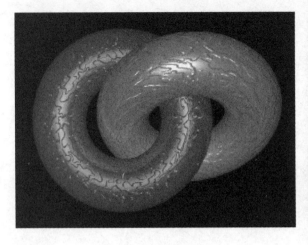
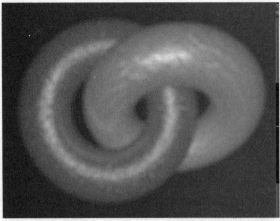
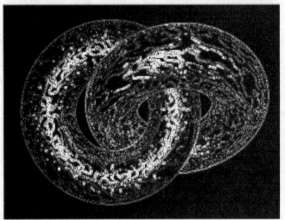

Figure 10.13
Two classic image processing filtering operations: low pass filtering which blurs because it removes high frequency components; and high pass filtering which emphasises detail by removing slow changing variations (low frequency components).

(10.6.3) **Fourier theory and sampled data**

Any computer algorithm that calculates a Fourier transform is by definition going to deal with discrete or sampled data and for such data the discrete Fourier transform (DFT) pair is given by:

$$F(s) = \frac{1}{N} \sum_{t=0}^{N-1} f(t) \exp\left(-i2\pi \frac{st}{N}\right)$$

$$f(t) = \sum_{f=0}^{N-1} F(s) \exp\left(i2\pi \frac{st}{N}\right)$$

where
N is the number of samples

(Note that these expressions are rarely used in this form in a program; instead the ubiquitous Fast Fourier Transform (FFT) is employed to calculate a DFT.)

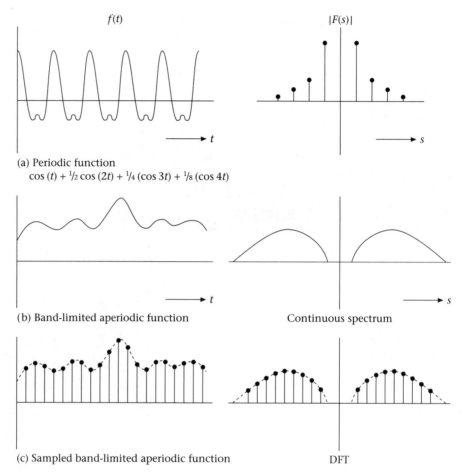

(a) Periodic function
cos (t) + ½ cos (2t) + ¼ (cos 3t) + ⅛ (cos 4t)

(b) Band-limited aperiodic function   Continuous spectrum

Figure 10.14
The difference between a line spectrum of a periodic function, a continuous spectrum of an aperiodic function and a DFT.

(c) Sampled band-limited aperiodic function   DFT

We can begin by viewing this transform as the discrete version of the Fourier integral transform, then move on to discuss the difficulties that arise with it. In Figure 10.14 we demonstrate the difference between a line spectrum of a periodic function, a continuous spectrum of an aperiodic function and a DFT. Figure 10.14(c) is identical to Figure 10.14(b) except that both $f(t)$ and $F(s)$ are made up of lines. In the case of $f(t)$ these represent the samples in the data. The DFT is a frequency spectrum that has N unique frequency components which ideally should be equivalent to a sampled version of the continuous spectrum of $f(t)$. $F(0)$ is the DC or average term as before.

There are two important practical issues associated with a DFT. First, the input data, by definition, has a finite length. In an application this may be a complete MoCap sequence or it could be a sample window from a much longer sequence. In either case we have to condition the data at either end of the sequence. If we simply start and stop the data abruptly we will introduce high

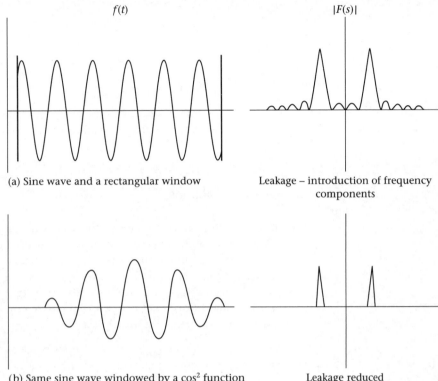

(a) Sine wave and a rectangular window

Leakage – introduction of frequency components

(b) Same sine wave windowed by a $\cos^2$ function

Leakage reduced

Figure 10.15
The DFT and leakage.

frequency components artificially. This phenomenon is known as leakage and is easily demonstrated by using a sine wave as a signal again. Figure 10.15 shows the effect of using a rectangular window – cutting of to the signal instantaneously. When the window interval is a multiple of the sine wave period the signal is zero at the window limits and there is no problem. If the window width is not equal to a multiple of the period then leakage occurs as shown.

In MoCap data this is relevant in two contexts. First, if we want to change the character of a (finite length) MoCap sequence then we need make sure that leakage does not occur. Another context is when the operation of cyclification or concatenation is required. This apparently simple process consists of taking a window of a periodic motion like walking and running and using it for a game action that is to last for a multiple of the window length. Here we simply need to concatenate the sequences together as often as required. However, if the end and beginning of the sequences do not match up we will introduce frequency components at the join, which do not exist in the original data.

To ameliorate the effects of leakage we use a non-rectangular window or a data weighting function. A popular choice is the Hanning or cosine weighting function given by:

$$f'(t) = f(t)\,w(t)$$
$$w(t) = \cos^2(\pi t/T_0) \qquad |t| \leq T_0/2$$
$$w(t) = 0 \qquad\qquad\ |t| > T_0/2$$

where
$$T_0 = NT \quad \text{(number of samples*time window)}$$

Another critically important consideration when working with MoCap data, and one that we shall now discuss in detail because it relates to time warping, is sampling.

10.6.4   Sampling and aliasing

The problem with sampling data is that if it is not done at a sufficiently high sampling frequency then aliasing occurs. Aliasing problems arise in MoCap data if we attempt to re-sample the original data, as we do, for example, in Section 10.4.1. There is also the problem in computer games that we often require a sample at unevenly spaced frame intervals. Aliasing is effectively loss of information. The quantification of this problem is given by Shannon's sampling theorem which we can state informally as:

> The sampling frequency must be at least twice as high as the highest frequency component contained in the signal.

Aliasing is easily demonstrated, as we show in Figure 10.16. Here we consider a signal to be a sine wave (of course, as a sine wave contains no information we are simply using its regularity to demonstrate a point). In Figure 10.16(a) the signal is adequately sampled – the sampling frequency is greater than twice the frequency of the sine wave. (Equivalently, the sampling interval is less than one half the period of the sine wave.) In Figure 10.16(b) the sampling frequency is exactly half of the sine wave frequency. The signal disappears. The other two examples show that when the sampling frequency falls below half that of the sine wave the amplitude of the resulting samples look as if they are sampling a lower frequency sine wave – an alias.

Under-sampling the sine wave and reconstructing a continuous signal from the samples (dotted line in the figure) produces an 'alias' of the original signal – another sine wave at a lower frequency than the one being sampled. We can say that this happens because the coherence or regularity of the sampling pattern is interfering with the regularity of the information. To avoid aliasing artefacts we have to sample at an appropriately high frequency with respect to the signal.

Now the example in Figure 10.16 can be generalised by considering these cases in the frequency domain for an $f(t)$ that contains information, that is not a pure sine wave. We now have an $f(t)$ that is any general variation in t and may, for example, represent a MoCap signal. The frequency spectrum of $f(t)$ will

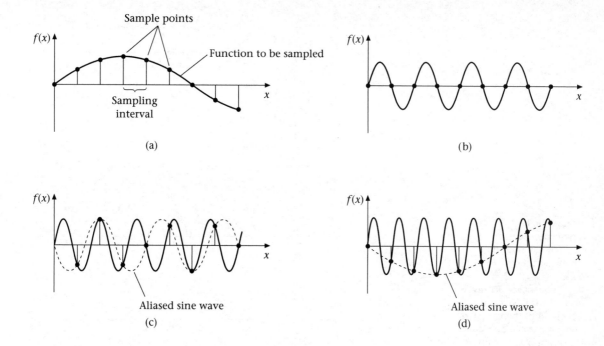

(a)

(b)

(c)

(d)

Figure 10.16
Space domain representation of the sampling of a sine wave. (a) Sampling interval is less than one-half the period of the sine wave. (b) Sampling interval is equal to one-half the period of the sine wave. (c) Sampling interval is greater than one-half the period of the sine wave. (d) Sampling interval is much greater than one-half the period of the sine wave.

exhibit some 'envelope' (Figure 10.17(a)) whose limit is the highest frequency component in $f(t)$, say, s_{max}. The frequency spectrum of a sampling function (Figure 10.17(b)) is a series of lines, theoretically extending to infinity, separated by the interval $s_{sampling}$ (the sampling frequency). Sampling in the space domain involves multiplying $f(t)$ by the sampling function. The equivalent process in the frequency domain is convolution (we will deal with convolution shortly; for now, you can accept the diagrammatic concept) and the frequency spectrum of the sampling function is convolved with $f(t)$ to produce the frequency spectrum shown in Figure 10.17(c) – the spectrum of the sampled version of $f(t)$. This sampled function is then multiplied by a reconstructing filter to reproduce the original function. A good example of this process, in the time domain, is a modern telephone network. In its simplest form this involves sampling a speech waveform, encoding and transmitting digital versions of each sample over a communications channel, then reconstructing the original signal from the decoded samples by using a reconstructing filter.

Note that the reconstruction process, which is multiplication in the frequency domain, is convolution in the space domain. In summary, the process in the space domain is multiplication of the original function with the sampled function, followed by convolution of the sampled version of the function with a reconstructing filter.

Now in the above example the condition:

$$s_{sampling} > 2s_{max}$$

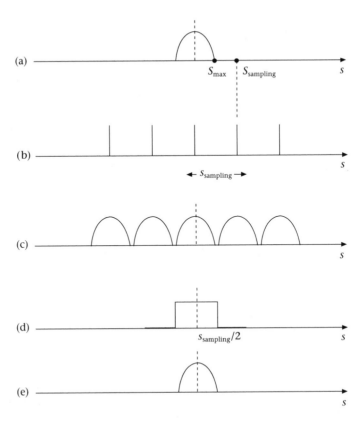

Figure 10.17
Frequency domain
representation of the
sampling process
when $s_{\text{sampling}} > 2s_{\text{max}}$.
(a) Frequency spectrum
of $f(x)$. (b) Frequency
spectrum of the sampling
function. (c) Frequency
spectrum of the sampled
function (convolution of
(a) and (b)). (d) Ideal
reconstruction filter.
(e) Reconstructed $f(x)$.

is true. In the second example (Figure 10.18) we show the same two processes of multiplication and convolution but this time we have:

$$s_{\text{sampling}} < 2s_{\text{max}}.$$

Incidentally, $s_{\text{sampling}}/2$ is known as the Nyquist limit. Here the envelopes, representing the information in $f(t)$, overlap. It is as if the spectrum has 'folded' over a line defined by the Nyquist limit (Figure 10.18(e)). This folding is an information-destroying process; high frequencies (detail in images) are lost and appear as interference (aliases) in low frequency regions.

10.6.5 Anti-aliasing filters

If we intend to sample a signal then we must obey the sampling theorem. In many practical applications we have a fixed sampling frequency and we ensure that aliasing does not occur simply by ensuring that the signal does not contain any frequency components higher than $2s_{\text{sampling}}$. This is achieved by passing the signal through a so-called anti-aliasing filter which is a low pass filter with a cut-off frequency equal to $2s_{\text{sampling}}$.

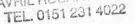
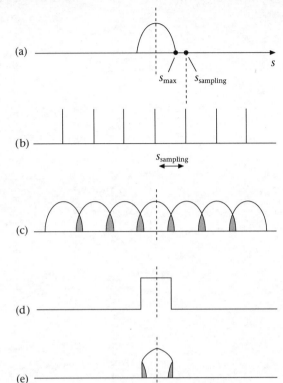

Figure 10.18
Frequency domain
representation of the
sampling process
when $s_{sampling} < 2s_{max}$.
(a) Frequency spectrum
of $f(x)$. (b) Frequency
spectrum of the sampling
function. (c) Frequency
spectrum of the sampled
function. (d) Ideal
reconstruction filter.
(e) Distorted $f(x)$.

This consideration must also be taken into account in speeding up or slowing down motion, as we discussed in Section 10.4.1. If we speed up the motion by skipping samples then we are effectively re-sampling the signal at a lower and lower frequency. When this operation reaches the Nyquist limit the motion will slow down, instead of speeding up, as aliasing occurs.

(10.6.6)   **Filtering in the time domain – convolution**

We now come to consider how we perform a single filtering operation in the time domain which is exactly equivalent to transforming the signal into the frequency domain, filtering and transforming the filtered version back into the time domain. Generally we would want to do this from an efficiency point of view. An example application is given in Section 10.6.1.

We remind ourselves that the filtering in the frequency domain is a scaling or multiplicative operation. We have already alluded to convolution and we will now examine this operation in more detail. The convolution theorem is:

$$f(t) \otimes h(t) \Leftrightarrow F(s)H(s)$$

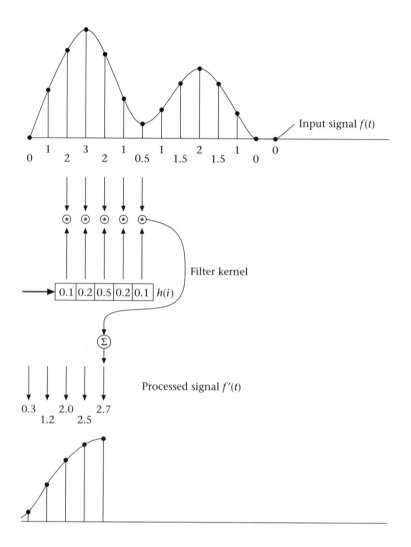

Figure 10.19
Illustrating a discrete digital convolution.

which, in words, states that to obtain the same effect as as multiplication of $F(s)$ by $H(s)$ in the frequency domain we must convolve $f(t)$ with $h(t)$, where $h(t)$ is the Fourier transform of $H(s)$.

Discrete convolution can be defined as:

$$f'(t) = \sum_{i=-w}^{w} h(i)f(t + i)$$

A good way to visualise this operation is shown in Figure 10.19. A so-called kernel moves along the signal, which we consider stationary, multiplying $(2w + 1)$ data samples by the filter weights $h(i)$. At each position these are summed and the result replaces the MoCap data sample on which the filter is currently centred.

10.7 Signal processing and MoCap data

As we mentioned at the beginning of Section 10.6, although signal processing applied to MoCap data has been a popular technique its basis is not entirely correct. The problem is the representation which, as we know, is the Euler angle representation. Conventional filtering techniques assume that the motion data $f(t)$ is linear. Euler angles are non-Euclidean – moving in any direction simply brings you back to the start point. However, for small movement the representation may be approximately linear. In a recent report Lee *et al.* [LEE02] address this problem and apply conventional filtering technology on transformed orientation data by employing exponential and logarithmic maps as a representation of angular displacement.

The other underlying assumption that legitimises the use of a Fourier transform in MoCap processing is that the Fourier parameters have physical meaning or relevance with respect to the data. This is the basis of the work reported in the next section where the authors associate the manipulation of Fourier parameters with 'emotion' in an action.

In the Fourier domain we have access to the amplitude, frequency and phase of the components. Consider first operating on the amplitude values. Applying a uniform scale factor to all components should alter the step length in a cyclic motion such as a walk. The MoCap data is the swing of a joint angle and if we increase all frequency components equally then we increase the amplitude of the swing. The normal filtering model is to alter the amplitude of frequency components by enhancing some and diminishing others. In this case the characteristics of the action alter. A snappy action should exhibit more energy in high frequency components and to make an action more jerky we should thus enhance such components. Bruderlin and Williams describe the effects of frequency filtering in the following terms (the method itself is described in Section 10.7.2):

increasing the middle frequencies of a walking sequence resulted in a smoothed but exaggerated walk. In contrast increasing the high frequency added a nervous twitch to the movement, whereas increasing the low frequencies generated an attenuated, constrained walk with reduced joint movement.

The number of frequency bands that we have to consider is low and depends on the sampling rate of the MoCap equipment. Unuma *et al.* [UNUM95] state that good results can be obtained with manipulating just three frequency components and that seven is a maximum.

The frequency of the fundamental can be altered and this changes the speed of the cyclic action. Another manipulation of the frequency variable is normalisation, which is employed in the next section.

We now look at two case studies which use classical signal processing techniques to operate on MoCap data.

10.7.1

Interpolation/extrapolation in the Fourier domain

In a study called 'Fourier principles for emotion-based human figure animation' Unuma *et al.* [UNUM95] use the Fourier domain for interpolation/extrapolation to generate new or modified motion sequences from existing ones. Here 'emotion' is considered as a secondary motion superimposed on a basic periodic motion for, say, a walk cycle. This assumption enables the authors to extract the difference between a sad and neutral walk (say) and apply this difference to a run.

Unuma *et al.* define a rescaled Fourier functional model as:

$$f(t) = a_0 + \sum_{i=1}^{n} a_i \sin(it + \phi_i)$$

which is a frequency or period normalised version of Equation 10.1. This aligns the frequency spectrum amplitude component of sequences that have different periods and enables interpolation or blending between two frequency spectra to produce a new motion. The effect of this operation should be equivalent to the alignment algorithm described in Section 10.4.3. Because of this normalisation operation the study is limited to cyclic (or near periodic motions).

Thus given two spectra a_i and b_i an interpolating function is formed as

$$f_{ab} = ((1 - s)a_0 + \sum_{i=1}^{n} ((1 - s)a_n + sb_n)\sin(it + (1 - s)\phi_{ai} + \phi_{bi}))$$

where
$0 \leq s \leq 1$ results in interpolation
$s > 1$ or $s < 1$ results in extrapolation of exaggeration

10.7.2

Multi-resolution filtering using the Laplacian

An efficient method of performing multi-resolution filtering for MoCap data was introduced by Bruderlin and Williams [BRUD95]. This is to construct a Laplacian or band pass hierarchy of the signal by convolution in the time domain. This concept is easy to understand using an image example. We consider two types of image pyramid, a low pass pyramid and a band pass or Laplacian pyramid. Examples of these are shown in Figure 10.20. A low pass image consists of the finest resolution image, followed by a half resolution version, followed by a quarter resolution version etc. Each version is formed from the previous one by using a low pass filter. The top of the pyramid is a single pixel which is the average of the entire image – its DC level.[3]

---

3. A mip map is the most common example of this type of image transform. Here a texture map is stored in this way and when the texture is to be mapped onto the object a metric that relates to the screen size or projection of the object is used to select a map at the appropriate resolution level. Objects far away from the user would select a small or coarse resolution map.

Figure 10.20
Low pass and band pass
image pyramids.

A band pass pyramid stores the difference between levels in the low pass pyramid. For example, if we have $m \times m$ pixels in the highest resolution image we generate a filtered version at $(m/2) \times (m/2)$ in the low pass pyramid. This filtered image is then 'expanded' back to $m \times m$ and subtracted from the original to form the band pass image.

If we notate the low pass pyramid as $G_0, G_1, \ldots, G_n$, where G_0 is the original image and G_n the single pixel average. Notating the band pass pyramid similarly as $L_0, L_1, \ldots, L_{n-1}$ then we have that the image is given by:

$$G_0 = L_0 \oplus (L_1 \oplus (L_2 \oplus \ldots \oplus (L_n \oplus (L_{n-1} \oplus G_n)$$

where

$\oplus$ indicates a dilation followed by a sum

That is, to generate the image we start with G_n, the single pixel average, dilate this to 2×2 pixels and add it to L_{n-1}. This gives G_{n-1}.

The hierarchy constructed by Bruderlin and Williams for MoCap data keeps the length of each sequence in the hierarchy the same, instead of reducing the length of each level by a factor of two. The hierarchy can then be expressed as a normal summation as:

$$G_0 = G_n + \sum_{k=0}^{n-1} L_k$$

This is done by packing the filter kernels with zeros. They use:

$$w_1 = [c\ b\ a\ b\ c] = [0.625\quad 0.25\quad 0.375\quad 0.25\quad 0.625]$$
$$w_2 = [c\ 0\ b\ 0\ a\ 0\ b\ 0\ c]$$
$$w_3 = [c\ 0\ 0\ 0\ b\ 0\ 0\ 0\ a\ 0\ 0\ 0\ b\ 0\ 0\ 0\ c]\ \text{etc.}$$

The low pass sequences are calculated by:

$$G_{k+1} = w_{k+1} \otimes G_k \quad k = 1,2,\ldots,n$$

where

$\otimes$ signifies the convolution operator

The Laplacian sequences are then given by:

$$L_k = G_k - G_{k+1}$$

These sequences can then be operated on according to the desired multi-resolution filtering requirements:

$$L_k = s_k L_k$$

and the processed motion signal given by:

$$G_0 = G_n + \sum_{k=0}^{n-1} L_k$$

Thus at the expense of expanding the MoCap data by a factor of n, L_k can be pre-calculated. A real-time implementation would then consist only of the weighting and summation.

If the approach is to be used to blend two sequences together, rather than altering the character of a single sequence, then time warping must be applied prior to the multi-resolution blend.

10.8 Motion editing: constraint-based approaches

We now come to look at constraint-based approaches to motion editing. These differ from the previous techniques we have examined in that they derive a new motion subject to the satisfaction of constraints that may be specified within a frame, over a number of frames or over the entire sequence. Motion

Figure 10.21
Re-targeting MoCap data means using the same data on a character whose scale is different to that of the actor who performed the motion. Note the change in joint angle for the elbow (courtesy of Kelseus.com).

transformations such as blending or filtering do not explicitly include constraints – they simply operate on motion data without regard to the geometric consequences of the new motion.

Most constraint-based methods use kinematic constraints, the most common being the desired position of the end effectors. There is no reason, apart from high cost, for not using dynamic constraints and indeed the originators of the so-called space–time constraint method – Witkin and Kass [WITK88], invoked dynamic constraints.

The most common application of constraint-based methods is motion fitting. Motion fitting or re-targeting is an important and difficult problem that has two common motivations. The first is reuse of MoCap data on a virtual character whose scale is different to the human character from which the data was collected. Common examples of this in a walking motion are the feet floating above the floor and the ubiquitous feet sliding problem. Consider Figure 10.21 which shows two characters of very different size being driven by the same 'switch on the light' MoCap data. Looking at the figure, we can see that joint angles have to change in a distinctly non-linear manner when the character size is changed. Also, some may have to be changed, others not. In this case it is clear that the elbow joint angle must be changed but the remainder of the pose could remain the same. However, it may be that if the motion is being re-targeted from the smaller character to the larger, other constraints may appear. The body pose of the larger character may have to be altered to prevent his nose colliding with the lamp.

Another common constraint application is to adapt MoCap data to cause new poses demanded by the game which did not appear in the original sequence. For example, we may want to alter a grasp motion if the position of the grasped

Figure 10.22
Problems with generic character/object interaction. If the same animation script is used to pick up similar large objects, then character/object penetration (visible in the image) should be handled. Alternatively a different script is required for each object (courtesy of Kelseus.com).

object or its size changes. In Figure 10.22 (also Colour Plate) a grasp MoCap sequence is applied to a new object (an object different from the one for which the motion was recorded). In this case hand/object penetration is visible. If the same MoCap sequence is to be used for a range of similar objects, then collision detection, or some other device, needs to be used to modify the MoCap sequence. Otherwise a different MoCap sequence will be required for each object. This particular problem is approached using an IK method in Section 10.8.3.

Motion fitting or re-targeting is usually seen as a constraint satisfaction problem. What is the best way to alter the motion so that the new constraints are met? In most applications constraints are usually satisfied by using IK (Chapter 11).

10.8.1 Dynamic constraints in motion

We will now briefly discuss the use of dynamic constraints. The motivation of dynamic constraints is not only their potential use in constraint-based motion transformations of MoCap data, but their potential for motion synthesis. If we could efficiently model the dynamics of the human figure in a way that produced convincing motion then we would obviate the need for MoCap technology. The aim of this section is to demonstrate both the use of dynamic constraints and also, with the example, to show why motion synthesis is so difficult for a figure of any complexity.

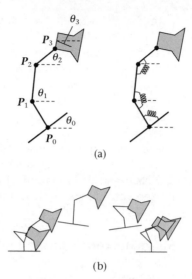

(a)

(b)

Figure 10.23
Witkin and Kass's simulation of *Luxo Jr.* (based on an illustration in [WITK88]). (a) A planar model constructed of rigid links and frictionless joints. (b) The simulation of a jump.

Witkin and Kass [WITK88] studied the problem of synthesising motion for a simple character – a planar model of *Luxo Jr.*[4] parameterised by four joint angles and translation (Figure 10.23). The aim of the project was to synthesise a motion for the character based on input such as 'jump from A to B'.

Commenting on the success of their approach, Witkins and Kass state:

> making a Luxo lamp execute a convincing jump just by telling it where to start and end. The results . . . show that such properties as anticipation, follow-through, squash and stretch, and timing indeed emerge from a bare description of the motion's purpose and the physical context in which it occurs.

A solution is enabled by introducing an objective function which is minimised together with the constraints, which in this case comprise the initial and final pose and position. The framework of the solution algorithm is then: find the set of joint angle motion curves that minimises the objective function subject to the constraints. The forces in the system are 'muscle' forces, the contact force between the floor and the base and gravity. Muscles are simulated by three angular springs joining the links at each joint, where the spring force is given by:

$$F_i = k_i(\varphi_i - \rho_i)$$

where

k_i is the spring stiffness
φ_i is the joint angle
ρ_i is the rest angle

---

4. *Luxo Jr.* is a famous animation short produced by John Lasseter for Pixar in 1987. The motivation for the work, described in [LASS87], was to incorporate the principles of traditional animation (squash and stretch, anticipation, follow-through etc.) in 3D computer animation.

Both the stiffness and rest angle are allowed to vary. The springs are used to build the objective function which optimises the motion's mechanical efficiency by ensuring that minimum power is consumed by the muscles at each time step, where muscle power is the product of the muscle force and the joint's angular velocity. The key point here is that the system solves for the character's motion and time-varying muscle force over the entire interval of interest rather than progressing sequentially through time. The system works by accepting space–time constraints as input, then searching for a solution that, say, minimises the power consumed by the muscles.

This example demonstrates both the potential of the space–time dynamics approach and its limitations. Essentially this is a simple model. The complexity and cost growth of the problem is severe for 'creatures'.

(10.8.2) Kinematic constraints in motion

In the previous section it was assumed that the desirable property was dynamic constraints defined by the physics of the system. As we discussed, the common approach to constraints in MoCap is kinematic. Geometric or spatial constraints are specified, or emerge in a game as it is played, and the motion must adapt accordingly. The most common constraints are joint limits and end-effector positions (or generally any point on a character). When constraints are used in motion fitting we have the situation that the original motion, by definition, has already satisfied all constraints. When re-targeting the motion it may be that all the original constraints can no longer be met. A simple example was given in Figure 10.21. In this case, clearly the position of the end effector must be maintained, but to meet this requirement the joint angle has to change. The image shows that it is generally impossible to meet end-effector constraints while maintaining joint angles. The question then arises: what is more important, end-effector positions or joint angles? Most schemes start from the basis that end-effector positions are predominant.

Shin *et al.* in [SHIN01] address this problem and assign an importance metric to the different constraints based on the following heuristics:

- The position of the root is most likely unimportant – this can move to accommodate the new posture required to satisfy the constraints.
- The position of an end effector is important if it is interacting with another object.
- The position of an end effector is important if it is near an object with which it will interact.
- Proximity needs to be qualified depending on whether an end effector is moving towards an object (important) or away from it (unimportant).

The idea of their importance-based approach is that the re-targeting system should find out what constraints are important and what are not. The system should then change aspects that are not important. For example, if an end effector is moving away from an object (with which it is to interact) then its importance value is diminished so that the captured posture of the corresponding limb is maintained.

The above heuristics are reflected in an importance value that relates an end effector to near objects as follows. A distance function is defined as:

$$D_{ij}(t) = \frac{d_{ij}(t) + d_{ij}(t + c\Delta t)}{2}$$

where
> D_{ij} is the average of the current distance and the predicted distance time $c\Delta t$ later
> d_{ij} is the distance from end effector i to object j
> c is a positive constant

This can be approximated as:

$$D_{ij}(t) = \frac{d_{ij}(t) + d_{ij}(t) + c\Delta t \dot{d}_{ij}(t)}{2}$$

$$= d_{ij}(t) + \lambda \dot{d}_{ij}(t)$$

where
> $\dot{d}_{ij}(t)$ is the first derivative of $d_{ij}(t)$

which is normalised as:

$$\bar{D}_{ij} = \frac{D_{ij}}{D_{ij}^{max}}$$

where
> D_{ij}^{max} is that maximum distance over which the end effector is influenced by the object. A large value makes for a sensitive interaction, a small value means that the end effector can move independent of the object unless it is very close.

An importance function, p, of the normalised distance is then defined as:

$$p(\bar{D}_{ij}) = \begin{cases} 2\bar{D}_{ij}^3 - 3\bar{D}_{ij}^2 + 1 & \text{if } \bar{D}_{ij} < 1 \\ 0 \text{ otherwise} \end{cases}$$

This cubic has the properties:

$$p(1) = 0 \quad p(0) = 1 \quad p'(0) = 0 \quad p'(1) = 1$$

Thus as the distance between an end effector and an object decreases to zero the importance becomes 1, and the rate of change of p becomes small at each of the extreme points.

Per frame re-targeting methods

The goal of motion fitting, explicitly addressed by constraint-based methods, is to find a new motion that satisfies the constraints and to do this in a way that preserves the characteristics of the original motion. The easiest way to do this is to operate within each frame, adjusting the pose of the figure to meet the constraints of the frame. This common approach is best suited to real-time work. Alternatively, as we describe in the next section we can consider the entire motion sequence when we look for a solution.

Now consider how we might use a simple IK approach to re-target a walk motion to a new character. The problems that we have to deal with are the prevention of foot sliding and penetration into the ground. We can either 'switch' the IK on only while the foot is on the ground; or we can use the IK to work out the new limb angles for every frame having the end effector – the foot – following the original foot motion through the sequence. The only difference between the two methods is the cost – the on/off solution being cheaper and so far the most popular approach.

Consider first applying IK in every frame. An example is shown in Figure 10.24.

The first image in Figure 10.24 shows the original motion. This can be compared with Figure 10.9 which, as we remarked, exhibits a near but not perfect periodicity. If the MoCap data used to produce this figure were perfectly periodic, then the ghost sequence, for each cycle, would repeat identically. It is apparent that this is not the case. In the second image the original motion is applied to a new character with different upper and lower leg limbs. Apparent in the figure is foot sliding and ground penetration. In the final image IK is applied in every frame, using the differential method described in Section 11.3.1. The foot or end effector takes its position from the ground during the strike phase of the cycle and follows the original positions during the 'foot off the ground' phase. The root, which takes the translation part of the MoCap data, also has its height adjusted. Note that although the method 'works', the final motion is somewhat unfeasible, with the angle of the lower limb approaching the horizontal. This defect can be cured by imposing joint angle limits as we describe in Section 10.8.2.

In the former approach, IK is used to plant or lock the feet at the step position while the body moves forward. The initiation of the IK is when the foot first strikes the ground; the foot remaining on the ground fixed in the same position in global space while the body moves forward. The IK is released when the time occurs for the foot to leave the ground.

Consider a scheme for a conventional walk cycle. At equal intervals it is specified that the foot must remain on the ground. When such a frame is reached, at time t_{left_on}, IK is turned on for that foot and the module calculates the relative orientation of the upper and lower leg so that the foot remains on the ground as the hip translates forward. For subsequent frames that the foot remains on the ground, the IK controller fixes the feet at the position of the **first** key of the foot on ground frames (t_{left_on}). This means that there is no discontinuity to

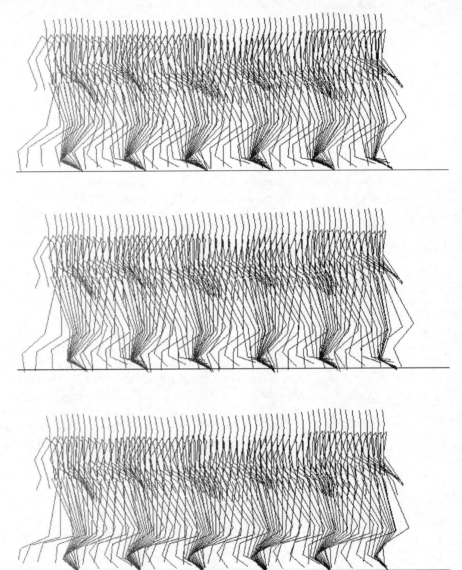

Figure 10.24
IK applied in every frame to re-target a walk cycle. The first image is the original MoCap sequence. The second is that sequence applied to a rescaled figure and the third is the sequence re-targeted to the new figure (courtesy of Michael Meredith).

handle when the IK is turned on. However, when the time comes for the IK to be turned off, the leg now needs to occupy its spatial position currently found on the animation at frame $t_{\text{left\_off}}$. This a spatial discontinuity which must be blended out.

The issue of high frequency components in MoCap data is extremely important – it contains the motion detail – the snap in a kick, for example. It is as important to retain this detail when re-targeting as it is *not* to introduce high frequency components which do exist in the original.

In an excellent insightful categorisation of constraint-based methods, Gleicher [GLEI01] terms the method addressed in this section as PFIK+F (Per Frame IK plus Filtering). Gleicher's approach is that constraints determined by the IK solver should be satisfied by using as low a frequency change to the motion as possible. An IK solver is invoked for each constraint frame, then the constraints are met by applying a displacement map (Section 10.4.4) which starts at a coarse level and refines. At each iteration the new motion is computed as the sum of the original and the current displacement level.

Lee *et al.* [LEE99] address the motion fitting problem by using a multi-resolution approach that combines hierarchical B-splines with an IK solver. MoCap data is represented using the exponential map. Hierarchical B-spline interpolation was introduced in Section 10.5.1 and Lee *et al.* use this approach to derive a (coarse to fine) hierarchical displacement map (Section 10.5.1) that incrementally adapts an original motion M_0 to the final motion M_h, where:

$$M_h = (\ldots ((M_0 + d_1) + d_2) + \ldots + d_h)$$

The displacement hierarchy is then defined as

$$\mathbf{d} = \sum_{k=1}^{h} d_k$$

For a particular frame t_j of the required motion the displacement is interpolated by a B-spline curve and propagated to neighbouring frames in the manner of Figure 10.6. For each constrained frame an IK solver (Chapter 11) gives the configuration $M(t_j)$ of the character that is required to meet the constraint. From the many available solutions, the one that minimises the difference between $M(t_j)$ and the previous motion is chosen. The algorithm transforms a motion M_0 into the M_h which satisfies a set of constrained frames notated by (t_j, C_j) and is as follows:

for $k = 1$ **to** h

    for each constrained frame (t_j, C_j)

        $M(t_j) = \text{IK\_solver}(C_j, M_{k-1}(t_j))$

        $d(t_j) = M(t_j) - M_{k-1}(t_j)$

        $D = D \cup (t_j, d(t_j))$

    Calculate d_k by curve fitting to D

        $M_k = M_{k-1} + d_k$

The advantages of hierarchical B-spline interpolation pertain when they are used in the context of MoCap. Finding the displacement map by going from a coarse level to a fine level should mean that the detail in the motion M_0 is preserved. Using single level B-spline interpolation can interfere with this detail by introducing undulations. The coarsest level of the displacement map has the largest spacing between knots and the largest range of influence. In subsequent levels of the displacement map the range decreases to fine-tune the motion. The authors quote good results with h set in the order of 4 or 5.

Lee *et al.* point out that a limitation of their method is its inability to handle interframe constraints that operate over many frames. This drawback is addressed in the work we describe in the next section.

Gleicher [GLEI01] adopts the same approach but couches it in standard signal processing terms and operates directly on Euler angle representation. Again the displacement map is computed iteratively as the difference between the new motion and the original. This is then conventionally filtered using a low pass filter. At each iteration the cut-off frequency of the filter is increased (implying smaller and smaller kernels). Thus again the constraints are met by the lowest possible frequency displacement map.

(10.8.4)   ### Space–time methods

The originating work that applied a space–time approach to MoCap data is [GLEI98]. Like the Witkin and Kass dynamic constraint method, this approach considers the entire motion sequence simultaneously. This is different to the PFIK+F method in the previous section which considered frames individually. It accomplishes this, like the PFIK+F approach, by minimising the changes required to achieve the new motion and by restricting their frequency content. The method considers the transformation as a constrained optimisation problem. It uses simple metrics to compare motions and spatial or geometric constraints. Because of its inherent cost, and the fact that it transforms one sequence into another by calculations on the entire sequence, the method is off-line.

As in the previous method, the concept of a displacement map is used. Also as in the previous method, a B-spline representation in conjunction with variable control point spacing is used to limit the high frequency content of introduced changes. Gleicher uses control point spacing of every 2, 4 or 8 frames, computes a bandpass decomposition of the original motion and chooses the key spacing that coincides with the lowest level of the hierarchy whose energy contribution exceeds a threshold.

Constrained optimisation methods require an objective function. The simplest example is:

$$g(M) = \sum_{i=1}^{n} (M(t_i) - M_0(t_i))^2 = \sum_{i=1}^{n} d(t_i)^2$$

where
$M_0(t)$ is the original motion sequence

The overall goal of the solution is to mimimise the effort required in the transformation to meet new constraints. An initial step in the algorithm is necessary because the positional offset of the root of the hierarchy is not independent of scaling (unlike angle MoCap data). Gleicher gives an example of a character approaching an object and picking it up. The constraint on the figure's position is that it must be sufficiently close to the object (in the centre frame) to be able to touch it. If the character is reduced in size then the entire motion sequence will move away from the object. This has to be corrected by interpolating the constant displacement and applying an offset to the translation data.

The steps in the algorithm are as follows:

(1) Define the constraints.

(2) Modify $M_0(t)$ to give $M_1(t)$ the initial solution by operating on the translational parameters of the motion.

(3) Choose a B-spline representation for the curve based on the frequency decomposition.

(4) Solve the constraint optimisation problem for a displacement which, when added to $M_1(t)$, results in a motion that satisfies the constraints.

(5) If step 4 does not satisfy the constraints sufficiently, replace $M_1(t)$ with $(M_1(t) + dt)$ and use the next denser set of control points.

An obvious advantage of the space–time approach over PFIK+F is that constraints that hold over many frames can be handled. In the PFIK+F approach these would be treated independently and separately as they arise. In [GLEI01] Gleicher points out that a major flexibility of the approach is that it can deal with 'don't care' constraints. He gives the example of foot plant constraints. Here the real constraint (in most cases) is that the foot strikes the floor – the exact position of the strike being unimportant.

Appendix 10.1 Demonstration

Wfft1D.exe is a one-dimensional FFT program. It accepts functional definitions via an equation parser. For example, Figure 10.15 was produced using:

abs(x) < 4.5? sin(4*x) : 0

abs(x) < 4.5? cos(x/4)*cos(x/4)*sin(4x) : 0

11 Inverse kinematics: the theory

11.1 An example – the two-link arm

11.2 The Jacobian

11.3 Approaches to IK

11.4 Practical approaches to inverse kinematics

Kinematic animation of a character embraces all those methods which do not take into account any dynamic considerations. This comprises almost all the current methods for animating a human-like character, be they off-line or real time. Within kinematic animation, forward kinematics is the norm. However, inverse kinematics is playing a more and more important role, particularly since the development of algorithms with real-time performance.

As we discuss throughout the text, simplified characters, represented by skeletons, are animated by forward kinematics using data which is either captured from live performers or interpolated from keys designed by animators. In forward kinematics we specify the pose of an articulated structure as a set of joint angles – a state vector θ together with a position and orientation for the root node (Section 10.8.2).

Many problems occur in forward kinematics – in particular it is time consuming and difficult to tune. And of course this is one of the motivations for the use of MoCap – it avoids many of these problems. In computer games inverse kinematics (IK) finds its main application in adapting MoCap data (Chapter 10).

We begin by considering the difference between forward and inverse kinematics by distinguishing between the spaces that they operate in:

(1) Joint space is the multidimensional space of joint angles. With a dimensionality equal to the number of DOFs of the computer graphics skeleton, the pose of a figure is a single point in this space. As a figure moves, a path is traced out in this space.

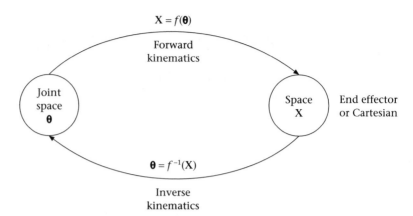

Figure 11.1
Forward and inverse
kinematics.

(2) End-effector space is the *m*-dimensional space of the end effector (where *m* = number of end effectors × their DOF).

(3) World space is the space in which the character is visualised.

Considering the first two spaces, this concept leads to a useful model of the relationship between forward and inverse kinematics (Figure 11.1).

Thus we write for forward kinematics:

$$X = f(\boldsymbol{\theta})$$

meaning that the position of any point on the skeleton (usually an end effector) is some function of the joint angles. This expression controls the pose of the skeleton and to visualise the character in world space we need to calculate the position of skin vertices associated with the skeleton (Chapter 8). We animate the character by injecting joint angles as a function of time into the forward kinematics equation, then transform the skeleton into a skinned character in world space using a skinning algorithm.

For IK we write:

$$\boldsymbol{\theta} = f^{-1}(X)$$

and here X is normally used to specify a required position for an end effector, in the case of character animation – the hands or feet. The expression models the notion: if the hands are to be moved to grasp an object, say, then we specify X as the goal and the IK calculates the $\boldsymbol{\theta}$ required to meet the goal. (Although for simplicity we will continually refer to $\boldsymbol{\theta}$ as determining the pose of the character, we also have to consider the position of the root node. In a grasping scenario, if the object is in range then only $\boldsymbol{\theta}$ need be altered; if it is out of range then the IK solution will also involve a change in position of the root node.)

In MoCap adaptation – the application of interest in computer games – the motivation of IK is modified as follows. Given a sequence captured for certain constraints, we would like to adapt the motion to meet new constraints. Most commonly these are that the scale of the game character is different from the live character, or a game event demands a sequence alteration – a run has to

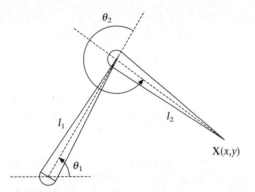

Figure 11.2
A simple two-link
structure.

be adapted because of change of terrain. Here the IK works out the required pose that meets the new constraint. There then follows some procedure which changes the original motion sequence to match the new requirements in a way that 'looks natural'. Precisely what this means is explained in Chapter 10. The important point is that the IK on its own is not a solution to MoCap adaptation. It is one phase of a two-phase approach.

To introduce the topic we will look at a simple example, the two-link arm (Figure 11.2). Although this may seem a ludicrously simple example, compared to a human skeleton, or even a computer graphics skeleton, we shall see in Section 11.1 how we can simplify a skeleton with two-link structures (albeit non-planar ones). In our two-link device one end is fixed, another is the end effector and the two links are joined by a single DOF (hinge) joint. IK is a difficult topic, and to start with the particular and generalise is as good a way as any of introducing the topic. The example is used to demonstrate the following points:

- The concept of an analytical or closed-form solution for IK. These are critically important in real-time applications. Although an analytical solution is impossible for a 50-DOF computer graphics skeleton, there are ways of using closed-form solutions on parts of the structure, as we shall see.

- The important notion of the Jacobian which leads to (possibly) the most common IK solution approach.

Most of the development of closed-form solutions comes from the robotics field where the interest is to control industrial robots such as the PUMA arm (see for example [CRAI88]). These tools have a low number of DOFs – usually 6. This compares with computer graphics structure (~50 DOFs) and the real human skeleton (> 250 DOFs). Closed-form solutions are only possible for low DOFs (≤ 6).

An example – the two-link arm

Simple link mechanisms are studied by setting up a coordinate frame at each joint and expressing the overall movement of a structure as a concatenation of a series of transformations that express the movement of the origin of frame *n* with respect to frame $n-1$. This enables us to express the motion of an end effector – the origin of frame n with respect to the base frame 0 as:

$$_n^0T = {}_1^0T\, {}_2^1T\, {}_3^2T \ldots {}_n^{n-1}T$$

(This expression is just a different way of notating the expression given as Equation 7.1.) The position and the orientation of the end effector is given by the concatenation of the individual link transformations.

Consider a simple example – the two-link planar mechanism. Here we set up four frames, frame 0 which is the base frame and cannot move, frame 1 which shares an origin with the base frame and can rotate in the plane of the paper, frame 2 which can also rotate in the the plane of the paper, and finally the end effector which we designate as frame 3. This is fixed to the end of the final link and cannot move. Thus the arm exhibits 2 DOFs, the same as the dimensionality of the space in which it moves.

We develop the transformation as follows. First we consider how frame 1 moves with respect to frame 0. It can only rotate and we have:

$$_1^0\mathbf{T} = \begin{bmatrix} c_1 & -s_1 & 0 & 0 \\ s_1 & c_1 & 0 & 0 \\ 0 & 0 & 1 & 0 \\ 0 & 0 & 0 & 1 \end{bmatrix}$$

Similarly

$$_2^1\mathbf{T} = \begin{bmatrix} c_2 & -s_2 & 0 & l_1 \\ s_2 & c_2 & 0 & 0 \\ 0 & 0 & 1 & 0 \\ 0 & 0 & 0 & 1 \end{bmatrix}$$

where:

c_1, c_2, s_1 and s_2 are abbreviations for $\cos\theta_1$, $\cos\theta_2$, $\sin\theta_1$ and $\sin\theta_2$

and

$$_3^2\mathbf{T} = \begin{bmatrix} 1 & 0 & 0 & l_2 \\ 0 & 1 & 0 & 0 \\ 0 & 0 & 1 & 0 \\ 0 & 0 & 0 & 1 \end{bmatrix}$$

reflects the fact that the end effector is rigidly attached to this link – the end effector has 2 DOFs only.

Inverse kinematics means calculating the change in configuration or pose of an articulated structure as the end effector moves from one position to another. This seems an ideal paradigm as we are, in most applications, interested in goal-directed motion. We require end effectors to move around in 3-space and perform tasks. If the joint animation can be derived from end-effector motion then we have a potential solution to the autonomous motion problem wherein we have a high-level process requesting motion from the end effectors of the structure, for example 'walk over to the table and pick up the glass'. (Note that this is a much more ambitious aim than the current game application of IK – adapting a MoCap sequence.) However, animation developed entirely from IK does not compare well with forward kinematics or MoCap data – visually it resembles the motion of a puppet and so we regard it as an important tool rather than a complete solution.

Much of the research in inverse kinematics has been conducted in the field of robot manipulators which are much less complex than human beings and in this respect the technique has been more successful in this application. IK solutions are used to control the joint motors and move the robot to a new goal. In the case of the two-link trigonometric manipulation gives the closed-form solution as:

$$\theta_2 = \cos^{-1}\left(\frac{x^2 + y^2 - l_1^2 - l_2^2}{2l_1 l_2}\right)$$

$$\theta_1 = \tan^{-1}\left(\frac{-l_2 \sin \theta_2 x + (l_1 + l_2 \cos \theta_2)y}{l_2 \sin \theta_2 y + (l_1 + l_2 \cos \theta_2)x}\right)$$

Finding a closed-form solution becomes progressively more difficult as the chain becomes more and more complex – that is, as the number of DOFs increases. Another problem with closed-form solutions is that they are difficult to generalise to multiple constraints, particularly if these are interacting. Their significant advantage is that they are fast. The application of a single formula results in a solution. This contrasts with all other approaches which are iterative.

11.2 The Jacobian

Now in the case of applications that do not have a closed-form solution we can implement inverse kinematics solutions by exploiting the fact that for small movements of the end effector we can assume a linear relationship between joint velocity and the velocity of the end effector. This is written as:

$$\dot{X} = J\dot{\theta}$$

J is known as the Jacobian and is a multidimensional derivative relating the end-effector velocity to the velocity of the joints. It is an $m \times n$ matrix, where n is the number of joint variables (the total number of DOFs) and m is the number of DOFs of the end effector. The ith column of J represents the incremental change in position and orientation of the end effector caused by an incremental change in θ_i. If the inverse of J exists then we can write:

$$\dot{\theta} = J^{-1}\dot{X}$$

We will now consider again the two-link arm and develop its Jacobian. We do this by developing an expression for the linear and rotational velocity of each frame, then expressing the velocity of the end effector with respect to the base frame. The base frame has zero linear and rotational velocity and we start with frame 1. This has zero linear velocity; it can only rotate and we have:

$$^1\omega_1 = \begin{bmatrix} 0 \\ 0 \\ \dot{\theta}_1 \end{bmatrix}$$

$$^1\mathbf{v}_1 = \begin{bmatrix} 0 \\ 0 \\ 0 \end{bmatrix}$$

To calculate the angular velocity of frame 2, we only augment its angular velocity with that of frame 1:

$$^2\omega_2 = \begin{bmatrix} 0 \\ 0 \\ \dot{\theta}_1 + \dot{\theta}_2 \end{bmatrix}$$

The linear velocity of the origin of frame 2 is that of the origin of frame 1 plus the component caused by the angular velocity of frame 1/link 1:

$$^2\mathbf{v}_2 = \begin{bmatrix} 0 \\ 0 \\ 0 \end{bmatrix} + \begin{bmatrix} c_2 & s_2 & 0 \\ -s_2 & c_2 & 0 \\ 0 & 0 & 1 \end{bmatrix} \begin{bmatrix} 0 \\ l_1\dot{\theta} \\ 0 \end{bmatrix} = \begin{bmatrix} l_1 s_2 \dot{\theta}_1 \\ l_1 c_2 \dot{\theta}_1 \\ 0 \end{bmatrix}$$

Finally we have:

$$^3\omega_3 = {}^2\omega_2 = \begin{bmatrix} 0 \\ 0 \\ \dot{\theta}_1 + \dot{\theta}_2 \end{bmatrix}$$

$$^3\mathbf{v}_3 = \begin{bmatrix} l_1 s_2 \dot{\theta}_1 \\ l_1 c_2 \dot{\theta}_1 \\ 0 \end{bmatrix} + \begin{bmatrix} 0 \\ l_2(\dot{\theta}_1 + \dot{\theta}_2) \\ 0 \end{bmatrix} = \begin{bmatrix} 0 \\ l_1 c_2 \dot{\theta}_1 + l_2(\dot{\theta}_1 + \dot{\theta}_2) \\ 0 \end{bmatrix}$$

Now we need to express the linear velocity of the end effector in the base coordinate system and for this we need the rotation matrix:

$$^0_3R = {}^0_1R\,{}^1_2R\,{}^2_3R = \begin{bmatrix} c_{12} & -s_{12} & 0 \\ s_{12} & c_{12} & 0 \\ 0 & 0 & 1 \end{bmatrix}$$

Giving

$$^0\mathbf{v}_3 = \begin{bmatrix} -l_1 s_1 \dot{\theta}_1 - l_2 s_{12}(\dot{\theta}_1 + \dot{\theta}_2) \\ l_1 c_2 \dot{\theta}_1 + l_2 c_{12}(\dot{\theta}_1 + \dot{\theta}_2) \\ 0 \end{bmatrix}$$

This leads directly to the Jacobian using the chain rule for differentiation:

$$J = \begin{bmatrix} -l_1 s_1 - l_2 s_{12} & -l_2 s_{12} \\ l_1 c_1 + l_2 c_{12} & l_2 c_{12} \end{bmatrix}$$

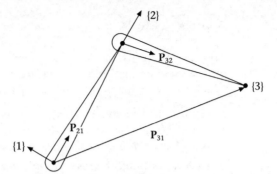

Figure 11.3
Vectors and frames for the
two-link arm.

Finding the Jacobian by differentiation becomes more and more difficult as the complexity of the structure increases and in practice it must be constructed geometrically. We will first state the general principles, then use the approach to evaluate the Jacobian for the two-link planar arm. The principle of this approach extends in a straightforward manner into 3-space and a more detailed treatment of the general case is given in [WATT92].

We consider the motion of the end effector in terms of velocities propagated from the base of the chain to the end. Each link in an *n*-link chain will in general be subject to a linear velocity (as its joint translates) and an angular velocity (as the link rotates about the joint). We state without proof that:

- the angular velocity at the end of the chain is equal to the sum of all local angular velocities (evaluated in the base frame);
- the linear velocity at the end of the chain is the sum over all intermediate frames of the cross-product of the local angular velocity with the vector from the end of the articulation to the origin of that frame.

A notationally simpler approach is shown in Figure 11.3. Accepting the above statement we can now write:

$$\mathbf{v}_{30} = \boldsymbol{\omega}_{10} \times \mathbf{P}_{31} + \boldsymbol{\omega}_{21} \times \mathbf{P}_{32}$$

The position vectors are given by:

$$\mathbf{P}_{31} = (l_1 c_1 + l_2 c_{12},\ l_1 s_1 + l_2 s_{12})$$
$$\mathbf{P}_{21} = (l_2 c_{12},\ l_2 s_{12})$$

The angular velocities are:

$$\boldsymbol{\omega}_{10} = \begin{bmatrix} 0 \\ 0 \\ \dot{\theta}_1 \end{bmatrix} \quad \boldsymbol{\omega}_{21} = \begin{bmatrix} 0 \\ 0 \\ \dot{\theta}_2 \end{bmatrix}$$

Substituting these values into the equation for $\mathbf{v}_{30}$ and rearranging gives us the same result as before.

Now before we move on we should point out that the Jacobian in this case is valid for all $\boldsymbol{\theta}$. In most cases of interest the Jacobian is a function of $\boldsymbol{\theta}$ and in an iterative approach it has to be continually re-evaluated.

11.3 Approaches to IK

Now, accepting the notion that most systems of interest are too complex to possess a closed-form solution, we look in general terms at the various ways in which the problem can be approached. These are:

- **Geometric/analytical** This generates a goal state in a single step and is hence fast. Although, as we have discussed, it cannot form a solution for a structure of any complexity, it can be used as part of a solution in a hybrid method.

- **Differential algorithms** We linearise the problem for small changes using the Jacobian and generate a solution by iteration. In other words, the Jacobian can be embedded in an iterative approach that, exploiting the linearity of small changes, moves the end effector towards a solution. The performance of any iterative approach is a function of its convergence properties.

- **Unconstrained optimisation methods** Instead of finding a solution which *must* satisfy the constraints, these methods operate by associating a cost or penalty with the non-satisfaction of a constraint.

- **Cyclic coordinate descent** This is an algorithm which again moves towards a solution in small steps. This time, however, the steps are formed heuristically.

- **Hybrid methods** These use a combination of approaches. Their motivation is usually real-time performance.

11.3.1 Differential methods using the Jacobian

We begin by restating the enabling equation:

$$\dot{\boldsymbol{\theta}} = J^{-1}(\dot{X})$$

which in an iterative framework becomes

$$\Delta\boldsymbol{\theta} = J^{-1}(\Delta x)$$

At each iteration we move the end effector ΔX nearer to its goal and calculate the corresponding change $\Delta\boldsymbol{\theta}$ in the state vector. The iteration is complete when the end effector reaches its goal. We can proceed as:

Δx = small movement in the direction of the goal

repeat

$\qquad \Delta\boldsymbol{\theta} = J^{-1}(\Delta x)$

$\qquad x = f(\boldsymbol{\theta} + \Delta\boldsymbol{\theta})$

$\quad$ calculate new value of J and invert

$\qquad x = x + \Delta x$

until goal is reached

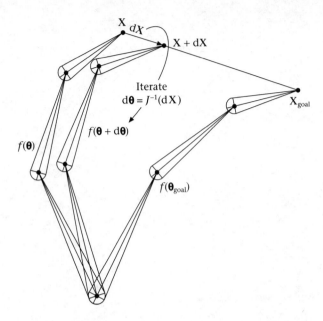

Figure 11.4
One iteration step towards the goal.

An iteration for a three-link arm is shown in Figure 11.4. Problems in the iteration can arise from tracking errors, which is when the desired change in $\mathbf{X}$ is different from the actual change. Tracking errors will occur when $\Delta \mathbf{x}$ is too large and are given by:

$$\| J(\Delta \boldsymbol{\theta}) - \Delta \mathbf{x} \|$$

A more intelligent iteration must then be employed which involves starting with a $\Delta \mathbf{x}$, evaluating the tracking error and subdividing $\Delta \mathbf{x}$ until the error falls below a threshold.

There are other difficulties inherent in this apparently simple approach. First, there is the problem of the behaviour of the system at or near singularities. Consider again the two-link arm fully extended (Figure 11.5). Changes in either θ_1 or θ_2 will both produce changes in the motion in exactly the same direction. We say that one DOF has been lost. Alternatively, we can describe the problem by stating that there is no set of state space velocities that will give an end-effector velocity towards or away from the base. Although singularities are a problem with this approach, we need to be able to handle them. After all, a fully extended arm or leg is not an unnatural pose. We shall see that other methods deal naturally with extended limbs.

Mathematically, as the pose changes we re-calculate the Jacobian and the singularity affects the rank of the matrix. The rank of a matrix is defined as the largest number of linearly independent rows or columns of a matrix. If the determinant of a matrix is zero then the matrix has lost its rank. In the case of the two-link arm we have

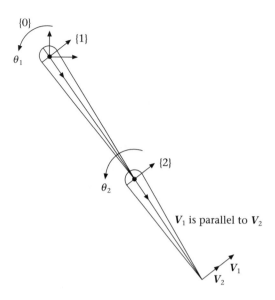

V_1 is parallel to V_2

Figure 11.5
Singularity at full
extension.

$$|J| = \begin{vmatrix} -l_1s_1 - l_2s_{12} & ls \\ l_1c_1 + l_2c_{12} & lc \end{vmatrix} = l_1l_2s_2$$

and this is 0 when θ_2 is 0 or π corresponding to full extension. Generally as singularities are approached, joint rates necessary to move the end effector in a direction along the current line of the link approach infinity. Thus we need to complicate the process further with heuristics to avoid singularities. The state of being near singularity can be detected by measuring how *ill-conditioned* J is. The most common strategy for dealing with it [MACI90] searches for a solution that minimises the sum:

$$\|J(\Delta\boldsymbol{\theta}) - \Delta\mathbf{X}\|^2 + \lambda^2\|\Delta\boldsymbol{\theta}\|^2$$

where the second term is a measure of the state space velocities. The strategy is to mimimise both the tracking error and the state space velocities. λ is a damping factor that defines the relative importance of the tracking error versus the state space velocity norm.

The final difficulty is that for any system of interest the Jacobian is not square – for practical structures the dimension of $\mathbf{X}$ is less than that of $\boldsymbol{\theta}$ – and hence it cannot be inverted. The practical reason for this is that skeletons are highly redundant – they possess more degrees of freedom than they require to reach their goal. A good example is the human arm. If we consider, without concerning ourselves with the complexity of the hand, that the end effector has 6 DOFs (for position and orientation), then this is one less than a simple 7-DOF skeleton for the arm. This consists of two spherical joints (shoulder and wrist) plus one hinge joint (the elbow). This is reflected in the physical situation that if we fix the hand and the shoulder in a desired position the elbow is free to swivel in an arc which is constrained by a plane normal to the line from

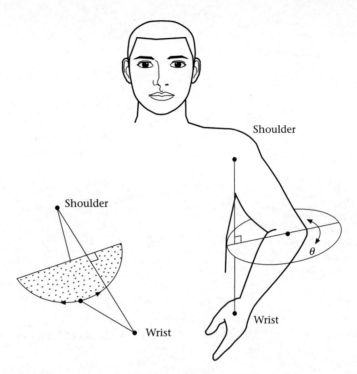

Figure 11.6
The elbow swivel angle θ. Elbow joint is free to move in a plane normal to the line from the shoulder to the wrist without affecting the position of the hand.

the shoulder joint to the wrist joint (Figure 11.6). This motion is caused by the redundant DOF in the shoulder joint. This is called the elbow circle.

The extra degree of freedom means that there is an infinity of solutions and we say that the structure can undergo self-motion. That is, the structure can move and take up a new pose without moving its end effector. Alternatively, we can say that the Jacobian transformation has a null space containing an infinite number of joint space rates that result in no end-effector motion. For a redundant structure, whatever method we use will result in a single solution out of an infinity of solutions. We exploit this by choosing a solution that satisfies some desirable constraints. In other words, we incorporate the constraints into the solution method.

Kinematically redundant manipulators offer certain critical advantages over non-redundant ones. In particular, we can include obstacle avoidance, self-collision avoidance and singularity avoidance into the solution. In general terms we say that a redundant structure is more dexterous.

This situation can be modelled mathematically as:

$$\Delta \boldsymbol{\theta} = J^+ \Delta X + (I - J^+ J) \Delta Z$$

where

J^+ is a square matrix known as the the pseudo-inverse
ΔX is referred to as the main task
I is the identity matrix of joint space dimension
ΔZ is known as the secondary task

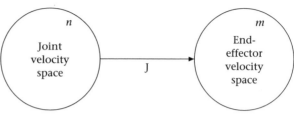

Jacobian relates joint velocity space
to end-effector space.

Figure 11.7
Pseudo-inverse relates m-dimensional end-effector velocity space to the m-dimensional subspace of the joint velocity space.

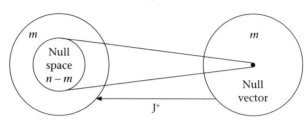

The pseudo inverse J^+ of the Jacobian J (an $m \times n$ matrix of rank r) is given by:

$$J^+ = \begin{cases} (J^T J)^{-1} J^T & \text{if } m > n = r \\ J^T (J J^T)^{-1} & \text{if } r = m < n \end{cases}$$

The first part of the solution is called the pseudo-inverse and the second part the homogeneous solution. The homogeneous component results in no end-effector velocity. This is shown in Figure 11.7. In the upper diagram the Jacobian J relates n-dimensional joint space to m-dimensional end-effector velocity space $(n > m)$. In the second diagram the pseudo inverse J^+ relates m-dimensional end-effector space to an m-dimensional subspace of the joint velocity space. $(I - J^+ J)$ is an operator that selects those components of ΔZ that lie in the set of homogeneous solutions. That is, we can set ΔZ as a secondary task because it projects into the null space and the end-effector motion is unaltered.

Secondary tasks can thus be used to satisfy constraints other than the goal. This is known as exploiting the redundancy. For example, we can change the pose of a figure without altering the end-effector position – precisely the requirement in Figure 10.21. To do this we proceed as:

evaluate $\Delta \boldsymbol{\theta} = J^+ \Delta \mathbf{X}$
evaluate $\boldsymbol{\theta}_t = \boldsymbol{\theta}_{t-1} + \Delta \boldsymbol{\theta}$
evaluate $\Delta \mathbf{Z}$ (see next section for an example)
project into null space by evaluating
            $(I - J^+ J) \Delta \mathbf{Z}$
add result to $\boldsymbol{\theta}_t$

Secondary tasks – joint limits

Possibly the most common secondary task is to ensure a good joint angle pose. For example, generate a pose that minimises the joint angle motion away from some desired configuration – say the mid-range angles. Set ΔZ to be the gradient:

$$\Delta Z = -2(\boldsymbol{\theta} - \boldsymbol{\theta}_M)$$

where

$\boldsymbol{\theta}$ is the current pose

$\boldsymbol{\theta}_M$ is the mid-range pose

More generally we can write:

$$\Delta Z = \nabla H$$

where

$$H = \sum_{i=1}^{\text{no\_of\_DOFs}} \alpha_i(\theta_i - \theta_i^M)$$

where

$\alpha_i \ (0 \leq \alpha_i \leq 1)$ is a gain value defining the stiffness of the joint

Figure 11.8 (also Colour Plate) shows the influence of joint angle constraints injected into a differential solution. The end effector (coloured blue) of the three-link planar structure is moved to simulate an animated goal and the constraints are:

$$-90° \leq \theta_1 \leq 90°$$
$$0 \leq \theta_2 \leq 140°$$
$$-10° \leq \theta_3 \leq 10°$$

Figure 11.9 (also Colour Plate) shows the same structure with its end effector placed in (approximately) the same positions but this time with the joint constraints removed.

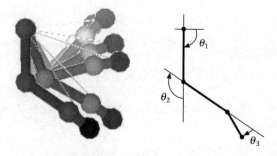

Figure 11.8
A differential IK solution for a three-link structure using joint angle constraints (courtesy of Michael Meredith).

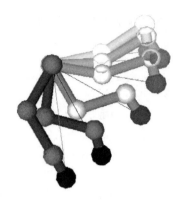

Figure 11.9
The three-link structure
with all joint constraints
removed. Compare with
previous solution.

11.3.2

Optimisation methods

IK can be cast in terms of a non-linear optimisation problem. This avoids many
of the problems of differential IK approaches. In particular, the methods are
more stable. Minimisation methods operate using standard iterative approaches
(see, for example, [PRES01]), to minimise an error function subject to constraints
as:

$$E(\boldsymbol{\theta}) = (\mathbf{X}_g - f(\boldsymbol{\theta}))^2$$

where
   $\mathbf{X}_g$ is the gaol or constraint position

The method can incorporate additional constraints or secondary goals such as
joint limits, in which case we write:

   Minimise $E(\boldsymbol{\theta})$ subject to the constraints $C(\boldsymbol{\theta})$

Iterative methods perturb $\boldsymbol{\theta}$ in such a way that $E(\boldsymbol{\theta})$ decreases. All such methods
suffer from the classic problem of local minima. That is, they may find a local
minimum instead of a global one.

   $E(\boldsymbol{\theta})$ is further elaborated depending on whether the goal of the end effector
is position or position plus orientation. Thus we have:

$$E(\boldsymbol{\theta}) = E_p(\boldsymbol{\theta}) + E_0(\boldsymbol{\theta})$$

If we define the goal of the end effector as $\mathbf{X}_g$, its current position as $\mathbf{X}_c$ and its
orientation goal and current orientation as (orthogonal) matrices R_g, R_c then we
can write $E(\boldsymbol{\theta})$ as:

$$E(\boldsymbol{\theta}) = \|(\mathbf{X}_g - \mathbf{X}_c)\|^2 + \sum_{j=1}^{3}((\mathbf{r}_{jg} \cdot \mathbf{r}_{jc}) - 1)^2$$

where
   $\mathbf{r}_j$ is a row of the matrix

The cyclic coordinate descent method (CCD)

The CCD algorithm was introduced in 1991 by Wang and Chen [WANG91] for industrial robotic manipulators. It is a fast algorithm that minimises error by operating on one joint angle at a time. Although the algorithm bears some relationship to optimisation methods, it is best described as a heuristic direct search method that uses a standard non-linear programming tool (CCD) to find a solution. The algorithm is not sensitive either to initial configurations or to singular configuration of the chain. The description we give is based on an interpretation by Welman [WELM93].

At each iteration the algorithm passes over the entire chain from the end effector to the root, minimising the position and orientation of the end effector for each joint angle. The algorithm is particularly straightforward if we are only interested in the position of the end effector. Figure 11.10 shows two iterations for a simple (planar) case. At each iteration we rotate the link i through angle ϕ_i, the angle between the link's current orientation and the line from the link's origin to the goal position.

Thus:

$$\phi_i = \cos^{-1}(\mathbf{P}_{ig} \cdot \mathbf{P}_{ic})$$

where

$\mathbf{P}_{ic}$ is the vector from the link i to the current end effector position
$\mathbf{P}_{ig}$ is the vector from the link i to the end effector goal position

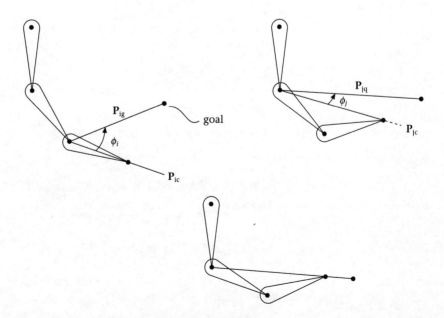

Figure 11.10
Two iterations in a CCD algorithm for a planar link.

Now, as can be seen from the diagram, we are free to rotate $\mathbf{P}_{ic}$ into a new position $\mathbf{P}'_{ic}(\phi)$, and as we must minimise the angle ϕ_i we maximise the expression:

$$g_1(\phi_i) = \mathbf{P}_{ig} \cdot \mathbf{P}'_{ic}(\phi_i)$$

In practice, we must define the rotation of $\mathbf{P}_{ic}$ about the particular DOF axis of the joint i and to rotate $\mathbf{P}_{ic}$ through angle ϕ about a joint axis we have:

$$\mathbf{P}'_{ic}(\phi) = R_{(XYZ)i}(\phi)\,\mathbf{P}_{ic}$$

where

$R_{(XYZ)i}(\phi)$ is the rotation matrix of angle (ϕ) about the joint's x, y or z axis (with respect to the base coordinate frame)

For a 6-DOF end effector we can define a similar expression as:

$$g_2(\phi_i) = \sum_{j=1}^{3} \mathbf{r}_{jg}\mathbf{r}_{jc}(\phi_i)$$

and combining these gives an aggregate expression to be maximised for joint i as:

$$g(\phi_i) = w_p g_1(\phi_i) + w_o g_2(\phi_i) \tag{11.1}$$

where

w_p and w_o are weighting factors for position and orientation

Wang and Chen suggest values for the weights as:

$$w_p = \alpha(1 + \rho)$$
$$w_o = 1$$

where

α is a scale factor based on the size of the world which ensures that the algorithm does not behave in a scale-dependent manner

$$\rho = \frac{\min(\|\mathbf{P}_{ig}\|,\|\mathbf{P}_{ic}\|)}{\max(\|\mathbf{P}_{ig}\|,\|\mathbf{P}_{ic}\|)}$$

Now equation 11.1 can be written as

$$g(\phi_i) = k_1(1 - \cos(\phi_i)) + k_2 \cos(\phi_i) + k_3 \sin(\phi_i) \tag{11.2}$$

where

$$k_1 = w_p(\mathbf{P}_{ig} \cdot R_{(XYZ)i})(\mathbf{P}_{ic} \cdot R_{(XYZ)i}) + w_o \sum_{j=1}^{3} (\mathbf{r}_{jg} \cdot R_{(XYZ)i})(\mathbf{r}_{jc} \cdot R_{(XYZ)i})$$

$$k_2 = w_p(\mathbf{P}_{ig} \cdot \mathbf{P}_{ic}) + w_o \sum_{j=1}^{3} (\mathbf{r}_{jg} \cdot \mathbf{r}_{jc})$$

$$k_3 = R_{(XYZ)i} \cdot [w_p(\mathbf{P}_{ig} \times \mathbf{P}_{ic}) + w_o \sum_{j=1}^{3} (\mathbf{r}_{jg} \times \mathbf{r}_{jc})$$

Taking the first derivative of the objective function (equation 11.2) and setting to zero

$$(k_1 - k_2) \sin \phi + k_3 \cos \phi = 0$$

and

$$\phi = \tan^{-1} \frac{k_3}{(k_2 - k_1)}$$

this gives a possible value for ϕ in the range $(-\pi/2 < \phi < \pi/2)$ together with the other two possible values $\phi + \pi$ and $\phi - \pi$. The objective function is maximised when its first derivative is zero and also its second derivative is negative A value is finally chosen which satisfies the second condition.

Because the method handles each joint individually, joint limit constraints are easy to incorporate. However, imposing joint limits can affect the convergence of the algorithm. The obvious behavioural drawback of the algorithm is that links near to the end effector are favoured. In particular, if a goal can be reached by moving only the end-effector link, then only that link will move. This effect may produce unnatural-looking results and can be ameliorated by limiting a joint swing to less than the calculated motion, even if it is within joint limits.

11.4 Practical approaches to inverse kinematics

As the following examples will demonstrate, practical approaches to IK are quite diverse. The most general practical simplification in IK for a figure is to apply the IK to only part of the structure. We do not have to solve for the entire skeleton but can divide and conquer, reducing the problem to sub-problems involving chains that we can handle. We can apply IK between any two joints in a skeleton and the obvious simplifications are the arms and legs as two-link mechanisms. The IK solver can operate only between these nodes and it may be that the end nodes are the input to or the output from another solver.

Consider an arbitrary skeletal structure which, as is the case in practice, will contain branches – a topic we have not yet considered. This is represented by a hierarchy or a network of nodes – one of which is the root node. We can apply IK between any two nodes in the skeleton; the only rule to be observed is that the node corresponding to the end effector is lower down the hierarchy than the node corresponding to the base node. We can have the concept of an IK algorithm as an attachable engine that can be attached to any part of the skeleton and whose function is to specify the orientation and position of all nodes between the end node and the base node (known as empty nodes). Clearly we can apply more than one IK engine to different parts of the structure. Figure 11.11 shows one obvious arrangement of engines for a simple human skeleton. The root (black triangle) is at the pelvis, base nodes (black squares) are at the hips and shoulders, end nodes (black circles) are at the hands and the feet; and the empty nodes (outlined circles) are at the elbows and knees.

Of course, other arrangements are possible; [PHIL91], for example, positions the root at one foot, making the other an end node in order to animate the motion of a standing figure. (Motions that include bending, shifting of weight

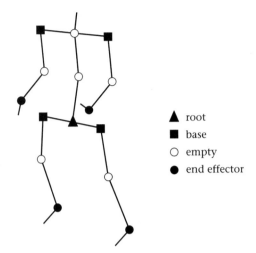

▲ root
■ base
○ empty
● end effector

Figure 11.11
Breaking a simple skeleton
into 4 × 2 link structure
each with a separate IK
control.

from one foot to another and turning.) Additional rules can be applied in the case where engines on a skeleton overlap. An obvious one would be to order them by assigning a priority to each – higher priority engines being evaluated before the lower ones which 'fill in' any remaining empty nodes.

The case studies are meant to be representative examples of current and recent practice; they are not put forward as a comprehensive review of the field.

(11.4.1) Hybrid methods – analytic + constrained optimisation

The advantage of algorithms that use a closed-form solution is that they are fast, avoiding the stability problems of differential algorithms and the local minima of optimisation methods. Closed-form solutions are, however, restricted to simple non-redundant structures. The motivation for hybrid methods, therefore, is to have an IK solver which includes a closed-form solution.

This is exactly the approach taken by Lee *et al.* in [LEE99] where they combine an analytical approach with a constrained optimisation method. In this work the redundant arm DOF – the elbow circle of Figure 11.6 – is used in both the knee joint and the elbow joint to reduce the overall DOF formulation of their figure (Figure 11.12). The model has a total of 37 DOFs – 6 DOFs for pelvis position and orientation, 3 DOFs for the spine and 4×7 for each limb. The motivation for the method is motion capture adaptation and this aspect of the work is described in Chapter 10.

Providing the position of the hands and feet are fixed by constraints then all possible poses of the figure are specified by four angles $(\theta_1, \ldots, \theta_4)$ plus the DOFs not included in the limbs linkage.

The IK solver divides into two phases – an analytical solution which results in θ_i, and the evaluation of a penalty method whose input is the DOFs not included in the limb linkage plus those links that are movable by altering θ_i.

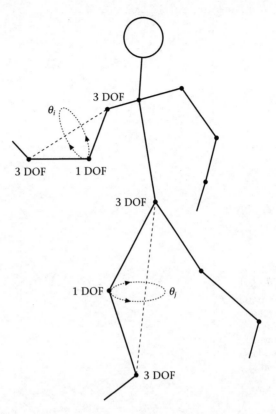

Figure 11.12
7-DOF limbs used in
[LEE99].

The algorithm proceeds by applying the analytical solution to fix the joint angles for the limb chains and provide swivel angles θ_i. The reduced constraint set is then input into the optimisation which finds the remaining (non-limb) DOFs and is also free to alter θ_i.

The analytic phase is shown in Figure 11.13 for an arm. Starting from an initial position, Lee *et al.* sequentially adjust the joint angles for the elbow, the shoulder and the wrist. First the elbow is rotated through ϕ to position the wrist at distance L from the shoulder. Where L is the distance from the shoulder to the goal position of the wrist. ϕ is given by:

$$\phi = \cos^{-1}\left(\frac{l_1^2 + l_2^2 + 2(l_1^2 - r_1^2)^{\frac{1}{2}}(l_2^2 - r_2^2)^{\frac{1}{2}} - L^2}{2r_1 r_2} \right)$$

where
   l_1 and l_2 are the lengths of the upper and lower arms
   r_1 is the distance from the elbow rotation axis to the shoulder
   r_2 is the distance from the elbow rotation axis to the wrist

The next step is to rotate the limb about the shoulder to bring the configuration into coincidence with the desired configuration. Finally the wrist angles are adjusted to match the desired orientation. The redundancy θ_i is then available.

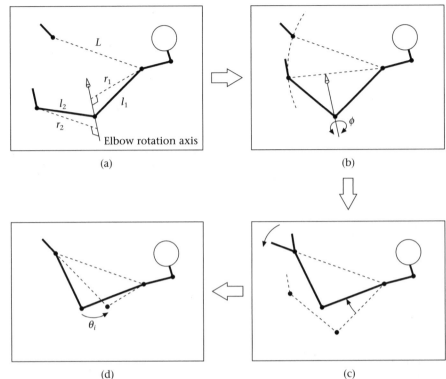

Figure 11.13
Adjusting the arm posture.
(a) Initial configuration;
(b) elbow rotation;
(c) shoulder and wrist
rotation; (d) redundancy
(after an illustration in
[LEE99]).

(a)

(b)

(d)

(c)

(11.4.2)

Hybrid method – three stage: analytic + constrained optimisation + analytic

Shin *et al.* [SHIN01] divide the IK problem into three sub-problems: root position estimation, body posture computation and limb posture computation. Again their motivation is motion adaptation – specifically computer puppetry which is, by definition, real-time motion adaptation. They note that in most problems the position of the root of a hierarchy is generally not important compared to other joints such as, of course, end effectors (see Section 10.8.2 for a discussion of the 'importance' property of pose attributes). Therefore they first move the end effector as close to the root as possible. Moving the root position is simple and efficient (compared to altering joint angles), a property that was also exploited by Gleicher in [GLEI98].

Given the current position of an end effector and a goal position defining a displacement vector, we can simply move the end effector by this displacement.[1]

---

1. Bear in mind here that the application is motion adaptation due to a difference in character scale. We are not talking about teleporting a game player so that he can successfully catch a ball that is 2 metres away from his outstretched hand.

 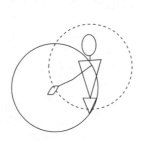 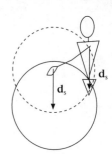

Figure 11.14
Reachable ranges (after an illustration in [SHIN01]).

If there is more than one goal then a weighted average can be used but that is not necessarily the best solution. The authors point out that that the root position should be chosen so that all end-effector goals are reachable by moving the root, then calculating a new posture.

To accomplish this they use the concept of reachable ranges, associated with the root position for each end effector's goal. This is illustrated in Figure 11.14 which develops the root sphere in three steps. The first sphere – the reachable range of the hand – is a sphere of radius equal to the arm extension and centred on the shoulder joint. The second sphere for the shoulder is of the same radius and shows for a given goal position that the shoulder must be positioned within this sphere. If the shoulder joint is anywhere within the sphere the goal can be reached by arm straightening. The equivalent sphere for the root is obtained by translating the shoulder sphere by vector $\mathbf{d}_s$ from the goal position. $\mathbf{d}_s$ is the vector from the shoulder to the root.

Now, since the character has four end effectors, there are four spheres associated with the root and the intersection of these spheres gives the range of the root position that makes all goals reachable. Calculating the best offset for the root position now becomes an analytical geometry problem, full details of which are given in [SHIN01]. In the case that there is no intersection between all the spheres, three spheres are discarded which do not intersect the one with the highest importance end effector (Section 10.8.2).

In the event that the root position estimation does not enable all end effectors to be able to reach their goal, the second stage adjusts the body posture. This consists of the root position, the pelvis orientation and the upper body posture. To do this an objective function is defined as:

$$E = E_g + \alpha E_p$$

The first term is similar to the first term in equation 11.2 – the objective function we defined in Section 11.3.3 except that now there are four joints that function as end effectors for this phase:

$$E_g = \sum_{i=1}^{4} E_i$$

where

$$E_i = \begin{cases} (\|\mathbf{x}_i^c - \mathbf{x}_i^g\| - l_i)^2 \\ 0, \quad \text{if } \|\mathbf{x}_i^c - \mathbf{x}_i^g\| < l_i \end{cases}$$

$\mathbf{x}_i^c$ and $\mathbf{x}_i^g$ are the current positions of the end effector (shoulder/coxa) and the associated goal position

l_i is the associated limb extension

Because the work is motivated by MoCap adaptation, E_p minimises the movement from the captured pose and is given by:

$$E_p = \sum_{j=1}^{n} \beta_j \|\ln(\mathbf{q}_j^{-1}\mathbf{q}_j^c)\|^2 + \gamma(\|\mathbf{p}_e - \mathbf{p}_e^c\|)^2$$

where

$\mathbf{q}_j^c$ is the captured orientation of the jth segment

$\mathbf{p}_e^c$ is the estimated root position

β and γ are weighting factors

The expression is the sum of two squared distances. The first part:

$$\ln(\mathbf{q}_j^{-1}\mathbf{q}_j^c)$$

is the geodesic or *slerp* distance between the two quaternions (see Appendix 7.1) and the second is a Euclidean distance. This factor keeps the new body posture as close to the captured posture as possible.

Given now the shoulder position has been set, the final step is to solve for an arm. This involves adjusting the shoulder joint to fix the wrist at the goal position. This changes the elbow swivel angle θ. This angle is then readjusted so that the arm posture deviates as little as possible from the captured posture. Shin *et al.* derive an analytical solution for this step (which compares with the method in the previous section which used an optimisation method).

We remind ourselves that the angle between two unit quaternions (Appendix 7.1) is given by:

$$\mathbf{q} \cdot \mathbf{q}' = \cos \theta$$

The minimum value for the elbow swivel is thus given by:

minimum_of($\mathbf{q} \cdot \mathbf{q}^c$)

where

$\mathbf{q}^c$ is the unit quaternion representing the elbow swivel at the captured posture

$\mathbf{q}$ is the required quaternion

The detailed formula is developed as follows. Beacuse of the equivalence of $\mathbf{q}$ and $-\mathbf{q}$ – both represent the same rotation, we write:

$$\theta = \text{minimum\_of}(\cos^{-1}(\mathbf{q}^c \cdot \mathbf{q})), \cos^{-1}(-\mathbf{q}^c \cdot \mathbf{q}))$$

which is maximised when $|\mathbf{q}^c \cdot \mathbf{q}|$ is minimised. Writing $\mathbf{q}$ as the rotation θ in the elbow circle from a reference quaternion $\mathbf{q}_0$ we have:

$$\mathbf{q} = \left(\cos\frac{\theta}{2}, \mathbf{n}\sin\frac{\theta}{2}\mathbf{q}_0\right)$$

where

      $\mathbf{n}$ is the unit vector in the line from the shoulder to the wrist (Figure 11.14)

and writing:

$$\mathbf{q}^c = (w^c, \mathbf{v}^c) \quad \mathbf{q}_0 = (w_0, \mathbf{v}_0)$$

then

$$|\mathbf{q}^c \cdot \mathbf{q}| = \left|(w^c, \mathbf{v}^c) \cdot \left(\cos\frac{\theta}{2}, \mathbf{n}\sin\frac{\theta}{2}\right)(w_0, \mathbf{v}_c)\right|$$

$$= \left|a\cos\frac{\theta}{2} + b\sin\frac{\theta}{2}\right|$$

$$= (a^2 + b^2)^{\frac{1}{2}}\left|\sin\frac{\theta}{2} + \alpha\right|$$

where

$$\alpha = \tan^{-1}\frac{a}{b}$$

$$a = w^c w_0 + \mathbf{v}^c \cdot \mathbf{v}_0$$

$$b = w_0 \mathbf{n} \cdot \mathbf{v}^c - w^c \mathbf{n} \cdot \mathbf{v}_0 + \mathbf{v}^c \cdot (\mathbf{n} \times \mathbf{v}_0)$$

Thus $|\mathbf{q}^c \cdot \mathbf{q}|$ is maximised at $\mathbf{q}(-2\alpha + \pi)$ or at $\mathbf{q}(-2\alpha - \pi)$ and:

$\mathbf{q}(-2\alpha + \pi)$ is the closest to $\mathbf{q}^c$ if $\mathbf{q}^c \cdot \mathbf{q}(-2\alpha + \pi) > \mathbf{q}^c \cdot \mathbf{q}(-2\alpha - \pi)$ otherwise
$\mathbf{q}(-2\alpha - \pi)$

Tolani *et al.* [TOLI00] adopt a similar approach and derive a closed-form solution for limb chains that includes joint limits. The method derives a formula for both the joint angles and their derivatives as a function of the elbow swivel angle θ_i. In this case their algorithm uses the extra elbow circle DOF to avoid joint limits or to place the elbow as close as possible to the desired position. If the goal is reachable the method finds a solution, otherwise an unconstrained optimisation is used together with the analytical form.

(11.4.3)

Preventing self-collision

A subsidiary problem in controlling arm links is the prevention of self-collision. For example, placing the hand in certain positions can cause the elbow to enter the trunk. An IK solver for an arm has no knowledge of the trunk part of the body and self-collisions can clearly occur. Huang in [HUAN96] suggests using a heuristic that is cast as a secondary task. This is to use virtual sensors – an oft-suggested heuristic for grasping objects. A hand grasp can be adapted to interact with objects of different shape and scale by using a standard grasp pattern which surrounds the object and closes when the fingers come into contact. Attaching spheres, which function as virtual sensors, enables this. As the grasp action is closing we collision-detect between the spheres and the object and control the finger-closing action accordingly.

In the self-collision context Huang uses spheres on the body at the elbows, wrists, knee joints and ankles. These are checked as:

> within the IK solver:
> **for** each pose θ
>   **for** each sphere collision
>   check between sphere and body
>   **if** collision detected **then** set up secondary task
>   **otherwise** accept current pose

For example, if the elbow sphere collides with the trunk the IK applied to the shoulder–elbow–wrist chain can move the elbow in the elbow circle which reflects the redundant DOF. The secondary task is set up by calculating ΔZ from a repulsion vector (a vector opposite to the collision direction). ΔZ is a joint space vector and has to be calculated from a displacement rate $\Delta \mathbf{d}$ in end-effector space. This is done by considering just the shoulder and elbow as an IK chain (the elbow as the end effector) and calculating:

$$\Delta Z = J^+ \Delta \mathbf{d}$$

Note that such a simple scheme will not suffice in all circumstances. It is possible for the lower arm to enter the trunk, even if the elbow and wrist spheres do not collide with the body.

11.4.4   IK and animated goals

In many applications the goal of the end effector is animated. For example, a character may have his direction of gaze controlled by an IK solver to which is input the position of a moving object of interest to the character. The object will itself be animated and inverse kinematics forms a method for enabling inter-action between two animated objects. All that we have to do to implement this scenario is to attach a virtual link from the head of the watcher to the reference point of the object. The reference point of the object then becomes the end effector for an IK chain that includes the virtual link and the head of the observer.

The relationship between forward and inverse kinematics (exemplified in Figure 11.1) is neatly exploited in an application for interacting agents described by Huang in [HUAN96], as would occur in a scenario involving autonomous agents. In this work two agents interact, for example, with a handshake. The sphere sensor grasp heuristic controls the hand grasping, after which one agent is deemed active and animated with forward kinematics, the other is deemed passive and activated by IK. The passive agent's hand is controlled by IK with the animated goal being the handshake motion of the active agent (Figure 11.15).

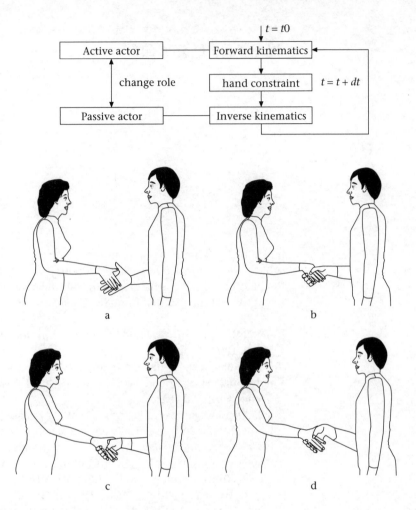

Figure 11.15
Two agents interacting with a handshake. In a and b the grasping is applied, in c and d, the woman actor actively moves with forward kinematics while the man follows with inverse kinematics (after an illustration in [HUAN96]).

References

[ASHI00] Ashikhmin, M., Premoze, S. and Shirley, P. (2000) A microfacet-based BRDF generator. *Proc. SIGGRAPH 2000*, pp. 65–74

[BADL99] Badler, N., Palmer, M. and Bindiganavale, R. (1999) Animation control for real-time virtual humans. *Communications of the ACM*, **42** (8), August, 64–73

[BANK94] Banks, D.C. (1994) Illumination for diverse codimensions. *Proc. SIGGRAPH 94*, pp. 327–34

[BARE94] Barequet, G. and Sharir, M. (1994) Piecewise linear interpolation between polygonal slices. *Proc. 10th Annual ACM Symposium on Computational Geometry*, pp. 93–102

[BIND00] Bindiganavale, R., Schuler, W., Allbeck, J., Badler, N., Joshi, A. and Palme, M. (2000) Dynamically altering agent behaviour using natural language instructions. *Autonomous Agents*, June, 293–300. http://www.cis.upenn.edu/~hms/publications.html

[BLIN76] Blinn, J.F. and Newell, M.E. (1976) Texture and reflection in computer generated images. *Comm. ACM*, **19** (10), 362–7

[BLIN77] Blinn, J.F. (1977) Models of light reflection for computer synthesised pictures. *Computer Graphics*, **11** (2), 192–8

[BLIN78] Blinn, J.F. (1978) Simulation of wrinkled surfaces. *Computer Graphics*, **12** (3), 286–92

[BLYT00] Blythe, D. (2000) Programming with OpenGL advanced rendering. *SIGGRAPH 2000 Course Notes*

[BRACE65] Bracewell, R.N. (1965) The Fourier Transform and its Applications. New York: McGraw-Hill Book Company

[BROO89] Brooks, R. (1989) A robust layered control for a mobile robot. *IEEE Journal of Robotics and Automation*, **2** (1), 14–23

[BRUD95] Bruderlin, A. and Williams, L. (1995) Motion signal processing. *Proc. SIGGRAPH 95*, pp. 97–104

[CABR87] Cabral, B., Max, N. and Springmeyer, R. (1987) Bidirectional reflection functions from surface bump maps. *Proc. SIGGRAPH 87*

[CASS00] Cassell, J. (2000) More than just another pretty face: Embodied conversational interface agents. *Communications of the ACM*, **43** (4), 70–8

[CASS01] Cassell, J., Nakano, Y., Bickmore, T., Sidner, C. and Rich, C. (2001) Non-verbal cues for discourse structure. Association for Computational Linguistics Joint EACL – 2001 ACL Conference

[CAVA99] Cavazza, M. and Palmer, I.J. (1999) Natrual language control of interactive 3D animation and computer games. *Virtual Reality*, **4**, 85–102

[CIGN98] Cignoni, P., Montani, C., Rocchinin, C. and Scopigno, R. (1998) A general method for preserving attribute values on simplified meshes. *IEEE Visualisation 98 conf. proc*, pp. 59–66

[COHE88] Cohen, M.F., Chen, S.E., Wallace, J.R. and Greenberg, D.P. (1988) A Progressive Refinement Approach to Fast Radiosity Image Generation, *Computer Graphics*, **22** (4) *Proc. SIGGRAPH 88*, pp. 75–84

[COHE93] Cohen, M.M. and Massaro, D.W. (1993) Modeling coarticulation in synthetic visual speech. In N.M. Thalmann and D. Thalmann (eds), *Models and Techniques in Computer Animation*. Tokyo: Springer-Verlag, pp. 139–56. http://mambo.ucsc.edu/psl/pslfan.html

[COHE96] Cohen, J., Varshney, A., Manocha, D., Turk, G., Weber, H., Agarwal, P., Brooks, F. and Wright, W. (1996) Simplification envelopes. *Proc. SIGGRAPH 96*, pp. 119–28

[COHE98] Cohen, J., Olano, M. and Manocha, D. (1998) Appearance-preserving simplification. *Proc. SIGGRAPH 98*, pp. 115–22, Orlando, Florida, July, 19–24

[COOK82] Cook, R.L. and Torrance, K.E. (1982) A reflectance model for computer graphics. *Computer Graphics*, **15** (3), 307–16

[COOK84] Cook, R.L. (1984) Shade trees. *Proc. SIGGRAPH 84*, pp. 137–44

[COOK87] Cook, R.L., Carpenter, L. and Catmull, E. (1987) The REYES image rendering architecture. *Proc. SIGGRAPH 1987*, pp. 95–102

[COQU90] Coquillart, S. (1990) Extended free form deformation. *Proc. SIGGRAPH 90*, pp. 187–96

[CRAI88] Craig, J. (1988) *Introduction to Robotics Mechanics and Control*. Reading, MA: Addison-Wesley

[DANA99] Dana, K.J., Ginneken, V., Nayar, S.K. and Koenderink, J.J. (1999) Reflectance and texture of real-world surfaces. *ACM Transactions on Graphics*, **18** (1), January, 1–34

[DEER95] Deering, M. (1995) Geometry compression. *Proc. SIGGRAPH 95*, pp. 13–20

[DESB00] Desbrun, M., Meyer, M. and Shroder, P. (2000) *Differential geometry operaors in nD*. Multiresolution Modelling Group, California Inst. of Technology, pre-print

[DOCA76] Do Carmo, P. (1976) *Differential geometry of curves and surfaces*. Upper Saddle River, NJ: Prentice-Hall Inc.

[DUCH97] Duchaineau, M.A., Wolinsky, M., Sigeti, D.E., Miller, M.C., Aldrich, C. and Mineev-Weinstein, M.B. (1997) ROAMing terrain: Real-time optimally adapting meshes. *Proc. IEEE Visualization 97*, October, 81–8

[DUFF86] Duff, T. (1986) Splines in animation and modelling. *SIGGRAPH Course Notes*, 15

[EAST01] Eastlick, M. and S. Maddock, S. (2001) Triangle-mesh simplification using error polyhedra. *Proc. 19th Eurographics UK Chapter Annual Conference*, UCL, 3–5 April, pp. 1–10

[ECK95] Eck, M., DeRose, T., Duchamp, T., Hoppe, H., Lounsbery, M. and Stuetzle, W. (1995) Multiresolution analysis of arbitrary meshes. *Proc. SIGGRAPH 95*, pp. 173–82

[EDGE01] Edge, J. and Maddock, S. (2001) Expressive visual speech using geometric muscle functions. *Proc. Eurographics UK 2001.*
http://www.dcs.shef.ac.uk/~jedge/

[EKMA73] Ekman, P. (1973) *Darwin and Facial Expressions*. New York: Academic Press

[FORS88] Forsey, D. and Bartels, R. (1988) Hierarchical B-spline refinement. *Proc. SIGGRAPH '88*, pp. 205–12.
http://www.cs.ubc.ca/nest/imager/contributions/forsey/dragon/facial.html

[FUNG99] Funge, J. (1999) *AI for Games and Animation: A modelling Approach*. AK Peters

[GARL97] Garland, M. and Heckbert, P. (1997) Surface simplification using quadric error metrics. *Proc. SIGGRAPH 97*, pp. 209–16

[GARL98] Garland, M. and Heckbert, P. (1998) Simplifying surfaces with colour and texture using quadric error metrics. *IEEE Visualisation 98 conf. proc*, pp. 263–9

[GARL99] Garland, M. (1999) Quadric based polygonal surface simplification. Ph.D. thesis, Tech. Rept. CMU-CS-99-105

[GLEI98] Gleicher, M. (1998) Retargetting motion to new characters. *Proc. SIGGRAPH 98*, pp. 33–42

[GLEI01] Gleicher, M. (2001) Comparative analysis of constraint based motion editing methods. *2000 Workshop on Human Modelling and Analysis*, Seoul, Korea

[GORA84] Goral, C., Torrance, K.E. and Greenberg, D. (1984) Modeling the interaction of light between diffuse surfaces, *Computer Graphics (ACM SIGGRAPH) Annual Conference Series*, **18** (3), pp. 213–22, Addison-Wesley

[GUIB85] Guibas, L. and Stolfi, J. (1985) Primitives for the manipulation of general subdivisions and the computation of Voronoi diagrams. *ACM Trans. on Graphics*, **4** (2), 74–123

[HANR90] Hanrahan, P. and Lawson, J. (1990) A language for shading and lighting calulations. *Proc. SIGGRAPH 90*, pp. 289–98

[HANR93] Hanrahan, P. and Kreuger, W. (1993) Reflections from layered surfaces due to sub-surface scattering. *Proc. SIGGRAPH 91*, pp. 197–206

[HEID98] Heidrich, W. and Seidel, H.-P. (1998) View-independent environment maps. *Proc. 1998 Eurographics/SIGGRAPH Workshop on Graphics Hardware*, Lisbon, August

[HEID99] Heidrich, W. and Siedel, H. (1999) Realistic hardware-accelerated shading and lighting. *Proc. SIGGRAPH 99*

[HEID00] Heidrich, W. (2000) Environment maps and their applications. *SIGGRAPH 2000 Course Notes: Approaches for Procedural Shading on Graphics Hardware*

[HOPP96] Hoppe, H. (1996) Progressive meshes. *Proc. SIGGRAPH 1996*, pp. 99–108

[HOPP97] Hoppe, H. (1997) View-dependent refinement of progressive meshes. *Proc. SIGGRAPH 1997*, pp. 189–98

[HOPP99] Hoppe, H. (1999) New quadric metric for simplifying meshes with appearance attributes. *IEEE Visualization 1999*, October 1999, pp. 59–66

[HUAN96] Huang, Z. (1996) *Motion Control for Human Animation*. Thesis No. 1601, Swiss Federal Institute of Technology, Lausanne

[KASS87] Kass, M., Witkin, A. and Terzopoulos, D. (1987) Snakes: Active contour models. *International Journal of Computer Vision*, **1** (4), 321–31

[KAUT99] Kautz, J. and McCool, M.D. (1999) Interactive rendering with arbitrary BRDFs using separable approximations. *Proceedings of the 10th Eurographics Workshop on Rendering*, June, pp. 281–92

[KILG99] Kilgard, M.J. (1999) A practical and robust bump-mapping technique for today's GPUs. GDC 2000 and www.nvidia.com

[KOBB98] Kobbelt, L., Campagna, S., Vorsatz, J. and Seidel, H. (1998) Interactive multiresolution modelling on arbitrary meshes. *Proc. SIGGRAPH 98*, pp. 105–14

[KURI91] Kurihara, T. and Arai, K. (1991) A transformation method for modelling and animation of the human face from photographs. In N.M. Thalmann (ed.), *Computer Animation '91*, Tokyo: Springer-Verlag

[LASS87] Lasseter, J. (1987) Principles of traditional animation applied to 3D computer animation. *Proc. SIGGRAPH 87*, pp. 35–44

[LEE98] Lee, A., Sweldens, W., Schroder, P., Cowsar, L. and Dobkin, D. (1998) MAPS: Multiresolution Adaptive Parameterisation of Surfaces. *Proc. SIGGRAPH 98*, pp. 95–104

[LEE99] Lee, J. and Shin, S.Y. (1999) A hierarchical approach to interactive motion editing for human-like figures. *Proc. SIGGRAPH '99*, pp. 39–48

[LEE00] Lee, A. (2000) Building your own subdivision surfaces. www.gamasutra.com/features

[LEE00] Lee, A., Moreton, H. and Hoppe, H. (2000) Displaced subdivision surfaces. *Proc. SIGGRAPH 2000*, pp. 85–94

[LEE02] Lee, J. and Shin, S.Y. (2002) General construction of time domain filters for orientation data. *IEEE Trans. On Visualization and Computer Graphics*, **8** (2), 119–28

[LEWI00] Lewis, J.P., Cordner, M. and Fong, N. (2000) Pose space deformation: A unified approach to shape interpolation and skeleton-driven animation. *Proc. SIGGRAPH 2000*, pp. 165–71

[LIND00] Lindstrom, P. and Turk, G. (2000) Image-driven simplification. *ACM Trans. on Graphics*, **19** (3), July, 204–41

[LIND01] Lindholm, E., Kilgard, M. and Moreton, H. (2001) A user-programmable vertex engine. *Proc. SIGGRAPH 2001*

[MACI90] Maciejewski, A. (1990) Dealing with the ill-conditioned equations of motion for articulated figures. *IEEE Computer Graphics and Applications*, May, 63–71

[MILL84] Miller, G.S. and Hoffman, C.R. (1984) Illumination and reflection maps: Simulated objects in simulated and real environments. *SIGGRAPH 84 Course Notes; Advanced Computer Graphics Animation* (long unavailable but see also http://www.debevec.org/ReflectionMapping/miller.html)

[PARK82] Parke, F.I. (1982) Parameterized model for facial animation. *IEEE Comp. Graphics and Applications*, **2** (9), November, 61–68

[PERL85] Perlin, K. (1985) An image synthesiser. *Proc. SIGGRAPH 85*, pp. 287–96

[PERL95] Perlin, K. (1995) Real-time responsive animation with personality. *IEEE Trans. on Visualization and Computer Graphics*, **1** (1), March, 5–15

[PERL96] Perlin, K. (1996) IMPROV: A system for scripting interactive actors in virtual worlds. *Proc. SIGGRAPH 96*

[PHIL91] Philips, C.B. and Badler, N.I. (1991) Interactive behaviour for bi-pedal articulated figures. *Proc. SIGGRAPH 91*, pp. 359–62

[PIGH98] Pighin, F., Hecker, J., Lischinski, D., Szeliski, R. and Salesin, D. (1998) Synthesizing realistic facial expressions from photographs. *Proc. SIGGRAPH 98*

[PIGH99] Pighin, F., Szeliski, R. and Salesin, D. (1999) Resynthesizing facial animation through 3D model-based tracking. *Proceedings of ICCV 99*

[PIXA88] The Pixar Corp. (1988) *The Renderman Interface v 3.0*. Pixar Corp., San Rafael, CA, May

[PRES01] Press, W.H., Teukolsky, S.A., Vetterling, W.T. and Flannery, B.P. (2001) *Numerical Recipes in C++*. Cambridge: Cambridge University Press

[PROU01] Proudfoot, K., Mark., W.R., Tzvetkov, S. and Hanrahan, P. (2001) A real-time procedural shading system for programmable graphics hardware. *Proc. SIGGRAPH 2001*

[RABI01] Rabin, S. (2001) A* Aesthetic optimisation. In Mark DeLoura (ed.), *Game Programming Gems*. Hingham, MA: Charles River Media, pp. 264–71

[REEV90] Reeves, W.T. (1990) Simple and complex facial animation: case studies. *AUSGRAPH 1990*, Melbourne, Australia

[REVE98] Reveret, L. and Benoit, C. (1998) A new 3D lip model for analysis and synthesis of lip motion in speech production. *Proc. Second ESCA Workshop on Audio-Visual Speech Processing, AVSP'98*, Terrigal, Australia, 4–6, December

[REVE00] Reveret, L., Bailly, G. and Badin, P. (2000) MOTHER: A new generation of talking heads providing a flexible articulatory control for video-realistic speech animation. *Proc. 6th Int. Conference of Spoken Language Processing, ICSLP'2000*, Beijing, China, 16–20 October

[REYN87] Reynolds, C. (1987) Flocks, herds and schools. *Proc. SIGGRAPH 87*, pp. 25–34

[ROSE98] Rose, C., Cohen, M.F. and Bodenheimer, B. (1998) Verbs and adverbs: Multidimensional motion interpolation. *IEEE Computer Graphics and Applications*, September, 32–40

[ROSS93] Rossignac, J. and Borrel, P. (1993) Multiresolution 3D approximation for rendering complex scenes. *Modelling in Computer Graphics: Methods and Applications*, pp. 455–65

[SAND00] Sander, P., Gu, X., Gortler, S., Hoppe, H. and Snyder, J. (2000) Silhouette clipping. *Proc. SIGGRAPH 2000*, pp. 327–34

[SEDE86] Sedeberg, T.W. and Parry, S.R. (1986) Free form deformation of solid geometric models. *Proc. SIGGRAPH 1986*, pp. 151–60

[SHIN01] Shin, H.J., Lee, J., Gleicher, M. and Shin, S.Y. (2001) Computer puppetry: An importance based approach. *ACM Trans. on Graphics*, **20** (2), 67–94

[SHOE87] Shoemake, K. (1987) Quaternion calculus and fast animation. *SIGGRAPH Course Notes*, 10

[SING98] Singh, K. and Fiume, E. (1998) Wires: A geometric deformation technique. *Proc. SIGGRAPH 1998*, pp. 405–14

[SING00] Singh, K. and Kokkevis, E. (2000) Skinning characters using surface oriented free-form deformations. *Proc. Graphics Interface 2000*, May, Montreal

[SLOA00] Sloan, P., Rose, C. and Cohen, M. (2000) *Shape and animation by example*. Microsoft Research Tech. Report, MSR-TR-2000-79. www.research.microsoft.com

[SLOA01] Sloan, P., Rose, C. and Cohen, M.F. (2001) Shape by example. *2001 Symposium on Interactive 3D Graphics*, March

[SUDA98] Sudarsky, S. and House, D. (1998) Motion capture data manipulation and re-use via B-splines. *CAPTECH '98*, Geneva, pp. 55–69, Published as: Lecture Notes in AI 1537. Berlin: Springer

[TAO99] Tao, H. and Huang, T. (1999) Explanation-based facial motion tracking using a piecewise Bézier volume deformation model. *Proc. IEEE Comput. Vision and Patt. Recogn., CVPR '99*. http://www.ifp.uiuc.edu/~tao/HTML/content.html

[TERZ93] Terzopoulos, D. and Waters, K. (1993) Analysis and synthesis of facial image sequences using physical and anatomical models. *IEEE Transactions on Pattern Analysis and Machine Intelligence*, **15** (6), June, 569–79. Special Issue on 3-D Modeling in Image Analysis and Synthesis. http://www.cs.toronto.edu/~dt

[TOLI00] Tolani, D., Goswami, A. and Badler, N. (2000) Real-time inverse kinematics techniques for anthropomorphic limbs. *Graphical Models*, **62** (5), 353–88

[UNUM95] Unuma, M., Anjyo, K. and Takeuchi, R. (1995) Fourier principles for emotion-based human figure animation. *Proc. SIGGRAPH 95*, pp. 91–6

[UPST89] Upstill, S. (1989) *The Renderman Companion*. Reading MA: Addison-Wesley

[WANG91] Wang, L. and Chen, C. (1991) A combined optimisation method for solving the inverse kinematics problem of mechanical manipulators. *IEEE Transactions on Robotics and Automation*, **7** (4), 489–99

[WATE87] Waters, K. (1987) A Muscle Model for Animating Three-Dimensional Faces. *Proc. SIGGRAPH '87*, July, pp. 17–24 http://www.crl.research.digital.com/projects/facial/facial.html

[WATT92] Watt, A. *Advanced Animation and Rendering Techniques*. Harlow: Addison-Wesley

[WATT00] Watt, A. *3D Computer Graphics*, 3rd edn. Harlow: Addison-Wesley

[WATT01] Watt, A. and Policarpo, F. (2001) *3D Games: Real-time Rendering and Software Technology*, Volume 1. Harlow: Addison-Wesley

[WEBE00] Weber, J. (2000) Run-time skin deformation. www.intel.com/ial/3dsoftware/inmdex.html

[WELM93] Welman, C. (1993) *Inverse Kinematics and Geometric Constraints for Articulated Figure Manipulation*. MSc. Thesis, Simon Fraser University, September

[WITK88] Wilkin, A. and Kass, H., Spacetime Constraints. *Proc. SIGGRAPH 88*, pp. 159–68

[WYNN00] Wynn, C. (2000) *Real-Time BRDF-based Lighting using Cube-Maps*. Technical Report, NVIDIA Corporation. www.nvidia.com

Index